Unknown and Unforgettable

A Guide to Canada's Prime Ministers

Unknown and Unforgettable

A Guide to Canada's Prime Ministers

Gary Schlee

Shorelawn Publishing
Toronto

Schlee, Gary
Unknown and Unforgettable: A Guide to Canada's Prime Ministers / by Gary Schlee
ISBN 978-1-7753780-0-6

Includes bibliographical references and index.

Cover and back designed by Riad.

Blog: canadianprimeministers.wordpress.com

Shorelawn Publishing
Toronto, Ontario, Canada
shorelawnpublishing@gmail.com

Printed in the U.S.

Table of contents

Introduction

Lester Pearson was Prime Minister when the idea for this book was conceived – more than 50 years ago. I bought *Facts About The Presidents* by Joseph Nathan Kane (a 75-cent pocket book – still have it) and couldn't help thinking it would be wonderful if a similar book about Canadian leaders existed.

It didn't. While books have been written about our Prime Ministers over the subsequent decades, more often than not our leaders have remained more unknown than unforgettable. And there still isn't a book with a concise, data-driven approach for every leader. It is my hope that this book helps to correct that. After all, 50-plus years of intermittent research and compilation has to count for something.

The 23 leaders portrayed here were and are individuals who sought to do what they felt was best for the people of Canada. They had their triumphs. They made mistakes. Like all of us. The book attempts to look at their lives objectively, recognizing that some leaders don't stand up as well under the prism of today's moral expectations.

How to use this Guide

Unknown and Unforgettable isn't designed to be tackled from start to finish, although readers are certainly welcome to do so. Instead, its value rests more when read in bite-size sections or used as a reference. Each chapter has three sections: key facts in the Prime Ministers' political and personal lives, brief stories that highlight significant moments, and extensive timelines that lay out their stories chronologically.

The brief stories may be arbitrary, but they reflect what resonated with one Canadian. I have little doubt that you and anyone else would likely come up with a different list, so I hope the accounts here cover areas of interest to you.

The timelines are written from the perspective of the leader profiled. That person is always the implied subject when items start with verbs. When someone or something else is the subject (often couldn't be helped), bear in mind that subsequent items will veer back to the Prime Minister's perspective. It is, after all, his or her chapter. Some timeline items are an action by the government, not the leader. Brevity has also required omitting explanations and definitions of the many terms and concepts that pop up over more than 150 years of Canada's history. If a reference or acronym is unfamiliar to you, please view it as an opportunity to find out more through an online search.

Countless sources were researched for this work – far too many to list in detail. You'll find many of the helpful ones in the Bibliography at the back, but capturing all individual references would double the size of this volume. Determining correct facts and dates was challenging. Sources would often disagree. Ultimately, errors in the information are mine.

Acknowledgements

There's nothing more encouraging than encouragement, and I've benefitted in a variety of ways from people like Roderick Benns who supported this project as it moved through its final decade. The advice or time given by Ted Barris, Sylvia McConnell, Avivah Wargon, Gillian O'Reilly and Paul Martin was also most welcome. Jonathan Scotland's editing of the manuscript made this a finer product. His uncanny grasp of Canada's rich political history and his composed, caring attention to improving the content helped to keep my mixed messages and conflicting facts to a minimum. Thanks, too, to Riad for his distinctive design and artwork for the book's cover. By the way, the four Prime Ministers found there are Thompson, Macdonald, Laurier and Meighen. I'll let you decide which are unforgettable or unknown. The luckiest break I received was the unwavering encouragement of my wife, Jan. A superb editor, she also tolerated my regular escapes into prime ministerial minutiae. Simply put, I've been blessed to have a family as supportive and loving as Jan and our daughter Laura. This book is dedicated to them.

Gary Schlee
July 2018

1

Sir John A. Macdonald

The Unstoppable Prime Minister

Considered the father of modern Canada, Macdonald was the persistent politician who stickhandled the country to creation. Even before he embraced Confederation, John A. supported collaboration between French- and English-Canadians, an approach that proved to be a founding principle for the new nation. The country's first Prime Minister was determined to see Canada grow. He raised tariffs to foster domestic industry and committed to building the world's longest railway to tie the coasts together. But doing so meant turning a blind eye to the plight of those in the path of his nation-building: First Nations and Métis in the west and burdened Chinese railway labourers.

Macdonald the Politician

Prime Minister of Canada: (1) July 1, 1867 – November 5, 1873; (2) October 17, 1878 – June 6, 1891
Length of terms: (1) 6 years, 4 months, 4 days; (2) 12 years, 7 months, 20 days; (Total) 18 years, 11 months, 26 days
Parliaments as Prime Minister: First; Second; Fourth; Fifth; Sixth; Seventh
Age on entering office: 52
Political party: Liberal-Conservative
Leader of party: July 1, 1867 – June 6, 1891
Member of Parliament: July 1, 1867 – June 6, 1891
Ridings represented: Kingston [Ont.] (1867-1878, 1887-1891); Victoria [B.C.] (1878-1882); Carleton [Ont.] (1882-1887)
Cabinet portfolios: Justice (1867-1873); Interior & Indian Affairs (1878-1883); Indian Affairs (1883-1887); Privy Council President (1883-1889); Railways & Canals (1889-1891)
Other political posts: Kingston alderman (1843-1844); Canada Assembly member (1844-1867); Receiver General, Canada West (1847); Commissioner of Crown Lands, Canada West (1847-1848); Attorney General, Canada West (1854-1858, 1858-1862, 1864-1867); Liberal-Conservative Party Leader (1856); Premier of Canada (1857-1858): Postmaster General, Canada West (1858); Militia Affairs (1861-1862, 1865-1867); Leader of the Opposition (1873-1878)
Knighted: June 29, 1867
Titles: Queen's Counsel (1846); Knight Commander of the Bath (1867);

Canadian Privy Councillor (1867); Imperial Privy Councillor (1879); Knight Grand Cross of the Bath (1884)
Quotes: "A British subject I was born; a British subject I will die." (declared during his last election campaign in 1891); "He shall hang though every dog in Quebec bark in his favour." (reaction in 1885 to possible clemency for Louis Riel)
Lived after term: Died in office

Macdonald the Man

Name: John Alexander Macdonald
Born: January 11, 1815, Glasgow, Scotland
Ancestry: Scottish
Religion: Presbyterian
Arrival in Canada: May 20, 1820
Education: did not attend school beyond age 14; admitted to the Upper Canada bar as a lawyer (1836)
Nicknames: Old Tomorrow; Old Chieftain
Military service: Sedentary Militia (1837 Rebellion, saw no action)
Occupation: lawyer; businessman
Publications: none
Appearance: "If he ever brushed his hair, he must have done so with his hands, for it burst about his face like black steel wool." (Patricia Phenix in *Private Demons*); "With his lumpy nose, his frizzy hair and his thin arms and legs, Sir John A. was a caricaturist's delight." (Lena Newman in *The John A. Macdonald Album*)
Personality: "He was self-assured, clever, funny, a delight for any woman to find seated beside her at a dinner table." (Richard Gwyn in *John A.: The Man Who Made Us*); "He drank openly and without apology." (Patricia Phenix in *Private Demons*)
First marriage: Isabella Clark – September 1, 1843, St. Andrew's Church, Kingston, Canada West (Ontario)
Age at first marriage: 28
Years married: 14
Second marriage: Susan Agnes Bernard – February 16, 1867, St. George's Church, Hanover Square, London, England
Age at second marriage: 52
Years married: 24
Died: June 6, 1891, Ottawa, Ontario
Age at death: 76
Cause of death: stroke
Buried: Cataraqui Cemetery, Kingston, Ontario

Macdonald was the:

- Only Prime Minister to win six majority governments (by cobbling together various Conservative groups)
- Only Prime Minister to win five consecutive elections
- Only Prime Minister to resign because of a scandal (Pacific Scandal, 1873)
- Only Prime Minister with a son who became a provincial premier (Manitoba)

- Oldest person to serve as Prime Minister (76)
- Winner of the most elections as a party leader (6)
- First Conservative Prime Minister
- First Prime Minister to be re-elected after losing office (1878)
- First Prime Minister to die in office
- First lawyer to become Prime Minister
- First Scottish-born Prime Minister
- First Presbyterian Prime Minister
- First Prime Minister to be a mason
- First Prime Minister to be knighted
- First Prime Minister to marry twice
- First Prime Minister to represent Ontario
- First Prime Minister to represent British Columbia
- First Prime Minister with a son who became a Member of Parliament
- First Prime Minister with a son who became a cabinet minister (Interior & Indian Affairs)
- First Prime Minister to have a child born while in office (daughter Mary)
- First Father of Confederation to be Prime Minister
- Second longest serving Prime Minister (after Mackenzie King)

Macdonald's legacy

- Founded the Canadian nation by making Confederation work
- Developed the English-French governance that became the nation's pattern
- Bought Rupert's Land and North-West Territories from Britain
- Brought Manitoba, British Columbia and Prince Edward Island into Confederation as provinces
- Built the Canadian Pacific Railway, the country's transportation backbone
- Formed the North-West Mounted Police (now the RCMP)
- Established protective tariffs as part of his party's National Policy
- Executed Louis Riel, alienating French Canadians
- Enacted policies designed to assimilate the Indigenous peoples

MACDONALD'S FAMILY

Macdonald's Parents

Father: Hugh Macdonald
Born: December 12, 1781, Dornoch, Sutherlandshire, Scotland
Arrival in Canada: May 20, 1820
Occupation: merchant; miller
Died: September 23, 1841, Kingston, Canada West (Ontario)
Age at death: 59

Mother: Helen Shaw
Born: 1777, Dalnavert, Inverness, Scotland
Married: October 21, 1811
Died: October 24, 1862, Kingston, Canada West (Ontario)

Age at death: 84

Macdonald's Brothers & Sisters (4 siblings; John the middle child)

Brother: William Macdonald (1812-1812)
Sister: Margaret 'Moll' Macdonald (1813-1876), no children
  Married: Rev. Dr. James Williamson (1852)
Brother: James Shaw Macdonald (1816-1822); murdered
Sister: Louisa 'Lou' Jean Macdonald (1818-1888), never married

Macdonald's First Wife

Name: Isabella Clark
Born: 1811, Scotland
Father: Alexander Clark (Scottish officer)
Mother: Margaret Shaw (half-sister of Macdonald's mother)
Arrival in Canada: Summer 1843
Age at marriage: 34
Children: 2 – John; Hugh
Died: December 28, 1857, Kingston, Canada West (Ontario)
Age at death: 46
Burial place: Cataraqui Cemetery, Kingston, Ontario
Older than Macdonald: 6 years
Died before Macdonald: 33 years

Macdonald's Second Wife

Name: Susan Agnes Bernard
Born: August 24, 1836, Dirty Pit, Jamaica
Father: Thomas James Bernard (attorney general of Jamaica)
Mother: Theodora Foulkes Hewitt
Arrival in Canada: 1854
Age at marriage: 33
Children: 1 – Mary
Title: Baroness Macdonald of Earnscliffe (August 4, 1891)
Died: September 5, 1920, Eastbourne, England
Age at death: 84
Burial place: Ocklynge Cemetery, Eastbourne, England
Younger than Macdonald: 21 years
Died after Macdonald: 29 years

Macdonald's Children (3 – 1 died in infancy)

Name: John Alexander Macdonald Jr.
Born: August 2, 1847, New York City, New York
Died: September 21, 1848, Kingston, Canada West (Ontario)

Name: Hugh John Macdonald
Born: March 13, 1850, Kingston, Canada West (Ontario)
Occupation: lawyer; federal Interior minister (1896); Premier of

Manitoba (1900)
Married: (1) Mary Jean Agnes Murray King (June 1, 1876); (2) Agnes Gertrude Vankoughnet (April 23, 1883)
Children: 2 – Isabella 'Daisy' Mary; John 'Jack' Alexander
Knighted: 1913
Died: March 29, 1929, Winnipeg, Manitoba

Name: Mary Theodora Margaret Macdonald
Born: February 7, 1869, Ottawa, Ontario
Died: January 28, 1933, Hove, East Sussex, England
Note: was an invalid with hydrocephalus; Macdonald's nickname for her was Baboo.

POLITICAL STORIES

The Liberal-Conservative Party

It's a party name that sounds, to today's ear, like an oxymoron. In fact, it was every bit as unusual when it was first coined in 1854. As a member of a rather weak Conservative Party, Macdonald succeeded in attracting some of the more moderate Liberals – along with old guard High Tories and Canada East Bleus – into a coalition government headed up Sir Allan MacNab.

Ironically, the group was first referred to as the Progressive Conservatives, a name that was revived again seven decades later when the Progressive Party merged with the Conservatives.

By 1873, there were no more former Liberals in the party, but some members of the Conservatives continued to run under the Liberal-Conservative banner until the close of the century. The first four Conservative Prime Ministers (Macdonald, Abbott, Thompson and Bowell) were officially Liberal-Conservatives.

The Double Shuffle

In the 20 years before Confederation, Canada was governed by an endless parade of coalition governments. That was the case in 1858, when the government combined Macdonald's Conservatives and Georges-Étienne Cartier's Bleus with a few Reformers and Hinckites.

During the debate on the bill to make Ottawa the capital, the Reformers succeeded in passing a motion to reject the choice. Their leader, George Brown, considered it to be a vote of non-confidence and had the house adjourned.

Four days later, Brown and Antoine-Aimé Dorion formed a Reform government, but the governor, Sir Edmund Head, refused to dissolve the house for an election. That made it necessary for the new cabinet members to resign their seats to seek re-election – a common practice at the time. Having temporarily given up their cabinet positions and seats in the Assembly, the Brown-Dorion administration collapsed two days later on a non-confidence vote.

Macdonald and Cartier returned to office armed with a clever strategy to save their seats. A cabinet minister could remain in the House by resigning as minister and accepting another office within 30 days. Macdonald shuffled every member of his cabinet into new portfolios (he became Postmaster General) and had them sworn in.

Once midnight passed, all cabinet ministers resigned and were sworn into their original cabinet portfolios. The opposition cried foul, but the double shuffle brought Macdonald's coalition back into power for the next four years.

The Great Coalition

Government in the United Province of Canada in 1864 had reached a stalemate. Almost no legislation could get past the 'double majority' that required majority votes in Canada East (Quebec) and in Canada West (Ontario). Over time, it almost became a matter of principle that a vote that passed in one part of the colony would be defeated in the other.

As a result, Canada had been hobbled by six governments in six years. Even Macdonald's coalitions between his Conservatives and Quebec's Bleus under Georges-Étienne Cartier were no longer working. A wobbly 1864 coalition government formed by Sir Étienne-Paschal Taché and Macdonald had collapsed in only a few months after the Assembly censured the finance minister, Alexander T. Galt, for his role in providing $100,000 of public money to the Grand Trunk Railway.

What was needed was a broader coalition, so Macdonald reached out to George Brown's Clear Grits in Canada West. They initially demanded four cabinet posts for their involvement – ending up with three. The coalition of Conservatives, Bleus and Clear Grits was committed to creating a federal union of all British North American colonies (Macdonald's plan), or, barring that, a tighter union of the two Canadas, bound by representation by population (Brown's plan).

The official leader of the coalition was Taché (and after his death, Sir Narcisse-Fortunat Belleau), but it was Macdonald, Brown and Cartier who made it work. Brown left the coalition after a year, but continued to support the government and Confederation.

The Quebec Conference

Delegates from the various British North American colonies met in Charlottetown in 1864 to explore a possible Confederation. The idea was endorsed unanimously that fall by those attending another conference, in Quebec City. Now it was time to get into the details of such a merger. For 18 days, politicians from five colonies debated 72 resolutions, over two-thirds of them written by Macdonald. Although the Canadian premier, Étienne-Paschal Taché, chaired the conference, it was Macdonald who dominated the proceedings. His background in constitutional law added weight to the major part he played.

The first issue to resolve was representation in the new Legislative Council or Senate. The Maritime colonies feared being overwhelmed by the more populous Canada colony to the west. Following five days of debate, they agreed to an equal split of Senate Seats for Canada West (Ontario), Canada East (Quebec) and the Lower Provinces (Nova Scotia, New Brunswick, Prince Edward Island) with an additional four seats going to Newfoundland.

The delegates also tackled the trickiest item on the agenda: the division of powers. Macdonald was a forceful advocate for a strong central government. He felt it was the strong state powers in the U.S. that contributed to the Civil War raging south of the border. However, the representatives from Canada East and the Lower Provinces feared that the loss of regional power would mean a loss of identity. In particular, delegates wrestled with the question: Who receives all the residual powers not specifically assigned to the federal government or the provinces?

In the end, Macdonald had his way advocating for a powerful federal system. A few days after the conference, the Quebec Resolutions were completed, awaiting approval by the governments of Canada, New Brunswick, Nova Scotia, Prince Edward Island and Newfoundland.

Appointed first Prime Minister

In the months leading up to Confederation, Macdonald was seen by most people – including himself – as the logical choice to be the first Prime Minister. The fact that the delegates to the London Conference in December 1866 had unanimously picked Macdonald to chair the meetings helped make it easier for the Governor General, Lord Monck, to handpick him for the Prime Minister's job prior to a first election being called.

By March 1867, Macdonald confided to his sister Louisa that he was already aware Monck "has charged me with the formation of the first government as Premier." It was confirmed on Queen Victoria's birthday, May 24, when Monck wrote to Macdonald to tell him that "In authorizing you to undertake the duty of forming an administration for the Dominion of Canada, I desire to express my strong opinion that, in future, it shall be distinctly understood that the position of First Minister shall be held by one person." The fractious results of having dual first ministers in the United Province of Canada were thankfully scrapped.

Red River Resistance

Louis Riel presented Macdonald and Canada with their first crisis. When Canada purchased Rupert's Land and the North-West Territories from the Hudson's Bay Company in 1869, the area's residents were angry that they'd never been consulted about the transfer.

Macdonald's Public Works minister, William McDougall, didn't help matters when he sent surveyors into the area to carve up the territory into arbitrary plots and townships before the transfer officially took place. McDougall's reward for his overzealous action was a posting as the acting governor of Canada's new acquisition.

The response in Red River, the territory's largest settlement, was to take things into their own hands. The Métis (half Indian, half French), along with some Canadian settlers, formed their own committee that sought to renegotiate better terms with Canada. When the committee, run by Louis Riel, occupied Fort Garry, Macdonald wisely postponed the takeover of the territory while a solution was sought to the western problem.

However, incidents continued to heat up the stalemate. Riel arrested 45 pro-Canadian settlers and formed a provisional government. Macdonald sent three negotiators to the settlement who failed to achieve a compromise. But they did convince Riel to send a delegation to Ottawa for further talks.

The crisis escalated further when Riel had one of his Canadian prisoners, Thomas Scott, executed for insubordination. Reaction was swift and strong. Canada and Britain responded to public demands to send troops to Red River to restore the peace and deal with Riel.

In the meantime, Macdonald's government continued discussions with the Red River negotiators (who were initially arrested for Scott's death), and by May 1870, a bill for the territory transfer was tabled in the House of Commons.

With legislation winding through Parliament and troops hurrying west to restore order, Macdonald was struck by a serious gallstone attack that nearly killed him. It meant he was slowly recuperating while the new province of Manitoba took official form and the troops arrived in Red River in late summer, sending Riel dashing south into Minnesota.

Macdonald had avoided a full-blown rebellion. It was a relief not only to the young new country of Canada, but to Macdonald himself – his son Hugh was with the troops sent to Red River.

The National Policy

Macdonald coined the term 'National Policy' in 1872 when he recognized that a desire for tariffs was often referred to as 'protectionism', while 'economic nationalism' had a more confident tone to it. However, the Pacific Railway Scandal broke that year and it would be another six years before his party aggressively used the National Policy as its campaign linchpin. It would continue to be the Liberal-Conservatives' primary platform in the following three elections.

Building a high tariff wall was a natural way for Macdonald to ensure less reliance on the neighbouring U.S. It also helped protect the business interests in Montreal and Toronto that had close ties to his party. After all, the U.S. had been busy building its own tariff barriers, higher than those suggested in the National Policy.

Introduced by the Finance minister, Samuel Tilley, in March 1879, the National Policy's tariffs were implemented for most Canadian manufactured products. At the same time, tariffs were lowered on the raw materials needed to create those products.

The National Policy was in effect for two decades and succeeded in fostering Canada's independence and strengthening its manufacturing base. However, it also resulted in higher prices, a slower rise in the cost of living and a tendency to favour the growth of monopolies.

The Pacific Scandal

On April 2, 1873, Liberal MP Lucius Seth Huntington rose in the House of Commons and called for the creation of a committee to delve into the questionable activities behind the transcontinental railway contract awarded to the Canada Pacific Railway Company. He not only accused the company of being privately backed by American funds, but denounced its president, Sir Hugh Allan, for contributing large sums of Canadian and U.S. money to Macdonald and colleagues Cartier and Langevin during the 1872 election campaign – before the contract was awarded.

For three months, Macdonald was able to prevent the 'Pacific Scandal' from crippling his government. But in early July, newspapers in Toronto, Montreal and Quebec City revealed additional details, including a devastating telegram Macdonald had sent to Allan's solicitor, John J.C. Abbott (later to become Canada's third Prime Minister) days before the election. In it, he told Abbott, "I must have another ten thousand. Will be the last time of calling. Do not fail me."

It was conclusive evidence that the Canada Pacific Railway was helping to fund a Conservative victory. Macdonald attempted to ride out the scandal with a stirring five-hour speech in the House of Commons. But when two Conservative MPs indicated they would support a Liberal vote of non-confidence, Macdonald avoided defeat in the House by visiting the Governor General and submitting the resignation of his government.

The North-West Rebellion

The North-West Rebellion of 1885 was actually two rebellions. The first was by Métis in the District of Saskatchewan who had moved west from Manitoba after the unsuccessful resistance in Red River under Louis Riel. Concerned about the growing number of settlers moving west and potentially destroying their way of life, the Métis convinced Riel to return from exile in the U.S. to again lead the resistance.

They formed a provisional government in the hope of winning concessions from the Canadians as they had done in 1869 in Red River. Macdonald had agreed to investigate the claims of the settlers and Métis, and was prepared to provide both land and grants as was belatedly done in Manitoba. But it was too late to prevent Riel's provisional government from starting to take action.

Under military leader Gabriel Dumont, the Métis won some early victories against Canadian militiamen and North-West Mounted Police at Duck Lake and Fish Creek. However, in a third battle on May 9 at Batoche, the Métis capital, Canadian forces under Major General Frederick Middleton defeated the Métis who ran out of ammunition. Riel surrendered and was taken to the Regina police outpost, while Dumont and others escaped to the U.S.

The second rebellion was launched by Cree warriors upset by the starvation facing their people. They were frustrated by the unsuccessful attempts to improve the terms of the treaty between the Cree and Canada to give them more access to food. Restless for a confrontation, they were encouraged by the early Métis victories at Duck Lake and Fish Creek.

On April 9, 1885, a Cree band attacked Frog Lake, killing nine settlers and the Indian agent, as well as taking three settlers captive. The Cree also defeated Canadian forces a month later in a battle at Cut Knife Creek, while a third battle between police and the Cree at Frenchman's Butte failed to stop the uprising.

Big Bear's Cree were pursued from Frenchman's Butte by a North-West Mounted Police detachment under Sam Steele. On June 3, Steele caught up with them at Loon

Lake and defeated the exhausted warriors after a short battle. Although Big Bear escaped, he surrendered a month later.

The quick defeat of the Métis and Cree was largely the result of a changing west. Macdonald's nearly completed Canadian Pacific Railway made it possible for troops to reach the prairies. There was also an effective local police force, the North-West Mounted Police, that had the support of the settlers.

Louis Riel hangs

Louis Riel objected to his lawyers' defense that he was insane when taking a leading role in the North-West Rebellion of 1885. A jury in Regina agreed with that objection and found him guilty of treason in August. Although they recommended mercy, the charge meant death by hanging and his execution was set for September 18. A week before that date, Macdonald's government granted Riel a reprieve of two months. It was responding to the growing number of petitions calling for clemency and the simmering anger in Quebec.

Macdonald was forced to make a decision after the British government refused to get involved. In October, his government called for an examination of Riel's sanity by three doctors. They found him to be a reasonable man, and on November 11 cabinet upheld the court decision to hang Riel.

Riel climbed the scaffold in the courtyard of the Regina jail on November 16. As the trapdoor was sprung, ending Riel's life in moments, it launched a backlash of outrage, particularly in Quebec, that would haunt Macdonald's Conservative party for 70 years.

A Roman Catholic, Riel was buried at St. Boniface Basilica across the Red River from Winnipeg. He became a martyr in Quebec where the Liberal leader Honoré Mercier capitalized on resentment of Protestant English Canada to win the 1886 election, becoming premier the following year.

Personal Stories

Family tragedies

Throughout his life, Macdonald faced recurring family and personal misfortunes. His only brother, James, (an older brother, William, died in infancy) was accidently killed at age five by an irate servant who had knocked him down.

Isabella, Macdonald's first wife and cousin, became ill within a year of their marriage. For nearly 14 years he took her to health resorts in the U.S., sat by her bedside, and watched her slowly die of tuberculosis. With difficulty, Isabella bore him a son, John A. Jr., who died a year later. A second son, Hugh, survived. His daughter Mary (by his second wife) was born with hydrocephalus, or water on the brain, and was never able to walk or look after her own affairs.

Macdonald himself suffered from weak health during most of his parliamentary career. A gallstone attack in 1870 nearly killed him and he suffered from cholera nine years later. In the 1880s, he tried to escape the political fray each summer by sailing to England or spending time at his summer home near Rivière-du-Loup, Que. He also found escape in alcohol. But, despite his unsteady health, Macdonald outlived most of his political colleagues.

Father and son in Parliament

The opening of the first session of the Seventh Canadian Parliament was capped by the glorious walk down the aisle of Macdonald arm in arm with his son Hugh. Despite the loud applause, they made an unlikely couple. Macdonald had dragged himself from his sick bed to enjoy the moment and was just over a month away from death; Hugh was the awkward, shy son, a reluctant politician who didn't want to run and ultimately resigned before his term was over.

Still, it was a poignant moment for two men whose relationship had usually been thorny. When Macdonald's first wife, Isabella, died in 1857, seven-year-old Hugh was sent to live with his aunt and uncle. Father and son had little regular contact, even when Hugh worked for his father's Toronto law firm, as Macdonald was often in Ottawa.

Despite his shyness, Hugh had a rebellious streak. It rose to the surface when, having signed up with the militia, he joined the troops heading west to put an end to Riel's Red River uprising. Later, he quit his father's law firm after Macdonald objected to his intention to marry a woman who was eight years older. But, Macdonald did adore his grandchildren Daisy and Jack, regularly encouraging Hugh's family to visit Earnscliffe in Ottawa.

When Hugh signed the register as an MP that day in 1891, he used his full name, capitalizing on the middle name he shared with his father. He'd done the same during the election campaign, and for the rest of his life he was known as Hugh John Macdonald.

John A. and Disraeli

When Macdonald accepted his honorary law degree at Oxford University in England, students in the hall struck up the chant "Dizzy! Dizzy!" The reaction wasn't surprising. He bore a striking resemblance to Benjamin Disraeli, Britain's former Chancellor of the Exchequer (and soon to go on to become Lord Beaconsfield and one of Britain's best known Prime Ministers). Both men had similarly unattractive features with wiry hair flanking high foreheads. Although Macdonald wouldn't meet the British titan for another 14 years, their likeness often sparked comments. Even Lady Dufferin, the wife of Canada's new Governor General, noted in her diary in 1873 that "The P.M. is the image of Dizzy."

During Macdonald's 1897 trip to England, the *London World* observed, "He wears his hair precisely as Lord Beaconsfield wears his, or rather as the Premier wore his when he was eight years younger. His face is closely shaven, and the whole shape, colour and expression are phenomenally like Lord Beaconsfield." The article noted that, like Disraeli, Macdonald was "witty and graceful in conversation, epigrammatic in Parliament and audacious in politics."

It was on this same trip that Macdonald met Disraeli for the first time, at the latter's manor outside London. Disraeli's assessment of his look-alike? "He is gentlemanlike, agreeable, and very intelligent, a considerable man, with no Yankeeisms except a little sing-song occasionally at the end of a sentence."

Macdonald attended the funeral of Lord Beaconsfield in 1881. A British official, seeing him in the crowd, thought he was looking at Disraeli's ghost.

John A. and alcohol

In an era when heavy drinking was an accepted norm, Macdonald's excesses still attracted the wrath of his political opponents and the wit of the cartoonists. Remembered as much for his bouts with alcohol as for his molding of Canada, he first started turning to the bottle for relief during the stressful decade of Isabella's illness.

On many occasions, Macdonald's binge drinking would send him into seclusion to recover. These lapses – usually referred to as 'attacks' or 'illnesses' in the newspapers and diaries of the time – would often last days. In 1873, as the Pacific Scandal was bringing the world down around him, he simply disappeared and not even Agnes knew where he was. When he re-emerged, it was probable that he spent most of the time in a stupor in Montreal and at his Rivière-du-Loup cottage.

His intoxicated bouts could have jeopardized his credibility during election campaigns, but his well-honed humour helped voters forgive his slip-ups. One popular story had Macdonald vomiting while standing at the podium. His apology was simple: whenever he heard his opponent's ranting, it turned his stomach.

Lady Agnes Macdonald

Despite a craving to be a part of Ottawa society, Agnes found her personality often clashed with her efforts. She didn't handle stress well and her hostess duties as the Prime Minister's wife made her uncomfortable. As a result, she often appeared humorless, stiff and averse to small talk.

Despite her solemn veneer in public, she was more relaxed around family. Agnes was devoted to her husband and invalid daughter, Mary. She eagerly followed political events that entangled Sir John A. and was not hesitant to comment on them.

Susan Agnes Bernard was born on her family's 500-acre inelegantly named Jamaican estate, Dirty Pit. It was an airy place to grow up and was probably sorely missed by four-year-old Agnes when the family moved into nearby, crowded Spanish Town. Life changed even more dramatically 10 years later when her father Thomas died in a cholera epidemic. She and her mother moved to England until, three years later, they joined Agnes's brother Hewitt who was a lawyer in Barrie, Ont.

When Hewitt became Macdonald's secretary in 1858, it wouldn't have been long before the Canadian premier and Agnes crossed paths. In fact, it's quite possible that Macdonald, who lost his first wife to tuberculosis in 1857, may have proposed to Agnes during this time.

But it was eight years later, when Agnes was again living in England and Macdonald was putting the finishing touches on Confederation at the London Conference, that the romance was rekindled. They were married in Hanover Square, London, in February 1867 with many of the Fathers of Confederation sitting in the pews.

Lady Macdonald's sense of adventure came to the fore in 1886 when, during a trip with her husband, she rode through the Rockies on a train's cowcatcher, seated on a candle box. In her diary, she wrote: "There is glory of brightness and beauty everywhere, and I laugh aloud on the cowcatcher, just because it is all so delightful."

Shortly after Macdonald's death in 1891, Agnes was elevated to the peerage as Baroness Macdonald of Earnscliffe. But the remainder of her life was not particularly aristocratic. She and Mary found Earnscliffe too big and too full of memories, preferring to spend time at the family cottage in Banff, Alta., then with Hewitt, who was in a sanitorium in Lakewood, New Jersey. There, Agnes's life was restricted to taking walks with Mary and Hewitt, both confined to wheelchairs.

Following Hewitt's death, she and Mary moved back to England, living at Sydenham in the summer and Italy in the winter. She died of a stroke in Eastbourne in 1920.

Macdonald's Timeline

1815: Born in Glasgow, Scotland, possibly on Brunswick Place (*January 11*).

1820: Sails to Canada with his family after the failure of his father's textile business, arriving in Quebec City (*May 20*). Settles in Kingston, Upper Canada, with his family (*July 17*).

1822: His five-year-old brother James is murdered by a family servant (*May 22*).

1824: Moves to Hay Bay where his father operates another store. Attends John Hughes's school in Adolphustown.

1825: Moves to Stone Mills (now Glenora) with his family where Hugh operates a gristmill.

1826: Attends Midland District Grammar School in Kingston.

1829: Transfers to John Cruikshank's new Presbyterian school in Kingston (*January*). Writes law exam in Toronto to become an apprentice.

1830: Articles as a law student in Kingston with George Mackenzie.

1832: Becomes manager of Mackenzie's branch law office in Napanee, Upper Canada (Ontario).

1833: Takes over law practice of his cousin Lowther Pennington Macpherson in Hallowell (Picton) (*Fall*).

1834: Becomes secretary of Prince Edward District School board for one year.

1835: Launches a law practice in Kingston following the death of George Mackenzie (*August 14*); moves to Rideau Street.

1836: Hires Oliver Mowat as a law student (*January 27*) who stays nearly five years. Admitted to the Upper Canada bar, following an examination in Toronto (*February 6*).

1837: Called into militia service in the Rebellion of 1837, marching up Toronto's Yonge Street to fight the rebels at Montgomery's Tavern (*December 7*).

1838: Serves as returning officer in Kingston's first municipal election (*March 24*). Successfully gains acquittals for seven farmers charged with treason as rebels attempting to take Fort Henry (*July*). Engaged as defense counsel for Nils Von Schoultz, Daniel George and Dorrephus Abbey, American sympathizers who attempted to invade Canada at Prescott on November 13, but was not permitted to take direct part in the court martial (*November 26*); all three were convicted and hanged a week later.

1839: Becomes solicitor for Commercial Bank of Midland District (*June*). Successfully defends Mohawk Abraham Brandt, getting the jury to reduce the conviction from murder to manslaughter (*Fall*). Seconds a motion to create a Presbyterian college (later Queen's University) in Kingston (*December*).

1840: Begins switching his law practice from criminal to commercial law (*Winter*).

1841: Takes over responsibility for his mother and unmarried sisters after his father's death (*September 23*).

1842: Uses £2,000 won gambling to visit England and Scotland for six months (*January*). Meets his cousin Isabella Clark in Scotland for the first time. Becomes a founding director of The Trust and Loan Company of Upper Canada.

1843: Elected alderman in Kingston (*March 28*) and serves three years. Marries Isabella Clark in Kingston and forms a law partnership with Alexander Campbell the same day (*September 1*).

1844: Becomes a Mason (*March 14*). Elected to the Legislative Assembly of the United Province of Canada, defeating Anthony Manahan in Kingston by a vote of 275 to 42 (*October 11*).

1845: Elected a director of Commercial Bank (*July 8*). Takes Isabella to southern U.S. to recover from illness (*July 18*); remains there for seven months.

1846: Becomes a Queen's Counsel (*December 19*).

1847: Visits Isabella in New York where she is awaiting the birth of their first child (*April*). Becomes Receiver General for Canada West (*May 11*). His son John Jr. is born in New York City (*August 2*). Re-elected in Kingston to the Canada Assembly, defeating John Counter (*September*). Becomes Crown Lands Commissioner (*December 8*).

1848: Resigns as Crown Lands Commissioner following the government's defeat (*March 10*). Moves into his Bellevue home in Kingston (*August*). His son John Jr. dies (*September 21*).

1849: Challenges Reform politician William Hume Blake to a duel for quoting passages out of context during the Rebellion Losses Bill debate; both men leave the Assembly, but the Speaker has them returned and ensures they guarantee to keep the peace (*February 16*). Serves as a director of Kingston Hospital upon its incorporation (*March 22*). His law partnership with Campbell ends (*September 1*). Moves from his Bellevue home to 180 Johnson Street.

1850: His second son Hugh is born in Kingston (*March 13*). Becomes a founding director of Kingston Fire and Marine Insurance Company (*August 10*). Visits England to secure capital for the Trust and Loan Company of Upper Canada (*August*) and returns the following year.

1851: Becomes a founding director of Wolfe Island Railway and Canal Company (*August 30*). Re-elected in Kingston to the Canada Assembly, defeating John Counter a second time (*December 17*).

1852: Moves to Brock Street in Kingston.

1854: Re-elected in Kingston, defeating John Counter a third time (*July 27*). Becomes Attorney General of Canada West in the MacNab-Morin government (*September 9*). Introduces a bill to secularize the clergy reserves set aside for the Church of England (*October 17*).

River lends name to future capital

An 1854 bill to rename the wilderness village of Bytown after the Ottawa River wasn't about to get Macdonald's support. He considered it absurd to name a town after a river. "How would it do," he asked, "to call Paris 'Seine' or London 'Thames'?" Other names suggested included By-zantium and By-copolis after founder John By, but the Ottawa bill passed.

1855: Pushes through a controversial separate schools bill, despite objections from Protestants in Canada West. Moves to Toronto, having members of his family stay at 194 Johnson Street in Kingston to maintain a local address.

1856: Joins Étienne-Paschal Taché as Canada West's leader in a Taché-Macdonald government after Allan MacNab resigns because of ill health (*May 24*).

1857: Hewitt Bernard becomes his chief clerk. Introduces legislation to allow Indigenous peoples to apply for Canadian citizenship, meaning they would lose their Indian status (*May*). Visits England where he fails to raise money for the Grand Trunk Railway (*July-September*). Becomes Premier of Canada at the head of a Macdonald-Cartier government with Georges-Étienne Cartier (*November 26*). Re-elected in Kingston, defeating John Shaw 1,189 to 9 (*December*). His wife Isabella dies in Kingston; suspected causes include tuberculosis, a mental disorder or multiple sclerosis (*December 28*).

1858: Resigns as Premier and Attorney General following defeat of a motion to make Ottawa the capital (*July 29*). The Reform government is defeated two days later because cabinet members are absent while contesting by-elections to regain their seats (*August 4*). Returns as Postmaster General in a Macdonald-Cartier government (*August 6*). Avoids a by-election by shifting the following day to his old Attorney General portfolio in a Cartier-Macdonald government (*August 7*).

1859: Narrowly avoids drowning after an anchor catches and prevents the Great Lake steamer *Ploughboy* from smashing into the rocks of the Bruce Peninsula during a heavy gale on Lake Huron (*July 1*).

1860: Invites 1,000 people to a large Valentine's party for $1 each at the St. Louis Hotel in Quebec City; 800 turn up including 23-year-old Susan Agnes Bernard, his clerk's sister (*February 14*). Accompanies the Prince of Wales (later Edward VII) on a boat tour along the St. Lawrence River (*August 10-September 3*).

1861: Re-elected in Kingston, defeating his former law colleague Oliver Mowat of the Reform party; his Conservatives win their first majority government (*July 2*). Becomes the first Militia Affairs minister (*December 28*).

1862: Cartier-Macdonald government's Militia bill is defeated (*May 20*). Resigns as Attorney General and Militia Affairs minister (*May 21*). His mother Helen dies in Kingston (*October 24*).

1863: Calls for a non-confidence vote in the Assembly, defeating the government of John Sandfield Macdonald and Louis-Victor Sicotte (*May 8*); Antione-Aimé Dorion replaces

Sicotte (*May 9*). Receives one of the first honorary Doctor of Laws degrees from Queen's University in Kingston. Re-elected in Kingston, defeating O.S. Gildersleeve (*July*), but his Conservative party is badly beaten in Canada West.

1864: Discovers his law firm is seriously in debt after his law partner Archibald Macdonnell dies (*March 27*). Again becomes Attorney General of Canada West in the coalition government of Sir Étienne Taché (*March 30*). Joins a broader coalition government of Liberal-Conservatives and Reformers, including George Brown, which commits itself to a policy of Confederation (*June 22*). Appointed president of St. Lawrence Warehouse, Dock and Wharfage Company, a British-owned firm in Quebec. Joins other Canadian delegates attending the Charlottetown Conference in Prince Edward Island to consider a British North American Confederation (*September 1-9*). Attends the Quebec Conference where delegates adopt a plan for Confederation; plays a major role drafting the plan (*October 10-27*).

1865: Passionately backs Confederation during the debates in the Canada Assembly (*March 7*). Visits England to discuss Confederation and defence matters (*April 20-July 7*). Receives an honorary Doctor of Civil Law degree from Oxford University (*June 21*). Again becomes Militia Affairs minister in the government of Sir Narcisse Belleau (*August 8*). Co-founds the Rideau Club with Cartier (*September*).

1866: The Battle of Limestone Ridge, Fort Erie, against invading Fenians, marks the first battle fought by Canadian soldiers accountable to a Canadian minister (*June 2*). Visits England (*November 14-April*) for the London Conference to discuss final Confederation terms (*December 4-February 10*). Badly burns his shoulder when his candle ignites his bed while he is reading in his London hotel room (*December 17*).

1867: Marries Susan Agnes Bernard, Hewitt's sister, in London (*February 16*). Honeymoons briefly in Oxford (*February*). The British North America Act is approved by the British House of Commons (*March 8*) and by Queen Victoria (*March 28*). Moves with his wife to 63 Daly Street in Ottawa. Appointed by Viscount Monck to be the first Prime Minister (*May 24*). Assembles his first federal cabinet (*May-July*). Knighted as a Commander of the Bath, becoming Sir John A. Macdonald (*June 29*). **Macdonald's first government (1867-1873).** Becomes the first Prime Minister and the first Justice minister of the new Dominion of Canada (*July 1*). His first cabinet includes 10 Fathers of Confederation. Canada's first federal election: elected as the first MP for Kingston; his Liberal-Conservatives form the government (*August 7-September 20*). Kingston's Commercial Bank folds, leaving him owing 10 times the amount he makes in a year as Prime Minister (*October*). Canada's First Parliament opens; nominates James Cockburn to be the first Speaker of the House (*November 6*). Appoints John Rose as Finance minister following the resignation of Galt (*November 18*).

1868: Sends Charles Tupper to England to counter the anti-Confederationists' effort in Nova Scotia (*March*); Britain refuses to allow Nova Scotia to secede. Helps carry the body of Thomas D'Arcy McGee (Conservative MP — Montreal West) indoors after he is shot on Sparks Street, Ottawa (*April 7*). Gives Langevin (Secretary of State) added cabinet responsibility as the first Superintendent General of Indian Affairs (*May 22*). First Session, First Parliament prorogued (*May 22*); longest parliamentary session in the 19th century: 198 days. Announces the appointment of Sir John Young (later Baron Lisgar) as the second Governor General, replacing Monck (*December 29*).

1869: Announces 'Better Terms' for Nova Scotia, including assuming most of the provincial debt (*January 25*). His daughter Mary is born in Ottawa (*February 7*); she has hydrocephalus (water on the brain). Newfoundland politicians vote to accept terms of union with Canada (*March*). A group of Métis and others led by Louis Riel take control of Fort Garry in the Red River settlement in opposition to Canada's proposed takeover (*November 2*). Postpones the takeover of Rupert's Land and the North-West Territories scheduled for December 1 until the unrest in Red River is resolved (*November 23*).

Coming to the aid of D'Arcy McGee

One of the people to arrive on the scene shortly after scrappy MP Thomas D'Arcy McGee was shot in front of his Ottawa boarding house in 1868 was Macdonald. He helped carry the body inside, but McGee died soon after. It was the last major Canadian political assassination until the October Crisis in Quebec over 100 years later. The man convicted of the murder, Fenian sympathizer Patrick Whelan, was hanged at the last public execution held in Canada.

1870: The Manitoba Act renames the Red River colony and makes Rupert's Land part of the North-West Territories (*May 2*). Suffers a severe gallstone attack (*May 6*); bedridden in his Parliament Hill office for nearly seven weeks, then spends part of the summer convalescing in Prince Edward Island. Canada acquires the North-West Territories for $1.5 million (*June 23*). Agrees to build a railway across the continent to the Pacific Ocean if the colony of British Columbia agrees to union with Canada (*July 1*). Manitoba becomes the fifth Canadian province, with Winnipeg (Red River settlement) as its capital (*July 15*). His son Hugh is among the Canadian troops arriving in Manitoba (*August 24*); Riel abandons Fort Garry and goes into hiding.

1871: Leaves for Washington for two months as Canada's representative on the Joint Commission to discuss U.S. fishing rights in Canadian waters, U.S. grievances over the *Alabama* affair, and Canadian grievances over the Fenian raids (*February 27*). Introduces a bill to build a transcontinental railway to the Pacific Coast (*March*). Signs the Treaty of Washington in the U.S. capital (*May 8*). British Columbia becomes the sixth province (*July 20*).

1872: Founds the Toronto *Mail* newspaper, which begins publication during a printers strike (*March 30*). Introduces the Trade Union Act to legalize unions (*April 18*). Announces the appointment of the Earl of Dufferin as the third Governor General, replacing Lisgar (*May 22*). Canada's First Parliament is dissolved, after five Sessions (*July 8*). Cables transcontinental railway solicitor John Abbott for an additional $10,000 for the election campaign (*August 26*). Carried by torchlight parade to Ottawa city hall where he pledges to take further steps to eliminate anti-labour legislation (*September 3*). Canada's second federal election: re-elected in Kingston, as is his Conservative government (*October 12*).

1873: Appoints Samuel Leonard Tilley (Customs) to replace Hincks as Finance minister (*February 22*). Changes the name of the proposed North-West Mounted Rifles at the last minute to North-West Mounted Police (NWMP) (*March 29*). Liberal opposition exposes the American backing of the proposed transcontinental railway and its contributions to the Conservative election campaign (*April 2*). Moves that a committee be formed to investigate the Liberal charges, marking the beginning of the Pacific Scandal (*April 8*). His colleague Georges-Étienne Cartier (Militia & Defence) dies of Bright's fever in London, England (*May 20*). Prince Edward Island becomes the seventh province (*July 1*). His telegram asking Abbott for campaign funds is published by several Canadian newspapers (*July*). Vacations for the first time near Rivière-du-Loup, Que. (*July*). Testifies at the Royal Commission into the Pacific Scandal (*September 17*). Implicated in the Royal Commission report tabled by

Charles Dewey Day (*October 1*). Asked by Dufferin to consider resigning because of the Pacific Scandal, but the Governor General leaves the decision to Parliament (*October 20*). Speaks for five hours in the House defending his government's involvement in the Pacific Scandal (*November 3*). Avoids a non-confidence vote by resigning (*November 5*). **Macdonald's first government ends.** Unsuccessful in his bid to step down and have the Liberal-Conservative party caucus choose a new leader (*November 6*).

1874: Canada's third federal election: re-elected in Kingston, beating John Carruthers by 38 votes; Conservatives lose to Mackenzie's Liberals (*January 22*). His Kingston re-election is disputed by Carruthers and declared void (*November 21*). Beats Carruthers by 17 votes in a second Kingston vote (*December 29*).

1875: Moves to Toronto from Ottawa, relocating his law office from Kingston (*September*).

1876: Unveils the Liberal-Conservative party's National Policy platform at a picnic in Uxbridge, Ont. (*July 1*).

1877: Offers to resign as party leader, but his caucus convinces him to stay (*Winter*).

1878: Hires his son Hugh to replace lawyer James Patton in his law firm (*April 15*). Threatens to punch Donald Smith (Conservative MP – Selkirk) during a debate in the House of Commons (*May 10*). Knocked unconscious during an unruly election rally in Montreal, but recovers to give his speech (*September*). Canada's fourth federal election: defeated in Kingston, but subsequently elected in Victoria, B.C., and Marquette, Man.; he chooses Victoria; his party is returned to power (*September 17*). **Macdonald's second government (1878-1891).** Becomes Prime Minister for the second time, as well as the fourth Interior minister, and the seventh Superintendent General of Indian Affairs (*October 17*). Moves to Stadacona Hall, on today's Laurier Avenue in Ottawa. The Marquess of Lorne becomes the fourth Governor General of Canada, replacing Dufferin (*November 25*).

1879: Fourth Parliament opens; nominates Joseph Blanchet to be the third Speaker of the House (*February 13*). MP Davin Flood's government report calls for public funding for a residential school system to separate Indigenous children from their families (*March* 14). Suffers a severe cholera attack in Montreal (*June 26*). Dominion Day is formally celebrated for the first time (*July 1*). Dismisses Luc Lutellier de St. Just, Lieutenant-Governor of Quebec, for his decision to dismiss the Quebec government in 1878 (*July 25*). Sails for England to establish a permanent Canadian agency in London and to raise funds for the proposed Canadian Pacific Railway (*July 26*). Enacts an Order-in-Council calling for the northern route of the CPR to pass through Fort Edmonton and the Yellowhead Pass, then along the Fraser River to the Pacific at Burrard Inlet (*October 14*).

1880: Prompted by ill health to resign (*March 21*); four days later, the cabinet persuades him to remain as leader. Sails for England to find a railway backer (*July 10-September 27*); meets with little success. Britain cedes nearly all its possessions in North America, primarily the Arctic Islands, to Canada; only Newfoundland remains British (*July 31*). The contract to build the Canadian Pacific Railway (CPR) is officially signed (*October 21*).

1881: CPR is incorporated, receiving $25 million and 25 million acres of right-of-way land from the government (*February 17*. Attends Benjamin Disraeli's funeral while visiting England (*April 27*). Sails to England again for medical advice (*May 21*); his doctor feared cancer, but the British doctor's diagnosis is "catarrh of the stomach, with a gouty state of body, not amounting to gout."

1882: Tells Parliament that all Indigenous peoples in the Assiniboia territory will be removed by force if necessary from land near the proposed railway (*March 24*). The Districts of Assiniboia, Athabaska, Saskatchewan and Alberta are established in the North-West Territories. (*May 8*). Supports black postal carrier Albert Jackson's efforts to be assigned related duties instead of menial tasks at the Toronto Post Office (*May 30*). Canada's fifth federal election: elected in Lennox and in Carleton; chooses to represent Carleton; his Conservative government is re-elected (*June 20*). Buys Les Rochers cottage near Rivière-du-Loup (*July*); has it renovated and moves in the following year. The Albany Club for Conservatives is founded in Toronto at his urging (*October*). Buys Earnscliffe home at 140 Sussex Drive in Ottawa (*November*).

1883: Fifth Parliament opens; nominates George Kirkpatrick to be the fourth Speaker of the House (*February 8*). Authorizes the creation of the first three residential schools, saying "Indian children should be withdrawn as much as possible from the parental influence, and the only way to do that would be to put them in central training industrial schools where they will acquire the habits and modes of thought of white men." Announces the appointment of the Marquess of Lansdowne as the fifth Governor General, replacing Lorne (*August 24*). Resigns as Interior minister and becomes Canada's 14th Privy Council President (*October 17*).

1884: Amendments to the Indian Act ban dances and traditional ceremonies and make attendance at residential schools compulsory (*April*). Artist Robert Harris completes and delivers his *Fathers of Confederation* painting to the government (*May 17*). A royal commission is appointed to examine Chinese immigration on the west coast (*June*). His only grandson, John 'Jack' Alexander Macdonald, is born (*August 7*). Sails to England for a rest (*October 10*); receives the Grand Cross of the Bath from Victoria (*November 21*); and attends a banquet held in his honour at London's Empire Club (*November 26*).

1885: Cabinet rejects the CPR's request for a further government loan (*March 18*). Riel establishes a provisional government at Batoche, North-West Territories (*March 19*). Belatedly appoints a commission to make land grants to the Métis in the North-West Territories (*March 30*). Riel surrenders to Middleton (*May 15*) and is taken to Regina. The fishing clauses in the Washington Treaty end, eliminating U.S. fishing rights in Canadian waters (*July 1*). The CPR receives additional government loans, prompted by its role in transporting troops to the west to help quell the rebellion (*July 10*). Grants Riel a reprieve of his sentence to hang (*September 11*). Appoints John S.D. Thompson as Justice minister (*September 26*). Sets up an inquiry to determine the degree of Riel's sanity (*October 22*). Cabinet upholds the court's decision to hang Riel (*November 11*). Riel is hanged in Regina (*November 16*). Sails to England for a rest (*November-January*). Six Cree and two Stoney involved in the North-West Rebellion are hanged in Battleford (*November 27*).

1886: Visits western Canada for the first time, traveling on the recently completed CPR (*July 10*); the trip includes his first visit to his son Hugh's home, Dalnavert, in Winnipeg. The government grants amnesty to most of those who fought in the North-West Rebellion (*July 17*). His wife Agnes creates excitement in the Rocky Mountains by riding the train's cowcatcher (*July 22*). Makes his first visit to Victoria, the riding he represented from 1878 to 1882 (*July 24*). Drives the last spike of the Esquimalt and Nanaimo Railway at Shawnigan Lake, B.C. (*August 13*). Invites Blackfoot chiefs Crowfoot and Red Crow to Earnscliffe (*October*); chiefs from the Cree, Salteaux and Assiniboine visit two weeks later.

1887: Appoints Tupper as Finance minister even though he still serves as High Commissioner to Britain (*January 27*). Canada's sixth federal election: elected in Carleton and Kingston; gives up the Carleton seat to represent Kingston once again; his Conservative government is re-elected (*February 22*). Sixth Parliament opens; nominates Joseph Ouimet to be the fifth Speaker of the House (*April 13*). Britain gives Canada the power to negotiate its own commercial treaties with foreign countries (*May 26*). Wilfrid Laurier becomes leader of the federal Liberal party, succeeding Edward Blake as Leader of the Opposition (*June 18*). Resigns as Superintendent General of Indian Affairs, and is succeeded by Thomas White (Interior) (*October 2*). Refuses to respond to the demands of the five provincial premiers attending the nation's first interprovincial conference held in Quebec; they demanded better financial terms from Ottawa, provincial selection of some Senators and control of railways (*October 28*). Becomes the founding president of the Manufacturers Life Insurance Company in Toronto. Helps found the *Empire* newspaper in Toronto after the *Mail* becomes too politically independent (*December 27*).

1888: Opposes unrestricted reciprocity with the United States, helping defeat the proposal in the House (*April 9*). Introduces a bill to end the CPR's monopoly in the west, bowing to Manitoba's pressure (*April 26*). Announces the appointment of Baron Stanley of Preston as the sixth Governor General, replacing Lansdowne (*May 11*). Becomes acting minister for Interior and Indian Affairs (*May 8*); steps down four months later.

1889: Announces that he doesn't intend to disallow the Jesuit Estates Act in Quebec to compensate the Society of Jesus for property confiscated nearly a century earlier (*January*). Becomes acting Railways & Canals minister (*April 10*). Steps down after 25 years as president of St. Lawrence Warehouse, Dock and Wharfage Company. Receives an honorary Doctor of Laws degree from Trinity College at the University of Toronto (*June 7*). Becomes Railways & Canals minister and resigns as Privy Council President (*November 28*).

1890: Attends the unveiling of his portrait on Parliament Hill by Henry Sandham (*February 27*). Manitoba creates one school system with instruction in English, eliminating tax support of its Catholic school system that was delivered mostly in French (*March 31*). The McKinley Act in the U.S. sets up a tariff wall between Canada and the U.S. (*October 6*). *Le Canadien* newspaper accuses Langevin (Public Works) of accepting kickbacks from government contractors (*November 19*).

Statue responsible for fatality

The first statue of Macdonald was unveiled in Hamilton by Prime Minister John Thompson in 1893. It sat in the middle of the busy King-John intersection until two fire wagons collided while trying to manoeuvre around it 12 years later. Fire Chief Alexander Aitchison was thrown from one of the wagons, fracturing his skull against the base of the statue. Soon after, the bronze Macdonald was moved into nearby Gore Park.

1891: Unable to attend his nomination meeting in Kingston because of illness (*February 7*); Tupper speaks in his place. Canada's seventh federal election: re-elected in Kingston and son Hugh elected in Winnipeg; his Conservative government is re-elected (*March 5*). Seventh Parliament, First Session opens; enters the House with son Hugh to sign the register; nominates Peter White to be the sixth Speaker of the House (*April 29*). Thomas McGreevy (Conservative MP – Quebec West), brother-in-law of Langevin (Public Works), is accused of accepting bribes from a contracting firm interested in Public Works contracts (*May 12*). Suffers a small stroke while meeting with Governor General Stanley (*May 12*). His government is defeated on a motion to adjourn because too many cabinet ministers are attending dinner parties hosted by Chapleau (Secretary of State) and Dewdney (Interior); but it survives the actual vote to adjourn (*May 21*). A Parliamentary hearing into the McGreevy-

Langevin scandal begins (*May 26*). Suffers a second stroke, which paralyzes his left side (*May 27*). Another severe stroke paralyzes his entire right side (*May 29*). Dies in Ottawa (*June 6*). **Macdonald's second government ends.** Lies in state in the Senate chamber (*June 9*). State funeral takes place in Ottawa (*June 10*). Buried in Cataraqui Cemetery near Kingston (*June 11*).

BOOKS ABOUT MACDONALD

- **1883**: Joseph Edmund Collins; *Life and Times of the Rt. Hon. Sir John A. Macdonald, Premier of the Dominion of Canada* (Rose)
- **1891**: James Pennington Macpherson; *Life of the Rt. Hon. Sir John A. Macdonald* (2 vols.) (Earle)
- **1891**: E.B. Biggar; *Anecdotal Life of Sir John A. Macdonald* (Lovell)
- **1891**: G. Mercer Adam; *Canada's Patriot Statesman: The Life and Career of the Right Honourable Sir John A. Macdonald* (Rose) (based on the 1883 Collins book)
- **1894**: Joseph Pope; *Memoirs of the Rt. Hon. Sir John A. Macdonald, First Prime Minister of the Dominion of Canada* (2 vols.) (Musson)
- **1909**: George R. Parkin; *Sir John A. Macdonald* (Jack)
- **1915**: Joseph Pope; *The Day of Sir John A. Macdonald: A Chronicle of the First Prime Minister of the Dominion* (Brook)
- **1921**: Joseph Pope; *The Correspondence of Sir John A. Macdonald* (Doubleday)
- **1924**: William Stewart Wallace; *Sir John Macdonald* (Macmillan)
- **1952**: Donald Creighton; *John A. Macdonald: The Young Politician* (Macmillan)
- **1955**: Donald Creighton; *John A. Macdonald: The Old Chieftain* (Macmillan)
- **1967**: Edwin C. Guillet; *You'll Never Die, John A.!* (Macmillan)
- **1969**: J.K. Johnson; *Affectionately Yours: The Letters of Sir John A. Macdonald and His Family* (Macmillan)
- **1971**: Donald Swainson; *Sir John A. Macdonald: The Man and the Politician* (Oxford University)
- **1974**: Lena Newman; *The John A. Macdonald Album* (Tundra)
- **1975**: Peter Waite; *Macdonald: His Life and World* (McGraw-Hill Ryerson)
- **1976**: Peter Waite; *John A. Macdonald* (Fitzhenry & Whiteside)
- **1978**: Stewart K. Dicks; *A Nation Launched: Macdonald's Dominion 1867-1896* (Prentice-Hall)
- **1989**: Cynthia M. Smith & Jack McLeod (eds.); *Sir John A.: An Anecdotal Life of John A. Macdonald* (Oxford University)
- **1995**: Richard A. Rohmer; *John A.'s Crusade: A Novel* (Stoddart)
- **2006**: Patricia Phenix; *Private Demons: The Tragic Personal Life of John A. Macdonald* (McClelland & Stewart)
- **2007**: Roy MacSkimming; *Macdonald: A Novel* (Thomas Allen)
- **2007**: Richard Gwyn; *John A.: The Man Who Made Us. The Life and Times of John A. Macdonald, Vol. 1 1815-1867* (Vintage)
- **2010**: Ged Martin; *Favourite Son?: John A. Macdonald and the Voters of Kingston 1841-1891* (Kingston Historical Society)
- **2011**: Richard Gwyn; *Nation Maker: Sir John A. Macdonald: His Life, Our Times, Vol. 2 1867-1891* (Random House)
- **2013**: Ged Martin; *John A. Macdonald: Canada's First Prime Minister* (Dundurn)

- **2015**: Lindy Mechefske; *Sir John's Table: The Culinary Life and Times of Canada's First Prime Minister* (Goose Lane)
- **2016**: Donna M. Ivey; *From Parlour to Parliament: Sir John A's Kingston House on Rideau Street* (Frontenac Heritage Foundation)
- **2017**: John Boyko; *Sir John's Echo* (J. Patrick Boyer)

Governors General of Canada

1.	4th Viscount Monck	1867-1868
2.	John Young, 1st Baron Lisgar	1869-1872
3.	1st Marquess of Dufferin & Ava	1872-1878
4.	Marquess of Lorne	1878-1883
5.	5th Marquess of Lansdowne	1883-1888
6.	Lord Stanley of Preston	1888-1893
7.	Earl of Aberdeen	1893-1898
8.	4th Earl of Minto	1898-1904
9.	4th Earl Grey	1904-1911
10.	Prince Arthur, Duke of Connaught & Strathearn	1911-1916
11.	9th Duke of Devonshire	1916-1921
12.	1st Viscount Byng of Vimy	1921-1926
13.	1st Marquess of Willingdon	1926-1931
14.	9th Earl of Bessborough	1931-1935
15.	John Buchan, 1st Baron Tweedsmuir	1935-1940
16.	1st Earl of Athlone	1940-1946
17.	1st Earl Alexander of Tunis	1946-1952
18.	Vincent Massey	1952-1959
19.	Georges Vanier	1959-1967
20.	Roland Michener	1967-1974
21.	Jules Léger	1974-1979
22.	Edward Schreyer	1979-1984
23.	Jeanne Sauvé	1984-1990
24.	Ray Hnatyshyn	1990-1995
25.	Roméo LeBlanc	1995-1999
26.	Adrienne Clarkson	1999-2005
27.	Michaëlle Jean	2005-2010
28.	David Johnston	2010-2017
29.	Julie Payette	2017-

2

Alexander Mackenzie

The Uncorruptible Prime Minister

He was lanky and dour, with a moral fibre that proved exactly what Canadians were looking for in the wake of Macdonald's Pacific Scandal. Alexander Mackenzie was an unlikely choice for leader. As a stonemason, he was the country's only Prime Minister who worked in the trades. Despite being a reluctant leader – he hadn't sought to head his party – Mackenzie introduced a series of reforms that included the secret ballot for elections that would now be held on a single day. The Supreme Court, the Auditor General, the North-West Mounted Police (today's RCMP), a military college, and free mail delivery were all created during his time in office.

Mackenzie the Politician

Prime Minister of Canada: November 7, 1873 – October 8, 1878
Length of term: 4 years, 11 months, 1 day
Parliaments as Prime Minister: Second; Third
Age on entering office: 51
Political party: Liberal (Reform)
Leader of party: March 5, 1873 – April 27, 1880
Member of Parliament: July 1, 1867 – April 17, 1892
Ridings represented: Lambton [Ont.] (1867-1882); York East [Ont.] (1882-1892)
Cabinet portfolio: Public Works (1873-1878)
Other political posts: Canada Assembly member (1861-1867); Ontario legislature member (1871-1872); Ontario Treasurer (1871-1872)
Title: Canadian Privy Councillor (1873)
Quotes: "Logic, sometimes, has very little to do with political action." (Parliamentary debate on the New Brunswick School Act, 1875); "Loyalty to the Queen does not require a man to bow down to her manservant, or her maidservant, or her ass." (his response to an accusation of disloyalty, 1867)
Lived after term: 13 years

Mackenzie the Man

Name: Alexander Mackenzie Jr.
Born: January 28, 1822, Logierait, Perthshire, Scotland
Ancestry: Scottish
Religion: Baptist
Arrival in Canada: May 6, 1842
Education: did not attend school beyond age 13
Nickname: Sandy (a common name for Scottish boys named Alexander)
Military service: Major, 27th Lambton Battalion Volunteer Infantry
Occupation: stonemason; contractor; newspaper editor; insurance executive
Publications: *Speeches in Scotland and Canada* (1876); *Reform Government in the Dominion* (1878); *Political Points and Pencillings* (1878); *The Life and Speeches of the Hon. George Brown* (1882)
Appearance: "Mackenzie's long, angular face with its naked upper lip and massive, reddish beard, looked stern, impassive and humourless." (Bruce Hutchison in *Mr. Prime Minister: 1867-1964*); "The weather-beaten, angular features and hard, thick hands contrasted sharply with the stiff, white collars and cuffs from which they protruded ..." (Dale C. Thomson in *Alexander Mackenzie: Clear Grit*)
Personality: "What Mackenzie lacked in personal magnetism, he supplied in hard facts and high principles." (Dale C. Thomson in *Alexander Mackenzie: Clear Grit*); "His humour wounded rather than healed." (William Buckingham, his secretary, in *Hon. Alexander Mackenzie, His Life and Times*)
First marriage: Helen Neil – March 28, 1845, St. George's Anglican Church, Kingston, Canada West (Ontario)
Age at first marriage: 23 years
Years married: 6
Second marriage: Jane Sym – June 17, 1853, Sarnia, Canada West (Ontario)
Age at second marriage: 31
Years married: 38
Died: April 17, 1892, Toronto, Ontario
Age at death: 70
Cause of death: paralysis caused by a stroke
Buried: Lakeview Cemetery, Sarnia, Ontario

Mackenzie was the:

- Only Prime Minister not knighted in the 50 years following Confederation
- Only Prime Minister who was a stonemason
- First Liberal Prime Minister
- First Prime Minister to serve a single term
- First to become Prime Minister without winning an election
- First Prime Minister who supported Confederation from the beginning
- First official Leader of the Opposition
- First Leader of the Opposition to become Prime Minister
- First Prime Minister who was a member of a provincial legislature (Ontario) and a provincial cabinet minister (Treasurer)

- First Prime Minister not appointed to the Imperial Privy Council (therefore not Right Honourable)
- First Prime Minister to live after his term
- First Prime Minister who was a newspaper editor
- First Baptist Prime Minister
- Last Prime Minister born in Scotland

Mackenzie's legacy
- Helped form the Liberal Party out of Liberals and Reformers
- Introduced same-day, secret-ballot elections
- Began free mail delivery in towns
- Established the Supreme Court of Canada
- Created the first Military College
- Created the Auditor General's office
- Pardoned followers of Louis Riel in the Red River resistance
- Introduced Hansard as the House of Commons unbiased record

Mackenzie's Family

Mackenzie's Parents

Father: Alexander Mackenzie Sr.
Born: April 11, 1784, Logierait, Perth, Scotland
Occupation: carpenter; ship builder; contractor
Died: March 7, 1836, Dunkeld, Perth, Scotland
Age at death: 52

Mother: Mary Stewart Fleming
Born: March 22, 1794, Logierait, Perth, Scotland
Married: November 16, 1817, Logierait, Perth, Scotland
Arrival in Canada: November 1847
Died: February 16, 1861, Sarnia, Canada West (Ontario)
Age at death: 66

Mackenzie's Brothers (9 siblings; Alexander was the third)

Brother: Robert Mackenzie (1818-1896), 3 children
  Occupation: cabinetmaker; Mayor of Sarnia (1864)
  Married: Mary
Brother: Hope Fleming Mackenzie (1820-1866), 4 children
  Occupation: cabinetmaker; Mayor of Port Sarnia (1857); Canada Assembly member for Lambton (succeeded by Alexander) (1860-1861); Canada Assembly member for North Oxford (1863-1866)
  Married (1): Vere McGregor (1847), 1 daughter
  Married (2): Helen Reid Young (1860), 3 children
Brother: Thomas Mackenzie (1824-1825)
Brother: Donald Mackenzie (1825-1825)
Brother: Daniel Mackenzie (1826-1827)
Brother: John A. Mackenzie (1828-1877), 9 children

Occupation: tinsmith; hardware merchant; farm implement manufacturer
Married (1): Mary Macrae (1843), 1 son
Married (2): Charlotte Watson, 8 children
Brother: Adam Stewart Mackenzie (1830-1919)
Occupation: cabinetmaker, druggist
Brother: James Mackenzie (1831-1887), 6 children
Occupation: cabinetmaker, oil and timber merchant
Married: Mary Dougall Gray (1861)
Brother: Charles Mackenzie (1833-1900), 11 children
Occupation: hardware merchant; Reeve of Sarnia (1888-1894); MPP for West Lambton (1889-1894)
Married: Agnes Young (1863)

Mackenzie's First Wife

Name: Helen Neil
Born: October 21, 1826, Irvine, Ayr, Scotland
Father: William Neil (stonemason)
Mother: Jean Gibson
Arrival in Canada: May 6, 1842
Age at marriage: 18
Children: 3 – Mary; Mary; William
Died: January 4, 1852, Port Sarnia, Canada West (Ontario)
Age at death: 25
Burial place: Lakeview Cemetery, Sarnia, Ontario
Younger than Mackenzie: 4 years
Died before Mackenzie: 40 years

Mackenzie's Second Wife

Name: Jane 'Jeannie' Sym
Born: March 22, 1825, North Sherbrooke Township, Lanark County, Upper Canada (Ontario)
Father: Robert Sym (farmer)
Mother: Agnes Wylie
Age at marriage: 28
Children: none
Died: March 30, 1893, Sarnia, Ontario
Age at death: 68
Burial place: Lakeview Cemetery, Sarnia, Ontario
Younger than Mackenzie: 3 years
Died after Mackenzie: 11 months

Mackenzie's Children (3 – two died in infancy)

Name: Mary Mackenzie
Born: June 25, 1846, Kingston, Canada West (Ontario)
Died: May 29, 1847, Kingston, Canada West (Ontario)

Name: Mary Mackenzie
Born: August 25, 1848, Port Sarnia, Canada West (Ontario)

Occupation: teacher
Married: Rev. John Thompson (November 1872)
Children: 3 – Helen; Alexander Mackenzie; Robert Fleming
Died: May 9, 1920, Guelph, Ontario
Note: Daughter Helen's son, Ian Strachan, was an Ontario MPP.
Note: Son Alexander was a Latin professor at McGill University.
Note: Son Robert was executive director of the Canadian Institute for the Blind.

Name: William Mackenzie
Born: April 3, 1850, Port Sarnia, Canada West (Ontario)
Died: April 29, 1850, Port Sarnia, Canada West (Ontario)

POLITICAL STORIES

Dual Representation

When Alexander Mackenzie was elected as a Reform member to Ontario's legislature in 1871, it didn't matter that he was already an MP in Ottawa. At Confederation, dual representation was possible for politicians in the new provinces of Ontario and Quebec, but not in Nova Scotia or New Brunswick.

The majority of cabinet members in the Ontario and Quebec provincial governments held seats in Ottawa as well. John Sandfield Macdonald, the first premier of Ontario, also sat in the Leader of the Opposition seat on Parliament Hill (although he didn't actually perform that role). Mackenzie added to those numbers when Ontario's second premier, Edward Blake – who also sat in Parliament – appointed him Treasurer.

The practice was particularly objectionable to Liberal MP David Mills who in the First Parliament introduced an unsuccessful private member's bill to abolish it. He kept at it for the next few years until the House finally ended the practice in 1873.

Before that, Mackenzie's 1872 provincial budget committed Ontario to eliminating dual representation. By the end of the year, both he and Blake left provincial politics and kept their federal seats. A year later, Mackenzie was Prime Minister and eventually brought Mills into cabinet as his Interior minister.

Mackenzie and Brown

From his earliest days in the Reform movement in Canada West, Mackenzie avidly followed the writing of George Brown in *The Globe*. So it wasn't surprising that as secretary of the Reform Party in Lambton-Kent, he actively encouraged Brown to run for election in 1851 in his riding.

After some dithering, a pattern with Brown, he decided to run and Mackenzie functioned as his campaign manager. Together they won the election and when Brown ran again in 1854 against local powerhouse Malcolm Cameron, they won once more. Three years later, Brown announced he was running in Toronto, leaving Lambton to hastily convince Mackenzie's brother, Hope, to run. Hope lost.

Brown's abandonment of Lambton didn't dampen Mackenzie's ardent support. Both men shared similar views on important issues of the day like representation by population and acquisition of the west. When Mackenzie became Prime Minister, he appointed Brown to the Senate. He would have made him Lieutenant Governor of Ontario had Macdonald not just filled the position.

Mackenzie's attempt to seek a title for Brown didn't sit well with Governor General Lord Dufferin who was fully aware of Mackenzie's own disdain for such designations. In later years, Mackenzie was actually able to offer Brown both the Lieutenant Governor position and a knighthood – Brown declined them both.

When Mackenzie's government was defeated at the polls, he retreated to Brown's house in Toronto to ponder his future. It was Brown who encouraged him to move from Sarnia to Toronto. Mackenzie was devastated when his close colleague died a year and a half later after being shot by a disgruntled former employee.

Mackenzie and Blake

In 1867 George Brown wrote to Mackenzie, telling him about the quirky genius who would be his new Reform colleague in the House of Commons – Edward Blake. "He has a great opinion of you and I am persuaded you will be immense helps to each other." For the next 15 years, the Mackenzie-Blake relationship would be a exasperating one.

Despite their ideological differences – Blake harboured more radical positions than Mackenzie – the two men initially worked well together. Mackenzie developed a 'great opinion' of Blake's political brilliance, if not his social quirkiness. When Blake was Premier of Ontario in the early 1870s, Mackenzie became his Treasurer. Both Reformers were founding partners of the Isolated Risk Fire Insurance Company in Toronto.

When it was time to officially anoint a leader of the Liberal party, each of them strenuously touted the attributes of the other for the post. Only hours before the Speech from the Throne to open Canada's second Parliament did Mackenzie emerge as leader. It wasn't because he wanted the job; he simply wasn't as forceful as Blake in refusing to accept it.

Within a year, Mackenzie was Prime Minister, thanks to the Pacific scandal. He would have preferred to see Blake assume the role, but at the very least he wanted the stocky genius in his cabinet. Pressure from colleagues prodded Blake to accept, but he did so reluctantly, putting minimal effort into the Justice portfolio.

In September 1874, he wrote to Mackenzie indicating he was now prepared to take on the role of Prime Minister. Barring that, he didn't see a role for himself in Mackenzie's government. Mackenzie attempted to bring Blake back into the cabinet in the spring without success. About a week later, Blake stunned colleagues at a Liberal gathering in Aurora, Ont., by criticizing the government's handling of trade negotiations with the U.S. and its railway negotiations with British Columbia.

In 1875 Mackenzie made another attempt to mend the fence by offering Blake the Chief Justice position on the new Supreme Court. But Blake didn't want to leave politics and instead accepted a role back in cabinet as Justice minister.

When the Mackenzie government was defeated in 1878, Blake went down with it. He blamed Mackenzie for his first personal defeat at the polls. When he contemplated seeking re-election in his original riding of Durham, he was hurt that Mackenzie seemed more interested in having his former Finance minister, Sir Richard Cartwright, contest the seat.

By the following year, Blake was back in Parliament, but the two men rarely spoke to each other. Blake continued to feel that he was the best qualified to lead the party, now in opposition. Mackenzie refused to yield, but by early 1880 he was tired of the pressure. A growing number of Liberal MPs finally convinced him that he no longer had the automatic loyalty of caucus and he resigned on April 29. Blake took over the next day. However, Mackenzie remained in the House, serving as Blake's unofficial lieutenant. In more than one debate, he vigorously defended his new leader, despite the circumstances.

PERSONAL STORIES

The Mackenzie Brothers

Not to be confused with the Second City comedy routine from the 1980s, these Mackenzie brothers – ten in all – were the children of Alexander and Mary Mackenzie of Perthshire, Scotland. Three died in infancy, but the remaining seven ended up moving to Canada where they left an indelible imprint on Sarnia, Ont.

Alexander Jr. was the first to emigrate, settling in Kingston in 1842. Shortly after arriving, he wrote his oldest brother Robert to say, "I only wish Mother and all the rest were out here with me." His brother Hope arrived the following year and soon moved further west to Port Sarnia at the south end of Lake Huron. Alexander joined him there two years later and they proved so successful that they soon had enough money to send Hope back to Scotland to bring over the rest of the family.

By the fall of 1847, Mary Mackenzie and her seven sons – Robert, Hope, Alexander, John, Adam, James and Charles – were reunited in Port Sarnia.

Robert began a cabinetmaking business with Hope and also worked with Alexander on major projects like the Essex County Courthouse, Sarnia's Episcopal Church and the Bank of Upper Canada. He served as mayor of Sarnia in 1864.

Of all the Mackenzie boys, Hope held the most promise. He'd had success as a carpenter, shipbuilder and cabinetmaker by the time he was appointed Sarnia's second mayor in 1857 – after the first mayor's election was declared invalid. In his short four-month term, he launched the town's farmers market. He was elected to Canada's legislative assembly in an 1860 by-election as the Reform member for Lambton. Business pressures and persistent illness convinced him not to seek re-election the next year; the seat was won by his younger brother Alexander (his first political office). Hope was persuaded to run again in 1863, representing North Oxford West riding. He supported the idea of Confederation but never saw it happen, dying of cancer at age 45 in 1866.

Younger brother John had some difficulty severing himself from his tinsmith apprenticeship in Scotland, but he put his experience to work in Sarnia making and selling stoves. The hardware business he started in 1848 with his brother Charles grew to become the largest hardware store in Canada west of Toronto. It's still operating today as Mackenzie Milne, Sarnia's oldest business. Adam, a Sarnia druggist, was the one brother who wasn't involved in partnerships with his siblings.

Love steers him to Canada

While constructing a bridge in Irvine, Scotland – his first job after completing his apprenticeship – Mackenzie met William Neil and his son Hugh. He became a regular visitor to their home where he met Neil's youngest daughter, 14-year-old Helen, and fell in love.

When the Neils decided there would be more building opportunities in Canada, Mackenzie readily agreed to accompany them. He was like a member of the family, sharing meals and worship with them on the trans-Atlantic crossing, then living with them in cramped quarters in Kingston, Ont., and even cozier conditions in a log cabin 35 km away in the backwoods.

The Neils were back in Kingston when Mackenzie secured a winter job supervising the cutting of stone on Wolfe Island for the Welland Canal. Each Saturday evening, Mackenzie would walk 5 km across the lake ice to visit Helen and other friends on the mainland in Kingston. One evening he turned up soaked and frozen after falling through the ice. It didn't stop his icy treks, but he did start carrying a pole to help him get out of the water. That was fortunate, because on at least one other occasion he turned up waterlogged.

Mackenzie's persistence paid off, because before all the ice was off the lake, he and Helen were married in Kingston. They spent their first summer near Morrisburg, where Mackenzie had another contract. Helen caught malarial fever in the marshy conditions. When the illness returned during her pregnancy the following year, she was accidently given an overdose of calomel by a drunken doctor. Plagued by tremors and numbness, Helen died six years later in Sarnia, never having recovered from the high levels of mercury that resulted in her poisoning.

Bid to build Parliament Buildings

As unhappy as Mackenzie was with the Province of Canada's decision to make Ottawa the new centre of government, it didn't deter him from submitting a tender to build the new capital's Parliament Buildings. The task suited him perfectly. As a successful Sarnia contractor he had constructed a variety of public buildings, and as a stonemason he had honed his craft on major public works projects like the Welland and Beauharnois canals.

Teaming up with his carpenter brother Robert, fellow Sarnia contractor James Stewart and Kingston plumber Neil McNeil, he spent a month in 1859 wandering over the craggy outcrop called Barrack Hill in Ottawa, studying its feasibility as the site for the proposed buildings.

The rocky base of Barrack Hill meant he didn't think the three proposed buildings could be constructed for the $540,000 suggested in the competition specifications. After careful planning, he submitted a tender to build the centre block of the proposed Parliament Hill for $450,000 and one for the east and west block buildings for $351,000. His bids were well above the winning ones submitted by Thomas McGreevy.

Work began, despite concerns about McGreevy's close friendship with Hector-Louis Langevin, a member of the legislative assembly, and the missing cost details in his tender.

Three years later and now a member of the assembly, Mackenzie was appalled at the status of construction. Only the foundation was in place. McGreevy had subcontracted most of the work and the price tag was already at $900,000 – $100,000 more than Mackenzie's original bid. Mackenzie demanded an inquiry, but the government initially dismissed his claim as the whining of a disappointed bidder.

By September 1861, the site had been closed down, with costs approaching $1.5 million. Mackenzie's sought-after inquiry was launched and construction resumed in 1863, with the Centre Block completed three years later. Mackenzie described the finished buildings as "one of he greatest examples of magnitude without convenience ever seen on the face of the earth."

He had his own opportunity to fine-tune the results once he was Prime Minister and Minister of Public Works. He added a tower – now called the Mackenzie Tower – to the West Block in 1875.

Jane Mackenzie

In 1852, Mackenzie was a 30-year-old widower with a five-year-old daughter and a thriving contracting business. The workload didn't stop him from making his regular Sunday hike east of Sarnia to the Baptist church. He often stayed after the service to enjoy the hospitality of another widower, Robert Sym.

During those visits he grew increasingly captivated by Sym's daughter, Jane, who had assumed the maternal role in the farmhouse raising the younger children. Although exhausted by the labour, she never seemed to lose her buoyant disposition. In June 1853, she and Mackenzie were married, and Mary once again had a mother.

Short and slim, Jane preferred to look after the household rather than tackle the hostess duties of a rising politician. Once Mackenzie became Prime Minister, however, 'Jennie' assumed the new role with diligence. Although never a comfortable chatelaine in Ottawa, she gracefully carried out the functions of a leading lady. The Mackenzies regularly invited people of all political stripes to their home for dinner or conversation.

Over the years, she grew rounder as he grew slimmer. He sadly missed her whenever she spent prolonged periods in Sarnia and later Toronto.

Mackenzie's Timeline

1822: Born in Logierait, Perthshire, Scotland (*January 28*). Baptized as a Presbyterian (*February 8*).

1825: Moves with family to Edinburgh, Scotland.

1827: Moves with family to Perth, Perthshire, Scotland (*November 26*).

1829: Moves with family to Pitlochry, Perthshire, Scotland, where he attends school in nearby Moulin (*May 15*).

1831: Attends private school in Perth.

1832: Looks after sheep and cattle on neighbouring farms.

1834: Moves with family to Dunkeld, Perthshire, Scotland (*Summer*).

1835: Concludes his formal education at age 13 to do farm work.

1836: His father Alexander Sr. dies (*March 7*).

1838: Apprentices with John Ireland in Dunkeld to become a stonemason in 1841.

1841: Builds a railway bridge at Irvine on the line being constructed between Glasgow and Ayr, Scotland (*Spring*). Stays with the Neil family.

1842: Sails to Canada with the Neil family on the *Monarch* (*April 5*), arriving in Montreal (*May 6*). Settles in Kingston, Canada West (*May 24*). Is not paid on his first construction job when the contractor goes bankrupt. John Mowat, father of Oliver, offers him the use of his original homestead 35 km north of Kingston (*Fall*). He and the Neils spend their first winter clearing land in the wilderness.

1843: Wins a contract to build a stone arch at Fort Henry (*Spring*). Works as a stonemason on the Beauharnois Canal. Older brother Hope arrives from Scotland.

1844: A falling stone on the Beauharnois project crushes one of his legs (*June*); it never completely regains its former strength. Works as a foreman building Lock 12 on the Welland Canal (*June*). Likely votes for Anthony Manahan in the election that first sends John A. Macdonald to the Canada Assembly for Kingston (*October 11*).

1845: Falls through the ice crossing from Wolfe Island to Kingston to visit fiancée Helen Neil (*January*). Marries Helen Neil in Kingston (*March 28*). Spends the summer near Morrisburg on a construction contract.

1846: Foreman of the Cedar Island Martello construction project near Kingston. His daughter Mary is born (*June 25*) but dies the following year. His Cedar Island crew capsizes while crossing Hamilton Cove (*September 12*); 17 of the 23 drown, so it is renamed Deadman's Bay. Stonemason for the Montreal harbour basin project.

1847: Moves to Port Sarnia and establishes a contracting business (*Summer*). His mother Mary and five remaining brothers arrive from Scotland and settle in the Sarnia area (*November*).

1848: Builds the Episcopal Church in Port Sarnia for $766. A second daughter, also named Mary, is born (*August 25*). Runs unsuccessfully as a Prohibitionist candidate for the Sarnia municipal council.

1850: His only son William is born (*April 3*), but dies later that month (*April 29*). Becomes secretary of the Central Reform Association of Lambton. Builds the Kent County courthouse and jail in Chatham.

1851: Convinces George Brown to run as the Reform candidate in Kent-Lambton riding; the campaign is successful (*December*).

1852: His wife Helen dies as a result of an overdose of calomel administered six years earlier (*January 4*). Publishes his first issue of *Lambton Shield* (*January 9*). Builds Sarnia's first bank, courthouse and jail.

1853: Marries Jane Sym in Sarnia (*June 17*).

1854: Sued for libel by Reform cabinet minister Malcolm Cameron of Sarnia (*April 27*); lack of funds causes the *Lambton Shield* to cease publication (*May 5*). Campaigns for Brown who is re-elected in Lambton defeating Cameron (*July*).

1856: Builds the Sandwich (Windsor) courthouse (now called Mackenzie Hall) and jail. Attends a meeting in Toronto that results in the formation of the Reform Alliance Party (*December*).

1857: Campaigns for his brother Hope who wants to replace Brown, now running in Toronto (*November-December*). Cameron is re-elected for Lambton, defeating Hope (*December 23*).

1858: Active in Sarnia activities as a member of the school board, the temperance society, the dialectic society, the agricultural society and the volunteer fire brigade.

1859: Appointed as an assessor by the Town of Sarnia; to 1861. Bids unsuccessfully on the contract to build the Parliament Buildings in Ottawa; five bids were lower than his to build the Centre Block (*Fall*).

1860: His brother Hope is elected to the Canada Assembly for Lambton (*November 16*).

1861: His mother Mary dies in Sarnia (*February 16*). Elected to Canada's Assembly as the Reform candidate for Lambton, succeeding his brother Hope who did not seek re-election because of ill health (*July*).

1862: Delivers his first speech in the Assembly in support of William McDougall's resolution to adopt representation by population (*March*). Succeeds in getting the government to set up a commission to review problems surrounding construction of Ottawa's Parliament Buildings (*May*); testifies before the commission (*August*).

1863: Chastised in the Assembly for leaking the Ottawa Commission report to the *Globe* (*February 27*). Returned to the Assembly by acclamation for Lambton (*June*).

Not above dirty tricks

Best remembered as a stoic pillar of integrity and honesty, Mackenzie wasn't totally above reproach. During one election campaign, his team and the Conservatives were staying at the same hotel. Because the Tories had partied late into the night, they weren't around early the next morning when Mackenzie spied a pile of his rival's campaign brochures in the hallway. They boasted juicy titles like 'Black Record of the Grit Party'. He burned them all.

1864: Reluctantly supports the move by Reformers George Brown, Oliver Mowat and William McDougall to join Macdonald's Great Coalition (*June 30*). Joins Thomas D'Arcy McGee's delegation to the Maritime colonies in support of Confederation (*July*).

1865: Refuses the offer to join the coalition cabinet as Privy Council president following Brown's resignation (*December 27*).

1866: Becomes a Major in Lambton's 27th Battalion Volunteer Infantry, which is preparing for possible attacks by the Fenians (*Spring*). His brother Hope dies of cancer in Sarnia (*June 2*).

1867: Attends the Reform convention in Toronto (*June 27*). Participates in the first Dominion Day celebrations in Sarnia (*July 1*). Canada's first federal election; elected as the first MP for Lambton, defeating Conservative banker Alexander Vidal by 688 votes. Sits in opposition with the leaderless Reformers (*August*). Recommends the creation of official reports of the Commons debates (*December 4*); idea is defeated.

1870: Visits the Maritimes to strengthen ties with the East Coast Liberals (*July*).

1871: Elected to the Ontario legislature for Middlesex West riding (*March 21*). Founds the Isolated Risk Fire Insurance Company (later Sovereign Fire Insurance) in Toronto with partners George Brown, Edward Blake, Alexander Campbell and others; becomes its first president (*July*). Becomes Treasurer of Ontario in Edward Blake's provincial government (*December 20*).

1872: Wins the by-election in Middlesex West by acclamation for his provincial cabinet seat (*January 5*). Introduces his first provincial budget (*February*). The Blake government in Ontario introduces legislation to abolish dual representation in both the federal and provincial parliaments (*February*). Becomes acting Ontario premier while Blake visits England (*February-October*). Debates with Macdonald in Sarnia (*August 21*). Canada's second federal election: re-elected in Lambton, again defeating Vidal; Liberals lose again to Macdonald's Conservatives (*September*). Resigns as Ontario Treasurer in favour of sitting only in the federal House (*October 25*). Daughter Mary marries Rev. John Thompson of Sarnia (*November*).

1873: Becomes leader of the Liberal Party – and by default Canada's first official Leader of the Opposition – following a vote of confidence in caucus (*March 5*). Two Conservative MPs indicate they will vote with the Liberals in a non-confidence vote over the Pacific Scandal (*November 4*). Asked by Governor General Lord Dufferin to form a government after Macdonald resigns (*November 5*). **Mackenzie government (1873-1878).** Becomes the second Prime Minister of Canada, and the third Public Works minister; prorogues the Second Session, Second Parliament (*November 7*). Steps down from his role as a Major in the volunteer infantry.

Secret staircase

As Minister of Public Works as well as Prime Minister, Mackenzie was able to indulge his stonemason expertise during renovations to the Parliament Buildings. He drew up plans for a hidden circular stairway to the grounds outside his West Block office. It was to provide his escape route when avoiding patronage seekers waiting in his outer office. Ninety years later, Pierre Trudeau used the same Mackenzie Tower concealed staircase to evade the media on his way to Rideau Hall to ask the Governor General to dissolve Parliament.

1874: After dissolving the Second Parliament, calls an election, which becomes Canada's shortest campaign at 20 days (*January 7*). Canada's third federal election: re-elected in Lambton by acclamation; his Liberal government is elected with a majority (*January 22*); it's the first federal election held on a single day. His request to appoint six additional Senators to offset the Conservative majority in the upper house is denied by the Queen (*January 26*). Becomes a grandfather after his daughter Mary gives birth to a daughter, Helen (*January 31*). Accepts Blake's resignation as Minister Without Portfolio who now sits as an independent member; Blake feels he should be Prime Minister instead of Mackenzie (*February 13*). Appoints George Brown to the British team in Washington discussing a possible reciprocity treaty with the U.S. (*February 26*). Third Parliament opens; nominates Timothy Anglin to be the second Speaker of the House (*March 26*). Louis Riel, recently elected to Parliament, turns up in Ottawa to sign the MPs roll then slips away before being detected (*March 30*). Riel is formally expelled from the House of Commons (*April 9*). Hansard begins to keep a record of Parliamentary sessions (*April 16*). Offers British Columbia financing for a railway between Esquimalt and Nanaimo in lieu of the 10-year guarantee for an intercontinental railway (*May*). The Dominion Elections Act formally enshrines single-day federal elections and the secret ballot (*May 26*). His Ottawa home at Kent and Wellington is destroyed by fire (*June*); rents Cliffside house (now the site of the Supreme Court). Arthur Meighen, Canada's ninth Prime Minister, is born in Anderson, Ont. (*June 16*). Forced to raise the protective tariff from 15% to 17.5% because of the economic depression. Riel is returned by acclamation in a Provencher by-election (*September 3*). Treaty #4 is concluded with the Cree and Chippewa (Salteaux) in the Qu'Appelle River Valley area who cede most of southern Saskatchewan (*September 14*). Blake criticizes Liberal policies in a speech in Aurora, Ont. (*October 3*); his comments come shortly after an unsuccessful attempt to convince Mackenzie to step down in his favour. William Lyon Mackenzie King, Canada's 10th Prime Minister, is born in Berlin (Kitchener), Ont. (*December 17*).

1875: Dufferin grants Riel amnesty without government approval (*January*). Mackenzie introduces a motion of amnesty for participants in the Red River uprising, providing that Riel and Ambroise Lépine accept a five-year exile (*February 10*). A bill is introduced to create a Supreme Court of Canada (*February 23*). Takes a tentative step to start the transcontinental railway by awarding a contract to build a railway 100 km west from Prince Arthur (Thunder Bay), Ont. (*April 3*). Appoints Blake as Justice minister (*May 19*). Offers to buy the remainder of the North-West Territories from the Hudson's Bay Company (*June 25*). Visits England, France and Scotland; sees his birthplace at Logierait, Scotland (*Summer*). Treaty #5 is concluded with the Saulteaux and Swampy Cree who cede the area around Lake Winnipeg (*September 24*). Appoints Ontario Chief Justice William B. Richards as the first Chief Justice of Canada (*October 8*). Visits New York City for medical advice on his failing health, then tours the Maritimes and Quebec (*October*).

Declines three offers of knighthood

Three times Mackenzie was offered a knighthood by Queen Victoria and three times he turned it down. His working-class pride meant he was the only Prime Minister of the first eight to go without 'Sir' in front of his name. The first overture was in 1877 along with Edward Blake. Both refused. Two years later, he again said no, and yet again in 1881. Nevertheless, he recommended George Brown for a knighthood. Brown declined.

1876: The North-West Territories Act establishes a territorial council and the District of Keewatin (*April 12*). The Indian Act is adopted, consolidating power under the Department of Indian Affairs (*April 15*). Military College of Canada opens in Kingston, Ont., with government support (*June 1*); two years later, Queen Victoria authorizes the addition of 'Royal' to the name. Intercolonial Railway officially opens from Quebec to Halifax (*July 1*); cost of the Confederation project is $34 million. Treaty #6 is signed with the Cree who cede what is today central Saskatchewan and Alberta (*September 9*). Prevents Dufferin from sending a report to Britain asking for Imperial assistance in resolving delays in building a railway to British Columbia (*November 18*).

1877: Prayers are introduced into the House of Commons (*February 19*). Refuses a knighthood, as does Blake (*May 17*). Agrees to allow experimental telephones to be installed between his West Block office and Rideau Hall (*July 17*). David Mills (Interior) visits Washington to discuss the implications of Sitting Bull's move to Canada; it is the first time Canada and the U.S. negotiate directly (*August*). Treaty #7 is concluded with the Blackfoot; Chief Crowfoot cedes claim to lands between the Cypress Hills and the Rocky Mountains: it is the last major treaty between western First Nations and the federal government (*September 22*). The first spike of the Canadian Pacific Railway is driven at Callander Station (now Bonfield), Ont. (*September 29*). Appoints Wilfrid Laurier to cabinet as Inland Revenue minister (*October 8*). The Fisheries Commission, meeting in Halifax, awards Canada $5.5 million for American rights in Canadian waters (*November 27*).

1878: Britain gives Canada the right to play a role in negotiated British treaties (*January 22*). His appointee as Lieutenant-Governor of Quebec, Luc Letellier du St. Just, dismisses Premier Charles Boucher de Boucherville, for opening the legislature without his consultation (*March 3*). A bill is passed clarifying Canada's sovereignty over the Arctic Islands (*May 1*). The Scott Act establishes the ability of municipalities to decide whether or not they wish to be alcohol-free (*May 10*). The government chooses a western route for the transcontinental railway to run along the Fraser River to Burrard Inlet (*July 12*). Appoints John McDougall as Canada's first auditor general (*August 2*). The British Columbia legislature passes a resolution threatening secession if Ottawa doesn't start the transcontinental railway by May 1879 (*August 9*). Canada's fourth federal election: re-elected in Lambton defeating J.A. Mackenzie by 146 votes; his government is defeated by the Conservatives; it is the first federal election to use the secret ballot (*September 17*). Announces the appointment of the Marquess of Lorne, Queen Victoria's son-in-law, as Governor General (*October 5*). Resigns as Prime Minister and Public Works minister (*October 8*). **Mackenzie government ends.** Moves to Toronto (*November*).

1879: Enters a well-publicized curling match in Ottawa against Governor General Lord Lorne (*March*). Isolated Risk Fire Insurance Company, of which he is president, changes its name to Sovereign Fire Insurance Company, reflecting an expansion of the business to avoid the unprofitability of isolated risk coverage (*April*). Refuses a knighthood for a second time (*May 24*).

1880: Reluctantly resigns as leader of the Liberal Party and Leader of the Opposition (*April 27*); refuses to sit in the Liberal caucus.

1881: Becomes the first president of the North American Life Insurance Company (now part of Manulife) in Toronto (*January*); holds the position until his death. Rejects a knighthood for a third time (*April 26*). Visits England, France, Switzerland, Germany, Belgium and Scotland (*May-September*). Refuses a trusteeship on CPR's board of directors (*September 7*).

1882: Publishes *The Life and Speeches of the Hon. George Brown*. Suffers a stroke while campaigning north of Toronto (*June 6*). Canada's fifth federal election; elected MP for York East, even though bedridden, defeating incumbent Conservative MP Alfred Boultbee by 108 votes (*June 20*). Visits Maine to restore his health (*August*).

1883: Visits Italy, England and Scotland (*May-September*).

1884: Visits western Canada (*August-September*).

1885: His cousin is killed in the Battle of Duck Lake, the opening skirmish of the North-West Rebellion (*March 26*).

1886: Buys a new house in Toronto on Wellesley Street between Yonge Street and Queen's Park. Visits Scotland (*May-September*).

1887: Urged to run for re-election even though in poor health (*January*). Canada's sixth federal election: re-elected MP for York East, again defeating Boultbee (*February 22*).

1891: Canada's seventh federal election: re-elected MP for York East, even though frail and barely able to talk, or to undertake any direct campaigning himself; de-feats Independent Conservative candidate William MacLean by 26 votes. (*March 5*).

1892: Slips and falls in front of his Toronto home (*February 2*). Dies on Easter morn-ing in Toronto (*April 17*). Funeral service at Jarvis Street Baptist Church in Toronto (*April 20*). Funeral service at St. Andrew's Presbyterian Church in Sarnia and burial at Lakeview Cemetery (*April 21*).

Books about Mackenzie

- **1892**: William Buckingham & George W. Ross; *The Hon. Alexander Mackenzie: His Life and Times* (Dent)
- **1930**: Thomas Marquis; *Hon. Alexander Mackenzie* (Ryerson)
- **1960**: Dale C. Thomson: *Alexander Mackenzie: Clear Grit* (Macmillan)

3

Sir John J.C. Abbott

The Unwilling Prime Minister

With Macdonald's death in 1891, the Conservatives were rudderless. John J.C. Abbott was the first coaxed to step up. He was one of two Senators to lead the country during this 'caretakers' period. Abbott never wanted the job and although Canadians had largely forgiven his part in the Pacific Scandal, from the moment he took office, he sought a way to leave it. Declining health gave him that chance after barely a year and a half in charge. However much he loathed the job, it didn't hamper his partisan political skills. During his short term, Abbott helped his party win 42 by-elections.

Abbott the Politician

Prime Minister of Canada: June 16, 1891 – November 24, 1892
Length of term: 1 year, 5 months, 4 days
Parliament as Prime Minister: Seventh
Age on entering office: 70
Political party: Liberal-Conservative
Leader of party: June 16, 1891 – November 24, 1892
Member of Parliament: July 1, 1867 – October 6, 1874; August 17, 1881 – February 22, 1887
Riding represented: Argenteuil (Que.) – 1867-1874, 1881-1887
Member of the Senate: May 12, 1887 – October 30, 1893 (for Quebec)
Cabinet portfolios: Minister Without Portfolio (1887-1891); Privy Council President (1891-1892)
Other political posts: Canada Assembly member (1860-1867); Solicitor General, Canada East (1862-1863); Mayor of Montreal (1887-1888); Leader of the Government in Senate (1887-1893)
Knighted: May 25, 1892
Titles: Queen's Counsel (1862); Canadian Privy Councillor (1887); Knight Commander of St. Michael & St. George (1892)
Quotes: "I hate politics, and what are considered their appropriate methods. I hate notoriety, public meetings, public speeches, caucuses, and every-

thing that I know of that is apparently the necessary incident of politics – except doing public work to the best of my ability" (written 12 days before he became Prime Minister); "I am here because I am not particularly obnoxious to anybody." (self-assessment about being chosen by caucus to succeed Macdonald)

Lived after term: 11 months

ABBOTT THE MAN

Name: John Joseph Caldwell Abbott

Born: March 12, 1821, St. Andrews, Lower Canada (Saint-André-d'Argenteuil, Quebec)

Ancestry: English

Religion: Anglican

Education: B.C.L. [Bachelor of Civil Law] (University of McGill College, 1854); D.C.L. [Doctorate of Civil Law] (McGill, 1867)

Nicknames: Great Poo-Bah; Lord High Everything Else; Sir John the Second

Military service: Ensign and Captain in Montreal Second Volunteer Regiment (1847-1849, 1849-1860s); created and commanded the Argenteuil Rangers (1862-1884), called out during threatened Fenian invasion (1866)

Occupation: lawyer; professor; businessman

Occupation after term: Senator

Publications: *The Argenteuil Case* (1860); *The Insolvent Act of 1864* (1864)

Appearance: "I would describe him as rather severe looking. He obviously never smiled in his photographs, but I think that was characteristic of most important men of the time, they weren't supposed to smile." (Christopher Plummer describes his great-grandfather in a CPAC documentary); "He had the appearance of being somewhat rumpled, perhaps academic..." (Carmen Miller, assistant history professor at McGill)

Personality: "He had an inherent dislike of publicity and a quiet and retiring nature." (cousin Maude Abbott in *Social History of the Parish of Christ Church, St. Andrews, Quebec*). "To serve a client's interests, he would turn night into day, unfortunately without the compensation of rest when day returned; so the wonder is not that he survived threescore and ten by only two years, but that, in spite of overwork, he reached the allotted term of well preserved old manhood." (former law partner Frederick Terrell in *Chronology of Montreal and Canada from A.D.1752 to A.D. 1893*)

Married: Mary Bethune, July 26, 1849, Christ Church Cathedral, Montreal, Canada East (Quebec)

Age at marriage: 28

Years married: 44

Died: October 30, 1893, Montreal, Quebec

Age at death: 72

Cause of death: stomach cancer

Buried: Mount Royal Cemetery, Montreal, Quebec

Abbott was the:

- Only Prime Minister who was a Canadian mayor (Montreal)

- Only Conservative Prime Minister who was not a member of Toronto's Albany Club (after all, he was a former mayor of Montreal)
- First Prime Minister born in Canada
- First Prime Minister born in Quebec
- First Prime Minister with a university education
- First Prime Minister to be fluent in English and French
- First Prime Minister to serve while sitting in the Senate
- First Prime Minister to serve in both the Senate and the House of Commons
- First Prime Minister to be knighted while in office
- First Prime Minister to marry only once
- First Prime Minister who was wealthy
- First Anglican Prime Minister (although Macdonald attended Anglican services with his wife)
- Second Conservative Prime Minister
- Great Grandfather of Canadian actor Christopher Plummer
- Great Great Grandfather of Canadian actress Amanda Plummer

Abbott's legacy
- Established a Department of Trade and Commerce
- Restored the Conservatives' confidence following Macdonald's death
- Increased the Conservative's majority by 13 seats, by winning 42 of 52 by-elections during his term
- An effective caretaker who cleaned up a backlog of paperwork

Abbott's Family

Abbott's Parents

Father: Joseph Abbott
Born: April 30, 1790, Little Strickland, Westmoreland, England
Arrival in Canada: 1818
Occupation: clergyman; educator; author
Died: January 10, 1862, Montreal, Canada West (Quebec)
Age at death: 71
Note: His brother William succeeded him as the minister at Christ Church in St. Andrews. William's widow, Frances, adopted two of Joseph's grandchildren, one being Dr. Maude Abbott, the renowned congenital heart disease doctor.

Mother: Harriet A. Bradford
Born: October 20, 1800, Woodstock Township, Ulster County, New York
Arrival in Canada: 1805
Married: August 10, 1820, Christ Church, Montreal, Lower Canada (Quebec)
Died: January 21, 1873, Montreal, Quebec
Age at death: 72

Abbott's Brothers & Sisters (9 siblings; John the oldest)

Sister: Jessie Sarah Isabella Abbott (1822-1893), never married

Brother: William Richard 'Dick' Hamilton Abbott (b.1824)
Occupation: farmer; slate quarry manager
Brother: Christopher Charles Abbott (1826-1827), died of measles
Brother: Christopher Charles Abbott (1827-1870), 1 son
Married: Isabella Thomasina Kains
Occupation: lawyer with his brother John at Abbott & Molson in 1850s
Note: Wrote *The Abbotts of Westmoreland.*
Brother: Henry 'Harry' Braithwaite Abbott (1829-1915), 3 children
Married: Marguerite Amelia Sicotte Freer (1868)
Occupation: civil engineer who oversaw the completion of the CPR in B.C.
Note: Abbotsford, B.C., was named in his honour by his friend and early settler, J.C. McClure.
Note: His great-granddaughter Elizabeth Abbott is author of *The Reluctant PM: Notes On the Life of Sir John Abbott, Canada's Third Prime Minister.*
Brother: Frederick Abbott (1831-1831)
Sister: Harriet Elizabeth Abbott (1832-1894), 2 children
Married: John C. King Houghton (lawyer)
Sister: Frances 'Fanny' Anne Abbott (1834-1845)
Brother: Frederick Abbott (1836-1837)

Abbott's Wife

Name: Mary Martha Bethune
Born: October 17, 1824 (on tombstone; some sources say 1823), Montreal, Lower Canada (Quebec)
Father: John Wadden Bethune (clergyman; acting principal of McGill)
Mother: Elizabeth Hallowell
Age at marriage: 25
Died: February 25, 1898, Montreal, Quebec
Age at death: 73
Burial place: Mount Royal Cemetery, Montreal, Quebec
Younger than Abbott: 3 years
Died after Abbott: 4 years
Note: Her grandfather John was also the great-great-grandfather of Norman Bethune, the Canadian physician who worked in the Spanish Civil War and the Chinese Revolution.

Abbott's Children (9 – one died in infancy)

Name: Frances 'Frankie' Maria Abbott
Born: June 17, 1850, Montreal, Canada East (Quebec)
Died: 1925

Name: John 'Jack' Betham Abbott
Born: December 23, 1851, Montreal, Canada East (Quebec)
Married: Lillian D. Young
Occupation: lawyer in father's firm; landscape painter; Director of the Art Association of Montreal (1900-1919)
Died: 1930

Name: William Hamilton Abbott

Born: 1853, Montreal, Canada East (Quebec)
Married: Mary Stukeley Gray (1888) (daughter of John Hamilton Gray, Father of Confederation)
Children: 1 – William Hamilton Jr.
Occupation: manufacturer
Died: 1930
Note: Son William Jr. was awarded the Military Cross in the First World War.

Name: Mary 'Minnie' Isabella Abbott
Born: July 18, 1855, Montreal, Canada East (Quebec)
Married: Rev. Arthur Phillips (1889)
Children: 3 – John A.; Mary; Charles C.
Died: 1932

Name: Henry 'Harry' Abbott
Born: October 5, 1857, Montreal, Canada East (Quebec)
Married: (1) Jane Ratcliffe Liddell (1882); (2) Bertha Pillans Stevenson (1897)
Children: 2
Occupation: lawyer in father's firm
Died: March 5, 1898, Montreal, Quebec

Name: Charles Alfred Abbott
Born: 1859, Montreal, Canada East (Quebec)
Died: 1860, Montreal, Canada East (Quebec)

Name: Alice Elizabeth Abbott
Born: 1861, Montreal, Canada East (Quebec)
Married: Richard Tuson Heneker (1885)
Children: 1 – Dorothy Alice
Died: 1945
Note: Daughter Dorothy wrote *The Seignorial Regime in Canada.*

Name: Arthur Edward Abbott
Born: 1863, Montreal, Canada East (Quebec)
Married: Marian Campbell
Children: 5 – Isabella Mary; John; Elizabeth; Phyllis; Arthur
Died: 1944
Note: Daughter Isabella's son is actor Christopher Plummer.
Note: Son John died of blood poisoning during the First World War.
Note: Daughter Phyllis lost her fiancé when he died in a car accident driving to their wedding.

Name: Harriet 'Baby' Ann Abbott
Born: 1867, Montreal, Quebec
Died: 1955 (never married)

Political Stories

Argenteuil: an election powder keg

Abbott's decision to enter politics by seeking election in his local Argenteuil riding was daring. The incumbent, Sydney Bellingham, had won the seat in 1854 amidst controversy. Accused of hiring Irish construction workers to intimidate French Canadian voters, Bellingham's victory was declared void. He immediately had the French parishes excised from the riding, which helped him win a second election. That too was quashed and he finally won by acclamation in 1856.

In the 1857 election, Abbott lost to Bellingham by 200 votes. His brother Harry was a scrutineer at a polling booth where six Irish brothers voted then hovered around the voting station with whipping sticks to ensure others voted for Bellingham. Abbott contested the result, saying Bellingham had attracted votes from citizens not owning property or living in Argenteuil. Two years later, a legislative committee agreed, giving the seat to Abbott. A few months later, Abbott published *The Argenteuil Election Case*, a 258-page review of the committee's deliberations in which he called for stronger enforcement of the existing election guidelines.

Bellingham was too bitter to contest the 1861 or 1863 elections, and, with Confederation, he opted to seek the Quebec provincial seat, which he won. Abbott now held the federal seat, but with the taint of the Pacific Scandal swirling around him, he managed to win the 1874 election by only four votes. The campaigning tables were turned on him when his challenger, Lemuel Cushing, accused Abbott of voting irregularities. The election was voided, and Cushing won the by-election. That too was declared void and the seat was subsequently won by acclamation by Thomas Christie.

Abbott was back for the 1878 election to challenge Christie. He lost, but, no surprise, contested the results. The election was declared void and Abbott beat Christie in the 1880 by-election. He was accused of bribing election officials and that vote too was declared void. However, Abbott took the seat by acclamation in the 1881 by-election. His last election fight never occurred when he retained the seat by acclamation in the 1882 federal vote. In fact, there were no contested results in Argenteuil (or voided elections) after 1881.

The Pacific Scandal's money handler

As solicitor to the Canada Pacific Railway that was looking for government approval to lay tracks to British Columbia, Abbott played a direct role in making corporate political contributions to Macdonald's Liberal-Conservative election campaign. The fact that Abbott was a Liberal-Conservative MP and that he was aware most of the money was coming from the company's American partners – against Macdonald's express wishes – put him in an awkward position.

When that position became public in April 1873 after the election, Abbott found himself in the middle of the firestorm. The Liberal opposition kept pounding away at the government, calling for an inquiry. When newspapers published the desperate telegram Macdonald sent to Abbott six days before the election ("I must have another $10,000. Will be the last time of calling. Do not fail me. Answer today."), the government was forced to call a Royal Commission.

The smoking-gun telegram was among papers stolen from Abbott's Montreal law office and copied. The thief, George Norris, was a law student articling with Abbott. He discovered there was better money to be made selling the incriminating information to the newspapers. About 130 years later, the *McGill News* named Norris "McGill's most influential law student."

The Royal Commission's report implicated Macdonald and he desperately tried to debate his way out of the morass in the House. It wasn't enough; the government fell. Abbott was now seeking re-election with the taint of scandal clinging to his coattails. He won the 1874 election in Argenteuil by four votes, but had the seat taken away when the results were challenged. It was seven years before he was able to regain the seat – doing it in the Argenteuil way: battling it out in a series of challenges and revotes.

A reluctant leader

When Macdonald died on June 6, 1891, the Conservatives faced a dilemma. As the party in power, it was the first Canadian government that needed to determine how to select a new Prime Minister. The official choice rested with the Governor General, Lord Stanley, but he left it to the politicians to sort it out before stepping in.

The obvious choice was Sir John Thompson, the able Justice minister. But the Conservative caucus knew, just as Macdonald did, that Ontario Protestants would never accept a convert (the word used in those days was 'pervert') to Roman Catholicism as the country's leader. When Stanley summoned Thompson to offer him the position, Thompson was smart enough to tactfully decline. Instead, he suggested Abbott, a man 23 years older, for the job.

Abbott probably saw this coming. He clearly did not want the job, but he also recognized that because "I am not particularly obnoxious to anybody" he was an ideal compromise. So, with reluctance, he accepted the position, and then went to work finding a way to extricate himself from it.

The answer turned out to be his health. Not well when he became Prime Minister, he learned he had stomach cancer after about a year in office. His doctors insisted that he rest to recover from exhaustion. He sailed for England to seek medical advice and, while there, wrote his letter of resignation. He urged Thompson, his Justice minister, to make the letter public as soon as it was convenient. That happened a month later. By this time, the country seemed better reconciled to accepting Thompson as the obvious leader, religious conversion notwithstanding.

Governing from the Senate

Abbott may have become Prime Minister in name, but it was Sir John Thompson, his Justice minister who acted the part. As Conservative House Leader, Thompson sat in the Prime Minister's chair (eventually) and conducted the government's day-to-day business. As a member of the Senate, Abbott was not an elected representative and did not have a seat in the House of Commons. In fact, he never used the Prime Minister's private office near the Commons.

Abbott's term had no sooner started than several Conservative MPs were on the defensive, facing charges of corruption and favouritism. Although he played a role in defusing the crisis, it was Thompson who traded daily barbs with the opposition. It was a role that Abbott, 70 years old and in declining health, was incapable of carrying out, even if he had been able to sit in the House.

A looming recession and the early twitches of the Manitoba schools question were other issues debated by Thompson and observed by Abbott. With Macdonald gone, factions within the Conservative and Liberal-Conservative ranks were beginning to flex their muscles. Despite being free from the daily fray in the House, Abbott was exhausted by the pressures of placating his party's divergent interests. When he left for England to try and recover his health, his last four months in office were completely turned over to Thompson.

Abbott resigned as Prime Minister in 1892, but he continued to serve as Government Leader of the Senate until his death the following year.

PERSONAL STORIES

Businessman and hobbyist

Abbott worked hard and played hard. As the top commercial lawyer in Canada, he sat on numerous boards and was a friend and advisor to Montreal's elite families, including the Molsons and Redpaths. His particular passion was railways and he bought and sold several of them. He survived the Pacific Scandal that sank the Canada Pacific Railway, and helped to bring about its successor, the slightly renamed Canadian Pacific Railway.

In addition to serving as president of the Citizens Insurance Company, the Canadian Central Railway and the Fraser Institute, Abbott was a founder of Montreal's Royal Victoria Hospital, the Montreal Museum of Fine Arts, and the Canadian Society for the Prevention of Cruelty to Animals. All of this was juggled alongside his 23 years as Dean of Law at McGill University and two years as Montreal's mayor. In politics, he was a member of the legislature for 21 years and Senate leader for six years.

He pursued his leisure interests, especially fishing, farming and raising orchids, with equal vigour. Abbott purchased a property in Quebec with its own river to ensure a reliable supply of salmon awaited him. On one fishing trip, his steam boat swamped near Anticosti Island in the St. Lawrence River. The island was owned by the eccentric French chocolate maker, Henri Menier, who happily encouraged Abbott's band of fishermen to stay with him until their boat was repaired.

Abbott's knowledge of animal husbandry nudged him into importing the first European Guernsey cattle to Canada. His care in breeding orchids made him one of the finest collectors in the country.

It's small wonder he was reluctant to take on the burden of being Prime Minister.

Lady Mary Abbott

She wasn't Canada's first lady long enough to make much impact on Canadians. As the wife of a successful Montreal lawyer-businessman, Mary Abbott spent much of her time tucked away at Boisbriant, the family estate on the west tip of the island of Montreal.

It was family that kept her occupied; she had eight children of her own and grew up with eight siblings. Born in 1824 (although some sources indicate it may have been 1823), Mary Martha Bethune was the daughter of Rev. John Bethune, the minister of

Montreal's Christ Church who went on to become principal of the University of McGill College.

Mary met Abbott through church. As a law student at McGill, he practised reading law with her brother, Strachan. When he became deputy registrar of McGill, Mary's father was not only his boss, but also his defender when Abbott's accounting practices were called into question.

Following their marriage at Christ Church in 1849, Mary and John became members of Montreal's elite, living comfortably at the foot of the mountain in a neighbourhood of imposing mansions. Two of Mary's daughters, Frankie and Baby, never left home, providing Mary with constant company while her husband's growing political commitments kept him increasingly in Ottawa. She also sang and played piano.

When Abbott became Prime Minister, the family rented Earnscliffe from Macdonald's widow. But the stay was short. Abbott resigned as Prime Minister after 17 months and died in 1893. Mary died in Montreal four years later.

Abbott's Timeline

1821: Born in Christ Church Anglican rectory in St. Andrews (Saint-André-d'Argenteuil), Lower Canada (Quebec); middle names were for his father Joseph and the delivering doctor, Hugh Caldwell (*March 12*). Christened in Christ Church, St. Andrews (*March 13*).

1822: His doctor Hugh Caldwell returns the naming favour by calling his first daughter Agnes Abbott Caldwell.

1825: Moves with family 160 km east to Yamaska Mountain where his father takes charge of the mission (*April*).

1826: Partly home tutored by his father who possesses a large personal library. Attends Yamaska school where the schoolteacher is his uncle, Charles Bradford (who later has a son named John Abbott Bradford). His brother Christopher is born at Yamaska, but dies of measles a year later.

1827: A second brother named Christopher is born at Yamaska (*June 18*).

1829: His brother Harry is born at Yamaska (*June 14*). His father Joseph attends the founding meeting of the Governors for McGill College in Montreal (*June 29*).

1830: Yamaska Mountain is renamed Abbottsford by his father, for the Abbott and Bradford families.

1831: His brother Frederick is born in Abbottsford (*March 14*); dies in September. His father Joseph is transferred to the mission in Grenville and serves as chaplain to the builders of the Grenville Canal between the St. Lawrence and Ottawa rivers (*June*). Relocates with family to St. Andrews while a house is built for them in Grenville. Attends St. Andrew's Academy in the old rectory (the family's former home) (*September*).

1832: Moves with family from St. Andrews to Grenville (*December*).

1833: Attends the Wanless Academy in Carillon, 40 km east of Grenville.

1834: Pulled out of school along with his brothers when the church cut his father's salary.

1837: His father Joseph takes part in the Battle of St. Eustache north of Montreal during the Rebellion of 1837 (*December 14*); armed only with a walking stick.

1838: Sails to Montreal with Archibald Kains to his first job; passes Fort Senneville at the west end of Montreal Island and boasts he will one day build his home there; does exactly that 27 years later. Works at Archibald Laurie & Company dry goods store in Montreal. Becomes ill after a few months from the foul air created by open sewage and returns home.

1839: Works for C. & J. McDonald merchants in Gananoque, Upper Canada (Ont.) for four years.

1843: Enrols at the University of McGill College in Montreal as one of the first three Arts students, one week after the official opening (*September*). Works as a deputy for his father who is McGill's bursar and Board of Governors secretary (*September*). Reads law with Strachan Bethune, son of McGill principal John Bethune and brother of Mary.

1844: Leaves McGill and finds work at a general store in Deseronto, Ont., and as a grain buyer in Oshawa (*Summer*).

1845: Returns to Montreal where the Abbott family now lives. His father takes on added duties as McGill's chaplain and first librarian. Accused, along with his father, of irregular accounting practices at McGill. Defended by Bethune, the college principal. Articles with Montreal law firm Meredith & Bethune.

1846: Begins reading law with Christopher Dunkin, the deputy provincial secretary for Canada East.

1847: Initiated as a freemason into St Paul's Lodge in Montreal (*January 26*); resigns and rejoins a few years later. Becomes an ensign in the 2nd Volunteer Regiment. Admitted to the bar (*October 25*). Buys stock in the Carillon and Grenville Railway, along with his father and brother Harry.

1848: Joins the law firm of William Badgely, Attorney General of Canada East and McGill's first law professor, as a partner; it becomes Badgley & Abbott. Studies vocal music with his sister Harriet and sings in the Christ Church choir; also directs a six-person choir at Christ Church.

Signing the Annexation Manifesto

Eighteen years before Confederation, a group of Montreal businessmen crafted a plea to citizens to support them in combating "the number and magnitude of the evils that afflict our country." One of the more than 300 signatories was lawyer John Abbott. It was a benefit-to-business solution that called for tariffs, free trade and a fond hope that the United States might accept the neighbouring British colonies into the fold. His signature cost him his commission in the local militia. While he would regain it before too long, his support for annexation caused him eternal embarrassment as he rose in Canadian business and politics.

1849: Marries Mary Martha Bethune at Christ Church in Montreal (*July 26*); they live with his parents. Signs the Annexation Manifesto, urging "a friendly and peaceful separation from the British connection and a union with the great North American confederacy of sovereign states." (*October 11*). Loses his commission with the 2nd Volunteer Regiment after signing the Manifesto; reinstated soon after.

1850: His first child Frances 'Frankie' Maria is born in Montreal (*June 17*).

1851: His first son John 'Jack' Betham is born in Montreal (*December 23*); middle name is from family friends living in England.

1852: Becomes Captain of the 4th Battalion of the 2nd Volunteer Regiment. His younger brother Christopher joins the law firm. Buys 70,000 acres of land near a slate quarry in Eastern Townships, with brothers Harry and Christopher.

1853: His second son William Hamilton is born in Montreal. Buys the slate quarry next to his Eastern Townships property; his brother Richard becomes the quarry manager. Begins lecturing in law at McGill; the Dean (Badgley) arranges for him to acquire a degree to teach. Moves into a semi-detached house on Saint Catherine Street; his parents live in the adjacent half (*October*).

1854: Receives his Bachelor of Civil Law degree from McGill. Given fishing rights over the Great Wacheeshoo River, 280 km east of Sept Iles; later, he and brothers Harry and Christopher buy a fishing schooner *Viking* to take them there. Becomes solicitor of the Carillon and Grenville railway and later becomes president.

1855: Assumes leadership of the law firm when Badgley is appointed to the Bench. Also succeeds Badgley as a Professor of Commercial and Criminal Law at McGill, until 1876. His second daughter Mary 'Minnie' Isabella is born in Montreal (*July 18*). Hires J.C. Baker as his law partner and the firm becomes Abbott & Baker.

1856: Becomes Dean of the Faculty of Law at McGill, until 1880.

1857: His brother Christopher leaves the law firm. Drops Criminal Law from his teaching duties to focus on Commercial Law. His third son Henry 'Harry' is born in Montreal (*October 5*). Runs for a seat in the Canada Assembly as the Liberal candidate in Argenteuil, losing against incumbent Sydney Bellingham (*December*).

1858: Contests the election results; an investigation takes place.

1859: Buys the troubled Montreal and Bytown Railway at a sheriff's sale for $21,000 (*January*). His third son Alfred is born in Montreal. Baker leaves the law firm and S.W. Dorman becomes his partner, creating Abbott & Dorman.

1860: Gains the Argenteuil seat following a two-year investigation into the 1857 election (*March 12*). Publishes *The Argenteuil Election Case* about his legal efforts to win the Argenteuil riding. Becomes a founding member of the Art Association of Montreal, now the Montreal Museum of Fine Arts. His year-old son Alfred dies.

1861: Becomes Deputy Grand Master of the Orange Order in Quebec. His third daughter Alice is born in Montreal. Re-elected in Argenteuil (*July*). Becomes president of the Canada Central Railway, chartered to build a railway from Quebec to Lake Huron. Meets first-year McGill law student Wilfrid Laurier (*Fall*).

1862: His father Joseph dies in Montreal (*January 2*). Organizes and commands the 11th Battalion of the Argenteuil Rangers, a cavalry militia battalion, following the Trent Affair between Britain and the U.S. (*Winter*). Becomes a Queen's Counsel. Becomes Solicitor General in the Sandfield Macdonald–Sicotte government (*May 24*).

1863: Carries on as Solicitor General in the Sandfield Macdonald-Dorion govern-ment (*March*). Resigns as Solicitor General after the defeat of the government (*May 30*). Re-elected in Argenteuil to the last assembly of the United Canadas (*July*). His youngest son Arthur is born in Montreal. Joins Louis-Victor Sicotte in opposing the new Sandfield Macdonald–Dorion ministry; begins to lean towards the Conservatives.

1864: Helps create the Insolvent Act passed by the Assembly (*June 30*). Sells the Montreal and Bytown Railway for a healthy profit. Sells his interest in the Carillon and Grenville Railway. Publishes the *Insolvent Act of 1864*, a primer on interpreting the legislation. Leaves Abbott & Dorman to set up his own firm, which specializes in commercial law related to bankruptcies. Defends 14 U.S. Confederate soldiers who crossed into St. Albans, Vermont, kidnapped several officials and stole $200,000 (*November*); succeeds in having them defined as soldiers committing an act of war, not criminals; they're set free, but rearrested following a backlash in the U.S. Succeeds in having the St. Albans case dropped on the grounds that a magistrate should not be allowed to handle an extradition case (*December*).

1865: Openly joins the Conservatives in support of Confederation. Buys the site of old Fort Senneville, on the west end of the Island of Montreal, to build a summer residence; eventually acquires 300 acres, calling the property Boisbriant. His brother Christopher buys a neighbouring property soon after.

1866: The Argenteuil Rangers battalion is sent to Cornwall, Ont., to repel a possible Fenian invasion (*April*); it actually shares a train with the Fenians, but there is no confrontation. Hires Edward Carter as his law partner, forming Abbott & Carter; the partnership dissolves within a year. His resolution calling on the Confederation delegates to protect the boundaries of the 12 English ridings in Quebec is endorsed by Alexander T. Galt and accepted at the London Conference as part of Article 80 of the British North America Act (*December*).

1867: Receives his Doctorate of Civil Law degree from McGill University, a designation automatically available without examination to any graduate 12 years after receiving a BCL degree. Canada's first federal election: elected as the first MP for Argenteuil riding, running as a Conservative for the first time and beating Benjamin Hutchins by 98 votes. (*August*). Elected chair of the House of Commons Banking Committee; serves until 1874.

Ties to McGill

Abbott's enrolment as one of McGill University's first arts students in 1843 marked the start of a relationship that lasted nearly a half-century. It's no surprise he went to McGill. His father was the bursar and Abbott assisted him part-time as well as sharing living quarters in the arts building. What was a surprise was being accused, along with his father, of improper accounting practices. It didn't dull the bond. Abbott went on to marry Principal John Bethune's daughter Mary, and served as a law lecturer (1853-1855), professor (1855-1876) and dean (1856-1880) before becoming a board governor in 1881. His close ties meant he was able to acquire bachelor and doctoral civil law degrees with minimum effort. Today's John Abbott CEGEP College in Montreal sits on land owned by McGill.

1868: His brother Harry marries Marguerite Amélie Sicotte, daughter of the former Joint Premier of the Canadas Louis-Victor Sicotte. Recommends the appointment of a commission to update his Insolvent Act of 1864.

1869: Helps found the Protestant Institution for Deaf-Mutes and for the Blind in Montreal. Becomes a founder of the Canadian Society for the Prevention of Cruelty to Animals. His brother Christopher rejoins his law practice.

1870: Christopher drowns in front of their homes at Boisbriant (*June 19*). Hires Melbourne M. Tait, and Ivan Wotherspoon to replace his brother; the latter opens a satellite law office in Ontario.

1871: Persuades his client, ship owner Sir Hugh Allan, to consider undertaking the project to build a transcontinental railway.

1872: Hires Fred Terrill to join Abbott, Tait & Wotherspoon as a partner; Terrill leaves within a year to set up his own practice. Unsuccessful in his attempts to forge a merger of the competing transcontinental railway proposals from Hugh Allan and Senator David MacPherson; Allan prefers to continue separately with quiet backing from the U.S. Witnesses Sir Georges-Étienne Cartier (Militia & Defence) asking Allan to contribute to the Conservative election campaign (*July 30*). Gives Hector-Louis Langevin (Public Works) $10,000 using Canada Pacific Railway money (*August 10*). Gives the Montreal Central Committee of Conservatives $20,000 and Macdonald $10,000 (*August 26*). Canada's second federal election: re-elected in Argenteuil by acclamation (*October 12*). Drafts the charter of the Canada Pacific Railway Company and becomes a provisional director (*October 15*).

1873: His mother Harriet dies in Montreal (*January 21*). Sails for England with Allan to seek money for the construction of the Canada Pacific Railway (*February*). Less able to attract British money after Liberal MP Lucius Huntington reveals American involvement in the railway project and the CPR's contributions to the Conservative election campaign (*April 2*); it becomes known as the Pacific Scandal. Canadian newspapers publish the telegram Macdonald sent to him asking for campaign money (*July*). On a Gaspé fishing holiday, uses one of the first split-cane fishing rods ever made, given to him by the inventor.

1874: Canada's third federal election: re-elected in Argenteuil by four votes over Lemuel Cushing (Liberal) (*January 22*). His son John joins his law firm. Removed from the board of Canada Central Railway. Unseated in Argenteuil by a petition originated by Dr. Thomas Christie (*October*). He does not seek re-election and Cushing wins the seat (*October 6*). This election, too, is declared void and Christie runs, winning the seat by acclamation (*December 31*).

1875: Joins his brother Harry in England to find funding for a new railway project; the Grand Trunk Railway thwarts their plans.

1876: Stops teaching at McGill but continues as Dean of Law.

1878: Begins importing Guernsey cattle, possibly the first brought to Canada, for his Boisbriant estate. A second son, Henry, joins his law firm. Canada's fourth federal election: defeated by 89 votes in his bid for re-election in Argenteuil against incumbent Christie (*September 17*); contests the results.

1879: Sails to England with Langevin (Public Works) to successfully secure Brit-ain's consent for the dismissal of Luc Letellier de St. Just as Quebec's Lieutenant-Governor; meets Queen Victoria during his stay in London.

1880: Results of the 1878 Argenteuil election are declared void (*January 9*). Wins the Argenteuil by-election against Christie by 67 votes (*February 12*), but the results are again declared void. Helps to attract George Stephen and Donald Smith as investors in the reconstituted transcontinental railway project, now called the Canadian Pacific Railway; becomes the railway's solicitor and draws up the contract (*October 21*). Retires as McGill's Dean of Law and is made a professor emeritus. Wotherspoon leaves the law firm, now called Abbott, Tait & Abbotts.

1881: Sails to England with Stephen and others to raise funds for the CPR (*February*). Wins the second Argenteuil by-election, by acclamation (*August 17*). Appointed to the Board of Governors of McGill University. Introduces the Insolvent Act of 1881 to replace the acts of 1864 and 1869.

1882: Moves his family to a larger house on Sherbrooke Street in Montreal; it includes a conservatory where he raises orchids. Canada's fifth federal election: re-elected by acclamation in Argenteuil (*June 20*).

1883: Appointed to three parliamentary committees: Banking and Commerce; Privileges and Elections; and Railways, Canals and Telegraphs (*February 8*).

1884: Sails to England with Stephen again to raise funds for the CPR. Steps down as commander of the Argenteuil Rangers.

1885: Becomes chair of the banking and commerce committee (*January 29*). Elected to the Canadian Pacific Railway board of directors. Becomes founder and president-for-life of the Fraser Institute: a free library, museum and art gallery in Montreal (*October 15*). Not present for the driving of the CPR's last spike at Craigellachie, B.C., but his brother Harry, a CPR executive, is (*November 7*).

1886: Appointed president of the Dominion Cartridge Company in Argenteuil; holds the position for two years. Also becomes president of Citizen's Insurance and the Canada Investment Company. Elected chairman of Guardian Fire & Life Insurance. Sons John and Harry take over the family law firm. Post office begins spelling Abbottsford, Que., with only one 't': Abbotsford; the new spelling sticks.

1887: Does not seek re-election to the House of Commons and is appointed to the Senate by Macdonald. (*February 22*). Elected Mayor of Montreal. Appointed Government Leader in the Senate (*May 12*). Becomes Minister Without Portfolio in Macdonald's cabinet (*May 13*). Resigns as solicitor of the CPR. Retires from his law practice. Becomes the first chairman of the proposed Royal Victoria Hospital in Montreal; it opens two months after his death.

1888: Re-elected as Montreal's mayor by acclamation, after accepting a request signed by every councillor to stand for a second term. Re-elected as a CPR director.

1889: Declines a request, signed by most Montreal council members, to run for a third term as mayor. Tells the Senate he fears a U.S. trade agreement could result in annexation – a complete reversal of his support for the Annexation Manifesto 40 years earlier (*March 15*). Encourages his cousin Maude Abbott who is pushing for women's rights at McGill. Visits England to discuss trade relations with Australasia and the Far East (*Summer*).

1891: Macdonald offers him the Privy Council President position in cabinet, seeing him as a possible successor; although not appointed, Abbott carries out the work (*May*). Macdonald tells Thompson (Justice) "When I am gone, you will have to rally around Abbott. He is your only man" (*May 20*). Macdonald changes his mind, telling Thompson that Abbott is "too damn selfish" to be leader; later in the day he has a massive stroke paralyzing his left side (*May 27*). Macdonald dies without indicating who should succeed him (*June 6*). Abbott named Macdonald's successor shortly after Thompson turns it down (*June 12*). Asks Macdonald's secretary Joseph Pope to remain and help with the transition (*June 14*). Unable to convince Quebec cabinet ministers to accept Ontario Conservative William Meredith as a cabinet member, creating fissures in cabinet solidarity (*June*). **Abbott's government (1891-1892).** Resigns as Minister Without Portfolio to become Canada's third Prime Minister and 15th Privy Council President (*June 16*). Unable to sit in the House of Commons as a Senator; appoints Thompson (Justice) as House leader. Retains all of Macdonald's cabinet ministers (*June 16*). Resigns as CPR solicitor and sells his CPR stock (*June*). Insists that Thompson use Macdonald's office near the House of Commons (*June*); Thompson declines but later relents. The Dominion Bank Act comes into effect (*July 1*). Rents Earnscliffe from Macdonald's widow who moves temporarily to Banff (*July*). Hector-Louis Langevin (Public Works) resigns in the face of charges that he and MP Thomas McGreevy received kickbacks at the end of Macdonald's administration (*August 11*). A parliamentary committee exonerates Langevin of corruption charges (*September 16*). Abbott supports Macdonald's opinion that the courts should decide the Manitoba schools question (*September 24*). McGreevy is expelled from the House of because of corruption charges (*September 29*); he is later sent to prison. The Supreme Court overturns the Manitoba court's decision denying guaranteed access to Catholic schools in the new provincial school system (*October 28*); Manitoba appeals to Britian's Imperial Privy Council.

1892: Canada begins using the red ensign as its official flag (*February 2*). George Foster (Finance) and Mackenzie Bowell (Militia & Defence) join Britain's U.S. ambassador in Washington for reciprocity discussions (*February 10*); nothing is resolved. A complete Criminal Code is introduced by Thompson (Justice) that includes a death penalty for abortions (*March 8*). A royal commission is established to examine the traffic of liquor and consider prohibition (*March 14*). Alexander Mackenzie, Canada's second Prime Minister, dies of paralysis in Toronto (*April 17*). Abbott knighted as a Commander of St. Michael and St. George; becomes Sir John (*May 25*). Imperial Privy Council upholds the Manitoba Schools Act (*June 30*). Has a dizzy spell on Parliament Hill, prompting doctors to insist he take a rest to recover from exhaustion (*August 6*); he never returns to his office. Barely able to take part in a cabinet meeting where tolls on the Welland Canal are eliminated in response to U.S. complaints (*August 15*). Canada's 2nd Chief Justice Sir William Richie dies in office (*September 25*). Visits England to seek medical assistance; he and Foster (Finance) travel to Paris (*October*). London doctors determine that stomach cancer is restricting blood circulation to his brain; writes a letter of resignation to Thompson, asking him to act on it at his convenience (*November 10*). Resigns as Prime Minister because of ill health (*November 24*). Resigns as Privy Council President (*December 4*). **Abbott government ends.** Retires to Boisbriant (*December*).

1893: Travels to Europe in an effort to restore his health. Dies in Montreal of stomach cancer (*October 30*). Funeral takes place at Christ Church Cathedral in Montreal; burial at Mount Royal Cemetery (*November 2*).

Book about Abbott

1997: Elizabeth L. Abbott, *The Reluctant PM: Notes On the Life of Sir John Abbott, Canada's Third Prime Minister* (manuscript)

4

Sir John S.D. Thompson

The Unpretentious Prime Minister

He was the obvious choice to succeed Macdonald, but John Thompson was a Catholic, a factor that wasn't acceptable to English Canada. When Abbott stepped down 17 months later, Thompson's performance as House leader made him a more tolerable choice. Respected as a former Justice minister, he spent much of his time as Prime Minister on a commission to open up the Bering Sea to international seal hunting. He died suddenly at 49 of a heart attack during lunch with Queen Victoria in England, never reaching his promising potential.

THOMPSON THE POLITICIAN

Prime Minister of Canada: December 5, 1892 – December 12, 1894
Length of term: 2 years, 7 days
Parliament as Prime Minister: Seventh
Age on entering office: 47
Political party: Liberal-Conservative
Leader of party: December 5, 1892 – December 12, 1894
Member of Parliament: October 16, 1885 – December 12, 1894
Riding represented: Antigonish [N.S.] (1885-1894)
Cabinet portfolio: Justice (1885-1892)
Other political posts: Halifax alderman (1871-1877); Nova Scotia legislature member (1877-1882); Attorney General of Nova Scotia (1878-1882); Premier of Nova Scotia (1882); Nova Scotia Supreme Court Justice (1882-1885); Conservative House Leader (1891-1892)
Knighted: September 10, 1888
Titles: Queen's Counsel (1879); Canadian Privy Councillor (1885); Knight Commander of the Order of St. Michael & St. George (1888); Imperial Privy Councillor (1894)
Quotes: "The one calamity above all others which stands before this country is that political divisions should follow the division of race or the division of religion." (House of Commons speech, September 7, 1892) "I detest the idea of being beastly rich." (appeared in several media eulogies, perhaps rationalizing his difficulty in staying out of debt)
Lived after term: Died in office

THOMPSON THE MAN

Name: John Sparrow David Thompson (he added the name Sparrow from his father's name)
Born: November 10, 1845 (he always maintained it was 1844), Halifax, Nova Scotia
Ancestry: Irish, Scottish
Religion: Roman Catholic (converted from Methodist in 1871)
Education: Free Church Academy, Halifax, 1859
Military service: none
Nicknames: Johnnie
Occupation: lawyer; premier; provincial chief justice
Publications: *Cadets of Temperance: Entertainment for the Christmas holidays* (a play; 1852)
Appearance: "A man of pleasant face, rather too plump, but unlined and intelligent. His curly hair descended in thick sideburns to exaggerate his heavy jowls (Bruce Hutchison in *Mr. Prime Minister, 1867-1964*). "… a wide mouth and full lips, and a well-shaped nose with flaring nostrils… Thompson had the look of controlled sensuality." (P.B. Waite in *The Man from Halifax*)
Personality: "He had a lively temper, an acute sensibility, a natural modesty, a powerful intelligence… He did not reveal himself easily; he detested the shallow arts by which men make themselves popular." (P.B. Waite in *The Man from Halifax*) "Thompson will never make a politician. He won't even consider whether a thing is good for the party until he is quite sure that it is good for the country." (an anonymous Conservative speaking to Sir Oliver Mowat's biographer, C.R.W. Biggar)
Married: Annie Emma Affleck, July 5, 1870, Portland, Maine
Age at marriage: 25
Years married: 24
Died: December 12, 1894, Windsor Castle, Windsor, England
Age at death: 49
Cause of death: heart attack
Buried: Holy Cross Cemetery, Halifax, Nova Scotia

Thompson was the:
- Prime Minister who died at the youngest age (49)
- Prime Minister to serve the shortest time as an MP
- Only Prime Minister married in the United States
- Only Prime Minister to lie in state at Windsor Castle, England
- First Prime Minister born in Nova Scotia
- First Prime Minister to represent Nova Scotia
- First Prime Minister who was a provincial premier (Nova Scotia)
- First Prime Minister to serve as a judge
- First Prime Minister of Irish descent
- First Roman Catholic Prime Minister
- First Prime Minister to die outside of Canada
- Second Prime Minister born in Canada

- Second Prime Minister from a provincial legislature (Nova Scotia)
- Second and last Prime Minister to die in office
- Third Conservative Prime Minister
- Third Prime Minister who was a lawyer

Thompson's legacy
- Represented Canada on the Bering Sea Tribunal, winning the decision to open up the sea to international seal hunting
- Developed the Canadian Criminal Code (as Justice minister)
- Separated the Exchequer Court (now the Federal Court) from the Supreme Court (as Justice minister)
- Reformed Canada's prison laws (as Justice minister)

THOMPSON'S FAMILY

Thompson's Parents

Father: John Sparrow Thompson
Born: 1795, Waterford, Ireland
Arrival in Canada: May 1827
Occupation: teacher; editor; civil servant; Queen's printer
Died: October 21, 1867, Halifax, Nova Scotia
Age at death: 72

Mother: Charlotte Pottinger
Born: 1801, Orkney Islands, Scotland
Arrival in Canada: 1804
Married: March 24, 1829, Halifax, Nova Scotia
Died: July 9, 1887, Barrington, Nova Scotia
Age at death: 85

Thompson's Brothers & Sisters (6 siblings; John the youngest)

Sister: Mary Thompson (1830-1848)
Sister: Jane Thompson (1832-1847)
Brother: William Thompson (1834-1882)
  Note: Moved to South Africa in 1859; died an alcoholic.
Sister: Charlotte Thompson (1836-1906); 1 daughter
  Married: Daniel Sargent, (1867)
Brother: Joseph Thompson (1838-1867)
  Married: Emma Hamilton
  Note: Moved to Galveston, Texas, in 1866 and died of yellow fever.
Sister: Elizabeth 'Bessie' Thompson (1842-1918); never married

Thompson's Wife

Name: Annie Emma Affleck
Born: June 26, 1845, Halifax, Nova Scotia
Father: James Affleck (sea captain)
Mother: Catherine Saunders

Age at marriage: 25
Died: April 10, 1913, Toronto, Ontario
Age at death: 67
Burial place: Mount Hope Cemetery, Toronto, Ontario
Older than Thompson: 5 months
Died after Thompson: 19 years

Thompson's Children (9 – four died in infancy)

Name: (infant) Thompson
Born: September 3, 1871, Halifax, Nova Scotia
Died: September 3, 1871, Halifax, Nova Scotia

Name: John Thomas Connolly Thompson
Born: October 20, 1872, Halifax, Nova Scotia
Occupation: lawyer; colonel in the infantry during First World War; Dominion Franchise Commissioner
Died: 1952, Toronto, Ontario
Note: Never married.

Name: Joseph Anthony Thompson
Born: August 6, 1874, Halifax, Nova Scotia
Occupation: lawyer
Married: Maud Eleanor Temple, (April 14, 1903)
Children: 2 – John Sparrow David; Eleanor Ann
Died: October 19, 1935, Toronto, Ontario

Name: Mary 'Babe' Aloysia Thompson
Born: March 22, 1876, Halifax, Nova Scotia
Married: Edmund Carlyon Wragge (September 28, 1905), lawyer
Children: 3 daughters
Died: June 13, 1917, Nelson, British Columbia

Name: Mary Helena 'Lena' Thompson
Born: March 29, 1878, Halifax, Nova Scotia
Married: Edwin Robert MacGregor (March 26, 1913)
Children: 2 – Ann Helena; Margaret Scott
Died: September 26, 1944, Toronto, Ontario

Name: Annie Mary Thompson
Born: November 19, 1879, Halifax, Nova Scotia
Died: September 17, 1880, Halifax, Nova Scotia

Name: (son) Thompson
Born: December 7, 1880, Halifax, Nova Scotia
Died: December 7, 1880, Halifax, Nova Scotia

Name: Frances 'Frankie' Alice Thompson
Born: December 17, 1881, Halifax, Nova Scotia
Died: 1947, Toronto, Ontario
Note: Suffered from a childhood hip disease.

Name: David Anthony Thompson
Born: 1883, Halifax, Nova Scotia
Died: 1885, Halifax, Nova Scotia

POLITICAL STORIES

Premier of Nova Scotia

John Thompson was Premier of Nova Scotia for just 54 days in 1882. Like most of his political jobs, it was one he neither sought nor wanted. But the previous premier, Simon Holmes, had alienated so many colleagues in cabinet with his preoccupation about consolidating Nova Scotia's railways that he was forced to resign shortly before the government went to the polls to seek re-election.

The previous fall, Thompson had struck an informal deal with Sir Charles Tupper, Railways & Canals minister in Ottawa. If he stayed on as the Nova Scotia Attorney General and agreed to act as party leader in the next provincial election, Ottawa would appoint him to the Nova Scotia Supreme Court. But, by May 1882, he was so fed up with politics, he handed in his resignation.

Before the month was up, Holmes was gone and Thompson was the obvious successor. So, instead of resigning, he found himself in the premier's chair embarking on a June provincial election. The results were disastrous. Thompson won his seat by a mere 63 votes. Province-wide, the Liberals tripled the number of seats they held in the legislature, giving them a comfortable majority over Thompson's Conservatives.

But the Liberals had no leader. Their caucus was such a loose cluster of politicians that Thompson immediately went to work to find enough of them to form a coalition government. For nearly a month he courted the most obvious in-name-only Liberals, but without luck. Everyone he approached suspected he was about to step down to accept a recent vacancy on the provincial court.

He resigned on July 18. His term as premier had been devoted entirely to waging a hard-fought re-election in Antigonish and undertaking a futile attempt to stay in office as leader of a coalition. The Liberals scrambled in caucus to come up with a premier, giving the job to William Pipes.

Almost immediately after his resignation, Thompson was appointed to the Nova Scotia Supreme Court. The Antigonish seat he fought so hard to keep was given up. He was out of politics and back into a field he enjoyed – law.

Enacting the Criminal Code

At the time of Confederation, Macdonald was determined Canada would have a set of uniform, codified laws. It took several decades before it happened, but by passing the task on to Thompson, his Justice minister, Macdonald's initiative ushered in a Criminal Code that remained largely unchanged for more than a century.

Thompson turned the task over to his deputy minister, Robert Sedgewick, and his former deputy minister, George Burbidge. Based on a draft codification of English law that was never enacted by Britain, the Canadian Code aimed to protect the community and the individual. The mammoth task called for the reclassification of offences based on their seriousness and attaching procedures to resolve them.

It was an equally daunting task for Thompson to maneuver the bill through committees and the House. When the House finally passed it on June 28, 1892, the Code boasted approximately 1,100 sections. It made it possible for prisoners to testify on their own behalf, offered stronger protection to girls and women attacked by males, raised the age of consent from 12 to 14, allowed minors under 16 to be tried separately, called for a stated number of strokes in whippings (and prohibited the whipping of women), and limited hanging to death sentences.

As society changed, Canada's Criminal Code was revised many times. Each revision addressed issues like drunk driving and gun control; other sections, including the death penalty and classification of abortion as an offence, were eliminated. In 1955, a larger overhaul reduced the number of sections from 1,100 to 753.

Turns down leadership

Macdonald's era as Prime Minister was coming to an end after he was incapacitated by a series of strokes in May 1891. As he lay dying, his caucus struggled to determine who would succeed him. Macdonald himself had indicated to Thompson that "when I am gone, you will have to rally around Abbott; he is your only man." But just before a third stroke left him mostly paralyzed and speechless, Macdonald told Thompson that Abbott was "too damned selfish" to make a good leader.

Nevertheless, Abbott remained the most logical choice. Thompson recognized that, at best, the aging Senator, who was not popular among French Canadians, would merely be a caretaker. Two other front-runners, Sir Hector-Louis Langevin and Sir Charles Tupper were mired in scandal. At Public Works, Langevin was implicated in accusations that contracts were being manipulated by his brother-in-law, Thomas McGreevey, MP. Tupper, then High Commissioner in London, was being chastised for campaigning for the Conservatives while holding a non-political position in Britain.

Thompson was clearly the ablest minister in cabinet and had kept the government going during Macdonald's illnesses, but his conversion to Catholicism made him unacceptable to Ontario Protestants voters. The Conservatives would need the province's vote in the next election and didn't want to antagonize the electorate. More importantly, Thompson didn't really want the job. He told his wife that the new leader would have a "devil of a time and yet they fancy it is a vast honour."

Macdonald died on June 6 and Governor General Lord Stanley put off appointing a new leader for a week while cabinet tried to come to a decision. Its members hoped a chosen successor might turn up in Macdonald's papers. They waited in vain. Stanley finally asked Thompson to form a government. He made a half-hearted effort to find enough support and potential cabinet appointees. But by June 12, he recommended that Stanley approach Abbott to lead a government.

Thompson had avoided the top job, but it didn't make much difference. With Abbott in the Senate, Thompson took on the role of House leader, which made him the prime minister in all but name. Seventeen months later, Abbott resigned and Thompson succeeded him.

Assumes leadership

From the moment Abbott became Prime Minister, he began hunting for a way to cede the responsibility. While his lieutenant, Thompson, busily handled pol-itical issues in the House of Commons, Abbott wearily watched from the Senate.

Then, 14 months into his term, Abbott suffered a dizzy spell and his doctors insisted he take a rest. Seeking further medical advice in England, he decided he must resign. Thompson had also been contemplating leaving politics. It appeared that wasn't going to happen.

Unlike the obvious scramble to find a replacement for Macdonald, the transition from Abbott to Thompson was a smooth one. What was different? Macdonald was a towering figure and no obvious successor proved able to match his mastery of House and party politics. Throughout Abbott's term, by contrast, Thompson had become the de facto leader in the House and done the job well. Abbott's cabinet had changed little in 17 months, and it was in-creasingly clear that no one was better suited than Thompson to take the helm.

It helped, too, that recent victories in a series of by-elections had boosted the Conservative majority from 27 to 60 seats. The party didn't need to be so worried about whether or not Ontario Protestants would accept a Catholic leader. As a result, cabinet quite readily embraced Thompson as the new Prime Minister. And he, with some reluctance, accepted.

Seals in the Bering Sea

Nothing dominated Canada's international agenda in the late 19th century as much as rights for fishing, whaling and sealing. For Prime Minister Thompson, seal hunting was his global issue.

In the 1870s, the U.S. had prohibited the seal hunt on the Pribilof Islands in the Bering Sea, and in "the waters adjacent thereto". Definitions of "adjacent" varied and often placed British Columbia seal hunters closer to the islands than accepted by the U.S. In the late 1880s, a handful of B.C. sealing vessels were seized and, in time, the U.S. claimed jurisdiction over most of the Bering Sea in the name of protecting the fur seal. Britain, representing B.C. interests, contested the claim and sought negotiation to solve the problem. Four years of talks, which included Russia, failed to break the impasse and the U.S. continued to exercise its jurisdiction.

In 1892, Britain – representing Canada – and the U.S. agreed to submit their concerns to a tribunal. The issues to be resolved included determining each country's right over the Bering Sea waters, and whether or not the U.S. had jurisdictional rights more than three miles beyond the Pribilof Islands' shores. The British-Canadian position was that the Bering Sea was no different than any other sea, therefore restricting Pribilof territorial waters to three miles.

The Bering Sea Tribunal talks began in Paris on March 23, 1893, with Thompson representing Canada as part of the British delegation. In fact, the British weren't very happy about having him take part. He had accepted the role when he was still Justice minister; it didn't seem appropriate to the Colonial Office that a Prime Minister take part. Thompson ignored their veiled suggestions that he step down.

When the arguments finally concluded five months later, Canada ended up winning on every point. A year later, Thompson turned down a U.S. offer of compensation of $400,000 for the rotting hulls of the seized B.C. sealing vessels. By the time the U.S. finally paid about $473,000 in 1898 (over $12 million in today's money), Thompson had already been dead more than three years.

PERSONAL STORIES

Heart attack at the Queen's luncheon

Although Thompson had been experiencing breathlessness while travelling in Italy and Britain, he was in good health on December 12, 1894, when he took the train to Windsor Castle to be inducted into the Imperial Privy Council by Queen Victoria.

Following the 20-minute ceremony, the participants adjourned to the castle's Octagon Room for a late lunch. Just before the meal, Thompson fainted and was helped into a nearby sitting room to recover. A few minutes later, a revived and embarrassed Thompson returned and sat down again, this time with the Queen's doctor, James Reid, seated beside him.

Thompson complained about a pain in his chest, then collapsed, falling towards the doctor. Reid administered brandy and checked Thompson's pulse. There wasn't one; Thompson had died.

His body was placed in the castle's Clarence Tower where a midnight mass was held. He was then moved to London. The Queen held a memorial service on December 14 that was attended by Thompson's daughter Helena, Sir Charles Tupper, Lord Tennyson, Cecil Rhodes, Secretary of State for the Colonies Lord Ripon, and others.

The *HMS Blenheim* carried Thompson's body back to Halifax where a state funeral was held at St. Mary's Cathedral on January 3, 1895. Dr. Reid, the Queen's physician was later knighted and attended to the Queen at her death in 1901, then at Edward VII's in 1910.

Lady Annie Thompson

In the year Nova Scotia became part of Canada, Thompson was dating Annie Affleck, the oldest daughter of a Halifax sea captain. Local gossips noted that Thompson was Methodist while Annie was Roman Catholic. When they were married in 1870, they required an episcopal dispensation for the ceremony. Because the Halifax archbishop was visiting the Vatican, it was necessary for the young couple to sail to Bangor, Maine, to get the bishop's permission. The ceremony took place there.

In contrast to Thompson's shyness, Annie was spirited and impulsive. Throughout his career, it was her strength he relied on. Annie was the one who would fortify Thompson to make the agonizing decisions to enter – or remain in – provincial and federal politics.

Urging him to accept Macdonald's offer of a cabinet position in 1885 resulted in their first extended separation. They doted on each other, a fondness that was evident in the letters they exchanged over the next three years until Annie and their youngest daughter finally joined Thompson in Ottawa.

Shortly after Annie's arrival, her husband was knighted and she became Lady Thompson. The new title, however, wasn't enough to usher Annie into the inner circle of Ottawa society. Local matrons had learned she might have once worked in a Halifax shop – simply not appropriate!

The Thompsons began to entertain regularly, usually every Monday and Tuesday. Just prior to becoming a Prime Minister's wife, she hosted one party for 250 guests, doing all of the cooking herself. Once she became the nation's first lady, she had two servants to help with the entertaining.

Two years later, Annie was suddenly a widow. The Thompsons had never had much money and a private subscription campaign was launched to take care of Annie and her daughter Frankie. In 1895, Parliament supplemented the fund.

She moved to Toronto where her two sons were studying law thanks to funding from Lord and Lady Aberdeen. She remained there until dying of cancer in 1913 and was buried in Mount Pleasant Cemetery where Prime Minister William Lyon Mackenzie King was later interred.

Thompson's Timeline

1844: Born John David Thompson in Halifax, N.S. (*November 10*).

1847: His older sister Jane dies of dropsy (internal fluid build-up) at age 15 (*November*).

1848: His oldest sister Mary dies of dropsy at age 18 (*July*).

1850: His father John becomes Halifax's school commissioner (*April 24*). Attends Royal Acadian School in Halifax where his father is a teacher.

1851: His family buys a house on Gottingen Street, Halifax (*June*).

1852: Writes play *Cadets of Temperance: Entertainment for the Christmas holidays* (*Fall*).

1858: Attends Free Church Academy in Halifax.

1859: His brother William is accused of fraud and fired as a Lunenburg surveyor (*December*); subsequently moves to South Africa, leaving the family to pay his debts.

1860: His family is forced to sell its home (*June 1*); but continues to live there as tenants. Begins using Sparrow as part of his name like his father, after his grand-mother Mary Sparrow. Leaves school to apprentice in the law office of Nepean Clarke (*Summer*). His father becomes a Nova Scotia Assembly reporter for the new Joseph Howe government (*September*).

1861: Articles as a law clerk with Henry Pryor, former mayor of Halifax.

1865: Called to the Nova Scotia bar (*July 5*).

1866: Meets Annie Affleck (*November*) and courts her for three years.

1867: Assists as a reporter of the debates about Confederation in the Nova Scotia assembly (*Spring*). His brother Joe dies of yellow fever in Galveston, Texas (*Summer*), as does Joe's wife, Emma. Transcribes the debates about separating from Canada after the anti-Confederationists win the Nova Scotia election (*Fall*); supports Joseph Howe's anti-Confederation stand. His father dies in Halifax (*October 21*). Begins to support his mother and sister Elizabeth.

1868: Serves as the primary reporter for Assembly debates, until 1873.

1869: Joins Joseph Combs's law firm as a partner (*April 1*).

1870: Marries Annie Affleck in Portland, Maine (*July 5*). Couple lives with his mother and sister Elizabeth.

1871: Converts to Catholicism (*April 21*); surprisingly loses no law clients because of the change. His first daughter dies in childbirth, following a difficult delivery (*September 3*). Elected as a Halifax alderman for Ward 5 (*October 2*); serves until 1877.

1872: Buys his first home, Willow Bank in Halifax (*May*); moves out of his mother's home. His first son John Thomas Connolly is born in Halifax (*October 20*).

1873: Ends his law partnership with Coombs and works as a sole practitioner (*August*). Becomes chairman of the city prisons committee and a commissioner for the new Point Pleasant Park. Appointed by council to the Board of School Commissioners (*November 1*).

1874: Represents Charles Tupper who was charged with corrupt election practices during the last federal election (*July 2*); succeeds in having the objections overruled. His second son Joseph is born in Halifax (*August 6*). Re-elected as a Halifax alderman by acclamation. Becomes chairman of the school board. Serves as president of the Young Men's Literary Association and as a president of the Charitable Irish Society.

1875: Becomes a director of the newly published Halifax *Morning Herald* (*January*).

1876: His daughter Mary 'Babe' Aloysia is born in Halifax (*March 22*). Appointed a Fellow at the University of Halifax (*July 20*).

1877: Assists U.S. lawyer Richard Dane during the International Fisheries Commission meeting in Halifax to reduce U.S. compensation to Canada by $9 million (*August-November*). Ends term as Halifax alderman (*October 1*). Elected to the Nova Scotia assembly in a by-election, representing Antigonish as a Conservative (*December 4*).

1878: Appointed as equity and real property examiner in the University of Halifax law faculty (*January*). His daughter Mary Helena is born in Halifax (*March 29*). Becomes chairman of the Halifax Board of School Commissioners (*May*). Re-elected to Nova Scotia's assembly in Antigonish by acclamation (*September 17*). Appointed Attorney General of Nova Scotia by Premier Simon Holmes (*October 22*). Steps down as School Commissioners chairman (*October*). Joins Wallace Graham as a law partner after Robert Weatherbe leaves to become a judge (*October*).

1879: Accompanies Holmes to Ottawa to seek better terms in Confederation (*January*); is unsuccessful. Becomes a Queen's Counsel (*June 18*). His daughter Annie is born in Halifax (*November 19*).

1880: His daughter Annie dies at 10 months (*September 17*). A son dies at birth (*December 7*).

1881: Helps draft legislation to eliminate the University of Halifax and retain the original six colleges (Acadia, Dalhousie, King's, Mount Alison, St. Francis Xavier, St. Mary's) (*March 3*). Tupper, a member of Macdonald's cabinet, agrees to appoint him to the Nova Scotia Supreme Court if he contests the coming provincial election as party leader (*October*). Thompson hires Tupper's son, Charles Hibbert, as his law partner, making it Thompson, Graham & Tupper. His daughter Frances 'Frankie' is born in Halifax (*December 17*).

1882: Resigns as a cabinet minister, feeling he can't in good conscience lead the party into another election if he then abandons it for a judge's seat (*May*). Premier Holmes loses party support and resigns (*May 23*). Thompson agrees to stay on and becomes Premier of Nova Scotia (*May 25*). Narrowly re-elected in Antigonish, but his government is defeated in the provincial election (*June 20*). Unsuccessfully attempts to form a coalition government. Resigns as Premier and Attorney General, ushering in a Liberal regime that becomes the longest in Canadian history: 43 years (*July 18*). Appointed a Puisne Judge of the Supreme Court of Nova Scotia (*July 27*); resigns his Antigonish seat in the assembly. Resigns from his law firm and is replaced by Robert Borden; the firm becomes Graham, Tupper & Borden.

1883: Visits U.S. law schools with Wallace Graham and Robert Sedgewick to determine the viability of starting a law faculty at Dalhousie University (*April*). Becomes one of the founders of the Dalhousie University Law School in Halifax, English Canada's first university law program (*October 30*). Lectures in the new law school about evidence (*November*). His youngest son David is born in Halifax.

1884: Approached by the provincial Liberal government to reorganize the Nova Scotia Supreme Court; simplifies many provincial legal procedures by introducing the Judicature Act, a document that remains largely unchanged until 1950. Actively courted by Macdonald, Tupper, Annie and others to enter federal politics (*June*).

1885: Wins the Confederation Medal. His youngest son David dies at age 2. Meets with Tupper and agrees to enter federal politics (*September 2*). Arrives in Ottawa and resigns as a Puisne Judge in Nova Scotia's Supreme Court (*September 25*). Enters Macdonald's federal cabinet as Justice minister (*September 26*). Elected to Parliament in an Antigonish by-election, defeating Alexander McIntosh by 228 votes (*October 16*). Suffers a kidney stone attack (*November 8*), removing him from most of the deliberations about the fate of Louis Riel, who is hanged before Thompson returns to his office.

Preferring law to politics

Thomson aspired to be a judge; being a politician got in the way. He attained his wish in 1882 when the Macdonald government appointed him to Nova Scotia's Supreme Court. But two years later that same government was actively trying to entice him back to politics. He enjoyed the legal rigour and family time in Halifax. Why give that up for Ottawa – unless, perhaps, he could be Justice minister? Macdonald agreed and he was back into politics only three years after leaving it.

1886: Introduced in the House by Macdonald at the opening of Parliament (*Feb-ruary 25*). Defends the hanging of Louis Riel in a speech to the House (*March 22*).

1887: Canada's sixth federal election: re-elected in Antigonish by 40 votes over Angus McGillivray, former Speaker of the Nova Scotia Assembly; Macdonald government re-elected (*February 22*). Returns to Halifax to visit his ill mother, Charlotte, who dies soon after (*July 9*). Rents a house for the family on Cooper Street in Ottawa (*Fall*). Appoints his deputy minister, George Burbidge, to the Exchequer Court and asks Robert Borden to be his new deputy minister; Borden declines (*Fall*). Becomes the first dean of the law school at the University of Ottawa; the school has trouble getting started and isn't successfully launched until 1953. Represents Canada in Washington with Tupper (Finance) and George Foster (Mar-ine & Fisheries) to negotiate a fishing rights settlement (*November 22-December 11*).

1888: A fishing settlement with the U.S. is reached (*February 15*), but is rejected six months later by the U.S. Senate. Joined by his family from Halifax in the first of four different houses he would rent on Metcalfe Street in Ottawa (*March*). Touted as a possible Supreme Court judge following the death of Justice William Alexander Henry (*May 3*); appoints Christopher Patterson of the Ontario Court instead. Knighted as Sir John for his role in the fisheries negotiations (*September 10*).

1889: Defends federal reluctance to disallow Quebec's Jesuit Estates Act that would compensate the religious order for lost properties (*March 27*). Approached, along with Macdonald (as acting Railways & Canals minister) by an inventor with a gadget to safeguard level railway crossings; his assessment of the pitch? "I think that he deserves to be killed on a level crossing." (*Spring*). Receives an honorary Doctor of Laws degree from the University of Ottawa. Moves to Lisgar Avenue in Ottawa (*September*).

1890: Refers Manitoba legislation for a single English-only school system with no tax support for the province's Catholic school system to the court rather than disallow the act (*Spring*). Called to the Ontario bar. Takes his first trip overseas to discuss a copyright act with Britain and visit his sons attending Stoneyhurst school (*June 25*). Becomes a lecturer at Dalhousie's law school. His youngest daughter Frankie begins a series of treatments to combat crumbling hip joints (*September 22*).

1891: Canada's seventh federal election: re-elected in Antigonish, beating Angus McGillivray by 228 votes; Macdonald government is re-elected (*March 5*). His daughter Frankie survives her strenuous orthopaedic treatments and an operation (*May 5*). Six days after Macdonald's death, Governor General Lord Stanley asks him to form a government; he recommends Senator John Abbott instead (*June 12*). Becomes Justice minister and Conservative House leader in Abbott's government (*June 16*). Takes over Macdonald's small office near the House of Commons after Abbott indicates he has no plans to use it (*Fall*). Writes the subcommittee report on the Langevin-McGreevy scandal, exonerating Langevin of corruption charges, but not McGreevy (*September 14*); two weeks later he moves that McGreevy be expelled from the House. His daughter Frankie continues to have hip problems, compounded by throat and lung difficulties that place her near death (*September*); she survives, but is lame (*December*). A challenge to his re-election in Antigonish is dropped, thanks to the efforts of Borden (*December*).

Halifax law fraternity

When Thompson teamed up with Halifax lawyer Wallace Graham in 1878, he became part of a small firm that turned out four Chief Justices of Nova Scotia and two Prime Ministers. In addition to Graham, the other future Chief Justices were Robert Weatherbe, whom he replaced in the firm, Robert Edward Harris, a law student, and his brother-in-law Joseph Chisholm, who arrived long after Thompson was gone. When he became a judge himself (but never a Chief Justice) in 1882, he was replaced in the firm by a newly minted lawyer, Robert Borden.

1892: Joins Foster (Finance) and Mackenzie Bowell (Militia & Defence) in Washington to discuss reciprocity and the Alaska boundary (*February 10*); the U.S. rejects reciprocity, but agrees to a joint survey into the Alaska dispute. Meets with U.S. President Benjamin Harrison whom he describes as "a contemptible nobody with all the airs of an emperor" (*February 13*). At Abbott's urging, assumes Macdonald's seat in the House (*February 25*). Introduces a complete Criminal Code that includes a death penalty for abortions (*March 8*).

Presents the Redistribution Bill in the House (*April 24*). Receives an honorary Doctor of Laws degree from Dalhousie University (*Spring*). Interrupts his family vacation in St. Andrews, N.B., after Abbott has a dizzy spell on Parliament Hill (*July*). Receives a letter of resignation from Abbott (*November 22*). Governor General Stanley asks him to form a government (*November 23*). Abbott formally resigns as Prime Minister because of ill health (*November 24*). Reviews the Manitoba schools question as part of a committee of the Privy Council that includes Bowell (Railways & Canals) (*November 25-26*). Department of Trade and Commerce is created (*December 3*). **Thompson government (1892-1894).** Becomes the fourth Prime Minister of Canada, and continues as the eighth Justice minister (*December 5*). Eliminates the Customs and Inland Revenue ministries in favour of a new Trade & Commerce ministry headed by Senator Mackenzie Bowell (*December 5*).

1893: Loses D'Alton McCarthy [Conservative-Simcoe North] who breaks with the government and its policy that recognizes a separate Catholic school system (*January 23*). Canada signs its first treaty with a European country: a commercial treaty with France (*February 6*). Sails for France with Annie and his three daughters (*March*). Takes part in the Bering Sea Tribunal to negotiate seal hunting in the Bering Sea (*March 23*). Meets with French President Sadi Carnot (*April 15*). Announces the appointment of the Earl of Aberdeen as Canada's seventh Governor General (*May 22*). Bering Sea Tribunal ends, with all recommendations in Canada's favour (*August 15*). His son John meets him in Ottawa after canoeing from North Bay, Ont., a 400-km trip (*August 27*). Greets Lord Aberdeen in Quebec City (*September 17*) A bust of Thompson, by Louis-Phillippe Hébert of France, is shipped to Canada (*September*); 42 years later, the Thompson family gives it to the Nova Scotia Archives. Unveils a statue to Macdonald in Hamilton, Ont. (*November 1*). Attends the funeral of Sir John Abbott, Canada's third Prime Minister, at Christ Church Cathedral in Montreal (*November 2*).

1894: Supreme Court rules that the Roman Catholic minority in Manitoba cannot appeal to the federal government against the School Act of 1890 (*February 20*). Thomas McGreevy, the former MP expelled from the House and sent to jail, is released by cabinet order because of ill health (*February 27*). Thompson's wife Annie is asked by Lady Aberdeen to be vice-president of the newly formed National Council of Women (*April*). The Imperial Privy Council overturns the Manitoba schools question decision, granting the right to appeal (*June 24*). Officially opens the Second Colonial Conference in Ottawa, the first one held outside Britain (*June 28*). The government creates Labour Day as an official holiday, moving it from May to September (*July 23*). Takes his only vacation while Prime Minister, to an island on Lake Rousseau, Muskoka, Ont. (*August*). Celebrates Canada's first Labour Day working in Ottawa (*September 3*). Advised by a Toronto doctor to get a full examination after evidence of heart disease is discovered (*September 4*). Opens the Canadian National Exhibition in Toronto (*September 5*). Unveils a monument in Springhill, N.S., to coal miners killed in the 1891 explosion (*September 12*). Doctors in Montreal and Ottawa discover problems with his kidneys; they and his wife urge him to take a rest and to consider quitting politics (*September*). Unveils a statue to Macdonald at Queen's Park, Toronto (*October 13*). Sails to France to spend time with his daughter Helena (*October 31*). Visits France, Monaco and Italy; climbs to the top of St. Peter's dome in Rome and suffers from breathlessness from that time on (*November*). Arrives in England but finds breathing difficult; the doctor indicates he has strained his heart and advises rest (*December 1*). Made a member of the Imperial Privy Council by Victoria, the only Canadian since Macdonald to be inducted (*December 12*). Faints during the luncheon after the swearing-in ceremony at Windsor Castle; after recovering, he returns to the table, then collapses, dying of a heart attack (*December 12*). **Thompson government ends.** Lies in state at Windsor Castle. Funeral service in London (*December 14*).

1895: Body arrives in Halifax on a British warship painted black (*January 1*). Lies in state at Province House in Halifax (*January 2*). Funeral at St. Mary's Cathedral, Halifax, and burial at Holy Cross Cemetery (*January 3*).

BOOKS ABOUT THOMPSON

- **1895**: J. Castell Hopkins; *Life and Work of the Rt. Hon. Sir John Thompson* (United)
- **1985**: P.B. Waite; *The Man From Halifax: Sir John Thompson, Prime Minister* (University of Toronto)

Leaders of the various Conservative parties

Liberal-Conservative (1867-1916)		
1.	Sir John A. Macdonald	1867-1891
2.	Sir John Abbott	1891-1892
3.	Sir John Thompson	1892-1894
4.	Sir Mackenzie Bowell	1894-1896
Conservative (1867-1917)		
5.	Sir Charles Tupper	1896-1901
Unionist (1917-1920)		
6.	Sir Robert Borden	1901-1920
National Liberal & Conservative (1920-1938)		
7.	Arthur Meighen	1920-1926
8.	R.B. Bennett	1927-1938
Conservative (1938-1942)		
9.	Robert Manion	1938-1940
	Arthur Meighen	1941-1942
Progressive Conservative (1942-2003)		
10.	John Bracken	1942-1948
11.	George Drew	1948-1956
12.	John Diefenbaker	1956-1967
13.	Robert Stanfield	1967-1976
14.	Joe Clark	1976-1983
15.	Brian Mulroney	1983-1993
16.	Kim Campbell	1993
17.	Jean Charest	1993-1998
	Joe Clark	1998-2003
18.	Peter MacKay	2003
Conservative (merger with Canadian Alliance) (2003-)		
19.	Stephen Harper	2004-2015
20.	Andrew Scheer	2015-

5

Sir Mackenzie Bowell

The Unscheduled Prime Minister

The third Prime Minister in three years, newspaper publisher and long-time politician Mackenzie Bowell was not a popular choice with his colleagues. He had been an able administrator in various cabinet portfolios, but wasn't a natural leader. Like those before him, he preferred to postpone making a decision to create a separate Catholic school system in Manitoba. He personally favoured doing so, a daring stand for the former Grand Master of the zenophobic Orange Lodge. But seven members of his cabinet, tiring of his equivocation, resigned, forcing Bowell to step down just before the 1896 election.

Bowell the Politician

Prime Minister of Canada: December 21, 1894 – April 27, 1896
Length of term: 1 year, 4 months, 6 days
Parliament as Prime Minister: Seventh
Age on entering office: 70
Political party: Liberal-Conservative
Leader of party: December 21, 1894 – April 27, 1896
Member of Parliament: July 1, 1867 – December 5, 1892
Riding represented: Hastings North [Ont.] (1867-1892)
Member of the Senate: December 5, 1892 – December 10, 1917
Province represented: Ontario
Cabinet portfolios: Customs (1878-1892); Railways & Canals (1891-1892); Militia & Defence (1892); Trade & Commerce (1892-1894); Privy Council President (1894-1896); Militia & Defence (1896); acting Finance (1896); Receiver General (1896)
Other political posts: Senator (1892-1917); Leader of the Government in the Senate (1893-1896); Leader of the Opposition in the Senate (1896-1906)
Knighted: January 1, 1895
Titles: Most Worshipful Grand Master and Sovereign of the Orange Association of British America (1870-1878); Canadian Privy Councillor (1878); Knight Commander of St. Michael and St. George (1895)

Quotes: "It is not my habit to boast, but you might conclude there is something in this old grey head of mine that justifies my rising to a position of that kind, notwithstanding the opinion of those men who left the cabinet over which I preside." (defending his government in a speech to the Senate, 1896); "nest of traitors" (his purported description of cabinet members who wanted him to step down as Prime Minster; but the phrase may actually have been coined by the media)
Lived after term: 21 years

BOWELL THE MAN

Name: Mackenzie Bowell
Born: December 27, 1823, Rickinghall, Suffolk, England
Ancestry: English
Religion: Methodist
Arrival in Canada: November 1832
Education: Printer's apprentice (1834); Sydney Normal School, Hastings, Ontario (teaching certificate, 1841)
Nicknames: Mack
Military service: Militia (1867-1872)
Occupation: editor; printer; publisher; businessman
Occupation after term: Senator; publisher
Publications: publisher of the *Belleville Intelligencer*
Appearance: "The crumpled face behind the whitening beard gave him the look of a bitter Santa Claus with crafty eyes." (Bruce Hutchison in *Mr. Prime Minister*); "…a tiny figure with a jagged grey beard and hooded eyes set in a parchment face." (Gordon Donaldson in *Fifteen Men*)
Personality: "An expert on patronage, vain, with little parliamentary panache, but faithful, hard-working and scrupulous." (P.B. Waite in *The Man from Halifax*); "His manner was quizzical and nagging. He seldom sweetened this language with compliments and, although not offensive, there was something in his tone of voice that aroused resentment even when his words did not betray any bitterness." (Betsy Dewar Boyce in *The Accidental Prime Minister*)
Married: Harriet Louise Moore, December 23, 1847, Belleville, Canada West (Ont.)
Age at marriage: 23
Years married: 36
Died: December 10, 1917
Place of death: Belleville, Ontario
Age at death: 93
Cause of death: pneumonia, old age
Buried: Belleville Cemetery, Belleville, Ontario

Bowell was the:
- Prime Minister with the longest previous experience in cabinet (18 years)
- Only Prime Minister forced from office by his cabinet
- Only Prime Minister who died in Canada without having a state funeral
- Only Prime Minister with a full beard
- First Prime Minister born in England

- First Prime Minister who was a widower while in office
- First Methodist Prime Minister
- First Conservative Prime Minister whose first name was not John
- Second Prime Minister who was an editor
- Second and last Prime Minister to serve while sitting in the Senate
- Second Prime Minister to be knighted while in office
- Fourth Conservative Prime Minister
- Last Prime Minister who was a Liberal-Conservative

Bowell's legacy
- Only Prime Minister to lose the confidence of his cabinet
- Tendency to waver prevented a clear solution to the Manitoba schools question

BOWELL'S FAMILY

Bowell's Parents

Father: John Bowell
Born: about 1799, Rickinghall, Suffolk, England
Arrival in Canada: 1833
Occupation: builder; farmer
Second marriage: Ann Mulligan, 1835
Died: October 16, 1883, Belleville, Ontario
Age at death: 84

Mother: Elizabeth Marshall
Married: March 19, 1824, Rickinghall, Suffolk, England
Died: October 5, 1834, Belleville, Upper Canada (Ontario) (in childbirth)
Note: Mackenzie was born a year before Elizabeth married John; he may have been called Mackenzie Marshall at first.

Bowell's Brothers & Sisters (4 siblings; Mackenzie the oldest)

Sister: Mahamah Bowell (1826-1919) several daughters
  Married: James Reid (November 23, 1844)
Sister: Mary Ann Elizabeth Bowell (1828-1906) 4 children
  Married: Jonas C. Canniff
Brother: Warwick Johnston Bowell (1832-1908)
  Married: Alice Frost
Sister: Elizabeth Bowell (1834-1834)

Bowell's Wife

Name: Harriet Louise Moore
Born: May 11, 1828, Upper Canada (Ontario)
Father: Jacob G. Moore (assessor; surveyor; constable)
Mother: Nancy Hickey
Age at marriage: 19
Died: April 2, 1884, Hermosa Beach, California
Age at death: 55

Burial place: Belleville Cemetery, Belleville, Ontario
Younger than Bowell: 4 years
Died before Bowell: 33 years

Bowell's Children (9 – 4 died young)

Name: Louise Mahamah Bowell
Born: November 29, 1848, Belleville, Canada West (Ontario)
Occupation: President of the *Belleville Intelligencer*
Married: James Coleman Jamieson (April 30, 1868)
Children: 5 – James Whiteford; John Lander; Mackenzie Bowell; Henry Lovell; Harriet Louisa
Died: October 22, 1919, St. Paul, Minnesota

Name: Caroline 'Carrie' Harriet Bowell
Born: May 22, 1850, Belleville, Canada West (Ontario)
Married: Charles Philip Holton (June 1872)
Children: 7 – Philip Clement; Lucy Louisa; Ezra Flint; Harriet Helen; Charles Mackenzie Bowell; George Harold; Albert Douglas
Died: January 1, 1939, Belleville, Ontario

Name: Elizabeth Nancy Bowell
Born: October 6, 1852, Belleville, Canada West (Ontario)
Died: July 12, 1854, Belleville, Canada West (Ontario)

Name: George Mackenzie Bowell
Born: April 23, 1855, Belleville, Canada West (Ontario)
Died: July 23, 1855, Belleville, Canada West (Ontario)

Name: John Moore Bowell
Born: October 1, 1856, Belleville, Canada West (Ontario)
Married: Alma Cecilia Patterson
Children: 2 – Mackenzie; Jean
Occupation: Civil servant; father's assistant in 1870s
Died: June 9, 1927, Vancouver, British Columbia

Name: Evalyn Margaret Bowell
Born: February 9, 1859, Belleville, Canada West (Ontario)
Married: George W. McCarthy (October 16, 1889)
Children: 1 – Evalyn Mary
Died: July 2, 1944, Belleville, Ontario

Name: Anna Mary Bowell
Born: May 15, 1861, Belleville, Canada West (Ontario)
Died: October 11, 1865, Belleville, Canada West (Ontario)

Name: Alice Maude Bowell
Born: July 14, 1865, Belleville, Canada West (Ontario)
Died: August 2, 1865, Belleville, Canada West (Ontario)

Name: Charles 'Charlie' James Bowell
Born: September 23, 1867, Belleville, Ontario
Occupation: Publisher, *The Intelligencer* newspaper; Customs officer

Married: Ida Mary Elizabeth Jerome, June 2, 1893 (divorced 1902)
Children: Hazel Steele (Stepdaughter)
Died: May 6, 1921, Belleville, Ontario

Political Stories

Leader by seniority

Bowell was quite happy to take on the role of acting Prime Minister while Thompson was in England being inducted into the Imperial Privy Council. Little did he know that Thompson would die of a heart attack while overseas. Governor General Lord Aberdeen felt bound by the tradition of asking the longest serving cabinet member to form the next government. That was Bowell – a cabinet fixture since Macdonald was re-elected to his second term in 1878.

But Aberdeen was concerned about Bowell's active involvement with the Orange Order. So he asked for Senator Frank Smith's advice. The Senator was not only a cabinet minister, but a Roman Catholic. He assured the Governor General that Bowell had made every effort to remain objective on religious issues, avoiding initiatives or comments that would offend Quebec and Catholic voters.

That evening, Aberdeen summoned Bowell. Although the acting Prime Minister suggested other cabinet members be approached to form a government, Aberdeen made up his mind to give Bowell the leadership.

He doubtlessly wanted the job, but knew it might be a dubious prize. Many cabinet ministers were not enthusiastic about serving under the fastidious, aging workhorse – as he was well aware. Since Aberdeen had already decided on Bowell, the existing cabinet members reluctantly acquiesced. Most were suspicious of each other and disliked Senator Bowell. It was a recipe for strife.

The Manitoba School Crisis

Manitoba's stubborn defiance of Ottawa's guarantees for schools that embraced French and Roman Catholicism stymied six Prime Ministers, but none so much as Mackenzie Bowell. With the support of an Imperial Privy Council decision, Bowell issued a remedial order that Manitoba redress the French Catholic minority that had been denied a constitutional right.

In July 1895, the province argued that the order was based on 'errors of fact and judgment' and should be reviewed by a government commission. Quebec members of Bowell's Conservative caucus became convinced that the government would cave in and not introduce remedial legislation. Three of his Quebec ministers – Sir Adolphe Caron, Joseph Ouimet and Senator Auguste Angers – threatened to resign. Bowell persuaded Caron and Ouimet to remain, but Manitoba's continuing refusal throughout the fall to accept the remedial order further polarized his cabinet.

Despite his Orange sensibilities, Bowell pushed ahead with remedial legislation in January 1896. Many of his cabinet continued threatening to resign. The Liberals stalled his bill in Parliament. His special envoys failed to budge Manitoba from its position. In the end, he simply ran out of time. He withdrew his legislation in April, dissolved

Parliament and stepped down to let Sir Charles Tupper fight the election.

"A nest of traitors"

Bowell spent most of his time as Prime Minister trying to persuade rebellious cabinet ministers not to jump ship. Trouble began when he changed his mind about immediately dissolving Parliament, preferring instead to brave out one final session. His Justice minister, Sir Charles Hibbert Tupper, resigned in protest but was cajoled into staying.

Three Quebec ministers resigned when they lost faith in Bowell's ability to introduce legislation that would force Manitoba to restore education rights for Roman Catholics and the Franco-Manitobans. Although two of them were persuaded to stay, Senator Auguste Angers didn't return.

At the beginning of 1896, Bowell faced his biggest threat when seven ministers resigned – Hibbert Tupper again, Sir George Foster (Finance), Arthur Dickey (Militia & Defence), William Ives (Trade & Commerce), John Haggart (Railways & Canals), Walter Montague (Agriculture) and John Wood (Customs). He filled the gaps with acting ministers, taking on Finance and Militia & Defence himself. The Prime Minister then attempted to step down, but Governor General Aberdeen wouldn't accept his resignation.

In a meeting with Sir Charles Tupper, who was back in Canada from his High Commissioner posting in England, Bowell agreed to turn over the government if the latter agreed not to reappoint Foster, Montague and Haggart. But after a week he conceded that demand as well. The crisis ended when all but one of the ministers returned. Hibbert Tupper accepted the post of Solicitor General outside of cabinet to make room for his father who finally resigned as High Commissioner to become Secretary of State.

Three months later, Bowell wearily and thankfully resigned and turned the government over to Tupper Sr. The embittered Senator denounced his seven former cabinet colleagues as a "nest of traitors".

PERSONAL STORIES

Bowell and *The Intelligencer*

When George Benjamin published the first edition of *The Belleville Intelligencer* in 1834, he included a small advertisement seeking "an intelligent lad" to help in his printing shop. It was answered by 10-year-old Mackenzie Bowell, whose mother had just died. So began a relationship with Belleville's first newspaper that lasted until Bowell's death over seven decades later.

Another *Intelligencer* apprentice, Rodney Moore, had a younger sister Harriet who eventually became Bowell's wife. When Benjamin sold the newspaper in 1848, it was the brothers-in-law Bowell and Moore who became the new owners. Within three years the paper belonged to Bowell alone and for the next 30 years neither Orange Order duties nor an emerging political career dampened his ability to tout Conservative issues in his paper.

In the end, it was his additional responsibilities as a federal cabinet minister that persuaded him to step away from his role as publisher and president. Those running the paper in his absence included his son-in-law James Jamieson and his own son Charles. When Bowell was eased out of his job as Prime Minister and Conservative party leader in 1896, he quickly reasserted his desire to help run the *Intelligencer*. After retiring from the Senate 10 years later, he again took over as the newspaper's publisher. Being in his 80s proved no deterrent to his love for printing and editorializing.

The Orange Order's Grand Master

It was Bowell's boss, George Benjamin, who urged him to join the Orange Order. Today, Orangemen are viewed as Protestant zealots marching along Northern Ireland streets in their orange sashes spoiling for a confrontation with the Catholics. In Bowell's time it was a powerful service organization that wielded political influence in Upper Canada.

Joining Belleville's Royal Scarlet Lodge in 1843, Bowell rarely missed a meeting as he climbed through the ranks to become the chapter's Worshipful Master. In Canada, you didn't have to be Irish to do well as an Orangeman.

He helped patch up a festering squabble in the Orange Order of British North America in 1856 between two competing Grand Masters. He suggested they both step down in favour of a neutral third candidate. It was a valiant move considering one of the Grand Masters was his mentor, George Benjamin. It also helped propel him into the role of Deputy Grand Master for Canada three years later. By 1870, he was Grand Master for British North America.

Throughout his years in the Order, Bowell tried to balance Orange stridency with his own sense of caution. When the Prince of Wales planned to visit Belleville in 1860, it was Bowell who assured local officials there wouldn't be the kind of boisterous Orange display that caused the Prince to bypass Kingston. But the arrival of an Orange contingent from Kingston persuaded him to reverse his stand and bring out the orange bunting. The Prince bypassed Belleville, too.

Although Orange pressure helped push Bowell into the federal cabinet, he often took positions that were not in the best interests of the Order. He had vehemently demanded restitution for Riel's execution of Thomas Scott, an Orangeman originally from his riding, but he also deftly avoided the Order's attempts to have the government incorporate it. One of the great ironies of his brief time as Prime Minister is that it was his support of Manitoba Catholic education that helped bring down his government. He came out squarely in favour of French language and Catholic education rights as intended in the British North America Act, even though it was a decidedly un-Orange thing to advocate.

Harriet Bowell

Bowell was the first, and only, widower to serve as Prime Minister. His wife, Harriet, died more than a decade before he assumed office, so it was his daughter, Evalyn McCarthy, who undertook hostess chores when necessary.

Harriet Louisa Moore was the younger sister of Bowell's apprentice colleague at the *Intelligencer*. A devout Methodist, she was upbeat and pleasant, a perfect foil for the sometimes crusty Bowell. It was an asset that became more valuable when he entered politics. But her preference was to remain at the large family home in Belleville, spending time with her children and grandchildren.

In 1883, her health began to decline, and Bowell convinced her to spend time in California to recuperate. Using his influence as a cabinet minister, he arranged to send her there on a private railway car. The change of climate didn't help and Harriet died the following March. Her funeral back in Belleville included a procession of 87 carriages to the cemetery.

Bowell's Timeline

1823: Born in Rickinghall, Suffolk, England (*December 27*).

1824: Baptized (*March 13*). His mother Elizabeth Marshall marries John Bowell in Rickinghall (*March 19*).

1825: Moves with family to nearby Walsham-le-Willows in Suffolk.

1832: Works for a Suffolk farmer scaring birds away from a field using a 'clapper'. Sails with family from Yarmouth, England, for Canada (*October*). Arrives in Canada and settles in Belleville, Upper Canada (*December*).

1833: Works in his father's Belleville carpentry shop. Attends Methodist Sunday School run by local prominent citizen Billa Flint.

1834: His sister Elizabeth is born in Belleville and dies shortly after (*September 25*); his mother dies as a result of the birth (*October 5*). *The Belleville Intelligencer* advertises for a print shop apprentice (*October 15*). Begins his apprenticeship as a printer, moving in with publisher George Benjamin's family above the office (*December*).

1835: His father remarries, to Ann Mulligan.

1837: Becomes a journeyman printer at *The Intelligencer*. Organizes and drills a boys militia to serve if needed in the Rebellion of 1837. Accused of being a Reformer and assaulting a Conservative with a fence board; the case of mistaken identity is quickly cleared up.

1838: His family moves to Hungerford Township, 22 km north of Belleville, but he continues to live and work for Benjamin at *The Intelligencer*.

1839: Becomes a master printer at *The Intelligencer*.

1841: Leaves *The Intelligencer* when denied a raise and enrols in Sydney Normal School in Foxboro, Ont., just north of Belleville.

1842: Receives his teaching certificate. Accepts a teaching position, but two days before he is to start, accepts Benjamin's offer of $10 a month to return to *The Intelligencer* as shop foreman (*September*).

1843: Joins the Royal Scarlet Lodge of the Orange Order in Belleville (*March 4*).

1846: His boss Benjamin becomes the Grand Master of Orange Lodges in British North America.

1847: Becomes a partner of *The Intelligencer* with Benjamin. Marries Harriet Moore (*December 23*).

1848: Buys *The Intelligencer* from Benjamin; his partner is former fellow apprentice Rodney Moore, now his brother-in-law.

1851: Becomes sole owner of *The Intelligencer*. Works on Benjamin's Conservative election campaign to become Assembly member for Hastings; Benjamin is defeated by another Conservative, Edmund Murney (*October*).

1856: Elected as a trustee to the Belleville common school board. Works on Benjamin's successful by-election campaign to become Assembly member for North Hastings.

1857: Becomes chairman of the Belleville common school board, until 1867. As an ensign, helps organize the Belleville Rifle Company militia.

1859: Family moves to William Street, their Belleville address for the rest of his life. Elected Deputy Grand Master of the Province of Canada Orange Order. Becomes a founding member of the Canadian Press Association (*September 28*).

1860: In Kingston to represent the Orange Order during the Prince of Wales's visit; the Prince refuses to come ashore because the Orange Order is banned in Britain (*September 4*). Respects Belleville's plea for no visible Orange displays during the Prince's visit, but changes his mind when Kingston Orangemen arrive by train to march; the Prince again refuses to disembark (*September 6*).

1862: Becomes Ontario's Grand Master of the British North America Orange Order; serves until 1877. Joins the executive of the Canadian Press Association (*September 23*). Moves *The Intelligencer* office to a new building next door to the old address (*Fall*).

1863: *The Intelligencer* building is destroyed by fire (*February 1*); buys new presses and is back in business on Front Street three weeks later. Seeks election to succeed Benjamin in the Canada Assembly, but is defeated by Reform candidate Campbell Wallbridge (*August*).

1864: Initiated into the freemasons at St. Lawrence Lodge in Montreal. Benjamin, who caught a chill while campaigning for Bowell and never fully recovered, dies (*September 7*)

1865: Takes a leave of absence as school board chairman because of militia duty. Stationed with the Belleville Rifle Company in Amherstburg to prevent Confederate soldiers, seeking refuge in Canada, from attacking the U.S. (*February-May*); he retires soon after. Elected president of the Canadian Press Association for one year (*September 6*).

1866: Launches *The Diurnal* newspaper, which features daily news from Europe via the Atlantic cable; at 10 cents, the expensive publication doesn't last long. A Fenian raid brings him out of militia retirement, as a captain at Prescott (*June*).

1867: Madoc Orange Lodge holds a banquet in his honour (*February*). Begins publishing *The Intelligencer* daily (*May 1*). Becomes a major in the 49th Hastings Battalion (*May*). Canada's first federal election: becomes the first MP for North Hastings as a Liberal-Conservative, beating Campbell Wallbridge (*September*). Steps down as Belleville school board chairman.

1869: Visits England and presides over the Orange Order's international meeting in Londonderry, Ireland. Visits Paris before returning to Canada.

1870: Thomas Scott, an Orangeman originally from Madoc in Bowell's riding, is executed by Louis Riel (*March 4*). Becomes Grand Master of the British North America Orange Order; serves until 1878. Votes against the act creating Manitoba because it allows for separate schools. Becomes a director of the Grand Junction Railway (*Fall*).

1871: Votes against the proposed transcontinental railway to the Pacific coast until the exact costs are known (*March*). Becomes brevet Lieut.-Col. in the 49th Battalion; retires soon after.

1872: Sits on the executive of the Native Canadian Society although he is neither Indigenous nor Canadian-born. Canada's second federal election: re-elected in North Hastings defeating Wallbridge; Macdonald's government is re-elected (*October 12*).

1873: Becomes president of the Hastings Mutual Insurance Company in Belleville. Defends the government in *The Intelligencer* during the Pacific Scandal, calling it the "Pacific Slander" (*April-July*).

1874: Canada's third federal election: re-elected in North Hastings defeating Liberal Edward O'Flynn by 95 votes; Macdonald government loses the election (*January 22*). Makes a motion in the House that Louis Riel, elected in Provencher, Man., be expelled; the vote passes (*April 9*). Doesn't refute an article in the Saint John, N.B., *Globe* that suggests he would be a worthy successor to Macdonald who is considering stepping down (*May*).

1876: Elected president of the Grand Triennial Orange Council of the World in Derry, Ireland (*July*). Joins Macdonald and Tupper speaking at a Conservative picnic in Belleville (*September 12*). Helps drive the Speaker, Timothy Anglin, from office for accepting a government printing contract (*September*); resists calls for his own resignation for accepting government ads in *The Intelligencer*.

1878: Becomes vice-president of the Moira Skating Club in Belleville (*January*). Canada's fourth federal election: re-elected in North Hastings, again defeating O'Flynn; Macdonald's government returns to power (*September 17*). Becomes Customs minister in Macdonald's cabinet (*October 19*) with some urging from the Orange Order. His son John becomes his assistant in Ottawa. Reduces his interest in *The Intelligencer*.

Icy water threat

Bowell could be mean-spirited in House debates and had a short fuse when opposition members returned the favour. Such was the case when a Liberal MP challenged one of his assertions. "Is the honourable member calling me a liar?" he shot back. When his challenger didn't deny it, Bowell grabbed his glass of ice water with the intention of hurling its contents across the floor. But as he raised it, the water arced out behind him and straight down the neck of his Cape Breton caucus colleague sleeping at his desk. With a yell, the man leaped up, frantically trying to reach the icy bits. The laughter in the House ended the confrontation between Bowell and his adversary.

1879: Joined by Tupper (Public Works) and Sir Samuel Leonard Tilley (Finance) for a tour of mines north of Belleville, where each minister gets to set off dynamite blasts (*December 10*). Ends up supporting construction of a transcontinental railway even though voters at a public meeting in Belleville overwhelmingly reject the project (*December*).

1881: Sends his son John to Winnipeg as a customs officer.

1882: Canada's fifth federal election: re-elected in North Hastings defeating Liberal William Coe; Macdonald government is re-elected (*June 20*).

1883: Does not actively support a motion in the House to incorporate the Orange Order; the initiative is defeated (*April*).

1884: Sends his wife Harriet to California to recuperate from illness (*February*). Harriet dies in Hermosa Beach, California (*April 2*). Goes to California to bring back his wife's body. Funeral for Harriet in Belleville (*April 30*). Hands in his resignation after Macdonald expresses concerns about the cabinet, but it is refused.

1885: Sends troops to the North-West to stop resistance by the Métis, acting for Tupper (Railways & Canals) who is raising railway funds in England (*April*). Announces a $20,000 reward to General Frederick Middleton for his role in the North-West Rebellion. Along with Senator Frank Smith, pleads with Macdonald to lend more money to the floundering Canadian Pacific Railway; the effort is unsuccessful, but the Bank of Montreal comes up with another loan to allow the CPR to carry on. Takes on Finance tasks while Tilley (Finance) visits England (*Summer*). Supports the hanging of Louis Riel (*November*).

1886: Accused by the Liberals of using his position to help his son-in-law James Jamieson acquire land in the North-West formerly occupied by the Métis (*March 31*); the charges are not proven. Writes to a friend that he is "weary of politics" and would be happy to retire (*November 12*).

1887: Canada's sixth federal election; re-elected in North Hastings defeating Liberal candidate Dr. H.H. Sutton by more than 1,000 votes; Macdonald's government is re-elected (*February 22*).

1888: Meets Mercy Stevenson of Napanee and within weeks proposes to her; she accepts (*August*). His daughters oppose the marriage and he discovers information about Stevenson that causes him to back out (*August*); the resulting rejection eventually persuades her to move to the U.S.

1891: Canada's seventh federal election: re-elected in North Hastings defeating Liberal Peter Vankleek; Macdonald's government is re-elected (*March 5*). Has his last conversation with Macdonald before a series of strokes leave the Prime Minister paralyzed and unable to speak (*May 22*). Visits Macdonald at Earnscliffe after his last stroke (*May 29*). Carries on as Customs minister in Abbott's government (*June 16*); serves as acting Railways & Canals minister. Misses three days of work to illness, something that rarely happened (*August*). A Bowell Orange Lodge chapter is established in Ottawa. Hands in his resignation to Abbott, but the Prime Minister refuses it (*November*).

1892: Becomes Militia & Defence minister in Abbott's cabinet (*January 25*). Joins Foster (Finance) in Washington to urge the U.S. to lift the McKinley tariff (*February 10-15*); they are unsuccessful. Joins Thompson (Justice) on another trip to Washington to protest proposed tolls on the Sault Ste. Marie Canal (*July*); again unsuccessful. Threatens to resign from cabinet if James Aikins, Lieutenant-Governor of Manitoba, isn't reappointed to the Senate as Macdonald had promised (*October*). Reviews the Manitoba schools question as part of a committee of the Privy Council (*November 25-26*). Appointed to the Senate instead of Aikins and becomes Government Leader in the Senate (*December 5*); resigns as MP for Hastings North. Becomes Canada's first Trade & Commerce minister in Thompson 's cabinet (*December 5*).

1893: Sails for Australia to promote trade with Canada (*September 17*). In Hawaii, suggests Britain annex an unoccupied island west of Hawaii to be used for a cable station (*September*); Britain ignores the idea. With Sandford Fleming, visits Queensland, Victoria and New South Wales to promote closer Canada-Australia ties and a Pacific cable.

Persuades Thompson to host a Colonial Conference in 1894. Arrives back in Canada (*December 23*).

1894: Participates in the Second Colonial Conference in Ottawa as a delegate (*June 28-July 9*). Tours Ontario, Quebec, New Brunswick and Nova Scotia with Foster (Finance) to promote the National Policy tariffs (*Summer*). Joins Thompson and his family on a vacation on Lake Rousseau, Muskoka, Ont. (*August*). Acts as deputy Prime Minister while Thompson sails to Europe to be sworn in to the Imperial Privy Council (*October 29*). Initially, doubts a telegram indicating the death of Thompson in London (*December 12*); joins Foster (Finance) and Thompson's secretary Douglas Stewart to visit Annie Thompson with the news. Governor General Lord Aberdeen asks him to form a government (*December 13*). Attempts to get cabinet backing to form a government (*December 14-19*). **Bowell government (1894-1896).** Becomes Canada's fifth Prime Minister, and 17th Privy Council President (*December 21*); he retains most of Thompson's cabinet. Premier Sir William Whiteway of Newfoundland expresses interest in bringing the colony into Confederation after both of its banks collapse (*December*).

1895: Knighted as a Commander of St. Michael and St. George (*January 1*). Attends Thompson's funeral in Halifax (*January 3*). The Imperial Privy Council rules that Canada's federal government has the power to resolve grievances in cases where a minority has lost previously held rights (*January*); the decision effectively contradicts the council's earlier decision overturning the Supreme Court of Canada's judgement opposing Manitoba's abolishment of Catholic school funding. His cabinet agrees to dissolve Parliament and call an election (*February 16*), but he's persuaded by some ministers to reverse the decision and hold another session in hopes that the Manitoba schools crisis will die down. Issues a remedial order calling on Manitoba to restore school rights to its Catholic minority (*March 12*); Manitoba avoids making any immediate response. His Justice minister Charles Hibbert Tupper resigns from cabinet to protest the switch on calling an election (*March 21*); convinces Hibbert Tupper to return to cabinet a few days later. The royal commission into liquor traffic concludes that prohibition does not prevent liquor sales (*March 29*). Offers to cover up to $10 million of Newfoundland's debt during the Canada-Newfoundland Confederation Conference in Ottawa (*April 16*); the colony asks Canada to assume the entire $16-million debt, but Canada refuses and Newfoundland turns Confederation down. A motion introduced by Manitoba MP Nicholas Flood Davin calling for women's suffrage is defeated (*June 5*). Manitoba rejects the federal remedial order to restore Catholic school rights, saying the request requires more study (*June 13*). Britain's Colonial Boundaries Act confirms Canada's sovereignty over the Arctic (*July 6*). Decides to give Manitoba time to reflect on its refusal to accept the remedial order, igniting a cabinet crisis (*July 6*); Senator August Angers (Agriculture), Sir Adolphe Caron (Postmaster General) and Joseph Ouimet (Public Works) resign in protest. Caron and Ouimet are persuaded to remain, with the latter also taking on Angers' Agriculture portfolio (*July 12*). Again calls on Manitoba to restore school rights to the Catholic minority (*July 26*). Travels west to vacation in Banff (with Lord Aberdeen) and British Columbia (with son John) (*July-August*). John Diefenbaker, Canada's 13th Prime Minister, is born in Neustadt, Ont. (*September 18*). The provisional districts of Yukon, Mackenzie, Ungava and Franklin are established in the North-West Territories (*October 2*). Visits Washington with Hibbert Tupper (Justice) to try to obtain the settlement negotiated in Paris in 1893 (*October 28*). Clark Wallace, Controller of Customs, resigns in protest over the government's action against Manitoba on the school question (*December 14*). Sir Charles Tupper, High Commissioner to London, arrives in Ottawa (*December 15*). Bowell makes Customs and Inland Revenue cabinet positions again (*December 24*). Manitoba refuses a third time to accept the remedial order to re-establish Catholic rights (*December 26*).

1896: At the opening of the Sixth Session, Seventh Parliament, Governor General Lord Aberdeen indicates Manitoba has rejected the remedial order (*January 2*); Parliament is adjourned for four days while cabinet develops remedial legislation to impose on Manitoba. Informed by seven cabinet ministers they intend to resign (*January 4*); they are Foster (Finance), Hibbert Tupper (Justice), Arthur Dickey (Militia & Defence), William Ives (Trade & Commerce), John Haggart (Railways & Canals), Walter Montague (Agriculture) and John Wood (Customs). Fills cabinet vacancies with acting ministers, with himself as acting minister in Finance and Militia & Defence; Thomas Daly (Interior & Indian Affairs) takes Justice and Secretary of State; John Costigan (Marine & Fisheries) takes Trade & Commerce; Joseph Ouimet (Public Works) takes Railways & Canals; Senator Donald Ferguson (Without Portfolio) takes Agriculture; and Senator Frank Smith (Without Portfolio) takes Customs (*January 7*). Tenders his resignation, but Governor General Lord Aberdeen refuses to accept it (*January 8*). Defends his position on the Manitoba schools question in the Senate (*January 9*). Meets with Tupper and agrees to step down only if Foster, Montague and Haggart are not part of a Tupper government (*January 11*). The cabinet crisis ends (*January 14*); Foster, Haggart, Ives and Wood return to their cabinet positions; Sir Charles Tupper resigns as High Commissioner to London and enters cabinet as Secretary of State; his son Sir Charles Hibbert Tupper accommodates him by becoming Solicitor General outside of cabinet. Another remedial bill, enforcing Catholic school rights in Manitoba, is introduced by Tupper in the House of Commons (*February 11*); Manitoba formally protests federal interference. The Liberal opposition begins a successful filibuster to delay final reading of the remedial bill until Parliament must dissolve (*March 19*). Dickey (Justice), Senator Alphonse Desjardins (Militia & Defence) and Sir Donald Smith are appointed commissioners to study the Manitoba schools issue (*March 21*). Talks with Manitoba collapse (*April 7*). Withdraws the remedial bill following a deadlock in the House debate (*April 15*). Canada's Seventh Parliament is dissolved at the very end of its five-year term (*April 24*). Resigns as Prime Minister and Privy Council President (*April 27*). **Bowell government ends.** Sails to England where he is a Canadian commissioner at the Pacific Cable Conference arranged by Sir Donald Smith, high commissioner to London (*May*). His successor, Tupper, loses the eighth federal election to Laurier after only 69 days as Prime Minister (*June 23*); Bowell becomes Leader of the Opposition in the Senate (*July 11*).

1897: Visits western Canada with Tupper (*September-October*). Attends Conserv-ative meeting in Toronto to try and rebuild the party (*October*).

1898: Leads a Belleville delegation to Grand Trunk Railway headquarters in Montreal to promote the reopening of its North Hastings line (*March*). Stops the Yukon Railway Bill in the Senate (*March*).

Dying in good company

On a 1911 visit to Toronto's Albany Club, bastion of all things Conserv-ative, the aging Senator had the misfortune to fall down the stairs. There was immediate concern that he was dead. Hearing the comment as he lay on the floor, Bowell gazed up at the photos on the wall of Macdonald, Tupper and Borden and replied: "Well, if I am, at least I am in good company."

1900: Introduces British Columbia's petition in the Senate to limit or stop Chinese immigration (*July 6*). Speaks out in Carleton Place, Ont., against the re-election of John Haggart, his former Railways & Canals minister who had quit cabinet (*October*).

1901: Becomes president of Belleville Hardware Manufacturing Company, serves for the next nine years.

1906: (*February 19*). Resigns as Leader of the Opposition in the Senate (*March 1*). Moves back to Belleville and resumes job as publisher of the *Intelligencer*, taking over from his son Charles.

1910: Becomes president of Springer Lock Manufacturing Company in Belleville until his death. Exposes the practice of the Belleville mayor and a councillor of selling unadvertised lots repossessed by the town to relatives who then resold them (*December*).

1913: Honored by 300 attending a banquet at Belleville's Masonic Moira Lodge to celebrate his 90th birthday (*December 27*).

1916: Gets bronchitis while visiting son John in Vancouver; persuaded not to travel on to the Yukon (*Summer*).

1917: Gets bronchitis again, at home in Belleville (*November*); dies two weeks later (*December 10*). Belleville stores close for his funeral at Bridge Street Methodist Church, but no leading politicians attend (*December 13*); buried at Belleville Cemetery

Book about Bowell

- **2017**: Betsy Dewar Boyce; *The Accidental Prime Minister: The Biography of Sir Mackenzie Bowell* (Kirby Books)

Kings and Queens of Canada

1.	Victoria	1867-1901
2.	Edward VII	1901-1910
3.	George V	1910-1936
4.	Edward VIII	1936
5.	George VI	1936-1952
6.	Elizabeth II	1952-

6

Sir Charles Tupper

The Untried Prime Minister

Dr. Charles Tupper spent only two months as Prime Minister, in spite of his 41-year apprenticeship as a politician. Brought in as a fixer after Bowell's departure, he was able to play the kind of troubleshooting role he had often performed successfully as a cabinet minister and diplomat during the Macdonald years. But it wasn't enough to stem the desire for change that defeated his Conservative party in 1896. His entire mandate as leader had been consumed fighting a losing election. Today, Tupper is better remembered as the Father of Confederation who brought (and kept) Nova Scotia into Canada.

Tupper the Politician

Prime Minister of Canada: May 1, 1896 – July 8, 1896
Length of term: 2 months, 7 days
Parliament as Prime Minister: none (Seventh already dissolved)
Age on entering office: 74
Political party: Conservative
Leader of party: May 1, 1896 – February 5, 1901
Member of Parliament: July 1, 1867 – May 28, 1884; November 9, 1887 – May 22, 1888; February 4, 1896 – November 18, 1900
Ridings represented: Cumberland [N.S.] (1867-1884, 1887-1888); Cape Breton [N.S.] (1896-1900)
Cabinet portfolios: Privy Council President (1870-1872); Inland Revenue (1872-1873); Customs (1873); Public Works (1878-1879); Railways & Canals (1879-1884); Finance (1887-1888); Secretary of State (1896)
Other political posts: Provincial Secretary of Nova Scotia (1857-1860, 1863-1867); Premier of Nova Scotia (1864-1867); High Commissioner to the United Kingdom (1883-1887, 1888-1896); Leader of the Opposition (1896-1901)
Knighted: May 24, 1879
Titles: Commander of the Bath (1867); Canadian Privy Councillor (1867); Knight Commander of St. Michael & St. George (1879); Grand Commander

of St. Michael & St. George (1886); Baronetcy (1888); Imperial Privy Councillor (1908)

Quotes: "A union of the North American provinces would elevate their position, consolidate their influence and advance their interests; and, at the same time, continue their fealty to their mother country and their Queen." (his observation after the 1864 Charlottetown Conference); "I do not at all regret having placed my services at the disposal of the party, as otherwise I would have been held responsible for its defeat." (his comments to the media after his government's loss to Laurier's Liberals in 1896).

Lived after term: 19 years

TUPPER THE MAN

Name: Charles Tupper

Born: July 2, 1821, Amherst, Nova Scotia

Ancestry: English

Religion: Baptist, Anglican

Education: Horton Academy, Wolfville, Nova Scotia (1840); M.D. [Doctor of Medicine] (University of Edinburgh, Scotland, 1843)

Nicknames: War Horse of Cumberland; Ram of Cumberland County; The Fighting Doctor

Military service: Surgeon Major of the Halifax Artillery First Brigade)

Occupation: doctor; premier

Occupation after term: politician

Publications: *Recollections of 60 Years in Canada* (1914); *Political Reminiscences of the Rt. Honourable Sir Charles Tupper, Bart.* (1914); *The Life and Letters of the Rt. Hon. Sir Charles Tupper, Bart., K.C.M.G.*, 2 vols. (1918)

Appearance: "... of medium height, straight, muscular, wiry, and had intense nervous energy which gave him quickness of movement and ceaseless mental activity." (E.M. Saunders in *The Life and Letters of the Right Hon. Sir Charles Tupper*); "... a short, overweight bulldog, humourless and caustic" (Vincent Durant in *War Horse of Cumberland*)

Personality: "He never wanted for language. His vocabulary was copious but not varied, and was more torrential than judicial." (George Ross, MP [1873-1883]); "Mr. Tupper is capable but too incisive; he makes bitter enemies for himself; he is ambitious and a gambler." (Hector-Louis Langevin, MP [1867-1892])

Married: Frances Amelia Morse, October 8, 1846, Amherst, Nova Scotia

Age at marriage: 25

Years married: 66

Died: October 30, 1915, Bexleyheath, Kent, England

Age at death: 94

Cause of death: heart failure

Buried: St. John's Cemetery, Halifax, Nova Scotia

Tupper was the:

- Prime Minister to serve the shortest term
- Prime Minister who held the second largest number of previous cabinet positions (7, tied with Meighen)

- Oldest Prime Minister to start a term
- First Prime Minister who wasn't in Parliament
- Only Prime Minister inducted into the Canadian Medical Hall of Fame
- Longest living Prime Minister (94)
- First Prime Minister educated at a foreign university (Edinburgh)
- First Prime Minister who was a post-graduate student (Doctor of Medicine)
- First Prime Minister who was a doctor
- First Prime Minister to write his memoirs
- First Prime Minister to serve as Finance minister
- Second Prime Minister who was a Father of Confederation
- Last surviving Father of Confederation
- Last Prime Minister who was also a provincial premier (for three days in Nova Scotia)
- Third Prime Minister who was a member of a provincial legislature (N. S.)
- Second Prime Minister whose son became a Member of Parliament
- Fifth Conservative Prime Minister
- First President of the Canadian Medical Association
- Longest serving President of the Canadian Medical Association – three years

Tupper's legacy
- Brought Nova Scotia into Confederation (as the colony's premier)
- Helped create the Conservative's National Policy

TUPPER'S FAMILY

Tupper's Parents

Father: Charles Tupper
Born: August 6, 1794, Cornwallis, Nova Scotia
Occupation: clergyman; educator; author
Second wife: Mary Miller (1852)
Third wife: Betsy Dimock Knowles (1868)
Died: January 19, 1881, Treemont, Nova Scotia
Age at death: 86

Mother: Miriam Knowlton Lockhart Lowe
Born: January 16, 1790, Parrsboro, Nova Scotia
First husband: John Smith Lowe (January 29, 1807) (they had 4 sons and 2 daughters)
Married: December 3, 1818
Children: 11 (6 with Lowe; 5 with Tupper)
Died: July 4, 1851
Place of death: Amherst, Nova Scotia
Age at death: 71

Tupper's Brothers & Sisters (4 siblings; Charles the second)

Sister: Charlotte Tupper (1819-1879); 2 children
Married: Thomas Bleakney (1840); clergyman

Brother: Nathan Tupper (1823-1888); 7 children
Married: Eleanor Jane Bent (September 18, 1847)
Occupation: physician
Brother: James (1825-1825)
Sister: Elizabeth (1829-1873); 6 children (with Baker)
Married: William F. McPhee (1847); Samuel Gates Baker (March 4, 1852)
Half-Brother: John Smith Lowe Jr. (1811-1895)
Married: Lucy Ann Rockwell
Half-Brother: Moses Amos Lowe (1812-1887)
Married: Mary Bent
Half-Brother: Thomas Lowe (b.1813)
Half-Sister: Margery Lowe (1814-1889)
Married: John Hillson
Half-Brother: George Lowe (1815-1820)
Half-Sister: Miriam Lavinia Lowe (1816-1891); 11 children
Married: Isaac Schurman (October 6, 1833)

Tupper's Wife

Name: Frances Amelia Morse
Born: May 11, 1828, Amherst, Nova Scotia
Father: Silas Hibbert Morse (law clerk)
Mother: Elizabeth Stewart
Age at marriage: 18
Died: May 13, 1912, Bexleyheath, Kent, England
Age at death: 86
Burial place: St. John's Cemetery, Halifax, Nova Scotia
Younger than Tupper: 6 years
Died before Tupper: 3 years

Tupper's Children (6 – 2 died young)

Name: Emma Tupper
Born: July 23, 1847, Amherst, Nova Scotia
Married: Maj.-Gen. Donald Roderick Cameron (July 22, 1869)
Children: 7 – Sophie Tupper; Nancie Sophia Ellis Tupper; Lily Tupper; Mary Tupper; Charles Stewart Tupper; Frances Melita Tupper; William Tupper
Died: November 5, 1925, London, England

Name: Elizabeth 'Lillie' Stewart Tupper
Born: April 23, 1849, Amherst, Nova Scotia
Died: November 30, 1850, Amherst, Nova Scotia

Name: James Stewart Tupper
Born: October 26, 1851, Amherst, Nova Scotia
Occupation: lawyer
Married: Marie Wilson Robertson (September 8, 1875); Ada Campbell Galt (June 9, 1880)
Children: 4 – Marie Stewart; Jessie Campbell; Frances; Charles Stewart
Died: April 29, 1915, Oxford, England
Note: Son Charles succeeded his grandfather to the baronetcy as Sir Charles.

Name: Sir Charles Hibbert Tupper
Born: August 3, 1855, Amherst, Nova Scotia
Occupation: lawyer; Marine & Fisheries minister (1888-1895); Justice minister (1895-1896)
Married: Janet McDonald (September 9, 1879) (sister Margaret married Charles's brother William)
Children: 7 – Charles Stewart; Sophie Almon; Frances Lillian; James Macdonald; Janet Miriam Grace; Reginald Hibbert; Victor Gordon 'Gordie'
Knighted: 1893
Died: March 30, 1927, Vancouver, British Columbia
Notes: Son Victor Gordon died at Vimy Ridge in the First World War. He was named for his grandfather's 1896 by-election victory and for the Governor General's family name: Gordon. His grandson Charles Merritt received the Victoria Cross and was MP for Vancouver-Burrard 1945-1949.

Name: Sophie Almon Tupper
Born: February 28, 1858, Amherst, Nova Scotia
Died: August 13, 1863, Halifax, Nova Scotia

Name: William Johnston Tupper
Born: June 29, 1862, Halifax, Nova Scotia
Occupation: lawyer; Lieutenant-Governor of Manitoba (1934-40)
Married: Abbie Margaret Wilhelmina Tulloch McDonald (July 6, 1887) (sister Janet married William's brother Charles)
Children: 7 – Catherine Gladys; Frances Amelia; Reginald; Emma Lillian; Edith Margaret; Charles William; Stewart McDonald
Died: December 17, 1947, Winnipeg, Manitoba

POLITICAL STORIES

Premier of Nova Scotia

When Tupper became premier in 1864, replacing James Johnston, he was already busy as provincial secretary pushing ahead on two of his favourite issues: expanding the railways and improving public education. As premier, he extended the Nova Scotia Railway to Pictou and pursued the creation of an Intercolonial Railway to Montreal.

He also introduced legislation for a non-denominational, state-subsidized education system. When many school districts refused to establish local taxation to pay for the public system, Tupper introduced a second act imposing compulsory local taxation.

These initiatives paled in comparison to the possibility of a maritime union that soon blossomed into a larger union with Canada. Tupper spent the remainder of his time as premier vigorously championing Confederation. In July 1867, he resigned as premier to run in Canada's first federal election, becoming the first MP for Cumberland, N.S.

29 years to get top job

The idea of a united British North America was first raised by Tupper in Saint John, N.B., in 1860. Three years later, as Nova Scotia's provincial secretary, he was able to advance the concept on a smaller scale when he secured the provincial assembly's approval for a conference to explore a union with other British Maritime colonies.

Tupper was Nova Scotia's premier by the time the 1864 conference took place in Charlottetown, P.E.I. His Nova Scotia delegation included both Conservatives and Liberals. When discussion expanded to consider a union of all British North America, Tupper was intrigued by its possibilities. After the conference, he kept the debate going by inviting interested delegates to continue working in Halifax. Canadian delegate George Brown stayed at the Tupper home that weekend.

He led the same Nova Scotia team to a second conference, held in Quebec City a month later. Again, he played the lead role among Maritime colonies in promoting Confederation.

For the next two years, Tupper fought vociferous opposition to the scheme in his province. When Nova Scotia joined the two Canadas and New Brunswick in 1867, he opted to become a member of the federal government. At first, he was the only Nova Scotia MP backing Confederation and he worked tirelessly with Macdonald to successfully keep Nova Scotia from opting out of the new union. It would be almost three decades before he became Prime Minister and at the time of his death, 48 years after Confederation, he was the last surviving Father of the great experiment.

The good life of a High Commissioner

Tupper's most satisfying job was likely that of Canada's High Commissioner to the United Kingdom, a position he held from 1883 to 1896 (except for a short interruption in 1887-1888). In addition to representing the nation's interests in the mother country, he also mingled with continental Europe's upper crust on a regular basis.

Initially, Tupper continued drawing a salary as a Canadian MP and Minister of Railways & Canals, so took no pay for the British posting. The opposition denounced him for holding two conflicting jobs. Although the government amended the legislation to permit the two roles if only one was paid, he soon resigned from cabinet and as an MP.

In 1887, Macdonald urged him to return home and serve as Finance minister. Tupper reluctantly agreed, but as his cabinet job dragged on into 1888, he was finally able to convince Macdonald to let him return to England and bring his son Charles Hibbert Tupper into cabinet. Before the end of the year, he was Baron Tupper and participating in trade negotiations with Spain.

Life was good. He wielded influence in Europe, although during negotiations with France in 1893 he over-extended himself by making decisions without consulting the Canadian government. Eventually, the seductive call of political duty resulted in his return to Canada, even though he now tended to see England as his home.

Another reluctant leader

Tupper's name was on a short list of logical successors to Macdonald as Prime Minister, even though his bully-style temperament made him unpopular with many of his colleagues. He told his son Charles Hibbert he was happy in his job as High Commissioner in Britain and supported Thompson for the leadership.

Over the next five years, he watched from London as Abbott, then Thompson, then Bowell attempted to navigate the Conservative government through the usual shoals of Canadian politics, dominated by the sensitive issue of minority religious and language rights in Manitoba.

The party wasn't happy with Bowell as leader. Tupper was continually being urged to come home and take over. He couldn't make his reluctance clearer when he told his son that assuming the leadership would be a death sentence. But, in late 1895, he unenthusiastically returned home on the pretext of promoting improved steamship service across the Atlantic. He used the opportunity to meet with Bowell, and during that meeting they learned that seven cabinet ministers (including Tupper's son) were planning to resign.

A few days later, Bowell asked Tupper to step in as Prime Minister. He declined. However, by agreeing to enter cabinet as Secretary of State, he helped defuse the cabinet rebellion. By then, the government's mandate was almost over and Bowell resigned when Parliament was dissolved. Lord Aberdeen, who had no love for Tupper, asked him to form a government – one that would last only 69 days.

PERSONAL STORIES

Sir Charles and Sir Charles Jr.

Tupper was the second Prime Minister to have a son in federal politics. Because father and son had the same name, references to the younger Charles usually included his middle name Hibbert, his grandfather's middle name. They not only shared a first name, they also had similar personalities. As Macdonald told Thompson in a note in the mid-1880s, Hibbert Tupper "has the bumptiousness of his father".

Before being elected as an MP in 1882, Hibbert Tupper had already solidified his political credentials by marrying Janet McDonald, daughter of the federal Justice minister James McDonald. In 1888, he entered Macdonald's cabinet as Marine & Fisheries minister – at 32, the youngest cabinet member in Canada's first 100 years.

Tupper Sr. managed much of his son's career, beginning by securing him a job with Thompson's Halifax law firm. Hibbert Tupper's first cabinet position was also dad's doing. It was the first of two times they swapped jobs in and out of cabinet. Charles Hibbert became Marine & Fisheries ministers after his father left Finance to return to England as High Commissioner. In 1895, Hibbert Tupper left cabinet to make room for his father as Secretary of State.

The arduous journey to Red River

After joining her husband who was posted to the Red River colony in 1869, Tupper's daughter Emma found herself stranded when the provisional government of Louis Riel barred them from entering. Tupper's wife urged him to bring Emma home, but it wouldn't be an easy trip for the 51-year-old politician. It was winter and there was no Canadian route to the west. With Canadian negotiator Donald Smith as his companion, Tupper took a variety of trains and sleds, arriving in Pembina, Minnesota territory, on Christmas Eve. Emma's reaction to the effort was, "What did you come for?"

But the trip wasn't over because Emma's luggage was in Riel's hands north of the border. Tupper had also agreed to Macdonald's request to try and meet with the Métis leader. The day after Christmas, he crossed into Red River territory, bundled onto a horse-drawn sled he described as "a large canvas shoe on a toboggan." His driver was a 17-year-old boy from Pembina. Frozen fog and 30-degrees-below-zero-Fahrenheit weather forced Tupper to get out and lead the horse through the snowdrifts. After losing the trail, they relied on occasional glimpses of the North Star. It was late at night when they staggered up to a remote Métis shack.

The next morning they pushed on to St. Norbert where Tupper met Riel's sister, one of the local nuns. The two continued to exchange letters until her death. Finally reaching Fort Garry, he met with Riel who agreed to return the luggage belonging to Tupper's daughter and her husband. Back in St. Norbert, he urged Father Richot to convince Riel to receive Canada's negotiators.

The trip back to Ottawa included a 10-day wagon trip and rides on nine railways. Leaving his daughter in the capital, he pushed on to New York, then sailed to Halifax on the *City of Boston*. After he disembarked, the ship set sail to Liverpool but disappeared in the Atlantic. It was last seen off Sable Island by a schooner called the *Charles Tupper*.

Lady Frances Tupper

Charles Tupper's diary entry about his proposal to Frances Morse reads more like a business arrangement than a profession of love. She was only 18 and recently back from private schooling in Massachusetts when she married the Amherst doctor. But, after 55 years of marriage, his written had taken a decided romantic turn. "I married her with the bloom of Cumberland on her cheek, and that bloom is in my heart now."

The in-between years were not always easy for Frances. She came to accept his domineering, bullying ways, pouring her energy instead into raising their four children (two others died young). She also seemed to accept that he was a rascal when it came to women, although she probably recognized most of it for what it was: embarrassing bluster rather than serial philandering.

Frances was the first lady for only 68 days, with little time to make her mark on Ottawa. She originally hadn't moved to the capital until her husband had already served as an MP for many years. However, her years of entertaining in London during Tupper's tenure as British High Commissioner made her a comfortable hostess during his short term as Prime Minister.

A telling glimpse into her secondary role in the marriage was confided in a letter to a friend. "It caused me a pang when my husband told me that he of-fered our house for sale not that I cared so much for Ottawa but it was our home."

Tupper's Timeline

1821: Born in East Amherst, N.S. (*July 2*). His parents build a log home on their recently acquired farm property in East Amherst.

1823: His brother Nathan is born in East Amherst (*July 18*).

1825: His brother James is born in East Amherst (*December 6*); dies 20 days later.

1826: Ill health forces his father Joseph to return to East Amherst after a short term as minister of the Baptist Church in Saint John, N.B. (*October 1*).

1827: Attends school in Amherst where one of the teachers is Jonathon McCully, a future Father of Confederation.

1828: Finishes reading the entire Bible to his father, a Baptist minister.

1829: His only sister Charlotte is born in East Amherst (*August 27*).

1833: Moves with family to Bedeque, P.E.I. (*May*).

1834: Moves with family back to Amherst where his father becomes principal of the Grammar School (*May*).

1837: Studies medicine with Dr. Benjamin Page in Amherst (*January*). Attends Horton Academy (now Acadia University) in Wolfville, N.S. (*August 12*).

1838: Helps plant ornamental trees on the Horton Academy grounds; some still standing in front of the old administration building. Saved from drowning by classmate Pat Hockney; asks Hockney to teach him to swim.

1839: Serves as a medical student to Dr. Ebenezer F. Harding in Windsor, Nova Scotia (*November 7*).

1840: Completes his apprenticeship with Harding (*August 27*). Sails for Scotland to attend medical school at the University of Edinburgh (*August*).

1841: While skating on a lake near Edinburgh, helps save a man who falls through the ice. Moves to a new rooming house where former classmate Daniel Parker lives (*August*); Parker prevents another roommate from shooting Tupper during an argument.

1842: Glimpses Queen Victoria on her first visit to Edinburgh; the crowd is so dense he was "lifted off my feet by the pressure and thus carried more than a hundred feet before I touched the ground." (*September 2*).

1843: Passes examinations to become a member of the Edinburgh Royal College of Surgeons (*April 20*). Receives his doctorate of medicine – MD – from the University of Edinburgh (*August 1*). Returns to Amherst to open a medical practice (*August*). Opens a pharmacy in Amherst that remains in business for the next 169 years (*Fall*).

1844: Attends a political meeting in Amherst featuring Nova Scotia cabinet minister Alexander Stewart and opposition leader Joseph Howe (*October 8*); sends a report of the meeting to the government leader, James W. Johnston.

1846: Marries Frances Morse – niece of former cabinet minister Stewart – in Amherst (*October 8*). Shares a house with his in-laws.

1847: Younger brother Nathan joins his medical practice. His first daughter Emma is born in Amherst (*July 23*).

1849: His second daughter Elizabeth 'Lillie' is born in Amherst (*April 23*). Their Amherst home burns down (*June*). Daughter Lillie dies of diarrhea (*November 30*).

1851: His mother Miriam dies in Amherst (*July 4*). Ill with typhus (*August*). His first son James Stewart is born in Amherst (*October 26*).

1852: Makes his first political speech nominating Thomas De Wolfe as the Conservative candidate opposing Joseph Howe in Cumberland County (*March*); Howe wins.

1855: Announces his candidacy in the colony's election as a Conservative can-didate with Alexander Macfarlane, running against Joseph Howe and Stephen Fulton (*May 1*). Elected along with Macfarlane (*May 22*). His brother Nathan takes on most of his patients. His second son Charles Hibbert is born in Amherst (*August 3*).

1856: Given a lead role in developing the Conservatives' policy by party leader James W. Johnston (*January 30*). Attends his first session of the legislative assembly (*January 31*). Announces in his maiden speech that the Conservatives have reversed their stand and now favour government involvement in railway construction (*February 5*). Takes on the project of having a railway built from the Atlantic colonies to the Canadas.

1857: Becomes Provincial Secretary in Johnston's government (*February 23*) and formally turns his medical practice over to his brother Nathan.

1858: Turns down appointment as Surgeon General of the Nova Scotia militia (*February 21*); had been Surgeon Major of the Halifax Artillery First Brigade. His third daughter Sophie is born in Halifax (*February 28*). Represents Nova Scotia in discussions in England seeking British support for an intercolonial railway; meets Queen Victoria, shipping magnate Samuel Cunard and colonial bureaucrat Lord Carnarvon, but fails to secure British funding.

1859: Re-elected in Cumberland County; the Johnston government continues in power even though the Liberals win a majority (*May 12*). Finishes 'perusing' the Bible in German, adding the accomplishment to his examination of the book in Hebrew, Syriac, Greek, Latin, Italian, French and English, as well as the New Testament in Spanish and Portuguese (*December 22*).

1860: Resigns as Provincial Secretary after the Conservatives lose a confidence vote (*February 7*). Becomes Halifax Medical Officer (*February*). Family moves to Halifax where he opens a medical practice. Becomes editor of the *British Colonist*, a Conservative newspaper published three times a week in Halifax. Speaks in Saint John, N.B., in favour of a British North America union (*November 9*).

1861: Receives his MRCS (Membership of the Royal Colleges of Surgeons) degree from Edinburgh. Seconds a motion in the Nova Scotia legislature presented by Premier Joseph Howe in favour of a British North America union (*April*).

1862: His third son William Johnston is born in Halifax; named after the former premier of Nova Scotia (*June 29*). Appointed a provisional governor of the new Dalhousie College (*August 19*).

1863: Re-elected in Cumberland County; the Conservative government is returned to power (*May 28*); again appointed Provincial Secretary. His five-year-old daughter Sophie dies of diphtheria (*August 13*). Visits Quebec to survey the Intercolonial Railway (*August*). Buys 'Armadale', his new home in Halifax. Becomes president of the Medical Society of Nova Scotia. Introduces a resolution to the Dalhousie College board to found a medical school (*November*).

1864: Brings a second doctor, William Wickwire, into his Halifax practice. Introduces a resolution in favour of union with other British Maritime colonies, suggesting a conference to discuss it (*March 28*). Becomes Premier of Nova Scotia replacing Johnston who becomes a judge (*May 11*). Leads the Nova Scotia delegation to the Charlottetown Conference in Prince Edward Island where he tables a motion for a possible Maritime union

(*September 1-8*); the motion is postponed while delegates explore possible union with Canada. Hosts the con-tinuation of the conference in Halifax after the discussion expands to explore a British North American union (*September 10-12*); Canada West delegate George Brown stays at his home. Leads the Nova Scotia delegation to the Quebec Conference where the concept of Confederation is approved (*October 10-27*). Visits Montreal, Ottawa, Kingston, Belleville, Coburg and Toronto after the conference (*October 28-November 5*). Maritime delegates meeting in Toronto agree to postpone Maritime union in favour of British North American Confederation (*November 3*).

1865: Tells Macdonald that Halifax merchants object to Confederation (*January 4*). Embarks on a Nova Scotia speaking tour to defend Confederation (*January*). Introduces the Act of Education, giving Nova Scotia the first free, non-denominational, tax supported school system in British North America. Joins New Brunswick Premier A.J. Smith in London, England, to complete the Intercolonial Railway contract (*June*); it is later cancelled by Nova Scotia when the company fails to carry it out. Has lunch with Queen Emma of Honolulu and explorer Dr. David Livingstone in London (*August*).

1866: Moves that Nova Scotia endorse Confederation and send delegates to a conference in England (*April 10*); it passes 31 to 19 eight days later in the face of a threatened Fenian invasion. Discovers a Halifax girl with cholera at the beginning of the epidemic and quickly sets up an isolation unit at the local hospital (*April 11*). Resigns as Halifax Medical Officer. Sails for England with the Nova Scotia delegation taking part in the London Conference (*July 19*). Visits Paris with his wife Frances and daughter Emma (*October 26*). Attends the London Conference for Confederation discussions (*December 4-February 10, 1867*).

1867: Attends the wedding of John A. Macdonald and Agnes Bernard; Emma, his daughter, is a bridesmaid (*February 16*). Meets Victoria, along with Macdonald, Cartier, Galt and Tilley (*February 27*). Returns to Nova Scotia for the opening of the legislative assembly (*March 16*). Gets Thomas D'Arcy McGee to agree that they both surrender spots in Canada's first cabinet in favour of a compromise candidate: Edward Kenny, a Nova Scotia Catholic (*June*). Victoria makes him a Companion of the Bath (*July 1*). Resigns as Premier of Nova Scotia and is succeeded by Hiram Blanchard (*July 3*). Canada's first federal election: becomes the first MP for Cumberland defeating William Annand by 94 votes; all other Confederationists are defeated; they also lose the first concurrent Nova Scotia provincial election (*September*). Elected the first president of the Canadian Medical Society (later Association) in Quebec City, serving for three years (*October 9*). William Annand of the anti-Confederation forces takes office as the second provincial Premier of Nova Scotia (*November 7*).

1868: Nova Scotia legislature passes a resolution to withdraw from Confederation (*February 21*). Tupper turns down Macdonald's offer to make him chairman of the Intercolonial Railway Commission (*March 14*). Sails for England to oppose the efforts of Annand and Howe to remove Nova Scotia from Confederation (*March*). Meets with Howe and offers him a possible federal cabinet position (*April 6*). Sails back to Halifax with Annand and Howe (*July 4*) after Britain rebuffs their appeal. Becomes one of the founders of Dalhousie University's Faculty of Medicine. Hosts the federal delegation visiting Halifax to try and win over the anti-Confederation politicians (*August 1-2*). Re-elected president of the Canadian Medical Society at its first annual meeting in Montreal (*September*). Establishes a medical practice in Ottawa.

1869: Offered a professorship at Dalhousie College (*July 1*); turns it down. His only daughter Emma marries Captain Donald H. Cameron (*July 22*). Re-elected president of the Canadian Medical Association for a third term (*September*). Leaves Toronto for the Red River Settlement with Donald Smith, one of the commissioners sent to study the Métis grievances and uprising. Plans to bring back his daughter who is stranded with McDougall's party in Pembina near the U.S. border (*December 13*). Arrives at Fort Garry and meets Louis Riel who agrees to return Emma's luggage (*December 28*).

1870: Arrives back in Halifax from Red River (*January 28*). Enters cabinet as Privy Council President, succeeding Kenny who returns to Nova Scotia to take over temporary administration of the provincial government (*June 21*). Declines re-election as president of the Canadian Medical Association for a fourth term.

1871: Leases a summer home in St. Andrews, New Brunswick. Buys a summer home in Parrsboro, Nova Scotia.

1872: Becomes Inland Revenue minister in Macdonald's cabinet (*July 2*). Declines a knighthood unless Howe also receives one (*July 16*). Canada's second federal election: re-elected in Cumberland County defeating Judge W.A.D. Morse by 1,260 votes; Macdonald government is re-elected (*August*). Asks Adams Archibald to resign as Lieutenant-Governor of Manitoba for agreeing to accept Louis Riel's assistance to repel a Fenian raid (*October*). Attends the opening of the international railway between Portland, Maine and Saint John, N.B., with Lord Lisgar, Tilley and U.S. President Ulysses S. Grant (*October*).

1873: Becomes Customs minister, succeeding Tilley who moves to Finance (*February 22*). Helps secure the post of Lieutenant-Governor of Nova Scotia for Joseph Howe, who dies on June 1 (*May*). Resigns as Customs minister after the fall of the Macdonald government because of the Pacific scandal (*November 5*).

1874: Canada's third federal election: re-elected in Cumberland, one of only two Conservatives elected in Nova Scotia as Mackenzie's Liberals easily win (*January 22*). Resumes his medical practice in Ottawa, moving it to St. Andrews, N.B., in the warmer weather. Becomes Finance and Public Works critic for the Conservative opposition (*March 26*). Charged by George Hibbard, his election opponent, with corrupt election practices; defended by lawyer John S.D. Thompson of Halifax (*July 2*) who succeeds in having the objections overruled (*August 17*).

1875: Tells a Halifax audience the Conservatives' National Policy would revive the economy (*November 16*); the speech is reproduced as a popular pamphlet.

1876: His daughter-in-law Marie, wife of son James, dies in Toronto following childbirth (*August 6*). Moves his medical practice from St. Andrews to Toronto, to be with his son James (*August*); returns to Ottawa within a year.

1877: Attends to Governor General Lord Dufferin who was thrown from his sleigh (*March*). Delivers a five-hour speech in the House proposing a non-confidence motion against the Mackenzie government (*April 21*); unsuccessful. Flagged by Macdonald as his possible successor at a picnic in Kingston (*June 6*).

1878: Canada's fourth federal election; re-elected in Cumberland defeating Liberal William Pipes (a future Nova Scotia premier); Macdonald's Conservatives return to power (*September 17*). Appointed Public Works minister in Macdonald's second government (*October 17*). Rents Cliffside house (on the site of today's Supreme Court) that was previously rented by Mackenzie.

1879: Presents a motion proposing the Canadian Pacific Railway (*May 10*). Becomes first Railways & Canals minister (*May 20*). Knighted with Samuel Tilley, Richard Cartwright and Alexander Campbell by Governor General Lord Lorne in Montreal (*May 24*). Sails to England with Macdonald to find funds for the proposed transcontinental railway (*July 26*).

Son Charles Hibbert marries Janet Macdonald, daughter of James Macdonald, Canada's Justice minister (*September 9*). Checks on railway progress in Winnipeg.

1880: Recommends that American backers be included in efforts to fund the railway (*June 15*). Visits England to complete the railway transaction with George Stephen's Canadian Pacific Railway syndicate (*July*). Contract to have Stephen's consortium build the Canadian Pacific Railway is signed (*October 20*). Checks again on railway progress in the west (*November*). Moves that the CPR be given a $25 million grant and 25 million acres of land in the North-West Territories as part of the agreement (*December 13*).

1881: His father Charles dies in Treemont, N.S. (*January 19*); Ottawa workload prevents his attendance at the funeral. Moves the third reading of the CPR incorporation bill (*February 1*). Suffers a severe bronchial attack (*February 12*). Sails to England for medical advice following concern he might have Bright's disease; gets advice from a young passenger Dr. William Osler to slow down (*March 9*); starts to improve. Attends the Monetary Conference in Paris with Sir Alexander T. Galt (*April*). Recommends that several provincial acts in Manitoba be disallowed for con-travening the CPR monopoly agreement (*November 2*).

1882: Absolved of any discreditable practices by a Royal Commission into the awarding of CPR contracts (*January*). Receives an honorary Doctorate of Civil Law degree from Acadia University. Moves the second reading of a bill to construct the Canadian Pacific Railway through a pass other than Yellowhead (*April 17*). Canada's fifth federal election: re-elected in Cumberland by acclamation and his son Charles Hibbert is elected as the Conservative member for Pictou; Macdonald's government is re-elected (*June 20*). Sails to England for a rest (*August*). Also visits Ireland where he meets a young man named Joyce (not James Joyce) in a poor house and brings him back to Canada to work.

1883: Appointed High Commissioner to London, England, succeeding Sir Alex-ander T. Galt; he receives no salary for the position and continues as Railways & Canals minister (*May 30*). Arrives in England (*June 20*), then visits Continental Europe. Represents Canada at an international conference on submarine cables, held in Paris (*October 15-24*). Leaves for Canada in response to the CPR financial crisis (*December 6*).

1884: Presents a motion in the House to loan $22.5 million to the CPR (*February 1*). Edward Blake, Leader of the Opposition, moves a resolution declaring Tupper's seat vacant, since he is serving as High Commissioner (*February 25*); the government passes an amendment to the Independence of Parliament Act permitting his dual role because he is not being paid to be commissioner. His bill authorizing a loan to the CPR is passed in the House (*February 28*). Argues with Macdonald during a cabinet meeting and storms out (*April*); Macdonald later apologizes, but the two are never again close friends. Visits New York City to sign a railway contract for Nova Scotia (*April 23*). Meets with U.S. president Chester A. Arthur in Washington (*April 30*). A special banquet is held in his honour in Ottawa (*May 8*), followed by one in Amherst (*May 22*). Sails to England (*May 24*). Resigns as Railways & Canals minister and as MP for Cumberland to concentrate on his duties as High Commissioner (*May 28*). Moves into a permanent London home on Cromwell Road (*June 17*). Negotiates a £3-million British loan to the CPR (*July 10*).

1885: Serves as executive commander for Canada at the Antwerp Exhibition. Sails to Canada (*July 31*). Receives $100,000 in CPR stock as a thank you for supporting the transcontinental railway (*August*). Helps talk Nova Scotia judge Sir John Thompson into entering Macdonald's cabinet as Justice minister; in return he agrees to re-enter government before the next election (*September 2*). Returns to England (*November 3*). Declines the

Grand Cordon of the Order of Leopold of Belgium as it's against British policy to accept foreign decorations (*November*).

1886: Receives the Knight Grand Cross of St. Michael and St. George (*February 1*). Represents Canada and helps run the Colonial and Indian Exhibition in London (*May 4*). Receives an honorary Doctor of Laws degree (LL.D.) from Cambridge University and is honoured by the London guild, Freedom of the Fishmongers' Company (*July 9*). Sails to Canada to visit his younger brother Nathan who is seriously ill in Amherst (*August 28*). Nathan dies (*September 15*). Returns to England (*October 14*).

1887: Re-enters cabinet as Finance minister (*January 27*); resigns as High Com-missioner to London. Canada's sixth federal election: elected once again in Cumberland defeating Pipes for a second time; Macdonald government is re-elected (*February 22).* Introduces his first federal budget, indicating a deficit of $5,834,572, largely caused by the North-West Rebellion of 1885 (*May 12*). Visits Washington to discuss fishing relations with the U.S. (*May 18*); agreement is reached to appoint an International Fishery Commission. Visits England for the summer to attract more CPR funding (*June*). Visits St. John's, Nfld., on his return from England and offers Canada's terms for Confederation; the colony begins negotiations that eventually falter in 1894 (*October*). His election in Cumberland is declared void after his campaign is accused of paying 50 cents to a Conservative supporter from another riding to take the train to vote in his riding (*October 12*). Wins the by-election against prohibitionist J.T. Bulmer (*November 9*). Represents Canada at the International Fishery Commission, with Thompson (Justice) as his legal advisor (*November 22-December 11*).

A Prime Minister without a Parliament

Sir Charles was the only Canadian Prime Minister never to preside over a parliamentary session. The Seventh Parliament had already run its full five-year course when it was dissolved and Bowell resigned. All Tupper was able to do was pull together a cabinet and fight an election he lost to the Liberals. It was Laurier who presided over the Eighth Parliament.

1888: Reaches a fishing settlement with the U.S. (*February 15*), but it is rejected six months later by the U.S. Senate. Asked by Macdonald to remain in cabinet and eventually replace him as Prime Minister; suggests Langevin should be the successor because he is French Canadian. Indicates he would prefer to return to England, so Macdonald agrees to appoint his son, Charles Hibbert, to cabinet (*April*). Introduces his second federal budget, indicating a surplus of $97,313 (*April 27*). Again appointed High Commissioner to London, resigns as Finance minister (*May 23*). His son Charles Hibbert enters cabinet as Marine & Fisheries minister (*June 1*). Arrives back in England (*June 4*) and spends the summer touring Scotland. Victoria makes him Baron Tupper (*August 24*). Represents Canada and Britain in trade negotiations with Spain (*October 27*). Becomes a director of the Bank of British Columbia (*October 31*).

1889: Visits Canada (*March 3*) and tours western Canada before returning to England (*May 5*). Suggests a conference of British colonies to discuss preferential trade and Empire unity (*June 22*).

1890: Tours Continental Europe (*March*); has his portrait painted in Florence. Becomes ill and is seen by Lord Dufferin's doctor.

1891: Arrives in Canada to help the Conservatives campaign during the election, at Macdonald's request (*February 6*); returns to England (*April 15*). Represents Canada at the International Conference on Postal Affairs in Vienna (*May 27-June 13*). Condemned by the Liberals for his role in the election while serving as High Commissioner (*May 29*); the motion is defeated. His son Charles Hibbert threatens to resign from cabinet if the dying Macdonald chooses Thompson to succeed him instead of his father (*June 1*). Tells his son he supports Thompson for leader (*June 4*). Declines an invitation by Kingston riding to contest the seat left vacant by Macdonald's death a day earlier (*June 7*). Writes an article supporting an Empire federation with the colonies being represented in the British cabinet (*October*).

1892: Receives an honorary Doctor of Laws degree (LL.D.) from his alma mater, the University of Edinburgh (*April 14*). Order-in-Council calls for his appointment to negotiate a trade treaty with France (*April 16*). While sailing to an international conference in St. Petersburg, Russia, his ship is quarantined when cholera breaks out in Russia (*August 12*). Attends the funeral of Lord Tennyson at Westminster Abbey (*October 12*).

1893: Signs the French trade treaty in Paris (*February 6*). Hands his resignation to Thompson after failing to consult with Canada during the commercial treaty negotiations with France (*March 22*); it isn't accepted. Meets with his son Charles Hibbert and new Canadian Prime Minister Thompson who are attending the Behring Sea Commission in Paris (*August*). His son Charles Hibbert is knighted.

1894: Hurries to Windsor Castle on learning that Prime Minister Thompson died there during his Imperial Privy Council investiture (*December 12*); arranges to have the body returned to Halifax for a state funeral, then ordered to bed because of heart problems. Possibility of being appointed Prime Minister is thwarted by Governor General Lord Aberdeen and his wife who don't like Tupper (*December 13*); Mackenzie Bowell becomes Prime Minister instead (*December 21*).

1895: Pressure starts to build to appoint him Prime Minister; he refuses (*January*). Urges his son Charles Hibbert not to resign from Bowell's cabinet in protest over the handling of the Manitoba schools crisis (*March*). Sails to Canada to promote faster steamship service to Britain (*December 7*). Dines with Bowell and requests a peerage for Sir Donald Smith (*December*).

1896: While meeting with Bowell, learns that seven cabinet members intend to resign (including Charles Hibbert) (*January 5*). Asked by Bowell to accept the role of Prime Minister; he refuses (*January 9*). Agrees to re-enter cabinet as Secretary of State, and Leader of the House, if the seven cabinet ministers agree to withdraw their resignations; Charles Hibbert becomes Solicitor General outside of cabinet to create a vacancy for his father (*January 14*). Accepts Dr. David MacKeen's offer to step down as Cape Breton's MP to open a seat (*January*). Elected MP for Cape Breton by acclamation in a by-election (*February 4*). Functioning as Leader of the House, he moves the second reading of the Manitoba remedial bill (*March 3*). Withdraws the remedial bill following a Liberal filibuster (*April 16*). Seventh Parliament, the longest ever held, is dissolved and an election is called (*April 24*). Looks on as Lady Aberdeen, a woman he detests, becomes the godmother of his grandson Gordie (*April 26*). Bowell resigns; Governor General Lord Aberdeen calls on Tupper to form a government; he accepts (*April 27*). **Tupper government (1896).** Becomes the sixth Prime Minister of Canada, and continues as the 12th Secretary of State (*May 1*). Keeps Bowell's cabinet except for John Costigan, Thomas Daly and Senator Donald Ferguson, who were staunch Bowell supporters; Hibbert Tupper and Senator Auguste Angers return to cabinet; only new member is Hugh John Macdonald,

Sir John's son (*May 1*). Presented with his portrait in Winnipeg painted by Victor Long (it now hangs on Parliament Hill) (*May 4*). Imperial Privy Council gives the federal government the exclusive right of absolute prohibition (*May 9*). Imperial Privy Council gives Canada rights over its fisheries (*May 26*). Tupper gives 42 speeches in 13 days while campaigning in Ontario (*June*). His friend John Beverly Robinson, with whom he'd had dinner, dies just before Tupper begins a campaign speech at Massey Hall in Toronto (*June 19*). Canada's eighth federal election: re-elected in Cape Breton riding; his Conservative government is defeated by Laurier's Liberals (*June 23*). Longtime colleague Sir Samuel L. Tilley, a Father of Confederation, dies in Saint John, N.B. (*June 25*). Delays turning over power to Laurier, likely to provide time to make final Senate and other political appointments; Governor General Lord Aberdeen refuses to approve his Order-in-Council for a steamship line and to sanction appointments (*July 2*); visits the Governor General to argue his case even though it's his 75th birthday. Order-in-Council extends Quebec's boundary north to Hudson Bay (*July 6*). Aberdeen forces the resignation of Tupper as Prime Minister and Secretary of State (*July 8*). **Tupper government ends.** Unanimously supported to stay on as Conservative leader (*July 27*). Becomes a member of the Selection and Railways, Canals & Telegraph Lines parliamentary committees (*August 19*). Officially chosen Conservative Leader, replacing Bowell who becomes Conservative Leader of the Senate (*August 27*). His article "Fast Atlantic Steamship Service" appears in *The Canadian Magazine* (*October*). Sails to England (*November 7*).

1897: Returns to Canada (*February 6*). Sails again to England (*July*); returns to Canada (*September 9*). Visits British Columbia (*September*). Sails to England yet again for meetings with the Gold Fields Company (*November*); returns to Canada (*December 15*).

1898: Visits western Canada with Hugh John Macdonald, son of John A. (*January*). His son Charles Hibbert moves to British Columbia. Sails for England (*June*); returns to Canada (*July 21*). Sails for England (*Fall*).

1899: Returns to Canada (*January 5*). Injured along with his wife when their sleigh overturns on the frozen Saskatchewan River in Strathcona (*Winter*). Receives an honorary Doctor of Laws (LLD) degree from Queen's University (*Spring*). Sails for England (*August 3*); returning to Canada in September. Campaigns in the west for the Conservatives (*December*).

1900: Tables a motion in the House against the government's preferential tariff with Britain; it's defeated (*March 30*). Formally apologizes to Clifford Sifton (Interior) for remarks accusing the government of corruption in managing the Yukon (*October*). Canada's ninth federal election; defeated in his bid for re-election in Cape Breton (*November 7*), his first defeat in 13 elections. Becomes the founding president of Crown Life Insurance in Toronto along with Borden.

1901: Resigns as leader of the Conservative party leader and Leader of the Op-position (*February 5*); succeeded by fellow Nova Scotian Robert Borden (*February 28*). Makes eight more trips to England, staying with his daughter Emma's family in Bexleyheath, Kent (*1901-1908*).

1905: Decides to learn Italian; able to "dream in Italian" within months (*Spring*).

1906: Invited to spend four days aboard the *HMS Prince of Wales* by Admiral Sir Reginald Tupper, a distant cousin.

1907: Visits Canada where he is feted in Cumberland County, then visits Vancouver. Publishes the article "The Problem with Empire" in *Nineteenth Century* magazine.

1908: Appointed to the Imperial Privy Council (*October 19*).

1909: Publishes articles in four British magazines. After a summer in Canada, sails to England to reside permanently; moves into The Mount at Bexleyheath where he continues to play on the neighbouring golf course well into his 90s.

1910: Attends the coronation of George V (*June 17*).

1911: Attends the unveiling of a plaque at London's Westminster Palace Hotel, commemorating the London Conference of 1866-1867 (*June 17*).

1912: Hit with a bad case of bronchitis (*Winter*). His wife Frances dies at Bexleyheath after a long illness (*May 13*). Accompanies Frances' body to Halifax where she is buried in St. John's Cemetery (*May 27*). Visits his sons William in Winnipeg and Charles Hibbert in Vancouver (*Summer*).

1913: Guests at a party in his honour in Amherst include Prime Minister Borden (*April 28*). Leaves Canada for England for the final time (*May 1*). Son James has a stroke at Bexleyheath.

1914: Publishes his memoirs: *Recollections of 60 Years in Canada*. Often visited by Canadian physician Sir William Osler.

1915: His grandson Reggie is wounded in the battle at Ypres (*April 24*); another grandson, Gordie, is killed at Vimy in 1917. His son James dies in Oxford, England (*April* 29). Suffers a heart attack (*September 22*). Dies at his home, Broomwood, in Bexleyheath (*October 30*). Funeral service held in Bexleyheath, followed by a memorial service at St. Margaret's in Westminster (*November*). His body is returned to Canada on warship *Metagama*. State funeral takes place in Halifax (*November 16*); buried in St. John's Cemetery, Halifax.

Books about Tupper

- **1883**: Charles Thibault; *Biography of Sir Charles Tupper*
- **1914**: Charles Tupper; *Recollections of 60 Years in Canada* (Cassell)
- **1914**: W.A. Harkin (ed.); *Political Reminiscences of the Rt. Honourable Sir Charles Tupper, Bart.* (Constable & Co.)
- **1916**: E.M. Saunders (ed.); *The Life and Letters of the Rt. Hon. Sir Charles Tupper, Bart., K.C.M.G.*, 2 vols. (Cassell)
- **1916**: James W. Longley; *Sir Charles Tupper* (Morang)
- **1985**: Vincent Durant; *War Horse of Cumberland: The Life and Times of Sir Charles Tupper* (Lancelot)
- **1999**: Jock & Janet Murray; *Sir Charles Tupper: Fighting Doctor to Father of Confederation* (Associated Medical Services/Fitzhenry & Whiteside)

7

Sir Wilfrid Laurier

The Unflappable Prime Minister

Canada's first French-Canadian Prime Minister radiated gentlemanly elegance and optimism, qualities that helped him retain power for the longest uninterrupted term of all Canadian leaders. Although Wilfrid Laurier's vision of the 20th century belonging to Canada didn't pan out, it did for his Liberal party, which held power for most of the next 100 years. His ability to compromise helped to resolve the Manitoba schools question. Determined to open the west to settlers, he presided over the creation of two prairie provinces, Saskatchewan and Alberta. He managed to keep Canada officially out of the Boer War, and later established the country's navy.

Laurier the Politician

Prime Minister of Canada: July 11, 1896 – October 6, 1911
Length of term: 15 years, 2 months, 25 days
Parliaments as Prime Minister: Eighth; Ninth; 10th; 11th
Age on entering office: 54
Political party: Liberal
Leader of party: June 18, 1887 – February 17, 1919
Member of Parliament: January 22, 1874 – February 17, 1919
Ridings represented: Drummond-Arthabaska [Que.] (1874-1877); Quebec East [Que.] (1877-1919)
Cabinet portfolios: Inland Revenue (1877-1878); Privy Council President (1896-1911)
Other political posts: Quebec legislature member (1871-1874); Mayor of Arthabaska (1882); Leader of the Opposition (1887-1896, 1911-1919)
Knighted: June 21, 1897
Titles: Canadian Privy Councillor (1877); Queen's Counsel (1880); Knight Grand Cross of St. Michael and St. George (1897); Imperial Privy Councillor (1897)
Quotes: "I pledge my honour that I will give the whole of my life to the cause of conciliation, harmony and concord among the different elements of this country of ours." (1864 student pledge to the Undergraduate Society of the

McGill University Faculty of Law); "Let me tell you, my fellow countrymen, that all signs point this way, that the 20th century shall be the century of Canada and Canadian development." (1904 speech at Massey Hall, Toronto).
Lived after term: 7 years

Laurier the Man

Name: Henry-Charles-Wilfrid Laurier
Born: November 20, 1841, St. Lin, Canada East (Quebec)
Ancestry: French
Religion: Roman Catholic
Education: B.C.L. [Doctor of Civil Law] (McGill University, 1864)
Nicknames: The Great Conciliator
Military service: none
Occupation: lawyer; editor
Occupation after term: Leader of the Opposition
Publications: none
Appearance: "He was tall, his hair a little greyer and less bountiful but still curly and cut close to his head, his face well shaved and pale, his eyes more penetrating and kind. He was always impeccably and immaculately dressed." (Laurier LaPierre in *Sir Wilfrid Laurier and the Romance of Canada*); "Tall, dapper in dress, and refined in manner, he was a handsome gentleman. Whatever doubts or insecurities he felt he hid beneath his elegant exterior." (Roderick Stewart in *Wilfrid Laurier: A Pledge for Canada*)
Personality: "Reserved in manner, often remote in thought, fastidious and something of a dandy in dress" (Christopher Ondaatje in *The Prime Ministers of Canada*); "… an expert in the softness of compromise and the hard use of power …" (J.L. Granatstein & Norman Hillmer in *Prime Ministers: Ranking Canada's Leaders*)
Married: Zoë Lafontaine, May 13, 1868, Montreal, Quebec
Age at marriage: 26
Years married: 50
Died: February 17, 1919, Ottawa, Ontario
Age at death: 77
Cause of death: stroke
Buried: Notre Dame Cemetery, Eastview (Ottawa), Ontario

Laurier was the:
- First French Canadian Prime Minister
- First Prime Minister fluent in both official languages
- First Prime Minister buried in Ottawa
- Prime Minister who served the longest uninterrupted years of office (15)
- Prime Minister who served longest as party leader (31 years)
- Only Liberal Prime Minister to accept a knighthood.
- Second Liberal Prime Minister
- Second Prime Minister born in Quebec
- Second Roman Catholic Prime Minister

- Second Prime Minister to win four consecutive majorities
- Third Prime Minister who was an editor
- Fourth Prime Minister who was a lawyer
- Fourth Prime Minister who was a member of a provincial legislature (Quebec)
- Longest serving Member of Parliament (nearly 45 years)

Laurier's legacy
- Prepared Liberals to rule Canada for most of the 20th century
- Established the prominence of French-Canadians participating in government
- Created compromises to diffuse the Manitoba schools question
- Created a Canadian Navy
- Populated the west through expansive immigration
- Created the provinces of Alberta and Saskatchewan

LAURIER'S FAMILY

Laurier's Parents

Father: Charles 'Carolus' Laurier
Born: March 17, 1815, St. Roch, Lower Canada (Quebec)
Occupation: farmer; land surveyor; mayor of St. Lin
Second wife: Adeline Ethier (1848)
Died: May 19, 1886, St. Lin, Quebec
Age at death: 71

Mother: Marie-Marcelle Martineau
Born: February 10, 1815, L'Assomption, Lower Canada (Quebec)
Married: April 8, 1834, L'Assomption, Lower Canada (Quebec)
Died: March 7, 1848, St. Lin, Canada East (Quebec)
Age at death: 33

Stepmother: Adeline Ethier
Born: February 11, 1823, St. Esprit, Quebec
Married: July 3, 1848, St. Lin, Quebec
Died: November 3, 1903, St. Lin, Quebec
Age at death: 80

Laurier's Brothers & Sisters (2 siblings; Wilfrid the second)

Sister: Marie-Honorine-Lidie Laurier (1836-1839), died before Wilfrid's birth
Sister: Honorine-Melina Laurier (1844-1855)
Half-Brother: Romuald-Charlemagne Laurier (1852-1906)
    Married: Marie-Euthalie Pauze (1875)
    Note: Liberal MP for L'Assomption (1900-1906)
Half-Sister: Honorine-Doctorée Laurier (1855-1921)
    Married: Moise Bricault dit Lamarche (1874), 11 children
Half-Sister: Marie Zoë-Honorine Laurier (1857-1859)
Half-Brother: Joseph Charles-Lyre 'Carolus' Laurier (b.1859)
Half-Brother: Joseph-Henri Laurier (1863-1906)
    Married: Marie-Louise Pépin (1889)

Note: Served as Laurier's secretary in the 1890s.
Half-Brother: Dr. Francois-Xavier-Ubald Laurier (1866-1899)

Laurier's Wife

Name: Marie Zoë Melinda Lafontaine
Born: June 26, 1842, Montreal, Quebec
Father: Napoleon-Godefoi Lafontaine (bailiff)
Mother: Zoë Tessier Lavigne
Age at marriage: 25
Children: none
Died: November 1, 1921, Ottawa, Ontario
Age at death: 79
Burial place: Notre Dame Cemetery, Eastview (Ottawa), Ontario
Younger than Laurier: 7 months
Died after Laurier: 2 years

POLITICAL STORIES

The eloquent orator

Already a practiced speaker thanks to his term in the Quebec legislature, Laurier's first speech in Parliament was a response to his government's Speech from the Throne in March 1874. Although his remarks were delivered in French, English-speaking Liberal MP James Young remembered the speech for its "charm of manner, a touch of dignity, an air of candour, a natural eloquence."

While Laurier was speaking, Louis Riel quietly and quickly entered the Parliament Buildings and signed the roll as the duly elected MP for Provencher. Over the next month, the battle lines were drawn between English Canada's outrage over the murdering rebel who dared to flout the warrant for his arrest and French Canada's view of Riel as a Métis hero merely ensuring his people's rights.

When Laurier rose in April to give his maiden English speech, he told the House that until the status of Riel's amnesty was clarified (was it granted or not?), Parliament had no right to expel him as an MP. Despite his unfamiliarity with English, the *Montreal Herald* judged it the best speech on the expulsion issue.

Twelve years later, Laurier would again defend Riel with an impassioned speech decrying his execution. "In the province to which I belong, and especially amongst the race to which I belong, the execution of Louis Riel has been universally condemned as being a sacrifice of a life, not to inexorable justice, but to bitter passion and revenge." His colleague Edward Blake christened it "the finest speech ever pronounced in the Parliament of Canada since Confederation."

Unwilling to lead

In 1887, Edward Blake recommended Laurier as his replacement as Liberal party leader. The 46-year-old Laurier believed his health was shaky and wasn't keen on the idea. The party was equally reluctant to have him at the helm, but there were no clear alternatives. He agreed to consider the role and eventually accepted it, even though everyone waited five days before making his leadership public.

A few months later, Laurier was threatening to resign and implored Blake to take back the leadership. Blake refused. The next year, Laurier tried again to resign and in the summer it's probable he again urged Blake to come back. Blake's election to the British Parliament in 1892 dashed the last hope Laurier may still have had to entice him back.

Laurier told the party treasurer in 1895 that he wanted to step down as leader so he could earn more money working as a lawyer. No one was really listening by this point.

Before the 1896 election, he offered the leadership to Ontario Premier Oliver Mowat, feeling the move would enhance the party's chances in that province. Again, no go. It was just as well, because, after nine years labouring as Leader of the Opposition and 22 years as an opposition MP, Laurier won a majority government to become Canada's seventh Prime Minister.

Diamond Jubilee in England

Laurier's impeccable manners and sartorial elegance made him a popular and natural fit at the festivities in England marking Queen Victoria's 60 years on the throne in 1897. It's a role few would have predicted for the ardent Quebecois patriot. But he and Zoë relished the adulation of thousands while riding London's streets in an open carriage directly behind the Queen.

He also surprised many in Quebec with his ready acceptance of a knighthood, feeling it would boost his appeal in English Canada. Yet, if Britain thought making him a 'Sir' would make him more pliable at the Colonial Conference after the celebrations, they were mistaken. Laurier pushed hard for preferential trade agreements between the colonies and England without sacrificing any of Canada's increasing independence.

Cambridge and Oxford universities presented him with honorary degrees. He also became the third Canadian Prime Minister to join the Imperial Privy Council (Thompson's membership lasted only minutes before he died).

After his time in Britain, Laurier was off to France, Italy and Ireland to be feted before returning to Canada. It represented the most glorious reception yet received by a Canadian leader abroad.

Alaska boundary dispute

Of all the disagreements between Canada and United States about boundaries, the vague border between British Columbia and Alaska was the most intense. It was also the most protracted, spanning most of Laurier's 15 years in power.

Ever since the U.S. bought Alaska from Russia, the thread of Alaskan territory along the Pacific coast tended to keep slithering southward, threatening to eventually eliminate most of B.C.'s ocean access. The Klondike gold rush inflamed the situation further, particularly in the Yukon where there was no ocean access at all.

A commission was established with six arbitrators – three American, two Canadian and one British – to hammer out a definitive border. It spent six years debating the issue, with Laurier acting as a panel member for several months in 1898. All the while, he worked hard behind the scenes to advance Canada's interests, including discussions with two U.S. presidents, William McKinley and Theodore Roosevelt.

It was all for nothing. The British panelist, anxious to maintain good relations with the United States, sided with the U.S. arbitrators, leaving Canada without nearly 1,000 km of coastline south of the Yukon.

The exercise influenced Laurier's determination later in his administration to gain control over Canada's own international affairs. He created a Department of External Affairs in 1909. After his successor Borden assumed the portfolio a few years later, all Prime Ministers until Diefenbaker in the 1950s spent some time as their own External Affairs minister.

South Africa's Boer War

Britain needed its colonies' help in 1899. The Boers in South Africa – that colony's original European occupiers – were resisting newer waves of British immigrants. The Empire asked the dominions and colonies to supply troops to teach the Boers a lesson. Laurier ignored the call to arms.

As the months passed, he did agree to help fund a contingent of Canadian volunteers willing to join the effort. The first group of over 1,000 soldiers soon left for South Africa. In all, 7,300 Canadian volunteers fought in the Boer War; 89 died, while another 135 succumbed to tropical diseases like typhoid.

The British captured Pretoria after eight months of fighting and, although guerilla warfare by the Boers continued for another two years, the Empire ultimately annexed both the Transvaal and Orange Free State.

Laurier's decision to ignore Britain's plea for battalions angered English Canadians who felt more was requied from Canada. Meanwhile, many French Canadians, influenced by Liberal MP Henri Bourassa, believed Laurier's response was too militant. When MPs celebrated Britain's victory in South Africa by spontaneously rising to sing God Save the Queen, Laurier remained sitting rather than break House rules that frowned on such outbursts. His most agonizing moment during the Boer conflict was likely learning that the son of his Defence minister, Frederick Borden, was killed during an assault.

Floating a Canadian navy

Canada had no navy at the beginning of the 20th century and the British were looking for significant naval support from the colonies as Germany ramped up its shipbuilding efforts. He had two choices: provide funding, sailors and supplies to the Royal Navy or create a Canadian navy. He picked the second option.

Supporting a 1909 motion from the Conservatives to establish a national navy, Laurier introduced his Naval Services Bill the following year. It was an ambitious plan to create a fleet of six destroyers and five cruisers, establish a naval board and open a naval college, all under the wing of a new Naval Services minister who was Laurier's current Marine & Fisheries minister.

The pejorative term 'tin pot navy' was almost literally true when the first cruiser, an obsolete Royal Navy hand-me-down adorned with flags and bunting, made its entrance into Halifax Harbour.

The whole undertaking was a hard sell for Laurier. French Canadians objected to funding a navy for Britain's use, while the Conservative opposition preferred to have the money sent to Britain so it could build its own ships. Laurier navigated through the differences and is remembered as the founder of the Royal Canadian Navy.

A shot at free trade

Early in his years as Liberal leader, Laurier convinced his party to adopt a policy of unrestricted reciprocity with the U.S. – no limits to free trade across the border. Canadians seemed receptive to the idea, despite the protectionism promised by Macdonald's National Policy. But Edward Blake, the former lead-er, was opposed to the idea and it quietly disappeared from the Liberal agenda.

After nearly 15 years as Prime Minister, Laurier felt ready to bring it back into play. He believed it would ultimately benefit Canadians and succeeded in securing a free trade deal. But businesses, particularly in Montreal, feared losing their protective tariffs. The Conservatives capitalized on that unease and opposed reciprocity in the 1911 election. It was a stand that contributed to the defeat of Laurier's Liberal government.

About 75 years later, free trade would be back and the tables would be turned. This time the Liberals under Turner would oppose the idea, while business and Mulroney's Tories would succeed in implementing a U.S. agreement.

PERSONAL STORIES

Frail health

When he was six, Laurier lost his mother to tuberculosis; seven years later, his sister Melina died of the same disease. It was perhaps only natural for him to suspect the worst when he starting spitting up blood during violent coughing fits three years later.

The spells, related to consumption and bronchitis, continued for years. His coughing was so bad that, when he first moved into his own Montreal apartment in 1866, his family moved in with him – although it's hard to see how all six of his family members fit into one space. Laurier's move to small-town L'Avenir to edit the *Le Défricheur* newspaper was done in part to bolster his rehabilitation. But his continuing ill health was a factor in the paper's demise a year later.

Perhaps politics was good for him. First elected as an MP in 1874, despite having to leave the campaigning to others on account of his bronchitis, he had his coughing mostly under control by the time he entered the House. He remained relatively healthy during his long tenure as Prime Minister. In his later years, the problem was not his lungs, but his teeth, many of which needed to be removed.

The other 'Mrs. Laurier' and Armand

When his law partner Joseph Lavergne married Émilie Barthe in 1876, Laurier was introduced to the vivacious, witty, perpetually cheerful woman who quite simply enchanted him. He spent a great deal of time with her over the next two decades.

The Lauriers moved to a new house in Arthabaska in 1878 – on the same street as the Lavergnes. Zoë Laurier and Joseph Lavergne seem to have reluctantly resigned themselves to the not-so-private arrangement between their respective spouses.

The birth of Émilie's son Armand in 1880 generated widespread gossip that Laurier was the father. The fact that Armand resembled Laurier didn't help, but there was never any evidence to support the idea.

By the time Laurier was Prime Minister, the relationship had begun to wane. The Lavergnes had followed the Lauriers to Ottawa in 1887 with Joseph serving first as an MP and then as a judge. In 1901, Laurier arranged to have Lavergne posted to Montreal, removing any temptation that might have still existed. He returned all the letters written by Émilie over the years and no doubt hoped she would do the same in return. His letters to her – intimate and tender – came to light in 1963.

Armand also became an MP, in 1904, but was expelled from the Liberals by Laurier three years later for defying party policy. Émilie spent the last years of her life as a recluse with the Grey Nuns of Montreal, far removed from her days as a bon vivant.

Lady Zoë Laurier

Montreal's Gauthier family took in boarders. They included McGill law student Wilfrid Laurier and piano teacher Zoë Lafontaine who looked after her bedridden mother. Zoë was Laurier's age and, as the two spent more time together, a romance inevitably began to blossom.

But Laurier's awkward courting and hypochondria eventually torpedoed the slow-developing relationship. After he moved out, she began dating Pierre Valois, ending it after her mother died. Laurier stepped back in, but his incessant coughing convinced him, once again, not to pursue her. The ardent Valois returned and was soon engaged to Zoë. It was the Gauthiers who connived to reverse the situation and rematch her with Laurier.

He and Zoë were about a decade into their marriage when Laurier embarked on his disturbing infatuation with Émilie Lavergne. However much it must have rankled, Zoë never publicly reacted to it. She disliked Laurier's entry into politics, but recognized it would move them away from the Lavergnes. However, when Joseph Lavergne also became an MP, Laurier and his intellectual mistress were together again, this time in Ottawa. The obsession eventually died out and Zoë was able to reclaim Laurier's devotion.

Her interest in Laurier's role as Prime Minister grew much stronger. She watched him in action from the visitors gallery of the House of Commons and became fluent in English. She also chaired an array of national organizations. The only public faux pas in her growing stature appears to be a traffic ticket issued to 'Lady Laurier' in 1910 for exceeding the speed limit of 10 miles (16 km) per hour.

Laurier's Timeline

1841: Born in St. Lin, Canada East (Quebec), and named after Wilfrid of Ivanhoe, a character in Sir Walter Scott's novel *Ivanhoe* (*November 20*). Baptized in St. Lin (*November 22*).

1844: His grandfather Charles Laurier dies in St. Lin (*January 22*). His sister Melina is born in L'Assomption, Que. (*January 23*).

1848: His mother Marcelle dies in St. Lin of tuberculosis (*March 7*). His father Carolus marries Adeline Ethier, Marcelle's caregiver (*July 3*).

1851: Sent 12 km away to Fort Rose School in New Glasgow, Canada East, to learn English (*September*); boards with the John Murray family, then the Kirks. Works part-time in Murray's tailor shop.

1854: Attends College de l'Assomption, in L'Assomption, Canada East, 33 km east of St. Lin (*September*).

1855: His father Carolus becomes the mayor of St. Lin. His sister Melina dies in St. Lin of tuberculosis at age 11.

1858: Suffers his first violent coughing spell, spitting up blood (*Winter*); the attacks reoccur for many years.

1861: Graduates from L'Assomption (*May*). Enters law school at McGill University in Montreal (*September*); meets law professor John Abbott. Boards with the Gauthiers, as does Zoë Lafontaine (*September*). Articles for Montreal lawyer Rodolphe Laflamme.

1862: Joins the library society Institut Canadien (*October*).

1863: Becomes president of McGill's Institut des lois. Becomes godfather to his step-brother Henri (*August 29*).

1864: Graduates from McGill with a Bachelor of Civil Law degree (*May 4*); is the valedictorian, giving his speech in French. Admitted to the bar. Begins law practice in Montreal as a partner with Oscar Archambault (*September*); they hire a third partner Henri Lesieur Desaulines (*December*).

1865: Becomes vice-president of Montreal's Institut Canadien; serves for two years. The Laurier, Archambault & Desaulines law firm dissolves (*April*). Forms a new partnership with Médéric Lanctôt (*April*). Helps with anti-Confederation activities.

1866: Leaves the Gauthier home and moves into a Montreal apartment (*June*). Suffers from health problems, prompting his father to move the family from St. Lin to Laurier's apartment for the summer. Suffers a severe bronchitis attack (*October*). Moves to L'Avenir to restore his health and edit the Rouge newspaper *Le Défricheur* following the death of editor Eric Dorion (*November 18*).

1867: Moves *Le Défricheur* to Victoriaville (*January 1*). His bronchitis, along with Catholic church opposition and a lack of money, causes *Le Défricheur* to fold (*March 28*). Forms a law partnership with Eugène Crépeau in Arthabaska (*June*). Spends many weekends in Montreal visiting Lafontaine. Is considered as a possible Liberal candidate in the first Quebec provincial election; he does not run (*August*). Moves to St. Christophe d'Arthabaskaville, commonly known as Arthabaska, and boards with the family of Dr. Modeste Poisson (*September*).

1868: Learns that Zoë Lafontaine plans to marry Pierre Valois in May (*January*). Hires Edouard Richard, a nephew of Poisson, to join the Laurier & Crépeau law firm (*May*). Hurriedly marries Lafontaine (*May 13*).

Marriage as a pre-emptive strike

Séraphin Gauthier, Laurier's former landlord, sent him a telegram in 1868 that urged him "Come at once. A Matter of urgent importance." When he arrived, he was given a physical examination by Dr. Gauthier and pronounced healthy except for his chronic bronchitis – nothing that should get in the way of marrying his on-and-off girlfriend, Zoë Lafontaine. She was to marry Dr. Pierre Valois in 10 days and was clearly unhappy about it. Gauthier prodded Laurier into meeting with Lafontaine, who lived with the Gauthiers, and they quickly embraced. That same evening the two were married in a double ceremony along with Emma Gauthier and Francois Coutu who had moved their wedding plans forward. Back at the house they encountered Valois who hadn't been told of the wedding. The jilted, morose suitor offered a toast to the couple.

1869: Becomes an ensign in the local militia; serves until 1878.

1870: Crépeau leaves the law firm (*Spring*).

1871: Agrees to run as a Rouge (Liberal) candidate for the provincial legislature (*May 28*) and is the only one elected to the Quebec legislature, representing Drummond-Arthabaska (*July 9*). Delivers his first speech, replying to the government's Speech from the Throne for more than an hour (*November 10*).

1872: Becomes a contributing editor to *Le Journal d'Arthabaska*, founded by his Rouge friend Ernest Pacaud (*March*).

1873: Hires Joseph Lavergne as a partner in the law firm, replacing Richard who moves to Mégantic to contest the federal election (*December*).

1874: Canada's third federal election: elected as the Rouge MP for Drummond-Arthabaska even though sick with bronchitis; Mackenzie's Liberals form a majority government (*January 22*); steps down as the provincial member. Delivers his first speech in the House of Commons (*March 30*); shortly after, Louis Riel slips onto Parliament Hill to sign the register as an MP and disappears again. Makes his first speech in English, supporting amnesty for Riel (*April 15*). Meets with Riel who is still in hiding in Quebec's Bois-Francs county (*Summer*).

1875: Recommended by George Brown as a possible cabinet minister (*November 15*). Passed over for a cabinet position in favour of Joseph Cauchon (*December 7*).

1876: Passed over again for a cabinet position, this time in favour of his first mentor, lawyer Rodolfe Laflamme (*October*). Law partner Lavergne marries Émilie Barthe in Arthabaska (*November 29*).

1877: Makes a speech in Quebec City emphasizing that Liberalism does not oppose the Roman Catholic church (*June 26*). Enters Mackenzie's cabinet as Inland Revenue minister (*October 8*). Bishop George Conroy, representing the Pope, tells Quebec Catholics that the church does not condemn the Liberal party and they are free to vote as they choose (*October 11*). Defeated in the by-election for his cabinet seat, losing by 87 votes in

Drummond-Arthabaska to Conservative Désiré Olivier Bourbeau (*October 27*). Agrees to contest a by-election in Quebec East where the Liberal MP steps down (*November 7*). Elected in Quebec East by-election, defeating former MP and Quebec City mayor Adolphe Guillet de Tourangeau by 314 votes (*November 28*).

1878: Canada's fourth federal election: re-elected MP for Quebec East; Mackenzie's government is defeated (*September 17*). Resigns as Inland Revenue minister (*October 9*). Moves out of the Poisson house in Arthabaska and into his newly built home in town, on the same street as his law office and the Lavergnes (*Fall*).

1880: Armand Lavergne is born to Joseph and Emilie, leaving some people wondering if he might be Laurier's illegitimate son (*February 21*). Becomes a Queen's Counsel. Joins a delegation of five Liberals who, with the support of caucus, ask Mackenzie to resign as Liberal leader (*April 27*); Edward Blake becomes leader of the party the next day. Laurier helps found *L'Electeur,* a newspaper edited by Ernest Pacaud (*July*). Speaks against the proposed Canadian Pacific Railway bill (*December 21*).

1881: Writes an article in *L'Électeur* charging Louis-Adélard Senécal with corrup-tion in Quebec politics (*April 16*). Senécal sues *L'Électeur* and Laurier for libel (*May 27*). Tours Nova Scotia with Blake and Pacaud (*August*). The Senécal libel trial ends as a mistrial, thanks to help from Laurier's lawyer, Honoré Mercier (*November 12*).

1882: Canada's fifth federal election: re-elected MP for Quebec East defeating J.P Rhéaume; Macdonald's government re-elected (*June 20*). Elected mayor of Arthabaska.

1883: Joins Blake on a speaking tour through Quebec's Eastern Townships (*Summer*).

1884: Minette Taschereau, Pacaud's niece, and Joseph Pope, Sir John A. Macdonald's secretary, marry and spend part of the summer at the Laurier's Arthabaska home.

1885: Speaks out in the House against the government's handling of the North-West Rebellion and its intention to hang Riel (*July 7*). Participates in a Montreal rally condemning the hanging of Riel (*November 22*).

1886: Speaks in the House against Riel's hanging (*March 16*). His father Carolus dies in St. Lin (*May 21*). Speaks in Toronto to try and smooth out the English-French divisions created by Riel's death (*December 10*).

1887: Canada's sixth federal election: re-elected MP for Quebec East defeating F.X. Drouin, while his law partner Joseph Lavergne is elected in Drummond-Arthabaska; Macdonald's government is re-elected (*February 21*). Blake announces his intention to resign as Liberal leader (*March 5*); officially resigns and suggests Laurier as his successor (*June 1*). Reluctantly nominated by caucus as leader; agrees to consider the nomination (*June 7*). Accepts leadership of the Liberal Party and becomes the fourth official Leader of the Opposition (*June 18*); the decision is officially announced five days later on the last day of the First Session of the Sixth Parliament. Indicates his tentative support for free trade with the U.S. at a Liberal picnic in Somerset, Que. (*August 2*). Asks Blake to take back the leadership of the Liberal party (*August*); turned down.

1888: His party officially adopts the policy of unrestricted reciprocity with the U.S. (*February 25*). Attempts again, unsuccessfully, to resign from the leadership (*March*). He and Zoë visit Blake in Murray Bay, Ont. (*Summer*). Embarks on a speaking tour of Ontario (*August*).

1889: Becomes president of the Arthabaska bar association. Speaks in Toronto against anti-French sentiments stirred up by MP D'Alton McCarthy (*September 30*).

1890: Represents Joseph Israel Tarte in a libel suit launched by Thomas McGreevy who had been accused of accepting political bribes (*October 1*); trial is postponed and Tarte leaves the Conservatives to join the Liberals.

1891: Speaks to the New York City Board of Trade about unrestricted reciprocity (*January 29*). Learns that Blake is prepared to publicly oppose reciprocity (*January 31*); Blake backs off. Canada's seventh federal election: re-elected MP for Quebec East by acclamation; Macdonald's government is re-elected (*March 5*). Introduces a motion condemning Tupper's role in the election while serving as High Commissioner (*May 29*); the motion is defeated. Delivers a heartfelt eulogy in the House for Macdonald (*June 8*); the seat opposite him in the House remains vacant for the next eight months. Attends Macdonald's state funeral (*June 10*). A Senate committee concludes that Laurier's friend Pacaud and Quebec premier Honoré Mercier were implicated in the Baie des Chaleurs Railway Scandal (*September 11*). Speaks at a banquet in his honour in Boston, Massachusetts, saying "I prefer the Yankee dollar to the British shilling, especially when the dollar is so near and the shilling is so far" (*November 17*).

1892: Pacaud resumes fundraising for Laurier and the federal Liberals after being largely exonerated in the Baie des Chaleurs Scandal (*April*). Laurier's hope that Blake would return as Liberal leader ends after Blake is elected to the British House of Commons and leaves Canada (*July*).

1893: Liberals hold the first national convention by a Canadian political party, at Rideau Rink in Ottawa (*June 20*).

1894: Makes his first visit to Western Canada (*August 22-October*); hears from a delegation of Catholics in Winnipeg, frustrated by Manitoba's restricted school system (*September 6*). Meets with a Governor General aide to discuss a national fund for Thompson's widow; some Conservatives fear this means Aberdeen might ask Laurier to form a government if a Tory leader isn't picked soon (*December 19*). Mackenzie Bowell succeeds Thompson as Prime Minister (*December 21*).

1895: Tells Liberal treasurer Charles Hyman he earnestly hopes to step down as leader so he can make an adequate living as a lawyer (*March 27*). Avoids taking a firm stand on the Manitoba schools question after the province rejects an Order-in-Council to rescind its legislation against Catholic and French language school instruction (*June 19*). Criticizes Bowell's government for its lack of Quebec representation in cabinet after its three Quebec ministers resign in protest over the handling of the Manitoba schools question (*July 9*). Tours Ontario indicating his support for a fair solution for all Manitobans without advocating specific solutions (*October 6-December*).

1896: While at a skating party at the Governor General's residence, indicates his willingness to form a government after seven of Bowell's ministers resign (*January 11*); Bowell hangs on with Tupper's support (*January 14*). Laurier launches a six-week filibuster to stop the government's Remedial Bill, coming out in favour of provincial rights (*March 3*). Refuses to become a commissioner to meet with the Manitoba government because Tupper refuses to give him access to all correspondence (*March 20*). Offers to let Ontario Premier Oliver Mowat take over the leadership to increase the Liberal party's federal chances in that province (*March*). Tupper withdraws the Remedial Bill (*April 16*). Seventh Parliament is dissolved and an election is called (*April 24*). Quebec's bishops issue a letter telling Catholics to support only candidates prepared to restore Catholic rights in Manitoba (*May 16*). Canada's eighth federal election; re-elected in Quebec East defeating Cléophas Leclerc (Conservative) and also elected in Saskatchewan Provisional District by 44 votes over James Mackay (Conservative); chooses the Quebec East seat; his Liberal party receives a majority (*June 23*). Tupper, who clings to power in order to make political appointments, is forced to resign by Aberdeen (*July 3*). **Laurier government (1896-1911).** Becomes the seventh Prime Minister of Canada and 19th Privy Council President (*July 11*). His cabinet includes three provincial premiers: Ontario's Sir Oliver Mowat (Justice), Nova Scotia's William S. Fielding (Finance), and New Brunswick's Andrew Blair (Railways & Canals) (*July 11*). Canada's Eighth Parliament opens; nominates James Edgar to be the seventh Speaker of the House (*August 19*). Sir Charles Tupper is officially chosen Conservative Leader, replacing Bowell who becomes Conservative Leader of the Senate (*August 27*). Appoints Clifford Sifton of Manitoba as Interior minister (*November 17*). Reaches an agreement with Manitoba Premier Thomas Greenway to allow for one hour of daily religious instruction for Catholic students in the province; French is placed on the same level as other second languages (*November 19*). Sifton (Interior) announces plans to promote immigration of farmers from Eastern Europe to help settle the west (*November 27*).

1897: Britain and the U.S. agree to set up a commission to settle the boundary claims between Alaska and the Yukon and British Columbia (*January 30*). A western wing of the Parliament Buildings in Ottawa burns (*February 11*). The Laurier-Greenway compromise passes in the Manitoba legislature (*March 30*). Lester B. Pearson, Canada's 14th Prime Minister, is born in Newtonbrook, Ont. (*April 23*). Laurier sails to England for Victoria's Diamond Jubilee (*June 5*). The Crow's Nest Pass Agreement is reached as a railway route through the Rockies (*June 10*). Knighted by Victoria (*June 21*), the day after her 60th year on the throne. Participates in the Queen's Diamond Jubilee parade through the streets of London (*June 22*). Attends the Colonial Conference in London (*June 24-July 29*); persuades Britain to set up preferential trade with the colonies. Receives an honorary Doctor of Civil Law degree from Oxford University (*June 30*), having already received an honorary Doctor of Laws degree from Cambridge University. Reintegrates the Customs and Inland Revenue cabinet portfolios (*June 30*). Addresses British Parliament (*July 5*). Becomes a member of the Imperial Privy Council (*July 7*). Establishes a 2% royalty on minerals from Canadian mines, including gold in the Klondike rush (*July 28*). Establishes a preferential tariff with members of the British Empire, representing a 25% reduced duty (*August 1*). His former law partner Joseph Lavergne is appointed to the Quebec Superior Court in Ottawa and gives up his seat as an MP (*August 4*). Laurier enforces the alien labour law against U.S. immigrants (*August 6*). Receives the Legion of Honour award in Paris from French President Félix Faure (*August 8*). Has an audience with Pope Leo XIII in Rome (*August 12*); returns to France, then travels to England and Ireland. Yukon District is created within the North-West Territories (*August 16*). Arrives back in Quebec (*August 27*). His family moves into 335 Theodore Street (later Laurier Avenue), an Ottawa house purchased for $9,500 by the Liberal Party (*September*); they leave the Russell Hotel where he has boarded since 1874. Sifton (Interior) takes a first-hand look at the Klondike gold rush and returns to propose a railway as well as encouraging an Alaska boundary settlement (*September-November*). Laurier meets with U.S. President William McKinley in Washington (*November 10*). Discusses the Alaska boundary dispute with U.S. Secretary of State John Sherman (*November 11*). Appoints Senator David Mills as Justice minister to replace the ailing Mowat (*November 18*). The Imperial Privy Council rules in favour of the provinces in granting the right to appoint Queen's Counsels (*December 8*). Rome issues a papal encyclical opposing the Manitoba's School Act, but urges the Catholic Church in Canada to accept the Laurier-Greenway agreement until the situation improves (*December 18*). The Bering Sea Commission, meeting in Ottawa, awards Canadian sealers $464,000 in damages from the U.S. (*December 22*).

1898: Yukon Railway Bill proposed by Sifton (Interior) is passed (*March 16*); stopped two weeks later in the Senate by a Conservative majority led by Bowell. Laurier receives an honorary Doctor of Laws degree from his alma mater McGill, but doesn't attend (*May*). Receives an honorary Doctor of Laws degree from Queen's. The Imperial Privy Council gives Canada sole power over implementing its own fisheries regulations (*May 26*). Joint high commission is set up to settle all outstanding Canadian-U.S. issues (*May 30*). The Federal Franchise Act, reinstating provincial control of the right to vote and voters' lists, takes effect (*June 13*). Yukon Territory is organized with Dawson City as the capital; Quebec's northern boundary is extended to Hudson Bay (*June 13*). One-penny postage (two cents) is established in many parts of the British Empire (*July 12*). Announces the appointment of the Earl of Minto as Canada's eighth Governor General (*July 25*). An Imperial military commission begins work on a confidential report about the condition of Canadian defences (*July 28*). The second half of the preferential tariff on British goods goes into effect (*August 1*). Hosts Lord and Lady Aberdeen at his Arthabaska home for a weekend (*August*). Represents Canada at the first joint high commission meeting held in Canada (in Quebec City) to discuss the Alaska boundary dispute (*August 23-October 10*). A federal referendum on prohibition is passed by 51.3% (*September 29*); chooses not to impose prohibition because the majority is too small. The joint high commission reconvenes in Washington (*November 9-February 20*).

All in the Grey family

The two Governors General for most of Laurier's lengthy term in office were brothers-in-law. Lord Minto's appointment was announced by Laurier in 1898. He already had experience in Canada as military secretary to Lord Lansdowne and chief of staff to General Middleton in the North-West Rebellion of 1885. He was married to Mary Grey, sister of Lord Grey who succeeded Minto as Governor General in 1905. The Greys' uncle was Lord Durham, the British North America Governor General whose 1839 report resulted in the union of Upper and Lower Canada.

1899: Begins receiving pressure from Britain and South Africa to send troops to fight the Boers in Africa (*February*). First celebration of Empire Day, which later becomes Victoria Day (*May 23*). Germany protests Canada's preferential tariff with Britain by depriving Canada of most-favoured-nation status in trading (*July 7*). Pacific Cable Bill is introduced (*July 25*). Laurier's electoral Redistribution Bill is blocked by the Senate (*July 29*). Presents a motion supporting the British fighting in the Transvaal, but offers no specific action (*July 31*). Nominates Thomas Bain to be the eighth Speaker of the House (*August 1*). Says Canada cannot send a contingent to fight in South Africa without approval from Parliament, which is prorogued (*October 3*). Visits Chicago to discuss the Alaska boundary dispute with U.S. President William McKinley (*October 7*); also meets with Mexican President Porfirio Diaz. Britain goes to war against the Boers (*October 12*). Cabinet agrees to provide funds for Canadian volunteers interested in fighting for Britain in the Boer War; it refuses to act on Britain's call for a Canadian contingent (*October 13*). Henri Bourassa resigns from the Liberal party to protest Canadian involvement in the Boer War (*October 18*). Britain and the U.S. agree on a provisional boundary between Canada and Alaska (*October 20*). The first group of 1,150 volunteer soldiers sails for South Africa (*October 30*), arriving in Capetown a month later. Hugh Macdonald, son of Sir John A. Macdonald, is elected premier of Manitoba (*December 7*). Laurier appoints the Ottawa Improvement Commission (*December 21*).

1900: Remains sitting while MPs stand to sing *God Save the Queen* to celebrate Britain's victory in South Africa, citing House rules as his reason (*June 7*). Dismisses Thomas

McInnes, Lieutenant-Governor of British Columbia, for supporting Premier Joseph Martin's government despite its defeat at the polls (*June 20*). Lieutenant Harold Borden, son of Sir Frederick Borden (Militia & Defence) is killed in action in South Africa (*July 16*). Appoints William Mulock to cabinet as Canada's first Labour minister (*July 19*). Lays the cornerstone for the new bridge across the St. Lawrence River at Quebec City (*October 2*). Eighth Parliament is dissolved (*October 9*). Asks Mulock (Postmaster General) to appoint nephew Wilfrid Laurier as postmaster of Laurentides to replace his step-brother Charlemagne who is running for Parliament (*October 16*). Canada's ninth federal election: re-elected in Quebec East defeating Joseph-Eugène Chapleau (Conservative); step-brother Charlemagne elected in L'Assomption; Liberals win another majority government (*November 7*).

1901: Tupper resigns as Leader of the Opposition and Conservative leader (*January 17*). Victoria dies in London, England (*January 22*); Edward VII becomes king. Robert Borden is chosen as leader of the Conservative party (*February 6*). Laurier nominates Louis Brodeur to be the ninth Speaker of the House at the opening of the Ninth Parliament (*February 6*). Has former law partner Lavergne's judicial appointment shifted to Montreal, with Émilie following him there; sends back all the letters she has written to him over the years, but she doesn't return the favour. Ottawa Mint Act is passed, giving Canada the ability to produce its own money (*May 21*). Attends reunion at L'Assomption College (*June 11-12*). Welcomes the Duke of York (later George V) and his wife Elizabeth to Canada then accompanies them on a trip to the west coast and back (*September 16-October*).

1902: Appoints Charles Fitzpatrick as Justice minister (*February 11*). A peace treaty in South Africa is signed at Vereeniging (*May 31*); 270 Canadians were killed of the 8,000 who went to South Africa during the Boer War. Sails for England (*June 14*). Edward VII's coronation is postponed after the new king gets appendicitis (*June 24*). Attends his second Colonial Conference in London (*June 30-August 11*). Receives an honorary Doctor of Laws degree from the University of Edinburgh (*July 26*). Attends the coronation of Edward VII in London (*August 9*). Visits France, Switzerland and Italy and becomes quite ill near the end of the trip (*August-October*). Dismisses Tarte (Public Works) for campaigning against the Liberal party's tariff policy (*October 21*). Leaves for Hot Springs, Virginia, with his wife in an effort to improve his rapidly declining health, diagnosed as asthma (*November 12*). Appoints Sir Henri Taschereau as Canada's fourth Chief Justice (*November 21*). Disallows British Columbia's legislation excluding Chinese and Japanese immigrants (*December 5*). Visits Washington to discuss the Alaska boundary dispute with U.S. President Theodore Roosevelt (*December*). Returns to Hot Springs, then on to Florida (*December*). Provincial premiers meet for the first time in 15 years in Quebec City (*December 18-20*).

1903: Returns to Ottawa (*January*). Government introduces a bill to set up a railway commission to study the feasibility of a second transcontinental railway north of the CPR (*March 20*); two weeks later a Grand Trunk Pacific Railway incorporation bill is introduced. Ottawa imposes a tariff against Germany in retaliation to its tariff. Accepts the resignation of Blair (Railways & Canals) who objects to the involvement of the Grand Trunk Railway in the second transcontinental railway scheme (*July 13*). Introduces his transcontinental railway bill in the House (*July 30*); it is passed on September 29. The Alaska Boundary Tribunal decides in favour of the U.S., ending Yukon's hope for an ocean outlet (*October 20*); Canadian representatives refuse to sign the agreement. The Grand Trunk Pacific Railway receives its charter on the last day of the Third Session, Ninth Parliament, the longest Session held to date, at 155 days (*October 24*). His stepmother Adeline dies in St. Lin (*November 3*).

1904: In a speech, says the 20th century belongs to Canada (*January 18*). Appoints Brodeur (Speaker of the House) as Inland Revenue minister (*January 19*). Appoints Blair chairman of the Dominion Railway Commission (*February 1*). Armand Lavergne, son of Émilie, is elected MP for Montmagny in a by-election (*February 16*). Nominates Napoléon Belcourt to be the 10th Speaker of the House at the opening of the Fourth Session, Ninth Parliament (*March 10*). His longtime friend Ernest Pacaud dies in Montreal of tuberculosis (*April 19*). Canada competes in the Olympics for the first time, in St. Louis, Missouri (*May 14*). Dismisses Lord Dundonald, Imperial commander of the Canadian militia, for his criticism of acting Militia & Defence minister Sidney Fisher (*June 7*); the practice of appointing British officers to command Canada's militia is discontinued. The preferential tariff is expanded to include South Africa (*July 15*). Announces the appointment of Earl Grey as Canada's ninth Governor General (*September 26*). Blair resigns as chairman of the Dominion Railway Commission to run as a Conservative candidate in the election (*October 18*). Canada's 10th federal election: re-elected in Quebec East defeating Michel Fiset (Conservative), but also wins election in Quebec's Wright riding, which he declines; Liberals win another majority government (*November 3*).

1905: Nominates Robert Sutherland to be the 11th Speaker of the House at the opening of the 10th Parliament (*January 11*). Introduces a bill to create two new provinces: Alberta and Saskatchewan; it allows for separate Catholic schools (*February 21*). Sifton (Interior & Indian Affairs) resigns in protest over the Alberta and Saskatchewan formula that accommodates Catholic education (*February 27*). Becomes acting Interior & Indian Affairs minister (*March 13*). The Alberta-Saskatchewan bill is amended to restrict Catholic education to the end of the school day (*March 22*). Steps down as acting Interior & Indian Affairs minister (*April 6*); Frank Oliver enters cabinet as minister the next day. Governor General Earl Grey becomes commander of the Canadian militia (*June 15*). Leader of the Opposition becomes the first in the British Empire to receive a salary: $7,000 (*July*). Visits the west with Earl Grey to inaugurate two new provinces (*August-September*). Alberta and Saskatchewan become the eighth and ninth provinces; Keewatin district is annexed to the Northwest Territories (government style removes the hyphen to make 'Northwest' one word) (*September 1*). Turns the first sod for the Lake Superior route of the Grand Trunk Pacific Railway (*September 11*).

1906: Becomes acting Marine & Fisheries minister, replacing Joseph Préfontaine who died of angina in Paris (*January 6*). British soldiers leave Canada; the Halifax garrison is turned over to Canada (*January 16*). Replaces himself in Marine & Fisheries with Brodeur (Inland Revenue) (*February 6*). Appoints Charles Fitzpatrick (Justice) as the fifth Chief Justice of Canada, succeeding Taschereau (*June 14*). Lord's Day Act comes into effect making Sunday a day of rest (*July 11*); remains on the books until 1985. Accepts the resignation of Charles Hyman (Public Works) who had been accused of election corruption (*August 29*). Chairs the first Conference of the Representatives of the Government of Canada and Various Provinces in Ottawa where the dominant topic is, predictably, financial subsidies to the provinces (*October 8-13*).

1907: Alienates Liberal MP Armand Lavergne following his consistent opposition to the party (*January 28*). The Dominion Railway Commission orders the CPR and GTR to reduce passenger fares to three cents a mile within 60 days (*March 18*). The Commissioner of the Northwest Territories is invested with executive powers (*March 22*). Accepts the resignation of Henry Emmerson (Railways & Canals) who is accused of alcoholism and affairs with women (*April 2*). Sails for England with Zoë (*April 5*). Attends his third Colonial Conference (*April 15-May 14*); suggests it be renamed the Imperial Conference, opposes the establishment of an Imperial military, and promotes an increase in the use of preferential trade. Visits Italy and Switzerland (*May-July*). Appoints William Templeman

(Inland Revenue) as the first Mines minister (*May 3*). The BNA Act makes further provision for provincial subsidies from Ottawa (*August 9*). The Alaska Boundary Commission releases its first report (*August 27*). Appoints former New Brunswick premier William Puglsey as Public Works minister and George Graham as Railways & Canals minister (*August 30*). The Quebec Bridge at Quebec City collapses, killing 75 workers (*August 29*). Anti-Japanese riots take place in Vancouver (*September 7-9*). A new commercial treaty is reached with France (*September 19*). Bourassa resigns as an MP to contest the Quebec provincial election (*October 28*).

1908: Yvonne Coutu, the daughter of Emma who was the other bride in the Laurier's double wedding ceremony, joins his household to help look after Zoë. Attends the celebrations marking the 300th anniversary of Quebec City, as does the Prince of Wales (*July 22*). Refuses a peerage (*July*). Recommends deputy Labour minister William Lyon Mackenzie King for a Companion of St. Michael and St. George, only to discover that it had already been conferred in 1906. The Dominion Lands Act comes into effect, opening up 30 million acres of land in the west (*September 1*). Civil Service Commission is created to handle government staff appointments (*September 12*). Canada's 11th federal election: re-elected in Quebec East where he again defeats Fiset; also wins a seat in Ottawa that he holds on to until the end of 1909; his Liberal government is re-elected (*October 26*). Bedridden with shingles and a muscle ailment (*October 30-November*). Indicates his intention to resign (*November*); Fielding (Finance), his designated successor, talks him out of it. The Alaska Boundary Commission releases its second report (*December 29*).

1909: Nominates Charles Marcil to be the 12th Speaker of the House at the open-ing of the 11th Parliament (*January 20*). Charles Murphy (Secretary of State) introduces a bill to establish a department of External Affairs (*March 14*). Supports Conservative MP George Foster's motion to establish a Canadian navy (*March 29*); the initiative, which is a response to Germany's aggressive shipbuilding program, is passed unanimously. Murphy (Secretary of State) becomes the first Secretary of State for External Affairs (*June 1*). Appoints King as Labour minister (*June 2*). Brodeur (Marine & Fisheries) and Sir Frederick Borden (Military & Defence) represent Canada at the Imperial defence conference in London, England (*June*). Captain J.E. Bernier, Arctic explorer, claims the Arctic Archipelago for Canada (*July 1*). Laurier visits the prairie provinces (*July-August*). Canada agrees to form a navy based on plans submitted by the British Admiralty (*September 18*). Announces the creation of the Conservation Commission, with Sifton as chairman (*September*). The Alaska Boundary Commission releases its third report (*December*).

1910: Introduces the Naval Services Bill to establish a Canadian navy that includes a naval board, a naval college, five cruisers, six destroyers and no compulsory naval service (*January 12*). King (Labour) introduces the Combines Act for limited control over mergers and combines in industry (*January 18*). Canada removes the surtax from German imports (*March 1*); Germany reciprocates. Naval Services Bill passes in the Commons (*April 10*). Appoints Brodeur (Marine & Fisheries) as the first Naval Services minister (*May 4*) and the Naval Service of Canada is established. Edward VII dies (*May 6*); his son becomes George V (*May 9*). The boundary between New Brunswick and Maine is settled by the Passamaquoddy Bay Treaty that gives Pope's Folly Island to the U.S. and the fishing grounds south of Lubec to Canada (*May 21*). Canada signs a commercial agreement with Italy (*June 6*). Tours western Canada (*July 9-September 2*). Chats with newsboy John Diefenbaker in Saskatoon (*July 29*). Thrown to the floor of his train when it collides with a freight train near Moose Jaw (*August*). Drives the first spike for the Alberta Central Railway in Red Deer (*August 10*). Opens the first Pacific Industrial (later National) Exhibition in Vancouver (*August 16*). Addresses the 20th Eucharistic Congress in Montreal, the first to be held in North America (*September 9*). Defends the Naval Bill in a rousing speech in

Montreal (*October 12*). Canada's first naval cruiser *Niobe* arrives in Halifax (*October 17*). Liberals lose a by-election in Drummond-Arthabaska, Laurier's former riding, because of fear surrounding the Naval Services Act (*November 3*). A delegation of 1,000 farmers demands tariff revisions (*December 16*). The Alaska Boundary Commission releases its fourth report (*December 28*). Canada and the U.S. agree to set up an international railway commission to regulate rates (*December 31*).

An unexpected chat with a future Prime Minister

At Saskatoon's railway station in 1910, Laurier began chatting with a newsboy. The Prime Minister was impressed with the 14-year-old's precociousness, referring to him later in his speech at the University of Saskatchewan's cornerstone ceremony. "You have some remarkable newsboys here," noted Laurier. "This one talked to me for half an hour at the railway station and then said, 'Well, Mr. Prime Minister, I can't waste any more time. I have to deliver my papers." The young, hustling newsboy was John Diefenbaker.

1911: Compulsory military training comes into force (*January 1*). Fielding (Finance) introduces a reciprocity agreement with the U.S. calling for the free trade of natural products and reduced tariffs on other items (*January 26*). Japan denounces its commercial treaty with Canada (*February 19*). Announces the appointment of the Duke of Connaught, George V's uncle, as Canada's 10th Governor General (*March 21*). Agrees to suspend debate on reciprocity until he returns from England (*May 5*). Sails to England (*May 12*). Attends his fourth Imperial (previously Colonial) Conference in London (*May 23-June 20*). Attends the coronation of George V (*June 22*). Arrives back in Canada (*July 10*). U.S. Senate ratifies the reciprocity agreement with Canada (*July 22*). The third transcontinental railway is completed with the branch line from Montreal to Port Arthur (*July 29*). Signs an Order-in-Council to ban Black immigration for one year (August 12); revoked two months later on a technicality. His car is jostled in Montreal and stones are thrown by Bourassa followers (*September 19*). Canada's 12th federal election: re-elected in Quebec East by acclamation, but his government loses to Borden's Conservatives; seven of his cabinet ministers, including King and Fielding, are defeated (*September 21*). Approached by King (Labour) who offers to write his biography (*September 29*); agrees but it's never pursued. **Laurier government ends** (*October 6*).

1912: Agrees to stay on as Liberal leader (*March 2*). His naval policy is dropped by Borden who does not offer an alternative (*March 18*). Attends the official opening of the Chateau Laurier hotel in Ottawa (*June 12*); unhappy with the look of the repaired broken nose on a marble bust of him at the hotel. Refuses to take part in a naval policy conference (*August 16*). Tours Quebec and Ontario (*September-October*).

1913: Launches a filibuster to stop the government's Naval Bill from passing (*March*). The government calls for closure to stop the Liberal filibuster (*April 9*).

1914: Commits the Liberal party's support to Britain after it declares war on Germany earlier in the month (*August 19*).

1915: Moves an amendment condemning the Conservative budget for increasing tariffs on British goods while war is being waged (*March 10*). A tooth infection causes his collapse in Napanee, Ont. (*September 2*); has the abscessed tooth removed. Tells Borden he won't support postponing the election until after the war (*November 8*). Conducts a war policy meeting with Ottawa's top 50 Liberals (*December 20*).

1916: Following a concert performance at Russell Hall, witnesses a fire on Parliament Hill that destroys the Centre Block (*February 3*); two who perish in the fire are longtime friends who had dinner at his home the previous evening; papers in his office are destroyed. Supports Borden's request to extend the 12th Parliament by one year (*February 8*). Supports Ernest Lapointe's resolution asking Ontario to revoke its motion against French schools in that province (*May 10*). Threatens to resign as Liberal leader if Lapointe's resolution isn't supported; the party endorses it (*May 11*), but it is defeated by the government. Has many of his remaining bad teeth removed (*June 2*).

1917: Asked by Borden to enter a coalition (*May 25*). Rejects Borden's offer because of the government intention to implement conscription (*June 6*). Western Liberals reluctantly endorse his stand against making conscription a party policy (*August 9*). Refuses Borden's second offer to form a coalition (*August*). Tells Parliament that one million women west of Quebec are being unfairly denied the vote despite having that right at the provincial level (*September*). Asked to resign by a delegation of English Liberals led by Fielding (*October 7*); he refuses, paving the way for the exodus of Liberals to Borden's coalition Unionist government (*October 12*). Begins his campaign against conscription (*November 9*). Campaigns in the west (*December 7*). Canada's 13th federal election; re-elected in Quebec East defeating Ferdinand Drouin (Conservative-Unionist); the Liberals take Quebec but are heavily defeated everywhere else (*December 17*).

1918: Votes against the government bill to give women the vote (*April 12*). His last day in the House (*May 24*). Vacations in Ste-Agathe, recovering from illness (*July*). Begins the work of reintegrating Liberals who had joined the Unionist coalition (*September*).

1919: Makes his last speech, in support of the formation of the Eastern Ontario Liberal Association (*January 14*). Suffers a mild stroke in his office (*February 15*). A second, more severe, stroke forces him to bed (*February 16*). Dies at 3 a.m. (*February 17*). Lies in state in the temporary House of Commons at Victoria Memorial Museum where every seat except his is removed (*February 20-21*). More than 100,000 people line the Ottawa route of the funeral procession to Notre Dame Basilica (*February 22*); buried in Ottawa's Notre Dame Cemetery.

BOOKS ABOUT LAURIER

- **1890**: Ulric Barthe; *Laurier On the Platform* (Turcotte & Menard)
- **1890**: Louis Fréchette; *Laurier* (Men of the Day series) (Louis N. Taché)
- **1903**: John Willison; *Sir Wilfrid Laurier and the Liberal Party*, 2 Vols. (Toronto)
- **1916**: O.D. Skelton; *The Day of Wilfrid Laurier* (Glasgow, Brook & Co.)
- **1919**: Peter McArthur; *Sir Wilfrid Laurier* (Dent)
- **1921**: Oscar D. Skelton; *The Life and Letters of Sir Wilfrid Laurier*, 2 Vols. (Oxford)
- **1922**: John Dafoe; *Laurier: A Study in Canadian Politics* (Thomas Allen)
- **1927**: Sir John Willison; *Sir Wilfrid Laurier* (Oxford)
- **1931**: Robert Rumilly; *Sir Wilfrid Laurier, Canadian* (Paris)
- **1935**: Lucien Pacaud; *Sir Wilfrid Laurier: Letters to My Father and Mother* (Ryerson)
- **1965**: Joseph Schull; *Laurier: The First Canadian* (Macmillan)
- **1967**: Raymond Tanghe; *Laurier: Architect of Canadian Unity* (Harvest House)
- **1971**: Barbara Robertson; *Wilfrid Laurier: The Great Conciliator* (Oxford University)

- **1973**: H. Blair Neatby; *Laurier and a Liberal Quebec* (Carleton Library)
- **1979**: Richard Clippingdale; *Laurier: His Life and World* (McGraw-Hill Ryerson)
- **1989**: Charles Fisher (ed.); *Dearest Émilie: The Love Letters of Sir Wilfrid Laurier to Madame Lavergne* (N.C.)
- **1996**: Laurier LaPierre; *Sir Wilfrid Laurier and the Romance of Canada* (Stoddart)
- **2002**: Roderick Stewart; *Wilfrid Laurier: A Pledge for Canada* (XYZ)
- **2013**: André Pratt: *Sir Wilfrid Laurier* (Extraordinary Canadians series) (Penguin)

Leaders of the Liberal Party

1.	Alexander Mackenzie	1873-1880
2.	Edward Blake	1880-1887
3.	Sir Wilfrid Laurier	1887-1919
4.	William Lyon Mackenzie King	1919-1948
5.	Louis St. Laurent	1948-1958
6.	Lester B. Pearson	1958-1968
7.	Pierre Trudeau	1968-1984
8.	John Turner	1984-1990
9.	Jean Chrétien	1990-2003
10.	Paul Martin	2003-2006
11.	Stéphane Dion	2006-2008
12.	Michael Ignatieff	2009-2011
13.	Justin Trudeau	2013-

8

Sir Robert L. Borden

The Unwavering Prime Minister

The First World War defined much of Robert Borden's time as leader. It pressed him to change his mind and give the vote to women (limited to wives, mothers and sisters of soldiers and women serving in the military). It convinced him to bring some Liberal MPs into cabinet to form a Unionist government. It shifted his thinking from staunch Imperialism to a drive to ensure Canada would have an independent voice at the peace talks. Ultimately, it persuaded Borden to use conscription to bolster the army's size as a way to counter staggering losses in Europe – a decision that further alienated Quebec.

Borden the Politician

Prime Minister of Canada: October 10, 1911 – July 10, 1920
Length of term: 8 years, 9 months
Parliaments as Prime Minister: 12th; 13th
Age on entering office: 57
Political party: Conservative
Leader of party: February 6, 1901 – July 10, 1920
Member of Parliament: July 11, 1896 – December 5, 1921
Ridings represented: Halifax [N.S.] (1896-1904, 1908-1917); Carleton [Ont.] (1905-1908); King's [N.S.] (1917-1921)
Cabinet portfolios: Privy Council President (1911-1917); External Affairs (1912-1920)
Other political post: Leader of the Opposition (1901-1911)
Knighted: July 22, 1914
Titles: Queen's Counsel (1891); Canadian Privy Councillor (1911); Imperial Privy Councillor (1912); Knight Grand Cross of the Order of St. Michael & St. George (1914)
Quotes: "Another able Cabinet Minister spoke of the shortage of guns, rifles, munitions, etc., but declared that the chief shortage was of brains." (1916 letter to Britain about the war); "Canada got nothing out of the war except recognition." (letter to his wife)
Lived after term: 16 years

BORDEN THE MAN

Name: Robert Laird Borden
Born: June 26, 1854, Grand Pré, Nova Scotia
Ancestry: English, Scottish
Religion: Anglican, Presbyterian
Education: did not attend school beyond age 18
Nicknames: Rob
Military service: Halifax Volunteers, 63rd Battalion of Rifles (1874-1876, 1878-1879)
Occupation: teacher; lawyer; business executive
Publications: *Canadian Constitutional Studies* (1929); *Canada in the Commonwealth: From Conflict to Co-operation* (1929); *Robert Laird Borden, His Memoirs, 2 Vols* (1938); *Letters To Limbo* (1971).
Appearance: "a sound, shaggy man" (Bruce Hutchison in *Mr. Prime Minister*); "his middle-parted hair looking like small wings" (George Bowering in *Egotists and Autocrats*)
Personality: "grim, unyielding, and sometimes inspired" (J.L. Granatstein & Norman Hillmer in *Prime Ministers: Ranking Canada's Leaders*); "an able, orderly, laborious and brave man" (Bruce Hutchison in *Mr. Prime Minister*)
Occupation after term: retired
Married: Laura Bond – September 25, 1889, St. Paul's Anglican Church, Halifax, Nova Scotia
Age at marriage: 35
Years married: 48
Died: June 10, 1937, Ottawa, Ontario
Age at death: 83
Cause of death: heart attack
Buried: Beechwood Cemetery, Ottawa, Ontario

Borden was the:
- Only Prime Minister to lead a coalition government (Unionist)
- First Prime Minister called Prime Minister and not Premier
- First Prime Minister who was a teacher
- First Prime Minister with no previous cabinet experience
- First Prime Minister to attend a British cabinet meeting
- First Conservative Prime Minister fluent in French
- First Prime Minister with a moustache (no beard)
- First Prime Minister of six in a row to serve as External Affairs minister
- Longest serving Leader of the Opposition before becoming Prime Minister
- Third Prime Minister from Nova Scotia
- Fifth Prime Minister who was a lawyer
- Sixth Conservative Prime Minister
- Last Prime Minister born before Confederation
- Last Prime Minister without a university education
- Last Prime Minister to be knighted

Borden's legacy

- Nudged Canada towards full sovereignty with his insistence the country play a full international role at the Paris Peace Conference
- Pushed for and achieved diplomatic status in the United States
- Gave women the right to vote federally
- Alienated Quebec after adopting conscription during the First World War

BORDEN'S FAMILY

Borden's Parents

Father: Andrew Borden
Born: February 14, 1816, Grand Pré, Nova Scotia
First wife: Catherine Sophia Fuller (Dec. 14, 1841)
Occupation: farmer; station master
Died: March 28, 1900, Grand Pré, Nova Scotia
Age at death: 84
Note: His nephew. Sir Frederick Borden, served in Laurier's cabinet.

Mother: Eunice Jane Laird
Born: May 1, 1825, Nova Scotia
Married: October 2, 1850, Horton, Nova Scotia
Died: March 29, 1915, Grand Pré, Nova Scotia
Age at death: 89

Borden's Brothers & Sisters (3 siblings; Robert the oldest)

Half-Brother: Thomas Andrew Borden (1842-1887)
Half-Sister: Sophie Amelia Borden (1844-1921), 8 children
  Married: Edward McLatchy (1865)
Brother: John William 'Will' Borden (1856-1937), no children
  Married: Annie Frances Brown (1892)
Sister: Julia Rebecca Borden (1858-1940)
Brother: Henry 'Hal' Clifford Borden (1870-1943), 3 children
  Married: Mabel Ashmere Barnstead (1898)
  Note: Youngest son Henry was close to Robert and Laura Borden.

Borden's Wife

Name: Laura Bond
Born: November 26, 1861, Halifax, Nova Scotia
Father: Thomas H. Bond (hardware merchant)
Mother: Catherine Atkinson
Age at marriage: 26
Children: none
Died: September 7, 1940, Ottawa, Ontario
Age at death: 78
Burial place: Beechwood Cemetery, Ottawa, Ontario
Younger than Borden: 7 years
Died after Borden: 3 years
Note: Her parents both died when she was 15.

POLITICAL STORIES

Another unwilling leader

Like a handful of party leaders before him, Borden didn't want the job. It was a pattern that started when he first entered politics. Tupper, who was about to become Prime Minister in 1896, asked him to run for Parliament. Borden said no, then backpedalled and agreed, if the Halifax incumbent John F. Stairs would return to take the seat back as soon as possible. Four years later, he told Tupper he wanted out. Not only did he end up running again, he managed the entire 1900 campaign for Nova Scotia.

That same year, Tupper and his son began encouraging Borden to assume the leadership. He wasn't interested. Despite that, he was nominated by caucus in 1901 to head the party. He refused. But it was unanimous, so he agreed to do it for a year while the party came up with a new leader. The party then convinced him that an 'interim' leader would lack clout, so he agreed to accept the permanent title.

Borden attempted unsuccessfully to resign in 1904, 1905 and 1910. Just before the 1911 election, he asked Richard McBride, premier of British Columbia, to take on the leadership. McBride and caucus turned him down and he ended up winning the election.

After the war and the peace negotiations, Borden again submitted his resignation. The party convinced him to stay one more year. But six months later, his declining health and his wife made it clear it was time to go. The party finally concurred.

Parliament on fire

While working in his office on the evening of February 3, 1916, shortly after leaving the House, Borden was confronted with a breathless messenger who told him the hall outside was on fire. Finding the corridor was indeed ablaze, he made a quick escape using a back staircase, leaving his coat and hat behind.

He and others watched helplessly as the fire spread. The House was still in session and many other MPs were in their offices, but nearly everyone escaped. Seven people perished, including Liberal MP Bowman Law, four government employees and two guests of the Speaker. Borden's Agriculture minister, Martin Burrell, was badly burned on his face and hands.

Adjourning to the Chateau Laurier with several cabinet ministers, Borden discussed their options, resolute that Parliament should continue meeting the next day. He returned to Parliament Hill around midnight and discovered the fire had spread to nearly all of the Centre Block. In fact, his chauffeur informed him that the Parliamentary Library was also lost. That proved to be false – an iron door saved it from the inferno.

The next morning, he visited several possible sites for the House to meet and decided on the Victoria Memorial Museum (today's Canadian Museum of Nature). He met with cabinet there at noon and three hours later MPs were back in session at that location. It was an incredibly rapid transformation turning the museum's auditorium into the House of Commons.

Tackling Sam Hughes

In his memoirs, Borden was candid about the difficulty in dealing with the "erratic temperament, countless indiscretions, absurd vanities, and lack of systematic administrative capacity" of his Militia & Defence minister Sir Sam Hughes. "His judgement was unbalanced and his temperament constantly led him into difficulty and controversy."

Soldiers in the First World War knew all about Hughes. He obstinately defended the use of the Ross rifle that tended to jam when used repeatedly in wet, muddy conditions. Military leaders finally had to overrule Hughes to replace the Ross with a better weapon. He also stoutly defended the MacAdam shovel, an entrenching tool he helped invent with a hole in the blade. It was neither effective for digging nor protective from gunfire. Eventually, all 23,000 shovels were sold for scrap.

Without cabinet approval, Hughes decided to move his department to England, closer to the warfront. Borden squashed the idea and appointed a minister of Overseas Military Forces instead. Hughes reacted emotionally in a series of meetings with Borden, whining about the humiliation. He followed these up with a formal letter chastising his boss. Borden finally had enough in 1916 and demanded his resignation.

Quebec and conscription

Borden's biggest challenge during the war was whether or not to impose compulsory enlistment (the same issue would plague King in the Second World War). On the one hand, the need for conscription was becoming dire. The British were clamouring for more soldiers and the Prime Minister estimated he'd need 100,000 more recruits. Despite enthusiastic recruiting in 1914 and 1915, there simply weren't enough volunteers to sustain the Canadian forces fighting overseas.

On the other hand, farmers and many in Quebec recoiled at the idea of conscription. French Canadians rejected the idea of fighting one of Britain's wars. Riots began in Quebec. One of Borden's Quebec cabinet ministers resigned and others threatened to follow, while the federal Liberal party split over the issue.

Borden held firm. A Military Services Bill was passed in the summer of 1917 and took effect the following January. The process rolled out acrimoniously over the next few months and by then the war was almost over. Some conscripts played a role in the war's final days and many others never made it to Europe to see action. But it was too late: conscription had hammered a nasty wedge between French and English Canada.

Forging a unified government

Borden felt that wartime conditions called for a united front that would benefit from a coalition government. He devoted much of the spring of 1917 to making it a reality. The key was to bring Laurier onside. Any hope of that evaporated because of the Liberal leader's opposition to conscription unless the govern-ment held a referendum.

But other Liberal MPs were open to the idea and, by October, nine of them had crossed the floor to join the cabinet of Borden's proposed Unionist party. There was even one Labour politician added to the mix. It was Canada's first – and still only – foray into coalition government.

Borden had asked his entire Conservative cabinet team to sign letters of resignation, giving him the flexibility to craft the new ministry. His belief in the coalition was so strong, he felt he should step aside and let Supreme Court Justice Lyman Duff become Prime Minister. His party refused to accept the proposal.

The Unionists won the 1917 election, but the need for a coalition faltered after the war. By 1920, most of the Liberals had returned to their former party and Borden's successor had renamed it the National Liberal and Conservative party. When Meighen lost the 1921 election, the party gravitated back to using only the Conservative name. The few remaining coalition Liberals joined the Tories outright.

A war, peace talks and a league

Throughout the war, Borden's tenacity never wavered in ensuring Canada played a meaningful role in decisions affecting its soldiers. In the subsequent peace talks, he succeeded in gaining a seat at the negotiation table for Canada rather than being relegated to a second tier of the British delegation.

Given his success at the Paris Peace Conference, it is hardly surprising that Borden pushed hard for Canada to be a full member of the League of Nations. The international organization, a proposal by U.S. President Woodrow Wilson, was enshrined in the Treaty of Versailles. Canada became a founding member on January 10, 1920.

Ten years after stepping down as Prime Minister, Borden served as Canada's representative to the international body. He was also president of the Canadian League of Nations Society.

PERSONAL STORIES

U.S. as a recovery destination

Politics didn't usually agree with Borden's health. He suffered a variety of ailments during his years as Prime Minister. The prescribed remedy was often relaxation, typically two-to-four weeks south of the border to play golf with Laura and perhaps 'take the waters'.

His destination of choice was often The Homestead in Hot Springs, Virginia, a luxury resort with an adjoining golf course that regularly welcomed several U.S. presidents. He also spent time in other southern U.S. states, as well as at White Sulphur Springs (now the Greenbriars) in West Virginia.

Being Statesside meant he could easily conduct business by taking quick trips to Washington or New York if needed. In his last year as Prime Minister, that scenario became the norm as he spent half the year in the U.S.

Lady Laura Borden

When Laura Bond Borden became a Prime Minister's wife in 1911, she moved easily and readily into the sphere of social functions and charity work, particularly the Red Cross during the Great War. It wasn't that she was bubbly; she was actually starchily reserved. But her years as the wife of one of Nova Scotia's most prominent lawyers had made her well practiced at entertaining high society.

At heart, Laura was a homebody. Not having children, she poured most of her time into reading and gardening. In Halifax, both took place at their elegant estate Pinehurst where she remained for years after politics took Borden to Ottawa. When she finally moved to Ottawa, the house she urged Borden to buy, Glensmere, was her refuge. She loved to watch the sunset over Macdonald Park at the front of the house; he preferred to watch the sunrise over the Rideau River in their backyard.

Laura shared her husband's passion for golf. In retirement, they got to play even more. Following Borden's death, she remained at Glensmere until her own death in 1940. The house later became the Chinese Embassy and was eventually replaced with the 21-storey unfortunately named Watergate Apartments.

Borden's Timeline

1854: Born in Grand Pré, N.S. (*June26*).

1858: Family moves to a new home in Grand Pré where his parents live until their deaths.

1863: Attends Acadia Villa Seminary, Grand Pré.

1869: Graduates and becomes an assistant teaching master at Acadia Villa Seminary (*April*).

1873: Hired as Professor of Classics and Mathematics at Glenwood Institute, Matawan, New Jersey (*September*).

1874: Returns to Nova Scotia (*June*). Passes the preliminary law examinations (*July*). Articles as a lawyer with Weatherbe & Graham in Halifax (*August*). Joins the Halifax Volunteers, 63rd Battalion of Rifles and undertakes military instruction in the evenings.

1877: Works on the Mackenzie government's case for the Fisheries Commission meeting in Halifax. Passes the law exam at top of the class (classmates include future cabinet ministers Charles Hibbert Tupper and Arthur Dickey), but too young to be admitted to the bar (*September*).

1878: Attends the militia's military school while articling at the law firm (*January*). Admitted to the Nova Scotia bar (*August*). Forms a law partnership with John Ross in Halifax.

1879: Tries his first case and is opposed by Nova Scotia Attorney General John S.D. Thompson (*Winter*); his *Memoirs* suggest he lost.

1880: Forms a law partnership with John Chipman in Kentville (*Winter*). Initiated into the freemasons at St. Andrew's Lodge, Halifax.

1881: Hears Wilfrid Laurier speak in Kentville as part of a Liberal party tour in the Maritimes (*August*).

1882: Makes a short speech to support his cousin Frederick Borden, a Liberal candidate in the federal election (*Spring*); he denounces Macdonald's National Policy in this first political endeavour. Joins the Halifax law firm of Wallace Graham and Charles Hibbert Tupper, to fill a vacancy left by the departure of Thompson to the Nova Scotia Supreme Court (*Summer*).

1884: Attends the second marriage of cousin Frederick, to Bessie Clarke, sister of Frederick's first wife Julia who died of tuberculosis (*June 12*).

1886: Objects to the Nova Scotia Liberals threat to secede from Confederation and switches his support to the Conservatives.

1887: Presents his first case in the Supreme Court in Ottawa. Turns down job offered by Thompson (Justice) to be federal deputy minister of justice (*Fall*).

1888: His law partner Hibbert Tupper leaves the firm to join Macdonald's cabinet in Ottawa (*May*). Visits England and France for the first time.

1889: Marries Laura Bond at St. Paul's Anglican Church in Halifax (*September 25*). His law partner Graham is appointed to the Nova Scotia Supreme Court and Borden becomes senior partner in Borden, Ritchie, Parker & Chisholm law firm in Halifax. (*October*)

1891: Presents a case before the Supreme Court in Ottawa as bells toll the death of Sir John A. Macdonald (*June 6*); hears Laurier in the House of Commons pay tribute to the country's first Prime Minister. Visits Europe with Laura. Becomes a Queen's Counsel.

1893: Visits Europe again with Laura (*Summer*). Sees the wedding procession for Victoria's grandson, the Duke of York (later George V) (*July 5*). Becomes godfather to Reginald Hibbert Tupper, son of Hibbert Tupper (*October 25*).

1894: Buys Pinehurst home in Halifax. Visits western Canada with Hibbert Tupper, the Marine & Fisheries minister (*Fall*).

1895: Visits England to appeal a judicial case (*July-August*).

1896: Becomes president of the Nova Scotia Barristers' Society. Sir Charles Tupper, about to become Prime Minister, asks him to consider running in the election (*April 27*). Wins Conservative nomination for Halifax riding, along with Thomas Kenny (Halifax has two seats in Parliament) (*April 30*). Canada's eighth federal election; elected as the Conservative candidate for Halifax, sharing the seat with Liberal Benjamin Russell (*June 23*). Hibbert Tupper rejoins the law firm (*August*). Moves into the Rideau Club in Ottawa (*August*). Delivers his first speech in the House, attacking the dismissal of public officials (*August 28*). Takes part in meetings in Montreal that result in the creation of the Canadian Bar Association.

1897: Moves from the Rideau Club to the newly opened Gilmour Hotel on Bank Street (*March*). Served on the Public Accounts committee of the House; later served on the Railways Committee and the Privileges and Election Committee. Begins riding a bicycle, never having learned to drive a car. Hibbert Tupper leaves the law firm and moves to Vancouver (*Fall*).

1899: Introduces a motion against corrupt election practices in two Ontario by-elections (*July 6*); devotes most of the session to the issue, with little success.

1900: His father Andrew dies in Grand Pré (*March 28*); helps to financially support his mother and sister Julia on the family farm. Makes two trips to New York City to see a specialist about stomach problems and starts a restrictive lifetime diet (*April-May*). Seeks Tupper's permission to resign from politics but is persuaded to stay. Canada's ninth federal election; re-elected in Halifax, sharing the seat with Liberal William Roche (*November 7*). Asked by Hibbert Tupper to consider assuming leadership of the party; indicates he's not interested (*November*). Becomes a founding member of Crown Life Insurance in Toronto along with Tupper.

1901: Reluctantly accepts his election as Conservative party leader by the caucus following the resignation of Tupper (*February 6*). Chooses MP Frederick Monk to be his Quebec lieutenant.

1902: Tours western Canada for seven weeks with Laura (*September 3-October 20*); meets Arthur Meighen and R.B. Bennett for the first time.

1903: First speech in French at a Montreal testimonial dinner for Monk (*January 29*). Rests at Caledonia Springs Resort east of Ottawa following a breakdown in health. Receives an honorary Doctor of Civil Law degree from Queen's University. Announces the Conservative policy to create a second transcontinental railway using existing rail lines (*August 18*).

1904: His Halifax home is damaged by fire (*January 8*). His Quebec lieutenant, Monk, resigns, protesting interference by fellow Quebec MP Joseph-Israel Tarte (*January*). Borden insists Canada should have played a more active role in the Alaska boundary dispute between the U.S. and Britain (*March*). Reveals leaked documents of a Grand Trunk Railway shareholders' meeting during a debate on government ownership of railways (*April 15*). Suggests that the new transcontinental railway be government-owned (*May 26*). Steps down as president of the Barristers' Society of Nova Scotia. Canada's 10th federal election; defeated by Liberal Michael Carney in his bid for re-election in Halifax (*November 3*). Takes a vacation in the U.S. until December. Urged by many members of caucus not to resign as leader (*December 4*).

1905: Informs caucus he intends to resign as leader (*January 7*). Talked into staying on; George Foster acts as House leader (*January 10*). Quietly gives his MP salary to Edward Kidd for the next three years after Kidd offers to open up his Carleton (Ont.) seat by resigning (*January 20*). Elected by acclamation in the Carleton by-election in (*February 4*). Rushes to Halifax to be with his brother Hal who is left with three small children following the death of his wife Mabel (*February 22*). Resigns from his Halifax law firm (*March*). Becomes the first Leader of the Opposition to receive a salary ($7,000) in addition to pay as an MP (*July*). Receives an honorary Doctor of Laws degree from St. Francis Xavier College in Antigonish (*September*). Moves permanently to Ottawa (*October*), living in rented houses for the next two years. Not invited to the Quebec Conservative convention in protest against his support to let Alberta and Saskatchewan disallow Catholic separate schools (*December*). Calls for a party convention, but is overruled (*December*).

1906: Commits the Conservatives to a policy of discrediting the Laurier government and unveiling its own 'purity in politics' campaign (*January 26*). Speaks out in favour of provincial rights over separate-school status for the new provinces of Alberta and Saskatchewan (*March 26*). Buys Glensmere home in Ottawa, previously rented by Justice minister Charles Fitzpatrick (*April 25*); it becomes his residence until his death.

1907: Calls for an inquiry into the 10-month Lethbridge coal miners' strike (*January 9*). Ignores a request from young Quebec Conservatives to restore Monk as the province's Tory chief (*January 24*). Attempts to hold a Conservative convention but is unsuccessful because of lack of support from Quebec (*April*). Unveils his Halifax Platform, which includes a call for honesty in government, Senate reform and civil service appointments by examination (*August 20*); begins a 10-week cross-Canada tour to promote the platform. Arrives in Quebec City the same day the Quebec Bridge collapses, killing 75 workers, making it the world's worst bridge construction disaster (*August 28*). Calls for government ownership or operation of public resources, but backtracks after some party members express alarm (*September 8*).

1908: Many of his Halifax Platform initiatives are adopted by the Liberal govern-ment. Civil Service Commission is created to hire government staff instead of relying on patronage appointments, partly in response to Conservative charges of corruption (*September 12*). Striking CPR employees attempt to disrupt his campaign speech in Montreal; Conservative supporters out-yell the strikers (*September 19*). Canada's 11th federal election; re-elected in Halifax, and in Carleton where he defeats Liberal James Caldwell; Laurier's Liberals retain power (*October 26*).

1909: Chooses to retain his Halifax seat (*January 25*), freeing up Carleton for its former member Edward Kidd who regains it by acclamation. Reappoints Monk as his Quebec chief (*January 28*). Calls for a committee to study the conservation of natural resources (*February 1*); eight months later a Commission of Conservation is created. Conservatives call on Canada to assume responsibility for its own naval protection; government supports the idea (*March 29*). Makes his first trip to England in 13 years (*June 29*). Meets with future Colonial Secretary and Prime Minister, New-Brunswick-born Bonar Law. Following visits to France and Switzerland, returns to Canada (*October 1*). Congratulates William Lyon Mackenzie King on his appointment to cabinet, noting it's the sixth time Laurier has reached outside the House to fill a position (*November 12*).

1910: Quebec Conservatives again oppose the idea of a national party convention (*March 1*). His amendment to reduce parliamentary control over the proposed navy is defeated (*March 9*). Opposed by a growing number of Conservatives over his shift towards providing emergency contributions to the Imperial navy without consulting the caucus (*March*). Hands his resignation to caucus, which rallies to his support (*April 6*). Holds open-air meetings in Ontario communities as part of an auto tour (*June*); then does the same in the Maritimes (*August*).

1911: Opposes the Liberals' proposed reciprocity treaty as a threat to Canada's nationhood (*February 6*). Gets promised support from several Liberals opposed to reciprocity with the U.S. (*March 1*). Majority of caucus members sign a petition urging him once again not to resign the leadership (*March 28*). Campaigns in the prairies for a month against reciprocity (*June 16*). Officially opens Calgary's new city hall (*June 26*). Canada's 12th federal election; re-elected in Halifax; his Conservatives win a majority (*September 21*). Persuades Toronto financier William Thomas White to become Finance minister; relegates Sir George Foster to Trade & Commerce (*October 4*). **Borden government (1911-1920).** Becomes the eighth Prime Minister and the 20th Privy Council President (*October 10*). Welcomes the Duke of Connaught, George V's uncle and Canada's 10th Governor General, to Quebec City (*October 13*). Re-elected by acclamation in Halifax to confirm his cabinet position (*October 27*). Canada's 12th Parliament opens; nominates Thomas Sproule to be the 13th Speaker of the House (*November 15*). Meets with former U.S. president Theodore Roosevelt at his home on Long Island, New York (*December 9*). Sets up the Public Service Commission to enable more effective government planning and procedures (*December*).

1912: Bill is passed to establish an independent Public Archives for Canada (*January 23*). Indicates he is dropping Laurier's naval policy, but offers no alternative (*March 18*). Conference with British West Indies delegates is held in Ottawa and Toronto; a preferential tariff is established (*March 29-April 10*). Becomes Secretary of State for External Affairs when the Department of External Affairs is separated from the Department of the Secretary of State; the portfolio is held by Prime Ministers for the next 34 years (*April 1*). The Board of Grain Commissioners is appointed to regulate grain trade (*April 10*). Vacations in Hot Springs (*April 23*). Addresses the Associated Press convention in New York City along with U.S. President William Howard Taft; guests include Alexander Graham Bell and Thomas Edison (*April 25*). Boundaries of Quebec, Ontario and Manitoba are extended north to Hudson Bay (*May 15*). Sails to England to discuss defence cooperation with the Imperial government (*June 26*). On his first day in London, meets with British Conservative Leaders Bonar Law and Lord Lansdowne (former Canadian Governor General), followed by Prime Minister Herbert Asquith and Lord of the Admiralty Winston Churchill (*July 5*). Sworn in as a member of the Imperial Privy Council at Buckingham Palace (*July 19*). Visits Paris (*July 27-31*). Returns to Canada (*August 29*). Suggests the government take over the Grand Trunk Pacific Railway (*September 11*); the proposal is rejected. Ontario rejects Borden's request to consider withdrawing Regulation 17 that limits French education in the public school system (*October 17*). Monk (Public Works) resigns to protest Canada's decision to support Britain's defence plans without a plebiscite (*October 18*). Moves his mother and sister Julia from Grand Pré to Ottawa for the winter (*November*). Attempts to win French Canadian support in caucus for emergency aid to Britain with limited success (*November 27*). Introduces the Naval Aid Bill calling for construction of three ships costing $35 million for Britain's use (*December 5*). Liberals begin a filibuster against naval aid that lasts for five months (*December*). Refuses a knighthood (*December*).

1913: Introduces the Agricultural Aid Bill to provide funding for agricultural education (*January*). Canadian Northern Railway asks the government for a $30 million loan (*January 17*); ends up receiving $15 million. Liberals increase the intensity of their filibuster against the Naval Aid Bill, resulting in round-the-clock debating for two weeks (*March 3-15*). Plagued by boils on his neck (*April*). Introduces a motion to close debate on the Naval Aid Bill (*April 8*). Motion to adopt rules for closure is passed (*April 23*). Naval Aid Bill passes without the need to enact closure (*May 15*). Senate refuses to pass the Naval Aid Bill without "the judgement of the country" (*May 30*); the bill dies. Borden announces that the government will pay for three British battleships, despite the Senate's opposition (*June 6*). Vacations in St. Andrew's, N.B., to recover from a carbuncle (*June 30-August 1*). Receives an honorary Doctor of Laws degree from McGill University (*September 1*). Lays cornerstone for Sir Georges-Étienne Cartier monument in Montreal (*September 2*). Introduces a new customs tariff with the U.S. offering lower rates (*October 4*). Appoints Duncan Campbell Scott Superintendent-General of Indian Affairs (*October*). Takes part in the opening of the provincial premiers conference in Ottawa (*October 27*). Vacations in New York City, White Sulphur Springs and Hot Springs, Virginia (*October-November*). His government's Order-in-Council that bars Hindus from entering British Columbia is ruled illegal by B.C. Chief Justice Gordon Hunter (*November 30*). A new Order-in-Council prohibits artisans and labourers from immigrating to British Columbia, virtually closing the country to Asian immigration (*December 8*).

1914: Louis Pelletier (Postmaster General) introduces bilingual postcards nationally without consulting cabinet (*January 19*); English Canadian reaction causes the government to again restrict bilingual cards to Quebec and Eastern Ontario the following year. Private members' bills to abolish honorary titles and capital punishment are rejected (*January 19*). Canadian Northern Railway requests another loan from Ottawa (*January 22*). Borden announces plan to consolidate all Canadian Northern Railway lines under one company, with government assuming a 40% interest, rather than providing more subsidies (*March*). Grand Trunk Pacific Railway borrows another $16 million from the government (*April 29*). Borden appoints Prince Alexander of Teck to be the next Governor General (*May 8*); but later indicates the Duke of Connaught will continue to serve instead. His former Public Works minister Frederick Monk dies in Montreal (*May 15*). Senate defeats the Naval Aid Bill approved earlier by the House. His government enforces its revised Order-in-Council of 1913 to refuse to let the Japanese steamer *Komagata Maru* dock in Vancouver because it is carrying 396 East Indians (*May 21*). CP steamer, *Empress of Ireland*, is rammed in the St. Lawrence River; more than 1,000 lives are lost (*May 29*). Bill introduced to increase the number of Senate seats from 72 to 96 (*June 11*); defeated in the Senate. Accepts a Grand Cross of St. Michael and St. George knighthood, becoming 'Sir' (*July 22*). Vacations in Muskoka (*July 23-31*). Begins a series of emergency cabinet meetings in Ottawa following outbreak of war in Europe (*August 1*). Canada acquires two submarines for the Pacific coast (*August 3*). Britain's declaration of war against Germany brings Canada into the war (*August 4*). Authorizes the mobilization of militia members volunteering to serve overseas (*August 6*). Parliament meets in a special war session for five days to approve the War Measures Act giving cabinet emergency powers (*August 18-22*). Formally declares war on Germany and Austria-Hungary (*August 19*). Canada's first troops, the Princess Patricia's Canadian Light Infantry, sail for England (*August 29*). Considers calling an election (*September 2*). Visits the quickly created soldiers' mobilization camp at Valcartier, Que. (*September 6*). Revisits Valcartier and decides to send all the volunteers to England (*September 21*). The first Canadian Expeditionary Force contingent of 33,000 sails for England (*October 3*). Appoints Pierre Blondin and Senator Thomas Casgrain to cabinet to replace Wilfrid Nantel (Inland Revenue) and Pelletier (Postmaster General) who oppose the war (*October*). Authorizes a program to train another 30,000 soldiers (*October 18*). Asks Meighen (Solicitor General) to investigate possible illegal war contracts between Britain and the U.S. through Canada (*October 19*). Decides against calling a wartime election (*October 21*). Vacations in Hot Springs, Virginia (*October 23-November 15*). A federal Order-in-Council calls for registration of alien enemies in Canada (*October 28*).

1915: Borden reminds the Grand Trunk Railway to honour its contract after the government is asked to buy the company (*January 13*). Canadian troops fight for the first time near Armentières, France (*February 24*). Second Canadian division of troops begins to arrive in Britain (*March 16*). Hurries to Grand Pré to see his mother Eunice the day before she dies (*March 28*). Extends voting privileges to all of the military, regardless of age, gender or length of residency in Canada (*April*). Expels MP William Garland (Carleton) and Arthur Foster (Kings) from caucus for profiting from army contracts (*April 13*). Again considers calling an election (*April 18*). Canadian troops gassed at Ypres, Belgium, by the Germans (*April 24*); the wounded include his godson, Reggie Tupper. Decides for the second time not to call an election (*May 6*). Takes a short holiday to Echo Beach Fishing Club in Quebec to relieve exhaustion (*May 6-22*). War Purchasing Commission is appointed to handle war contracts (*May 8*). Arranges to have the ineffective Ross rifles of Canadian soldiers replaced with British Lee-Enfields (*June*). Discussions about Newfoundland's interest in joining Confederation continue, but the war effort postpones any action (*June 25*). Shares train ride to New York City with William Lyon Mackenzie King (*June 28*). Sails to England with R.B. Bennett (*June 30*). Increases the size of the Canadian force to 150,000 (*July 8*). Meets with George V (*July 13*). Attends British cabinet meetings, first Canadian Prime Minister to do so (*July 14*). Visits troops in France (*July 20-26*). Receives France's Grand Cross of the Legion of Honour (*August 10*). Visits Sir Charles Tupper at Bexleyheath, England (*August 14*). White (Finance) seeks Canada's first international loan, $45 million from New York (*August*). Learns that Britain won't be able to throw its full effort into the war for another 18 months (*August 21*). Returns to Canada, having visited 52 soldiers hospitals in England and France (*September 3*). Canada's two army divisions combine to become the Canadian Corps under General E.A.H. Alderson (*September*). Brings Meighen and his portfolio (Solicitor General) into cabinet (*October 2*). Prepares an Order-in-Council to expand Canada's military force to 250,000 (*October 29*). Tupper, sixth Prime Minister, dies in England (*October 30*). Laurier makes it clear that he won't support any effort to postpone having an election until after the war (*November 8*). Canada declares war against Bulgaria and Turkey (*November 20*). White (Finance) issues domestic war bonds (later called Victory Loans) to raise $50 million; ends up attracting $100 million (*November 22*). Agrees to protect Canadian Northern Railway by providing more money

(*November 26*). Appoints Sir Joseph Flavelle chairman of the Imperial Munitions Board (*November 29*). Ill health forces Speaker Thomas Sproule to retire and accept a Senate seat (*December* 2). Takes a Christmas holiday in the U.S. (*December 12-27*). Bedridden with lumbago (*December 28*).

1916: Announces intention to increase the military force to 500,000 (*January 1*); more than 13,500 Canadians have been killed or are missing in action since the war began. At the opening of the 12th Parliament's Sixth Session, nominates Albert Sévigny to be the 14th Speaker of the House (*January 12*). Manitoba gives women the right to vote, ostensibly meaning they could also vote federally (*January 26*). Crawls out of his office to avoid smoke inhalation in a Parliament Buildings fire that destroys the Centre Block, killing seven (*February 3*). Holds an emergency cabinet meeting in the middle of the night at the Chateau Laurier to decide where Parliament will meet next (*February 4*). House of Commons meets in the Victoria Memorial Museum 15 hours after the fire (*February 4*). Asks the House for an extension of the 12th Parliament to October 17, 1917 (*February 8*). White (Finance) presents his sixth budget that includes a Business War Profits Tax, the government's first foray into direct taxation (*February 15*). Nearly 5,000 protesters in Ottawa ask him to repeal Ontario's legislation against education in French (*February 24*). Charles Doherty (Justice) introduces a bill to prevent transport of alcohol into prohibitionist provinces, indicating federal support on the issue (*March 20*). A Royal Commission is established to examine charges of corruption in the Militia & Defence department (*March 30*). Assumes control of Militia & Defence while Sir Sam Hughes is involved with the inquiry (*April 19*). Three Quebec cabinet members threaten to resign because of cabinet's refusal to intervene against legislation in Ontario and Manitoba restricting French instruction in schools (*April 25*. Vacations at Echo Beach Fishing Club in Quebec (*May 20-29*). 12th Parliament is extended for one year (*May 25*). Lt.-Gen. Julian Byng replaces Alderson as commander of the Canadian Expeditionary Force (*May 28*). Canadian troops play a major role in the Battle at Mount Sorrel that results in 8,000 casualties (*June 2-14*). Receives an honorary Doctor of Laws degree from McMaster University. One soldier dies, 35 suffer heat exhaustion and many boo Hughes (Militia & Defence) during his visit to the hastily created Camp Borden near Barrie, Ont. (*July 11*). Announces the appointment of the Duke of Devonshire as Canada's 11th Governor General (*August 19*). Cornerstone of the new Centre Block is laid by Governor General Duke of Connaught (*September 1*). Hughes (Militia & Defence) forms the Canadian Military Council in London, England, without consulting the government (*September 6*); he is recalled. National Service Board established (*October 5*). Appoints R.B. Bennett director general of National Service Board (*October 16*). Sir George Perley (Without Portfolio) becomes the first Overseas Military Forces minister (*October 31*); to be based in London, England. Hughes (Militia & Defence) objects to Perley's appointment (*November 1*). Demands Hughes's resignation (*November 9*); gets it two days later. Appoints Albert Edward Kemp (Without Portfolio) as Militia & Defence minister (*November 23*). National Research Council is established (*November 29*). Tours the country with Bennett to stimulate military recruitment (*December 6-21*). Thomas Casgrain (Postmaster General) dies of pneumonia in Ottawa (*December 29*).

1917: His cousin Sir Frederick Borden dies in Canning, N.S. (*January 6*). Seventh Session, 12th Parliament opens; nominates Edgar Rhodes to be the 15th Speaker of the House (*January 18*). Temporary tax legislation is introduced as a war measure (*January 18*). At cabinet, discusses the possibility of a wartime coalition government with the Liberals; no decision is reached (*February 2*). Leaves for England with the Premier of Newfoundland, Sir Edward Morris (*February 14*). Discusses the war with George V (*February 24*). Visits military hospitals in England and on the Western front (*March 7-11*). Attends Imperial war cabinet meetings in London (*March 20-May 2*). Attends Imperial war conference (*March*

21-April 27); in Resolution 9, calls for a postwar imperial conference to reexamine the relationship between Britain and its Empire, moving more towards a commonwealth of nations. Presented with a new mace for the House of Commons to replace the one lost in the fire (*March 28*). Vimy Ridge, France, is captured by four Canadian divisions and one British brigade (*April 9-12*); Canadians sustain nearly 10,000 casualties during the fighting. Suggests Canada annex the Caribbean's Turks & Caicos Islands; rejected by Britain (*April*). Recommends that any thought of an Imperial government be postponed until after the war (*April 16*). Receives an honorary Doctor of Laws degree from the University of Edinburgh. Returns to Canada (*May 15*). Informs cabinet of his intention to implement conscription (*May 17*). Announces conscription in the House, saying as many as 100,000 more men will be needed for the war effort (*May 18*). Riot in Quebec City against conscription (*May 24*). Asks Laurier to join a coalition government (*May 25*); 12 days later, Laurier refuses since he wasn't consulted about implementing conscription (*May 25*). Borden's proposal for a wartime coalition government is endorsed by caucus (*June 7*). Esioff Patenaude (Secretary of State and Mines) resigns in protest over conscription (*June 9*). Military Service Bill is tabled, introducing conscription (*June 11*). All cabinet ministers submit their resignations to prepare for the formation of a coalition government (*June 12*). Informs Sir William Mackenzie that the government plans to take over the Canadian Northern Railway (*June 14*); Mackenzie breaks down. Maj.-Gen. Sir Arthur Currie succeeds Byng as commander of the Canadian troops (*June 19*). Military Service Bill is passed following a lengthy, heated debate (*July 24*). White (Finance) introduces the income tax bill (*July 25*) and announces plans to nationalize Canadian Northern Railway, with the government buying the remaining 60% it doesn't already own (*August 1*). Attempts to sell the idea of a coalition government at a secret meeting hosted by Governor General Lord Devonshire (*August 9*). His suggestion that Justice Lyman Duff be the leader of a coalition government is rejected by his caucus (*August 10*). Robert Rogers (Public Works) resigns in protest over efforts to form a coalition government (*August 17*). Asks Liberal Frank Carvell to join a coalition government (*August 22*). Military Voters Act is passed, allowing British subjects in the Canadian armed forces to vote during the war (*August 29*). Montreal protest against conscription attracts 5,000 demonstrators (*August 29*). Collapses from overwork and nervous prostration (*September 4*). Asks Liberal Hugh Guthrie to join a coalition government (*September 7*). Notes that women aren't considered 'persons' in the 1898 legislation that gives provinces control of federal voters' lists, even though many provinces now permit women to vote (*September*). Wartime Elections Act is passed, giving the vote to women with relatives in the armed forces and taking it away from conscientious objectors and enemy aliens naturalized after 1902 (*September 14*); the legislation also returns control of federal voters' lists to Ottawa. Liberals Arthur Sifton, James Calder and Thomas Crerar agree to join a coalition government after initially refusing unless there was a new leader (*September 22*). Conscription is upheld by the Supreme Court (*September 26*). Liberal Charles Ballantyne enters cabinet as Public Works minister (*October 3*). Liberal Hugh Guthrie enters cabinet as Solicitor General (*October 4*). 12th Parliament is dissolved (*October 6*). Announces the formation of a Unionist government (*October 12*); remains as Prime Minister and Secretary of State for External Affairs, while the new cabinet is made up of 13 Conservatives and nine Liberals. First conscripts called into service (*October 13*). Becomes chairman of the War Committee and the Reconstruction and Development Committee (*October 23*). Appoints Labour politician Gideon Robertson to the Unionist cabinet as Minister Without Portfolio (*October 23*). Second Battle of Passchendaele begins in France, killing or wounding over 15,000 Canadian soldiers (*October 26*). Refused a chance to speak by an election audience in Kitchener (*November 24*); mayor later apologizes. Collision of two ships in Halifax harbour kills 1,530, leaves 25,000 homeless and causes $20 million damage (*December 6*). Visits the site of the Halifax explosion and calls for $500,000 in immediate aid (*December 7*). Bowell, fifth Prime Minister, dies in Belleville, Ont. (*December 10*). Canada's 13th federal election: elected in Kings defeating James Sealy (Laurier Liberal); his Unionist government wins a majority (*December 17*). Vacations in Hot Springs, Virginia (*December 22*).

Shuffling the military vote

Borden's Unionist party had overwhelming support from the armed forces during the war. That's why the Military Voters Act included a wrinkle that allowed the military to vote for a party instead of a candidate. Those votes could then be moved by the party to whichever riding might most benefit. For the Unionists, it meant shifting soldiers' votes to Liberal strongholds in Quebec. The practice helped them win an additional 14 ridings in 1917.

1918: Conscription law takes effect (*January 1*). Visits Washington (*January 7*). Returns from vacation in Hot Springs, Virginia (*January 10*). Soldier Settlement Board is appointed (*February 1*). Order-in-Council establishes the Canadian War Mission in Washington to handle trade (*February 2*). War Purchasing Board is empowered to make all purchases for the government (*February 7*). War Trade Board is established with Foster (Trade & Commerce) as chairman (*February 8*). Food Board is absorbed by the Agriculture department (*February 11*). Asked by western premiers to shift natural resources to provincial jurisdiction (*February 18*). Appoints Senator Sir James Lougheed (Without Portfolio) to be the first Soldiers' Civil Re-establishment minister (*February 21*). Albert Sévigny (Inland Revenue) resigns in protest over conscription (*March 26*); Inland Revenue is combined with Customs. Conscription riots in Quebec (*March 28-April 1*); four civilians killed in the gunfire. Order-in-Council requires all males, ages 16 to 60, to be regularly engaged in some useful occupation (*April 4*). Another Order-in-Council gives the government the power to declare martial law and send in troops to curb rioting (*April 4*). Overseas Military Council is formed, with Albert Kemp (Overseas Military Forces) as chairman (*April 11*). Bill to give women the vote is passed (*April 12*). His initiative to standardize Daylight Savings Time nationally occurs for the first time as clocks across Canada move ahead one hour (*April 14*). Order-in-Council removes exemptions from conscription (*April 19*); men, ages 20 to 22, to be called for military service. Farmers demonstrate against the removal of exemptions to conscript their sons (*May 14*). Order-in-Council abolishes use of titles unless approved by the Prime Minister (*May 21*). Attends a Royal Society of Canada meeting to hear the country's first radio program, broadcast by XWA Montreal (later CFCF-AM) (*May 20*). Statistics Act calls for the creation of the Dominion Bureau of Statistics (*May 24*). Sails for England with Meighen (Interior & Indian Affairs) (*May 24*). Speaks out in Imperial cabinet against disorganization at the front (*June 13*). Receives a new Black Rod for the Senate from the Empire Parliamentary Association to replace the one destroyed in the 1916 fire (*June 21*). Receives an honorary Doctor of Laws degree from Cambridge University. Visits military bases and hospitals in France (*June-July*). Watches the Canadian Corps championship baseball game in Tincques, France (*July 1*). Proclaims an amnesty to deserters and defaulters who report for military service by August 24 (*August 2*). Canadian troops attack German positions near Amiens, beginning its Hundred Days offensive that lasts until the war's end (*August 8*). Borden returns to Canada (*August 21*). Public Instruction department is formed to promote the war effort (*September 12*). Receives an honorary degree from Dalhousie University. Authorizes sending troops to Murmansk, Russia, to fight the Bolsheviks (*September*); 4,000 are deployed, but none see action. Vacations in Hot Springs, Virginia (*September 21-October 15*). Another Order-in-Council bans strikes and lockouts during the war (*October 11*). First cases of Spanish influenza reported in Edmonton (*October 19*); the six-month worldwide epidemic is the worst since the Black Death during the Middle Ages, eventually killing 65,000 Canadians. Urged by British Prime Minister Lloyd George to sail to England for probable peace talks (*October 27*). Austria signs the armistice (*November 4*). Canadian Trade Mission established in London (*November 7*). Sails for England with Foster (Trade & Commerce), Sifton (Customs & Inland Revenue) and Robertson (Labour) (*November 8*). Still aboard the *Mauritania* on Armistice Day when Germany's surrender takes place at 11 a.m. (*November 11*); of Canada's 619,636 enlisted soldiers, approximately 424,000 served overseas, nearly 61,000 were killed and about 172,000 were wounded. Meets with Lloyd George about the peace conference (*November 17*). All of Canada's government railways are combined (*November 19*). White (Finance) hosts the second Dominion-Provincial conference in Ottawa to discuss soldier resettlement issues (*November 19-22*). Borden indicates intention that Canada be represented at the peace conference (*December 4*). Britain agrees to promote the idea that the dominions have separate representation (*December 31*). Wartime boosted the public debt from $350 million to $1.5 billion. Becomes Chancellor of McGill University, Montreal, until 1920.

The vote for women

He was the man who noted in September 1917 that Canada's laws didn't recognize women as persons, even if some provinces were letting them vote. In spite of that, Borden extended the franchise that same month to women serving in the war or having close relatives involved in the fight. With the war winding down the following year, his government opened the vote to all women with the Women's Franchise Act.

1919: Opens an exhibit of war memorial paintings in London (*January 4*). Arrives in Paris (*January 11*). U.S. agrees to accept representatives from the dominions in the peace talks (*January 13*). First meeting of the British Empire delegation at the Paris Peace Conference includes Britain, Canada, Newfoundland, Australia, India and South Africa (*January 13*). Begins to take French lessons in Paris and arranges to have his portrait painted. Laurier, seventh Prime Minister, dies in Ottawa (*February 17*); Liberal MP D.D. McKenzie becomes interim Leader of the Opposition. Grand Trunk Pacific Railway unable to meet payments and is placed in receivership by the government with John Reid (Railways & Canals) as receiver (*March 7*). Riot of Canadian troops awaiting repatriation at Kimmel Park base in England; 12 killed, 21 wounded (*March 8*). Visits French battle sites (*March 23*). Turns down offer by Lloyd George to be Britain's ambassador to the U.S. (*March 26*). Succeeds in having British dominions officially represented at the Paris Peace Conference (*May 6*). Is present when the Treaty of Versailles is given to Germany; considers it too severe (*May 7*). Leaves the peace talks after Thomas Crerar (Agriculture) and White (Finance) threaten to resign from cabinet over budget proposals that would alienate western farmers (*May 14*); makes plans to return home. Winnipeg general strike begins (*May 15*). Visits George V and the Prince of Wales (*May 16*). Resolution is passed to cease the awarding of British knighthoods in Canada (*May 22*). Federal legislation forces Winnipeg strikers back to work (*May 26*). Calder (Immigration & Colonization) introduces legislation permitting the deportation of British subjects not born in Canada (*June 6*); used to charge leaders in the Winnipeg strike. Two demonstrators killed during rioting in the Winnipeg general strike (*June 21*). Convinces Conservative caucus to continue its support of the Unionist government (*June 26*). Doherty (Justice) and Sifton (Secretary of State, Public Works) sign the Treaty of Versailles for Canada (*June 28*). War Purchasing Commission bill is blocked by opposition on both sides of the House (*July 3*). Canadian Nation Railway, the new government amalgamated rail company, receives its charter (*July 7*). His wife Laura insists he resign from politics (*July 13*). Visits Quebec to find support for the Unionist government (*July 17-26*). Appoints Sir Henry Drayton as Finance minister to replace White who resigns for health reasons (*August 1*). Carvell (Public Works) resigns to become chairman of the Board of Railway Commissioners and is replaced by Sifton (Customs; Inland Revenue). William Lyon Mackenzie King is elected Liberal leader, becoming Leader of the Opposition (*August 7*). Accompanies Edward, Prince of Wales, on his Royal visit through the Maritimes and Quebec to Ottawa (*August 15-September 1*). Receives an honorary Doctor of Laws degree from Dalhousie University. Prince of Wales lays the cornerstone of the new Centre Block and opens the Third Session, 13th Parliament (*September 1*). Suffers a flu attack (*September 6*). Canada ratifies the Treaty of Versailles (*September 12*). Recuperates in White Sulphur Springs, West Virginia (*October 3-31*). Meighen (Interior & Indian Affairs) introduces a bill to nationalize the Grand Trunk Railway and merge it with the Canadian National Railway (*October 10*). Pierre Trudeau, Canada's 15th Prime Minister, is born in Montreal (*October 18*). Grand Trunk Bill passes (*November 5*). Meets with Meighen (Interior & Indian Affairs), Newton Rowell (Privy Council) and James Calder (Immigration & Colonization) in New York (*November 12*). Accompanies the Prince of Wales by boat from New York to Halifax, then returns to Ottawa (*November 26*); involved in a train collision en route. Urged to retire from politics by doctors in Montreal (*December 9*). Informs Governor General Lord Devonshire of his decision to retire (*December 16*). Cabinet convinces him to stay for another year and take an extended vacation (*December 18*).

1920: The Districts of Mackenzie, Keewatin and Franklin form the Northwest Territories (*January 1*). Leaves for Florida with Viscount Jellicoe, Britain's Admiral of the Fleet (*January 2*). Canada becomes a founding member of the League of Nations (*January 10*). Tours Cuba and the West Indies (*January*). Visits England (*January-February*). Royal Northwest Mounted Police merges with the Dominion Police to become the Royal Canadian Mounted Police (*February 1*). Eleven MPs formally declare themselves as members of the new National Progressive Party, with former Agriculture minister Thomas Crerar as leader (*February*). Grand Trunk Railway sale to the government is ratified by shareholders (*February 19*). Fourth Session, 13th Parliament opens in the rebuilt Centre Block (*February 26*), with Foster (Trade & Commerce) serving as acting leader. Spends time in South and North Carolina (*March-May*). Unionist caucus approves a new party policy developed by Reid and Calder (*March 11*); postpone announcing it until Borden returns. Canada empowered to appoint a minister plenipotentiary to serve in Washington under the British ambassador (*May 10*). Returns to Ottawa (*May 12*). Again informs Governor General Lord Devonshire of his decision to retire (*June 21*). Hands his resignation to Conservative caucus (*June 30*). Dominion Elections Act creates a universal franchise for voting and makes it possible for women to become MPs (*July 1*). Resignation is accepted and party is renamed National Liberal and Conservative party (*July 1*). Oversees the task of choosing his successor by a ballot vote in caucus; Meighen receives 68 votes, White 42 (*July 1*). Asks Meighen to form a government, but he declines, still preferring White (*July 3*). Asks White to form a new government, but he declines for health and business reasons (*July 7*). Meighen (Interior & Indian Affairs, Mines) agrees to a form a government (*July 7*). Refuses to accept a portfolio in Meighen's government (*July 9*). Resigns as Conservative leader and steps down as Prime Minister (*July 10*). **Borden government ends.**

1921: Emphasizes the importance of Dominion autonomy in a speech in the House prior to the approaching Imperial Conference (*April 27*). Represents Canada at the Washington Conference on Limitations of Armaments (*November 12-February 6*). Steps down as MP for Kings (*December 5*). Signs the Four-Power Treaty at the Washington Conference as Canada's representative (*December 13*).

1922: Signs the Five-Power and Nine-Power treaties at the Washington Conference as Canada's representative (*February 6*).

1924: Becomes Chancellor of Queen's University, Kingston, until 1930.

1925: Addresses the Institute of Politics in Williamstown, Virginia, about the status of dominions (*August 17*).

1926: Encourages Conservative leader Meighen to form a government following King's resignation during the King-Byng Affair (*June 28*). Turns down Meighen's offer of a Senate seat (*June*).

Three pitches, three strikes

The three Prime Ministers who succeeded Borden all attempted to appoint him to the Senate. The first offer came from his protégé Meighen during his second, very brief term as Prime Minister in 1926. The second was from political opponent King in 1929. A third came the next year from Bennett. He said no to each.

1927: Speaks at the Conservative convention in Winnipeg where R.B. Bennett is elected leader to succeed Meighen (*November 10-12*). Becomes chairman of the Canadian Institute of International Affairs.

1928: Elected a Fellow of the Royal Society of Canada. Begins dictating his memoirs to his secretary (*October 15*). Becomes president of Crown Life Insurance (*November*).

1929: Turns down the offer of a Senate seat by King (*January 11*). Becomes president of Barclay's Bank. His 1928 Oxford lectures are published as *Canadian Constitutional Studies* and *Canada in the Commonwealth: From Conflict to Co-operation.*

1930: Serves as Canada's representative at the League of Nations, replacing Senator Raoul Dandurand. Becomes president of the Canadian League of Nations Society. Becomes president of the Canadian Historical Association. Turns down Bennett's offer of a Senate seat (*August*). Attends the Imperial Conference in London as part of Bennett's delegation (*October 1-November 14*).

1932: Becomes chairman of the Canadian Investment Fund, Canada's first mutual fund (*October*).

1933: Begins writing *Letters To Limbo* as a memorial to Canadian lawyer John S. Ewart and to refute his anti-Commonwealth beliefs; not published until 1971. Attends British Commonwealth Relations Conference in Toronto (*September 11-14*).

1934: Works on his *Memoirs.*

1936: Attends the unveiling of the Vimy Memorial in France (*July 26*).

1937: Vacations in Georgia and suffers a heart attack (*February-March*). Returns to Ottawa (*April*). Suffers a severe angina attack after climbing up the embankment from the Ottawa River to his Glensmere home (*May 13*). Dies in Ottawa (*June 10*). Funeral at All Saints Church; buried at Beechwood Cemetery (*June 12*).

BOOKS ABOUT BORDEN

- **1938**: Henry Borden (ed.); *Robert Laird Borden, His Memoirs*, 2 Vols. (Macmillan)
- **1971**: Henry Borden (ed.); *Letters to Limbo* (University of Toronto)
- **1975**: Robert Craig Brown; *Robert Laird Borden, A Biography*, 2 Vols. (Macmillan, Vol. 2, 1980)
- **1977**: John English; *Borden: His Life and World* (McGraw-Hill Ryerson)
- **1978**: Kathleen Saunders; *Robert Borden* (The Canadians, Fitzhenry & Whiteside)
- **2010**: Martin Thornton; *Sir Robert Borden: Canada* (Makers of the Modern World series, Haus)

9

Arthur Meighen

The Unemotional Prime Minister

He may have been a passionate orator, but Arthur Meighen's business-like approach to policy often left colleagues, opponents and Canadians in general feeling cold. It was a trait that often hampered the political ambitions of the brilliant, uncompromising idealist. As Borden's adroit fixer in cabinet, he was the logical person to replace his leader. Defeated soon after by King's Liberals, he returned to power in 1926 when Governor General Lord Byng offered him a chance to form a government. But King orchestrated a non-confidence vote that ended Meighen's second term of office after less than three months.

Meighen the Politician

Prime Minister of Canada: (1) July 10, 1920 – December 29, 1921; (2) June 29, 1926 – September 25, 1926
Length of terms: (1) 1 year, 2 months, 15 days; (2) 2 months, 26 days; (Total) 1 year, 5 months, 5 days
Parliaments as Prime Minister: 13th; 15th
Age on entering office: 46
Political party: Conservative
Leader of party: July 10, 1920 – September 25, 1926; November 18, 1941 – December 11, 1942
Member of Parliament: October 26, 1908 – September 25, 1926
Ridings represented: Portage La Prairie [Man.] (1908-1921, 1925-1926); Grenville [Ont.] (1922-1925)
Cabinet portfolios: Solicitor General (1915-1917); Secretary of State (1917); Mines (1917), Interior & Indian Affairs (1917-1920); Mines (1919-1920); External Affairs (1920-1921); Privy Council President (1926); Minister Without Portfolio (1932-1935)
Other political posts: Leader of the Opposition (1921-1926); Senator (1932-1942)
Titles: King's Counsel (1915); Canadian Privy Councillor (1915); Imperial

Privy Councillor (1920)
Quotes: "Let there be no dispute as to where I stand. When Britain's message came then Canada should have said: "Ready, aye ready; we stand by you." (criticizing King's stand during the Chanak crisis, 1922); "One great secret of successful debate: when you have a man under your hammer, never be tempted into doubtful ground and give him a chance to digress." (1943)
Lived after term: 33 years

Meighen the Man

Name: Arthur Meighen
Born: June 16, 1874, near Anderson, Ontario
Ancestry: Irish
Religion: Presbyterian (later United)
Education: B.Sc. [Bachelor of Science] (University of Toronto, 1896); Teaching Certificate (Ontario School of Pedagogy, 1897)
Nicknames: The gramophone of Mackenzie and Mann (refers to railway promoters; coined by R.B. Bennett), The father of railway nationalism in Canada (used by some MPs during the GTR nationalization debates)
Military service: none
Occupation: teacher; lawyer; businessman
Publications: *The Greatest Englishman in History* (1936); *Unrevised and Unrepented* (1949)
Appearance: "…the massive bald dome of his head, the lean, wedge-shaped face and hard, piercing eyes, the upright skeletal body with arms akimbo or hands tightly clasped" (Bruce Hutchison in *Mr. Prime Minister*); "a very thin, fragile-looking figure…but it was the face, with its rather pronounced cheek bones, its long straight nose and, rising over deep-set blue eyes with sharply creased crow's-feet at the corners, its high dome of thought from which the graying hair had begun to recede." (Roger Graham in *Arthur Meighen, Vol. 2: And Fortune Fled*)
Personality: "intelligent but blinkered … a master of everything but politics" (J.L. Granatstein & Norman Hillmer in *Prime Ministers: Ranking Canada's Leaders*); "…despite his reserve and aloofness, despite his deficiencies in the small, personal arts of politics, and despite the essentially intellectual nature of his public personality, he could arouse feelings of passionate enthusiasm by the very power of his mind, the perfection of his speech, the manifest sincerity of his beliefs." (Roger Graham in *Arthur Meighen, Vol. 1: The Door of Opportunity*)
Occupation after term: businessman
Married: Jessie Isabel Cox, June 1, 1904, St. George's Anglican Church, Birtle, Manitoba
Age at marriage: 29
Years married: 56
Died: August 5, 1960, Toronto, Ontario
Age at death: 86
Cause of death: heart failure
Buried: St. Mary's Cemetery, St. Mary's, Ontario

Meighen was the:

- Only Prime Minister to represent Manitoba (Macdonald was elected in Manitoba in 1878 but declined the seat)
- First Prime Minister born in the Dominion of Canada
- First Prime Minister born in Ontario
- First Prime Minister under 50
- First Prime Minister who was a member of the United Church (formerly Presbyterian)
- First Prime Minister defeated by a non-confidence vote
- Second Prime Minister to lead a minority government
- Second longest living Prime Minister after his term (33 years)
- Seventh Conservative Prime Minister
- Prime Minister to hold the second highest number of cabinet positions (8, tied with Tupper)

Meighen's legacy

- A Parliamentary debater without rival
- Convinced Britain to broaden its ties with Japan to create a multilateral alliance with Pacific countries
- Created the Canadian National Railway (Interior Minister)
- Implemented conscription in the First World War that alienated Quebec (Solicitor General)

MEIGHEN'S FAMILY

Meighen's Parents

Father: Joseph Meighen
Born: July 20, 1846, St. Mary's, Canada West (Ontario)
Occupation: farmer
Died: April 26, 1924, Ottawa, Ontario
Age at death: 77

Mother: Mary Jane Bell
Born: November 30, 1848, Blanchard Township, Perth County, Canada West (Ontario)
Married: January 23, 1871
Died: April 10, 1931, Toronto, Ontario
Age at death: 82

Meighen's Brothers & Sisters (5 siblings; Arthur the second)

Sister: Annie Meighen (1872-1940)
  Married: Samuel Wesley White (1894)
Sister: Sara Meighen (b.1877)
Brother: William Meighen (b.1878)
Brother: Edward Meighen (1881-1951)
  Married: Myra Rose

Note: Managed several farms around Portage La Prairie owned by Arthur.
Sister: Jennie Meighen (b.1883)
Married: John A. Anderson

Meighen's Wife

Name: Jessie Isabel Cox
Born: April 18, 1883, Granby, Quebec
Father: Charles Cox
Mother: Lillian Mary Booth
Age at marriage: 21
Died: September 6, 1985, Toronto, Ontario
Age at death: 102
Burial place: St. Mary's Cemetery, St. Mary's, Ontario
Younger than Meighen: 9 years
Died after Meighen: 25 years
Note: Her Uncle Palmer Cox wrote the *Brownie* books and built Brownie Castle in Granby, Quebec.

Meighen's Children (3)

Name: Theodore 'Ted' Roosevelt O'Neil Meighen
Born: October 1905, Portage La Prairie, Manitoba
Occupation: lawyer; philanthropist
Married: Margaret 'Peggy' deLancey Robinson (1937); she remarried in 1990 to Senator Hartland Molson, becoming the only Canadian to have both a son and a husband in the Senate
Children: 2 – Michael Arthur; Edward Arthur
Died: 1979, St. Andrews, New Brunswick
Note: First English Canadian to study law at Laval University.
Note: Son Michael was a Senator and Chancellor of McGill.

Name: Maxwell Charles Gordon Meighen
Born: June 5, 1908, Portage La Prairie, Manitoba
Married: Jane McWhinnie
Occupation: corporate executive
Died: February 5, 1992, Toronto, Ontario

Name: Lillian Mary Laura Meighen
Born: June 21, 1910, Portage La Prairie, Manitoba
Married: Donald Wright (June 29, 1935)
Children: 3 – Timothy A.J.; Priscilla J.M.; Patrick O.G.
Occupation: philanthropist
Died: January 12, 1993, Toronto, Ontario
Note: Husband Donald was a musician; music buildings are named after him at Western and Victoria universities.
Note: Daughter Priscilla was a singer who had a hit *Man in a Raincoat* in 1955.

POLITICAL STORIES

Conservative workhorse

Meighen was addicted to work. He fixated on efficiency and doggedness and his leader, Borden, was delighted to use it to advantage. The first major challenge he faced was during the debate over the Naval Aid Bill of 1913. Meighen drafted the rules to impose closure, a first in the Canadian House of Commons, and then lead the debate for the Conservatives.

His next major challenge was developing legislation and the terms of sale for the Canadian Northern Railway. Then, when war broke out, he was kept busy drafting bills to put the country on a military footing, starting with the War Measures Act. He also helped establish the War Purchasing Commission.

With all this activity, he still wasn't sitting at the management table. That changed in 1915 when Borden appointed him to cabinet and cycled him through five portfolios in five years. He was the mastermind behind the legislation for conscription and for the nationalization and merging of two railways to create the Canadian National Railway. He also stepped in to deal with the Winnipeg General Strike.

Unfortunately, his workaholic ways meant he didn't get to know his three children very well until he resigned as leader in 1926.

The great debater

Best remembered for his oratorical skills, Meighen was revered by colleagues and, later, by biographers for his turn of the tongue. Civil servant (and future Prime Minister) Lester Pearson felt that, "Few Canadians in all history have surpassed him in intellectual brilliance and … above all, in parliamentary debate." Biographer Roderick Benns agreed. "He was unbeatable in debate. Yet for all his skills in winning arguments, he didn't win the hearts of Canadians."

That knack for successful argument was honed in debates across the kitchen table with his father and expanded with the high school Literary Society. Debating also figured heavily in his university years, capped by a losing argument "that the government should have full control of the railways" – an ironic topic considering the key role he played 24 years later in nationalizing two Canadian railways.

His collection of speeches published in 1949, *Unrevised and Unrepented*, was one of the few times he garnered consistently positive press. He was surprised and genuinely grateful for the response.

A two-month term

There was every reason for Meighen and the Conservatives to celebrate on election night in 1925. They'd won 15 seats more than the Liberals and boosted their popular vote by more than 16% since the last election. But King clung to power – "like a lobster with lockjaw," noted Meighen – with the help of the Progressives.

Seven months passed before a Customs scandal in the King government forced his resignation. Governor General Byng turned to Meighen to form a government and he readily agreed. But King was incensed and determined to topple the Conservatives' minority government.

Protocol required Meighen to step down and seek re-election to his cabinet position. He tried to dodge the same fate for his cabinet colleagues by appointing them to acting positions. King pounced, denouncing them as not truly being a cabinet. Without Meighen in the House to counteract King's claims, the power-broker Progressives began swinging back to the Liberals.

On July 2, King's non-confidence vote about the "unconstitutional" cabinet passed by one vote. It shouldn't have happened. Progressive MP Thomas Bird supported the motion even though he was paired with an absent MP and not eligible to vote. It would have resulted in a tie to be broken by the Speaker.

But the vote was upheld and Meighen resigned the same day. Byng agreed to an election and the Conservatives lost.

Meighen and King

Few party leaders detested each other as much as Meighen and his Liberal nemesis William Lyon Mackenzie King. Only Diefenbaker and Pearson came close to sharing the same kind of animosity.

Besides stark differences in appearance (long, lanky Meighen vs. pudgy King) and personality (severe Meighen vs. convivial King), the two politicians were extraordinarily wary of each other. King felt Meighen was somehow behind Governor General Byng's refusal to grant him a dissolution of Parliament. Meighen was subsequently manoeuvered out of power by King.

He considered King "the most contemptible charlatan ever to darken the annals of Canadian politics," according to biographer Roger Graham. Proud of his values, he recoiled at the repulsive tactics used by King. Precision of language and candor were his hallmarks; King specialized in ambiguity.

King feared Meighen's intellect and brilliant, acid tongue. But, while Meighen would become easily mired in his morals and rectitude, King was the better strategist. It typically left King on the winning end of most issues, to Meighen's lasting resentment.

Party leader again

Meighen had been through with politics for 15 years. But the Conservatives were leaderless in 1941 and there was growing pressure on him to return and help bring the party back to power. Comfortable with his Toronto investment career, he had no desire to return.

As the entreaties grew, he visited Manitoba Premier John Bracken in an effort to recruit him as leader. It didn't work. At the party's Ottawa convention in November, he firmly refused to consider the offer and left to catch a train back to Toronto. A delegation of politicians caught up with him at the station, but he again refused.

Over the next few days, the media, friends in the party and even Isabel urged him to reconsider. He finally capitulated and became leader for a second time. Early in 1942, he lost the by-election that would have returned him to the House. Embarrassed by the result, he resigned as leader and never again sought political office.

PERSONAL STORIES

Bay Street businessman

Having tackled careers as a teacher, lawyer and politician, Meighen embarked on a corporate job after his unceremonious exit from government in 1926. He was actively courted by a large respected law firm, but opted instead to join Canadian General Securities in Winnipeg as general counsel.

The following year, he helped launch CGS's Toronto operation. Each day, he'd walk from his posh Rosedale home to his Bay Street headquarters. He took a financial hit in the 1929 stock market crash, but by the early 1930s was president of the company.

His lifestyle was more relaxed and he found he was more appreciated. Meighen also had time to indulge in his passions of politics (as Conservative Leader in the Senate) and community service (on the advisory board of the Salvation Army). By the time he retired, he had built an impressive, wealthy estate.

Isabel Meighen

Meighen was a law student articling in Portage La Prairie and earning extra cash as an occasional real estate agent. A possible sale took him to Winnipeg, but the client failed to show. As he waited in the hotel lobby, he met a friend who urged him to come upstairs to meet some people he knew. That was too frivolous for Meighen, so the friend brought the group down to the lobby, which was when he met Isabel Cox for the first time.

That same evening, he invited her to see the play *Still Waters Run Deep*, launching a long-distance relationship that lasted for several years (he was studying law in Portage La Prairie, she was teaching in Birtle). After their marriage in 1904, the upbeat, sociable Isabel continued to be the antithesis of the reserved Meighen.

When politics took the Meighen family to Ottawa, Isabel's poise effectively masked an intimidating feeling she had that she was just a 'small town girl'. It was a gracefulness that served her well as a Prime Minister's wife, meeting heads of state like George V and Belgium's Albert I.

She was more comfortable during Meighen's later career in the corporate world of Toronto. Isabel died at 102.

MEIGHEN'S TIMELINE

1874: Born near Anderson, Ont. (*June 16*).

1879: Attends Blanchard School #1 in Anderson (*September*).

1885: Sells subscriptions to *The Farmer's Advocate*, winning a gold watch that didn't actually work.

1886: Family moves to a farm near St. Mary's, Ont. (*Spring*). Attends St. Mary's Collegiate (*September*).

1890: Elected councillor of the school's Literary Society debating club (*September*); again in 1891.

1892: Elected secretary of the Literary Society (*January*). Enrols in Mathematics at the University of Toronto (*September*).

1893: His debates at university likely included several with student William Lyon Mackenzie King, his future political adversary.

1895: Joins a boycott of classes to protest the dismissal of Professor William Dale (*February 15*); one of the boycott leaders was King. Wins a university debate arguing in favour of the government owning all railways (*November*).

1896: Receives a Bachelor of Science degree in Mathematics (*May*). Hired by a general store in Woodham, Ont. (*June*); soon loses interest in merchandising. Attends the Ontario School of Pedagogy (teachers college) in Toronto (*September*),

1897: Becomes a high school teacher in Caledonia, Ont. (*September*).

1898: Resigns following a vote of non-confidence from the school board after disciplining the board chairman's daughter (*March*). Moves to Winnipeg, Man., to launch a dried fruit cleaning venture that fails to find customers (*August*). Becomes a teacher at the Winnipeg Business College to pay off the dried fruit debts (*September*).

1900: Articles as a law student with Edmund Taylor in Winnipeg (*January 2*). Moves to the Munsen & Allan law firm (*June*).

1901: Moves to the Howard, Johnston & Loftus law firm (*Winter*).

1902: Takes charge of S.R. Wright's law office in Portage La Prairie, Man.; articles with W.J. James. Meets Isabel Cox, a Birtle schoolteacher, in Winnipeg (*August*).

1903: Passes law exams and is admitted to the Manitoba bar (*Spring*). Opens his own practice in Portage La Prairie.

School principles

As a novice teacher, Meighen disciplined a student in his Caledonia high school class by sending her home. The student's parent, who was chair of the school board, visited him in class to berate him publicly. Meighen requested a chance to make his case to the board members, giving them an ultimatum that either the chair or the teacher must go. The board surprisingly backed Meighen five votes to three, but two members were absent. The crafty chair brought the two absent trustees around to his way of thinking, then called a second meeting without Meighen's knowledge. The chair ended up voting twice – once for the motion and then a second time to break the resulting tie. Meighen immediately resigned, although he continued to tutor many of the class in a rented room at his own expense.

1904: Buys his first home, on Campbell Street (*Spring*). Marries Isabel Cox in Birtle, Man. (*June 1*). Honeymoons in New England and eastern Canada, including St. Mary's and

Granby, their hometowns (*Summer*). Forms a law partnership with Ewan McPherson in Portage La Prairie.

1905: His son Theodore is born in Portage La Prairie (*October*).

1907: Nominated to run as the Conservative candidate for Portage La Prairie in the next federal election (*December*).

1908: His second son Maxwell is born in Portage La Prairie (*June*). Hogg becomes a partner with the firm. Canada's 11th federal election: elected Conservative MP for Portage La Prairie, defeating incumbent Liberal John Crawford by 250 votes; Laurier's Liberals are re-elected (*October 26*).

1909: Family moves to Ottawa for the Session, residing at Russell House, then the Alexandra Hotel (*January*).

1910: First speech in the House supports an investigation into the National Transcontinental Railway Commission (*January*). His daughter Lillian is born in Portage La Prairie (*June 2*). W.J. Cooper replaces Hogg in the law firm (*Spring*).

1911: Canada's 12th federal election: re-elected MP for Portage La Prairie defeating Liberal Robert Patterson; the Conservatives win a majority (*September 21*).

1913: Chairs the Conservative committee drafting rules to close debate on Borden's Naval Aid Bill and writes the closure legislation (*February*). Leads the debate in the House (*April*). Joins R.B. Bennett in opposing his own party by objecting to Senate amendments to the Bank Act (*June 2*). Becomes Solicitor General, not an official cabinet position (*June 26*). Re-elected by acclamation in a by-election in Portage La Prairie following his quasi-cabinet appointment (*July 19*). W.R. Sexsmith becomes his final law partner, following the death of Cooper.

1914: Drafts legislation to bail out Canadian Northern Railway by giving the government a 40% interest in the business (*March*). Presented with a gold watch by caucus for his work on the railway bill; this watch works (*June*). Drafts the mortgage for the Canadian Northern Railway (*July 10*). Joins cabinet sessions at which Canada follows Britain's decision to declare war on Germany (*August 4*). Helps draft the War Measures Act (*August*). Convinces Borden to countermand an order by Sir Sam Hughes (Defence) that prohibited recruits from Portage La Prairie from joining the first contingent of soldiers to Europe (*September*). Asked by Borden to investigate possible illegal war contracts between Britain and the U.S. funnelled through Canada (*October 19*).

1915: Becomes a King's Counsel. Moves permanently to Ottawa, buying a house at 21 Cooper Street near the Rideau Canal. His investigation of war contracts results in the introduction of the War Purchasing Commission (*May 8*). Suggests Borden consider a coalition wartime government with the Liberals (*May 12*). His Solicitor General portfolio is elevated to the cabinet table (*October 2*). Offered a position as quartermaster in a new regiment of Grenadier Guards commanded by his second cousin Lieut.-Col. Frank Meighen; Borden refuses to allow him to leave cabinet to go overseas (*November*).

1917: Presents a draft of conscription legislation to cabinet (*May 24*). Approached by Liberal MPs Frank Carvell and A.K. MacLean who are considering joining a coalition government (*May 29*). Speaks out against Laurier's amendment to call a referendum on conscription (*June 21*). Sons Ted and Max begin a business raising chickens in the family backyard for the war effort (*Summer*). Plays a leading role in the government's intention to nationalize Canadian Northern Railway (*August*). Becomes Mines minister and Secretary of State, replacing Esioff Patenaude who resigned in opposition to conscription (*August 25*).

Introduces the Wartime Elections Bill (*September 6*). Reluctantly vacations with Borden at his Quebec fishing camp (*September 21-25*). Threatens to resign if Borden creates a coalition government including four powerful Liberal politicians (*October 10*); Borden promises him a senior cabinet post. Becomes Interior minister and Superintendant General of Indian Affairs in the Unionist government (*October 12*). Campaigns for the Unionists in western Canada (*October-November*). Canada's 13th federal election: re-elected in Portage La Prairie with over 80% of the vote, defeating Liberal Frederick Shirtliff; Borden's Unionist government is elected (*December 17*).

1918: Sails for England with Borden; seasick most of the way (*May 24*). Attends Imperial War Cabinet meetings (*June*). Visits Canadian troops and hospitals in southern England (*June 15-16*). Attends the Imperial War Conference (*June 17*). Meets with Alfred Smithers to discuss the terms of the acquisition of the Grand Trunk Railway (*June 17*). Visits troops and battle sites in France, including Vimy (*June 30-July 3*). Returns to Canada (*July*). Rests in Florida with cabinet colleagues John Reid (Railways & Canals) and Martin Burrell (Mines) following a bout of influenza (*December 31*).

1919: Returns to Ottawa (*January 11*). Tours the west to gain support for the Unionist government (*January*). Takes daughter Lillian to Laurier House to pay his respects on the death of Sir Wilfrid Laurier (*February 18*). As acting Justice minister, arrives in Winnipeg with cabinet colleague Senator Gideon Robertson (Labour) to deal with the General Strike (*May 22*); federal postal workers are legislated back to work (*May 26*). Introduces amendments to the Criminal Code to outlaw organizations advocating change by force (*June 27*). Accused of marshalling soldiers' votes in the west during the 1917 election, but is cleared when the incriminating telegram is attributed to a lesser figure in the party (*October*). Introduces a bill to nationalize the Grand Trunk Railway (*October 10*); the bill passes (*November 5*). Meets with Borden, who is recuperating from a heart attack, in New York City (*November 12*). Borden tells cabinet he intends to retire (*December 14*); persuaded to stay on for another year, although Meighen feels he should retire.

1920: His parents move from St. Mary's to an apartment on Cooper Street in Ottawa. Tells Borden twice he doesn't wish to be Prime Minister, preferring former Finance minister Thomas White. Rejects federal health support to deal with tuberculosis outbreaks sweeping through Indigenous reserves, indicating the move would duplicate efforts being done locally (*June 8*). Is the caucus favourite to be the next leader after Borden submits his resignation; cabinet prefers White (*June 30*). Receives 68 votes in a caucus ballot to choose a new leader; White receives 42 votes (*July 1*). Unionist party changes name to National Liberal and Conservative party (*July 1*). Asked by Borden to form a government, but declines, still preferring White (*July 3*). Accepts another request to form a government after White declines (*July 7*). **Meighen's first government (1920-1921).** Becomes the ninth Prime Minister of Canada and second Secretary of State for External Affairs (*July 10*); 11 other Borden cabinet members continue to serve. Receives Sir John A. Macdonald's office chair from Borden (*July 13*). Tours Ontario and Maritimes, including hometown of St. Mary's (*August-September*). Unveils a monument to Sir Georges-Étienne Cartier in Quebec City (*September 6*). Tours the west (*October*). Becomes a member of the Imperial Privy Council (*October 13*). Canada is represented at the first League of Nations meeting in Switzerland by Sir George Foster (Trade & Commerce), Charles Doherty (Justice), and Newton Rowell (*November 15-December 18*). New law requires immigrants to possess at least $250 (*December 15*).

1921: Arthur Sifton (Secretary of State) dies (*January 22*). Arbitration board begins to examine nationalization of Grand Trunk Railway (*February 1*). Introduces legislation to extend the Grand Trunk Railway arbitration deadline in return for government control of all company directorships (*April 11*). Government calls for a debate on agenda items for the approaching Imperial Conference, the first time this is done (*April 27*). Shareholders of Grand Trunk Railway agree to terms of the government bill (*May 13*); headquarters moves from England to Canada. Customs & Inland Revenue department becomes Customs & Excise (*June 4*). Sails for England with wife Isabel and mother Mary Jane (*June 7*). Attends Imperial Conference (*June 20*). Sworn in as a member of the Imperial Privy Council at Buckingham Palace (*June*). Receives the freedom of London from the Lord Mayor (*June*). Receives the freedom of Edinburgh (*June*). Receives an honorary Doctor of Laws degree from the University of Edinburgh (*June*). Meets Viscount Byng of Vimy, the soon-to-be-named Governor General, at Belgrave Square (*June*). Speaks at Imperial Conference against renewal of the Japanese alliance (*June 29*); succeeds in having a Pacific conference established to discuss the alliance (*July 1*). Unveils the Cross of Sacrifice at Vimy Ridge, France (*July 3*). Announces the appointment of Lord Byng of Vimy as Canada's 12th Governor General (*August 2*). Arrives back in Canada (*August 6*). Greets Lord Byng at Quebec City (*August 10*). Receives an honorary Doctor of Laws degree from the University of Toronto. Shuffles his cabinet to bring in eight new ministers including R.B. Bennett (Justice) and Henry H. Stevens (Trade & Commerce) (*September 21*). Appoints Robert Manion as Soldiers' Civil Re-establishment minister (September 22). Calls for the wheat board to become voluntary for use by farmers (*October*). Succeeds in mollifying a Quebec City crowd unhappy about the use of conscription during the war (*November 8*). Almost hit by a rock thrown through a window in Sherbrooke (*November 9*). Red and white are declared Canada's official colours by George V (*November 21*). Canada's 14th federal election: defeated in Portage La Prairie by Harry Leader of the Progressives; King's Liberals win the most seats, with Meighen's Conservatives polling third behind the Progressives who win the greatest number of seats ever won by a third party (*December 6*); six provinces elect no Conservative candidates. Progressive Agnes Macphail becomes the first woman elected to the House of Commons (*December 6*). Announces he will contest a by-election in Grenville, Ont., where the newly elected Conservative, A.C. Casselman, resigns to accept a minor post in the Soldiers' Civil Re-establishment department – a post he resigns from the following day without ever collecting a salary (*December 27*). Meighen resigns as Prime Minister (*December 29*). **Meighen's first government ends.** Becomes Leader of the Opposition when Thomas Crerar of the Progressives turns it down (*December 29*).

1922: Elected MP for Grenville in a by-election defeating Progressive Arthur Patterson (*January 26*). Offered a position in the law firm of Robert MacKay in Toronto (*March 3*); declines. Spends three weeks with his family in Tadoussac, Que., in order to improve his French (*July*). Tells the Toronto Liberal-Conservative Business Men's Club that Canada should stand by Britain and keep the Dardanelles neutral (*September 22*).

1923: *Montreal Herald* runs story suggesting corporate interests in the Conservative party no longer support his leadership (*May 8*). His cousin Edna, wife of Gordon Edwards, moves into 24 Sussex Drive, the house that becomes the official Prime Minister's residence about three decades later. Tours Atlantic Canada (*Summer*) and the west (*September-October*).

1924: His father Joseph dies in St. Mary's (*April 26*). As a Presbyterian, speaks in the House in favour of the proposed church union with the Methodists and Congregationalists to create the United Church (*July*).

1925: Publishes a Conservative private member's resolution favoring protective tariffs (*February 4*); later defeated in the House. His son Ted enrols at the Royal Military College in Kingston (*September*). His former Justice minister and Quebec lieutenant, Esioff Patenaude, agrees to run for the Conservatives, but makes it clear that Quebec Conservatives will conduct a separate campaign without Meighen's involvement

(*September 20*). Canada's 15th federal election: re-elected MP in Portage La Prairie defeating incumbent Harry Leader; his Conservatives win 15 more seats than the Liberals (*October 29*). King plans to stay in power by getting the Progressive party to support the government (*November 4*). Calls King's clinging to power a "usurpation of power and contempt of the popular will" (*November 9*). Outlines a policy, in a Hamilton speech, of calling an election before imposing conscription, a policy opposed by many members of his party (*November 16*). Vacations at Highland Pines, North Carolina (*November*).

1926: Makes no concessions in Conservative agricultural and labour policies when canvassed for his views by Progressive and Labour MPs (*January 6*). His non-confidence amendment following the Speech from the Throne motion is defeated; the government wins by three votes a subsequent amendment justifying its decision to retain power (*January 15*). Patenaude and other Quebec MPs agree to firmly rejoin the Conservatives (*May 26*). King's government is defeated on three motions relating to the Customs smuggling scandal (*June 25-26*). Agrees to form a government when King resigns because Governor General Lord Byng refused to dissolve Parliament (*June 28*). **Meighen's second government (1926).** Becomes Prime Minister and Secretary of State for External Affairs for the second time (*June 29*). Appoints six acting cabinet ministers who aren't paid, which means they don't have to seek re-election (*June 29*). Progressive party agrees to support Meighen's government until the end of the Session (*June 29*). King challenges the constitutionality of the new government (*June 30*). A Liberal amendment to avoid censure in the Customs department scandal is defeated; a Conservative amend-ment of censure passes (*June 30*). Two-cent postage is restored and the gold standard is re-established (*July 1*). A Liberal motion protesting the unconstitutionality of appointing acting ministers is passed 96 to 95; the deciding vote mistakenly cast by Thomas Bird (Progressive) who had actually been paired with an MP not present in the House (*July 2*). Asks Byng to dissolve the 15th Parliament after only one session (*July 2*); launching what becomes Canada's longest election campaign to date at 74 days. Presents his cabinet (*July 13*). Announces the appointment of Viscount Willingdon to be Canada's 13th Governor General (*August 5*). Canada's 16th federal election: defeated again in Portage La Prairie, by Liberal Ewan McPherson, his first local law partner; King's Liberals win a plurality of votes (*September 14*). Resigns as Prime Minister (*September 24*). **Meighen's second government ends.** Announces intention to retire as leader and not seek re-election (*September 25*). Calls a caucus meeting to discuss the election of a new Conservative leader; Hugh Guthrie is chosen temporary leader in the House (*October 11*). Becomes vice-president and general counsel of Canadian General Securities Limited, an investment banking firm in Toronto (*November*).

1927: Buys a house on Castle Frank Crescent in the Rosedale area of Toronto (*September*). Addresses the first Conservative leadership convention where he un-expectedly defends his divisive 1925 Hamilton speech about conscription (October 10). The convention elects Bennett to succeed him as party leader (*October 12*).

1928: Co-founds Third Canadian General Investment Trust Limited, one of the oldest closed-end funds in North America.

1929: Stock market crash seriously affects his investments (*October 29*).

1930: Turns down the Conservative nomination in the Long Lake, Sask., riding, preferring to stay in business (*April*). Speaks at the Good Will Congress of the World Alliance for International Friendship in Washington, expressing disappointment in the lack of success by the League of Nations (*November*).

1931: Turns down a request from Lester Pearson of the External Affairs department to speak to the Ottawa chapter of the Canadian Institute of International Affairs, although Pearson provided him with research notes for a presentation in Toronto (*February 26*). Turns down the chairmanship of the Board of Railway Commissioners offered by Prime Minister Bennett (*March*). His mother Mary Jane dies in Toronto (*April 10*). Becomes a member of the Ontario Hydro-Electric Power Commission (*June*). Resumes his law practice on a limited basis (*Fall*).

1932: Appointed as a Senator by Bennett and becomes Conservative Leader in the Senate (*February 2*). Enters Bennett's cabinet as Minister Without Portfolio (*February 3*). Succeeds in getting Senate approval for the report into the Beauharnois scandal (*May 3*). Becomes president of Canadian General Securities (*July*). Is a delegate to the Imperial Economic Conference in Ottawa (*July 20-August 20*).

1934: Resigns from the Ontario Hydro-Electric Power Commission following Liberal allegations he was using the position to political advantage (*April*). The Ontario government's Latchford-Smith Commission accuses Meighen of poor judgment and impropriety while serving on the power commission (*July 10*). Sails for Australia to represent Canada at the State of Victoria's centennial (*October*). Visits Hawaii and Fiji; sits in on a session of the Fiji Parliament (*October*). Writes his speech *The Greatest Englishman of History* about William Shakespeare while en route (*October*). Returns to Canada while Isabel and Lillian continue to travel in the Far East (*December*). Delivers his *Greatest Englishman* speech to the Vancouver Canadian Club, and later presents it in Ottawa, Montreal, Toronto and Pittsburgh (*December*).

Shakespeare from memory

Thrilled that Meighen had agreed to be a speaker, the Vancouver Canadian Club was rather surprised that his topic would be *The Greatest of All Englishmen*. More startling was the Englishman he picked: Shakespeare. But, the former politician was an acknowledged expert on the English bard and he proved it with a flourish. The entire speech, laced with quoted passages from plays and poems, was developed while Meighen was sailing the Pacific with no access to any of Shakespeare's works. Repeating the speech in Ottawa, he was asked by the media for a hard copy. He didn't have one and promptly recited the entire speech again from memory.

1935: Resigns as Minister Without Portfolio and Government Leader in the Senate following the Conservative loss in the election; continues as Conservative leader in the Senate (*October 14*).

1936: Lawsuit against him and others for inappropriately hiring detectives at the Hydro commission to investigate the source of anti-commission propaganda is dismissed (*December 4*).

1938: Refuses efforts to have his name suggested for the leadership of the Conservative party (*July 5*); Gives keynote speech at the Conservative leadership convention, speaking against the government's opposition to having British pilots trained in Canada during peacetime (*July 5*). Encourages Bennett not to pursue a last-minute decision to run again for the leadership (*July 6*). Robert Manion succeeds Bennett as leader (*July 7*).

1939: Becomes chairman of the Toronto advisory board for the Salvation Army, then chairs the national advisory board (*Fall*); holds latter position until his death.

1940: Refuses to accept the leadership after Manion resigns,; R.B. Hanson becomes acting leader (*May 13*). Both his sons enlist as soldiers in the Second World War.

1941: Receives an honorary Doctor of Laws degree from Queen's University. Asks Manitoba premier John Bracken to seek the party's leadership (*October*). Declines the leadership at the party convention in Ottawa (*November 7*). Refuses a formal request to lead the party (*November 8*). Pressure from the party, the media and his wife convince him to accept the leadership (*November 18*); Hanson continues as House leader and acting Leader of the Opposition. MP Lieut.-Col. Allan Cockeram resigns from his South York seat to open it for Meighen (*November 27*).

1942: Resigns from the Senate to contest the South York by-election (*January 16*). His stand favouring possible conscription is undercut by the Liberal Throne Speech calling for a plebiscite before it would be considered (*January 22*). Defeated in the South York by-election by high school teacher Joseph Noseworthy (CCF) (*February 9*). Calls for a leadership convention (*September*). Visits Winnipeg to encourage Bracken again to accept the leadership (*November*). Resigns as Conservative leader (*December 11*). New leader Bracken insists the party name be changed to Progressive Conservative (*December 11*). Attends the unveiling of his portrait on Parliament Hill by Ernest Fosbery (*December*).

1949: *Unrevised and Unrepented*, containing 38 Meighen speeches, is published.

1953: Afflicted with Ménières disease, an ear infection and uncontrollable hiccups that last for more than a month (*June*).

1955: An original recording of his *Greatest Englishman* speech is pressed as a record and distributed to friends. His son Max launches the Morgan Meighen investment firm in Toronto. *The Man in the Raincoat*, sung by his granddaughter Priscilla Wright peaks on the U.S. *Billboard* chart at #11 (*August 6*); she is only 14.

1956: Urges Canada to support Britain during the Suez crisis, just as he urged support during the 1922 Chanak crisis (*November 5*).

1957: Honoured at the 60th anniversary banquet of the Canadian Club of Toronto; Prime Minister Diefenbaker attends to pay tribute (*December 3*).

1958: Salvation Army opens Toronto's Isabel and Arthur Meighen seniors home.

1959: Audience with Queen Elizabeth II and Prince Philip aboard the Britannia in Toronto as the Queen's senior privy councillor in Canada (*June*).

1960: Dies in his sleep in Toronto following a short illness (*August 5*). Funeral service at St. Andrew's United Church in Toronto; burial in St. Mary's . (*August 7*).

Books about Meighen

- **1949**: Arthur Meighen; *Unrevised and Unrepented* (Clarke, Irwin)
- **1960**: Roger Graham; *Arthur Meighen: The Door of Opportunity* (Clarke, Irwin)
- **1963**: Roger Graham; *Arthur Meighen: And Fortune Fled* (Clarke, Irwin)
- **1965**: Roger Graham; *Arthur Meighen: No Surrender* (Clarke, Irwin)
- **1977**: John English; *Arthur Meighen* (Fitzhenry & Whiteside)
- **2012**: Roderick Benns; *Arthur Meighen: A Way With Words* (Fireside)

10

William Lyon Mackenzie King

The Unending Prime Minister

Rather than confront dilemmas or conflicts, William Lyon Mackenzie King preferred to let time erode their impact. The strategy worked; he was Canada's longest-serving Prime Minister. Often accused of banality, his shrewd use of delay turned his low-key approach to problem solving into a strength. It served him well as the intermdiary between Britain's Churchill and the U.S.'s Roosevelt during the Second World War. It helped deflect headaches like military conscription and idiosyncratic premiers. King's 30 years of private diaries were made public after his death, revealing the minutae of his life, including his interest in seances and a strong affection for his mother.

KING THE POLITICIAN

Prime Minister of Canada: (1) December 29, 1921 – June 28, 1926;
(2) September 25, 1926 – August 7, 1930;
(3) October 23, 1935 – November 15, 1948
Length of terms: (1) 4 years, 5 months, 30 days; (2) 3 years, 10 months, 13 days; (3) 13 years, 23 days; (Total) 21 years, 4 months, 5 days
Parliaments as Prime Minister: 14th; 15th; 16th; 18th; 19th; 20th
Age on entering office: 47
Political party: Liberal
Leader of party: August 7, 1919 – August 6, 1948
Member of Parliament: October 26, 1908 – September 21, 1911; October 20, 1919 – October 29, 1925; February 15, 1926 – April 30, 1949
Ridings represented: Waterloo North [Ont.] (1908-1911); Prince [P.E.I.] (1919-1921); York North [Ont.] (1921-1925); Prince Albert [Sask.] (1926-1945); Glengarry [Ont.] (1945-1949)
Cabinet portfolios: Labour (1909-1911); External Affairs (1921-1926, 1926-1930, 1935-1946); Privy Council President (1921-1926, 1926-1930, 1935-1948)
Other political post: Leader of the Opposition (1919-1921, 1926, 1930-1935)
Titles: Companion of St. Michael and St. George (1906); Canadian Privy Councillor (1909); Imperial Privy Councillor (1922); Grand Cross of the Order of the Netherlands Lion (1949); Belgium's Insignia of the Grand

Cross of the Order of Leopold (1949); Luxembourg's Grand Cross of the Oaken Crown (1949); France's Legion of Honour, Grand Cross (1949)
Quotes: "Conscription if necessary, but not necessarily conscription." "It is what we prevent, rather than what we do that counts most in Government." (three years before Second World War begins)
Lived after term: 1.5 years

King the Man

Name: William Lyon Mackenzie King
Born: December 17, 1874, Berlin (Kitchener), Ontario
Ancestry: Scottish
Religion: Presbyterian
Education: B.A. [Bachelor of Arts] (University of Toronto, 1895); LL.B. [Bachelor of Law](Toronto, 1896); M.A. [Master of Arts](Toronto, 1897); M.A. [Political Economy](Harvard University, 1898); Ph.D. [Doctor of Philosophy](Harvard, 1909)
Nicknames: Willie (family name); Billy (boyhood name); Rex (university name; Latin for *king*)
Military service: none
Occupation: civil servant; industrial counsellor
Occupation after term: retired
Publications: *The Secret of Heroism* (1906); *Industry and Humanity* (1918); *The Message of the Carillon and Other Addresses* (1927); *Canada at Britain's Side* (1941);
Canada and the Fight for Freedom (1944)
Appearance: "short and chubby; there was a certain softness about his appearance" (Roger Graham in *Arthur Meighen, Vol. 1: The Door of Opportunity*); "a pale, colourless little man, clad in the aura of indestructibility." (Dalton Camp in *Gentlemen, Players and Politicians*)
Personality: "intelligent, politically astute, strategic, compassionate, insightful, deferential, and respectful … frequently over-shadowed by his other side, the one that was self-righteous, egotistical, petty, vain, moralistic, paranoid, selfish, self-centred and vindictive." (Allan Levine in *King*). "Sly and tough, a master of timing and applied ruthlessness." (J.L. Granatstein & Norman Hillmer in *Prime Ministers: Ranking Canada's Leaders*)
Married: no
Died: July 22, 1950, Kingsmere, Quebec
Age at death: 75
Cause of death: pneumonia
Buried: Mount Pleasant Cemetery, Toronto, Ontario

King was the:
- Longest serving Prime Minister (21 years, 5 months, 1 day)
- Longest serving Prime Minister in the British Commonwealth
- Only Prime Minister to serve three terms
- Only Prime Minister to lead three minority governments
- Only Prime Minister to serve under three monarchs
- Only Prime Minister to serve as an MP for five different ridings

- Only Prime minister who was an industrial counsellor
- Only Prime Minister to earn a PhD degree
- Prime Minister to earn the most degrees (5)
- First Prime Minister educated at a U.S. university
- First Prime Minister who never married
- First Prime Minister who was a civil servant
- First Prime Minister to represent Saskatchewan
- First Prime Minister to lead a minority government (1925)
- First Prime Minister to lead two minority governments (1926)
- First Prime Minister to lead three minority governments (1945)
- Second Prime Minister to oversee six Parliaments
- Second Prime Minister born in Ontario
- Third Liberal Prime Minister
- Third Prime Minister with a Scottish background
- Third Presbyterian Prime Minister

King's legacy

- Created a Liberal party that became the 'government party'
- Ushered Canada into actual nationhood
- Introduced the old age pension, unemployment insurance, family allowance support and legitimate collective bargaining
- Kept the country together during the Second World War, often by avoiding making decisions
- Helped bring Roosevelt and Churchill together during the war
- Carved out a spot in the political middle ground for the Liberals
- Remembered by some, because of his diary entries, as a spiritualist who conversed with his dead mother and his dead dogs

KING'S FAMILY

King's Parents

Father: John King
Born: September 15, 1843, Toronto, Canada West (Ontario)
Occupation: editor; lawyer; lecturer
Died: August 30, 1916, Toronto, Ontario
Age at death: 72

Mother: Isabel Grace Mackenzie
Born: February 6, 1843, Rochester, New York
Married: December 12, 1872, Toronto, Ontario
Died: December 18, 1917, Ottawa, Ontario
Age at death: 74
Note: Daughter of William Lyon Mackenzie, 1837 activist.

King's Brothers & Sisters (3 siblings; Willie the second)

Sister: Isabel 'Bella' Christina Grace King (1873-1915)
Sister: Janet 'Jennie' Lindsey King (1876-1962), 4 children

Married: Harry Morrison Lay (1906)
Brother: Dougall Macdougall 'Max' King (1878-1922), 2 sons
Married: May Wookey (1911)

POLITICAL STORIES

Wins Liberal leadership

The Liberal's first leadership convention took place in August 1919 and King had to hustle home from England to be there for it. He was not favoured to win the contest; that role was comfortably held by former Finance minister William S. Fielding who had the support of many in caucus and most provincial premiers – even though he didn't want the job.

Fielding had also supported conscription and it wasn't certain the Quebec delegates could ignore his abandoning of the Laurier Liberals. As it turned out, they couldn't. On the first ballot, King polled 47 votes ahead of Fielding, with former cabinet minister George Graham and acting Leader of the Opposition Daniel D. McKenzie tied for third. There was no requirement that candidates with the least votes be dropped from the next ballot.

King kept inching his way to the needed majority in the following three ballots as Graham withdrew during the third round and McKenzie did the same in the fourth. King then took the fifth ballot with 52% of the vote, becoming Liberal leader at the same age as Laurier: 44.

King and Lapointe

They made an unusual team. King was short and pudgy while his Quebec lieutenant, Ernest Lapointe, was tall and swarthy. But together, they forged a powerful partnership that lasted two decades, sharing similar views on most issues.

Lapointe helped define the role of Quebec lieutenant in the Liberal party, moving it beyond its original function in the old Canada East-Canada West days. It became an integral part of the party's solid grasp on French Canada until the 1990s, keeping the province's patronage machine well oiled and maintaining order in the often unruly political ranks. It was no surprise that the Progressive Conservatives adopted a similar post in the province.

If King was not in the House, Lapointe was in charge. He served initially as Marine & Fisheries minister but soon moved to Justice. A confident debater in both languages, he had an intellect that King relied on without hesitation, especially in gauging the mind of Quebec. Losing Lapointe to cancer in 1941 devastated King. "No man had a truer friend," he noted, seeing to it that Lapointe had a state funeral.

Finding someone to take Lapointe's place could have been an exhausting, even futile task. But, as was often the case, luck was with the Prime Minister, who was able to attract another Quebec City lawyer to the role: Louis St. Laurent.

The King-Byng Affair

Losing the 1925 election to the Conservatives by 17 seats didn't necessarily mean losing power. King sought the help of the Progressive party to give him a slim majority. Governor General Lord Byng reluctantly accepted the scenario although he would have preferred to ask Conservative leader Meighen to form a government.

A customs scandal brought down the King government eight months later and the Prime Minister asked Byng to dissolve Parliament so an election could be called. Byng reminded him that the Conservatives had the most seats in the House and deserved a chance to try and form a government.

King was outraged at what he considered regal interference. He eagerly waited for his chance in Parliament. When several of Meighen's cabinet members stepped down to seek re-election to their new positions, as required, King pushed through a successful non-confidence vote against Meighen's strategy of filling the remaining cabinet posts with acting ministers.

This time, Byng granted Meighen's request to end Parliament. King was annoyed that Byng offered Meighen the very thing he had wanted. But he still got his election and received a majority, campaigning against the 'meddling' of the Governor General.

Four maverick premiers

Prime Ministers have always had to contend with premiers pushing hard for provincial rights, but King had to endure a handful of particularly uncon-ventional premiers – quirky, authoritarian men used to having their own way.

Ontario's Mitchell Hepburn – brash, independent-minded, unpredictable – was a Liberal, but that didn't dull his hatred for King, which stemmed from the Prime Minister's refusal to back the premier's anti-union campaign in 1937. With his rural-roots appeal, Hepburn attempted to win over the hearts of all Canadian Liberals and when King planned to extend the term of Ontario's Lieutenant Governor H.A. Bruce, Hepburn announced a preference for a new appointment. Two days later, Hepburn agreed to extending Bruce's term. Five days after that, he was against it again. Nine days later, he swung back to Bruce. Three weeks later, he was opposed. King finally appointed a new representative, avoiding Hepburn's choice.

Quebec's Maurice Duplessis – lusty, dictatorial, determined – was a demagogue adored by the voters. He dared the federal government to disallow his Padlock Law that gave police unlimited powers to ferret out communism and got away with it. Only the threat of King's Quebec cabinet members resigning helped to oust Duplessis in the 1939 provincial election. But he was back at the end of the war and ruled Quebec until 1959.

Alberta's William Aberhart – controversial, autocratic, altruistic – ushered in Social Credit dogma with its unusual economic theories. The radio evangelist chipped away at federal powers, attempting to gain control of the banks and media as well as waiving personal debt. In each case, either the Supreme Court or the federal government had to step in to disallow the initiatives.

British Columbia's Duff Pattullo – brash, loud, confident – joined Hepburn in stonewalling Ottawa's attempt to let the federal government distribute revenues from richer provinces to poor ones. He also pushed hard for 'socialized capitalism', coaxing a variety of social programs from the federal government. Pattullo wasn't as successful when it cam to getting approval for his fanciful relief programs.

The Roosevelt-Churchill go-between

Canada played a significant role in the Second World War, both militarily and financially, but it also took on a meaningful mediation role. King served as a 'middleman', helping to grease the wheels that brought leaders Winston Churchill of Britain and Franklin D. Rossevelt of the U.S. together into a bilateral relationship as wartime allies.

Unimpressed when he first met Churchill in 1900, King revised that assessment over the years and, by wartime, admired the British leader's decisiveness. Churchill relied on King's thoughts about the Americans' perspective before the U.S. entered the conflict.

King's first meeting with Roosevelt was two years before the war, but once combat started, King became the intermediary who allowed the two world leaders to test out their relationship while the U.S. remained resolutely neutral.

Although he met clandestinely with Churchill and Roosevelt once or twice, King set up two key summits with all three leaders in Quebec City in 1943 and 1944. It was a struggle for King to carve out a meaningful role at these summits and he often agonized over the reasons for not being invited to other summits. Given Canada's limited clout on the world stage, King's go-between function tended to raise the country's role beyond its size.

Conscription becomes necessary

King was a master at juggling Canada's various interests, putting off making decisions that would tilt those interests in divisive ways. The most glaring example was whether or not to make enlistment mandatory during the conflict – the same dilemma faced by Borden in the First World War.

Quebec was adamantly opposed to conscription and remained bitter about its introduction by Borden in 1917. But as the number of volunteer recruits dropped, English Canada began clamouring for mandatory service.

The Prime Minister bought time by conducting a national plebiscite on the issue, which yielded the predictable results and gave him the mandate to call for conscription. Its implementation played out in slow motion as King hoped the war or recruitment would somehow preempt the need. In the meantime, cabinet ministers on both sides of the conscription debate resigned or threatened to, protesting that the pace was too fast or too slow. Even King threatened to resign, suggesting he be replaced with a pro-conscription leader.

By the end of 1944, he had persuaded most of his own MPs to accept conscription and won a confidence vote in the House. But by then, the war was winding down and the new conscripts were not needed. It played out almost as King had famously promised: "Conscription if necessary, but not necessarily conscription."

Personal Stories

King and Henry Albert Harper

As good friends on the university debating team, King and Henry Albert Harper kept in touch after graduation. When King became Canada's first Deputy Minister of Labour in 1900, he hired Bert Harper as his assistant and the two rented a room in Ottawa. Harper began dating King's sister Jennie and was cycling with King in the Gatineau Hills when they discovered the enchanting property that would become Kingsmere.

On December 6, 1901, Harper drowned in the Ottawa River attempting to save Bessie Blair, daughter of Railways & Canals minister Andrew Blair, after she fell through the ice while skating. Both were swept downriver under the ice.

King was part of the committee to mark Harper's heroism by erecting a statue on Parliament Hill. The memorial, a bronze casting of Sir Galahad, was dedicated by Governor General Lord Grey in 1905. The following year, King published *The Secret of Heroism*, his tribute to close friend Bert Harper.

First bachelor Prime Minister

He may have never married, but King had an array of women friends throughout his life. Most of them – like Joan Patterson, Marjorie Herridge and Violet Markham – were primarily confidents, easy to talk or write to. Comforting. Attentive. Platonic.

But whenever a closer relationship developed, King began agonizing and over-analysing, rationalizing why the affair simply couldn't proceed. Much of this angst was committed to his diary. The biggest hurdle was finding a mate who could remotely match the standard of perfection reserved for his mother.

King's courtships tended to be private affairs, especially as he grew older. He also had a particular affinity for American women (Chicago's Mathilde Grossert and Rosa Humpal, Newport's Julia Grant and New York's Jean Greer). One of his Canadian dates was at the urging of Laurier's wife, Zoë, who set him up with Martha Sheriff, a wealthy 24-year-old Ottawa widow. But, as often happened, he didn't pursue the relationship.

For King, the thought of marriage was never strong enough to overcome his caution, his professional ambition and his attachment to his mother.

Industrial counsellor

Had the political bug not taken hold, it's likely King would have enjoyed a distinguished career in industrial relations. It was, after all, his chosen field. He had studied the subject as a graduate student and had published articles about trade unions. His work as a civil servant in Ottawa's new Labour Department focused on resolving worker-management disputes.

After his first stint in politics, King and the Liberals were defeated in the 1911 election. His reputation as an industrial relations expert gained the attention of John D. Rockefeller who was trying to contain a violent strike by his miners in Colorado.

King's successful push to get the Rockefellers to underwrite a company union cemented his U.S. credentials.

Setting himself up as an industrial counsellor, he worked with John D. Rockefeller Jr. and various corporations throughout the States for the next year and a half. But the death of Laurier in 1919 and the prospect of leading the Liberal party proved too strong a lure, which abruptly and ultimately ended King's vocation in industrial relations.

Talking with the dead

It started with fortune telling. Rachel Bleaney of Kingston predicted that King would run into trouble in the 1925 election, but that the situation would improve after that. It turned out to be an astute prophecy.

Bleaney's suggestion that he call an election in 1930 didn't go so well; he ended up out of power for the next five years. However, he was starting to move on to the pithier world of spiritualism. He was already familiar with the powers of Etta Wreidt of Detroit when he was invited to one of her séances taking place in Brockville (the hostess was the mother of Martha Sheriff whom he had dated many years earlier).

King was hooked. He immediately invited Wreidt to Ottawa to conduct more séances and he was soon in otherworldly conversations with Laurier, Bert Harper and, of course, his mother. For the next decade, until Wreidt's death in 1942, King regularly sought her powers to talk with the dead.

Table rapping expanded his ability to converse with deceased family members and friends. Numerology and tealeaf readings were also added to the mix. Although he sometimes sought answers to pressing affairs of state, there is no evidence that government policy was influenced in any meaningful way by these gatherings.

57 years of diaries

"After having been told by many that I could never keep a diary, I decided to make, at least, an attempt," wrote King on September 6, 1893. It was an undertaking that would continue and flourish for nearly six decades, almost 30,000 pages and about 7.5 million words.

That first diary in 1893 had the word 'Private' penned in several places on the cover. It was never King's intention to make his diaries public. After retiring as Prime Minister in 1948, he relished the thought that he had a gigantic source of material for his autobiography. But the memoir project was barely underway when he died less than two years later.

King's four literary executors knew that he wanted to have the diaries destroyed, but it wasn't easy for them to obliterate such a treasure trove of information. In 1955, an Archives employee microfilmed and sold parts of the diary, forcing the executors' hands. Between 1971 and 1981, they released the entire contents in three lots, hoping that most of the protagonists mentioned would be gone.

The release of the diaries shone a bright light on King's various private dalliances, including chats with his dead mother and handwringing about his relationships with other women. The private side of his life began to define him as the diaries were released. Today, his private thoughts and words are readily available on the Internet.

KING'S TIMELINE

1874: Born on Benton Street, Berlin (Kitchener), Ont. (*December 17*).

1879: Attends Central School (now Suddaby) on Frederick Street (*September*).

1882: Hears Sir John A. Macdonald campaigning in Berlin (Kitchener) and is impressed that the girl who gave him flowers received a hug (*Spring*).

1886: Family moves to Woodside home on the edge of Berlin. Taught by student teacher William Diefenbaker, future father of John.

1887: Attends Berlin High School (now Kitchener-Waterloo Collegiate) (*September*).

1891: Enrols in Arts at University College, University of Toronto (*September*). Elected class president. Acquires the nickname Rex, Latin for 'king'. Begins Sunday visits to Hospital for Sick Children to read to patients.

1892: Enrols in Political Science on a Blake scholarship at the University of Toronto (*September*).

1893: Enters debates at university; some possibly with student Arthur Meighen, his future political adversary. Family moves to Toronto where his father John becomes a lecturer at Osgoode Hall law school (*Summer*). Begins writing a diary, which he keeps up daily until just before his death (*September 6*). Initiated into the Kappa Alpha fraternity (*October 30*). Decides he will become a Presbyterian minister (*December 15*). Sings with the university Glee Club for Governor General Lord Aberdeen in Ottawa (*December 21*); wrote accounts of the trip for the *Globe* and *Saturday Night*.

1894: Influenced by the death of Katie Cameron at the Hospital for Sick Children where he volunteers each Sunday; decides to dedicate more time to saving souls (*January 7*). Acts as an usher to Governor General Lord Aberdeen during a Toronto visit (*February 16*). Volunteers at the Haven for homeless people in downtown Toronto (*February*). During a riot at the university's convocation exercises at Massey Hall, he pushes down the registrar, James Brebner (*October 5*); no action seems to have been taken.

1895: Helps lead a boycott of university classes to oppose the administration's attempt to stop publication of the student newspaper, and calling for the dismissal of Professor William Dale who questioned the hiring of a staff member for political reasons (*February 15*). Seconds a motion to end the strike after the university agrees to set up an inquiry (*February 20*). Called as a witness during the inquiry where he tends to defer to the administration (*April 17*). Receives his Bachelor of Arts degree from Vice-Chancellor William Mulock (*June 11*). Turns down an economics scholarship at the University of Chicago in favour of taking law at the University of Toronto (*June 21*). Articles for his father, deciding that a law career is not for him (*June-August*). Hears Jane Addams speak about her settlement work at Hull House in Chicago (*July 20*). Has a short relationship with Kitty Riordan after meeting her in Muskoka (*August*). Loses his law fellowship at the University of Toronto (*September 30*). Becomes a police court reporter for the *Toronto News*, then later for the *Globe* (*October*).

1896: Receives his Bachelor of Law degree (LL.B.) from the University of Toronto (*June 12*). Turned down for the political science master's program at the university (*June*). Leaves his job as a *Globe* reporter (*September 4*). Enrols in a master's program at the University of Chicago (*October 1*). Moves into Hull House as a resident member (*October 31*).

1897: Leaves Hull House, unable to handle settlement house demands and graduate work (*January 7*). Develops typhoid symptoms and enters St. Luke's Hospital where he meets nurse Mathilde Grossert; they begin dating (*March 8*). Publishes a story about trade unions in the *Journal of Political Economy* (*March*) and one on the International Typographical Union six months later. Submits his thesis on the International Typographical Union to the University of Toronto (*April 26*) and receives his Master of Arts degree in political economy. Turned down for a doctoral program at the university (*June*). Ends his relationship with Rosa Humpal of Chicago, but continues dating Grossert (*June 23*). Interviews socialist (and future British Prime Minister) Ramsay Macdonald who is on his honeymoon in Toronto, for the Toronto *Globe* (*August 24*). Writes a series of four articles for the Toronto *Mail & Empire* on immigrants, housing and labour (*September-October*). With his father, confronts Postmaster General William Mulock about unfair wages and demands placed on textile workers making postal uniforms; asked to prepare a report about it (*September 18*). Enrols in political economy at Harvard University in Cambridge, Massachusetts (*October 2*).

1898: Presents his textile workers report to Mulock (*January*); it results in a fair wages clause being added to government contracts. Writes the first of two articles about sweatshops for the *Montreal Herald* (*April 16*). Visits Chicago to tell Grossert he doesn't want to become engaged (*April 20*); they maintain a lifelong connection. Receives his Master of Arts degree from Harvard (*June 29*). Spends the summer house-sitting at Shady Hill, the home of noted Harvard fine arts professor, Charles Eliot Norton (*June-August*); years later he names one of his Kingsmere cottages Shady Hill. Joined by his sister Bella who studies nursing in Boston for half a year (*July*). Begins doctoral work on clothing industry sweatshops (*Fall*).

Kingsmere ruins

With an appreciation for grand European architecture, King began to pepper his Kingsmere summer estate lawns with exotic ruins, cobbled together in stonework taken from other ruins. The centrepiece of his Abbey Ruins, resembling a Greek temple, is a large bay window rummaged from a Sandy Hill home slated for demolition. The Arc de Triomphe is actually the entrance pillars of Ottawa's former British North American Bank Note Company. Many of his carvings came from Europe, including gargoyles from the Big Ben tower. When Britain's Westminster building was bombed in 1941, King dispatched civil servant Lester Pearson to the site to acquire more bric-a-brac for his gardens.

1899: Passes the oral exam for his doctorate at Harvard (*March 30*). Meets Julia Grant with whom he continues a lifelong correspondence (*September 8*). Wins the Henry Lee fellowship allowing him to travel to Europe (*September*). Attends the London School of Economics and does some lecturing (*October 9*); lives in the Passmore Edwards Settlement complex.

1900: Visits Paris, Brussels, Berlin, Switzerland and Rome (*March-June*). Offered a job by Mulock (Postmaster General) as editor of the *Labour Gazette* in the new federal Labour department (*June 26*). Offered an instructor position at Harvard University (*June 29*). Harvard suggests he accept Mulock's offer (*July 5*). Accepts the *Labour Gazette* job and moves to Ottawa (*July 24*). Appointed Deputy Minister of Labour in addition to his responsibilities as editor (*September 15*). Publishes the first issue of the *Labour Gazette*

(*September 20*). Rents a room at 202 Maria (Laurier) Street with college friend Bert Harper, whom he hired as his assistant (*October 9*). Discovers Kingsmere on a cycling trip with Harper in the Gatineau Hills (*October*). Acts as conciliator in a labour dispute in Valleyfield, Que., where he succeeds in bringing striking spinning operators and excavators back to work (*October*). Meets British politician Winston Churchill for the first time in Ottawa and isn't impressed (*December*).

1901: His sister Jennie begins dating Harper. Boards at Mrs. McMinn's in Kingsmere (*Summer*). Meets Marjorie Herridge in the Gatineau, who is married to a Presbyterian minister; they have a relationship (*Summer*). In a letter to his mother, indicates he hopes to eventually become Prime Minister (*September 2*). Buys his first property at Kingsmere for $200 (*September 8*). Unsuccessful in ending a miners' strike in Rossland, B.C. (*November 19*). Harper drowns in the Ottawa River while attempting to save Bessie Blair, daughter of Andrew Blair (Railways & Canals), who fell through the ice (*December 6*). Takes an active part on the committee to erect a memorial statue to Harper (*December*). Establishes a Human Resources library in Ottawa, the government's second federal library.

1902: William S. Fielding (Finance) suggests King's youth and the low profile of the Labour department doesn't entitle him to a full deputy minister's salary of $3,200 (*February 8*); King threatens to quit and two days later cabinet agrees to pay the salary.

1903: Leaves for British Columbia as secretary of the royal commission examining CPR's strike-breaking tactics during a miners strike (*April 23*). Becomes a founder and first vice-president of the Ottawa Canadian Club (*October 7*).

1904: Builds a cottage on his Kingsmere property (*Summer*). Rules in favour of management in a steel workers strike in Sydney, N.S. (*July*). Named president of the Ottawa Canadian Club (*October 12*). Mulock (Labour) suggests King enter politics (*November 18*).

1905: His mother Isabel has her portrait painted by artist J.W.L. Foster with the book *Life of Gladstone* in her lap open at the chapter *Prime Minister*. Investigates fraudulent claims made to entice British workers to replace Canadian workers on strike. Allen Aylesworth becomes Labour minister after Mulock is appointed an Ontario judge (*November 3*). Gets support from Laurier for his desire to enter politics and become Labour minister (*November 4*). Lord Grey unveils the statue of Sir Galahad on Parliament Hill in memory of Harper (*November 18*). Meets Violet Markham at a Governor General's party; becomes a lifelong friend (*December*).

1906: Publishes *The Secret of Heroism* about Harper (*January*). Aylesworth (Labour) becomes Justice minister and is replaced by Rodolphe Lemieux (*June 14*). Sails for England with his father on a government mission to discuss the emigration of British strikebreakers (*September 21*). Becomes a Companion of the Order of St. Michael and St. George, bestowed by Edward VII (*September*). Visits Scotland (*October 4-16*). Works to help settle a coal miners strike in Lethbridge, Alta. (*November-December*). Returns to Ottawa (*December 4*).

1907: His Industrial Disputes Investigation Act is passed (*March 22*). Appointed to the commission looking into the telephone operators dispute in Toronto (*June*) Finishes the telephone commission report calling for improved working conditions (*August 27*). Urged by Laurier to consider courting wealthy 24-year-old widow Martha Sheriff (*August 27*); takes her out, but nothing develops. Mentioned as a possible leadership candidate for the Ontario Liberal party; isn't interested (*September 9*). Arrives in Vancouver to investigate the riots protesting Japanese and Chinese immigration (*October 20*).

1908: Visits Washington to discuss U.S. support in limiting Japanese immigration; meets with President Theodore Roosevelt and Secretary of State Elihu Root who both favour limited immigration (*January 25*). Visits England to negotiate the restriction of immigrants from India to Canada; the agreement is similar to the Canadian-Japanese agreement (*March-April*). Serves as a British delegate at the Opium International Commission in Shanghai, China. Recommended by Laurier for a Companion of St. Michael and St. George that had already been conferred in 1906. Negotiates with China to restrict Chinese immigration; China agrees to consider it, but the government collapses in 1910. His legislation to ban opium use across Canada is approved (*July 20*). Appointed to the commission looking into the Quebec textile workers dispute; the report results in stricter laws on child labour (*August*). Told by Laurier of plans to set up a separate Labour department with him as minister (*September 9*). Resigns as deputy minister of Labour to seek election as the Liberal candidate for Waterloo North (Ont.) (*September 21*). Canada's 11th federal election: elected MP for Waterloo North defeating schoolteacher Richard Reid by about 250 votes; Laurier's Liberal government is re-elected (*October 26*). Sails for India to promote an international conference on emigration (*December 14*); he is unsuccessful.

1909: Attends the International Opium Commission meeting in Singapore as one of the five British delegates (*February*). Discusses controls on Chinese emigration to Canada (*March*); returns to Canada (*May 9*). Appointed by Laurier to be Canada's fourth Labour minister, the first one to handle it as a separate portfolio (*June 2*). Re-elected MP by acclamation in the Waterloo North by-election for his cabinet seat (*June 21*). Receives his Doctor of Philosophy degree from Harvard after submitting his Labour department papers as his thesis; speaks at the commencement dinner in Cambridge, Massachusetts (*June 30*). Hires Fred McGregor as a Labour department secretary, beginning a lifelong friendship (*July 5*).

1910: Introduces the Combines Investigation Act to regulate trusts and monopolies (*January 18*); the legislation is used once to little effect and is repealed nine years later. Visits Europe to attend labour conferences in The Hague, Brussels, Paris and Lugano (*August-October*). A strike by Grand Trunk Railway employees ends, but his handling of negotiations allows the company to avoid rehiring many of the workers, putting the onus on the government to hire them (*August 2*).

1911: Canada's 12th federal election: loses his Waterloo North seat to William Weichel (Conservative), mayor of Waterloo; the Laurier government is defeated by Borden's Conservatives (*September 21*). Offers to write Laurier's biography; Laurier agrees but it's never pursued (*September 29*). Resigns as Labour minister (*October 6*). Becomes president of the Ontario General Reform Association, although he was again considered as possible leader of the Ontario Liberal party (*October 31*). Helps campaign for the Liberals in the Ontario provincial election; the Conservatives win (*December 11*).

1912: Visits New York City to discuss becoming editor of *Outlook* magazine (*January*). Attempts to have Humboldt (Sask.) seat vacated so he can seek the nomination, but the incumbent decides not to step down (*March 16*); similar efforts in Regina (Sask.) and East Kent (Ont.) are unsuccessful. Appointed director of the Liberal Information Office in Ottawa (*February*). Visits England on a speaking tour about conciliation legislation (*July 24*). Investigates the possibility of running for the British House of Commons. Returns to Canada (*November*).

1913: Nominated as the Liberal candidate for North York (Ont.) (*March 8*). Publishes his first issue of *Liberal Monthly* (*September*).

1914: Becomes chairman of the Canadian Association of International Conciliation, a peace group. Explains the Industrial Disputes Investigation Act of 1907 to the U.S. Commission on Industrial Relations meeting in Washington (*April*). Approached by the Rockefeller family for help resolving labour violence in the Colorado mineworkers strike (*June 1*). Becomes director of research for the Rockefeller Foundation (*October 1*). Resigns as president of the Ontario General Reform Association (*November 27*).

1915: Accompanies John D. Rockefeller Jr. to a meeting with Colorado union leaders in New York to propose a separate company union; the idea is rejected (*January 27*). Visits Colorado to deal with the miners problem first-hand (*March 19*). His older sister Bella dies in Toronto (*April 4*). Testifies before the U.S. Commission on Industrial Relations, which ultimately tables a report condemning the Rockefeller plan as a "substitute for trade unions that will deceive, mollify and sooth public opinion while bulwarking the employer's arbitrary control." (*May 25*). Works at Kingsmere to develop Rockefeller's company union plan (*July*). Visits Colorado with Rockefeller to promote the union plan (*September-October*). Colorado workers vote in favour of the Rockefeller union plan (*October 25*).

1916: Proposes a book to Rockefeller about the need for humanity in labour (*May*); removes the telephone from Kingsmere to eliminate distractions while beginning the book (*Summer*). His father John dies in Toronto (*August 30*). Suffering from nervous exhaustion, King seeks medical help from noted psychiatrist Adolf Meyer at John Hopkins Hospital in Baltimore, Maryland (*October*); Dr. Lewellys Barker becomes his doctor for nearly three decades. His mother Isabel moves in with him in Ottawa (*December*).

1917: Changes his views on conscription, supporting it as a "fair method of defensive necessity" (*May 10*). Canada's 13th federal election: defeated by York North Conservative incumbent John Armstrong; Borden's Unionist government is elected (*December 17*). His mother Isabel dies in Ottawa (*December 18*).

1918: Ends association with the Rockefeller Foundation, becoming an industrial counsellor for John D. Rockefeller Jr. (*January 18*). May have proposed by letter to Jean 'Daisy' Greer of New York (*February 24*); she doesn't reply and marries someone else the following year. Drafts an agreement to help solve labour problems at two cola companies in Maryland (*April*). Visits mines in Colorado with the Rockefellers (*May-June*). Drafts a representation plan to help solve labour problems at Bethlehem Shipbuilding Corporation in Pennsylvania (*August*). Meets neighbours Joan and Godfroy Patterson at his Roxborough apartment in Ottawa; the friendship lasts more than 30 years (*September*). Declines an invitation to sit in Borden's Unionist cabinet (*September 18*). Completes his book *Industry and Humanity*, based on his work with the Rockefellers (*October 3*). Spends six months working as an industrial consultant for companies in Ohio, Indiana, Illinois and Colorado (*October*). Declines a directorship with the Carnegie Corporation in New York (*December*).

1919: Attends Wilfrid Laurier's funeral (*February 22*). A study for Consolidated takes him to mining camps in West Virginia, Pennsylvania, Maryland and Kentucky (*March-April*). Gives his first public speech in French to the Trades and Labour Council in Quebec (*March 28*). Sails for England (*May 15*) where he visits industrialists and war-torn parts of France and Belgium. Sails for Canada to be back in time for the Liberal leadership convention in Ottawa (*July 15*). Elected leader of the Liberal party on the fifth ballot (*August 7*). Declines an offer to run in a Glengarry-Stormont (Ont.) by-election (*August 18*). Attends the National Industrial Relations Conference in Ottawa (*September 15-20*). Seeks a seat in a Prince (P.E.I) by-election (*September 20*). Receives an honorary Doctor of Laws degree from Queen's University (*October 16*). Elected by acclamation in Prince (*October 20*). At his suggestion, Rockefeller Jr. donates $5 million to further Canadian medical education and research (*December 25*).

1920: Defends himself in the House about his time with the Rockefellers during the war years (*March*). Helps oversee the reconstruction of the Leader of the Opposition office in the Centre Block, complete with frescoes including his mother as an angel; he refuses to vacate the office later after becoming Prime Minister. Makes Ernest Lapointe his Quebec lieutenant (*September 4*).

1921: Zoë Laurier, widow of Wilfrid, dies, willing Laurier House to King (*November*); the house is renovated. Canada's 14th federal election: elected as MP in York North defeating incumbent Armstrong; his Liberals win a minority (*December 6*). Progressives Thomas Crerar and A.B. Hudson refuse seats in King's cabinet (*December 12*). **King's first government (1921-1926).** Becomes Canada's 10th Prime Minister, third Secretary of State for External Affairs, and 24th Privy Council President (*December 29*).

Other people's names

In the 1921 election that made King Prime Minister, the York North candidates all carried the illustrious names of others. There was, of course, King who proudly wore the name of his famous, rebel grandfather William Lyon Mackenzie. He was running against the Conservative incumbent John Alexander Macdonald Armstrong whom he beat by more than 1,000 votes. Representing the Progressives was Ralph Waldo Emerson Burnaby.

1922: Visits Denver, Colorado, to be with his brother Max who is seriously ill with muscular dystrophy (*January 2*). 14th Parliament opens; nominates Rodolphe Lemieux to be the 16th Speaker of the House (*March 8*). Thomas Crerar, leader of the Progressive party, refuses to sit as Leader of the Opposition; Meighen assumes the role (*March 8*). King is informed by Crerar that the Progressives are willing to cooperate with a Liberal government, giving it the majority needed to govern (*March 14*). His brother Max dies in Denver, Colorado (*March 18*); travels to Colorado to bring the body back to Toronto. Becomes a member of the British Privy Council (*June 3*). Takes part in a Washington conference looking at armaments on the Great Lakes (*July 13*). First visit to his hometown Kitchener as Prime Minister where 10,000 turn out to hear him speak (*September 13*). Asked by British Prime Minister David Lloyd George for troops for a possible conflict with the Turks in the Dardenelles strait (*September 15*). Cabinet opposes sending troops to Turkey; tells Lloyd George such a decision would require the approval of Parliament, which is not in session (*September 18*). Britain signs an armistice with Turkey, ending the Chanak crisis (*September 29*). Canadian National Railway lines are consolidated (*October 4*). Bonar Law, born in New Brunswick, becomes British Prime Minister (*October 23*). Crerar resigns as Progressive party leader (*October*); succeeded by Robert Forke. Commerce treaty signed with Italy (*November 5*). Encourages former Unionist Liberals to rejoin the Liberal ranks in a Toronto speech (*November 9*). Progressive MP W.J. Hammell joins the Liberal party (*November*); Joseph Binette joins the following month. Commercial treaty signed with France (*December 15*).

1923: Militia & Defence department is renamed National Defence; all military forces are under one minister for the first time (*January 1*). Britain agrees to allow Canada to sign its own treaties (*January 16*). William Kennedy (Railway & Canals) dies in Florida (*January 17*). Lapointe (Marine & Fisheries) signs the Halibut Fisheries Treaty in Washington; no British signatures required for the first time (*March 2*). Governor General Lord Byng and

Lady Byng become some of the first official guests to visit King's new home, Laurier House (*March 11*). Cannabis is added to the list of drugs in his government's proposed legislation prohibiting the use of opium, morphine and heroin (*April 23*). Receives an honorary Doctor of Laws degree from the University of Toronto. Sails to England (*September 22*), where he receives the Freeman of the City of London. Attends the Imperial Economic Conference (*October 1-November 8*); unsuccessful in setting up preferential trade tariffs. Pushes for more control over foreign relations; supported by Ireland, but opposed by Britain, Australia and New Zealand (*October 8*). Meets with George V (*October 9*). Sworn in as a member of the British Privy Council (*October 11*). Bonar Law, the only Canadian to be British Prime Minister, dies in London of throat cancer (*October 30*). Arrives back in Ottawa (*December 1*). Williams Fielding (Finance) suffers a paralytic stroke that ends his political career (*December 4*). Sir Jean-Lomer Gouin (Justice) resigns for health reasons (*December 6*).

1924: A manufacturers sales tax comes into effect (*January 1*). The Red Ensign becomes the official flag (*January 26*). Shuffles cabinet, moving Lapointe (Marine & Fisheries) to Justice and appointing Pierre Cardin to Marine & Fisheries (*January 30*). Progressive leader Forke pledges his party's support for the Liberals to reduce taxes, balance the budget and make tariff changes (*February 27*). Joan Patterson gives him an Irish terrier he names Pat. The Royal Canadian Air Force is formed (*April 1*). Ten Progressive MPs oppose supporting the Liberals and join Labour MPs to create the Ginger Group (*June*). Receives honorary degrees from Oxford University, the University of Edinburgh and Yale University. As a Presbyterian, suggests in the House that the Supreme Court should rule on the church's reservations about a proposed union with the Methodists and Congregationalists (*July*); instead, the House favors going ahead with the union the following year. O.D. Skelton is appointed counsellor of External Affairs (*July*), becoming deputy minister a year later, a post he holds until his death in 1940. Trade agreement signed with Australia (*September 25*). Prince of Wales visits Canada (*October 15*). The Board of Railway Commissioners revokes the Crow's Nest Pass Act (*October*); an Order-in-Council overrides the decision and restores the act until the Supreme Court rules on the decision. British Columbia opposes further Asian immigration to Canada (*December 17*).

1925: Supreme Court upholds Order-in-Council to maintain the Crow's Nest Pass Act (*February*). Has his fortune read for the first time by Rachel Bleaney of Kingston (*March 1*). Opposes the League of Nations' Geneva Protocol for Pacific Settlement in International Disputes (*March 10*). United Church of Canada is formed by the union of Methodists, Congregationalists and some Presbyterians (*June 10*). Nova Scotia Liberals nearly wiped out in a provincial election after 43 years in power (*June 25*). Canada House in London, England, is opened by George V (*June 29*). After Jacques Bureau (Customs) profits from border smuggling and rum running (instead of stopping it), King appoints him to the Senate to remove him from cabinet (*September 4*). Appoints James Robb (Immigration & Colonization) as Finance minister after he'd been acting in the role since Fielding's death (*September 5*). Appoints five new cabinet ministers, including Vincent Massey, former president of the Massey-Ferguson Company, and Walter Foster, former premier of New Brunswick (*September 5-26*). Senator Raoul Dandurand elected president of the Assembly of the League of Nations (*September 7*). Tells an Erindale, Ont., audience that he will ask the Governor General to dissolve Parliament and call an election again if he doesn't receive a majority (*September 9*). Consults fortune teller Bleaney, who predicts a troubled election with a rosier future (*October 20*). Canada's 15th federal election: defeated in North York by Conservative Thomas Lennox, along with eight of his cabinet ministers; wins 17 fewer seats than Meighen's Conservatives, but retains power with support from the Progressives who have 24 seats (*October 29*). Asked to consider resigning by Governor General Lord

Byng (*October 30*). Decides to carry on at the urging of his cabinet (*November 2*); announces his decision two days later.

1926: Progressive and Labour MPs confront King and Meighen for their views on agriculture and labour issues (*January 6*). 15th Parliament opens; Lapointe (Justice) becomes leader of the House until King finds a seat (*January 7*). Agrees to introduce unemployment insurance and a pension as a demand for support from Labour MPs J.S. Woodsworth and A.A. Heaps (*January 7*). A motion justifying the Liberal decision to retain power carries by three votes after a week of debate (*January 15*). Liberal MP Charles Macdonald resigns from his Prince Albert, Sask., seat, to free up a riding (*January 16*). Conservative MP Harry Stevens accuses the government of being aware of smuggling activities in the Customs & Excise department and doing nothing to stop it (*February 3*). Georges Boivin (Customs & Excise) agrees to set up a committee to investigate Stevens's charges (*February 5*). King wins the by-election in Prince Albert (*February 15*). Appoints Premier Charles Dunning of Saskatchewan to cabinet as Railways & Canals minister (*February 20*). Progressive party announces it will support Liberal legislation, but won't join ranks with the government (*March 4*). The Old Age Pensions Bill to provide pensions in provinces signing agreements with Ottawa passes in the House (*March 26*). The Senate defeats the pensions bill (*June 8*). A motion is passed to postpone the transfer of natural resources rights to Alberta until the Supreme Court rules on it (*June 15*); Progressive MPs reluctantly support the motion rather than defeat the government. Customs & Excise inquiry committee finds smuggling is widespread in the Montreal area (*June 18*). Stevens introduces an amendment to the Customs & Excise report censuring the government for inaction (*June 22*) CCF leader J.S. Woodsworth adds another amendment that the minister's name be deleted from the report; it is defeated, the Liberals' first loss on a vote since the election. Another amendment is ruled out of order by the Speaker; the House is in favour of tabling it, representing a second Liberal defeat. Decides to dissolve Parliament and avoid a vote on the Stevens amendment; Byng refuses to grant a dissolution, saying Meighen deserves a chance to form a government since the Conservatives have the most seats (*June 26*). Byng refuses to grant a dissolution for a second time (*June 27*). Byng refuses to grant a dissolution for a third time (*June 28*); King resigns and tables a motion in the House to adjourn. **King's first government ends.** Challenges the constitutionality of the new government (*June 30*). Liberals lose an attempt to prevent a vote of censure on the Customs department scandal (*June 30*). Liberals win a vote 96 to 95 protesting the unconstitutionality of appointing acting ministers (*July 2*). Meighen successfully asks Byng to dissolve the 15th Parliament after only one session (*July 2*); Canada's longest election campaign begins. King invites fortune teller Bleaney to predict the election outcome; she predicts a Liberal victory (*July 26*). Canada's 16th federal election: re-elected in Prince Albert defeating Conservative John Diefenbaker; Liberals win another minority, although the Conservatives garnered more of the popular vote (*September 14*). Attends a send-off dinner for the Byngs (*September 23*). **King's second government (1926-1930).** Becomes Prime Minister, Secretary of State for External Affairs and Privy Council President for the second time (*September 25*). Appoints eight new cabinet ministers, including James Ralston and Progressive party leader Robert Forke (*September 25*). Byng lays the cornerstone in the Memorial Chamber of the Peace Tower to mark his departure from Canada as Governor General (*September 27*). Viscount Willingdon becomes Canada's 13th Governor General (*October 2*). King sails for England with Lapointe (Justice), Massey and Skelton (*October 10*). Meighen resigns as Conservative leader (*October 11*). Attends the Imperial Conference (*October 19-November 22*); South Africa wants more autonomy and threatens to secede, and Ireland supports the move; avoids the conflict by suggesting Governors General represent the Crown instead of the British government. Conference approves the Balfour Declaration of 1926 that declares Dominions to be autonomous states (*November 15*).

Massey becomes the first Canadian ambassador to the U.S. (*November 26*). Arrives back in Canada (*December 8*). 16th Parliament opens (*December 9*). Canada formally requests direct communication with the British gov-ernment (*December 29*); past communication was always through the Governor General.

1927: First U.S. Ambassador to Canada, William Phillips, is appointed (*February 3*). Vacations in Atlantic City, New Jersey (*February 22-March 7*). The Imperial Privy Council rules in favour of Newfoundland's claim for 12,000 square miles (31,000 square kilometers) of territory in Labrador (*March 1*). Old Age Pensions Bill passes, proposing a monthly pension of $20 to needy persons over 70 (*March 21*); costs are to be shared equally with the provinces, but only British Columbia signs up. Customs & Excise department becomes National Revenue (*March 31*). Cabinet backs British decision to end trade relations with Russia (*May 25*). Speaks on Parliament Hill as part of Canada's 60th birthday; it is the first speech by a Prime Minister broadcast over radio (*July 1*); celebrations include a visit by the Prince of Wales (later Edward VIII), Prince Albert (later George VI) and British Prime Minister Stanley Baldwin. Direct communication with the British government comes into effect (*July 1*). Welcomes Charles Lindberg to Ottawa; the American pilot stays at Laurier House (*July 2*). Canada rejects U.S. invitation to discuss a St. Lawrence seaway (*July 16*). Canada is elected to a non-permanent seat on the League of Nations Council (*September*). Inaugurates transatlantic telephone service with Britain, making a call to Baldwin (*October 3*). R.B. Bennett is elected Conservative leader and becomes Leader of the Opposition (*October 12*). First pension cheques issued, in British Columbia (*October 15*). Chairs the third Dominion-Provincial Conference in Ottawa (*November 3-10*); discussions on Senate and constitution reform remain unresolved; subsidies to the Maritime provinces become permanent; British Columbia is given control of its railway lands.

1928: First national assembly of Liberal Women meets in Ottawa (*April 17-18*). Supreme Court rules that the BNA Act doesn't permit women to sit in the Senate (*April 24*). Ottawa agrees to give Manitoba control of its natural resources (*July 3*); comes into effect two years later. Officially opens Prince Albert National Park in his riding (*August 10*). Visits France, Italy and Britain (*August 17-October 29*). Meets and briefly dates Beatrix Henderson Robb in Paris (*August*). Empire Parliamentary Association meets in Canada (*August 24-October 5*). Signs the Briand-Kellogg Pact in Paris (*August 27*). Accepts Canada's membership on the Council of the League of Nations in Geneva (*September 7*); also elected as one of its vice-presidents. Meets with Italian Prime Minister Benito Mussolini in Rome (*September 26*). Opens the Canadian legation in Paris (*September 29*). Visits Vimy (*October 5*). Has lunch with George V and Queen Mary (*October 11*). Imperial Privy Council confirms a Supreme Court decision that mineral rights on Hudson's Bay Company lands belong to Canada (*November 9*). Appoints the Aird Commission to recommend a public policy for radio (*December 6*); ends up shelving the report that calls for the creation of seven publicly-owned radio stations.

1929: Signs agreement with U.S. to preserve Niagara Falls (*January 2*). Order-in-Council approves project by the Beauharnois Syndicate of Montreal to develop hydroelectric power and build a canal on the St. Lawrence River (*March 8*). Canadian rumrunner *I'm Alone* is sunk by the U.S. Coast Guard in the Gulf of Mexico, creating an international incident (*March 22*); Ambassador Massey protests the imprisonment of the crew in New Orleans. John Turner, Canada's 17th Prime Minister, is born in Richmond, England (*June 7*). Welcomes Winston Churchill to Kingsmere (*August 14*). Meets with Ramsay Macdonald, British Prime Minister, in Ottawa (*October 17*). The Judicial Committee of the Imperial Privy Council in England (the appeals court for the Supreme Court of Canada) rules that women are legally 'persons' (*October 18*). Tours western Canada (*October 30-December

6). James Robb (Finance) dies of pneumonia (*November 11*). Appoints Dunning (Railways & Canals) to be Finance minister (*November 26*). Canada resumes diplomatic relations with the U.S.S.R. (*December 20*). Thomas Crerar, former Progressive leader, enters cabinet as Railways & Canals minister (*December 30*).

1930: Discusses water-power rights with Ontario Premier Howard Ferguson and Quebec Premier Louis Taschereau (*January 24*). Appoints Cairine Wilson as the first woman to the Senate (*February 5*). Convinced by fortune teller Bleaney to call an election (*February 8*). Indicates he will not give federal money to insurance schemes in provinces with Conservative governments: "I would not give them a five-cent piece." (*April 3*). Vacations in Bermuda (*April 11-21*). Marine & Fisheries depart-ment is split, with Cardin continuing as Marine minister (*June 14*); Cyrus Macmillan enters cabinet three days later as Fisheries minister. James Ralston (National Defence) becomes the first Pensions & National Health minister (*June 19*). Appoints Vincent Massey as High Commissioner to Britain (*July 24*). Canada's 17th federal election: re-elected in Prince Albert defeating George Braden (Conservative); loses government to Bennett's Conservatives (*July 28*). Resigns as Prime Minister (*August 6*). **King's second government ends.**

1931: A House committee investigating the Beauharnois hydro-electric agreement finds that his friend W.L. McDougald may have used his influence to get the agreement approved (*June 10*). Denies knowledge that McDougald used Beauharnois funds to pay for their Bermuda hotel (*July 22*). Appoints Massey acting president of the National Liberal Federation to centralize campaign donations, a lesson learned from the Beauharnois scandal (*October 20*).

1932: Attends his first séance in Brockville, Ont., conducted by Etta Wreidt of Detroit (*February 21*); later invites her to Ottawa and Kingsmere so he can speak to his departed family members and Laurier. McDougald resigns from the Senate over the Beauharnois scandal (*May 3*). Announces the Liberal policy favouring the creation of a central federal bank (*September 9*).

1933: Establishes the Liberal party as holding the middle ground between the Conservatives on the right and the new Co-operative Commonwealth Federation on the left (*February 27*); also formally endorses the creation of unemployment insurance. Kingmere escapes unscathed following a Gatineau fire (*July 5*). Tours the West (*July 20-August 22*). Reluctantly attends a Liberal summer school organized by Massey in Port Hope, Ont., to discuss party policy (*September 3-9*). Experiences table-rapping spiritualism and begins engaging in it regularly with Joan Patterson (*November 13*).

1934: Unveils a Centennial plaque in Toronto listing the city's first council led by his grandfather, William Lyon Mackenzie, in 1834 (*March 6*). Loses 40 pounds following a strict diet begun the previous November (*July 24*); regains it within a few years. Visits England, France and Italy (*September 29-November 23*).

1935: Refuses to move a non-confidence vote against the Speech from the Throne, convinced that Bennett's government doesn't yet have its 'New Deal' legislation ready (*January 21*). Turns down a knighthood offered to him by Bennett (*April 18*). Buys his first ruins for Kingsmere: a round bay window from a house being demolished in Ottawa (*May 9*). Attends a memorial service for former governor general Lord Byng at Ottawa's Capitol Theatre (*June 9*). His biography is published by Norman Rogers, an update of a 1925 book by John Lewis; largely overseen by King (*August 1*). Broadcasts the first of three radio speeches as a response to Bennett's winter broadcasts (*August 1*). Canada's 18th federal election: re-elected in Prince Albert defeating Alexander Bedard (Social Credit); his Liberals win a majority (*October 14*). **King's third government (1935-1948).** Becomes

Prime Minister, Secretary of State for External Affairs and Privy Council President for the third time (*October 23*). Skelton, External Affairs deputy minister, recommends economic sanctions against Italy for its invasion of Ethiopia (*October 25*); endorsed by cabinet. John Buchan, now Lord Tweedsmuir, becomes Canada's 15th Governor General (*November 2*). W.A. Riddell, Canada's representative at the League of Nations in Geneva, makes a motion to include oil supplies in the sanctions against Italy; his action is contrary to the government's directive that he take no active part in the debate (*November 2*); League of Nations decides to let Italy occupy Ethiopia rather than risk a European war with Mussolini. Appoints James Gardiner, former Saskatchewan premier, as Agriculture minister (*November 4*). Visits Washington to finalize a Canadian-U.S. tariff agreement with President Franklin D. Roosevelt and Secretary of State Cordell Hull (*November 8-10*). Returns to Washington to sign tariff agreement (*November 15*). Vacations in Georgia with Skelton (*November 16*). Publically disavows Riddell's support for oil sanctions against Italy (*November 28*). Chairs the eighth Dominion-Provincial Conference in Ottawa (*December 9-13*); the provinces receive larger relief grants and all agree to set up procedures to amend the constitution.

1936: George V dies (*January 21*); his son becomes Edward VIII. 18th Parliament opens; nominates Pierre Casgrain as 19th Speaker of the House (*February 6*). Lapointe (Justice) meets with eight provincial attorneys general to discuss a procedure to amend the BNA Act (*February*); New Brunswick doesn't attend, scuttling the amendment efforts. Norman Rogers (Labour) introduces the National Employment Commission to advise government on dealing with unemployment (*March 30*). Lapointe (Justice) introduces an amendment to the BNA Act giving provinces the power to levy indirect taxes (*May 14*); later defeated in the Senate. Section 98 of the Criminal Code, which made it a crime to advocate the use of force in changing governments, is eliminated (*June 19*). Closes the relief camps created by the Conservatives (*June 30*). Canadians enlist to fight in the Spanish civil war (*July*). Sails for Europe (*September 13*). Tells the League of Nations in Geneva that Canada would not enter a European war without approval of Parliament (*September 20*). Visits Paris, Vimy and London (*October*). Meets with Edward VIII (*October 27*). Returns to Canada (*November*). Appoints C.D. Howe (Railways & Canals, Marine) the first Transport minister (*November 2*). Canadian Radio Broadcasting Commission (CRBC) becomes Canadian Broadcasting Corporation (CBC) (*November 2*). Tells British Prime Minister Stanley Baldwin that voluntary abdication would be the honorable way out for Edward VIII if he marries commoner Wallis Simpson (*November 28*). Appoints Crerar (Immigration & Colonization, Interior & Indian Affairs) as the first Mines & Resources minister (*December 1*). Edward VIII abdicates so he can marry Simpson (*December 11*); succeeded by his brother George VI. Cabinet agrees to add $15 million to the $20-million defence budget (*December 18*).

1937: Supports a Supreme Court decision that most of the Conservative legislation in the mid-1930s is invalid because it infringes on provincial jurisdiction (*January 28*). Meets with Ontario Premier Mitchell Hepburn in Toronto and learns that Ontario isn't interested in a St. Lawrence seaway until a dispute over use of Quebec hydro power is resolved (*March 4*). Visits Washington to meet with President Roosevelt who hopes to improve U.S.-British relations (*March 5*). Vacations in New York City and Virginia (*March 8-18*). Quebec passes the Padlock Law permitting the government to lock any building suspected of harbouring Communist sympathizers (*March 24*). Ottawa's refusal to support Hepburn's campaign against unions causes the premier to split with the federal Liberals. Trans-Canada Airlines is created by an act of Parliament (*April 10*). Sails for England (*April 23*). Takes part in the coronation procession of George VI (*May 12*). Attends the Imperial Conference (*May 14-June 24*); refuses to commit Canada to Commonwealth foreign and defence policies without the approval of Parliament. Meets with Adolf Hitler, German Chancellor, in Berlin; telling him that Canada would support Britain in the event of a war (*June 29*). Opens the Canadian pavilion at the Paris Exposition (*July 2*). Appoints a Royal Commission on Dominion-Provincial relations (known as the Rowell-Sirois Commission), prompted by the grants given to Manitoba and Saskatchewan to help avoid economic default (*August 15*). Ottawa disallows Alberta legislation requiring banks to lend money at provincially determined rates (*September 5*). Indicates he will extend H.A. Bruce's term as Ontario's Lieutenant-Governor, but Hepburn prefers another candidate (*September 28*); following more than a month of flip-flopping by Hepburn, King appoints Albert Mathews to the position. Governor General's awards for literature are established (*November 24*). Denies Hepburn's request to export hydroelectricity to the U.S. (*November 25*); Hepburn confronts the federal cabinet and complains to the media, without success. Ontario's Hepburn and Quebec's Duplessis oppose the continuation of federal subsidies to western farmers (*December 10*).

1938: Supreme Court upholds Ottawa's disallowance of Alberta's banking legislation (*March 4*). Unemployed workers occupy Vancouver's post office and art gallery to protest B.C. Premier Duff Pattullo's restriction of relief funds (*May 20*); Ottawa authorizes the RCMP to evict the workers using tear gas. Unveils a plaque on Parliament Hill to the Famous Five, Alberta women who fought to have women legally defined as persons (*June 11*). Ottawa disallows Alberta's legislation to waive debts (*June 13*); the move is not contested by Premier William Aberhart. Officially opens the Mackenzie Heritage Printing Museum, his grandfather's print shop in Queenston, Ont. (*June 18*). Another unemployment riot, Bloody Sunday, breaks out in Vancouver (*June 19*). Robert Manion is elected Conservative leader, replacing Bennett; the party changes its name from Liberal-Conservative to National Government (*July 7*). Advised by Lapointe (Justice) to avoid disallowing Quebec's Padlock Law or risk alienating Liberal voters in the province (*July 5*). Joins U.S. President Roosevelt to open the Ivy Lea bridge across the St. Lawrence River; Roosevelt promotes the idea of a St. Lawrence seaway in his speech (*August 18*). Paul Martin, Canada's 21st Prime Minister, is born in Windsor, Ont. (*August 28*). Sets up an inquiry into the government's bren gun weapons contract with Hahn that did not go to tender (*September 1*); government is exonerated. Seriously ill at Kingsmere with sciatica (*September 1-19*). Cabinet refuses to comment on Germany's occupation of the Sudetenland in Czechoslovakia, without Parliament's consent (*September 23*). Vacations in New York, followed by a cruise to Bermuda, Jamaica and Cuba with Skelton (*October 8-November 7*). Signs a trade agreement with Britain and the U.S. (*November 17*). Learns that Hepburn intends to campaign against the Liberals in the next federal election (*November 21*). Opposes Crerar's (Mines & Resources) wish to admit 10,000 Jewish refugees to Canada (*December 1*). King's leadership is endorsed by the party, effectively ending Hepburn's influence (*December 17*). Refuses to let the British Royal Air Force set up training schools in Canada or train Canadian pilots for the RAF unless under the auspices of Canada (*December 31*); RAF is permitted to send its pilots to Canada for training.

1939: Writes Adolf Hitler asking him "not to imperil or destroy what you have already accomplished" (*January*); receives a conciliatory response six months later. *Globe & Mail* publisher George McCullagh forms Leadership League, calling for a coalition federal government and a return to traditional values (*February12*); membership grows to over 100,000 but it folds less than three months later. King indicates the government would recommend Canada's involvement in a possible war between Britain and Germany (*March 20*). Brian Mulroney, Canada's 18th Prime Minister, is born in Baie Comeau, Que. (*March 20*). The Wheat Board Amendment Act is introduced, setting the minimum wheat price at 60 cents a bushel (*March 27*); opposition from western farmers results in raising the minimum price to 70 cents. Mackenzie (National Defence) says $6 million will be used to train pilots, including 50 British pilots (*April 26*). National Film Board is launched (*May 2*). George VI becomes the first reigning monarch to visit Canada (*May 17*). Accompanies the King and Queen through Quebec, Ontario, western Canada, Washington, New York and the Maritimes (*May 17-June 16*). George VI addresses the Houses of Parliament (*May 19*). Joe Clark, Canada's 16th Prime Minister, is born in High River, Alta. (*June 5*). Indicates he is not interested in accepting Jewish refugees fleeing Nazi Germany aboard a ship, responding the same way as most countries in North and South America (*June 8*). Cabinet agrees that Canada will likely have to go to war if Germany invades Poland (*August 24*). Order-in-Council is passed to buy up to $7 million worth of U.S. airplanes (*August 25*). Cabinet implements the War Measures Act after Germany invades Poland (*September 1*). Britain and France declare war on Germany (*September 3*). Wartime Prices and Trade Board established to prevent hoarding and profiteering (*September 3*). Tells U.S. President Roosevelt that Canada is still neutral, which means the U.S. can still send weapons to Canada without affecting its own neutrality (*September 5*). Appoints Ralston, who has returned to politics, to replace an ailing Dunning as Finance minister (*September 6*). During the war debate, CCF leader J.S. Woodsworth is the only MP to speak against entering the war (*September 7*). A $100 million War Appropriation Bill is passed (*September 9*). Canada declares war on Germany (*September 10*). Assures Manion there will be another parliamentary session before a federal election (*September 13*). First meeting of cabinet's emergency council (*September 15*); military chiefs recommend a budget of $491,689,000 to equip three divisions for the war; cabinet nearly halves the amount for two divisions. Announces that one Canadian division will be sent overseas (*September 19*). Appoints Rogers (Labour) as National Defence minister (*September 19*) who recommends General A.G.L. McNaughton, chairman of the National Research Council, as commander of the expeditionary force to Europe (*September 22*). Advised by Quebec ministers Lapointe, Cardin and Chubby Power that the only way to prevent Duplessis' election as Quebec premier is the threat of their cabinet resignations; their absence from Ottawa would raise the fear of conscription in Quebec (*September 25*). Asked again by Britain to participate in an air force training program (*September 26*). Duplessis defeated in Quebec by Adelard Godbout (Liberal) with the help of federal Liberals (*October 25*). Cabinet's emergency council becomes the war committee (*December 5*). Signs an agreement with Britain to create the British Commonwealth Air Training Plan, with Canada's cost being $313 million (*December 17*); it's expected to be Canada's primary war contribution as part of King's effort to wage a war of limited liability. First Canadian Division of troops arrives in England (*December 17*).

1940: Considers calling an election in reaction to Hepburn's resolution in Ontario criticizing the federal government's war effort (*January 18*). Sixth Session, 18th Parliament opens; Lord Tweedsmuir surprisingly announces the dissolution of Parliament; King decided that morning to call an election, despite his promise to Manion there would be another session (*January 25*). Tweedsmuir suffers a stroke (*February 6*); dies five days later. Chief Justice Sir Lyman Duff becomes Admin-istrator (*February 11*). Canada's 19th federal election: re-elected in Prince Albert defeating Robert Manville (Nationl-Unity-Conservative); his government wins the largest majority since Confederation (*March 26*). Suggests to cabinet that the Earl of Athlone be appointed the next Governor General; feels wartime prevents the consideration of a Canadian appointment (*March 28*). Munitions & Supply department is established with Howe (Transport) as minister (*April 9*). Vacations in Virginia Beach, Virginia (*April 12-23*). Meets with Roosevelt at Warm Springs, Georgia (*April 23-24*). Visits John D. Rockefeller Jr. at Williamsburg, Virginia (*April 24-26*). Meets with U.S. Secretary of State Cordell Hull and Roosevelt in Washington (*April 27-29*). Returns to Ottawa (*May 1*). Richard Hanson chosen as Conservative House leader to replace defeated party leader Manion (*May 13*). War Measures Act bans communist and fascist groups (*May*). Rowell-Sirois Commission tables its report on federal-provincial relations (*May*). 19th Parliament opens; nominates James Glen to be the 20th Speaker of the House (*May 16*). Asks Roosevelt for U.S. training aircraft (*May 19*); Roosevelt says no, but indicates the U.S. will enter the war if Britain is defeated. Agrees to send all of Canada's destroyers to Britain's aid (*May 23*). Appoints Power (Postmaster General) as the first National Defence for Air minister (*May 23*). Asked by Roosevelt to approach Churchill about sending the British fleet to the U.S. in the event of a British surrender (*May 25*); Churchill replies he has no intention of surrendering. About 338,000 allied soldiers, including Canadians, are evacuated from Dunkirk, France (*May 27-June 4*). Announces the appointment of the Earl of Athlone as Canada's 16th Governor General (*June 2*). Rogers (National Defence) killed in an airplane crash while travelling to speak at the Empire and Canadian Clubs in Toronto (*June 10*); his loss is a major blow to King. Canada declares war on Italy (*June 10*). France surrenders to Germany (*June 16*). Suggests to Churchill that Canada might use the Royal Navy in the event of a British defeat (*June 17*); Churchill again insists that Britain is not going to surrender. Introduces the National Resources Mobilization Act requiring Canadians to register for service within Canada (*June 18*). Attempts unsuccessfully to attract Montreal and Toronto businessmen to join cabinet; instead, only Nova Scotia Premier Angus L. Macdonald agrees to serve (*June 26*). Moves Ralston (Finance) to National Defence (*July 5*). Conservatives refuse to sit on the cabinet war committee (*July 11*). Appoints Angus Macdonald as the first National Defence for Naval Services minister, Gardiner (Agriculture) as the first National War Services minister, and Power (National Defence for Air) as the first National Defence associate minister (*July 12*). Supports U.S. interest in establishing air facilities in Newfoundland (*July 13*). Camillien Houde, mayor of Montreal, publicly opposes registering Canadians, calling it the first step towards conscription; urges Quebecers not to register (*August 2*) and is arrested three days later by the RCMP, then placed in an internment camp where he spends the next four years. King meets with Roosevelt in Ogdensburg, New York, and agrees to establish a Permanent Joint Board of Defence to discuss common defence programs; known as the Ogdensburg Agreement (*August 17*). Registration of Canadians takes place (*August 19-21*). U.S. leases air and naval bases in Newfoundland for 99 years; in exchange, Britain receives 50 destroyers (*September 3*). Germany, Italy and Japan form an alliance (*September 27*). Cabinet agrees to pursue the development of a St. Lawrence seaway if agreement can be reached with U.S., Ontario and Quebec (*October 8*). First 30,000 home defence conscripts report for their 30-day term of service (*October 9*). Cabinet war committee opposes sending Canadian troops in England to Africa to gain battle experience (*December 4*). Howe (Munitions & Supply) is rescued after his ship is sunk near Iceland by the Germans (*December 14*).

1941: Chairs the ninth Dominion-Provincial Conference in Ottawa (*January 14-15*); no agreement reached on recommendations in the Rowell-Sirois report. Cabinet war committee agrees to a 1941 defence budget of $1.3 billion, extending compulsory military training from one to four weeks, and creating a tank brigade (*January 28*). Skelton, Canada's top diplomat at external affairs and a close friend of King, dies in Ottawa (*January 28*). Asks Roosevelt to postpone St. Lawrence seaway talks until after the war (*January 29*). Rejects a suggestion from CPR President Sir Edward Beatty that R.B. Bennett be asked to join the cabinet (*February 19*). Lays the cornerstone of Ottawa's Lord Elgin Hotel, a building with pillars and cladding he suggested (*February 27*). Signs the St. Lawrence seaway agreement with U.S. (*March 19*). Visits Washington for talks with Roosevelt, Hull and U.S. Treasurer Henry Morgenthau (*April 16-17*). Visits Roosevelt at Hyde Park where Canada agrees to sell defence materials to the U.S. to help pay for the war effort (*April 20*). Requests stones for his ruins from London's Westminster Hall after it is damaged by bombs (*May 11*).

Appoints Joseph Thorson to cabinet as National War Service minister who is also responsible for public information (*June 11*). Helps launch the first of nine Victory Loan campaigns that raise approximately $12 billion to help pay for the war (*June 15*). Speaks at Princeton University commencement ceremony and to the Canadian Society in New York City (*June 17*). Tours the West (*June 24-July 12*). The Unemployment Insurance Act comes into effect (*July*). His Irish terrier, Pat, dies (*July 15*). Not invited to meet with Churchill and Roosevelt near Newfoundland where the Atlantic Charter is announced (*August 9*). Takes the first overseas air flight by a Prime Minister, to England with diplomats Norman Robertson and Georges Vanier (*August 19*). Visits Canadian troops at Aldershot (*August 23,26*). Visits (and dances!) with the Churchills at Chequers (*August 23-24*). Stays with George VI at Balmoral Castle (*August 30-31*). Meets with British General Montgomery at Dover (*September 5*). Returns to Ottawa (*September 7*). Etta Wreidt, his favourite spiritual medium, dies (*September 15*). The Pattersons' terrier, Pat II, comes to live with him (*October 11*). Announces wage and price freezes by the Wartime Prices & Trade Board (*October 18*). Meets with Roosevelt at Hyde Park, New York (*November 1-2*). Regrets learning his old adversary Meighen has agreed to return as Conservative party leader to replace Hanson (*November 8*). Lapointe (Justice) becomes seriously ill with cancer (*November 8*); dies in Montreal 18 days later. Canadian troops arrive in Hong Kong to support the British garrison (*November 16*); Japan invades a month later. Attends the centenary of Laurier's birth in St. Lin, Que. (*November 20*). Canadian Institute of Public Opinion, founded by U.S.'s George Gallop, publishes the results of its first poll, indicating voters would release the government from its pledge to avoid conscription (*November 29*). Attends Lapointe's funeral in Quebec City (*November 29*); asks Quebec premier Adélard Godbout to enter cabinet as Justice minister, but he declines; Cardin (Transport) suggests Quebec lawyer Louis St. Laurent for the job. Following another refusal from Godbout, King asks St. Laurent to become Justice minister (*December 5*). Canada declares war on Japan, prior to Britain and the U.S., following the Japanese attack on Pearl Harbor and Manila (*December 7*). Threats of Japanese air raids black out British Columbia cities for three nights (*December 8*). Uses Manitoba's resolution calling for conscription as a reason to consider a national plebiscite on the issue, thus avoiding a potential split in cabinet and the House (*December 17*). St. Pierre and Miquelon off the Newfoundland coast are taken over by Free French troops (*December 24*); Canada discouraged the takeover, but accepts it. Two Canadian battalions fall to the Japanese in Hong Kong (*December 25*). Meets with Churchill and Roosevelt in Washington (*December 26*). Returns to Ottawa with Churchill, who becomes a member of Canada's Privy Council (*December 29*). Churchill addresses Parliament with his famous "Some chicken … Some neck" speech and poses for portraits by photographer Yousef Karsh (*December 30*).

1942: In by-elections, Meighen is defeated in York South and steps down as Conservative leader while St. Laurent (Justice) is elected in Quebec East (*February 9*). Announces an Order-in-Council for the detention of all persons of Japanese origin on the west coast (*February 26*). Plebiscite Bill about conscription is passed (*March 4*). Visits Washington to meet with Roosevelt and the Pacific Council (*April 15*). Canadians vote in favour of conscription (*April 27*). Introduces an amendment to the Mobilization Act removing restrictions against conscription (*May 11*); Cardin (Public Works, Transport) resigns in opposition to conscription. Persuades Ralston (National Defence) to remain in cabinet after he threatens to resign if conscription isn't implemented (*June 12*). Visits Washington to meet with Roosevelt, Churchill and the Pacific Council (*June 25*). House votes in favour of the Conscription Bill (*July 23*). Over 5,000 Canadian troops take part in the raid on Dieppe, France; 900 are killed and 2,000 wounded (*August 19*). Churchill requests that General McNaughton be sent to Moscow to discuss a northern European military plan favoured by Churchill; Canada refuses to place its commanding officer in such a vulnerable position

(*September 22*). Canadian warplanes make first attacks against Japanese forces on Kiska Island in the Aleutians (*September 28*). Canada ceases to recognize the Vichy government in France (*November 9*). Visits Washington for talks with Roosevelt (*December 4-6*). Manitoba premier John Bracken is elected Conservative party leader; succeeds in having the party renamed Progressive Conservative (*December 11*).

Namesake dies in WW2

The Second World War became very personal for King on September 27, 1943, when he learned that his nephew, named William Lyon Mackenzie King, was lost and presumed dead after his ship was torpedoed by the Germans. Lyon, a doctor and naval officer, had been particularly close to King after the death of his own father, King's brother Max. Despite the loss, King was comforted by "the honour which one feels in having one's own do what is heroic and right."

1943: Declares Ottawa Civic Hospital extraterritorial so that Netherlands Queen Juliana's newborn daughter, Margriet, could claim her mother's Dutch nationality (*January 19*). Hanson resigns as Conservative House leader following a heart attack and is succeeded by Gordon Graydon (*January 27*); Bracken is still waiting to contest a by-election. Cabinet War Committee reluctantly agrees to Churchill's request to allow the U.S. to take over Canada's shipping space in Britain to bring in American pilots (*March 17*). Meets with Churchill and Roosevelt in Washington to discuss the invasion of Sicily (*May 18-21*). Reprimands the Joint Defence Board for planning a joint attack on the Aleutian Islands without approval from each government (*May 27*). Meets with Czechoslovakian President Eduard Benes who addresses Parliament (*June 3*). Manion, former Conservative leader, dies in Ottawa (*July 2*). Canadian troops participate in the invasion of Sicily (*July 9*). Meets with Churchill in Quebec City (*August 10-11*). Takes part in the Quebec Conference at the Citadel in Quebec City with Churchill and Roosevelt (*August 17-24*). Welcomes Roosevelt to Parliament Hill (*August 25*). Meets with Churchill and the Cabinet War Committee in Quebec City (*August 31*). Learns that his nephew, Dr. William Lyon Mackenzie King, is missing in action in the Mediterranean and presumed dead (*September 27*). His leadership is reaffirmed at the Liberal convention in Ottawa (*September 27-28*). General McNaughton submits his resignation to protest Ralston's (National Defence) suggestion he is no longer able to command troops in actual combat; later apologizes to Ralston after learning he hadn't made the remarks, but still asks to retire as soon as a new Canadian commander is appointed (*November 10*). Canadian legation in Washington becomes an embassy (*November 11*). Meets with writer Emil Ludwig who begins work on the Prime Minister's biography (*November 23*). Broadcasts a speech called 'The Fight Against Inflation' (*December 4*). Meets with Hull (U.S. Secretary of State) in Washington (*December 6*). Vacations in Williamsburg, Virginia, then visits John D. Rockefeller Jr. and Mrs. Andrew Carnegie in New York (*December 7-15*). Canadian victory at Ortona, Italy (*December 28*).

1944: Appoints Thibaudeau Rinfret as the ninth Chief Justice of the Supreme Court, succeeding Duff (*January 7*). Cabinet endorses the concept of a family allowance (*January 11*). Celebrates Sir William Mulock's 100th birthday in Toronto (*January 19*). Cabinet agrees that Canadian pilots in the Royal Air Force should form Royal Canadian Air Force squadrons that would be controlled by Canada (*February 9*). Labour Relations Code is introduced (*February 17*). Howe (Munitions & Supply) reaffirms the government's intention of maintaining control of international aviation through Trans-Canada Airways, scuttling a bid by CPR to enter aviation (*March 17*). General Harry Crerar appointed

Commander-in-Chief of the Canadian Army, replacing an ailing McNaughton (*March 20*). Flies to England (*April 26*). Attends the Prime Ministers Conference (*May 1-15*). Meets with George VI (*May 3*). Spends a weekend with the Churchills at Chequers (*May 6-7*). Becomes the first Canadian Prime Minister to address British Parliament (*May 11*). Views the Normandy invasion fleet at Portsmouth with Churchill (*May 12*). Visits the Canadian bomber group at Goldborough (*May 16*), and the Canadian army the next day. Meets with General Montgomery (*May 18*). Arrives back in Canada (*May 21*). Receives a thunderous welcome in the House for his efforts in England (*May 22*). Meets with Australian Prime Minister John Curtin who addresses Parliament the following day (*May 31*). Tells the nation that nearly 30,000 Canadian troops are taking part in the D-Day invasion (*June 6*). Tommy Douglas becomes the first CCF leader to win an election, becoming Saskatchewan's 10th premier (*June 15*). Conservatives begin to press for conscription (*June 19*). Checks final proofs of *Canada and the Fight for Freedom*, a book of his wartime speeches (*June 21*). Reconstruction and Veterans Affairs departments are established (*June 30*). Meets with New Zealand Prime Minister Peter Fraser who addresses Parliament (*June 30*). General Charles de Gaulle of the Free French government visits Ottawa (*July 11*). National Health & Welfare department is established (*July 24*). Family Allowance Bill receives unanimous approval on its second reading (*July 28*). Celebrates his 25th anniversary as Liberal leader at a Chateau Laurier dinner in his honour in Ottawa (*August 7*). Meets with Churchill and Roosevelt again in Quebec City, but plays a smaller role (*September 12-16*). Tells a Liberal gathering in Quebec City that conscription probably won't be necessary as the war is going well (*September 14*). General Kenneth Stuart requests an additional 15,000 soldiers and recommends conscription (*October 15*). Appoints Brooke Claxton as the first National Health & Welfare minister (*October 18*). Launches the 7th Victory Loans drive with U.S. actress Shirley Temple on Parliament Hill *(October 21*). Ralston, Macdonald, James Ilsley, William P. Mulock and Colin Gibson threaten to resign after cabinet votes 13 to 8 against imposing conscription (*October 31*). Asks General McNaughton to become National Defence minister, then informs Ralston at a cabinet meeting that his two-year-old resignation letter has been accepted; other dissenters remain in cabinet (*November 1*). Members of cabinet demand a deadline date for conscription if volunteers can't be found (*November 20*). Offers to resign in favour of a pro-conscription leader (*November 21*); cabinet rejects the suggestion. Decides conscription will be necessary to avoid a cabinet split after McNaughton (National Defence) indicates there is no hope of finding enough volunteers (*November 22*). Chubby Power (National Defence associate, National Defence for Air) resigns in protest against his party's switch to conscription (*November 23*). Appeals to the House and to Quebec members of his party to support the reluctant switch to conscription (*November 27*). Wins a confidence vote in the House; 19 of his Quebec members support him (*December 8*). Becomes a life member of Ottawa's Parliamentary Press Gallery on his 70th birthday (*December 17*).

1945: McNaughton (National Defence) loses by-election in Grey North (*February 5*). The Prime Minister speaks the first words over the CBC's new international broadcasting service (*February 25*). Visits Washington to discuss Yalta Conference with Roosevelt (*March 9*). Attends Roosevelt's funeral in Hyde Park, New York (*April 15*). Appoints seven new cabinet ministers, including Paul Martin Sr. (Secretary of State), Lionel Chevrier (Transport) and Douglas Abbott (National Defence for Naval Services) (*April 18*). Cabinet War Committee is abolished; war decisions to be made by the entire cabinet (*April 19*). Attends the founding conference of the United Nations in San Francisco, California (*April 25-May 14*). His former Public Works minister, Cardin, announces the formation of Le Front National party in Quebec (*April 27*); lack of support causes Cardin to run as an Independent Liberal. Germany surrenders (*May 7*). V-E (Victory in Europe) celebrations on Parliament Hill; King and St. Laurent broadcast from San Francisco (*May 8*). Spends four days campaigning in Prince Albert where he fears he may lose (*May 19-22*). Canada's 20th federal election: loses seat in Prince Albert by 129 votes to Edward Bowerman; barely wins a majority government (*June 11*). Returns to San Francisco (*June 22*) with St. Laurent (Justice) to sign the United Nations charter (*June 26*). First Family Allowance 'baby bonus' cheques issued under the Family Allowance Bill (*July 20*). William MacDiarmid offers his Glengarry seat to him (*July*). Wins the by-election in Glengarry (*August 6*). Chairs the 10th Dominion-Provincial Conference in Ottawa to discuss post-war reconstruction and centralized taxation (*August 6-10*). Broadcasts his announcement of Victory in Japan Day (*August 12*), but Japan doesn't actually surrender until two days later. Appoints Abbott (National Defence for Naval Services) as National Defence minister, replacing the twice-defeated McNaughton (*August 21*). General Charles de Gaulle makes a second visit to Ottawa (*August 28*). Canada's first nuclear reactor begins operation at Chalk River, Ont. (*September 5*). 20th Parliament opens; nominates Gaspard Fauteux to be the 21st Speaker of the House (*September 6*). Igor Gouzenko, a cipher clerk at the Soviet embassy in Ottawa, unsuccessfully asks to see St. Laurent (Justice) with documents implicating the Russians of espionage in Canada (*September 6*). Gouzenko is picked up by police and makes a statement to the RCMP about Russian agents in the External Affairs department and the National Laboratories in Ottawa and Montreal (*September 7*). King tells St. Laurent (Justice) he wants him to assume leadership of the Liberal party (*September 19*). Visits Washington to brief Truman on the Gouzenko affair (*September 30*). Sails for England (*October 1*). Cabinet passes a secret Order-in-Council empowering the RCMP to detain and interrogate persons suspected of giving information to a foreign power (*October 6*). Briefs British Prime Minister Clement Attlee on the Gouzenko affair (*October 7*). Discusses the possibility of Pearson in External Affairs serving as Secretary General of the United Nations (*October 12*). Begins sitting for his portrait by Frank Salisbury (*October 13*). Canada hosts a conference in Quebec City to establish a United Nations Food and Agricultural Organization (*October 16-November 1*); Pearson is chair. King learns that Britain would like to see Newfoundland join Canada (*October 18*). Atlee agrees to have all Canadian soldiers returned to Canada by April 1946 (*October 21*). Has lunch with George VI (*October 23*). Attends a dinner in his honour in the British House of Commons (*October 24*). Sails for New York (*November 3*). Lays wreaths at Arlington Cemetery, Virginia, with U.S. President Harry Truman and Atlee (*November 11*). Discusses use of the atomic bomb with Truman and Atlee (*November 12-15*). Meets in Ottawa with Atlee who addresses Parliament (*November 15-19*). An agreement is reached at the Dominion-Provincial Conference to set up an economic committee (*November 26-29*).

1946: Meets with U.S. General Dwight D. Eisenhower in Ottawa (*January 9-10*); tells him Castle Mountain near Banff is being renamed Mount Eisenhower. Creates the Central Housing and Mortgage Corporation to help house families of returning soldiers (*January*). Gouzenko affair is made public; a royal commission is set up investigate (*February 15*); as a result, four civil servants and MP Fred Rose are arrested for giving information to the Soviet Union (*March 4*). Canada agrees to loan Britain $1.25 billion for post-war reconstruction; Britain's $425 million balance owing on the Air Training Plan is cancelled (*March 6*). Agrees with Britain's willingness to grant India complete independence (*March 15*). Announces the appointment of Viscount Alexander of Tunis as Canada's 17th Governor General (*March 21*). Sails for England (*May 13*). Canadian Citizenship Act passes, making Canada the first Commonwealth country to establish its own nationality (*May 14*). Attends the Prime Ministers Conference (*May 20-23*). Meets with George VI twice (*May 24, 30*). Attends one of his most 'remarkable' séances, led by medium Helen Hughes (*May 30*). Becomes Canada's longest-serving Prime Minister, passing Macdonald; honoured with a supper at 10 Downing Street in London (*June 7*). Rides in London's Victory parade (*June 8*). Saskatchewan introduces the first program of socialized medicine

(*July 1*). Rejects a proposal for a national flag that would be a White Ensign with a maple leaf and Union Jack, knowing that Quebec would oppose the latter (*July 12*). Meets Gouzenko for the first time (*July 16*). Sails for England (*July 19*). Canada agrees to send 600 million bushels of wheat to Britain over the next four years (*July 24*). Becomes a member of the Bench at Gray's Inn law court in London (*July 26*). Attends the Paris Peace Conference (*July 29-August 23*). Visits Normandy battlefields (*August 10-11*). Atomic Energy Control Act is passed (*August 13*). Made an honorary citizen of Dieppe, as is Vanier (*August 18*). Observes the Nuremberg war trials (*August 22*). Sails for Canada (*August 26*). Resigns as Secretary of State for External Affairs (*September 3*). Appoints St. Laurent (Justice) as the first full-time Secretary of State for External Affairs; Pearson becomes under-secretary (*September 4*). Arranges to have F.W. Gibson classify his personal papers (September 10). Attends the opening session of the United Nations General Assembly in Flushing Meadows, New York (*October 23*). Visits John D. Rockefeller Jr. in Tarrytown, New York (*October 26-27*). Meets with Truman in Washington (*October 28*). Offered the chancellorship of McGill University; declines since he doesn't know when he'll retire (*November 13*). Appoints Abbott (National Defence) as Finance minister to replace Ilsley who becomes Justice minister (*December 10*). Cabinet discusses the feasibility of Newfoundland joining Confederation; tells Britain it wants to settle affairs with the nine existing provinces first (*December 27*).

1947: Receives Canadian citizenship certificate 0001 at the first citizenship ceremony for 26 new Canadians (*January 3*). Maj.-Gen. Georges Vanier signs Canadian peace treaties with Italy, Romania, Hungry and Finland (*February 10*). Becomes ill with bronchitis, influenza and pneumonia (*February 18-March 10*). Announces that the Canadian garrison will be withdrawing from Germany (*March 10*). Kim Campbell, Canada's 19th Prime Minister, is born in Port Alberni, B.C. (*March 10*). Recuperates from illness in Virginia Beach and Williamsburg, Virginia (*March 26-April 21*). Meets with Truman and Hull in Washington (*April 21-23*). Government announces immigration policy giving priority to relatives and refugees; Asian immigration is restricted, but restrictions on Chinese immigration in B.C. are repealed (*May 1*). Attends the unveiling of his and Borden's portraits on Parliament Hill (*June 10*). Truman addresses Parliament (*June 11*). Newfoundland delegation comes to Ottawa to discuss possibility of joining Confederation; Joseph Smallwood is the delegation secretary (*June 24-October*); cabinet generally favours it although he questions the financial burden. Bennett, Canada's 11th Prime Minister, dies in England (*June 26*). Asks St. Laurent (External Affairs) again about succeeding him (*July 18*); St. Laurent expresses a desire to return to law practice. Hedley Bridges (Fisheries) dies of throat paralysis in Ottawa (*August 10*). His second terrier, Pat II, is put down following an illness (*August 11*). Canada accepts a seat on the United Nations Security Council (*September 8*). Becomes a member of the Bench of the Law Society of Upper Canada (*September 18*). St. Laurent (External Affairs) indicates an interest in succeeding him (*October 1*). Governor General is given authority to fully act for the Crown in Canada (*October 1*). Canada signs the international General Agreement on Tariffs and Trade (GATT) with 22 other nations in Geneva, Switzerland (*October 30*). Trip to England (*October 31-December 4*). Canada agrees to consider giving Newfoundland full provincial status and absorbing much of its $63 million debt if a majority of Newfoundlanders approve the settlement (*November 6*). Visits Paris (*November 8*). Receives an honorary degree at the University of Brussels in Belgium (*November 10*). Visits Netherlands (*November 12*). Becomes the first Canadian to receive Britain's Order of Merit, from George VI (*November 17*). Attends the Royal wedding of Princess Elizabeth and Philip of Mountbatten at Westminster Abbey (*November 20*). Canada supports the UN resolution to partition Palestine into Jewish and Arab states (*November 29*).

1948: Becomes the longest serving prime minister in Commonwealth history, with 7,825 days in office (*January 8*). General McNaughton becomes Canada's delegate on the United Nations Security Council (*January 9*). G.S. Patterson represents Canada on the United Nations Temporary Commission for Korea, in Seoul (*January 12*); opposes Canada's involvement in the conflict. Announces intention to retire in the fall and calls for a leadership convention to choose his successor (*January 20*). Informs Britain that Canada is willing to consider a defence alliance of Atlantic countries after the Soviet Union takes over Czechoslovakia (*March 11*). Fears the introduction of compulsory military service in the U.S. could revive concerns about conscription in Canada (*March 17*). Receives an honorary degree from the College of William and Mary in Williamsburg (*April 2*). Canada becomes a founding nation of NATO, the North Atlantic Treaty Organization (*April 4*). Newfoundland holds a referendum to determine its form of government; responsible government receives 44.55 per cent of the vote, followed by joining Confederation with 41.13 per cent and government by commission at 14.32 per cent (*June 3*); there is no majority, requiring a second referendum between the top two choices. Introduces his last bill in the House, a plan for improvements in the capital region (*June 28*). Makes his final speech in the House of Commons that includes a suggestion for an official Prime Minister's residence in Ottawa (*June 30*). Ilsley (Justice) resigns to return to law practice (*June 30*). Bracken announces his resignation as Conservative leader for health reasons (*July 19*). Newfoundland's second referendum favours Confederation with 52.34 per cent of the vote, followed by responsible government at 47.66 (*July 22*); Canada announces that Newfoundland will become the 10th province. Attends the Liberal leadership convention in Ottawa where St. Laurent (External Affairs) is elected leader (*August 5-7*); receives an Irish terrier, Pat III, as a parting gift. Visits John D. Rockefeller Jr. in Seal Harbor, Maine (*August 14-20*). Irish Prime Minister John Costello announces in Ottawa that his country is ending its membership in the Commonwealth and becoming a republic (*September 7*). Appoints Lester Pearson as Secretary of State for External Affairs, moving St. Laurent (External Affairs) back to Justice (*September 10*). Visits Europe (*September 13-November 7*). Attends the third United Nations General Assembly in Paris (*September 21*). George Drew, Ontario premier, is elected leader of the Conservatives, becoming Leader of the Opposition (*October 2*). Becomes a member of the Institut de France (*October 5*). Illness prevents him playing a role at a Prime Ministers Conference while in London; St. Laurent (Prime Minister designate) flies over to take his place (*October 14*). Visited by George VI (*October 21*). Visited by Liaquat Ali Khan of Pakistan and Jawaharlal Nehru of India (*October 25*). Receives an honorary Doctor of Laws degree from London University (*October 25*). Resigns as Prime Minister and Privy Council President (*November 15*). **King's third government ends.** Given $100,000 by John D. Rockefeller Jr. to ease any retirement financial concerns and to write his memoirs (*December*).

1949: Receives the Grand Cross of the Order of the Netherlands Lion (*March 11*). Sits for his last day as an MP (*April 30*). Becomes an honorary member of the Canadian Society of Landscape Artists and Town Planners (*October 15*). Learns of plans to rebuild his boyhood home 'Woodside' in Kitchener (*November 24*). Governor General Earl Alexander hosts a 75th birthday party for him at Rideau Hall (*December 17*). Suffers a mild heart attack (*December 26*).

1950: Makes out his will, calling for most of his diaries to be destroyed (*February 28*). Listens to radio coverage of the opening of his grandfather's home, Mackenzie House, in Toronto as a museum (*May 9*). An Ottawa bridge across the Rideau Canal is named Mackenzie King Bridge (*June 10*). Suffers a chill, acute pneumonia and a second heart attack at Kingsmere (*July 20*). Dies at Kingsmere (*July 22*). Funeral is held at St. Andrew's

Presbyterian Church in Ottawa after the body lies in state on Parliament Hill (*July 26*). Buried in the family plot at Mount Pleasant Cemetery, Toronto (*July 27*).

BOOKS ABOUT KING

- **1922**: Owen McGillicuddy; *The Making of a Premier, An Outline of the Life Story of the Right Hon. W. L. Mackenzie King, C. M. G.* (Musson)
- **1925**: John Lewis; *Mackenzie King, The Man, His Achievements* (Morang)
- **1930**: Andrew Haydon; *Mackenzie King and the Liberal Party* (T. Allen)
- **1935**: Norman McLeod Rogers; *Mackenzie King* (Morang)
- **1944**: Emil Ludwig; *Mackenzie King, A Portrait Sketch* (Macmillan)
- **1945**: Paul Martin; *A Lifetime of Public Service, A Brief Biographical Sketch of Mackenzie King* (Mortimer)
- **1949**: H. Reginald Hardy; *Mackenzie, King of Canada, A Biography* (Oxford University)
- **1952**: Bruce Hutchison; *The Incredible Canadian, A Candid Portrait of Mackenzie King, His Works, His Times and His Nation* (Longmans, Green)
- **1952**: Frank Grierson; *William Lyon Mackenzie King, A Memoir Presented for the Earnest Consideration of All Patriotic Canadians*
- **1955**: H.S. Ferns & Bernard Ostry; *The Age of Mackenzie King, The Rise of the Leader* (W. Heinemann)
- **1958**: R. MacGregor Dawson; *William Lyon Mackenzie King (Vol. 1), A Political Biography, 1874-1923* (University of Toronto)
- **1960**: J.W. Pickersgill; *The Mackenzie King Record* (4 volumes) (University of Toronto)
- **1961**: R. MacGregor Dawson; *The Conscription Crisis of 1944* (University of Toronto)
- **1962**: F.A. McGregor; *The Fall and Rise of Mackenzie King, 1911-1919* (Macmillan)
- **1963**: H. Blair Neatby; *William Lyon Mackenzie King (Vol. 2), The Lonely Heights, 1924-1932* (University of Toronto)
- **1967**: Roger Graham; *The King-Byng Affair, 1926, A Question of Responsible Government* (Copp Clark)
- **1976**: C.P. Stacey; *A Very Double Life, The Private World of Mackenzie King* (Macmillan)
- **1976**: H. Blair Neatby; *William Lyon Mackenzie King (Vol. 3), The Prism of Unity, 1932-1939* (University of Toronto)
- **1976**: C.P. Stacey; *Mackenzie King and the Atlantic Triangle* (Macmillan/Maclean-Hunter)
- **1977**: J.L. Granatstein; *Mackenzie King, His Life and World* (McGraw-Hill Ryerson)
- **1977**: John English & J.O Stubbs (ed.); *Mackenzie King: Widening the Debate* (Macmillan)
- **1980**: Joy Esberey; *Knight of the Holy Spirit: A Study of William Lyon Mackenzie King* (University of Toronto)
- **1982**: Bernard Saint-Aubin; *King et son époque* (La Presse)

- **1988**: Brian Nolan; *King's War: Mackenzie King and the Politics of War 1939-1945* (Random House)
- **1998**: Paul Roazen; *Canada's King: An Essay in Political Psychology* (Mosaic)
- **2000**: Robert Wardhaugh; *Mackenzie King and the Prairie West* (University of Toronto)
- **2003**: Lian Goodall; *William Lyon Mackenzie King: Dreams and Shadows* (The Quest Library, XYZ)
- **2011**: Allan Levine; King: *William Lyon Mackenzie King: A Life Guided by the Hand of Destiny* (Douglas & McIntyre)
- **2012**: Terry Reardon; *Winston Churchill and Mackenzie King: So Similar, So Different* (Dundurn)
- **2014**: Allen Wells; *The First Canadian: William Lyon Mackenzie King 1874-1950* (Xlibris Self Publishing)
- **2014**: Julie Gilmour; *Trouble on Main Street: Mackenzie King, Reason, Race, and the 1907 Vancouver Riots* (Allen Lane Canada)
- **2017**: Christopher Dummitt; *Unbuttoned: A History of Mackenzie King's Secret Life* (McGill-Queen's University)

Leaders of the Progressive Party

1.	Thomas Crerar	1920-1922
2.	Robert Forke	1922-1926

11

R.B. Bennett

The Unrepentant Prime Minister

It was Richard Bedford Bennett's bad luck to kick off his term as Prime Minister just as Canadians started to confront the Great Depression. A wealthy millionaire comfortable inhabiting Canada's boardrooms, R.B. was ill- equipped to play the role of compassionate champion for those struggling to survive financial collapse. Seen as an out-of-touch, uncaring Conservative, he nevertheless played out of character as his mandate came to a close. His new deal promised a minimum wage and unemployment insurance – neither of which happened during his term. But his creation of two other government-intervention entities did: the Bank of Canada and the CBC.

Bennett the Politician

Prime Minister of Canada: August 7, 1930 – October 22, 1935
Length of term: 5 years, 2 months, 16 days
Parliament as Prime Minister: 17th
Age on entering office: 60
Political party: Conservative
Leader of party: October 12, 1927 – July 6, 1938
Member of Parliament: October 10, 1911 – October 6, 1917; December 6, 1921 – January 28, 1939
Ridings represented: Calgary (Alta.) 1911-1917; Calgary West (Alta.) 1921-1939
Cabinet portfolios: Justice (1921); Minister Without Portfolio (1926); Finance & Receiver General (1926, 1930-1932); Mines, Interior & Indian Affairs (acting) (1926); External Affairs (1930-1935); Privy Council President (1930-1935)
Other political posts: Town Councillor, Chatham [N.B.] (1896); North-West Territories Assembly member (1898-1905); Alberta MLA (1909-1911); Leader of the Opposition (1935-1938); British House of Lords member (1941-1947)
Titles: Canadian Privy Councillor (1921); Imperial Privy Councillor (1930); Viscount Bennett of Mickleham in the County of Surrey and of Calgary and Hopewell in the Dominion of Canada (1941)

Quotes: "To hold convictions and principles is more important than power." (speech after being chosen Conservative leader in 1927). "The old order is gone…I am for reform. And, in my mind, reform means government intervention." (first 'new deal' radio broadcast in 1934).
Lived after term: 11 years

Bennett the Man

Name: Richard Bedford Bennett
Born: July 3, 1870, Hopewell Hill, New Brunswick
Ancestry: English
Religion: United (formerly Methodist)
Education: Teaching certificate (New Brunswick Normal School, 1886); LL.B. [Bachelor of Law] (Dalhousie University, 1893)
Nicknames: Dickie, Dick, Bonfire Bennett (based on his bombastic debating style), Iron Heel Bennett (based on a 1932 anti-communism speech)
Military service: none
Occupation: teacher; lawyer; business executive
Occupation after term: retired
Publications: none
Appearance: "He was an imposing figure, six feet tall, dressed impeccably, and with the solid girth almost de rigueur among successful businessmen." (P.B. Waite in *In Search of R.B. Bennett*); "Bennett was the perfect cartoon capitalist—a top-hatted, carnationed exploiter of the masses—a Marxist's dream villain." (Gordon Donaldson in *The Prime Ministers of Canada*).
Personality: "He was a sublime egotist, clever, irascible, unsparing of himself or of others; wound up in the coils of his own nature" (P.B. Waite in *In Search of R.B. Bennett*); "He acted as though he was the smartest person in the room because he usually was." (John Boyko in *Bennett: The Rebel Who Challenged and Changed a Nation*)
Married: no
Died: June 26, 1947, Juniper Hill, Surrey, England
Age at death: 76
Cause of death: heart failure
Buried: St. Michael's Church Cemetery, Mickleham, England

Bennett was the:

- Only Prime Minister to hold four cabinet positions at one time (Prime Minister, Privy Council, Finance, External Affairs)
- Only Prime Minister who was a member of a territorial legislature (North-West Territories)
- Only Prime Minister born in New Brunswick
- Only Prime Minister who did not have a state funeral
- First Prime Minister to represent Alberta
- Second and last Prime Minister who never married
- Second Prime Minister to serve as Finance minister
- Second Prime Minister who was a member of the United church

- Third Prime Minister who was a teacher
- Fifth Prime Minister who was a member of a provincial legislature (Alberta)
- Seventh Prime Minister who was a lawyer
- Eighth Conservative Prime Minister
- Last Prime Minister to die outside Canada
- Last Prime Minister to authorize the awarding of knighthoods

Bennett's legacy
- Launched the Bank of Canada
- Created the forerunner of the Canadian Broadcasting Corporation (CBC)
- Set up the Canadian Wheat Board
- Developed the first version of employment insurance

BENNETT'S FAMILY

Bennett's Parents

Father: Henry John Bennett
Born: April 3, 1842, Hopewell Cape, New Brunswick
Occupation: shipbuilder; merchant; farmer; blacksmith; justice of the peace
Died: March 10, 1905, Hopewell Cape, New Brunswick
Age at death: 62

Mother: Henrietta Stiles
Born: July 13, 1844, Hopewell, New Brunswick
Occupation: schoolteacher
Married: January 22, 1869, New Brunswick
Died: October 1, 1914, Hopewell Cape, New Brunswick
Age at death: 70

Bennett's Brothers & Sisters (5 siblings; R.B. the oldest)

Brother: Henry 'Harry' A. Bennett (1872-1876)
Sister: Evelyn Read Bennett (1874-1929), 1 son
    Married: Dr. Horace Weldon Coates (1915)
Brother: Ronald Vivian Bennett (1876-1961), 2 sons
    Married: Elva Inch Machum; Marion Harrison Machum (Elva's sister)
Brother: George Horace Bennett (1881-1938), 1 daughter
Sister: Mildred Mariann Bennett (1889-1938), 1 son
    Married: William Duncan Herridge (1931)
Note: W.A.C. Bennett, premier of British Columbia third cousin once removed.

Bennett never married.

POLITICAL STORIES

Bennett becomes leader

The Conservatives' Winnipeg leadership convention – their first one – opened in October 1927 with two party titans considered potential leaders. The first was

Meighen, the leader who had recently stepped down. But he scuppered his chances to retain his position as party leader when he delivered a speech defending his intention to invoke conscription in any future war, a stand that needlessly infuriated the party's Quebec wing. The second was Ontario's premier, Howard Ferguson. He bungled things just as badly, however, when he pilloried Meighen's misstep with a caustic diatribe that irked the convention's delegates.

Without a clear frontrunner, six party members let their names stand for the leadership contest. Two were old Borden cabinet members who weren't seen as strong contenders: Sir Henry Drayton and Robert Rogers. Two more were Liberals who had crossed the floor and joined the Unionist coalition 10 years earlier: interim leader Hugh Guthrie and Robert Manion. The remaining two were Bennett and Montreal MP Charles Cahan.

Bennett's strong speech helped give him a commanding lead on the first ballot, but not enough for a majority. On the second ballot, he was able to draw votes from all five other candidates, giving him a majority of two votes and the leadership.

The Great Depression

Bennett came to power along with the 1930s Depression. It haunted his entire term and re-formed his ideas of welfare. Unfortunately, despite scrambling to find solutions for the imploding economy, he failed to address the suffering caused by poverty and widespread unemployment.

His first effort was to boost protective tariffs. He also tried taking over powers in the struggling provinces that weren't in a financial position to shore up their economies. Neither policy worked. Efforts to assist the unemployed without resorting to 'handouts' failed as well. The result was the creation of relief camps operated by National Defence; they functioned more like holding pens for young, single men who worked long hours on the land for little money while living in shabby conditions.

His proposed New Deal came too late to contain the frustration of those in the camps. In April 1935, hundreds of unemployed young men in British Columbia camps began leaving, coming together in Vancouver where they paraded and rallied for several months. About 1,000 decided to board boxcars and take their case to the federal government.

The enormous undertaking became known as the 'On to Ottawa Trek'. Although Bennett wasn't happy with it, he was convinced it would melt away as the trains moved east. But the protesters, who were initially feared in each town they passed through, came to represent a flashpoint for the nation's discontent over government inaction amidst economic desolation.

Bennett had the RCMP stop the trek in Regina while a small delegation was allowed to move on to Ottawa. He met with them in an angry exchange, confirming his intention to maintain law and order at all costs. On July 1, that cost was paid in Regina when the RCMP attempted to arrest the trek's leaders, sparking a riot that killed two.

Three months later, after King defeated Bennett at the polls, the economic picture slowly began to brighten and the relief camps were shuttered.

Bennett's New Deal

Demonstrating his government's conviction to aggressively tackle the Depression, Bennett went on-air with his first radio broadcast in January 1935 outlining his surprising New Deal for Canadians. He laid out a framework in five broadcasts that called for government intervention, regulations on business, unemployment and health insurance, a tax on the rich, and a minimum wage. It was a radical departure from Conservative values and his own moral compass, borrowing profusely from Roosevelt's vigorous New Deal in the U.S.

It was Bennett's brother-in-law, William Herridge, Canada's ambassador to the U.S., who helped bring the Prime Minister around to the idea. Herridge's job put him in the front row as Roosevelt rolled out his New Deal two years earlier. He kept working on Bennett to take the significant plunge, then began working on the script four months before the first broadcast.

There was one catch: Bennett hadn't consulted his cabinet before the broad-casts, so the legislation to support his promises didn't yet exist. Most of it had yet to take effect before his government came to an end in the 1935 election.

Bennett and Stevens

Harry Stevens, a west coast MP, worked hard behind the scenes to ensure Bennett's election as party leader. Clearly they were simpatico. He was picked to be Trade & Commerce minister in Bennett's cabinet.

However, Stevens's role in the fight to improve working conditions in the textile industry began to drive a wedge between the men. Bennett reminded him that making the needed changes was a provincial responsibility. That didn't stop Stevens from suggesting publicly that Ottawa would take action. He'd overstepped and offered to resign, but Bennett kept him on the team. In fact, he mollified Stevens by handing him the Price Spread Committee (later a Royal Commission) to investigate the issue.

As Stevens amassed more information on working conditions, he veered back towards injudicious comments, accusing Simpson's retail chain and its owner Sir Joseph Flavelle of price-fixing and unhealthy working conditions. Bennett demanded he apologize. Instead, Stevens again tendered his resignation. This time it was accepted.

Although out of cabinet, Stevens had hoped to find his way back to the management table. It was a desire not shared by most of his cabinet colleagues. Bennett had lost a powerful Conservative voice in western Canada. Stevens went on to form the Reconstruction party, which fared even worse than the other two new parties in the 1935 election – Social Credit and the Co-operative Commonwealth Federation (CCF). He won its only seat.

Personal Stories

Bennett and Beaverbrook

The two met on a brief ferry trip up New Brunswick's Miramichi River. Bennett was a dapper 19-year-old school principal. Max Aitken was a precocious 10-year-old. Yet, despite their differences in age and demeanor, the two struck up a friendship that would last until the day Bennett died.

The Aitkens often invited Bennett to their home for dinner. When Max was 16, his older friend brought him into his law firm. The following year, Aitken served as Bennett's campaign manager in his successful bid for a seat on Chatham's town council. And when Bennett moved to Calgary, Aitken followed a year later and began working at the Lougheed Bennett law firm.

Aitken soon returned to the Maritimes, but as his business star ascended he brought Bennett in on many of his ventures. Bennett became president of two of them: Canada Cement and Calgary Power. The two remained close after Aitken moved to England in 1910, still dabbling in business schemes and sharing political gossip.

When Bennett retired to England in 1938, he bought an estate near Aitken's (who was now Lord Beaverbrook, the name borrowed from another area along the Miramichi). The Second World War began a year later and Beaverbrook asked Bennett to assist him in his new role as Aircraft Production minister. After the war, they visited each other often; Beaverbrook dropped by to see Bennett on June 26, 1947, several hours before Bennett's death.

The generous business tycoon

The expansion of Bennett's law career into a sideline of business ventures began in 1899. He had already been buying up real estate in Calgary and now had a chance to rent some of his property to the Western Pacific Exhibition Company for its annual fair. Two years later, he sold the property to the company and it is still the site of today's Calgary Stampede. His land-selling activities bore bigger fruit in 1904 when he sold a parcel to the CPR for a terminal on its new rail line.

Two childhood friends, Max Aitken and Jennie Shirreff, played a role in propelling his business career forward. Aitken introduced him to a variety of investment opportunities that resulted in control of several companies. When Shirreff died in 1921, one-third of her estate passed to Bennett. It made him a major shareholder in the E.B. Eddy match company because Sheriff was Eddy's widow. Bennett eventually ended up owning the Eddy empire.

By the time he became Prime Minister, he was vice-president of the Alberta Pacific Grain Company, a partner in Canada Cement (and former president), a director of Imperial Tobacco and Canada Packers, chief solicitor of the CPR, and a shareholder in E.B. Eddy (as well as its former owner), Imperial Oil, Royal Bank and countless other petroleum and mining companies.

He turned down the presidency of the Bank of Montreal after he left politics, focusing instead on England where he became chairman of BOAC (British Overseas Airways Corporation, now British Air).

Canada's wealthiest Prime Minister, he was a multi-millionaire before age 30. But he was also the most philanthropic Canadian leader. He rarely publicized his giving, but organizations like Dalhousie University and other institutions, charities and individuals all benefitted. The reason his net worth was down to $1.2 million at his death was that he'd given much of his wealth away.

Viscount Bennett

Did Bennett hope that by resurrecting Britain's ability to grant titles to Canadians – a practice quashed by Borden in 1918 – he would gain one himself? Probably. A year before reinstating the practice, he told a British colleague about his desire to eventually retire to England and receive a peerage.

With the policy back in place, he offered a knighthood to King, which was rejected. In fact, King ignored the new policy when he returned to power, reverting to Borden's decision. Despite that, he didn't object to Winston Churchill offering Bennett, now living in England, a peerage in 1941. Viscount Bennett of Mickleham in the County of Surrey and of Calgary and Hopewell in the Dominion of Canada represented the highest rank yet granted to a Canadian.

The title nicely captured Bennett's history. Mickleham was the world of his retirement, Calgary the world of his career success, and Hopewell the world of his formative development. As a Lord, he was entitled to a seat in the British House of Lords and he delighted in the airs and the decision-making that took place in its historic red-plush, stained-glass hall.

Bennett's Timeline

1870: Born in Hopewell Hill, N.B. (*July 3*).

1876: His brother Ronald is born in Hopewell Cape (*May 13*); dies seven months later.

1886: Attends Normal School (teachers college) in Fredericton (*September*).

1887: First teaching job at Irishtown, N.B., at $160 a year (*January*). Campaigns for Liberal-Conservative federal candidate Richard Weldon who wins the Albert County riding (*February 22*).

1888: Returns to Normal School in Fredericton for his senior certificate (*January*). Becomes principal of four small schools in Douglastown, N.B. (*October*). Joins the Sons of Temperance Lodge, becoming its secretary (*Fall*).

1889: Meets Max Aitken who later becomes Lord Beaverbrook (*Spring*). Joins the local New Brunswick militia.

1890: Campaigns for independent provincial candidate Lemuel Tweedie, who becomes premier of New Brunswick 10 years later (*February*). Complains to the education ministry that local trustees never visited his school. Works part-time in Tweedie's law office in nearby Chatham (*Winter-Spring*); then full-time in the summer. Enters Dalhousie University Law School in Halifax (*September*). Works part-time in the university law library (*Fall*). Meets Sir John A. Macdonald, Sir John Thompson and Sir Charles Tupper at a Halifax Conservative picnic (*October 1*).

1891: Campaigns for his dean, Richard Weldon, federal Conservative incumbent for Albert (*February-March*). Works at Tweedie's law firm (*March-August*).

1892: Works at Tweedie's law firm (*Summer*). Elected 'premier' of Dalhousie's mock parliament (*Fall*).

1893: Graduates from Dalhousie with a law degree (*April 25*). Becomes the junior partner of Tweedie & Bennett in Chatham, N.B. (*April*). First meets Jennie Shirreff, a lifelong friend who later marries industrialist E.B. Eddy.

1895: Law student Max Aitken becomes office boy at the firm.

1896: Initiated as a freemason into Miramichi Lodge. Elected alderman in Chatham's first municipal election by one vote; Aitken, 17, is his campaign manager (*September*). Resigns from council three months into his two-year term because of a lack of support for his initiatives and his plans to move west (*December*).

1897: Moves to Calgary, Alberta District, North-West Territories (*January*). Begins work as a junior partner in Senator James Lougheed's law firm (*January*). Contests a case about an illegal billiard table, opposing lawyer Arthur Sifton; marks the start of a long-standing personal and political rivalry with Sifton and his brother Clifford (*February*). Speaks at meetings in Alberta District pushing for prohibition of alcohol. Returns to New Brunswick for Christmas as he does for the next 16 years (*December*).

1898: Joined by Aitken who begins working at Lougheed Bennett (*Spring*). Wins a seat in the North-West Territories legislative assembly as the Conservative candidate for West Calgary (*November 4*).

1899: Speaks out against Premier Frederick Haultain on the first day of the new assembly (*April 5*). One of his clients becomes E.B. Eddy Co. Rents his property in southern Calgary to the Western Pacific Exhibition Company for its annual fair (today's Calgary Stampede) (*Summer*).

1900: His brother George joins him in Calgary, sharing his rooms at 222 Reinach (now Fourth) Avenue (*January*). Resigns his territorial seat to run federally. Canada's ninth federal election; loses to the Liberal incumbent Frank Oliver in the Alberta-Provisional District riding (*November 7*).

1901: Sells his southern municipal property to the city for $7,000, the site of today's Calgary Stampede (*February 14*). Wins the West Calgary by-election to regain his territorial seat (*March 22*).

1902: Re-elected in West Calgary, defeating Thomas Riley (*May 21*). Hires H.A. Allison to join the Lougheed Bennett law firm. Speaks out in favour of unions at a rally of striking carpenters (*July 6*). Meets Conservative leader Robert Borden who is on a tour of the West (*September*).

1903: Gives a keynote speech at the Conservative convention in Yorkton (*January*); does so again in Calgary a week later. Attends the Moose Jaw convention where he backs policies in favour of party politics and provincial status for Alberta and Saskatchewan (*March 25*).

1904: Drives his brand new Rambler car into a light pole, causing Calgary's first traffic accident (another story has him hitting the Imperial bank with his brand new Oldsmobile); subsequently relies on a chauffeur. Buys land in Wetaskiwin and later sells it for a substantial profit when the CPR, his client, chooses it as the terminal for a new rail line.

1905: His father Henry dies in Hopewell Cape (*March 10*); returns to New Brunswick for the funeral. Acclaimed at a Red Deer convention as the first leader of the Conservative party in the proposed province of Alberta (*August 16*). Alberta becomes a province (*September 1*). Hires W.P. Taylor to join the Lougheed Bennett law firm. Takes over the senior role at his law firm. Loses the Calgary seat by 16 votes to Liberal William Cushing in the first Alberta provincial election (*November 9*). Informs Borden that he is quitting politics and steps down as leader of the Alberta Conservatives (*November*).

1906: Helps Jennie Eddy handle her estate following the death of her husband E.B. Eddy (*Winter*). Leads an unsuccessful campaign to establish a university in Calgary.

1907: Hires William McLaws to join the Lougheed Bennett law firm.

1908: Becomes a founding member of the Calgary library board (*May 18*). Begins his association with the E.B. Eddy Company in Hull.

1909: Nominated without his knowledge as a Conservative candidate in the second Alberta provincial election. Wins the junior Calgary seat in Alberta's election; Cushing retains the senior seat (*March 22*). Invests in the Canada Cement Company with Aitken; later becomes the firm's president.

1910: Censures the Alberta government in the legislature for railway fraud (*March 2*); Premier Alexander Rutherford resigns before a commission completes its inquiry. Becomes president of the Calgary Power Company organized by Aitken; holds the position for 10 years. Unable to condemn the new Liberal premier after the commission finds the government inept but not criminal in its railway decisions (*November 10*). Resigns as party leader and is succeeded by Independent member Edward Michener.

1911: Hires J.E. Brownlee (later premier of Alberta) to article at Lougheed Bennett. Lougheed forms the Lougheed & Taylor brokerage firm, siphoning some of the Lougheed Bennett business (*April*). Canada's 12th federal election: wins the Calgary West seat, the only Alberta Conservative in the new Borden government (*September 21*). Resigns as vice-president of CPR's Irrigation Colonization Company (*September 22*). Fails to gain a cabinet seat, losing out to his law partner Senator James Lougheed (*October*). Represents the Royal Bank in its court case against the Alberta government over railway transfer payments (*October*); loses the case, but wins on appeal to the British Privy Council in 1913. Resigns as Calgary's member in the Alberta legislature (*October 31*). As a rookie MP, asked to reply to the Speech from the Throne (*November 20*).

1912: Helps organizers of the first Calgary Stampede to allow Indigenous peoples on reserves to participate in the parade. Visits England and speaks in Ashton-under-Lyne where Aitken is now MP (*August 3*). Successfully argues the Royal Bank case before the British Privy Council. His grain elevators and a flour mill become the Alberta Pacific Grain Company (*September 21*); sells his stock in 1923 for a profit of nearly $1.35 million.

1913: Member of Arthur Meighen's committee that drafts the closure rules on the Naval Aid debate (*February*). Joins Meighen in opposing his own party by objecting to Senate amendments to the Bank Act (*June 2*).

1914: Breaks rank by opposing the Borden government's support of the Mackenzie-Mann Canadian Northern Railway (*May 14*). Owns shares in the Calgary Petroleum Company (later Royalite, still later Imperial Oil) that strikes oil in Turner Valley (*May 14*). Unable to enlist at the outbreak of the First World War, so works for the Alberta Red Cross, becoming its president (*August*). Helps fund Calgary soldiers heading to Quebec for training (*August*). His mother Henrietta dies in Hopewell Cape (*October 1*). Hires Alice Millar as an office stenographer; she later becomes his secretary for 30 years. Joins the board of the Southern Alberta Patriotic Fund supporting the war effort.

1915: Sails to England as parliamentary secretary to Borden for war cabinet meetings (*June 30*). Returns to England to retrieve his brother George who was released from the army suffering intestinal problems (*November*). Tells Borden he thinks a year-end proposal to expand Canada's fighting force to 500,000 is unrealistic (*December*). Spends Christmas with his two sisters in Vancouver, his holiday pattern for the next 12 years (*December*).

1916: Proposes an amendment to the government's prohibition bill, leaving it to the provinces to restrict the sale of alcohol (*March*). Irked at not being offered a cabinet position and contemplates running in the British election (*June*). Becomes director general of the National Service Board following the resignation of Sir Thomas Tait (*October 16*). Lougheed asks to have the law firm dissolved, but both agree to postpone it (*November*). Tours Canada with Borden to promote military recruitment (*December 6-21*).

1917: Oversees the national registration census to determine the pool of possible military recruits (*January*). His resignation from the National Service Board, since the government is considering the use of conscription, is refused (*January*). Railway commission vindicates his opposition to subsidizing the Canadian Northern Railway (*April*). Undergoes abdominal surgery in Montreal (*June*). Decides not to seek re-election under the assumption that Borden will offer him a Senate seat. His term as director general of the National Service Board ends (*September 20*). Criticizes the formation of the Unionist government in caucus (*September*). Term ends as MP for Calgary (*October 6*).

1918: Is not on Borden's list of Senate appointments (*February 5*). Criticizes Borden in a letter for not making him a Senator (*April 18*); his name is dropped from a list of nominations for an Order of the British Empire (OBE). Successfully defends Norman Lewis, who claimed a farmer's exemption from military conscription before the Alberta Supreme Court (*June 28*); a month later, the Supreme Court of Canada overrules a similar decision in Ontario.

1919: Ill with erysipelas, a bacterial infection leaving him covered with red rashes (*January*). Represents Alberta at Red Cross conferences in Winnipeg and Toronto (*Fall*). Receives an honorary Doctor of Laws degree from Dalhousie University (*Fall*).

1920: Represents Canada at an international Red Cross conference in Geneva, Switzerland (*March*). Becomes a member of the Board of Governors of Dalhousie University. Chairs a session at the Canadian Bar Association annual meeting for speaker Louis St. Laurent (*September 20*).

1921: Turns down an offer to be Chief Justice of Alberta (*April*). Accepts Meighen's request to serve as Justice minister, after turning down earlier cabinet positions (*May 23*). Helps oversee the transformation of Calgary Petroleum Products into Royalite Oil. Jennie Shirreff Eddy, longtime friend, dies and leaves 500 shares of her husband's match company fortune to him; it represents one-third of her estate (*August 9*). Appointed Justice minister and Attorney-General (*October 4*). Canada's 13th federal election: elected in Calgary West by six votes over Liberal candidate Joseph Shaw; Meighen's government is defeated (*December 6*). Shaw appeals to district court for a recount and wins by 16 votes (*December 23*). Appeals to Alberta Supreme Court without success; launches an appeal to the Supreme Court (*December*). Resigns as Justice minister (*December 29*).

1922: Sets up a scholarship fund for Calgary high schools. Supreme Court rejects his appeal to overturn the district court's decision on the election results (*June*). Sails to England to appeal the Calgary West election results before the British Privy Council (*June*); again unsuccessful. His law partnership with Lougheed ends with the launch of Lougheed McLaws Sinclair & Redman (*July 29*). Hurries back from England to salvage his portion of the firm (*August 24*); places the original firm in receivership until gaining a settlement several years later. Bennett, Hannah & Sanford law firm is formed. Moves to the Ranchman's Club in Calgary from his longtime residence at a Fourth Street rooming house; maintains his book collection at Fourth Street for another seven years.

1923: His marriage proposal to Edith Cochrane, daughter of former Railways & Canals minister Frank Cochrane, is turned down. Moves to a large suite at the Palliser Hotel in Calgary. Settles his brother George, who is combating a problem with alcohol, in a house in Fort McMurray, Alta.

1924: Visits England to help negotiate a takeover of the Alberta Pacific Grain Company by Spillers Milling and attends the British Empire Festival at Wembley Stadium (*July-August*). Begins to anonymously fund the upbringing and education of his niece, Joan Bennett (daughter of George) in Toronto (*September*). Royalite Oil well #4 blows and boosts his shares (*October 14*). Creates the Dalhousie Oil Company from a collection of small independent operators (*Fall*).

1925: Turns down Meighen's request to return to politics and the promise of a cabinet seat if the Conservatives get elected (*June 10*); later changes his mind. Canada's 15th federal election: elected MP for Calgary West by a healthy majority; Conservatives win the most seats, but Liberals hang on to power (*October 29*).

1926: Serves on the committee that examines corruption charges in the Customs department of the King government (*February 9*). Becomes president of Royalite Oil. Acquires controlling interest in the E.B. Eddy Co. after receiving the shares of Harry Shirreff who dies (*May 20*). Customs committee releases report castigating the Liberals for corruption in the Customs department (*June 18*). Byng prevents King from dissolving Parliament, asks Meighen to form a government (*June 28*). Meighen loses a confidence vote and dissolves Parliament (*July 2*). Appointed Minister Without Portfolio by Meighen (*July 7*). Appointed Finance minister as well as acting minister of Interior, Indian Affairs and Mines (*July 13*). Canada's 16th federal election: re-elected in Calgary West, but Meighen's government is defeated (*September 14*). Resigns as Finance minister and from his acting portfolios (*September 24*). Receives an honorary Doctor of Laws degree from Queen's University. Refuses to let his name stand as interim party leader; the caucus chooses Hugh Guthrie (*October 11*).

1927: Purchases chimes for the bell tower of his church, Central United in Calgary. The sale of the E.B. Eddy match production subsidiary to Swedish match monopolist Ivar Kreugaer falls through (*October 10*). Elected Conservative leader at the party convention in Winnipeg, winning on the second ballot (*October 12*). E.B. Eddy match company sold to Bryant and May, an English firm (*December*). Moves from Ottawa's Rideau Club to the Chateau Laurier, having decided against buying homes like Earnscliff and Montebello (*December*). Resigns as a director of Metropolitan Life (*December 30*) and from most boards except E.B. Eddy.

1928: Resigns as president of Royalite Oil. Establishes National News Service to promote the Conservative party. Raises visibility by touring Quebec (*June*) and the Maritimes (*July-August*). Helps launch the *Regina Daily Star*, which he secretly owns (*July*). Visits England, Czechoslovakia and Austria (*December-January*).

1929: His sister Evelyn dies of cancer in Vancouver (*May 1*). His other sister Mildred moves into his suite with him at the Palliser Hotel in Calgary. Begins national speaking tour (*June*). Becomes president of the Canadian Bar Association (Louis St. Laurent is vice-president) (*September*). Visits England (*October*).

1930: Moves a non-confidence vote against the Liberal's budget, but is pre-empted by King's decision to call an election (*May 6*). Opens his election campaign in the Winnipeg Amphitheatre where he was elected leader three years earlier (*June 9*). Canada's 17th federal election: re-elected in Calgary West defeating Liberal Colin McLaurin; his

Conservatives win a majority (*July 28*). **Bennett Government (1930-1935)**. Becomes Canada's 11th Prime Minister, fourth Secretary of State for External Affairs, 13th Finance minister and 26th Privy Council President (*August 7*). Cabinet expands the Prime Minister's power to call meetings and to dissolve Parliament (*August 7*). Rejects the desire of caucus to eliminate the External Affairs department (*August*). Attends the Canadian Bar Association annual conference in Toronto (*August 15-16*). Attends a banquet in his honour in Calgary (*August 22*). Canada's 17th Parliament opens; nominates George Black to be the 17th Speaker of the House and introduces the Unemployment Relief Act (*September 8*). Introduces a protective tariff on an array of household items (*September 16*). Attends the Imperial Conference in London (*October 1-November 14*); tells the delegates he is adopting a Canada-first policy and encourages each dominion to establish preferential tariffs with the others. Lunenburg's shipyards launch the fishing schooner *R.B. Bennett* (*October*). Becomes a member of the British Privy Council (*October 27*). Norway recognizes Canada's sovereignty over the Sverdrup Islands in the Arctic (*November 12*). Receives honorary Doctor of Laws degrees from Dublin's Trinity College, Belfast's Queen's College, and the University of Edinburgh (*November*). Visits Vimy Ridge in France (*November*). Returns to Ottawa (*December 13*).

A chance to live in Macdonald's house

When Bennett became leader, there was no official Prime Minister's residence. But that was about to change. The government had been wanting to buy Earnscliffe, Macdonald's former home, for years and it was back on the market again. What better house in Ottawa to serve as the leader's home? But Bennett wasn't remotely interested in the costs attached to such a rash move. He was happy living in his suite at the Chateau Laurier. Later that year, the British bought the home making it their High Commission headquarters.

1931: Stops propping up the Conservative central office with his own funds and shuts it down (*January 6*). Meets with U.S. President Herbert Hoover in Washington to discuss a deep waterway along the St. Lawrence River (*January 30*). Appoints William Herridge ambassador to the U.S. (*March 8*). Appoints Sir Josiah Stamp as chair and Lester Pearson as secretary of the Royal Commission on grain futures (*March*). Announces the appointment of the Earl of Bessborough as Canada's 14th Governor General (*March 20*). Hosts the fourth Dominion-Provincial Conference in Ottawa to discuss Britain's proposed Statute of Westminster that will ensure full-government for the Empire's dominions (*April 7-8*). Attends the marriage of his sister Evelyn to William Herridge, Canada's U.S. ambassador; gives his sister $2 million (*April 27*). Proposes contributory unemployment insurance (*April 29*); later thwarted by an inability to reach an acceptable formula with the provinces. As Finance minister, introduces a budget forecasting a deficit of more than $80 million (*June 1*). Committee formed to investigate Mackenzie King's 1929 agreement with the Beauharnois Syndicate (*June 10*). Eliminates the law requiring cabinet appointees to seek re-election (*June*). Unemployment and Family Relief Bill is introduced to combat the Depression (*July 1*). Senator Gideon Robertson (Labour) returns from a cross-country trip convinced that the Depression is temporary (*July*). Supports a Relief Bill provision that permits the federal and provincial governments to take any steps necessary to quell dissent by the unemployed (*July 29*). Police raid Communist offices, charging leader Tim Buck with sedition (*August 11*). Beauharnois' president and general manager are forced to resign following the tabling of the government committee report in the summer (*September*). Receives an honorary Doctor of Laws degree from the University of Toronto. Pledges that

Canada "will pay her obligations in gold" after Britain goes off the gold standard, sending the market into disarray (*September 21*). Sails to England (*November-December*). British Parliament passes the Statute of Westminster (*December 12*).

1932: Resigns as Finance minister, succeeded by Senator Edgar Rhodes (Fisheries) (*February 3*). Former prime minister Arthur Meighen enters cabinet as Minister Without Portfolio (*February 3*). British Privy Council upholds a Supreme Court decision that granting of radio licences is a federal power, not a provincial one (*February 9*). Proposes a 10% cut in MP and civil service salaries to cut costs (*February*). Re-meets and falls in love with Hazel Colville (*February*). Sir George Perley (Without Portfolio) and Maurice Dupré (Solicitor General) represent Canada at the first World Conference on Disarmament in Geneva, Switzerland (*February*). Hosts the fifth Dominion-Provincial Conference in Ottawa to tackle unemployment relief (*April 8-9*). Receives the Senate's report into the Beauharnois scandal (*May 3*). Establishes the Canadian Radio Broadcasting Commission (*May 26*). Plays a role in forcing Sir Henry Thornton to resign as the first president of the Canadian National Railway (*July 19*). Brother-in-law William Herridge, ambassador to the U.S., signs the St. Lawrence Seaway treaty in Washington (*July 15*); not ratified by the U.S. Senate. Chairs the Imperial Economic Conference held in Ottawa (*July 20-August 20*); it fails to establish a preferential tariff, but does result in bilateral agreements with various Commonwealth countries. The Co-operative Commonwealth Federation is formed in Calgary; (*August 1*); J.S. Woodsworth, MP, becomes the first party leader. Officially opens the fourth Welland Canal (*August 6*). Railways royal commission, chaired by Sir Lyman Duff, recommends that the CPR and CNR remain separate, but work more cooperatively (*September*). An Order-in-Council calls for work camps to be set up across Canada for the unemployed (*October 8*); they serve more than 170,000 men over the next four years. Officially opens the Winnipeg Auditorium (*October 15*). Exemption from Britain's 10% tariff ends (*November 15*). His affair with Colville ends; sails to England (*November*) and returns a month later.

MP not dead yet

No one ever accused Bennett of being a team player. Many of his Conservative MPs probably wondered if the leader knew they were there at all. That was certainly the case for one MP whose wife received a letter from Bennett expressing his condolences on the death of her husband. The husband was rather miffed that Bennett didn't seem to be aware that he had been sitting in caucus and in the House earlier that same day.

1933: Hosts the sixth Dominion-Provincial Conference in Ottawa to discuss unemployment relief and old age pensions (*January 17-19)*). Threatens to cut off aid to those provinces unable to balance their budgets (*January*). Introduces the Unemployment and Farm Relief Bill, extending the provisions of the 1932 Relief Act (*February*). His new Tariff Board hires Phyllis Turner whom he later dates (*Winter*); her son John will become Canada's 17th Prime Minister. Introduces a bill to give the Canadian Radio Broadcasting Commission more autonomy (*March*). Visits Washington to meet with new U.S. President Franklin D. Roosevelt (*April 29*). Reintroduces the policy allowing Britain to grant titles to Canadians (*May 24*). Attends the International Monetary and Economic Conference in London (*June 12-July 27*). Urges France not to leave the conference after the U.S. objects to reliance on the gold standard (*July 6*). The Co-operative Commonwealth Federation adopts its Regina Manifesto in Regina (*July 19-21*). Vacations at Harrowgate spa in Yorkshire

(*July 30-August 12*). Chairs the International Wheat Conference in London that establishes a uniform base price for wheat (*August 21-26*). Begins speaking about a desire to step down as leader (*September*). Tells Harry Stevens (Trade & Commerce) that it is up to the provinces to do something about unjust working conditions in the garment industry (*September*). Macmillan Royal Commission on Banking and Currency recommends the establishment of a central bank (*September 27*). Loses three by-elections to the Liberals (*October 23*). Has the Canadian Labour Defence League delegation forcibly removed from his office (*November*).

1934: Jean Chrétien, Canada's 20th Prime Minister, is born in Shawinigan, Que. (*January 11*). Stephens (Trade & Commerce) vaguely commits the government to action in addressing injustices in the garment industry (*January 15*). Keeps Stevens in cabinet even though the minister has handed in his resignation (*January 17*). Hosts the seventh Dominion-Provincial Conference in Ottawa to discuss employment and provincial financial stability (*January 18-19*). Stevens's Price Spread Committee inquiry into the garment industry begins (*February 16*). Unveils a centenary plaque in Toronto to mark the city's 100th anniversary (*March 6*). The Bank of Canada Act receives second reading in the House (*March 8*). Talks Rhodes (Finance) into staying in cabinet after his wife suddenly dies (*May 6*). Introduces the Farmers' Creditors Arrangement Act to help farmers avoid bankruptcies (*June 4*). The Natural Products Marketing Act is passed, allowing provinces to regulate marketing and control prices (*June 7*). Delivers the convocation address at Rensselaer Polytechnic in Troy, New York, using a speech written by Pearson (*June 16*). Stevens's committee becomes a Royal Commission (*July 7*). Opens the Calgary Stampede. A confidential speech by Stevens is published in which he accuses Simpson's retail store of being involved in garment industry injustices (*August 2*). Brother-in-law William Herridge, Canadian Ambassador to Washington, is unsuccessful in interesting Roosevelt in a trade agreement (*August 7*). Leads the delegation to the General Assembly of the League of Nations in Geneva (*August-October 19*). Appoints Graham Towers the first Governor of the Bank of Canada (*September 8*). Asks Stevens to retract his statements about Simpson's and its chairman, Sir Joseph Flavelle (*October 25*). Stevens resigns from cabinet and as chair of the Royal Commission on Price Spreads (*October 26*). Appoints W.W. Kennedy to take over the Price Spreads Commission (*October 26*). Shuffles cabinet to fill Stevens's position and bring in Grote Stirling as National Defence minister (*November 17*). Announces intention to carry on as Conservative leader beyond the next election and plans to introduce unemployment insurance (*December 5*). His former secretary, Andrew MacLean, publishes *R.B. Bennett* prior to the coming election (*December 10*).

1935: Broadcasts the first of five radio messages on 38 stations offering a new deal similar to Roosevelt's to combat the Depression (*January 2*). Speaker George Black resigns following a nervous breakdown (*January 16*). Canada's 17th Parliament opens; nominates James Bowman to be the 18th Speaker of the House (*January 17*). King refuses to move a non-confidence vote on the Speech from the Throne, calling the government's bluff that it doesn't yet have 'New Deal' legislation to table (*January 21*). Introduces the Employment and Social Insurance Act in the House (*January 29*); presents the Minimum Wages Act a few days later. Becomes Rector of Queen's University. Suffers a respiratory infection following a speaking tour outlining his new deal (*February 24*); confined to his Chateau Laurier suite. Suffers a mild heart attack while convalescing (*March 7*). The Bank of Canada begins operation (*March 11*). Weekly Day of Rest Act introduced in the House to ensure a day off work, preferably Sunday (*March 14*). Walkout begins at B.C. relief camps and men head for Vancouver (*April 4*). Price Spreads Commission submits its report (*April 12*). Appears at a press conference for the first time since his heart attack (*April 16*). The Prairie Farm Rehabilitation Administration is established (*April 17*). Leaves for England to attend George V's Silver Jubilee (*April 18*); returns in May. The Macdonald Royal Commission on Relief Camps tables a report that criticizes the government for not paying unemployed men at the camps (*May 23*). Hundreds of unemployed men in Vancouver board boxcars heading east, beginning the On To Ottawa Trek (*June 3-4*). Cabinet agrees the trek must be stopped; Regina is picked as the place to end it (*June*). Invokes the Railway Act to move Saskatchewan's RCMP to federal jurisdiction (*June 12*). Stevens invited to caucus in an effort to patch up his differences with the government; his presence is overlooked and he leaves shortly after arriving (*June*). Bennett indicates he has no intention of stepping down as leader, quelling Stevens's supporters (*June 19*). Turns down a request for work and wages by a trekkers' delegation from Regina (*June 22*). The Dominion Housing Act introduced in the House to provide mortgage loans (*June 24*). Regina Riot breaks out when police try to arrest the trekkers' leaders at a demonstration and stop the march (*July 1*). Sixth Session, 17th Parliament prorogued; King crosses the House to shake hands and everyone sings *Allouette* and *Auld Lang Syne* (*July 5*). Stevens creates the Reconstruction party (*July 7*). Bennett turns down requests from a group of Toronto marchers, the only ones to successfully make it to Ottawa (*July 17*). Appoints Edgar (Finance) to the Senate after he turns down an offer to succeed Bennett as leader (*July 20*). Announces the appointment of author John Buchan (becomes Lord Tweedsmuir) as Canada's 15th Governor General (*August 10*). Joins other nations in condemning Italy's invasion of Ethiopia (*October 10*). Asks League of Nations representative, Dr. W.A. Riddell, to support sanctions against Italy for invading Ethiopia, reversing an earlier decision to stall on the matter (*October 13*). Canada's 18th federal election: re-elected in Calgary West defeating Robert Reid (Social Credit); his government loses to King's Liberals (*October 14*). Resigns as Prime Minister (*October 22*). **Bennett's government ends.** Travels to California, Panama Canal, Cuba and New York (*November 18-December*).

1936: Refuses to support the nomination of Pierre Casgrain as Speaker because of his premature firing of 120 House employees (*February 6*). Exonerated by the Regina Riot Inquiry Commission in Saskatchewan for his role in the confrontation between trekkers and the RCMP (*April 23*). Steps down as Rector of Queen's University. Sails for Fiji and New Zealand (*August 19*), to Australia (*September 27*), and to South Africa (*November 9*). Visits Victoria Falls (*December 3*) and Madeira (*December 30*).

Belated wedding gift

In a conversation with fellow MP John Diefenbaker, Bennett asked if he was married. The future prime minister responded: "eight years." Bennett wondered if he'd given the Diefenbakers a gift at the time. "No reason you should," responded Dief. Bennett subsequently sent a cheque for $2,500 to Dief's Prince Albert home.

1937: Arrives back in Ottawa four days after the resumption of Parliament (*January 18*). The Liberal government agrees with a Supreme Court decision that most of the Conservative legislation enacted in the mid-1930s is invalid because it infringes on provincial jurisdiction (*January 28*). Sails for England with his sister Mildred to attend the coronation of George VI (*May*); later visits Germany to seek medical advice and receive spa treatments (*June-July*).

1938: His brother George dies in Fort McMurray, Alta. (*January 27*). Tells caucus he is resigning as leader (*February*). Opposes parts of the government's Throne Speech, with little support from his own party (*January 31-February 11*). Announces his resignation as leader of the Conservative Party (*March 5*). Visits his sister Mildred who is fighting breast cancer in New York City (*May*); she dies a few days after his return to Ottawa. Resigns as MP for Calgary West (*July 1*). Supports Murdoch MacPherson's bid to succeed him as leader, but Robert Manion is chosen on the second ballot at the party convention in Ottawa (*July 7*). Sails to England to purchase a home (*August*). Buys the Juniper Hill estate near Mickleham, Surrey, next to Beaverbrook's Cherkley Court estate (*November 1*). Returns to Canada (*November 19*).

1939: Takes a last tour of the West; followed by send-offs in Toronto, Ottawa and Saint John (*January*). Sails to England (*February*). Declines to contest the British riding of Marylebone in London (*June*). Alice Millar continues as his secretary by moving from Ottawa to Juniper Hill (*Summer*). Bennett's speaking tour of northern Europe is sidelined by Germany's invasion of Poland (*September 1*). Turns down an offer to become president of the Bank of Montreal (*September*). Moves to Juniper Hill (*October 1*). Sells nearly $1.8 million of his E.B. Eddy shares to protest the company's lack of strong management (*November*); remains a major shareholder. Becomes chairman of the London advisory committee of the Canadian Red Cross in the Second World War. Returns to Canada to sell nearly $750,000 in securities and donates money to Britain for the war effort (*December*).

1940: Undertakes a speaking tour of Canada to support the war effort and enlistment. Becomes a Surrey justice of the peace (*January*). Britain considers using him as an advisor on Canadian matters, but the High Commissioner opposes the idea and it is dropped (*February*). His rescheduled speaking tour of northern Europe is cancelled after Germany invades Denmark and Norway (*April 9*). Becomes Lord Beaverbrook's assistant at Britain's Ministry of Aircraft Production (*May*). Joins the board of the British Manufacturing and Research Company and begins to reorganize it for wartime (*July*). Chairs an inquiry into an aircraft factory collapse that killed six workers; determines it was an accident, not human error (*August*).

1941: Suggestion by CPR President Sir Edward Beatty that he be given a cabinet position in Canada is rejected by King (*February 19*). Becomes Viscount Bennett of Mickleham, Calgary & Hopewell (*June 12*). Takes his seat in the British House of Lords (*July 23*). Flies to Canada to sell the family home in Hopewell Cape (*August*).

1942: Creates the Viscount Bennett Scholarship at the University of Alberta. Attends the Conservative convention committee in Ottawa and agrees that John Bracken is the best man to succeed Meighen as leader (*October*).

1943: Sells his remaining E.B. Eddy shares to George Weston Limited and joins its board (*March*). Becomes chairman of the British Overseas Airways Corporation (*April 16*). Donates $725,000 to Dalhousie University for four endowed faculty chairs (*April*).

1944: Discovers he has diabetes. Steps down from the Weston board. Ronald Bennett, his nephew, is killed in action in Normandy (*August 5*); Ronald's brother Harrison is killed in Normandy nine days later.

1946: Begins insulin shots for diabetes (*March*). Becomes chairman of the Box Hill Trust near his estate, and a member of the Men of the Trees council. Moves to Sidmouth, Devon, to improve his health (*December*).

1947: Returns to Juniper Hill (*March*). Attends a luncheon for Princess Elizabeth who presents him with the City of London Medal of Freedom (*June 11*). Questions the constitutionality of Alberta's Bill of Rights Act before Britain's Privy Council judicial committee (*June 24*). Re-elected president of the Royal Society of the Arts (*June 25*). Dies in his bath (*June 26*). Buried in Mickleham, England (*June 30*). His memorial service is held at Westminster Abbey in London (*July 4*).

Books about Bennett

- **1935**: Andrew MacLean; *R.B. Bennett: Prime Minister of Canada* (Excelsior)
- **1959**: Lord Beaverbrook; *Friends: Sixty Years of Intimate Personal Relations with Richard Bedford Bennett* (Heinemann)
- **1963**: Ernest Watkins; *R.B. Bennett: a biography* (Kingswood House)
- **1964**: Michael David Swift; *R.B. Bennett and the Depression, 1930*-1935 (unpublished thesis)
- **1975**: Stanley Gordon; *R.B. Bennett, M.L.A., 1897-1905: The Years of Apprenticeship* (University of Calgary)
- **1979**: Robert Saunders; *R.B. Bennett* (Fitzhenry & Whiteside)
- **1991**: James H. Gray; *R.B. Bennett: The Calgary Years* (University of Toronto)
- **1992**: P.B. Waite; *The Loner: Three Sketches of the Personal Life and Ideas of R.B. Bennett, 1870-1947* (University of Toronto)
- **1992**: Larry Glassford; *Reaction and Reform: The Politics of the Conservative Party Under R.B. Bennett, 1927-1938* (University of Toronto)
- **2010**: John Boyko; *Bennett: The Rebel Who Challenged and Changed a Nation* (Key Porter)
- **2012**: P.B. Waite; *In Search of R.B. Bennett* (McGill-Queen's University)

Chief Justices of Canada

1.	Sir William Richards	1875-1879
2.	Sir William Ritchie	1879-1892
3.	Sir Samuel Strong	1992-1902
4.	Sir Henri Taschereau	1902-1906
5.	Sir Charles Fitzpatrick	1906-1918
6.	Sir Louis Davies	1918-1924
7.	Francis Anglin	1924-1933
8.	Sir Lyman Duff	1933-1944
9.	Thibaudeau Rinfret	1944-1954
10.	Patrick Kerwin	1954-1963
11.	Robert Taschereau	1963-1967
12.	John Cartwright	1967-1970
13.	Gérald Fauteux	1970-1973
14.	Bora Laskin	1973-1984
15.	Brian Dickson	1984-1990
16.	Antonio Lamer	1990-2000
17.	Beverley McLachlin	2000-2017
18.	Richard Wagner	2017-

12

Louis St. Laurent

The Unassuming Prime Minister

Despite his reputation as kindly Uncle Louis, St. Laurent was an astute lawyer and, aided by his external affairs minister, Lester Pearson, was the architect of Canada's halcyon days in global relations. He actively supported the UN's role in Korea, but refused to back Britain's bid to reclaim the Suez Canal. Newfoundland joined Canada and Canada joined NATO during this period. Domestically, St. Laurent introduced old age pensions, equalization payments and the Canada Council. By the time his government pushed through the unpopular Trans-Canada Pipeline, he was simply worn out.

ST. LAURENT THE POLITICIAN

Prime Minister of Canada: November 15, 1948 – June 21, 1957
Length of term: 8 years, 7 months, 6 days
Parliaments as Prime Minister: 20th; 21st; 22nd
Age on entering office: 66
Political party: Liberal
Leader of party: August 6, 1948 – January 16, 1958
Member of Parliament: February 9, 1942 – February 1, 1958
Riding represented: Quebec East (Que.) 1942-1958
Cabinet portfolios: Justice (1941-1946, 1948); External Affairs (1946-1948); Privy Council President (1948-1957)
Other political post: Leader of the Opposition (1957-1958)
Titles: King's Counsel (1915); Canadian Privy Councillor (1941); Imperial Privy Councillor (1946); Companion of the Order of Canada (1967)
Quotes: "I didn't know at first that there were two languages in Canada. I just thought that there was one way to speak to my father and another to speak to my mother." "We shall be theoretically and practically in full possession of our autonomy…We shall be masters in our own house." (1949 speech to Young Liberals)
Lived after term: 16 years

ST. LAURENT THE MAN

Name: Louis-Étienne (Stephen) St. Laurent
Born: February 1, 1882, Compton, Quebec
Ancestry: French, Irish
Religion: Roman Catholic
Education: B.A. [Bachelor of Arts] (St. Charles Seminary, Sherbrooke, 1902); LL.L. [Bachelor of Civil Law] (Laval University, 1905)
Nickname: Uncle Louis (coined by Norman Campbell of the *Toronto Telegram* during the 1949 campaign, after viewing St. Laurent's special attention to children in Trail, B.C.)
Military service: none
Occupation: lawyer; professor
Occupation after term: businessman; executive
Publications: *The Foundations of Canadian Policy in World Affairs* (1947)
Appearance: "Though in manner he was a shy, rather stiff corporate lawyer, he still had a kindly, grandfatherly appearance enhanced by his immaculate attire and white moustache." (Robert Bothwell in *Dictionary of Canadian Biography, Vol. 20*); "benign and courtly – Good Uncle to the nation" (J.M.S. Careless in *Canada: A Story of Challenge*)
Personality: "Highly intelligent, serene, fluently bilingual … he did it all with an avuncular style that inspired trust." (J.L. Granatstein & Norman Hillmer in *Prime Ministers: Ranking Canada's Leaders*); "He had none of Laurier's mystical impulses and none of his vanity either. He had all of Borden's integrity and a larger mind." (Bruce Hutchison in *Mr. Prime Minister*)
Married: Jeanne Renault – May 19, 1908, Église de Saint-François-d'Assise, Beauceville, Quebec
Age at marriage: 26
Years married: 58
Died: July 25, 1973, Quebec City, Quebec
Age at death: 91
Cause of death: natural
Buried: Saint Thomas d'Aquin Cemetery, Compton, Quebec

St. Laurent was the:

- First Prime Minister to live at 24 Sussex Drive, the official residence
- First Prime Minister who was previously External Affairs minister
- First Prime Minister to receive the Order of Canada
- First Liberal Prime Minister who represented only one riding
- Second French Canadian Prime Minister
- Second oldest serving Prime Minister (75)
- Third longest-living Prime Minister
- Third Prime Minister with a son who became a Member of Parliament
- Fourth Liberal Prime Minister
- Fourth oldest Prime Minister on assuming office
- Eighth Prime Minister who was a lawyer

St. Laurent's legacy

- Directed Canada through a period of economic prosperity and global unrest
- Presided over the golden age of Canadian foreign policy
- Engineered Newfoundland's admission to Canada
- Brought Canada into NATO, 1949
- Abolished appeals to the Imperial Privy Council (1949)
- Introduced equalization payments to provinces
- Appointed the first Canadian Governor General
- Permitted married women to work in the federal civil service
- Created the Canada Council (1956)
- Introduced universal old age pensions

St. Laurent's Family

St. Laurent's Parents

Father: Jean-Baptiste-Moise St. Laurent
Born: September 18, 1839, Trois-Rivières, Quebec
Occupation: merchant
Died: July 9, 1915, Compton, Quebec
Age at death: 76

Mother: Mary Ann Broderick
Born: September 2, 1852, Poppyhill, Galloway, Ireland
Occupation: teacher
Married: April 27, 1881, Église Saint Thomas d'Aquin, Compton, Quebec
Died: April 8, 1933, Compton, Quebec
Age at death: 81

St. Laurent's Brothers & Sisters (5 siblings; Louis the oldest)

Sister: Lora St. Laurent (1883-1972)
Sister: Marie-Louise St. Laurent (1885-1917)
Brother: Jean-Baptiste-Maurice St. Laurent (1887-1967)
  Married: Marie Joséphine Albertine Goyette (1914)
Sister: Kathleen C. St. Laurent (Sister Maria Teresa) (b.1889)
Brother: Nil Joseph St. Laurent (1893-1930)
  Note: Priest

St. Laurent's Wife

Name: Jeanne Marie Renault
Born: October 22, 1886, Beauceville, Quebec
Father: Pierre-Ferdinand Renault (merchant)
Mother: Amanda Montminy
Age at marriage: 21
Children: 5 – Marie Marthe; Renault; Jean-Paul Stephen; Thérèse; Madeleine Eva
Died: November 14, 1966, Quebec City, Quebec
Age at death: 80

Burial place: Saint Thomas d'Aquin Cemetery, Compton, Quebec
Younger than St. Laurent: 4 years
Died before St. Laurent: 7 years

St. Laurent's Children (5)

Name: Marie Marthe St. Laurent
Born: March 31, 1909, Quebec City, Quebec
Married: Dr. Matthieu Samson (1931)
Children: 3 – Louise; Thérèse; Monique

Name: Renault St. Laurent
Born: September 12, 1910, Quebec City, Quebec
Occupation: lawyer
Married: Louise Badeaux (May 30, 1942)
Children: 6 – Pierre; Monique; Michel; Paul; Louise; Robert
Died: May 13, 1977, Quebec City, Quebec

Name: Jean-Paul Stephen St. Laurent
Born: April 23,1912, Quebec City, Quebec
Occupation: lawyer; MP for Témiscouata (1955-1958)
Married: Madeleine Hamel (1936)
Children: 4 – Hélène; Louis S. II; Marie; Françoise
Died: December 22, 1986, Quebec City, Quebec

Name: Thérèse Sylvie St. Laurent
Born: December 7, 1914, Quebec City, Quebec
Married: G. Frank Lafferty (1940)
Children: 2 – Jean; Louise

Name: Madeleine Eva St. Laurent
Born: April 3, 1917, Quebec City
Married: Hugh O'Donnell (1945), William John Alexander Veitch (1963)
Children: 2 – Michael; Mary (adopted)
Died: April 1, 2002

POLITICAL STORIES

The Call from Ottawa

The telephone call from the Prime Minister that interrupted the St. Laurent family dinner on December 4, 1941 was not unexpected. King wanted to meet with him the next day and St. Laurent knew why. Ernest Lapointe, the Justice minister and Quebec lieutenant for the Liberals had died of cancer eight days earlier and the Liberals needed to fill his important shoes.

St. Laurent was not unknown to the federal party. It had hired him to determine the validity of the previous government's legislation to curb the Depression. He convinced the Supreme Court that many of Bennett's policies were unconstitutional. Next came the Rowell-Sirois commission examining dominion-provincial relations, on which he served as legal counsel. And now he was co-chairing the Victory Loan campaign in

Quebec to support the war effort. Former cabinet minister Pierre Cardin had suggested St. Laurent's name to King while heading to Lapointe's funeral.

In Ottawa, King appealed vigorously to St. Laurent's sense of wartime duty. The Quebec lawyer, nearly 60, asked for a few days to consider it. He canvassed his family, his partners, the archbishop, the premier and a Supreme Court judge while trying to deflect what was stacking up to be a foregone conclusion.

Then, two days into his deliberation, the Japanese bombed Pearl Harbor and the U.S. entered the war. This was now much more than an 'Imperial' war and St. Laurent felt compelled to play his part. The decision was made. He would enter cabinet for the duration of the war – a commitment that eventually stretched 12 years beyond that.

Bringing Newfoundland into the fold

In the 1930s, during the worst of the Great Depression, Newfoundland averted financial collapse by agreeing to give up self-government in favour of being governed by Britain through a commission government. But after the war, the colony was back on a stronger fiscal footing and needed to make a decision. Should it remain under Britain's wing or revert to a self-governing colony? Other options included joining Canada as a province or even possibly becoming a U.S. state.

As External Affairs minister, St. Laurent was in charge of negotiations with Newfoundland about joining Canada. This was the preferred option in both Canada and Britain, offsetting strong opposition from the St. John's business community.

While the costs of providing services to the colony seemed steep, there was never much doubt that the merger would take place. St. Laurent bartered with Newfoundland's Gordon Bradley (who later joined cabinet) and Joey Smallwood (who became the first premier) to hammer out an agreement.

Presiding over the official union on April 1, 1949, St. Laurent (now Prime Minister) noted that the inkwell used at the signing was the same one used at Confederation in 1867. Similarly, a 10th stone plaque purposely left blank at the entrance to the Peace Tower would now portray Newfoundland's coat of arms.

Sending troops to Korea

The surrender of Japan in 1945 brought Korea under the trusteeship of two world powers: the Soviet Union in the north of the peninsula and the U.S. in the south. As the new Koreas – emphatically communist north of the 38th parallel and equally capitalist to the south – constantly skirmished, the United Nations stepped in to keep the peace.

St. Laurent (External Affairs) was thoroughly in favour of Canada's participation in the UN's 1948 Korean commission and had publicly committed to the initiative while he was acting Prime Minister. But King objected and refused to sign off. The stalemate between King and St. Laurent lasted several weeks, with both threatening to resign. That forced a more detailed examination of the issue with each agreeing Canada would 'observe' the election process in Korea rather than 'enforce' it.

The UN's efforts crumbled two years later when North Korea invaded the south. St. Laurent was now the leader and agreed to send troops to Korea only if they were part of a UN force. When that didn't happen, he expressed a willingness to participate in an

American-led alliance endorsed by the UN. There was surprisingly little resistance to the idea, particularly in Quebec.

Canada sent 26,000 troops to Korea over the next two years, losing over 500 in the conflict. The Korean War did little more than retrench the status quo along the 38th parallel. Canadian troops stayed another three years as observers and were visited by St. Laurent as part of his 1954 world tour. He recalled them at the end of the year.

A NATO godfather

After the Second World War, St. Laurent felt Canada needed to step up its international presence. In his speech to the UN General Assembly in September 1947, he first broached the idea of a North Atlantic alliance.

Seven months later, amid increased talks with the U.S. and European countries, he was the first leader to publicly declare the need for such a collective. Britain, France, Belgium, the Netherlands and Luxembourg had already agreed to collective security and it did not take long before most of Western Europe signed on. Soon, the scope of the new defence organization was about to stretch even further.

St. Laurent pushed hard to get Canada to join the alliance to be called the North Atlantic Treaty Organization (NATO). Parliament endorsed Canada's participation with only two dissenting votes and, on April 4, the country became the first to ratify the treaty. In 1951, St. Laurent hosted the NATO Council for the first time in Ottawa.

The St. Laurent world tour

At age 72, St. Laurent hopped a plane in Ottawa, becoming the first Prime Minister to tackle an around-the-world trip. The boom in commercial air travel made it possible for him to visit 12 countries in 42 days.

The trip gave him a chance to review Canadian troops in France and Germany and raise the profile of the recently created NATO. He flew next to the region that was the original intent of the trip: India and Pakistan. Not there to patch up conflicts between the two nations, he hoped to improve their relations with Canada.

St. Laurent spent a week in India and didn't strike up a rapport with Prime Minister Jawaharlal Nehru until the second last day in New Delhi. It came at the urging of their daughters, Madeleine O'Donnell and Indira Gandhi. They each chastised their fathers for not making an effort, resulting in a hastily organized final meeting characterized by candid, rich conversation that made the trip worthwhile. Then it was on to Ceylon, Indonesia, Philippines, South Korea and Japan.

Sir Winston Churchill had warned him he would find the pace exhausting. It was. By the time he reached Tokyo, St. Laurent was suffering from dysentery, weeks of unfamiliar food and shifting time zones. Back in Ottawa, he looked his age and never regained his vitality as he tackled three more years of gruelling challenges.

Closing the spigot on the Pipeline Debate

With his Transportation minister C.D. Howe taking a lead role, St. Laurent hammered out an agreement with the U.S. company TransCanada PipeLines to build a pipeline that would move natural gas from the West to eastern markets. However, to ensure the pipe travelled a more expensive all-Canadian route, the government agreed to provide loans to cover the extra costs.

Debate on the pipeline began in mid-May 1956. To meet its summer deadline with TransCanada, however, the government imposed closure. The opposition parties did everything in their filibuster power to slow down the debate, concerned about American control of the project during construction.

Howe aggressively pushed the bill forward, but St. Laurent stayed out of the fray, sometimes appearing to read at his desk while MPs sparred around him. On June 5, the opposition convinced the Speaker, Beaudoin, to permit debate on a matter of procedure. It tied up the rest of the day, but the next morning he backtracked, claiming it was a mistake and that it was time to vote. Tempers soared – Liberal MP Lorne McDougall actually died of a heart attack just outside the House – but the vote was forced and the pipeline was approved.

Imposing closure, a tactic rarely used in Parliament, was considered by many to be an over-reaction to the pipeline issue and contributed to the party's election defeat two years later. In an interview with CBC journalist Jeanne Sauvé (later Governor General), St. Laurent admitted, "I didn't say as much as I should have; people do make mistakes, you know."

Personal Stories

Quebec lawyer with a national perspective

In 1914, St. Laurent, then a successful Quebec City commercial lawyer, helped resurrect the Canadian Bar Association, becoming an active member for the next two decades. Most of his activity was initially in Quebec where the national association was considered a threat to the province's French civil code.

Then, in 1920, he gave his first national speech at a CBA meeting in Ottawa. Calgary lawyer, R.B. Bennett, a colleague he would often work with through the 1920s, introduced him. After becoming a life member of the association in 1927, St. Laurent served as Quebec's vice-president, then hosted the national convention in his hometown the following year.

At that meeting he was elected national vice-president, serving under Bennett. In 1930, he became president, then was re-elected to a rare, second one-year term. He continued to attend annual meetings of the association after entering politics and becoming Prime Minister. In 1962, his son Renault became CBA president.

Jeanne St. Laurent

If St. Laurent was warm and fuzzy – 'Uncle Louis' to Canadians – his wife Jeanne was the fond 'Aunt'. She played the role primarily from Quebec City, reluctant to leave her family or the familiar neighbourhood. It wasn't until 24 Sussex Drive was thrust on the couple in 1951 that she moved to Ottawa.

Jeanne Renault's first sight of St. Laurent was seeing him catch the sleeve of his graduation gown on the chair of Lady Grey, the Governor General's wife, at Laval's convocation. A year later, they met through friends at the Winter Carnival and he took her for several walks, letting another year go by before actually dating.

Coming from a wealthy, small-town family, Jeanne wanted to be sure she ended up with a husband able to sustain her lifestyle. By the time they married in 1908, he was was a promising lawyer able to ensure her comforatable life . Her time revolved around their growing family and a love of playing cards.

St. Laurent's move into politics in 1941 shattered her comfortable home life. She was just getting over illness and valued having a husband, almost 60, who was home for dinner each evening. So she remained in the large Grand Allée home for as long as she could – 10 years as it turned out.

In 1949, she became the first wife of a Prime Minister in 22 years. Canadians weren't used to having a first lady and that was fine with her; she was far more interested in maintaining a quiet profile in Quebec. She refused to fly, which meant staying home during St. Laurent's global tour. Attending the wedding of Princess Elizabeth in England meant a round-trip passage on the *Queen Elizabeth* liner. When her husband was defeated in the 1957 election, she happily returned to the Grand Allée house where she died in 1966.

St. Laurent's Timeline

1882: Born in Compton, Que. (*February 1*); baptized two days later.

1890: Attends Catholic school in Compton (*September*).

1896: Hears Laurier speak in Sherbrooke during the eighth federal election campaign (*Spring*). Becomes the first French Canadian student from Compton to attend a classical college, St. Charles Seminary in Sherbrooke, Que. (*September*).

Father runs for the Liberals

St. Laurent was 12 when his father became the first French Canadian to seek election as the provincial Liberal candidate in Compton. But the riding always supported an English Conservative candidate and this particular by-election was no different. Ten years later, Jean St. Laurent tried again and his son was happy to help. Political chicanery in Quebec City meant the provincial Liberal party had no intention of supporting the Compton candidate and Jean lost again. The experience soured both father and son on politics for many years to come.

1902: Receives his Bachelor of Arts degree from St. Charles Seminary, standing top of the class (*June 20*). Enters law school at Laval University in Quebec City (*September*).

1904: Campaigns for his father running in the provincial election; his father loses largely because he has no support from the Liberal party (*November 25*); father and son lose interest in politics.

1905: Receives his law degree at Laval from Governor General Lord Grey (*June 19*). As the top student in his graduating class, he is offered the first Rhodes Scholarship given to a Laval student; he turns it down in favour of opening a law practice. Joins the law firm of Drouin, Pelletier & Baillargeon in Quebec City as a clerical assistant (*June*).

1906: Meets Jeanne Renault at a Carnaval party (*February*).

1907: Pleads his first major case in court to help his friend Marius Barbeau reclaim his inheritance (*Fall*).

1908: Marries Jeanne Renault in Beauceville, Que. (*May 19*). Rents an eight-room flat on Rue St. Jean in Quebec City (*Spring*). Forms a law partnership with Antonin Galipeault in Quebec City (*Fall*).

1909: Law partner Galipeault wins a provincial by-election for the Liberals in Bellechasse (*February 2*). His first daughter Marthe is born in Quebec City (*March 31*).

1910: His father Jean has a stroke, leaving him partially paralyzed. His first son Renault is born in Quebec City (*September 12*).

1911: Pleads his first case in the Supreme Court in Ottawa.

1912: His son Jean-Paul is born in Quebec City (*April 23*). First major client becomes newsprint buyer *New York World.*

1913: Builds a three-storey house on Grand-Allée in Quebec City.

1914: Adds three more lawyers to his Quebec City law firm and moves to a larger building. Succeeds Louis-Philippe Pelletier as Professor of Law at Laval. Becomes a founding member of the re-formed Canadian Bar Association (*March*). His daughter Thérèse is born in Quebec City (*December 7*).

1915: His father Jean dies in Compton,(*July 9*). Receives his Doctor of Law degree from Laval. Becomes a King's Counsel.

1916: Develops swollen neck glands, which doctors fear might be tuberculosis. His mother begins to learn French so she can communicate with her sons.

Couldn't dance

Growing up next door to the Methodist church in St. Lin had its drawbacks. St. Laurent's mother was determined her children would be brought up as well as those attending the nearby church. That included no dancing, a Methodist no-no. As a result, Canada's 12th Prime Minister never learned to dance.

1917: His daughter Madeleine is born in Quebec City (*April 3*). His sister Louise dies of tuberculosis (*April*). Spends the spring and summer at Métis in the Gaspé where he bathes regularly in salt water; the swelling in his neck slowly disappears. Acquires a strong interest in fishing.

1920: Sails to England with Jeanne to plead a case before the Imperial Privy Council. Visits Paris and Rome. Gives his first national speech, at a Canadian Bar Association meeting in Ottawa (*September*); introduced by R.B. Bennett.

1923: Establishes his own law firm in Quebec City after dissolving his partnership with Galipeault; veers away from commercial law in favour of constitutional law.

1925: Buys a summer home on Isle of Orleans near Quebec City; his family spends summers there until it burns down in 1928.

1926: Discreetly approached to serve in Meighen's Conservative cabinet (*June*); makes it clear he has no interest in politics, but reaffirms his Liberal ties by speaking for local Liberal candidate, C.G. Power.

1927: Becomes a life member of the Canadian Bar Association.

1928: Becomes Quebec vice-president of the Canadian Bar Association. Makes his first trip west to attend the CBA convention in Regina.

1929: Becomes president of the Canadian Club in Quebec City. Chairs the Canadian Bar Association convention in Quebec (*September*). Becomes national vice-president of the Canadian Bar Association (*September*); Bennett is the president. The stock market crash is a disaster for St. Laurent who is heavily invested in stocks (*October*); it leaves him buried in debt for years.

1930: Receives honorary Doctor of Laws degrees from Queen's University and the University of Victoria. Refuses attempts to get him to run for office to succeed his former law partner Galipeault, who is appointed to the Court of Appeal (*June*). Becomes the first French Canadian president of the Canadian Bar Association, succeeding Prime Minister Bennett (*August*). Attends the American Bar Association convention in Chicago (*September*). Brother Nil dies of a heart attack in Carcassonne, France.

1931: Accepts a second term as Canadian Bar Association president, only the second person asked to serve more than one year. Serves on the National Council of the Canadian Radio League advocating for public radio.

1933: His mother Mary Ann dies of cancer in Compton, Que. (*April 8*).

1935: Hired by the federal Liberals to contest the validity of various Conservative government bills used to combat the Depression. Receives an honorary law degree from the University of Manitoba (*May*). His son Jean-Paul is called to the bar and joins the firm.

1936: Pleads a case before the British Privy Council in London, with Jeanne, Renault, Thérèse and Madeleine in the gallery (*Fall*).

1937: Supreme Court invalidates many of the Conservative bills (*January 28*). Begins his work as legal counsel for the Rowell-Sirois commission investigating federal-provincial relations (*November 29*).

1939: Visiting England when Britain declares war against Germany; quickly flies back to Canada (*August*).

1941: Co-chairs the Quebec Victory Loan campaign to raise money for the war effort. At the funeral of Ernest Lapointe (Justice), Pierre Cardin (Transport) suggests St. Laurent as his possible successor (*November 29*). King asks him to be Justice minister (*December 5*). Decides he needs to help the war effort after the Japanese bomb Pearl Harbor (*December 7*). Enters cabinet as Canada's 22nd Justice minister (*December 10*).

1942: Indicates he will support conscription if it becomes necessary (*February 5*). Elected in a by-election in Quebec East to replace Lapointe, defeating Paul Bouchard (Canadian party) (*February 9*). Orders the removal of 30,000 Japanese Canadians from the Pacific coast area (*February 26*). Is the only remaining French Canadian cabinet minister after the resignation of Pierre Cardin (Public Works) over the conscription issue (*May 11*). Helps persuade pro-conscriptionist Ralston (Defence) to stay in cabinet (*June*). First major speech in the House supports conscription if it is necessary (*June 16*).

1943: Receives an honorary degree from the University of Lennoxville (Bishop's). Releases Communist party leader Tim Buck from jail (*October 7*).

1944: Introduces the family allowance bill. Appointed acting Secretary of State for External Affairs during King's absence in England (*April 26*). Attends the United Nations Monetary Conference in Bretton Woods, New Hampshire (*July*). Votes for conscription (*November 22*). Publicly explains his reluctant support for conscription, despite probable backlash in Quebec (*December 6*).

1945: Attends the founding conference of the United Nations in San Francisco, California, as a member of the Canadian delegation (*April 25*). Broadcasts from San Francisco with Prime Minister King on V-E Day (*May 8*). Canada's 20th federal election: re-elected in Quebec East defeating Noel Dorion (Independent) (*June 11*). Signs the United Nations Charter in San Francisco (*June 26*). Takes part in the Federal-Provincial Conference on Reconstruction (*August 6-10*). Refuses to see Soviet embassy employee Igor Gouzenko who defected with papers revealing Soviet espionage (*September 6*). Asked by King to be his successor; he feels he is too old at 65 to take on the job (*September 19*). Presents the United Nations Charter to Parliament for approval (*October 19*). Successfully asks the House to extend the Liberal government's wartime emergency powers for one more year beyond war's end (*November 19*). Becomes a member of the British Privy Council, along with Finance minister James Ilsley (*December 31*).

1946: Attends United Nations First General Assembly in London, England (*January 10*). Presides over the 11th Federal-Provincial Conference in Ottawa; discussions include old age pensions and unemployment assistance (*April 29-May 3*). Appointed acting Prime Minister during King's absence in England (*May-June*). Appointed acting Prime Minister and acting Secretary of State for External Affairs during King's absence in France (*July 19-August*); also serves as acting House leader. Reluctantly agrees to remain in King's cabinet, moving from Justice to become the first full-time Secretary of State for External Affairs (*September 4*). Attends the opening session of the United Nations General Assembly in Flushing Meadows, New York (*October 23*). Makes his first speech in the United Nations as External Affairs minister (*October 29*).

1947: Delivers the Gray Lecture at the University of Toronto, outlining the importance of national unity to Canada's increasingly independent foreign policy (*January 13*). Appointed acting Prime Minister during King's illness and recuperation (*February 18*). Receives an honorary Doctor of Laws degree from Dalhousie University (*May*). Receives an honorary Doctor of Laws degree from the University of Ottawa (*June*). Asked again by King to succeed him as Prime Minister; insists he wants to return to his law practice (*July 18*). Advances the idea of a North Atlantic Alliance in a speech to the UN General Assembly (*September 18*). Indicates a willingness to seek the leadership of the Liberal party, following pressure from colleagues and friends (*October 1*). Appointed acting Prime Minister during King's absence in Europe (*October 30*).

1948: Threatens to resign from cabinet if King repudiates Canada's involvement in the United Nations Commission in Korea (*January 7*); Canada's participation is made official the following week. King announces his retirement to take place in the fall and calls for a leadership convention (*January 20*). St. Laurent's speech asking democratic nations to form a "closer association for collective self-defence" becomes the first international reference to what will become the North Atlantic Treaty Alliance (NATO) (*April 29*). Receives an honorary degree from Dartmouth College in New Hampshire. Publicly indicates he is considering running for the leadership (*June 22*). Wins the leadership on the first ballot with 848 votes, defeating James Gardiner (323) and Chubby Power (56) (*August 7*). Appointed acting Prime Minister during King's absence in Europe (*September 13*). Welcomes the Newfoundland delegation to Ottawa to hammer out the last details of union with Canada (*October 5*). Flies to London to represent Canada at the Common-wealth Conference, following King's illness (*October 14*). His return flight to Canada is delayed, prompting the RCAF to provide an aircraft for future flights by the Prime Minister (*October 23*). Publicly calls for a security pact among north Atlantic nations (*November 11*). **St. Laurent's government (1948-1957).** Becomes Canada's 12th Prime Minister (*November 15*). Signs the terms of reference to admit Newfoundland into Confederation (*December 11*). George Drew, Leader of the Opposition, is elected in a by-election (*December 20*).

1949: The 32-year-old Income War Tax Act drops the word 'War' (January 1). Meets with U.S. President Harry Truman in Washington to discuss the St. Lawrence Seaway project and the proposed North Atlantic Treaty Organization (NATO) (*February 11*). Parliament passes the NATO proposal (*March 28*). Newfoundland becomes Canada's tenth province (*March 31*); welcomes Premier-elect Joey Smallwood to Ottawa the next day. Appoints Gordon Bradley as Secretary of State, the first Newfoundlander in cabinet (*April 1*). Canada signs the North Atlantic Treaty, becoming a member of NATO (*April 4*). Appoints Vincent Massey to chair the Royal Commission on the Arts, Letters and Sciences (*April 8*). Tours Western Canada, picking up the media nickname 'Uncle Louis' along the way (*April 8-24*). The British Commonwealth becomes the Commonwealth of Nations (*April 26*). Announces that India will remain a member of the Commonwealth (*April 27*). Launches his election campaign at his former seminary school in Sherbrooke, Que. (*May 10*). Canada formally recognizes Israel (*May 17*). Receives an honorary Doctor of Civil Law degree from McGill University (*May 30*). Receives an honorary doctorate from Rensselaer Polytechnic Institute in Troy, New York. Loses his voice for a week during the campaign (*June 7*). Canada's 21st federal election: re-elected in Quebec East defeating Conservative Mark Drouin; his Liberal government is re-elected with a strong majority (*June 27*). Takes his first real holiday in years with his children and grandchildren at Kent Lodge near Bathurst, N.B. (*July*). 21st Parliament opens; nominates W. Ross Macdonald to be the 22nd Speaker of the House (*September 15*). Introduces legislation to make the Supreme Court of Canada the court of final appeal, a role formerly held by the British Privy Council (*September 16*). Douglas Abbott (Finance) devalues the dollar by 10 per cent in response to devaluation in Britain and other Commonwealth countries (*September 19*). Meets with India's Prime Minister Jawaharlal Nehru who addresses Parliament (*October 23-24*). Britain empowers Canada to amend the British North America Act (*December 2*). The Trans-Canada Highway Act becomes law, calling for a two-lane road across Canada (*December 10*).

A Drouin repeat

In the 1949 election, St. Laurent defeated Conservative candidate Mark Drouin by 18,000 votes in Quebec East. By then, the Drouins were used to getting clobbered by Prime Ministers. Thirty-two years earlier, Drouin's grandfather Ferdinand Omer Drouin ran against Prime Minister Laurier in the same riding, receiving one vote to every 12 for Laurier. Yet another Drouin, François-Xavier tackled Laurier even earlier in the 1887 election receiving only 22% of the vote. Mark Drouin was not entirely unlucky, however – he was later appointed Speaker of the Senate by Diefenbaker.

1950: Chairs the 12th Federal-Provincial Conference in Ottawa; there is agreement to repatriate the constitution, but no solution on how to do it (*January 10-11*). Pearson (External Affairs) indicates an interest in recognizing China (*January 14*); public outcry and

Chinese indifference squelch the initiative. Establishes the Department of Citizenship & Immigration, with his Parliamentary Assistant, Walter Harris, becoming the first minister (*January 18*). Splits the Department of Mines & Resources into Mines & Technical Surveys and Resources & Development (*January 18*). Supreme Court rules that federal government controls in an emergency are legitimate (*March 1*). Ratifies the Colombo Plan to help raise living standards in Asia over the next six years (*March 10*). Ottawa's Stornoway is purchased as the Leader of the Opposition's residence (*March 21*). Construction begins on the $95 million interprovincial pipeline to carry oil from Edmonton to Lake Superior (*May 1*). Buys a summer home in St. Patrick, Que., two doors away from the former summer residence of Macdonald (*Spring*). Meets with Pakistani Prime Minister Liaquat Ali Khan who addresses Parliament (*May 31-June 2*). Receives an honorary doctorate from St. Louis University in Missouri (*June 6*); warns students to avoid Communist witch hunts like the one being carried out by U.S. Senator Joe McCarthy. C.D. Howe (Trade & Commerce) introduces a proposal for an official Prime Minister's residence (*June 7*). Receives an honorary doctorate from St. Lawrence University in Canton, New York (*June*). Supports the UN's censure of North Korea after it invades South Korea (*June 25*). Announces Canada's decision to send troops to Korea only as part of a UN force (*June 30*). Canada's Inuit gain the right to vote (*June 30*). Tours western Canada (*July*); opens the Calgary Stampede in a downpour. William Lyon Mackenzie King, 10th Prime Minister of Canada, dies at Kingsmere (*July 22*). Attends King's funeral in Ottawa and his burial in Toronto (*July 26-27*). Humphrey Mitchell (Labour) dies suddenly in Ottawa (*August 1*); is given a state funeral. Announces recruitment for a special armed UN force in Korea (*August 7*). Meets unsuccessfully with rail workers in an attempt to end Canada's first national strike (*August 26*). Emergency session of Parliament opens to deal with the railway strike (*August 29*); workers are legislated back to work. Gives up hope of repatriating the constitution after unsuccessful negotiations at the 13th Federal-Provincial Conference in Quebec City, the first conference not held in Ottawa (*September 25-28*). The government unties the Canadian dollar from the gold standard and lets it float free against other currencies (*September 30*). Canada and U.S. agree on possible joint defence production (*October 26*). Receives an honorary Doctor of Laws degree and addresses convocation at the University of Toronto (*October 27*). Extends Governor General Earl Alexander's term for one year (*October 28*). Attends the UN General Assembly in New York (*November*); proposes a UN force for Korea, but is turned down. Hosts the Canadian Film Awards. Chairs the 14th Federal-Provincial Conference in Ottawa to propose extending the federal-provincial tax-rental agreement (*December 4-7*); all premiers sign on except Maurice Duplessis of Quebec. Meets with British Prime Minister Clement Atlee in Ottawa (*December 11*). First Canadian troops arrive in Korea (*December 18*). Takes the first trip to Europe on an official government plane by a Prime Minister (*December 31*).

1951: Attends the Commonwealth Prime Ministers Conference in London (*January 4-12*). Visits Paris (*January 13-14*). Engine problems delay his flight in Iceland (*January 14*); continues the next day on a TCA flight. Announces a $5-billion defence program (*February 5*). Six Princess Pats become the first Canadian casualties in the Korean conflict (*March 2*). Agrees to compensate western farmers for $65 million after Britain backs out of an agreement to buy wheat (*March 2*). Receives an honorary Doctor of Civil Law degree from the University of Western Ontario (*March 7*). Government approves the formation of TransCanada PipeLines to build a natural gas pipeline from Alberta to Montreal (*March 9*). Vacations in Bermuda (*March*). Becomes the first occupant of the official Prime Minister's residence at 24 Sussex Drive (*March*). Appoints Howe (Trade & Commerce) as minister of the new Department of Defence Production (*April 1*). Meets with French President Vincent Auriol who addresses Parliament (*April 5*). Canadian troops defend Kapyong Valley in Korea against a Chinese attack (*April 24-25*). Britain amends the BNA Act to allow federal-provincial control of old age pensions (*May 31*). Massey's Royal Commission releases its report on culture recommending the creation of the National Library of Canada and the Canada Council (*June 1*). Universal pension legislation is passed to provide pensions to citizens over 70 in participating provinces, and pensions to those in need between 65 and 70 (*June*). Indian Act of 1876 is amended to eliminate the ban on potlatches and other ceremonies and on drinking in public (*June*). Proposes federal grants for universities, as suggested by the Massey commission (*June 19*). Ends Canada's war status with Germany (*July 10*). Vacations at his new St. Patrick summer residence (*July*). Dispels rumours that he is planning to retire (*September 6*). Pearson (External Affairs) signs the peace treaty with Japan in San Francisco (*September 8*). NATO Council meets in Ottawa for the first time (*September 15-20*). Meets with U.S. President Truman in Washington to discuss the St. Lawrence Seaway project (*September 28*). Greets Princess Elizabeth in Montreal who is visiting Canada for the first time with her husband, Philip, the Duke of Edinburgh (*October 8*). Commits Canada to a NATO pledge to maintain military bases in Europe (*October 18*). House approves St. Lawrence Seaway Authority (*December 12*). Conservatives filibuster against proposed legislation to prohibit price-fixing by manufacturers, but the bill eventually passes (*December 17-27*).

1952: Universal pension plan comes into effect for those over 70 (*January 1*). Meets with British Prime Minister Winston Churchill in Ottawa (*January 11-15*); agrees to a request that Canada give up Governor General Earl Alexander to Churchill's cabinet. Announces the appointment of Vincent Massey as the first Canadian-born Governor General (*January 25*). Proclaims Elizabeth II as the new Queen following the death of George VI several hours before she is proclaimed Queen of the United Kingdom (*February 6*). Receives honorary doctorates from Laval, Montreal and Mount Allison universities. Agrees to stay on as leader rather than risk a government defeat (*July*). Fire damages the Parliamentary Library (*August 4*). Receives an honorary Doctor of Laws degree from the University of British Columbia (*September 4*). Pearson (External Affairs) is elected president of the 7th UN General Assembly (*October 14*). James Sinclair (father of Margaret) enters cabinet (*October 15*). Canadian troops fight to take Hill 355 in Korea (*October 17-23*). Visits England (*November 27-December 11*) to attend the Commonwealth Prime Ministers Conference and meet the new Queen. Announces the construction of a National Library (*December 22*).

1953: Brings railway management and labour representatives to Ottawa to negotiate a contract and avert a strike (*January 29*). Introduces bill to have the Queen identified as the Queen of Canada (*February 3*). Yukon's capital moves to Whitehorse from Dawson City (*April 1*). Meets with U.S. President Dwight Eisenhower in Washington (*May 7-9*). Sails to England (*May 19*) to attend the coronation of Elizabeth II (*June 2*). Attends the Commonwealth Prime Ministers Conference (*June 3-9*). Receives an honorary degree from Oxford University (*June 6*). Returns to Canada (*June 10*). Appoints his assistant, Jack Pickersgill, as Secretary of State (*June 12*). Fighting in Korea ends (July 27). Canada's 22nd federal election: re-elected in Quebec East defeating Raymond Maher (Conservative); his Liberal government gets another majority (*August 10*). Receives an honorary degree from St. Francis Xavier University. Appoints Jean Lesage as Resources & Development minister (*September 17*). Announces that Canada and the U.S. are building an early-warning system to defend against possible air attack (*September 30*). Authorizes the 1st Canadian Infantry Division, the first in peacetime (*October 16*). 22nd Parliament opens; nominates Louis-René Beaudoin to be the 23rd Speaker of the House (*November 12*). Meets with U.S. President Eisenhower who addresses Parliament (*November 14*).

1954: Leaves on a 45-day world tour (*February 4*) of England, France, Germany, Italy, Pakistan (*February 12-21*), India (where he addresses Parliament) (*February 23*), Ceylon,

Indonesia, Philippines, Canadian troops in South Korea, Japan, Hawaii and back to Canada (*March 9*). Canada's most northerly Arctic islands are named Queen Elizabeth Islands (*February 5*). Woodside, Mackenzie King's boyhood home in Kitchener, becomes a national park (*April 1*). Meets with Ethiopia Emperor Haile Selassie in Ottawa (*June 4*). Meets with British Prime Minister Winston Churchill in Ottawa (*June 29*). Appoints Walter Harris (Citizenship & Immigration) as Finance minister after Abbott (Finance), Brooke Claxton (National Defence) and Lionel Chevrier (Transport) retire from cabinet (*July 1*). Board of Transport Commissioners approves in principle a TransCanada PipeLines application to build a natural gas pipeline from Alberta to eastern Canada and the U.S. Midwest (*July*). Canada serves on the international commission to supervise the Indo-China armistice (*July 28*). Turns sod for the St. Lawrence Seaway with New York Governor Thomas Dewey at Cornwall, Ont. (*August 10*). Meets with Duplessis to discuss taxation; agrees to give Quebec an alternative to the federal-provincial tax-rental agreement that only Quebec had adopted (*October 5*). Calls for a Royal Commission to look into the devastation caused by Hurricane Hazel that killed 83 people in southern Ontario (*October 19*). Elizabeth II and the Queen Mother visit Ottawa (*November 12-17*). Recalls the remaining Canadian troops from Korea (*December 5*). Ottawa celebrates it centennial (*December 30*).

1955: Parliament is televised for the first time for the Speech from the Throne (*January 7*). TransCanada PipeLines begins negotiations asking the government to guarantee a $295-million mortgage (*January 7*); rejected. Announces plan to build Canada's first atomic power plant near Des Joachims, Ont. (*January 24*). Attends the Commonwealth Prime Ministers Conference in England (*January 31-February 9*). Becomes a Freeman of London (*February 1*). TransCanada PipeLines abandons its plan to start construction in 1955 (*March 17*). Chairs the 15th Federal-Provincial Conference, a preliminary meeting to discuss unemployment relief and tax sharing with the provinces (*April 26-27*). Conservatives begin a filibuster in the House to stop the Defence Production Bill (*June 13*). Visits son Renault, who is recovering from a heart attack, in Toronto (*June 15*). Agrees to changes in the Defence Production Bill to end Conservative opposition (*July 11*); the Defence Production department becomes permanent, but parts of its work will expire within four years. Announces the appointment of MP David Croll as Canada's first Jewish Senator (*August 4*). Alcide Côté (Postmaster General) dies and is given a state funeral (*August 7*). Howe (Transport) opens the Canso Causeway between Nova Scotia's mainland and Cape Breton Island (*August 13*). Breaks a lower leg bone while fishing at Knob Lake, Labrador (*August 19*). Agreement is reached that Canada and Ontario will build the natural gas pipeline and lease it to TransCanada PipeLines (*September 1*). Attends 50th anniversary celebrations in Alberta and Saskatchewan (*September 4*). His son Jean-Paul becomes an MP after winning a by-election in Temscouata, Que. (*September 26*). The Canadian Unemployment Act comes into effect (*October 2*). Chairs the 16th Federal-Provincial Conference at which a plan is developed to share the cost of unemployment insurance (*October 3-6*). Receives an honorary Doctor of Laws degree from McMaster University (*October*). First of 14 new naval destroyer escorts is to be named *St. Laurent* (*October 29*).

1956: A federal agreement with TransCanada PipeLines is announced (*January 10*). Accompanies his son Jean-Paul into Parliament (*January 10*). Meets with British Prime Minister Sir Anthony Eden who addresses Parliament (*February 4-6*). Discovers he has an ulcer (*February*). Meets with Italian President Giovanni Gronchi who addresses Parliament (*March 4*). Chairs the 17th Federal-Provincial Conference in Ottawa to explore tax sharing (*March 9*). The pipeline bill is introduced, but debate is postponed to May (*March 15*). Meets with U.S. President Eisenhower and Mexican President Adolfo Ruiz Cortines at White Sulphur Spring, Virginia (*March 26-27*). Howe (Trade & Commerce) expands the government's construction role on the pipeline (*May 14*) and imposes closure of debate to end in early June. Opposition attempts to tie up debate on the pipeline bill (*May*). Receives an honorary degree from the University of Sherbrooke, his alma mater. Meets with Indonesian President Achmed Sukarno who addresses Parliament (*June 5*). Pipeline bill is passed following closure (*June 6*); receives Royal Assent five days later. Attends Commonwealth Prime Ministers Conference in London with Pearson (External Affairs) (*June 27-July 6*). Persuades Beaudoin, Speaker of the House, not to resign over his handling of the pipeline debate (*July 2*). Introduces legislation for equalization payments to the provinces (*July 16*). The Female Employees Equal Pay Act guarantees equal pay for equal work for federal government female workers (*August 14*). Drew, Leader of the Opposition, resigns for health reasons (*September 18*), and rejects a Senate seat offer. Government agrees to sell 24 F-86 jet fighters to Israel (*September 21*); order cancelled a month later when Israel attacks Egypt. His first great-grandchild is born (*September*). Tells Britain that Canada does not support the attack on Egyptian airfields following Egypt's nationalization of the Suez Canal (*October 30*). Pearson (External Affairs) flies to New York to push for a UN peacekeeping force in Egypt (*November 1*). UN votes for a peacekeeping force, but Britain and France invade Egypt anyway (*November 3*); Britain later withdraws because of lack of international support. Offers Canadian soldiers for the Middle East peacekeeping force (*November 7*); Egypt feels Canada's military is too similar to British troops. Announces formation of the Canada Council to financially assist the arts, humanities and social sciences (*November 12*). First Canadian military presence in a UN peacekeeping force arrives in Egypt (*November 24*). Grants $1 million to provide victims of the Hungarian revolution free passage to Canada (*November 28*). John Diefenbaker is elected leader of the Progressive Conservative party (*December 10*); becomes Leader of the Opposition four days later.

1957: Intervenes to settle the Canadian Pacific Railway strike (*January 8*). Parliament proclaims Thanksgiving to be a national holiday on the second Monday of October (*January 31*). About 1,400 people attend a Quebec City banquet to celebrate his 75th birthday (*February 1*). Meets with French Premier Guy Mollett who addresses Parliament (*March 4*). Supreme Court nullifies Quebec's Padlock Law (*March 6*). UN emergency force takes over the Gaza Strip in the Middle East (*March 7*). Gordon (Finance) tables a budget that introduces the Registered Retired Savings Plan (RRSP) (*March 14*). Meets with British Prime Minister Harold Macmillan in Bermuda to discuss the Common Market and the Middle East (*March 25-26*). Formula for equalization payments from rich to poor provinces comes into effect (*April 1*). Herbert Norman, Canada's Ambassador to Egypt who had been falsely accused of communist sympathies, jumps to his death in Cairo (*April 4*). Chevrier re-enters cabinet as Privy Council President (*April 25*). Paul Hellyer enters cabinet as Associate National Defence minister (*April 26*). Canada's 23rd federal election: re-elected in Quebec East defeating Louis Gagnon (Conservative); Diefenbaker's Conservatives defeat the Liberals by six seats (*June 10*). **St. Laurent's government ends** (*June 21*). Becomes director of six corporations: Rock City Tobacco, Industrial Acceptance Corp., Investors Syndicate of Canada, Famous Players Canadian Corp., Rothmans of Pall Mall Canada, and La Compagnie Miron. Holidays at St. Patrick's (*Summer*). Son Renault and son-in-law Mathieu Samson urge him to consider stepping down (*September*). Pearson and Chevrier convince him he should retire as party leader (*September 4*); announces his retirement two days later. Moves into the Chateau Laurier, declining to use Stornoway (*September*).

1958: Pearson is elected leader of the Liberal party (*January 16*). St. Laurent resigns as party leader and Leader of the Opposition (*January 16*). Seconds Pearson's motion in Parliament that the government resign (*January 20*); instead, Prime Minister Diefenbaker lashes back and calls another election. Vacations in Florida (*February*). Announces his retirement from active politics (*February 17*). His son Jean-Paul is defeated in the federal election (*March 31*) and moves to Florida.

1959: Attends the unveiling of his portrait on Parliament Hill by Audrey MacNaughton (*March 4*). Has a prostate operation in Boston to improve his health (*Spring*). Rejoins the family law firm after his son Renault suffers a second heart attack. Becomes chairman of the board for a carpet company. Becomes president of the Canadian Heart Foundation.

1961: Speaks at a Liberal rally in Ottawa honoring the late C.D. Howe (*January*).

1962: Son Renault becomes president of the Canadian Bar Association.

1963: Receives an honorary Doctor of Laws degree from the University of Sask-atchewan (*May 14*).

1964: A peak in the Rocky Mountains is named Mount Louis Saint Laurent (*October 6*).

1966: His wife Jeanne dies in Quebec City following a short illness (*November 14*). Attends the launching of the *Louis St. Laurent* icebreaker in Montreal (*December*).

1967: Privately endorses Pierre Trudeau as his choice to succeed Pearson as leader. Receives the Order of Canada. His brother Maurice dies (*September 26*).

1968: Confined to a wheelchair after breaking his hip.

1972: His closest sibling Lora dies (*January 23*).

1973: Dies in Quebec City (*July 25*); buried in Compton following a state funeral at Notre-Dame Cathedral.

Books about St. Laurent

- **1967**: Dale C. Thomson; *Louis St. Laurent: Canadian* (Macmillan)
- **1975**: Jack W. Pickersgill; *My Years With Louis St. Laurent: A Political Memoir* (University of Toronto)
- **1981**: Jack W. Pickersgill; *The Canadians: Louis St. Laurent* (Fitzhenry & Whiteside)
- **1982**: Magella Quinn & Claude Marcil; *Louis-S St. Laurent: Jurist, Politician and Statesman* (Parks Canada)

13

John Diefenbaker

The Unabashed Prime Minister

John Diefenbaker's lengthy path to leadership was littered with seven rejections at the polls or on convention-room floors. Through it all, he built a growing base of Canadians who warmed to his homespun eccentricities. Ultimately, 'Dief' won the largest majority ever in a federal election. He appointed Canada's first female cabinet minister (Ellen Fairclough), first Indigenous Senator (James Gladstone) and first French-Canadian Governor General (Georges Vanier). But he also foundered by scrapping the Avro Arrow and firing Bank of Canada Governor James Coyne. Rejected by his own party in the 1967 leadership race, he faced defeat yet again.

Diefenbaker the Politician

Prime Minister of Canada: June 21, 1957 – April 22, 1963
Length of term: 5 years, 10 months, 1 day
Parliaments as Prime Minister: 23rd; 24th; 25th
Age on entering office: 62
Political party: Progressive Conservative
Leader of party: December 14, 1956 – September 9, 1967
Member of Parliament: March 26, 1940 – August 16, 1979
Ridings represented: Lake Centre [Sask.] 1940-1953; Prince Albert [Sask.] 1953-1979
Cabinet portfolios: External Affairs (1957); Privy Council President (1962-1963)
Other political posts: Wakaw, Saskatchewan, councillor (1920-1923); Saskatchewan Conservative Party Leader (1936-1940); Leader of the Opposition (1956-1957, 1963-1967)
Titles: King's Counsel (1929); Canadian Privy Councillor (1957); Imperial Privy Councillor (1957)
Quotes: "Freedom is the right to be wrong, not the right to do wrong." (1958) "[New MPs] do one of two things – they grow or they swell." (1974 in *The Globe & Mail*)
Lived after term: 16 years

DIEFENBAKER THE MAN

Name: John George Diefenbaker
Born: September 18, 1895, Neustadt, Ontario
Ancestry: German, Scottish
Religion: Baptist
Education: B.A. [Bachelor of Arts] (University of Saskatchewan, Saskatoon, 1915); M.A. [Master of Arts in Political Science and Economics] (Saskatchewan, 1916); LL.B. [Bachelor of Law] (Saskatchewan, 1919)
Nickname: Dief the Chief
Military service: Canadian Army (1916-1917)
Occupation: lawyer
Occupation after term: Leader of the Opposition; MP
Publications: *Those Things We Treasure* (1972); *One Canada: Memoirs Vol. 1: The Crusading Years 1895-1956* (1975); *One Canada: Memoirs Vol. 2: The Years of Achievement 1956-1962* (1976); *One Canada: Memoirs Vol. 3: The Tumultuous Years 1962-1967* (1977); *My First Prairie Christmas* (1988)
Appearance: "this man with the shock-wave hair and saxophone voice was no silk-tie Conservative (George Bowering in *Egotists and Autocrats*); "With eyes flaming, arms flailing and shoulders and jowls aquiver" (Knowlton Nash in *Kennedy and Diefenbaker*)
Personality: "He was large, loud and rambunctious, humorous and churlish, sanctimonious and savage, magnificently obtuse and devastatingly incisive (Gordon Donaldson in *Sixteen Men*); "transformed himself into an icon, a national treasure, a loveable, old curmudgeon." (J.L. Granatstein & Norman Hillmer in *Prime Ministers: Ranking Canada's Leaders*)
First marriage: Edna May Brower, June 29, 1929, Walmer Road Baptist Church, Toronto, Ontario
Age at first marriage: 23
Years married: 21
Second marriage: Olive Evangeline Freeman Palmer, December 8, 1953, Park Road Baptist Church, Toronto, Ontario
Age at second marriage: 58
Years married: 23
Died: August 16, 1979, Ottawa, Ontario
Age at death: 83
Cause of death: heart failure
Buried: Diefenbaker Canada Centre, University of Saskatchewan, Saskatoon, Saskatchewan

Diefenbaker was the:

- First Prime Minister to win more than 200 seats
- First Progressive Conservative Prime Minister
- First Prime Minister from Saskatchewan
- First Prime Minister of German ancestry
- First Prime Minister to serve in a World War
- First Prime Minister to use Harrington Lake as a summer residence
- Second Prime Minister with no previous cabinet experience

- Second Prime Minister to lead two minority governments
- Second Prime Minister to be defeated by a non-confidence vote
- Third longest serving Member of Parliament (over 39 years)
- Third Prime Minister to lead a minority government
- Third Prime Minister born in Ontario
- Only deceased Prime Minister not to have a mountain named after him
- Ninth Prime Minister who was a lawyer

Diefenbaker's legacy
- Enacted the Bill of Rights
- Introduced the first non-racist immigration policy
- Extended the vote to Indigenous peoples
- Appointed the first woman to cabinet (Ellen Fairclough)
- Recommended the appointment of the first French Canadian Governor General (Georges Vanier)
- Recommended the first Indigenous Senator (James Gladstone)
- Scrapped the Avro Arrow aircraft project

Diefenbaker's Family

Diefenbaker's Parents

Father: William Thomas Diefenbaker
Born: April 6, 1868, Hawkesville, Ontario
Occupation: teacher; civil servant
Died: February 12, 1945, Saskatoon, Saskatchewan
Age at death: 76
Note: Only teacher to have two future PMs in his classes: William Lyon Mackenzie King in Berlin (Kitchener) when he was a student teacher, and his own son at Plains Road school in Todmorden (Toronto).

Mother: Mary Florence Bannerman
Born: October 26, 1872, Port Elgin, Ontario
Married: May 2, 1894, Port Elgin, Ontario
Date of death: February 20, 1961, Saskatoon, Saskatchewan
Age at death: 88

Diefenbaker's Brother (1 sibling; John the oldest)

Brother: Elmer Clive Diefenbaker (1898-1971), never married

Diefenbaker's First Wife

Name: Edna Mae Brower
Born: November 30, 1899, Wawanesa, Manitoba
Father: Chauncey Brower (teacher)
Mother: Maren 'Mary' Knutson
Occupation: teacher
Age at marriage: 29
Children: none

Died: February 7, 1951, Saskatoon, Saskatchewan
Age at death: 51
Burial place: Woodlawn Cemetery, Saskatoon, Saskatchewan
Younger than Diefenbaker: 4 years
Died before Diefenbaker: 28 years

Diefenbaker's Second Wife

Name: Olive Evangeline Freeman Palmer
Born: April 14, 1902, Roland, Manitoba
Father: Dr. Charles Bradford Freeman (Baptist minister)
Mother: Angie Alicia Eaton
Occupation: teacher; education administrator
Age at marriage: 51
First husband: Harry F. Palmer (1898-1936), 1933
Children: 1 – Carolyn (from first marriage)
Died: December 22, 1976, Ottawa, Ontario
Age at death: 74
Burial place: Ottawa; moved in 1979 to the Diefenbaker Canada Centre, University of Saskatchewan, Saskatoon, Saskatchewan
Younger than Diefenbaker: 7 years
Died before Diefenbaker: 2 years

Diefenbaker's Stepdaughter

Name: Carolyn Diefenbaker (1934-2010); married Donald Weir; 5 children – John, Michael, Victoria (Fitzgerald), Sarah (Donnelly) and Sandy

Political Stories

Five losses in 15 years

Diefenbaker had his first taste of elected office in 1920 when he won by 12 votes to become a member of council in Wakaw, Sask. He served for three years, but then endured 15 years of political rejection. Luck wasn't with him from 1925 to 1940. He was defeated twice federally, twice provincially and once municipally, before capturing a seat in the House of Commons.

His first federal attempt was in Prince Albert where he garnered less than a quarter of the votes and a third-place finish behind local pharmacist Charles McDonald (Liberal) and incumbent Andrew Knox (Progressive) in the 1925 election. Months later, McDonald stepped down to open the seat for Prime Minister King. Diefenbaker opted not to challenge him. But he did take King on the following year when another election was called, receiving about one-third of the vote.

Anything but frustrated, Diefenbaker turned his energy to provincial politics where Conservatives were barely making an imprint. In 1929, he lost by a mere 145 votes against Saskatchewan Attorney General T.C. Davis. No matter; time to try city politics. He ran for mayor of Prince Albert in 1933, losing by 48 votes to H.J. Fraser.

Moving back to the provincial level, he accepted the leadership of the Saskatchewan Conservatives, a position no one wanted, then tried his luck again in the 1938 election in Arm River. He lost to Liberal incumbent Herman Danielson by 190 votes. Not a single Conservative won across the province.

By 1939 he wasn't so keen to do it all again, but the Conservatives in Lake Centre thought otherwise. They manoeuvered him into the nomination when all the other candidates endorsed him. Running under Meighen's temporarily named National Government, he beat Liberal incumbent John Johnston by more than 1,000 votes. Diefenbaker was finally on his way to Ottawa.

Three cracks at party leadership

It was a good thing that Diefenbaker was used to losing. His burning desire to be federal party leader pitted him against strong rivals and it was not until his third try that he finally succeeded.

He'd only been an MP two years when he first ran in 1942 after Meighen stepped down. He knew he didn't have a chance, but his ardent Saskatchewan supporters wanted him on the ballot. The Tories had their hearts set on long-time Manitoba Premier John Bracken. It didn't matter that he was a Liberal-leaning Progressive; he won elections in Manitoba. He also won the Conservative leadership (now Progressive Conservative at his request) with over 60% of the votes on the second ballot. Diefenbaker came third, behind M.A. MacPherson who was contesting his second leadership race.

Bracken was gone by 1948 and Diefenbaker was back on the ballot again, this time against another popular premier, Ontario's George Drew. His hope was that his experience and vision for the country would be enough to help him buck the party machine. They weren't. It only took one ballot to confirm Drew with two-thirds of the votes. Diefenbaker polled third again, this time behind Donald Fleming.

Despite enthusiastic support for Fleming who was back again for the 1956 leadership campaign, Diefenbaker ran and won on the first ballot at the convention with 60% support from the delegates.

Winning by a landslide

When Diefenbaker's Conservatives took power for the first time since the Great Depression, they could hardly believe their luck. Ironically, they would go on to score an even greater electoral achievement thanks to the Liberals' newly minted leader, Lester Pearson, who gave Diefenbaker an opportunity he couldn't ignore.

Pearson's maiden speech as Leader of the Opposition in January 1958, naively demanded that the government resign because of economic mismanagement. The charge wasn't a surprise; the economy was in a recession. But when Pearson arrogantly demanded that the House let the Liberals re-form a government without an election, the Conservatives pounced.

Brandishing documents, Diefenbaker declared the St. Laurent government had been aware of the possibility of an economic recession. Then, the Prime Minister accepted the opposition's bluff and called a snap election.

The timing proved masterful. The Conservatives ended up winning the largest majority in Canadian history, attaining the highest popular vote ever in peacetime (53.6%). And they did it in an election that tops the list for voter turnout (79.4%).

Diefenbaker had more than Liberal bungling to thank for the feat. Two provinces proved to be key to the boost in Conservative fortunes. The retirement of Liberal leader St. Laurent robbed Quebec of a 'favourite son' on the federal scene, and Premier Maurice Duplessis threw his electoral machine behind the Tories. The result netted Diefenbaker 50 Quebec seats, up from nine the previous year.

In the West, the Social Credit party imploded, losing every one of its 19 seats, eliminating the alternative choice for right-wing voters. Thirteen of those seats were in Alberta and they all went to the Conservatives. In fact, the entire province turned blue, establishing Alberta as an unassailable Tory stronghold until the Reform party emerged 35 years later.

The Diefenbunkers

At the height of the Cold War, Diefenbaker knew he needed to tackle the threat of a potential nuclear attack by the Soviet Union. He had 50 bomb shelters built across the country to protect the political and military leadership. Referred to by a bewildering series of abbreviations (CEGHQ, REGHQ, MEGHQ, ZEGHQ, RU), the underground shelters were quickly dubbed Diefenbunkers.

Central headquarters was located in Carp, Ont., 38 km west of Parliament Hill. It was a four-storey underground warren of rooms designed to protect and sustain the country's governing elite for several weeks. The complex wasn't expected to deflect a direct hit, but none of the Diefenbunkers were ever put to the test. The sites were decommissioned in the mid-1990s and the Carp complex is now a tourist attraction.

The Diefenbunker in Penfold, Alta., suffered a more ignoble end. Sold privately, it was rumoured that an outlaw motorcycle gang was interested in acquiring it. To prevent such a possibility, the Chrétien government bought it back and had it destroyed.

The Prime Minister and his wife had an alternative to the standard bunkers, if needed. In the 1950s, the Emergency Measures Organization insisted on adding a bomb shelter to 24 Sussex Drive. One wonders how effective the finished sanctuary would have been; it cost $450 to build.

The Coyne Affair

The Bank of Canada's second governor, James Coyne, was a cautious spender with a firm hand on the country's financial levers; controls that might have relaxed the financial pains of the late 1950s recession. Appalled by the government's tendency to spend beyond its means, he started peppering his public speeches with his concerns about budget deficits in 1959.

Diefenbaker's Finance minister, Donald Fleming, put up with the criticisms for a year and a half before demanding that Coyne stop publicly chastising the government. Coyne agreed. But the public spat needed a firmer resolution and Fleming requested Coyne's resignation. The governor refused, even after his own board reluctantly voted for his dismissal. So, Fleming introduced legislation to remove him from office. In an attempt to stop its passage, Coyne wrote MPs to tell them, "Mr. Diefenbaker has been the evil genius behind this whole affair." The House passed the bill.

But the Senate, with its Liberal majority, did not. Minutes after rejecting the bill, Coyne submitted his resignation, saying the Senate action vindicated his stand. He was gone, and so was the shield of infallibility wrapped around the Diefenbaker government after winning its huge majority.

A fourth, humiliating leadership bid

Many Conservatives felt Diefenbaker had squandered his hold on power. The party's sense of dissatisfaction only increased when the Liberals returned to power in 1963. Several Quebec MPs bolted from caucus to protest his leadership. The party's president pushed for a review, finally succeeding in having a leadership convention called for 1967.

Most party members expected Diefenbaker would resign, but he wasn't saying either way. They knew he was upset that the Conservatives had endorsed a two-nation, French-English policy over his protestations that there was only "one Canada". The convention was already underway when he allowed his name to stand on the ballot so he could fight the two-nation concept.

His speech to delegates was short and off-the-cuff, a last plea for one Canada. In a vote littered with 11 candidates and five ballots, Diefenbaker never managed to move beyond fifth place. After the third ballot, he stepped down and moved his support to Manitoba Premier Duff Roblin. But it was too late to beat Nova Scotia Premier Robert Stanfield who maintained a lead throughout.

Although Diefenbaker threatened to walk out of the convention if the two-nation policy remained, he didn't follow through. In fact, he stayed on the Hill as a Conservative MP until his death 12 years later.

PERSONAL STORIES

Caught in a snowstorm

The winter of 1907-08 was one of the most brutal for homesteaders in Saskatchewan. Dressing warmly and not getting lost were essential, but the weather wasn't always predictable. That was the case on March 11, 1908, when Diefenbaker and his Uncle Ed, who was also his teacher, left for school in somewhat balmy (a mere minus 15 degrees Celsius) conditions.

The two decided to stay after school for a concert. But it ended early when a fierce blizzard descended on the endless prairie landscape. In their rapid run home in an open sled, the Diefenbakers' horse lost its way, moving forward aimlessly until the sled became stuck.

Forced to spend the night in the sled, John had no boots and only two blankets to ward off the blowing snow. His uncle kept nudging him to stop him from falling into a fatal sleep. The next morning, the storm was still in full howl, but suddenly it ended. Once the sled was unburied, it took them another hour to reach home.

Diefenbaker's legs were frozen from the knees down. His parents tended him for the next three weeks in an effort to stop the spread of gangrene and restore his ability to walk. Eventually he was able to return to school, but never overcame his chronic aversion to blizzards.

Olive Diefenbaker

After returning from overseas service during the First World War (he was hit with a shovel while digging trenches), Diefenbaker, a 22-year-old law student, resumed attending youth gatherings at the local Baptist church in Saskatoon. He was particularly smitten by the minister's daughter, Olive Freeman, and began to muster the courage to ask her out – until he discovered she was only 15.

Diefenbaker went on to build his law career, marrying Edna Brower in 1929. Olive's family moved to Brandon, Man., and she later became a teacher in Ontario. In 1933 she married Harry Palmer, but three years later she was a widower with a two-year old daughter, Carolyn.

Specializing in vocational guidance, Olive eventually became Ontario's Assistant Director of Vocational Guidance in Toronto. In 1953, she was asked to become Director, but turned it down. The reason was a growing, but secret, relationship she was having with Diefenbaker who had lost his wife two years earlier. The two were married in December.

She had become the wife of a seasoned and ambitious MP. Within three years, Diefenbaker was Conservative party leader. Olive refused to move into Stornoway because she was confident Diefenbaker would require the Prime Minister's residence shortly. She was right.

Olive was Diefenbaker's anchor, his advisor, his hostess, his confidante, his defender. Her ability to present a public persona of grace and warmth helped to offset the crusty edges of her husband.

Diefenbaker's Timeline

1895: Born in Neustadt, Ont. (*September 18*).

1897: His family moves to Greenwood, Ont., north of Whitby.

1898: His brother Elmer is born (*April 21*).

1899: Attends Greenwood school at age 4; his father is the teacher (*Winter*).

1900: His family moves to Todmorden (now in Toronto), Ont. (*Summer*). Attends Plains Road School at Todmorden where his father is the teacher (*September*).

1903: His family moves to Fort Carlton, North-West Territories (now Saskatchewan) because of his father's failing health (*August 15*). Lives in one-half of the Fort Carlton school (*September*). Meets Gabriel Dumont who often visits the Carlton area (*Fall*).

1904: His family buys land north of Borden (Sask.); $10 for 160 acres (*December 15*).

1905: Spends the summer on the Borden property (*July-August*). His family moves to Hague, Saskatchewan district (*August*). The district becomes Saskatchewan, Canada's ninth province (*September 1*).

1906: His family moves to a farm near Borden (*August*). Attends school in Halcyonia (*September*); his teacher is his uncle, Ed Diefenbaker.

1908: Caught in a snowstorm with his Uncle Ed (*March 11*); both suffer frostbite after a night sleeping in an open sleigh.

1909: Fails his year at school, having unsuccessfully written an exam in Saskatoon after eating too much ice cream (*June*).

1910: His family moves to Saskatoon so he will be able to attend university; attends Saskatoon Collegiate (*February*). As a newsboy, sells a newspaper to Laurier who is visiting Saskatoon to lay a cornerstone at the University of Saskatchewan (*July 29*).

1911: Captivated by the federal election campaign and decides to become a Conservative (*September*).

1912: Graduates from Saskatoon Collegiate (now Nutana) (*June*). Enrols at the University of Saskatchewan (*September*).

1913: Acts as Conservative leader and Leader of the Opposition in the Boys Parliament in Regina (*Spring*). Works as a farm labourer south of Blaine Lake (*Summer*). Joins the debating club and is later elected to the student council.

1914: Teaches Doukhobor children, Grades 1 to 5, at Wheat Heart School (*Summer*); does not receive his teaching certificate after the inspector finds him shooting gophers instead of being in the classroom.

1915: Receives his Bachelor of Arts degree from the University of Saskatchewan (*May*). Sells illustrated Bibles and war books by bicycle in northern Saskatchewan with little success; arrested in Hanley for selling without a licence (turns out the company did have a licence) (*Summer*). Enrols in the master's program in economics and political science at the University of Saskatchewan (*September*).

Yearbook predicts opposition

The University of Saskatchewan's 1915 yearbook predicted that graduate John Diefenbaker would be Canada's Leader of the Opposition by 1955. The forecast was only out by one year. He assumed the job in 1956.

1916: Enlists in the army in the First World War (*March*); takes a six-week training course in Winnipeg. Receives his Master of Arts degree in political science and economics, in absentia (*May*). Briefly articles with Saskatchewan lawyer Russell Hartney (*May*). Sent overseas as a lieutenant in the 39th Battalion of the Saskatoon Fusiliers (*September 23*). Stationed at Shorncliffe, England (*October*), later transferred to the Canadian Military School at Crowborough, Sussex.

1917: Invalided home after being hit in the back with a shovel while digging trenches in Crowsborough; psychological trauma may have contributed to his return to Canada. Enrols in the University of Saskatchewan's law school (*Fall*). Meets Olive Freeman in Saskatoon whom he marries 36 years later (*Fall*). Articles with the Saskatoon law office of Ferguson & MacDermid (*Fall*). Campaigns in the federal election for Conservative James Wilson (*November-December*).

1919: Articles with the Saskatoon law firm of T.A. Lynd & Yule. Receives his Bachelor of Laws degree (*May*). Called to the Saskatchewan bar (*June*). Opens a law practice in

Wakaw, Sask., along with law student Michael Stechishin (*July 1*). Wins his first case; the jury reputedly acquits his client because it is the young lawyer's first – as well as his birthday (*September 18*). Publicly opposes the firing of professors at the University of Saskatchewan (*Fall*).

1920: Elected councillor in Wakaw by 12 votes; serves for three years. Asks Olive Freeman in Saskatoon for a date just before her family moves to Brandon.

1921: Turns down an offer to join the Liberal party. Takes a driving trip to Vancouver.

1922: Handles a successful appeal for two rural school trustees convicted of permitting French to be taught beyond the first grade. Buys a summer cottage on Wakaw Lake. Initiated as a freemason into Wakaw Lodge (*September 11*).

1923: Takes a driving trip to Los Angeles. Becomes engaged to Beth Newell, but she is diagnosed with tuberculosis and dies the following year. Operated on after suffering a hemorrhage caused by laughing when an auto racer accidently drove into the South Saskatchewan River.

1924: Moves his law practice to Prince Albert, Sask., maintaining an office in Wakaw.

1925: Forms a law partnership with F.C. Cousins and R.B. Godfrey (who runs his Wakaw office); Cousins dies soon after. Wins the Conservative nomination for the Prince Albert federal riding by acclamation (*August 6*). Canada's 15th federal election: polls third behind Liberal Charles McDonald and Progressive Andrew Knox (*October 29*).

1926: Decides not to contest the by-election after McDonald resigns to open up a seat for King who lost his North York seat (*January 16*); King wins. Diefenbaker becomes chairman of the Eclectic Club; introduces Arctic explorer Roald Amundsen at one of the men's club meetings in Saskatoon. Canada's 16th federal election: polls second to King in Prince Albert (*September 14*).

1927: Supports Hugh Guthrie at the first Conservative leadership convention in Winnipeg (*October 12*); R.B. Bennett wins.

1928: Heckles the Saskatchewan Premier James Gardiner at a provincial Liberal rally and ends up being invited to speak (*October*).

1929: Polls second in the provincial election to Attorney General T.C. Davis in Prince Albert, losing by 145 votes (*June 6*). Marries Edna Brower in Toronto, a teacher from Langham, Saskatchewan (*June 29*). Closes his Wakaw satellite law office. Named King's Counsel (*December 31*).

1930: Declines the Conservative federal nomination for Long Lake (Saskatchewan) riding because of an ulcer.

1932: Elected vice-president of the Saskatchewan Conservative Party.

1933: Hires Jack Cuelenaere to article with his law firm (*June*). Runs for mayor of Prince Albert; defeated by H.J. Fraser by 48 votes.

1935: Becomes president of the Saskatchewan Conservative Party. Declines the Conservative federal nomination for Prince Albert.

1936: Visits Europe and attends the unveiling of the Canadian Memorial at Vimy Ridge (*July 26*) as well as the Olympic Games in Berlin (*August*). Wins the leadership of the Saskatchewan Conservative party by default (*October 29*).

1938: Polls second in the provincial election to Liberal Herman Danielson in Arm River (*June 8*). Receives a wedding gift of $2,500 from R.B. Bennett, eight years after his marriage (*July*). Represents Grey Owl's daughter in the court case to settle her father's estate. Leadership is endorsed at the Saskatchewan Conservative convention in Moose Jaw (*October 26*).

1939: Declines the Conservative nomination in Lake Centre [Sask.] but members of the riding's party vote him in anyway (*June 15*).

1940: Canada's 19th federal election: elected in Lake Centre defeating the Liberal Deputy Speaker of the House Fred Johnson (*March 26*). Moves into the Chateau Laurier with Edna (*Spring*). Richard Hanson becomes interim party leader in Ottawa, replacing Robert Manion (*May 13*). Begins his career in Parliament; colleagues include three Conservative MPs who were in his 1903 class at Plains Road School: Joe Harris, R.H. McGregor and George Tustin (*May 16*).

1941: Tells King and Hanson he will not support Hanson's agreement with the Liberals about the war expenditures committee (*February 24*). Meighen again becomes Conservative party leader (*November 8*), but is defeated in a York South by-election. Diefenbaker becomes Justice critic for the Conservatives after St. Laurent is appointed Justice minister (*December*).

1942: Polls third at the Conservative leadership convention in Winnipeg, behind John Bracken and Murdo MacPherson (*December 11*).

1943: Defeated by one vote by Gordon Graydon in his bid to succeed Hanson as Conservative House leader (*January 27*).

1944: Succeeds in getting Conservative MPs to support the government's Family Allowance Bill (*July*).

1945: His father William dies in Saskatoon (*February 12*). Attends the United Nations San Francisco Conference as advisor to Conservative delegate Gordon Graydon. Canada's 20th federal election: re-elected in Lake Centre defeating Leslie Bright (CCF) (*June 11*).

1946: His wife Edna spends several months at a Guelph sanitorium receiving treatment for depression (*January-March*). Attends Commonwealth-U.S. meetings in Washington and Bermuda. Attempts unsuccessfully to have a Canadian Bill of Rights considered as part of the proposed Canadian Citizenship Act (*May*). Becomes External Affairs critic for the Conservatives after St. Laurent is appointed External Affairs minister (*September*).

1947: Buys a house on 19th Street West in Prince Albert, which he later outfits with a bed and couch belonging to Sir John A. Macdonald.

1948: Polls second at the Conservative leadership convention in Ottawa, behind George Drew (*October 2*).

1949: Dumps the party's campaign literature in Lake Centre's lake, feeling it is counterproductive (*June*). Canada's 21st federal election: re-elected in Lake Centre defeating Delmar Valleau (CCF) (*June 27*).

1950: Attends the Commonwealth Parliamentary Association conference in Australia (*December*). Learns that Edna has acute lymphatic leukemia.

1951: Grants his wife's wish to take on the manslaughter case of Jack Atherton, a railway telegraph operator accused of causing a train collision. His wife Edna dies of leukemia

(*February 7*). Joins the B.C. bar to take on the Atherton case (*March*). Atherton trial begins (*May 9*), which he later wins.

1952: Lake Centre riding disappears in redistribution; abandons his thoughts of possible retirement from politics after he decides to contest another election in a new riding. Attends the U.S. Republican Convention in Chicago where Eisenhower wins the nomination (*July*).

1953: Agrees to run in Prince Albert, since Lake Centre was being dismantled (*May*). Canada's 22nd federal election: wins in Prince Albert riding defeating David Corney (CCF) (*August 10*). Passed over for the deputy House leader position in favour of Earl Rowe. Marries Olive Freeman Palmer in Toronto (*December 8*); honeymoons in Mexico.

1954: Visits Israel.

1956: Drew resigns as leader because of ill health; Earl Rowe becomes House leader (*September 18*). Elected leader of the Progressive Conservative party in Ottawa, defeating Donald Fleming and Davie Fulton on the first ballot (*December 14*); retires from his active law practice.

1957: Allister Grossart, Diefenbaker's leadership campaign manager, becomes national director of the party and manager of the election campaign (*January*). Launches his campaign at Massey Hall in Toronto, first articulating his vision of northern Canada as the New Frontier (*April 25*). Canada's 23rd federal election: re-elected in Prince Albert defeating Robert Gooding (CCF); Conservatives defeat the Liberal government winning a minority government with 111 seats (*June 10*). Drives to Saskatoon to visit his mother in hospital with the news he will finally be Prime Minister (*June 12*). St. Laurent announces his decision to resign after the military vote is counted (*June 17*). **Diefenbaker government (1957-1963).** Becomes Canada's 13th Prime Minister and seventh Secretary of State for External Affairs (*June 21*); no one in his cabinet has previous experience. Appoints first woman to cabinet: Ellen Fairclough (Secretary of State) (*June 21*). Flies to London for the Commonwealth Prime Ministers Conference (*June 23*); the plane suddenly drops about 1,000 feet, crushing three of Olive's vertebrae. Visits Elizabeth II and British Prime Minister Winston Churchill. Speaks to the London Club on Canada's 90th birthday (*July 1*). Returns to Canada (*July 5*). Canada signs an agreement with the U.S. to conserve and regulate salmon fisheries in the Juan de Fuca-Fraser River area on the Pacific Coast (*July 3*). The Distant Early Warning (DEW) radar line, a joint Canada-U.S. defence project, begins operation in the Arctic (*July 31*). Announces the formation of the North American Air Defence Command (NORAD) with Marshall Roy Slemon of the RCAF as deputy commander (*July 31*). Speaks at a Canadian Bar Association banquet in Banff, Alta. (*September 6*), then flies to Dartmouth College in New Hampshire to deliver his first U.S. speech and receive an honorary degree (*September 7*). Turns down a British free-trade proposal (*September 9*). Resigns as Secretary of State for External Affairs (*September 12*) and appoints Sidney Smith, president of the University of Toronto, to the position, the first person to hold the portfolio who was never a Prime Minister (*September 13*). Appointed to the Imperial Privy Council (*September 15*). Speaks to the United Nations General Assembly in New York City (*September 23*). 23rd Parliament is opened by Elizabeth II; he nominates Roland Michener to be the 24th Speaker of the House (*October 14*). Visits U.S. President Eisenhower in Washington with Elizabeth II. Chairs the 18th Federal-Provincial Conference in Ottawa to discuss hospital insurance (*November 25-26*). Attends the first NATO Summit in Paris where he proposes a World Food Bank (*December 16-19*). Celebrates Christmas at the Saskatoon railway station where he sold a newspaper to former Prime Minister Wilfrid Laurier 47 years earlier (*December 25*).

1958: Pearson elected leader of the Liberal party, succeeding St. Laurent as Leader of the Opposition (*January 16*). Diefenbaker tables a document indicating the Liberals were aware of a possible economic recession, after being challenged by Pearson to resign (*January 20*). Greeted by 3,000 in Winnipeg, including Isabella Gainsford, granddaughter of Sir John A. Macdonald (*January 27*). Receives an honorary doctorate from St. Mary's University in Halifax (*January 30*). Appoints James Gladstone (Akay-na-muka) as Canada's first Indigenous Senator (*February 1*). Begins his election campaign in Winnipeg, introducing his 'Vision of the North' (*February 12*). Speaks to 8,500 voters packed into Vancouver's Exhibition Forum; fights take place outside (*March 13*). Attends the first test flight of the Avro Arrow in Malton, Ont. (*March 25*). 24th federal election: re-elected in Prince Albert defeating Thora Wiggens (CCF); wins 208 seats, the largest majority ever in Canada and the highest voter turnout (79.4%) (*March 31*). Meets with West German President Theodor Heuss who addresses Parliament (*June 2*). Meets with British Prime Minister Harold Macmillan who addresses Parliament (*June 13*). First official observance of Dominion Day takes place on Parliament Hill (*July 1*). Meets with U.S. President Eisenhower who addresses Parliament the next day (*July 8*). Introduces the Canada Conversion Loan program, encouraging Canadians to cash in wartime Victory bonds and reinvest them (*July 14*). Meets with Ghana's Prime Minister Kwame Nkrumah who addresses Parliament (*July 19-22*). Signs the South Saskatchewan River project agreement (*July 25*). Receives an honorary doctorate from the University of British Columbia (*August*). The air defence department recommends the Avro Arrow project be stopped because the technology is becoming obsolete (*August 8*). Introduces simultaneous translation into the House (*August 11*). Becomes the first Prime Minister to visit the Yukon (*August*). Announces plans to stop production of the Avro Arrow, but the airplane's development will continue (*September 23*). Introduces the use of the U.S.-built SAGE (semi-automatic ground environment) computer defence system (*September 23*). The TransCanada PipeLines natural gas pipeline from Alberta to Quebec is completed (*October 10*). Appoints Canada's first woman ambassador, Blanche Margaret Meagher to Israel (*October 22*). Leaves with Olive on a world tour of 15 countries (*October 28*); meets with Dag Hammarskjold at the United Nations (*October 29*); meets with British Prime Minister Macmillan in London (*November 3*); speaks at Royal Albert Hall (*November 4*); meets with General Charles de Gaulle in Paris (*November 6*); meets with Belgium Premier Paul-Henri Spaak and General Lauris Norstad of NATO in Brussels (*November 6*); meets with West German Chancellor Konrad Adenaur in Bonn (*November 7*); meets with Italy Premier Amintore Fanfani and Pope John XXIII in Rome (*November 11-12*); meets with Pakistani President Ayub Khan in Karachi (*November 15*); visits the Khyber Pass (*November 18*); meets with India's Prime Minister Jawaharlal Nehru in New Delhi (*November 19*); receives an honorary degree from the University of Delhi; takes part in a Bengal tiger hunt, but catches no tigers; meets with Ceylon's Prime Minister Solomon Bandaranaike in Colombo; meets with Malaya's Prime Minister Tunju Abdul Rahman in Kuala Lumpur (*November 28*); visits Singapore and Djarkarta, Indonesia (*December 2*); visits Australia and New Zealand; made an honorary Maori chief; returns to Canada (*December 19*).

1959: The Federal-Provincial Hospital Plan comes into effect in Ontario and Nova Scotia (*January 1*); other provinces join the plan later. Formally recognizes the new Cuban government of Fidel Castro, despite objections from the U.S. (*January 8*). The Royal Canadian Air Force takes over the DEW (Distance Early Warning) stations in the Arctic from the U.S. (*February 1*). Scraps the contract to build the Avro Arrow; A.V. Roe company in Toronto dismisses 11,800 employees (*February 20*); announces an alternative defence program to install U.S. Bomarc anti-aircraft nuclear missiles. Takes over as acting External Affairs minister following the death of Smith (External Affairs) (*March 17*). Meets with British Prime Minister Macmillan in Ottawa (*March 18*). The St. Lawrence Seaway opens to navigation (*April 25*). Stephen Harper, Canada's 22nd Prime Minister, is born in Toronto (*April 30*). Receives an honorary Doctor of Laws degree from the University of Toronto. Resigns as acting External Affairs minister (*June 3*) and appoints Howard Green (Public Works) the next day. Receives an honorary degree from the University of Montreal (*June*); during the convocation, he considers for the first time the possibility of making General Georges Vanier the next Governor General. Joins Elizabeth II and U.S. President Eisenhower to open the St. Lawrence Seaway (*June 26*). Announces the formation of the National Energy Board with powers over oil, natural gas and hydroelectric energy (*July 18*). Work begins on the Diefenbunker in Carp, Ont.. Announces the appointment of Georges Vanier as Canada's 19th Governor General, the first French-Canadian in the post (*August 1*). Unveils plans for a \$60-million nuclear plant at Point Douglas, Ont. (*September 9*). Presides over a Federal-Provincial Conference in Ottawa (*October 15-16*); rejects an increase in equalization payments.

Acidic response letter

Diefenbaker had a form letter to reply to writers who annoyed him: "Dear Sir, This is to inform you that some crackpot is using your name and has recently written to me over your signature putting forward views so eccentric in nature and so much at variance with your usual logical style that the letter could not possibly be from you. I felt I owed it to you to bring this to your attention."

1960: Presides over a Federal-Provincial Conference on centennial celebrations for 1967 (*February 8*); agreement is reached to support Montreal's bid for the 1967 World's Fair. Opens the National Gallery of Canada in Ottawa (*February 17*). Donald Fleming (Finance) presents his fourth budget, becoming the first minister to buy a new pair of shoes for his budget speech (*March 29*). Signs a trade deal with the U.S.S.R. in which the Soviets will spend \$25 million annually on Canadian goods (*April 18*). French President Charles de Gaulle visits Canada (*April 18-21*). Visits Mexico as a guest of President Adolfo López Mateos (*April 21*). Attends the Commonwealth Prime Ministers Conference in London (*May 3-13*); suggests a Colombo Plan for Africa. Attends the wedding of Princess Margaret to Anthony Armstrong-Jones (*May 6*). Officially opens the South Saskatchewan River Dam project (*May 30*). Meets with U.S. President Eisenhower in Washington (*June*). The Quebec Liberals under Jean Lesage defeat the Union Nationale in the provincial election (*June 22*). Opens Ottawa's new airport terminal (*June 30*). Indigenous peoples on reserves gain the right to vote without losing their status (*July 1*). Chairs the 19th Federal-Provincial Conference in Ottawa to discuss equalization payments and shared-cost programs (*July 25-27*). His Bill of Rights is passed (*August 4*). Authorizes sending troops to the Congo as part of a UN peacekeeping operation (*August 5*). Hazen Argue is elected leader of the CCF party, succeeding M.J. Coldwell (*August 11*). Receives honorary Doctor of Laws degrees from Queen's and Ottawa universities. Establishes a Royal Commission on Government Organization (*September 16*). Addresses the UN, speaking on behalf of nationalities in Eastern Europe controlled by the U.S.S.R. (*September 26*). Meets with Eisenhower and former president Herbert Hoover (*September 27*). The Forestry Department is established (*October 1*). Shuffles his cabinet, moving Douglas Harkness (Agriculture) to National Defence (*October 11*). Cuba nationalizes its banks except the Royal Bank and the Bank of Nova Scotia (*October 14*); Diefenbaker plans to continue trade with Cuba despite the U.S. embargo against the Caribbean nation (*October 19*). Opens the Sir John A. Macdonald Hall law school at Queen's University (*October 20*). Chairs the 20th Federal-Provincial Conference in Ottawa to discuss equalization payments (*October 26-28*). The Medical

Research Council is established (*November 14*). Provincial premiers meet in Quebec City to set up a permanent secretariat (*December 1-2*). Legislation prevents a national strike by 111,000 non-operating railway workers (*December 2*). Told by the RCMP about an affair between Pierre Sévigny (Associate National Defence) and suspected spy Gerda Munsinger; decides not to make it public (*December 7*). Introduces legislation that requires Superior and Supreme Court judges to retire at age 75 (*December 14*).

1961: His wife Olive receives an honorary Doctor of Laws degree from her alma mater, Brandon College in Brandon, Man. (*January*). Attorneys-General reach a general agreement on amending the BNA Act (*January 12-13*). Signs the Columbia River Treaty with Eisenhower in Washington (*January 17*). Announces the sale of 40 million bushels of grain to China for $60 million (*February 2*). Becomes the first leader to meet with new U.S. President John F. Kennedy in Washington (*February 20*). His mother Mary dies in Saskatoon (*February 20*). Chairs the 21st Federal-Provincial Conference in Ottawa to discuss equalization payments (*February 23-24*). Becomes the first Prime Minister to visit Ireland and Northern Ireland (*March 4-7*). Attends the Commonwealth Prime Ministers Conference in London (*March 8-17*); opposes the apartheid policy of South Africa. Fleming (Finance) tells the Governor of the Bank of Canada, James Coyne, that his speeches are embarrassing the government (*March 18*); Coyne indicates he will accept no more speaking engagements. The Royal Commission on Transportation tables its report, recommending the government subsidize both major railways (*April 5*). Meets with British Prime Minister Macmillan in Ottawa (*April 9-10*). Meets with U.S. President Kennedy who addresses Parliament (*May 17*). Bank of Canada Governor Coyne is asked to resign (*May 30*). South Africa leaves the British Commonwealth (*May 31*). Earnscliffe, the former home of Sir John A. Macdonald in Ottawa, is declared a historic site (*June 5*). Calls Kennedy to demand the release of unloaders needed to complete the grain shipment deal with China (not recognized by the U.S.) (*June 5*). Canada orders 64 U.S. Voodoo jet interceptors without nuclear warheads (*June 12*). Coyne refuses to resign as Governor of the Bank of Canada (*June 13*). Royal Commission on Publications tables its report (*June 15*). Receives an honorary Doctor of Laws degree from Dalhousie. Announces plans to restore the Louisbourg Fortress on Cape Breton Island as a Centennial project (*June 17*). Establishes a Royal Commission on Health Services chaired by Emmett Hall (*June 26*). Robert Thompson is elected leader of the federal Social Credit party, succeeding Solon Law (*July 6*). A bill forcing Coyne's dismissal passes in the House (*July 7*); the Senate grants him a hearing. Briefed, along with cabinet, about Britain's possible entry into the European Common Market (*July 13*). Senate rejects the Coyne bill (*July 13*); Coyne resigns, saying he has been vindicated. Diefenbaker becomes the first Prime Minister to travel north of the Arctic Circle to open Inuvik (*July 21*). Inaugurates the $25-million microwave communications network in Whitehorse, Yukon (*July 22*). Appoints Louis Rasminsky to be Governor of the Bank of Canada (*July 24*). Opposes Britain's application for European Common Market membership as detrimental to Commonwealth trade (*July 31*); France's opposition effectively guts the initiative. Premier Tommy Douglas of Saskatchewan is elected federal leader of the New Democratic party, which replaces the CCF (*August 3*). Opens the Hockey Hall of Fame on the CNE grounds in Toronto (*August 26*). The first Canada Council Medals are awarded (*September 6*); recipients include Vincent Massey. Fleming (Finance) elected chair of the new international Organization for Economic Co-operation and Development (OECD) (*October 1*). Presented with a 141,000-signatures petition against nuclear weapons (*October 6*). Responds to a letter from U.S. President Kennedy that expresses distress that Canada is going to oppose nuclear testing. Visits Japan (*October 24-30*). Agrees to pay 60% of the cost to build a floodway around Winnipeg (*November 17*). Saskatchewan passes legislation to create a pre-paid medical care plan (*November 18*). Talks with Elizabeth II on the round-the-world Commonwealth cable (*December 19*).

Bringing Champagne

The first Prime Minister to visit Northern Ireland, Diefenbaker arrived in Belfast to find a truck on the tarmac waiting to accept his wine. It was in response to a telegram from Canada that the "PRIME MINISTER WILL BE BRINGING CHAMPAGNE." Joining him was his confidential messenger Gilbert Champagne (also messenger for five previous Prime Ministers: Borden, Meighen, King, Bennett and St. Laurent).

1962: Becomes a member of the National Press Club (*January 20*). Announces a 33% increase in university grants (*January 22*). Announces a pension increase of $10 a month (*January 23*). The Royal Commission on Transportation tables its second report, indicating that competition, not government, should determine prices (*January 24*). Hazen Argue, the NDP House leader, resigns after criticizing his party's policies and joins the Liberals (*February 18*). Cabinet approves in principle the construction of a causeway to P.E.I. (*February 27*). Bomarc missiles are installed in North Bay (*March*). Canada is elected to the UN Commission on Human Rights, beginning in 1963 (*April 17*). Asks cabinet to support a provincial conference to develop a national flag (*April 23*); the initiative stalls. The government re-ties the Canadian dollar to the gold standard, pegging it at 92.5 U.S. cents (*May 2*). Liberals produce the 'Diefenbuck', a Canadian dollar worth 92.5 cents (*May*). Sparks a near riot by a rowdy crowd at the Vancouver Forum during an election rally; several Doukhobor women disrobe to protest discrimination (*May 30*). Canada's 25th federal election: re-elected in Prince Albert defeating Roger Carter (NDP); left with a minority government after losing 92 seats, five cabinet ministers and 17% of the popular vote (*June 18*). Announces austerity measures (*June 24*). Saskatchewan begins introducing its medical care plan (*July 1*). His close friend Senator William Brunt is killed in an automobile accident (*July 7*). Breaks a bone in his ankle stepping off the patio at Harrington Lake (*July 23*). New cabinet ministers sworn in at 24 Sussex Avenue in his bedroom (*August 9*). Appoints the Royal Commission on Taxation, chaired by Kenneth Carter (*August 27*). Officially opens the Trans-Canada Highway in Rogers Pass, B.C, near the spot where the CPR's last spike had been driven in 1885 (*September 3*). The Royal Commission on Government Organization tables the first of five reports (*September 6*). Attends the Commonwealth Prime Ministers Conference in London; again opposes Britain's entry into the European Common Market (*September 10-18*). Opens the Garden of the Provinces in Ottawa (*September 24*). Appoints Dalton Camp as Conservative National Director (*September 25*). 25th Parliament opens; nominates Marcel Lambert to be the 25th Speaker of the House (*September 27*). Announces government spending cuts of $228 million (*October 18*). Backs U.S. President Kennedy's blockade of Cuba until the U.S.S.R. removes missiles (*October 22*). Davie Fulton (Public Works) announces his intention to leave cabinet and seek the B.C. Conservative leadership (*November 29*). The Royal Commission on Unemployment Insurance tables its report (*December 20*). Becomes Privy Council President (*December 21*). Meets with U.S. President Kennedy and British Prime Minister Macmillan in the Bahamas (*December 21*).

1963: Opposition Leader Pearson reverses his stand, coming out in favour of nuclear arms (*January 12*). Turns sod for 300-acre Sheridan Park research community west of Toronto (*January 18*). Indicates he likely won't put nuclear warheads on $685- million worth of Bomarc surface-to-air missiles; part of a defence agreement with the U.S. (*January 25*). Britain loses effort to join the European Common Market (*January 29*). Recalls Canada's Ambassador in Washington after the U.S. contradicts his comments about joint defence plans (*January 30*). Parliament criticizes the U.S. for publicizing the disagreement about

Canada's nuclear policy (*January 31*); the U.S. apologizes. Turns sod for the Fathers of Confederation Memorial Building in Charlottetown, P.E.I., with Nova Scotia Premier Robert Stanfield (*February 2*). Harkness (National Defence) resigns in protest over plans to not use nuclear warheads (*February 3*). Loses two non-confidence votes in the House over nuclear weapons policy (*February 5*); George Hees (Trade & Commerce) fails to get party support for the Prime Minister's resignation; subsequently supports the leader publicly (*February 6*). Hees (Trade & Commerce) and Sévigny (Associate National Defence) resign in protest over defence policy (*February 9*). Meets with Macmillan in London (*February 22-25*). Becomes a Freeman of the City of London (*February 25*). A Front de Libération du Québec (FLQ) bomb is discovered on CN railway tracks near Lemieux, Que., before Diefenbaker's train is scheduled to pass over them (*April 1*). Canada's 26th federal election: re-elected in Prince Albert defeating Henry Apps (NDP); Liberals defeat the government, but fail to win a majority (*April 8*). Six Social Credit MPs agree to support the Liberals, allowing Pearson to form a government (*April 12*); three of them subsequently withdraw their support, but Pearson retains a majority of one. Diefenbaker decides to resign (*April 13*); the three remaining Social Credit MPs withdraw their backing of Pearson, eliminating his majority. Vincent O'Neill becomes the first fatality of an FLQ bombing (*April 20*). **Diefenbaker's government ends** (*April 22*). Visits Egyptian President Gamel Nasser in Cairo, and Israeli Prime Minister David Ben Gurion in Tel Aviv (*September*).

1964: Wins a leadership vote of confidence at the Conservative annual meeting in Ottawa; appoints Léon Balcer as Quebec lieutenant while Dalton Camp is elected party president (*February 1-5*). A Conservative Thinkers Conference in Fredericton adopts a two-nation policy opposed by Diefenbaker (*September 12*). Receives a letter from Pearson who indicates he is aware that a former Conservative cabinet member was involved with suspected spy Gerda Munsinger (*December 4*); the two argue about the issue in Pearson's office (*December 10*).

1965: Visits Tobago and Caracas, Venezuela (*January*). The Conservative executive supports his leadership, despite Quebec's agitation for a review (*February 6*). MP Rémi Paul becomes an Independent in protest over his leadership (*February 18*). Tells several close friends he intends to resign (*March 14*). Resignation rumour becomes public and he changes his mind (*March 22*). Celebrates 25 years in federal politics (*March 26*). Balcer becomes an Independent in protest over his leadership (*April 7*). Canada's 27th federal election: re-elected in Prince Albert defeating Peter Kachur (NDP); party loses to Pearson's Liberals (*November 8*). Takes a Caribbean cruise (*December*).

1966: Questions Lucien Cardin (Justice) who mentions the Munsinger affair (*March 4*). Dalton Camp, Conservative party president, begins a campaign to elect a new Conservative leader (*September 20*). The Spence Commission tables its report, criticizing Diefenbaker's handling of the Munsinger affair and not removing Sévigny from cabinet (*September 23*). Attends a Quebec meeting where a resolution is passed calling for a leadership convention (*October*). Faces heckling at the Conservative annual meeting; Camp is re-elected national president; vote taken to hold a leadership convention before 1968 (*November 16*). Visits Florida (*December*).

1967: Calls for a Conservative leadership convention (*January 18*). Attends the dedication of Diefenbaker Lake created by the South Saskatchewan dam (*July*). Nova Scotia Premier Stanfield enters the leadership race (*July 19*). Diefenbaker's boyhood homestead at Borden is moved to the legislature grounds in Regina. Opposes the two-nation policy adopted by the Conservatives at their Thinkers Conference in Montmorency, Que. (*August 7-10*). Announces his last-minute bid to hold on to the leadership based on his opposition to the two-nation policy (*September 8*). Loses the leadership vote to Stanfield, never polling better than fifth place on three ballots (*September 9*). Resigns as leader of the Conservative party (*September 20*). Tells a Parliamentary Press Gallery dinner in his honour that he will not speak in the House again; a rash promise never kept. Moves out of Stornoway and rents a house in Rockcliffe Park; later buys a house near Stornoway. Receives the Shevchenko Freedom Award from the Ukrainian Congress Committee of America in New York City (*November 19*). Speaks on freedom, along with Michael Starr, at a Ukrainian rally in Madison Square Gardens, New York City (*December*).

1968: Calls on the Liberal government to resign following its defeat in the House on a motion to add a 5% surcharge on income tax (*February 19*). Canada's 28th federal election: re-elected in Prince Albert defeating Al Hartley (NDP) (*June 25*). Unveils a monument to Sir John A. Macdonald's parents at his ancestral home in Scotland (*July 13*). Attends the unveiling of his portrait on Parliament Hill by Cleeve Horne (*October 8*).

1969: Receives a human relations award in Winnipeg from the Canadian National Council of Christians and Jews (*September 18*). Becomes chancellor of the University of Saskatchewan (*October 26*).

1970: Suggests Parliament create an Environment Week each year; the idea is pursued and enacted the following year.

1972: *Those Things We Treasure: A Selection of Speeches on Freedom and in Defence of Our Parliamentary Heritage* is published. Canada's 29th federal election; re-elected in Prince Albert defeating W.J. Berezowsky (NDP) (*October 30*).

1973: Donates the Diefenbaker family homestead in Borden to the University of Saskatchewan (*May 18*).

1974: Canada's 30th federal election: re-elected in Prince Albert defeating Thora Wiggens (NDP) for a second time (*July 8*).

1975: *One Canada: The Crusading Years*, the first of his three-volume autobiography, is published. His wife Olive suffers a stroke (*December*).

1976: Appointed a Companion of Honour by Elizabeth II (*January 1*). His wife Olive is admitted to hospital with a heart condition (*September*); she dies in Ottawa after prolonged heart trouble (*December 22*).

1978: David Crombie, mayor of Toronto, speaks at Diefenbaker's successful Prince Albert nomination meeting, touching off speculation that he is his chosen successor (*April 19*).

1979: Suffers a stroke while campaigning (*April 13*). Canada's 31st federal election: re-elected in Prince Albert defeating Stan Hovdebo (NDP); Conservatives defeat the Liberals (*May 22*). Is given a larger office by Prime Minister Clark after 16 years in a cramped space on Parliament Hill (*August 8*). Dies in his Ottawa study (*August 16*). Lies in state at the Parliament Buildings (*August 17-19*). State funeral held at Christ Church Cathedral in Ottawa (*August 19*). A second funeral takes place beside the South Saskatchewan River in Saskatoon (*August 22*) and he is buried at the city's Diefenbaker Canada Centre on the University of Saskatchewan grounds.

Books about Diefenbaker

- **1962**: B.T. Richardson; *Canada & Mr. Diefenbaker* (McClelland & Stewart)
- **1963**: Peter C. Newman; *Renegade in Power, The Diefenbaker Years* (McClelland & Stewart; revised 1989)

- **1965**: Peter Regenstreif; *The Diefenbaker Interlude: Parties and Voting in Canada, an Interpretation* (Longman)
- **1968**: Thomas Van Dusen; *The Chief* (McGraw Hill)
- **1968**: Patrick Nicholson; *Vision and Indecision* (Longman)
- **1971**: James Johnston; *The Party's Over* (Longman)
- **1975**: Peter Stursberg; *Diefenbaker, Leadership Gained, 1956-1962* (University of Toronto)
- **1975**: John G. Diefenbaker; *One Canada, The Crusading Years, 1895-1956* (Macmillan)
- **1975**: Margaret Wente (ed.); *I Never Say Anything Provocative: Witticisms, Anecdotes and Reflections by Canada's Most Outspoken Politician* (Peter Martin Associates)
- **1976**: Peter Stursberg; *Diefenbaker, Leadership Lost, 1962-1967* (University of Toronto)
- **1976**: John G. Diefenbaker; *One Canada, The Years of Achievement, 1957-1962* (Macmillan)
- **1977**: John G. Diefenbaker; *One Canada, The Tumultuous Years, 1962-1967* (Macmillan)
- **1995**: Denis Smith; *Rogue Tory: The Life and Legend of John G. Diefenbaker* (MacFarlane, Walter & Ross)

Leaders of the New Democratic Party

Co-operative Commonwealth Federation (1932-1961)

1.	J.S. Woodsworth	1932-1942
2.	M.J. Coldwell	1942-1960
3.	Hazen Argue	1960-1961

NDP (1961-)

4.	Tommy Douglas	1961-1971
5.	David Lewis	1971-1975
6.	Ed Broadbent	1975-1989
7.	Audrey McLaughlin	1989-1995
8.	Alexa McDonough	1995-2003
9.	Jack Layton	2003-2011
10.	Thomas Mulcair	2012-2017
11.	Jagmeet Singh	2017-

14

Lester B. Pearson

The Unconfrontational Prime Minister

Despite never leading a majority government, Lester Pearson's five-year mandate ushered in significant changes to Canada's political landscape. These included the introduction of a Canadian flag, medicare, the Canada Pension Plan, a unified armed forces, an auto pact with the U.S. and an immigration strategy based on skills instead of ethnic restrictions. With all of that, Pearson is best remembered as either the minister of, or a civil servant in, the department of external affairs. His global activity included a term as president of the United Nations General Assembly and a role as broker in the 1957 Suez Crisis that earned him the Nobel Peace Prize.

Pearson the Politician

Prime Minister of Canada: April 22, 1963 – April 20, 1968
Length of term: 4 years, 11 months, 28 days
Parliaments as Prime Minister: 26th; 27th
Age on entering office: 65
Political party: Liberal
Leader of party: January 16, 1958 – April 5, 1968
Member of Parliament: October 25, 1948 – June 25, 1968
Riding represented: Algoma East [Ont.] 1948-1968
Cabinet portfolio: External Affairs (1948-1957)
Other political posts: Ambassador to U.S. (1945-1946); Chairman of NATO (1951-1952); President of UN General Assembly (1952-1953); Leader of the Opposition (1958-1963)
Titles: Officer of the Order of the British Empire (1935); Canadian Privy Councillor (1948); Nobel Laureate (Peace Prize) (1957); Imperial Privy Councillor (1963); Companion of the Order of Canada (1968)
Quotes: "The grim fact is that we prepare for war like precocious giants and for peace like retarded pygmies." (accepting the Nobel Peace Prize in Oslo, 1957); "Prime ministers require the hide of a rhinoceros, the morals of St. Francis, the patience of Job, the wisdom of Solomon, the strength of Hercules, the leadership of Napoleon, the magnetism of a Beatle and the

subtlety of Machiavelli." (to a Liberal rally, 1964)
Lived after term: 4 years

PEARSON THE MAN

Name: Lester Bowles Pearson
Born: April 23, 1897, Newtonbrook (Toronto), Ontario
Ancestry: Irish
Religion: United (formerly Methodist)
Education: B.A. [Bachelor of Arts] (University of Toronto, 1919); B.A.Hon. [Honours Bachelor of Arts in Modern History] (Oxford University, 1923); M.A. [Master of Arts] (Oxford, 1925)
Nicknames: Mike (acquired in the Royal Flying Corps, 1917); Michael Macdonald (pseudonym used for his weekly BBC broadcasts to Canada during the First World War)
Military service: Canadian Army Medical Corps (1915-1917); Canadian Reserve Battalion (and Royal Flying Corps) (1917-1918)
Occupation: professor; civil servant; diplomat
Occupation after term: professor; chancellor
Publications: *Canada and Post-War Organization* (1945); *Democracy in World Politics* (1955); *The Crisis in the Middle East, October-December 1956* (1957); *The Crisis in the Middle East, January-March 1957* (1957); *Where Do We Go From Here?* (1957); *Diplomacy in the Nuclear Age* (1959); *A Critical Evaluation of the United Nations* (with Ernest Gross and Sir Patrick Dean, 1961); *The Control of Proliferation: Three Views* (with Sir Solly Zuckermann and Alva Myrdal, 1966); *Peace in the Family of Man: Reith Lectures* (1968); *The Crisis of Development* (1970); *The Commonwealth, 1970* (1971); *Mike, Memoirs Vol. 1: 1897-1948* (1972); *Mike, Memoirs Vol. 2: 1948-1957* (1973); *Mike, Memoirs Vol. 3: 1957-1968* (1975)
Appearance: "A man of average size…with hazel eyes, thinning gray hair that tends to drift down over his forehead when he speaks, and a pleasant Irish face." (John Beal in *The Pearson Phenomenon*) "Pearson, with his trademark grin … and his bow tie, became a political icon … Rumpled, respected, reliable, identifiably Canadian" (Robert Bothwell in *Pearson: The Unlikely Gladiator*)
Personality: "His manner was easy, his wit gentle and increasingly self-deprecating, and he exuded an apparent candour…" (John English in *The Worldly Years*) "He was the antithesis of a stuffy bureaucrat." (Mitchell Sharp quoted in Peter Stursberg's *Lester Pearson and the Dream of Unity*)
Married: Maryon Moody, August 22, 1925, Winnipeg, Manitoba
Age at marriage: 28
Years married: 47
Died: December 28, 1972 (lapsed into coma December 27), Ottawa, Ontario
Age at death: 75
Cause of death: cancer of the liver
Buried: MacLaren Cemetery, Wakefield, Quebec

Pearson was the:
- Only Prime Minister to receive a Nobel Prize

- Only Prime Minister to represent northern Ontario
- Only Prime Minister who was President of the UN General Assembly
- First Prime Minister who never led a majority government
- First Canadian government official to fly across the Atlantic (1939)
- Second Prime Minister who was a civil servant
- Second United Church Prime Minister
- Fourth Prime Minister who was a teacher
- Fourth Prime Minister born in Ontario
- Fifth Liberal Prime Minister
- Last Prime Minister born in the 19th century
- Last Prime Minister appointed to the British Privy Council
- Last Prime Minister to serve in the armed forces

Pearson's legacy

- Established universal free medicare
- Implemented the Canada Pension Plan
- Signed the Auto Pact with the United States
- Gave Canada its own flag
- Unified the armed forces
- Created the zenith of Canada's welfare state
- Introduced a colour-blind immigration policy based on points system
- Sparked the creation of a bilingual civil service

PEARSON'S FAMILY

Pearson's Parents

Father: Edwin Arthur Pearson
Born: May 21, 1868, Uxbridge, Ontario
Occupation: Methodist (later United) minister
Died: September 6, 1931, Toronto, Ontario
Age at death: 63

Mother: Anne 'Annie' Sarah Bowles
Born: July 3, 1878, Eramosa, Ontario
Married: July 13, 1892, Orangeville Methodist Church, Orangeville, Ontario
Died: August 2, 1962, Southampton, Ontario
Age at death: 84

Pearson's Brothers (2 siblings; Lester the second)

Brother: Marmaduke 'Duke' Pritchard Pearson (1894-1982)
  Married: Constance Reid Bell (December 1918)
Brother: Vaughan Whittier Pearson (1898-1982)
  Note: bond trader

Pearson's Wife

Name: Maryon Elspeth Moody
Born: December 13, 1901, Winnipeg, Manitoba

Father: Arthur William Moody (physician)
Mother: Elizabeth Jane Holland
Age at marriage: 23
Died: December 26, 1989, Toronto, Ontario
Age at death: 88
Burial place: MacLaren Cemetery, Wakefield, Quebec
Younger than Pearson: 4 years
Died after Pearson: 17 years

Pearson's Children (2)

Name: Geoffrey Arthur Holland Pearson
Born: December 24, 1927, Toronto, Ontario
Occupation: diplomat; Canadian Ambassador to the Soviet Union (1980-1983); Executive Director, Canadian Institute for International Peace and Security (1985-1991); President, United Nations Association of Canada (1999-2003)
Married: Landon 'Lucy' Carter Mackenzie (December 26, 1951) (Senator 1994-2005)
Children: 5 – Hilary Maryon; Katharine Alice; Anne M.; Michael; Patricia Margaret
Died: March 18, 2008, Ottawa, Ontario
Note: Daughter Hilary is President and CEO of Philanthropic Foundations Canada and married Michael Sabia, former president of BCE.
Note: Daughter Patricia is an author and journalist.

Name: Patricia Lillian Pearson
Born: March 9, 1929, Ottawa, Ontario
Occupation: nurse
Married: Dr. Walter Hannah (1950)
Children: 5 – Paul; Barbara, Robin, David, Jonathan

POLITICAL STORIES

The United Nations activist

The Second World War was still raging when Pearson joined a U.S. initiative to explore the creation of a replacement for the League of Nations. For the next two years, he played a central role in discussions that culminated in the United Nations; he also helped develop two of its agencies: the FAO (UN Food and Agricultural Organization) and UNRRA (UN Relief and Rehabilitation Administration).

It was Prime Minister King who first suggested Pearson serve as Secretary-General of the UN. The U.S. agreed and nominated him in 1946 to be the first person to occupy the position. But the Soviet Union threatened to veto the idea and a compromise candidate was found in Norway's Trygve Lie. King was just as happy since he had been pushing Pearson to consider entering politics and join cabinet.

Pearson was External Affairs minister when he was elected president of the 7th UN General Assembly in 1952, meeting at its brand new headquarters in New York City. Secretary General Lie was planning to step down and wanted him to seek that position.

Again, Pearson was willing to let his name stand and, again, the U.S.S.R. opposed the choice. This time the compromise candidate was Sweden's Dag Hammarskjöld.

The two rejections didn't sour Pearson on the United Nations. A week after his second unsuccessful attempt, he officially presented Canada's gift to the new headquarters building: seven large main doors. Three years later, he relied on the UN to help craft a solution to the crisis in Egypt.

Suez Crisis and Nobel Prize

When Egyptian President Gamal Abdel Nasser suddenly nationalized the Suez Canal in July 1956, the waterway's administrators, Britain and France, were outraged. They threatened to take it back by force. Ever the peacemaker, Pearson headed for London to urge the British to avoid military action. He had the same message for the NATO Council meeting in Paris.

In the meantime, Israel invaded Egypt to protect its interests, further inflaming the situation by occupying the Sinai and the Gaza strip. Pearson convinced cabinet to endorse a solution calling for a UN peacekeeping force at the Suez, then flew to New York that afternoon to promote the idea at the UN.

Washington called for a cease-fire, but Pearson knew there was no way to enforce it. The peacekeeping proposal he successfully presented to the General Assembly didn't stop Britain and France from invading Egypt the next day. However, international pushback forced them to bow out after one day, deferring to the UN initiative.

Pearson's role during the Suez predicament earned him the Nobel Peace Prize the following year in Oslo, Norway. He is the first and only Canadian to win the honour.

Making Bilingualism official

Calling for greater efforts to encourage French-English bilingualism across the country, Pearson set up the Royal Commission on Bilingualism and Biculturalism chaired by journalist André Laurendeau and former CBC chair Davidson Dunton. Its work helped shift Canada from its status quo of French in Quebec and English-only almost everywhere else.

The commissioners warned that the language issue had driven a large rift between the two cultures. As a start, they urged the government to promote bilingualism in the civil service, particularly at senior levels. They also asked Ontario and New Brunswick to extend the same rights to French that were already extended in Quebec to English.

Within a year, Pearson was sending the first 20 senior bureaucrats off to Quebec for language training. New Brunswick became the first (and still only) official bilingual province in 2002; French-language schools were formally recognized in Ontario in 1968. The national landscape began to shift with many English families sending their children to French immersion classes.

The rough road to a new flag

Pearson promised Canadians their own flag and discovered the path to getting one was far rockier than anticipated. He had his personal favourite, designed by artist Alan

Beddoe, that he presented to the nation on May 14, 1964. It featured three red maple leaves on a white background, flanked by two vertical blue bars.

A few days later, a room full of Legion members who were partial to the British-inspired Red Ensign loudly booed the Prime Minister and his new flag proposal. Despite that, Pearson brought his prototype to Parliament, ensuring a summer of heated debate. To deflect the growing angst about the design, he agreed to let a parliamentary committee of 15 MPs look into it further.

The team came back with a modified design based on a suggestion by George Stanley of the Royal Military College – one red maple leaf centred between two red bars. The acrimonious debate resumed; Diefenbaker did everything he could to scuttle the revised design. The Liberals imposed closure, forcing a final vote on December 15. Two-thirds of the House endorsed the new flag, which replaced the Red Ensign atop the Peace Tower on February 15, 1965. "Under this flag," concluded Pearson in his remarks that day, "may our youth find new inspiration for loyalty to Canada."

Canada's 100th birthday

Pearson's plan was to remain in office until Canada's 100th birthday party was over. And what a party it was! Pearson kicked it off on Parliament Hill by lighting the Centennial Flame, a temporary monument that the public wanted kept in place. It still burns today.

The birthday centerpiece was Montreal's world fair, Expo 67, that was host to over 50 million visitors. Centennial trains and vans crossed the country with displays. A 5,000-km voyageur canoe trip by 10 canoes finished at Expo. Winnipeg hosted the first Pan American Games held in Canada. Thousands of Canadian communities had their own centennial projects ranging from the poignant to the wacky.

The Order of Canada was created and the Public Archives building was opened. Pearson was kept busy and happy for the year, except for one blemish. Visiting French President Charles de Gaulle proclaimed his shocking "Vive le Québec libre", prompting Pearson to reply, "Canadians do not need to be liberated. Indeed, many thousands of Canadians gave their lives in two world wars in the liberation of France and other European countries."

Ushering in Medicare

Saskatchewan introduced public health care in 1947 and Alberta followed three years later. St. Laurent established national public health insurance in 1957, but it was Pearson who agreed with the findings of the Royal Commission on Health Services to create 'medicare' for the whole country.

The hard work had just begun. Attempting to sell publicly subsidized universal health care to the premiers and the medical community was slow, arduous toil. Two years of intense negotiations convinced the Liberals they wouldn't be able to launch medicare on July 1, 1967. So, it was delayed a year. British Columbia and Saskatchewan were the first provinces to sign on a few months after Pearson stepped down as Prime Minister. The last province aboard was Quebec in 1970.

PERSONAL STORIES

Excelling at sports

Pearson was the most avid athlete among Canada's Prime Ministers. Four sports were the focus of most of his efforts and successes: baseball, hockey, lacrosse and tennis. The passion for baseball came from his father and grandfather. As he got older, he joined teams at the amateur and semi-pro levels in Ontario cities like Hamilton, Chatham and Guelph before and after the First World War.

As much as he enjoyed baseball, he never aspired to be a professional player. Once he was a civil servant, he reverted to the role of spectator. In 1969, he threw the first pitch for the Montreal Expos at the first major league baseball game held outside the U.S.

On ice, Pearson was most active at Oxford where Canadians were typically viewed as natural aces. The university team was undefeated in its 1921 tour of Switzerland and the next year he was playing with the Swiss hockey club in Davos helping it qualify for the European championship. He was later offered, but had to turn down, a spot on Britain's Olympic hockey team to play at the Winter Games in Chamonix, France.

When it wasn't winter, Pearson was winning awards playing lacrosse. In the spring of 1922, he joined the Oxford-Cambridge lacrosse team on its tour of eastern U.S. colleges. Playing gave way to coaching lacrosse after returning to Canada.

On the tennis court, he reached the second round in Canada's pairs championship in 1924 with his partner Roland 'Roly' Michener (future Governor General) and in the mid-1930s won the Rockcliffe Lawn Tennis Club's singles championship – twice. In 1967, he rejoined Michener to defeat King Constantine of Greece and one of the Governor General's aides in a recreational match.

Maryon Pearson

In her final year at the University of Toronto's Victoria College, Manitoba's Maryon Moody decided to take a history course being offered for the first time by new lecturer Mike Pearson. There was a mutual attraction and the two began dating secretly. In 1925, they were married in a double ceremony with her sister Grace – it was the only way to wed quickly without beating her older sister to the altar.

As Maryon evolved from being an academic's wife to a diplomat's wife, she found sacrificing her desire for privacy was challenging. But being a politician's wife was the mightiest trial of all. She simply didn't have the personality to be a model political wife. Maryon could be blunt and up-front. Canadians were used to the smiling warm grace of a Madame St. Laurent or Olive Diefenbaker and didn't easily take to Maryon's unexpected candour.

What was on her mind was what was spoken. At the end of a busy day of campaigning, she was asked if there was anything she would like to bring up. "Yes, the last five cups of coffee." In the 1958 election, she watched her husband's party go down to humiliating defeat and her hope to have him leave politics thwarted. "We've lost everything. We've even won our own seat."

After Pearson's death, she continued to live in Rockcliffe to the end of the 1970s, then moved to Toronto where she spent most of the '80s immobile in a nursing home.

PEARSON'S TIMELINE

1897: Born in the Methodist parsonage in Newtonbrook (Toronto), Ont. (*April 23*); his given names are the surnames of his maternal grandparents. His family moves to the Methodist parsonage in Davisville, Ont. (Toronto) (*Summer*).

1900: His family moves to the Methodist parsonage in Aurora, Ont.

1901: Begins school in Aurora (*September*).

1902: His family returns to Toronto to the Methodist parsonage of Centennial Church. Attends Dewson Street Public School.

1904: Experiences his first political thrill when visiting his uncle, Marshall Green, who had just been elected mayor of Orangeville, Ont. (by acclamation).

1907: His family moves to the parsonage of George Street Methodist Church in Peterborough, Ont. Attends Central Public School.

1910: Attends Peterborough Collegiate (*September*).

1911: His family moves to the parsonage of Central Methodist Church in Hamilton, Ont. Attends Hamilton Collegiate.

1912: Delivers the *Toronto World* newspaper in Hamilton.

1913: Spends a last summer at his grandparents' farm northwest of Toronto and with other relatives in Orangeville (*Summer*). Enters Victoria College at the University of Toronto to study history; lives in Burwash Hall where the residence dean is Vincent Massey (*October*).

1914: Begins a summer job as a timekeeper for Hamilton civic project workers and plays baseball in the City League (*July*). Joins his family in the move to the parsonage at Park Street Methodist Church in Chatham, Ont. (*July*). Joins Chatham's City League baseball team (*July*). Enrols in the University Officers Training Corps commanded by Massey. Becomes a medical orderly in the University of Toronto Hospital Unit shortly after the outbreak of the First World War (*Fall*).

1915: Leaves university to enlist in the First World War as a private on his 18th birthday; joins the University of Toronto Hospital Unit of the Canadian Army Medical Corps (*April 23*). Leaves for Plymouth, England (*May 15*). Becomes a night orderly at the Shorncliffe camp hospital (*Spring*). Sails to Alexandria, Egypt, as a quartermaster of No. 4 General Hospital Corps (*September*). Arrives in Salonica, Greece (*November 12*).

1916: Unaffected by malaria sweeping through the Salonica camp (*Summer*).

1917: Returns to England after his father intercedes with family friend Sir Sam Hughes (Militia & Defence) (*March*). Enters an officer training course at Oxford University (*March 30*). Sets a record by throwing a cricket ball 114 yards. His family moves to the parsonage at Norfolk Street Methodist Church in Guelph (*June*). Posted to the 4th Canadian Reserve Battalion (*July*). Transfers to pilot training with the Royal Flying Corps at Reading and Hendon (*October 10*). Squadron leader dislikes the name Lester, so calls him Mike. Hit by a bus in London during an air raid (*December*); leg wounds and shattered nerves end his active war service.

1918: Arrives back in Canada after recuperating in hospital (*April 6*). Becomes an aerial navigation instructor for pilot cadets at the University of Toronto and joins the RAF rugby team (*Spring*).

1919: Re-enters the University of Toronto in fourth year honours history (*January*). Receives his Bachelor of Arts degree in history (*June 5*). Articles with the law firm McLaughlin, Johnson, Moorehead & Sinclair in Toronto for less than a week (*June*). Plays semi-professional baseball in Guelph, Ont., and works at Partridge Tire and Rubber (*Summer*). Works as a sausage stuffer at Fowler Packing in Hamilton (*September*); his uncle Edson White is president of the parent company in Chicago.

1920: Transfers to the Armour Fertilizer Company in Chicago (*February*).

1921: Returns to Toronto (*Spring*). Receives a Massey Foundation Fellowship from Vincent Massey to enrol at St. John's College, Oxford University (*May*). Hired by The *Christian Guardian* of the Canadian Methodists as a contributing writer (*Summer*). Sails to England and begins modern history studies at Oxford (*August*). Plays on the Oxford hockey team during its tour of Switzerland; team is undefeated (*December*).

1922: Wins an international cap playing on the winning English team in lacrosse. Joins the Oxford-Cambridge lacrosse team on a tour of eastern U.S. colleges (*March 13-May 7*). Spends the summer in Heidelberg, Germany, with two classmates: Roland Michener (later Governor General) and Dick Bonnycastle (later publisher of Harlequin romance novels). Returns to Switzerland with the Oxford hockey team (*December*). Plays with the Swiss hockey club in Davos to qualify for the Swiss team in the European championship.

1923: Receives an honours modern history degree from Oxford (*Spring*). Joins the Oxford-Cambridge lacrosse team on an Ontario tour (*Summer*); at the Oshawa game he retrieves the opening pitch thrown by Prime Minister King. Appointed as lecturer of modern history at the University of Toronto (*September*); also becomes a don at Burwash Hall residence and coaches football, hockey and basketball. One of his history students is Maryon Moody (*September*). Turns down a chance to play for England's hockey team in the 1924 Winter Olympic Games in Chamonix, France.

1924: Becomes secretly engaged to student Maryon Moody (*March*). Reaches the second round of the Canadian national tennis pairs championship playing with Michener. Visits Maryon at her family home in Winnipeg (*August-September*).

1925: Marries Maryon in Winnipeg, in a double ceremony including Maryon's sister Grace and Norman Young (*August 22*). Moves into the top floor of 12 Admiral Road near the university (*September*).

1926: While doing research in Ottawa, witnesses the King-Byng affair.

1927: His father Ed receives an honorary doctorate of divinity from Victoria College, Toronto (*April*). Pearson becomes an assistant professor at the University of Toronto (*June*). His son Geoffrey is born in Toronto, delivered by his friend from war days in Macedonia, Dr. William Dafoe (his brother Dr. Roy Dafoe delivered the Dionne quintuplets eight years later) (*December 24*).

1928: Writes the qualifying examination for a job with the Department of External Affairs (*June*). Appointed first secretary of External Affairs in Ottawa (*August 10*). Turns down job offer to be athletics director for the University of Toronto (*October*).

1929: His daughter Patricia is born in Ottawa (*March 9*). Moves to 20 Russell Avenue, Ottawa (*May*). Takes temporary charge of the Canadian legation in Washington for three months (*June*).

1930: Attends the Naval Conference in London, England, as External Affairs advisor to James Ralston (National Defence) (*January 19-April*); the National Defence advisor is Georges Vanier. Attends a League of Nations law conference in The Hague (*March*). Bennett replaces King as External Affairs minister (*August 7*). Attends the Imperial Conference in England with Bennett's Canadian delegation (*October-November*).

Gallery seats to watch King resign as Prime Minister

Even though recently married in 1926, Pearson left his wife in Toronto and headed to Ottawa to carry out research for a book about the United Empire Loyalists. He soon became distracted by the potboiler antics of the King-Byng affair unfolding on Parliament Hill. Encountering one of his former students, Paul Martin (a former classmate of Maryon's and future External Affairs minister in his cabinet), he dragged him off to the Diplomatic Gallery where they witnessed King abruptly resign as Prime Minister to protest the Governor General's refusal to dissolve Parliament. Pearson and Martin then managed to have lunch with J.S. Woodsworth, founding leader of the CCF. No wonder Pearson never completed his Loyalists research.

1931: Becomes secretary of the Royal Commission on Grain Futures examining the impact of the Depression on wheat farmers (*April 10*). His father Ed dies in Toronto (*September 6*); his brother Vaughan, a Toronto stockbroker, moves in with their mother Annie for the remainder of her life.

1932: Attends the first World Conference on Disarmament in Geneva, Switzerland (*February 2*); the conference bogs down, so he returns home in the summer. Attends the Imperial Economic Conference in Ottawa as press relations assistant (*July 20-August 20*).

1933: Returns to the Disarmament conference for several weeks in Switzerland. Wins the singles tennis championship at the Rockcliffe Lawn Tennis Club (*Summer*); repeats the feat two years later.

1934: Becomes secretary of the Royal Commission on Price Spreads, chaired by Harry Stevens, examining companies overcharging for products (*July 7*). Recommended by Bennett to be an Officer of the Order of the British Empire (OBE) for his role on the Price Spreads commission. Accompanies Bennett to the Royal Jubilee and Commonwealth talks in London, as well as to the League of Nations meeting in Europe (*August-October*).

1935: Completes work on the Price Spreads commission (*April*). Attends George V's Silver Jubilee with Bennett (*May 6*). Receives his OBE while playing tennis at Ottawa's Rockcliffe Club. Appointed counsellor to Canada House in London, England (*August*). Takes part in the Special Assembly of the League of Nations in Geneva to discuss economic sanctions against Italy following its invasion of Ethiopia (*September 11-October 9*). Begins his appointment in London (*October*). King once again becomes External Affairs minister replacing Bennett and confirms the London appointment (*October 23*). Massey becomes Pearson's boss as the new High Commissioner to London; the first secretary is Vanier (*October 23*). His family moves to a house in Hampstead, England (*November*). Appointed to the League of Nations Co-ordination Committee and Committee of Eighteen to debate sanctions against Italy (*December 12*); they are never imposed.

1936: Attends the funeral of George V (*January 28*). Relays the actual moment of Edward VIII's abdication and accession of George VI, first to Massey, then to King (*December 10*).

OBE hoisted over the fence

Feeling queasy on a ship bobbing in the middle of the Atlantic, Pearson was summoned by Prime Minister Bennett, whom he was accompanying to George V's Royal Jubilee, to review the list of Canadians slated for British honours. Surprised to find his own name on the list for an Order of the British Empire because of his work with the Price Spreads commission, he quietly suggested he'd rather have a pay raise than an OBE. Bennett wasn't amused and Pearson let his name stand. He received his OBE from a Governor General's aide who tossed it over the fence while he was playing tennis back in Ottawa.

1937: Approached by the CBC about a job (*February*); considers it for over a year but turns it down. Serves as an usher at the coronation of George VI (*May 1*). Attends the Imperial Conference in London (*May 14-June 24*).

1938: His family moves to Fairacres in Roehampton, England.

1939: Becomes First Secretary at Canada House, following Vanier's appointment as Minister to France (*January*). Sails to Canada for a holiday at Lac du Bonnet, Man., with his in-laws (*June 30*). In anticipation of war, he returns to Ottawa, leaving his family in Manitoba (*August*). Becomes the first government official to take a trans-Atlantic flight to England (*August*). Writes Canada's declaration of war that is approved by George VI at Windsor Castle (*September 10*). Rents an apartment close to Trafalgar Square with Brigadier Harry Crerar (*October*). Meets the first troops arriving from Canada at Greenock, England (*December 18*).

1940: His wife Maryon joins him in London (*January*). Begins weekly broadcasts for the BBC that are beamed to Canada under the pseudonym Michael Macdonald. Asked by Prime Minister King to obtain several bricks from recently bombed Westminster Hall for his Kingsmere ruins (*May 11*). Visits Dover to witness the evacuation of troops across the English Channel from Dunkirk (*June 2*). His wife returns reluctantly to Ottawa (*June*). German firebombs ignite part of his Fairacres apartment, but the flames are quickly extinguished (*October*).

1941: O.D. Skelton, deputy minister of External Affairs, collapses and dies while driving in Ottawa (*January 28*). Passed over in favour of Norman Robertson to be the new deputy minister (*January 28*). Returns to Canada to work for Robertson (*June*); marks the beginning of a close association with King. His daughter, Patsy, 13, is the first to tell General Crerar about the Japanese bombing of Pearl Harbour (*December 7*).

1942: Becomes minister counsellor in Washington to Canada's U.S. Minister, Leighton McCarthy (*Spring*). His brother-in-law, Captain Norman Young, is killed at Dieppe (*August 19*). Ghostwrites a letter signed by Roosevelt to be sent to King congratulating him on the British Commonwealth Air Training Plan (*December*).

1943: Member of the Canadian delegation at the first United Nations meetings sponsored by the U.S. at Hot Springs, Virginia (*May 18-30*). Becomes chairman of the UN Interim Commission working in Washington (*June*). Helps ensure that Canadian troops are acknowledged in the U.S. announcement of the invasion of Sicily (*July*). Elected permanent chair of the working group creating a UN Food and Agricultural Organization (FAO) (*July*). The Canadian legation in Washington becomes an embassy with McCarthy as Ambassador (*November 11*). Attends the first UNRRA (United Nations Relief and Rehabilitation Administration) meeting in Atlantic City, New Jersey, serving as chair of the supply committee (*November 10-December 1*).

1944: Job title in Washington is revised to Envoy Extraordinary & Minister Plenipotentiary (*Summer*). Chairs an UNRRA meeting in Montreal (*September*).

1945: Succeeds McCarthy as ambassador to the U.S., becoming the first career civil servant to be an ambassador (*January 1*). Attends Franklin Roosevelt's funeral at the White House (*April 14*). Attends the founding conference of the UN in San Francisco, California, as a member of the Canadian delegation (*April 25-June 26*). Receives an early morning phone call about Victory in Europe (V-E) being declared that day; waits until daylight before letting King know (*May 9*). Represents Canada on the executive committee planning the first meetings for the UN General Assembly (*August 16*). Receives an honorary Doctor of Laws degree from the University of Toronto. Welcomes King to Washington for a meeting with President Truman to talk about the Gouzenko affair (*September 29*). His name is raised by King as a possible candidate to be the UN's first Secretary-General (*October 12*). Chairs the Quebec Conference to establish the FAO (*October 16-November 1*); declines election as its first director-general. Joins atomic energy talks with King, Truman and British Prime Minister Clement Attlee in Washington (*November 10-15*); helps draft final memorandum on using atomic energy for peaceful purposes.

1946: Reviews Churchill's Iron Curtin speech at King's request (*March 2*). Receives an honorary Doctor of Laws degree from Yale University. Attends his last UNRRA conference in Geneva; tours UNRRA activities in Germany and Poland with U.S. delegate Fiorello La Guardia (*Summer*). Called to Paris Peace Talks by King (*August 3*); King suggests he might succeed him as External Affairs minister. Nominated by the U.S. to be the first UN Secretary-General; vetoed by the U.S.S.R.; compromise candidate is Trygve Lie of Norway. Becomes Under-Secretary of State for External Affairs; St. Laurent (Justice) becomes External Affairs minister (*September 4*). Completes his posting in Washington (*October 6*). Rents a house on Augusta Street in Ottawa's Sandy Hill neighbourhood.

1947: Chairs a UN sub-committee that draws up a plan for the partition of Palestine into Arab and Jewish states (*May-September*); plan is passed on November 29, but partition is torpedoed by a pre-emptive strike by the Zionists. Offered the position of president of the Rockefeller Foundation, but turns it down (*September 19*).

1948: Meets with President Truman in Washington to convey King's concern about Canada's involvement in peacekeeping in Korea (*January 2*); personally supports such involvement. Attends his first meeting of the UN Security Council of which Canada is a member (*January 3*). Attends a meeting in Washington with U.S. and British delegates to discuss the feasibility of a North Atlantic defence alliance (*March 22*). Writes a speech for St. Laurent (External Affairs) that includes the first international reference calling on democratic nations to form a "closer association for collective self-defence" (*April 29*). Attends expanded meetings in Washington to discuss a North Atlantic defence alliance (*July 6-7*). St. Laurent is chosen to replace King as Prime Minister (*August 8*). Pearson is appointed by King to be Secretary of State for External Affairs (*September 10*). Nominated as the Liberal candidate for Algoma East (*September 24*). Elected in the by-election, then flies to England and Paris for the UN General Assembly (*October 25*). St. Laurent becomes Prime Minister (*November 15*). Pearson receives financial support after his friend Walter Gordon and others start a fund called the Algoma Fishing and Conservation Society.

1949: Breaks with tradition in his first speech in the House by making a partisan remark about the Conservatives not supporting NATO (*February 4*). Signs the North Atlantic Treaty for Canada in Washington (*April 4*). Meets with British Prime Minister Clement Atlee, then visits Oxford where he spends the night in his old residence room (*April 20*). Represents Canada at the Commonwealth Prime Ministers Conference in London (*April 22-29*); agreement is reached to accept India in the Commonwealth despite it being a republic. Attends Foreign Ministers Conference in Paris (*May 23*). Canada's 21st federal election: re-elected in Algoma East with an increased majority even though he was facing a Conservative candidate for the first time (*June 27*). Attends the first NATO Council meeting in Washington (*September 17*). Leads the Canadian delegation to the 4th UN General Assembly (*September 19*). Elected chairman of the political committee of the 4th UN General Assembly (*September 20*). Opts not to recognize the newly declared People's Republic of China (*October 1*).

1950: Begins a trip around the world (*January 2*), with stops in the Azores, Gibraltar, Malta, Suez Canal and Pakistan before attending the Commonwealth Foreign Ministers Conference in Colombo, Ceylon (*January 9-14*) where the Colombo Plan is approved, providing aid to Asia. Indicates an interest in recognizing China (*January 14*); public outcry and Chinese indifference squelch the initiative. His trip continues with stops in Pakistan, India (during the last few days before becoming a republic), Burma, Singapore, Hong Kong and Japan (*January-February*). Attends King's funeral in Ottawa and his burial in Toronto (*July 26-27*). Creates a special force to be available to the UN for the defence of South Korea (*August 7*). Leads the Canadian delegation to the 5th UN General Assembly (*September 19-December 15*). Feels betrayed by the U.S. after it decides to push its fight in Korea across the border into North Korea, but feels compelled to support the move (*October 7*). Serves on the UN Korea Cease-Fire Committee with Nasrullah Entezam of Iran and Sir Bengel Rau of India (*December 15-19*); fails to find a solution to the conflict, although some recommendations are adopted later.

1951: His former assistant and Canada's permanent delegate to the UN, Gerry Riddell, dies of a heart attack (*March 17*). In a Toronto speech, says Canada has a right to criticize U.S. actions "if we feel it necessary" (*April 10*); encounters backlash from Washington. Accused of passing on information to Soviet agents by American spy Elizabeth Bentley testifying at U.S. security hearings (*August*); she is unable to support the claim. Signs the Japanese peace treaty for Canada in San Francisco (*September 8*). Attends NATO meeting in Ottawa (*September 15-20*); becomes chairman of the NATO Council.

1952: Attends NATO meeting in Lisbon, Portugal (*February 20-25*); his name is raised as a possible first Secretary-General of the organization, but he declines. UN Secretary-General Trygve Lie informs him he intends to resign and would like to see him succeed (*September 11*). Elected president of the 7th UN General Assembly at the new headquarters building in New York City (*October 14*). Begins negotiations to find a Korean armistice resolution acceptable to the U.S. and India (*October 27*). The Korean resolution is passed by the UN (*December 3*). Informs St. Laurent he will accept the UN Secretary-General post if drafted by the Security Council (*December 30*).

1953: Told by St. Laurent he would be frontrunner to succeed as party leader because both St. Laurent and Douglas Abbott (Finance) intend to retire after the next election (*February 6*). Meets with the new U.S. Secretary of State John Foster Dulles in Washington (*February 15*). Pearson's UN Secretary-General nomination is vetoed in the Security Council by the U.S.S.R. (*March 19*). Appoints his former under-secretary Arnold Heeney to be Ambassador to the U.S. (*Spring*). Canada's 22nd federal election: re-elected in Algoma East defeating George Bishop (Conservative) (*August 10*). Appoints Hume Wrong as under-secretary in External Affairs (*November*).

1954: Hume Wrong dies in Ottawa (*January 24*). Represents Canada at the Far Eastern Conference in Geneva to settle the Korea question (*April 26*). Appoints Jules Léger, Ambassador to Mexico, as his new under-secretary (*July*). Attends a nine-nation conference in London to discuss issues including re-armament of West Germany (*September 28-October 3*). Signs the agreement in Paris to admit West Germany to NATO (*October 23*).

1955: Attends the Commonwealth Conference in London with St. Laurent (*January 28*). Buys the Ottawa house his family has been renting for nine years on Augusta Avenue. Attends the 10th anniversary of the UN in San Francisco as the Canadian delegate (*June*). Begins a world tour that includes London (*September 30*), Paris (*October 1-4*), Berlin (*October 4*), Moscow (first foreign minister of a NATO country to visit the U.S.S.R.) (*October 5*), Leningrad (*October 8*), Stalingrad (*October 11*), Sebastopol, and Yalta where he has dinner with Soviet Party Secretary Nikita Khrushchev and Chairman Nikolai Bulganin and signs an agreement for favored trade status and Arctic cooperation (*October 11*). Visits India (*October*). Opens Canada Dam in West Bengal, India (*November 1*). Meets with Prime Minister Gamal Abdel Nasser in Cairo, Egypt (*November 10*).

1956: Attends meetings with St. Laurent, Eisenhower and Mexican President Adolfo Ruiz Cortines in White Sulphur Springs, West Virginia (*March*). Makes his most partisan speech to date, defending the TransCanada PipeLines bill (*June 5*). Receives an honorary degree from Princeton University (*June*). Attends the Commonwealth Conference in London with St. Laurent (*June 22-July 2*). Visits London to urge Britain to avoid force in trying to reclaim the Suez Canal from Egypt (*September 3*); repeats the message a few days later to the NATO Council in Paris. Successful in urging cabinet to support efforts to end the Suez Crisis through the UN (*November 1*). Flies to New York to push for a UN peacekeeping force in Egypt (*November 1*). Abstains from voting on a U.S. proposal for a cease-fire in the Suez that can't be policed (*November 2*). His proposed UN motion for a peacekeeping force is passed (*November 4*). Britain and France invade Egypt (*November 5*); Britain announces a ceasefire the next day because of lack of international support. His name is raised again as possible NATO Secretary-General; he again declines and nominates Paul-Henri Spaak of Belgium (*December*).

1957: Visits Bermuda with St. Laurent for talks with British Prime Minister Macmillan and U.S. President Eisenhower (*March 25-26*). Canada's 23rd federal election: re-elected in Algoma East defeating Merton Mulligan (Conservative); Liberals defeated by Diefenbaker's Conservatives (*June 10*). Briefs Diefenbaker on the approaching Commonwealth Prime Ministers Conference (*June 20*). Told by Diefenbaker that many people suggested he join the Conservative cabinet as External Affairs minister (*June 20*). Resigns as Secretary of State for External Affairs (*June 21*). Joins Lionel Chevrier (former Privy Council president) to convince St. Laurent to resign as party leader, as requested by the St. Laurent family (*September 4*); writes the resignation announcement. Announces his intention to seek the Liberal party leadership (*December 4*). Receives the Nobel Peace Prize from Dr. Gunner Jahn at University Aula in Oslo, Norway (*December 10*).

1958: Elected Leader of the Liberal party in Ottawa, defeating Paul Martin Sr. on the first ballot (*January 16*). On his first day as Leader of the Opposition, moves that the government resign and turn power over to the Liberals (*January 20*); Diefenbaker responds by verbally tearing him to shreds. Diefenbaker calls for another election (*February 1*). Receives financial assistance through the fund raised by party members; John Turner, a Montreal lawyer, is one of the trustees. Canada's 24h federal election: re-elected in Algoma East defeating Conservative Basil Scully; Liberals win the fewest seats since Confederation, while Conservatives win the most (*March 31*). Vacations in Palm Beach, Florida (*April*). Moves into Stornoway.

1959: Becomes chairman of the Council on World Tensions.

1960: His wife Maryon and daughter Patsy join the anti-nuclear weapon group, Voice of Women. Attends the Liberal Study Conference on National Problems, at Queen's University in Kingston (*September 6-10*). Receives the Medallion of Valor of the State of Israel for his role during the Suez crisis (*November 16*).

1961: Endorses an expansive economic program that includes tax cuts and lower interest rates (*January 20*). Hires Keith Davey to direct Liberal party headquarters (*May 15*). Agrees to hire U.S. pollster Lou Harris, the first time polling is used extensively in Canadian politics.

1962: Attends a banquet in Washington for Nobel Prize winners hosted by President Kennedy (*April 29*). Canada's 25th federal election: re-elected in Algoma East defeating Alex Berthelot (Conservative); Liberals again defeated by Diefenbaker's Conservatives (*June 18*). His mother Annie dies in Southampton, Ont. (*August 2*). Calls for equal status for Quebec and a study of bicultural and bilingual issues in Canada (*December 17*).

1963: Comes out in favour of nuclear arms, reversing his earlier stand (*January 12*). Moves a non-confidence motion against the Diefenbaker government for its anti-nuclear policy (*February 4*); passes the next day. 25th Parliament is dissolved (*February 5*). Makes a pledge of "60 Days of Decision" if elected (*March 25*). Endures pea-shooter attacks during a campaign speech in Vancouver (*March 30*). Canada's 26th federal election: re-elected in Algoma East defeating Paul Jewell (Conservative); Liberals win a minority (*April 8*). Six Social Credit MPs indicate they will support the Liberals (*April 12*). **Pearson's government (1963-1968)**. Becomes the 14th Prime Minister of Canada (*April 22*). Appoints Robert Taschereau as the 11th Chief Justice of the Supreme Court (*April 22*). Visits London to meet with British Prime Minister Macmillan and Elizabeth II (*April 30-May 4*). Appointed a member of the British Privy Council (*May 3*). The Social Credit party reprimands the six members who 'defected' to the Liberals (*May 9*). Visits U.S. President Kennedy in Hyannisport, Massachusetts; announces intention to have Roosevelt's home on Campobello Island, N.B., used by both countries for public purposes (*May 10-11*). 26th Parliament opens; nominates Alan Macnaughton to be the 26th Speaker of the House (*May 16*). Survives a non-confidence vote related to nuclear arms (*May 21*). Announces establishment of a 12-mile coastal fishing zone (*June 4*). Receives an honorary degree from Notre Dame University (*June 9*). Walter Gordon (Finance) presents his first budget that proposes a tax on Canadian businesses taking over U.S. firms (*June 13*), part of the Liberals' 60 Days of Decision. Eric Kierans, president of the Canadian Stock Exchange, blasts the new tax, threatening to encourage brokers to short sell Canadian stocks (*June 18*). Takeover tax is withdrawn (*June 19*). Rejects Gordon's (Finance) offer to resign (*June 20*). His government survives a Conservative non-confidence motion (*June 24*). The U.S. exempts Canada from its new equalization tax that threatened Canada's stock market (*July 21*). Establishes the Royal Commission on Bilingualism and Biculturalism, chaired by André Laurendeau and Davidson Dunton (*July 22*). Appoints Bud Drury (Defence Production) as Canada's first Industry minister (*July 25*). The Federal-Provincial Conference includes discussion about a federal pension plan (*July 26-27*). Establishes the Economic Council of Canada (*August 2*). Signs a nuclear test ban treaty with the U.S., Britain and the U.S.S.R. (*August 8*). Inaugurates the Montreal World Fair site (*August 12*). Canada signs an agreement about the use of U.S. nuclear warheads in Canada (*August 16*). The Social Credit party splits into Social Credit, still led by Robert Thompson, and Ralliement Créditistes, led by Réal Caouette (*September 9*); they reunite eight years later. A trade agreement to sell $500 million of wheat to U.S.S.R. is Canada's biggest trade deal (*September 16*). Addresses the opening of the 18th UN General Assembly in New York (*September 19*); speaks about the importance of peacekeeping forces. Announces the U.S. will be able to store defensive nuclear warheads in Canada (*October 9*). The Old Age Pension is raised to $75 a month (*October 16*). Martin (External Affairs) recommends a significant increase in Canada's foreign aid program (*November*). Attends the funeral of assassinated U.S. President John F. Kennedy in Washington (*November 25*). Hosts the federal-provincial conference in Ottawa about finance (*November 26-29*). Inaugurates the world's longest underwater telephone cable, from British Columbia to Australia, with the prime ministers of Britain, Australia and New Zealand by phone (*December 2*). Chevrier (Justice) resigns to become High Commissioner in London (*December 27*); replaced by Guy Favreau (Citizenship & Immigration).

1964: Becomes the first Prime Minister to officially visit France (*January 14-18*); meets with President Charles de Gaulle. Signs Columbia River Treaty, a hydro-electricity and flood-control project, with U.S. President Lyndon Johnson in Washington (*January 22*). Opens Toronto International Airport; it is renamed Lester B. Pearson International Airport 20 years later (*February 28*). Begins to mobilize peacekeeping troops to Cyprus, then gets Parliament's approval (*March 13*); it becomes Canada's longest UN peacekeeping mission. John Garland (National Revenue) dies in North Bay at age 46 (*March 14*); replaced by Edgar Benson. Introduces the Canada Pension Plan Bill (*March 17*). Paul Hellyer (National Defence) announces intention to unify the Army, Navy and Air Force into the Canadian Forces (*March 26*); bill passes four months later. Federal-Provincial Conference held in Quebec City (*March 31-April 1*); Quebec presents its own pension plan. Government introduces the Social Insurance Number (SIN) to help administer federal pension and employment programs (*April*). Announces significant tax-sharing concessions to the provinces because of a pension compromise with Quebec (*April 20*); the move alienates Judy LaMarsh (National Health & Welfare). Makes Favreau (Justice) his Quebec deputy (*April 25*). Attends the Commonwealth Prime Ministers meeting in London (*May 8-15*). Plans to proceed with legislation for a Canadian flag, expressing a preference for a design with three red maple leaves flanked by blue borders (*May 14*). Booed at Canadian Legion convention in Winnipeg when raising his flag proposal (*May 17*). UN Secretary-General U Thant addresses both Houses of Parliament (*May 26*). Announces proposed flag design in Parliament (*May 27*). Meets with U.S. President Johnson in New York (*May 28*). Parliament approves the Columbia River Treaty (*June 5*). His cabinet sanctions talks with the U.S. about shared auto production that eventually result in the Auto Pact (*June 11*). Flag debate begins (*June 15*). His appointee to the International Control Commission (ICC), Blair Seaborn, meets with North Vietnamese Prime Minister Pham Van Dong in an unsuccessful attempt to end the hostilities with the U.S. (*June 18*). The Hall Royal Commission on Health Services recommends the creation of medicare (*June 19*). Is the subject of a documentary shot by D.A. Pennebaker that the CBC refuses to air because it is unflattering (*June*). Announces plans to study the implications if Quebec was to secede (*June 28*). Attends the Commonwealth Prime Ministers Conference in London (*Jul 8-15*); proposes a declaration of racial equality. Conservatives plan to filibuster the flag debate (*July 22*). The Student Loan Act is created to provide university students with loans up to $5,000 (*July 28*). Appoints Frank Miller as Canada's first Chief of Defence Staff who commands all three branches of the armed forces (*August 1*). His wife Maryon and 'Lady Bird' Johnson open Roosevelt Campobello International Park in New Brunswick (*August 20*). A protester throws a carton of beef blood from the gallery onto the floor of the House of Commons (*August 24*). Federal-Provincial Conference in Charlottetown marks the 100th anniversary of the Charlottetown Conference (*August 31-September 2*); discussion of the Fulton-Favreau formula for amending the BNA Act. The flag debate is suspended with the issue sent to committee to come up with a proposal (*September 10*). Meets with U.S. President Johnson and British Columbia Premier W.A.C. Bennett in Great Falls, Montana, to sign the Columbia River Treaty (*September 16*). Gordon (Finance) tables legislation to prevent foreign takeovers of some financial institutions (*September 23*). Elizabeth II visits Canada to celebrate the centenary of the Charlottetown and Quebec City conferences (*October 5-12*); encounters separatist demonstrations in Quebec. Parliamentary committee recommends a new flag design with one red maple leaf flanked by red bars (*October 29*). His parliamentary secretary, Guy Rouleau, resigns after being implicated in a charge of bribery to help Lucien Rivard make bail (*November 24*). Dorion enquiry is established to look into the Rivard affair (*November 25*). Keeps Maurice Lamontagne (Secretary of State) and René Tremblay (Citizenship & Immigration) in cabinet despite Conservative charges that they accepted furniture without payment in Quebec (*November 30*). Closure imposed on the flag debate (*December 14*); house approves the flag at 2:13 a.m. the next morning. House votes to main-tain the Union Jack flag as a symbol of Commonwealth membership (*December 17*).

1965: Meets with Quebec Premier Jean Lesage in Florida and unsuccessfully attempts to entice him back to federal politics (*January*). Visits U.S. President Johnson at his ranch in Texas (*January 15*). Signs the Canada-U.S. Automotive Agreement, or Auto Pact, with Johnson, eliminating tariffs on new cars and parts crossing the border (*January 16*). Yvon Dupuis (Without Portfolio) is fired following charges of accepting $10,000 to help a racetrack franchise in his riding (*January 20*); convicted and later acquitted on appeal. Flag receives Royal assent (*January 28*) and is officially raised (*February 15*). Announces old-age pensions will kick in at age 65 instead of 70 (*February 17*). Civil servants will now have the right to collective bargaining and arbitration (*February 23*). The Royal Commission on Bilingualism and Biculturalism's preliminary report warns of the "deep gulf of awareness dividing French and English Canada" (*February 25*). Quebec and France sign a cultural agreement, without input from Canada (*February 27*). Speaks at the Canadian Society of New York about Vietnam (*March 5*). Parliament passes legislation for a Canada Pension Plan (*March 29*). Receives Temple University's World Peace Award in Philadelphia (*April 2*); in his remarks he suggests bombing of Hanoi should end. Meets with U.S. President Johnson who criticizes him for his Hanoi remarks (*April 3*). Second Session, 26th Parliament prorogued, ending the longest session to date at 248 days (*April 3*). New Senators now required to retire at age 75 (*June 2*). Receives an honorary law degree from Queen's University. Turns sod for Expo 67 in Montreal (*June 15*). Attends the Commonwealth Prime Ministers Conference in London (*June 17-25*); Canadian Arnold Smith becomes the first Secretary-General of the newly formed Commonwealth Secretariat. Parliament exempts *Time* and *Reader's Digest* from advertising tax on its Canadian editions (*June 28*). Dorion inquiry report is tabled, implicating various Liberal politicians; Favreau (Justice) is moved to Privy Council as a result (*June 29*) and is replaced by Lucien Cardin (Public Works). Announces the building of a causeway to Prince Edward Island (*July 8*); idea abandoned four years later. Governor General Vanier's term is extended indefinitely (*July 15*). Hosts a Federal-Provincial Conference in Ottawa that includes representatives from Yukon and Northwest Territories (*July 19-22*); introduces a medical health insurance program to the premiers. Tours western Canada (*August 19-29*). Gérard Pelletier, Jean Marchand and Pierre Trudeau decide to run as Liberals in the election (*September 10*). Provincial health ministers meet in Ottawa to discuss medicare (*September 23*). The Canadian Film Development Agency is created as a Crown corporation (*October 13*). Opens the Macdonald-Cartier Bridge between Ottawa and Hull (*October 15*). Indicates that Gordon (Finance) will remain in the portfolio after the election, despite objections from MP Robert Winters (*October 26*). Canada's 27th federal election: re-elected in Algoma East defeating broadcaster Joel Aldred (Conservative); wins another Liberal minority (*November*

8). Gordon (Finance) resigns because of his advice to call an election (*November 11*). Refuses to recognize the proclaimed independence of Rhodesia (*November 11*). Receives the Family of Man Award from the Protestant Council of Churches in New York (*November 17*). Becomes the first Prime Minister to visit Jamaica, for talks with Prime Minister Donald Sangster (*November 28*); also visits Trinidad and Tobago. Appoints John Turner to cabinet as Minister Without Portfolio and moves Mitchell Sharp (Trade & Commerce) to Finance. Canada imposes an oil embargo on Rhodesia (*December 20*).

Ignatieff's first name

George Ignatieff, a colleague of Pearson's in the High Commissioner's office in London, also became a friend. A close enough friend that Ignatieff named his first son after Pearson. Michael Ignatieff grew up to be an academic and leader of the Liberal party, 2009-2011. Even though 'Mike' was merely a nickname, it's not surprising that Ignatieff Sr. opted for it rather than calling his son Lester Ignatieff.

1966: Canada Pension Plan and Quebec Pension Plan come into effect (*January 1*). Appoints Pierre Trudeau to be his parliamentary secretary (*January 9*). Attends the Commonwealth Prime Ministers Conference in Lagos, Nigeria (*January 11-13*); sanctions against Rhodesia are approved. 27th Parliament opens; nominates Lucien Lamoureaux to be the 27th Speaker of the House (*January 18*). Opens the 13-km, $200-million, east-west subway in Toronto (*February 25*). Forty students arrested during Vietnam protest on Parliament Hill (*March 4*). Agrees to set up an inquiry into the handling of spying allegations against George Victor Spencer, a Post Office employee, reversing a decision by Lucien Cardin (Justice) not to press charges (*March 4*). France asks Canada to move its NATO forces to Germany (*March 10*). Establishes a Royal Commission to investigate Gerda Munsinger's relationship to the former government, to be chaired by Justice Wishart Spence (*March 14*). Sharp (Finance) presents his first budget, introducing a Guaranteed Income Supplement to accompany the pension for those in need (*March 29*). Parliament votes to retain capital punishment (*April 5*). Announces plan to promote bilingualism in the civil service, including higher pay for two-language positions and language training (*April 6*). Former postal worker Spencer dies of natural causes in Vancouver (*April 9*). A day after trying to see the Prime Minister at his residence, Paul Chartier of Alberta is killed when his homemade bomb explodes prematurely in a Parliament washroom (*May 18*). Receives the Atlantic Union Pioneer Award in Springfield, Illinois, for his role in creating NATO (*June 11*). Martin (External Affairs) indicates Chester Ronning of his department is involved in possible peace negotiations in North Vietnam (*June 15*). The Company of Young Canadians, inspired by the U.S. Peace Corps, is created (*June 28*). Hosts the Canadian Caribbean Conference in Ottawa (*July 6-8*). The Wells enquiry finds Spencer guilty of gross misconduct in supplying information to the USSR. Six premiers reject the proposed federal medicare plan at a conference in Toronto (*August 2*). Lays the visitors pavilion cornerstone at Roosevelt-Campobello International Park with U.S. President Johnson (*August 21*). Parliament legislates 118,000 striking railway employees back to work (*August 29*). Créditiste MP Gilles Grégoire sits as an Indpendent after becoming president of a Quebec separatist party (*August 29*). Attends the Commonwealth Prime Ministers Conference in London (*September 4-15*); proposes that Britain ask the UN to impose sanctions on Rhodesia if the Commonwealth effort fails. Postpones the medicare plan for one year (*September 8*). Martin (External Affairs) chairs the opening session of the 21st UN General Assembly (*September 20*). Spence commission censures Diefenbaker for retaining Sévigny and censures Fulton for not investigating further in the Munsinger affair (*September 23*).

The Commonwealth Parliamentary Association Conference is held in Ottawa (*September 28-October 5*). Appoints Marchand (Citizenship & Immigration) as the first Manpower minister and Benson (National Revenue) as president of the proposed Treasury Board (*October 1*). Liberals reject Gordon's economic proposals to reduce foreign ownership at a Liberal Policy Conference in Ottawa (*October 12*). Federal-Provincial Conference in Ottawa results in an agreement to raise equalization grants by $150 million (*October 24-28*). His wife Maryon opens the Canadiana Room in the official residence, using the family's early art, handicrafts and furniture (*November 1*). Canada is elected to a two-year term on the UN Security Council (*November 11*). The Medical Care Act is passed (*December 21*).

1967: Lights the Centennial Flame on Parliament Hill (*January 1*). Pauline Vanier, the Governor General's wife, dedicates the Centennial Train in Ottawa (*January 1*); it makes 83 stops across Canada. Reappoints Gordon to cabinet as Minister Without Portfolio (*January 9*). Appoints Marchand (Manpower & Immigration) as his Quebec deputy, replacing Favreau (*January 18*). Yellowknife becomes the official capital of the Northwest Territories (*January 18*). Appoints Gordon (Without Portfolio) to chair a special committee to study foreign ownership (*January 23*). Announces the formation of the Royal Commission on the Status of Women, (*February 3*). Twenty senior civil servants sent to Quebec for French language training (*February*). Carter Royal Commission on Taxation tables its report, proposes a capital gains tax (*February 24*). Meets with Vanier who offers to stay on as Governor General until the end of Centennial year (*March 4*). Vanier dies in Ottawa (*March 5*); Chief Justice Taschereau becomes administrator to replace Vanier. Civil servants are given collective bargaining rights and the Treasury Board is created (*March 13*). Robert Thompson resigns as Social Credit leader (*March 17*). Announces the appointment of Roland Michener as Canada's 20th Governor General (*March 29*). Favreau (Privy Council) resigns to become a Quebec Supreme Court judge (*April 3*). Appoints Trudeau as Justice minister and Jean Chrétien as Minister Without Portfolio; moves Turner (Without Portfolio) to Registrar General (*April 4*). Parliament recommends *O Canada* as the National Anthem, with *God Save the Queen* as the Royal Anthem (*April 12*). Announces the creation of the Order of Canada award (*April 17*). Uses NORAD hotline phone to summon a tow truck after his car breaks down on the way to Harrington Lake (*April 21*). Armed Forces Unification Bill passes (*April 25*). Expo 67 opens in Montreal, with Ethiopia Emperor Haile Selassie as the first visitor (*April 27*); attendance in the first three days is nearly 1.5 million. Peacekeeping force in the Middle East ends after 11 years (*May 19*); Canadian forces begin emergency withdrawal from Gaza Strip a week later. Centre Block is locked for the first time during a demonstration by 10,000 diary farmers seeking higher milk prices (*May 24*). Macdonald's Bellevue House in Kingston officially opens (*May 24*). Meets with Johnson at Harrington Lake after the U.S. president's visit to Expo 67 (*May 25*). Receives an honorary Doctor of Science in Politics degree from the University of Ottawa. Receives an honorary Doctor of Laws degree from Dalhousie University. Opens the $13-million National Library and Archives Building in Ottawa (*June 20*). Officiates at Canada's 100th birthday celebrations in Ottawa (*July 1*). Elizabeth II addresses Parliament for the second time (*July 1*). Governor General Michener receives the first Order of Canada (*July 1*); 90 Canadians are named to the list two days later. Accompanies Elizabeth II and Prince Philip to Expo 67 (*July 3*). Former Justice minister Favreau dies in Montreal (*July 11*). Pan-American Games held in Canada for the first time, in Winnipeg (*July 23-August 6*). Rebukes French President Charles de Gaulle for shouting "Vive le Québec libre" during a state visit; the French leaders cuts his visit short (*July 24*). Meets with the 10 competing provincial teams in the Centennial Voyageur Canoe Pageant that began at Rocky Mountain House, Alta., in May and will end 5,000 km later at Expo 67 (*August 29*). Jack Pickersgill (Transport) resigns to become first president of the Canadian Transport Commission (*September 5*). Conservatives choose Premier Robert Stanfield of Nova Scotia to replace Diefenbaker as leader (*September 9*). Former Quebec cabinet minister René Lévesque declares his support for Quebec independence (*September 18*). Joins tennis partner Governor-General Michener to defeat King Constantine of Greece and Michener's aid Marc Landry on the court (*September 21*). Martin (External Affairs) calls on the U.S. to stop bombing in North Vietnam (*September 27*). Expo 67 closes; total attendance is 50,306,648 (*October 29*). Officially opens Pearson Park in St. Catharines (*November 3*). 100th anniversary of Canada's first Parliamentary session (*November 6*). Stanfield wins by-election in Colchester-Hants (*November 6*). Supreme Court rules that west-coast off-shore mineral rights are a federal jurisdiction (*November 7*). Visits England where he receives an honorary degree from the University of London and the Freedom of the City of London (*November 21-27*). House votes for a partial ban on capital punishment for five years (*November 23*). The New Bank Act is passed by the Senate, officially allowing foreign banks to operate in Canada (*November 26*). Turns down an offer to attend the Confederation For Tomorrow Conference of premiers discussing provincial issues, held in Toronto (*November 26-30*). Describes de Gaulle's press conference in France calling for Quebec to become a sovereign state as "intolerable" (*November 27*). Bilingualism & Biculturalism report asks Ontario and New Brunswick to extend the same rights to French in their provinces as are extended to English in Quebec (*December 5*). Benson (Revenue) announces $1.2 billion in government spending cutbacks (*December 7*). Announces his intention to resign (*December 14*). Trudeau (Justice) outlines changes in the Criminal Code related to homosexuality, abortion, lotteries and possession of weapons (*December 21*). Department of Consumer & Corporate Affairs is established with Turner (Registrar General) as the first minister (*December 21*). Vincent Massey, the first Canadian-born Governor General, dies in London, England (*December 30*).

1968: Appoints Chrétien (Without Portfolio) as Finance minister, replacing leadership hopeful Sharp (*January 13*). The Divorce Act receives Royal Assent, expanding grounds for divorce beyond adultery (January 25). Special committee established to discuss a proposed national capital region (*January 31*). Presides over the Federal-Provincial Constitutional Conference in Ottawa that recognizes national French language rights (*February 5-8*). Gordon (Privy Council) tables report on foreign investment, recommending a policy to protect national sovereignty over Canadian subsidiaries of foreign companies (*February 15*). Receives an honorary degree from the University of the West Indies in Jamaica (*February 17*). Vacations at Senator Harland Molson's in Jamaica (*February 17-19*). Canada suspends diplomatic relations with Gabon after it invites Quebec to an international conference on education (*February 19*). Government loses a vote on the third reading of an income tax bill (*February 19*). Forced to cut his vacation short following the defeat in the House (*February 20*). Wins a confidence vote after the Conservatives decide not to oppose it (*February 28*); Conservative MP Gordon Churchill resigns from caucus in disgust. Accepts Gordon's (Privy Council) resignation (*March 11*); replaces him on an acting basis with Trudeau (Justice). Removes MP Ralph Cowan from caucus for opposing government policy (*March 15*). Suspends gold trading for three weeks because of rapidly rising demand (*March 15*). The Canadian Radio-Television Commission (CRTC) is created (*April 1*). Delivers his farewell speech to delegates at the leadership convention in Ottawa (*April 4*). Trudeau (Justice) wins the Liberal leadership (*April 6*). Moves to Harrington Lake retreat with Maryon (*April*). **Pearson government ends** (*April 20*); unable to deliver a farewell speech because Trudeau dissolves Parliament. Visits Ireland (*April*). Appointed professor of international affairs at Carleton University in Ottawa (*May 9*). Moves to Montague Avenue in Ottawa's Rockcliffe neigh-bourhood. Awarded the Companion of the Order of Canada (*June 28*). Becomes honorary president of the Institute of Strategic Studies, a British disarmament and defence research centre (*July 17*). Becomes chairman of the Commission on International Development to determine the effectiveness of World Bank aid programs (*August 19*). Becomes honorary board chairman of the Ottawa Rough Riders football team. Attends the unveiling of his portrait on Parliament Hill by Hugh Mackenzie (*October 24*). Begins around-the-world travel for the Commission on International Development. Broadcasts the first of six Reith Lectures on international politics for the BBC (*November 18*).

1969: Pennebaker documentary *Mr. Pearson* is finally aired by the CBC (*April 20*). Becomes chancellor of Carleton University. Begins teaching a weekly seminar course on International Relations at Carleton (*September*). His Commission on International Development report is published calling for an affirmative partnership of rich and poor countries to make aid programs work (*October*).

1970: Becomes honorary chairman of the Montreal Expos baseball team. Visits the Expos training camp in West Palm Beach, Florida (*March*). Becomes honorary president of the World Federalists of Canada. Tumorous right eye is removed at Ottawa General Hospital and replaced with a glass one. Becomes the first chairman of the International Development Research Centre to research problems facing developing countries (*October 22*).

1972: Becomes honorary chairman of United World College of the Pacific, a Canadian/U.S. educational venture to build a college on Vancouver Island (*January 29*). Presented with Britain's Order of Merit by Elizabeth II at Buckingham Palace, London (*June 8*). Awarded the Victor Gallancz Humanity Award in London (*June 13*). First volume of his memoirs, *Mike, Memoirs Vol. 1, 1897-1948* is published (*October*); tours to promote it. Vacations in Florida (*December*); cancer of the liver brings him back to Ottawa before Christmas (*December 24*). Lapses into a coma at his Rockcliffe home and dies soon after (*December 27*). Lies in state on Parliament Hill where 12,000 file past (*December 30*). Funeral held at Christ Church Anglican Cathedral; buried in the Gatineau Hills near Wakefield, Que. (*December 31*).

BOOKS ABOUT PEARSON

- **1964**: John R. Beal; *The Pearson Phenomenon* (Longman)
- **1968**: Peter C. Newman; *The Distemper of Our Times: Canadian Politics in Transition, 1963-1968* (McClelland & Stewart; revised 1990)
- **1972**: Lester B. Pearson; *Mike, The Memoirs of the Right Honourable Lester B. Pearson, Volume One, 1897-1948* (University of Toronto)
- **1973**: Lester B. Pearson; *Mike, The Memoirs of the Right Honourable Lester B. Pearson, Volume Two, 1948-1957* (University of Toronto)
- **1974**: Bruce Thordarson; *Lester Pearson: Diplomat and Politician* (Oxford University)
- **1975**: Lester B. Pearson; *Mike, The Memoirs of the Right Honourable Lester B. Pearson, Volume Three, 1957-1968* (University of Toronto)
- **1978**: Robert Bothwell; *Pearson: His Life and World* (McGraw-Hill Ryerson)
- **1978**: Peter Stursberg; *Lester Pearson and the Dream of Unity* (Doubleday Canada)
- **1980**: Peter Stursberg; *Lester Pearson and the American Dilemma* (Doubleday Canada)
- **1989**: John English: *Shadow of Heaven: The Life of Lester Pearson, Vol. 1, 1897-1948* (Lester & Orpen Denys)
- **1992**: John English: *The Worldly Years: The Life of Lester Pearson, Vol. 2, 1949-1972* (A.A. Knopf)

- **1993**: Geoffrey Pearson; *Seize the Day: Lester B. Pearson & Crisis Diplomacy* (Carleton University)
- **1999**: Norman Hillmer (ed.); *Pearson: The Unlikely Gladiator* (McGill-Queens University)
- **2006**: Gordon R. Gibb; *Lester B. Pearson: The Geek Who Made Canada Proud* (JackFruit;) (juvenile) (re-released by Five Rivers in 2015)
- **2008**: Andrew Cohen; *Lester B. Pearson* (Extraordinary Canadians, Penguin)
- **2009**: Michael Carroll; *Pearson's Peacekeepers: Canada and the United Nations Emergency Force, 1956-67* (UBC)
- **2012**: Yves Engler; *Lester Pearson's Peacekeeping: The Truth May Hurt* (RED/Fernwood)
- **2015**: Antony Anderson; *The Diplomat: Lester Pearson and the Suez Crisis* (Goose Lane)

Leaders of the Social Credit Party

1.	John Blackmore	1935-1944
2.	Solon Low	1944-1961
3.	Robert Thompson	1961-1967
4.	Réal Caouette	1971-1976
5.	André-Gilles Fortin	1976-1977
6.	Lorne Reznowski	1978-1979
7.	Fabien Roy	1979-1980
8.	Martin Hattersley	1981-1983
9.	Harvey Lainson	1986-1990
10.	Ken Campbell	1990-1993
Créditistes		
1.	Réal Caouette	1963-1971

15

Pierre Trudeau

The Unconventional Prime Minister

Pierre Trudeau was an intellectual and a contrarian, qualities Canadians hadn't previously experienced in their leaders. They either loved or hated the man as he moved the country further to the left than ever before. His toughness revealed itself with the imposition of the War Measures Act during the October Crisis, and again when he patriated the Canadian Constitution without Quebec's participation. His indifference to popularity made it possible for him to introduce wage and price controls, the metric system, and a national energy program despised by the West. Perhaps his most enduring legacy remains the Charter of Rights, which altered Canada's judicial landscape.

Trudeau the Politician

Prime Minister of Canada: April 20, 1968 – June 4, 1979; March 3, 1980 – June 30, 1984
Length of terms: (1) 11 years, 1 month, 15 days; (2) 4 years, 3 months, 27 days; (Total) 15 years, 5 months, 12 days
Parliaments as Prime Minister: 27th; 28th; 29th; 30th; 32nd
Age on entering office: 48
Political party: Liberal
Leader of party: April 6, 1968 – June 15, 1984
Member of Parliament: November 8, 1965 – July 9, 1984
Riding represented: Mount Royal [Que.] 1965-1984
Cabinet portfolios: Justice (1967-1968); Privy Council President (acting) (1968)
Other political posts: Parliamentary Secretary to the Prime Minister (1966-1967); Leader of the Opposition (1979-1980)
Titles: Canadian Privy Councillor (1967); Commonwealth's Companion of Honour (1984); Companion of the Order of Canada (1985)
Quotes: "I have never denied the existence of the French-Canadian nation; nor do I deny the aboriginals … the status of a nation in the sociological sense. What I rejected … is the doctrine that claims that every sociological nation must have political sovereignty and independence." (1993 in *Memoirs*).

"Just watch me." (1970 response to a reporter about how far he would go to resolve the October Crisis)
Lived after term: 16 years

Trudeau the Man

Name: Joseph Philippe Pierre Yves Elliott Trudeau
Born: October 18, 1919, Montreal, Quebec
Ancestry: French, Scottish
Religion: Roman Catholic
Education: B.A. [Bachelor of Arts] (College Jean de Brébeuf, 1940); LL.D. [Doctor of Laws] (University of Montreal, 1943); M.A. [Master of Arts in Political Economy] (Harvard University, 1945)
Nicknames: Toto; PET; Ti-Pet
Military service: Canadian Army (Canadian Officers Training Corps); Home Service (1941-1945)
Occupation: lawyer; civil servant; professor; journalist
Occupation after term: lawyer
Publications: *La Grève de l'Amiante (Asbestos Strike)* (editor) (1956); *Two Innocents in Red China* (with Jacques Hébert) (1960); *Federalism and the French Canadians* (1968); *Approaches to Politics* (1970); *Conversation with Canadians* (1972); *Pierre Elliott Trudeau: Portrait in Time* (1977); *Lifting the Shadow of War* (1987); *Speaks Out on Meech Lake* (1990); *Fatal Tilt: Speaking Out about Sovereignty* (1991); *Memoirs* (1993); *The Canadian Way* (with Ivan Head) (1995); *Against the Current: Selected Writings 1939-1996* (1996); *The Essential Trudeau* (1998)
Appearance: "The graven elegance of the high cheekbones and the big nose; the sudden animation, the deprecating smile and the depth of the huge eyes. It should have been an ugly face – it was furrowed and pockmarked but the parts are masterfully assembled for the lens. From any angle it was alive and compelling." (Gordon Donaldson in *Fifteen Men*, 1969) "The manner is unaffected and instantly attractive; the light blues eyes ironical and amused, but they can change expression, and almost colour, to a chillier, cooler tone." (Charles Ritchie in *Storm Signals*, 1983)
Personality: "The key elements … are self-discipline, sensitivity, and an almost obsessive sense of independence or freedom" (George Radwanski in *Trudeau*); "He is a litany of contradictions. A shy egocentric. 'A solitary sort of fellow' in his own words, who yearns for the spotlight. A populist aristocrat." (Richard Gwyn in *The Northern Magus*)
Married: Margaret Joan Sinclair, March 4, 1971, St. Stephen's Roman Catholic Church, North Vancouver, British Columbia
Age at marriage: 51
Years married: 13
Separated: May 27, 1977
Divorced: April 2, 1984
Died: September 28, 2000, Montreal, Quebec
Age at death: 80
Cause of death: prostate cancer
Buried: Saint-Rémi-de-Napierville Cemetery, Saint-Rémi, Quebec

Trudeau was the:

- Only Prime Minister who married while in office
- Only Prime Minister with a son who became Prime Minister
- First Prime Minister to win a majority after losing a non-confidence vote
- First Prime Minister born in the 20th Century
- First Prime Minister to be divorced
- First Prime Minister never to serve as External Affairs minister (since the department's creation in 1912)
- Second Prime Minister to have children born while in office
- Third longest serving Prime Minister
- Third French Canadian Prime Minister
- Fourth Prime Minister under 50
- Fourth Prime Minister born in Quebec
- Fourth Roman Catholic Prime Minister
- Sixth Liberal Prime Minister
- Tenth Prime Minister who was a lawyer

Trudeau's legacy

- Patriated the constitution
- Created a Charter of Rights
- Introduced official bilingualism and multiculturalism
- Introduced wage and price controls
- Invoked the War Measures Act against separatist violence in Quebec
- Joined the G7 nations
- Moved the country from Imperial to metric measure
- Helped defeat the 1980 Quebec independence referendum
- Introduced the national energy program

TRUDEAU'S FAMILY

Trudeau's Parents

Father: Joseph Charles 'Charley' Émile Trudeau
Born: July 5, 1887, St. Rémi de Napierville, Quebec
Occupation: lawyer; business owner
Died: April 10, 1935, Deland, Florida
Age at death: 47

Mother: Grace Elliott
Born: August 23, 1890, Soulanges, Quebec
Married: May 11, 1915, Montreal, Quebec
Died: January 16, 1973, Montreal, Quebec
Age at death: 82

Trudeau's Brothers & Sisters (3 siblings; Pierre the third)

Brother: Jacques Charles Elliott Trudeau (1916-1916)
Sister: Suzette Trudeau (1918-2008), 3 children
Married: Pierre Rouleau (1945)

Brother: Charles 'Tip' Elliott Trudeau (1922-1994)
Married: Andrée Lavigne (1945)

Trudeau's Wife

Name: Margaret 'Maggie' Joan Sinclair
Born: September 10, 1948, Vancouver, British Columbia
Father: James Sinclair (businessman; MP; cabinet minister)
Mother: Doris Kathleen Bernard
Occupation: author; speaker
Age at marriage: 22
Second marriage: Fried Kemper (April 19, 1984)
Children with Kemper: Kyle James Joachim (November 17, 1984); Alicia 'Ally' (February 2, 1989)
Second divorce: 1999
Younger than Trudeau: 29 years

Trudeau's Children (3)

Name: Justin Pierre James Trudeau (*see Chapter 23*)
Born: December 25, 1971, Ottawa, Ontario
Occupation: teacher; MP; Liberal party leader; 23rd Prime Minister of Canada
Married: Sophie Grégoire (May 28, 2005)
Children: 3 – Xavier James; Ella-Grace Margaret; Hadrien Grégoire

Name: Alexandre 'Sacha' Emmanuel Trudeau
Born: December 25, 1973, Ottawa, Ontario
Occupation: journalist; filmmaker
Married: Zoë Bedos (2007)
Children: 3 – Pierre-Emmanuel; Gala Simone; Ariane Lea

Name: Michel 'Micha' Charles-Émile Trudeau
Born: October 2, 1975, Ottawa, Ontario
Died: November 13,1998, Kokanee Lake, British Columbia

Name: Sarah Elisabeth Coyne
Born: May 5, 1991, St. John's, Newfoundland
Mother: Deborah Coyne (ran for Liberal leadership, 2012)

POLITICAL STORIES

Three Wise Men

Highly visible in Quebec, Jean Marchand, Gérard Pelletier and Pierre Trudeau were virtually unknown in English Canada when they agreed to run as Liberal candidates in 1965. Quickly dubbed the three wise men by the media, they represented Pearson's new-wave, federalist front to raise the nation's awareness about the *indépendiste* feelings growing in Quebec.

They were a package deal. Trudeau first met journalist Pelletier in the mid-1940s who in turn introduced Trudeau to union organizer Marchand. The three maintained a close bond over the years, arguing at regular house gatherings of intellectuals and contributing to the journal *Cité libre*. The federal Liberals wanted Marchand as a candidate in 1963, but he wouldn't commit unless Pelletier and Trudeau came along, too. Then Pearson came out in favour of nuclear arms, reversing his stand, and all three Quebecers quickly backed out.

Wooing the three men began again in the lead-up to the next election two years later. It was still Marchand the Liberals wanted; the other two were a harder sell. But Marchand made it clear it was all three or none. All three were elected.

When Trudeau became Prime Minister in 1968, both colleagues ended up in cabinet, with Marchand as Secretary of State until he moved to Manpower & Immigration to make room for Pelletier. Never happy as a politician, Marchand resigned as Environment minister in 1976, while Pelletier had left a year earlier to become Ambassador to France.

The Trudeaumania phenomenon

Something unusual was happening in the lead-up to Trudeau's decision to seek the Liberal leadership. It first surfaced clearly at the Ontario Liberal convention where Trudeau was mobbed by fans. A week later, he became a leadership candidate and the wild enthusiasm and adoration kept building. Two months later, he was Prime Minister. The media – drawing on the Beatlemania phenomenon – dubbed it Trudeaumania.

He was swarmed everywhere by Canadians wanting to get his autograph, touch him, hug him, kiss him. What was the attraction? There was no simple answer to explain the star-quality buzz. Some found him sexy; he was single, wore sandals, liked beautiful women and was athletic (a flip into a pool became major news). He represented change to young people wanting to shake up the system. They adored him every time he flouted the system.

Trudeaumania didn't last, but it survived until his marriage to Margaret Sinclair in 1972. Forty-three years later, it returned with the aura surrounding his son Justin. The same inexplicable mix of good looks and a compelling change in 'how to do government' gave him a majority – only, this time, Trudeaumania was characterized by selfies instead of signatures.

Handling the October Crisis

The growing violence of the Front de libération du Québec (FLQ) crossed a line in October 1970 when one of the movement's cells kidnapped James Cross, the British Trade Commissioner. While Trudeau's government was still deciding how to respond to the threat, a second kidnapping hit closer to home. Pierre Laporte, Quebec's labour minister and a lifelong friend of Trudeau (they'd played together as boys in Montreal's Outremont area), was also taken.

Not knowing the extent of the crisis, Trudeau and cabinet imposed the War Measures Act, sending federal troops into Montreal with the blessing of the city and the province. Nearly 500 people were arrested and detained, but most were eventually released. Canada's swinging Prime Minister could be tough when needed. Asked by the media how far he was prepared to go to deal with the trouble, he responded with his baiting, "Just watch me."

Laporte was assassinated by the FLQ, but Cross was released in early December. By then, Trudeau had replaced the War Measures Act with less invasive legislation. Before the end of the year, Laporte's captors surrendered and were tried.

Wage and Price Controls

Inflation was running unchecked in 1975 and Trudeau knew he had to do something about it. In the last election, Robert Stanfield's Conservatives had proposed bringing in controls over wage and price increases. Trudeau blat-antly grabbed the idea and began trying to sell it to labour and the provinces.

Then, on October 13, he surprised Canadians by implementing mandatory wage and price controls to last for three years. An Anti-Inflation Board was created to police the initiative and caps were slammed onto salary increases and price hikes.

The nation wasn't happy. A year after their launch, nearly one million workers demonstrated on Parliament Hill against the controls. By 1978, the rate of inflation was ebbing and Trudeau began removing the constraints.

The first Quebec Referendum

It was a grim scenario. The Parti Québecois – committed to taking Quebec out of Canada – won the 1976 provincial election and the new premier was Trudeau's close-but-detested acquaintance, René Lévesque. While the Prime Minister maintained a business-as-usual attitude on the international stage, he had limited options in influencing Quebec's next steps.

Over the next three years, both governments postured about what the other side couldn't do. Quebec's Charter of the French Language made the province's prevalent language it's dominant one, and a growing number of corporations and English-speaking residents were leaving the province. Finally, a referendum on Quebec's place in Canada was set for May 1980. The weighty question, over 100 words long, asked Quebecers whether or not they favoured "sovereignty – and, at the same time, maintain with Canada an economic association."

Trudeau was not prepared to negotiate with Quebec should the vote be 'Yes'. He dispatched Jean Chrétien (Justice) to lead the federal forces on the 'No' side and spoke at several rallies in Quebec City and Montreal.

On May 20, 59.9% of Quebecers voted against the question. It was a satisfying majority, but it also revealed that Trudeau would need to get serious about embarking on constitutional reform. That took two years and Quebec did not sign the new Canada Act. Another, even closer, referendum took place in 1995 with the same result. But Trudeau had retired from politics by this time and played no role in the vote.

Bringing the Constitution home

Few issues made Canadians' eyes roll as readily as the prospect of constitutional talks. The sheer challenge of getting all the provinces and interest groups together to forge a new framework for governing was one that overpowered most leaders. Still, Trudeau was ready to tackle it.

Throughout his term in office, numerous federal-provincial constitutional conferences were convened. At times, he threatened to create a new constitution without input from the provinces unless they were prepared to cooperate. The 1980 Quebec referendum boosted the effort to find a way through the impasse. The Supreme Court said Ottawa could patriate the contitution unilaterally, but warned that doing it without the provinces went against conventional practice.

A final push by Trudeau and the premiers took place in Ottawa in November 1981. Ontario and New Brunswick agreed with Ottawa's proposed constitution. Quebec was prepared to agree if the package went to the voters in a referendum. The remaining seven provinces were ready to give up their preferred amending formula if given the ability to use the veto power of a 'notwithstanding' clause.

A deal was reached, but Quebec didn't sign it. The Canada Act, along with the Charter of Rights and an amending formula, was passed by the House and the Senate before the end of the year. Britain approved it three months later and, on April 17, 1982, Trudeau and Elizabeth II signed the homegrown consti-tution in Ottawa.

PERSONAL STORIES

Trudeau and the Canoe

In 1941, 21-year-old Trudeau talked three friends into canoeing over 1,200 km from Montreal to Moosonee. It was the beginning of his infatuation with the canoe, developed as a summer camper and paddler in Algonquin Park. The epic journey up the Ottawa and down the Harricana to Hudson Bay became the subject of his *Exhaustion and Fulfillment: The Ascetic in a Canoe* which appeared in a Catholic youth magazine three years later.

Trudeau paddled the Mackenzie River in 1956 with poet and constitutional expert Frank Scott, the first of many trips on Arctic rivers over the next 40 years. Political leadership ended his trips for a decade, but after being defeated by Clark's Conservatives he returned to his annual river journeys with an existing group of voyageurs that included MPs John Godfrey and Peter Stollery, and CTV's Craig Oliver. Trudeau was 85 when he took his last canoe trip.

He was able to indulge his love of canoeing with his family at the Prime Minister's summer residence at Harrington Lake. A neighbour on Meech Lake was naturalist Bill Mason, Canada's canoe guru. His one unconventional boating experience was at age 40 when he joined several other thrill-seekers in an unsuccessful attempt to row from Key West, Florida, to Cuba.

Only Prime Minister to marry in office

As Canada's most eligible bachelor when he became Prime Minister, Trudeau enjoyed dating celebrities and other intriguing women. Shortly before winning the leadership, he encountered a vivacious 19-year-old who was vacationing at the same Club Med in Tahiti. Margaret Sinclair entranced him, but two and a half years would pass before they started dating.

Talk drifted towards marriage by the summer of 1970, almost to Trudeau's surprise. In fact, he proposed one final, futile time later that summer to another girlfriend Carroll Guérin before moving forward on plans with Margaret.

Their relationship had been largely private and they kept marriage plans absolutely secret. Even Trudeau's assistant Marc Lalonde knew nothing until he dropped his boss off at the airport for the flight to Vancouver on March 4, 1971. They were married at a small Catholic Church in North Vancouver before the nation became aware of the union. After a short honeymoon at the Sinclair's mountain cabin, Maggie and Pierre returned to Ottawa.

Margaret Trudeau

She was 29 years younger than the Prime Minister, a flower-child who clearly had a mind of her own. Margaret Trudeau was the first person to marry a sitting Prime Minister and, from the outset, almost physically bristled at the constraints of being the leader's spouse.

But she was attractive and the media loved her naïve charm. Margaret Sinclair was the fourth of five daughters of St. Laurent's former Fisheries minister, Jimmy Sinclair. In the late 60s and early 70s, she delved into the counter-cultural world of drugs and free sex. But by the beginning of 1974, she was a wife of two years with two sons, heavily medicated to combat depression.

The tension between the two Trudeaus increased over the next three years until Margaret separated on a trial basis, indulging her free spirit by joining Ron Wood of the Rolling Stones in Toronto and at New York discos. The separation became permanent with the Prime Minister gaining custody of Justin, Sacha and Michel. Margaret continued to live at 24 Sussex until the proximity became too toxic.

Divorced in 1984, Margaret married real estate developer Fried Kemper and had two more children, Kyle and Ally. After divorcing Kemper, she moved to Montreal to be closer to her Trudeau sons. Her life – and battles with bipolar disorder – were shared publicly through her books *Beyond Reason*, *Conse-quences*, *Changing My Mind* and *The Time of Your Life*.

TRUDEAU'S TIMELINE

1919: Born at home on Durocher Street in the Montreal borough of Outremont, Que. (*October 18*).

1920: Spends first of many summers at Lac Tremblant.

1922: Attends École Notre-Dame de Bonsecours, run by nuns in Outremont.

1924: Attends Académie Querbes in Outremont; asks the principal to move him from the first to second grade so he can be with his friend Gerald O'Connor – his request is granted (*September*).

1927: Switched by his parents from Querbes' English stream to French stream.

1930: His family moves to 84 McCulloch Avenue in Outremont.

1931: His father Charles sells his chain of service stations for $1.4 million, making the family wealthy.

1932: Attends College Jean de Brébeuf run by the Jesuits (*September*).

1933: His family tours Europe by car (*Summer*); meets his uncle's neighbours in France: painters Georges Braque and Joan Miró.

1935: His father Charles dies of a virus while visiting his baseball team training in Orlando, Florida (*April 10*).

1937: Begins his relationship with American Camille Corriveau at Old Orchard Beach, Maine (*August*).

1938: Loses the Academic Council election to Jean de Grandpré (later CEO of Bell Canada) (*February*). Writes and appears in a college play, *Dupés* (*May 16*). Attends Camp Ahmek in Algonquin Park, Ont., for the first time (*July*). Vacations at Old Orchard Beach and is visited by Corriveau (*August*).

Trudeau the separatist

Asked as a 13-year-old Brébeuf student to write an essay envisioning the future, Trudeau predicted, tongue-in-cheek: "I return to Montreal sometime around the year 1976: the year is ripe to declare Quebec's independence...I take command of the troops and lead the army to victory." The Parti Québécois formed a government in 1976, but Trudeau was firmly on the federalist side in the real independence scenario.

1939: Breaks his leg skiing (*Winter*). Visits the New York World's Fair (*June*). Returns to Camp Ahmek (*July*). Vacations at Old Orchard Beach, spending time with Corriveau (*August*). Becomes editor of the student newspaper *Brébeuf* (*September*). Visits Corriveau at Smith College in Massachusetts (*November*).

1940: Fails to win a Rhodes Scholarship (*February*). Seeks career advice from fabled politician and publisher Henri Bourassa (*Winter*). Receives his Bachelor of Arts degree from Brébeuf, finishing first in his class (*May*). Vacations at Old Orchard Beach, again spending time with Corriveau (*June*). Travels with his family on a train and car trip across Canada and down the U.S. west coast (*June-July*). Enters law school at the University of Montreal (*September*).

1941: Required to join the Canadian Officers Training Corps and undertake training (*Summer*). Canoes the Ottawa River then up to Hudson Bay along a route used by Radisson & Des Grosseillers (*Summer*). Treks around the Gaspé (*Summer*).

1942: Begins actively reading political works and develops an admiration for Marshall Pétain, leader of France's Nazi-controlled Vichy government. Develops a close friendship with Gabrielle, the wife of Quebec painter Paul-Émile Borduas. Speaks as a witness in the defence of Maurice Riel, a student protester opposed to conscription (*April*). Takes part in officers' training at Farnham (*June 21-July 4*). Joins several friends in releasing *Our Plan of the Revolution* to create "a sovereign French Canadian state" (*July 14*); within a year he leaves the group and it dies out. Travels the Maritimes by motorcycle, then hikes a 175-km route inspired by a character in *Maria Chapdelaine* (*August*). Campaigns unsuccessfully for classmate Jean Drapeau (later mayor of Montreal), an Independent candidate in a federal by-election in Outremont. (*November*).

1943: As a prank, shoots blanks during a university debate on gallantry (*January 8*). Joins the reserve unit of Les Fusiliers Mont-Royal. Declines to attend Corriveau's U.S. wedding (*May*). Receives his law degree from the University of Montreal, winning the Governor General's Medal for excellence and the Lieutenant Governor's Medal for coming first (*June*). Enrols at a Nova Scotia military camp (*July*). Masquerades with friends as a German soldier to frighten Quebecers (*Summer*). Joins the Montreal law firm of Hyde & Ahern (*September*). Denied permission by the federal government to do post-graduate work in the U.S. that was available in Canada (*October 27*). Begins dating Thérèse Gouin, daughter of Senator Léon-Marcier Gouin (*Fall*). Joins the Bloc Populaire Canadien to oppose conscription (*Fall*).

1944: Called to the Quebec bar. Leaves Hyde & Ahern and defers his military service (*Spring*). His story about his 1941 canoe trip *Exhaustion and Fulfillment: The Ascetic in a Canoe* is published in the Catholic youth magazine *Journal JEC* (*June*). Travels on a goodwill group trip to Mexico to learn Spanish and hitchhikes across the country (*June 15-July 25*). After receiving permission from the military to leave the country, begins studying political economy at Harvard University in Boston (*November 1*).

1946: Receives his Master's degree from Harvard (*June 26*). Works in the Sullivan gold mines of Val d'Or, Que. (*July 9-August 2*). Leaves for Paris to take courses on a scholarship at the Sorbonne's École Libre des Sciences Politiques (*September 21*). Rushed to a Paris hospital for an emergency appendectomy (*December 10*).

1947: Begins five months of psychoanalysis (*February*). Returns to Quebec (*June*). Gouin ends their relationship (*June 22*). Begins lessons for his pilot's licence (*August 1*). Attends the London School of Economics in England for doctoral studies in political science (*October 6*). Speaks about Canadian politics as part of a speaker series at the Cité Club de Paris (*December 20*).

1948: Travels by motorcycle through France and Spain for three weeks with friend Andrée Desautels (*March-April*). Travels around the world to do doctoral research on the "interplay" between Christianity and Marxism; visits Germany, Austria (attending a socialist youth camp in Ebensee), Hungary (using fake papers), Poland (interpreter at the trade fair of the Communist International Union of Students), Yugoslavia (jailed for illegal entry into the country), Bulgaria, Greece, Turkey (swims the Bosphorus Strait), Syria (detained as a suspected spy), Lebanon, Trans-Jordan, Jerusalem (arrested as a spy during the Arab-Israeli conflict, returned to Amman and later released), Iraq (avoids robbery by shouting poetry and faking insanity), Pakistan (avoids being robbed by pirates), India, Afghanistan (through the Khyber Pass), Burma (during a civil war), Thailand, Indo-China, China (another civil war), Hong Kong and Japan (*July-April 1949*).

1949: Arrives back in Quebec and *Le Devoir* immediately publishes an interview 'Five Minutes with Pierre Trudeau – Around the World in 580 Days' (he was gone less than a year) (*April 13*). Accompanies Gérard Pelletier of *Le Devoir* to Asbestos, Que., to witness the asbestos workers strike; delivers a militant speech (*April 21*) and is arrested for demonstrating with the workers. Meets Jean Marchand of the Confédération des Travailleurs Catholiques du Canada union who asks him to join as a legal advisor; he refuses, but Pelletier joins as public relations director. Unable to secure a teaching position at the University of Montreal (*Summer*); subsequent attempts over the next decade also fail, often thwarted by Quebec Premier Maurice Duplessis. Becomes junior clerk in the Privy Council office in Ottawa (*September 14*). Begins meeting almost weekly with a group of Montreal intellectuals including Pelletier and Pierre Laporte (*Fall*).

1950: Attends the 12th Federal-Provincial Conference in Ottawa, taking notes about suggestions for constitutional change (*January 10-11*). Plays an active role in the first issue of *Cité Libre* (*June 15*). Disagrees with the Liberals' participation in the Korean conflict (*August 31*). Begins dating Helen Segerstrale, a clerk at the Swedish Embassy (*Fall*).

1951: Summoned, along with Pelletier, to meet with Montreal Archbishop Paul-Émile Léger about anti-clerical articles in *Cité libre* (*Spring*). Serves as secretary during a meeting when a proposed bill of rights is presented to Prime Minister St. Laurent and Pearson (External Affairs) (*May 8*). Quits his Privy Council job, partly because of the conflict writing for *Cité libre* (*October 6*). Joins the CCF (Co-operative Commonwealth Federation) party. Begins nine months of travel, starting in France, Italy and Greece (*October 24)*.

1952: Visits Egypt and Sudan (*January-February*). Segerstrale breaks off their engagement (*January 26*). Visits Stockholm in an unsuccessful attempt to revive his relationship with Segerstrale (*February*). Returns to Paris (*March 13*). Attends a world economic conference in Moscow, reporting for *Le Devoir* (*April*). Returns to Paris (*May 5*), then Stockholm. Returns to Canada (*July 23*). Criticizes the foreign policy work of Pearson (External Affairs) in a presentation at the Couchiching Conference in Ontario (*August 11*). Runs his law practice out of his home on Avenue McCulloch in Outremont.

1953: Begins working on arbitration boards for labour unions and lecturing at labour colleges. Begins taking judo, eventually achieving his brown belt. Speaks on CBC-Radio Canada about Methods of Economic Stabilization (*December 6*).

1954: Begins writing for Jacques Hébert's *Vrai* in addition to *Cité libre*. Helps found the French-Canadian Institute of Public Affairs (*February 28*). Drafts a brief for La Féderation des unions industrielles du Québec to present to the province's Royal Commission of Inquiry on Constitutional Problems (*March 10*). Attends a Commonwealth relations conference in Lahore, Pakistan (*March 17-27*), then visits Bali, Australia, New Zealand and Hawaii (*April-May*). Helps found *Écrits du Canada Français* journal with Claude Hurtubise.

1955: Visits Europe (*Summer*). Moves to a Trudeau-owned apartment at 518 Sher-brooke West, Montreal.

1956: Has an audience with Pope Pius XII (*January 25*). Lives in London and Paris for six months while editing *La Grève de l'amiante*, a book about the Asbestos Strike. Canoes the Mackenzie River with poet and constitutional expert Frank Scott (*August 9-29*); witnesses the first session of the Northwest Territories Council held north of the Arctic Circle. Becomes vice-president of the newly formed Le Rassemblement to promote democracy in Quebec (*September 8*). His study on the Asbestos strike, *La Grève de l'amiante,* is published (*October*).

1957: Attends the International Student Service seminar in Ghana (*June 16-July 7*), then visits London and Paris (*July*). Joins picketers at the lengthy Gaspé Copper Mines strike in Murdochville, Que. (*August 19*).

1958: Covers the Quebec Liberal Convention that elects former MP Jean Lesage as leader, for *Vrai* (*May 31*). Supports an unsuccessful attempt to turn Le Rassemblement into an active political coalition to defeat Duplessis; the initiative fades when Duplessis dies the following year. His article 'Some Obstacles to Democracy in Quebec' is published in the *Canadian Journal of Economic and Political Science* (*August*). Announces the formation of L'Union des forces démocratques that largely replaces Le Rassemblement (*October*).

1959: Breaks his leg skiing (*Winter*). His scholarly 'Some Obstacles' article wins the President's Prize at the University of Western Ontario. Becomes president of Le Rassemblement not long before its demise (*April*). Visits Japans, Taiwan, Vietnam, India, Nepal, Iran, Israel and Europe (where he attended July's Socialist International Congress in Hamburg) (*April-September*).

1960: Attempts to paddle from Key West, Florida, to Cuba; only gets 50 km in three days (*April 30*). Regularly dates artist-model Carroll Guérin as well as maintaining relations with Madeleine Gobeil who later becomes a Carleton professor. Tours China for six weeks with Jacques Hébert and three others; among the first Westerners to be admitted since the Revolution (*September 18-October 22*).

1961: Castigates separatism in a *Cité libre* article 'The New Treason of the Intellectuals' (*February*). Publishes *Two Innocents in Red China* with Hébert (*March 28*). Becomes an associate professor of law and founding member of the Institut de recherches en droit public (Public and Research Institute) at the University of Montreal (*May 29*). Spends the summer in Europe where he runs with the bulls in Pamplona, Spain (twice, *July 7 & 9*) and meets Guérin in Italy. Begins meeting every second Friday with Quebec's natural resources minister René Lévesque, André Laurendeau, Pelletier and Marchand for political discussions (*October*); continues for two years.

1962: Opposes Lévesque's intention to nationalize Quebec's hydro-electricity companies (*February*).

1963: Joins Marchand and Pelletier in agreeing to run as federal Liberal candidates (*January*). Pearson reverses his nuclear arms stand; Trudeau, Marchand and Pelletier back out as possible candidates (*January 12*). Campaigns unsuccessfully for Mount Royal NDP candidate Charles Taylor (*March*). Condemns Pearson in a *Cité Libre* article for coming out in favour of nuclear arms (*April*). Meeting with friends at Pelletier's when they hear an FLQ bomb go off in a Westmount mailbox (*May 17*). Travels to Europe and North Africa (*Summer*). Hired as a research consultant for the Royal Commission on Bilingualism and Biculturalism, but teaching commitments prevent any active involvement (*Fall*). Begins meeting weekly with a group of intellectuals organized by civil servant Marc Lalonde (*Fall*). Unsuccessful in his bid to co-host CBC's *This Hour Has Seven Days*; the job goes Laurier LaPierre (*December*).

1964: Elected a Fellow of the Royal Society of Canada (*April 4*). Joins Pelletier in reorganizing *Cité libre* by removing separatist editor Pierre Vallières (*April*). Endorses the Canadian Manifesto that supports federalism, drafted by the Lalonde group and published in *Cité Libre* and *Canadian Forum* (*May*). Travels in Italy with Guérin (*August*), then in Europe with Gobeil (*September*).

1965: Maurice Sauvé (Forestry) suggests he run with Marchand and Pelletier in the next election (*August 29*); agrees to consider it. Meets with Favreau and other Quebec federal politicians to overcome objections to his and Pelletier's candidacies on the Liberal ticket (*September 9*). Joins Marchand and Pelletier to announce they will run; immediately dubbed "The Three Wise Men" (*September 10*). Wins the Liberal nomination over Victor Goldblum for Mount Royal, Que. (*October 7*). Canada's 27th federal election: wins in Mount Royal defeating Charles Taylor, the NDP candidate he campaigned for in 1963 (*November 8*). Takes a ski trip in Europe (*November*); while there he initially turns down Pearson's offer to be his parliamentary secretary, but relents with urging from Marchand.

1966: Appointed parliamentary secretary to the Prime Minister (*January 9*). Helps re-establish the Quebec wing of the federal Liberal party at the Quebec City convention

(*March 24-26*). Attends the Canada-France Parliamentary Group meeting in Paris (*April*) followed by a Jurists conference in Paris, followed by official visits to the emerging African countries of Togo, Cameroon, Ivory Coast, Senegal and Tunisia. Helps develop strategies to oppose Premier Daniel Johnson's desire to give Quebec 'special status'. Takes a wilderness canoe trip along the Coppermine River; helps rescue an American couple from their overturned canoe (*Summer*). Serves as a member of Canada's delegation at the UN in New York (*Fall*).

1967: Marchand replaces Favreau as Quebec lieutenant, giving the reformers a dominant role (*January 18*). Enters cabinet as Justice minister (*April 4*). Supports the idea of a constitutional conference after initial reluctance (*September 4*). Meets with Walter Gordon (Privy Council) who sounds him out as a possible party leadership candidate (*November*). Introduces the Divorce Bill (*December 4*). Pearson announces his retirement and meets with Marchand and Trudeau, telling them there must be a French Canadian candidate in the leadership contest (*December 14*). Introduces revisions to the Criminal Code, an Omnibus Bill including a relaxing of legislation about homosexuality, abortion, lotteries and weapons possession (*December 21*); says "there's no place for the state in the bedrooms of the nation." Leaves for a two-week vacation in Tahiti (*December 26*); meets Margaret Sinclair at the resort.

1968: Meets individually with seven premiers prior to the constitutional conference (*January 19-26*). Is the keynote speaker at the Quebec Liberal Federation meeting in Montreal, adding strength to speculation he should run for leader (*January 28*). Introduces legislation to broaden the grounds for divorce (*February 1*). Plays a central role at the Federal-Provincial Constitutional Conference in Ottawa that recognizes national French language rights; jousts verbally with Quebec's Johnson (*February 5-8*). Mobbed by fans at the Ontario Liberal Association convention in Toronto (*February 9*). Pearson urges him to contest the leadership since Marchand refuses (*February 13*). Announces he will run for the Liberal leadership (*February 16*). His book *Federalism and the French Canadians* is published by Macmillan (*February*). Becomes acting Privy Council President after Walter Gordon resigns (*March 11*). Pelletier edits *Réponses de Pierre Elliott Trudeau*, outlining Trudeau's stand on major issues (*March 21*); sells 13,000 copies. Leadership candidate Mitchell Sharp withdraws and backs Trudeau, bringing Chrétien and others with him (*April 3*). Wins the leadership convention (*April 6*). Begins dating Jennifer Rae, sister of Bob Rae who was later an interim Liberal leader (*April 11*). Working vacation in Fort Lauderdale, Florida, to form a cabinet (*April 12-17*). Second place leadership candidate, Robert Winters, informs him he is leaving politics and returning to business (*April 18*). **Trudeau's first government (1968-1979).** Becomes 15th Prime Minister of Canada (*April 20*). Makes Montreal lawyer Marc Lalonde his principal secretary. 27th Parliament is dissolved (*April 23*). Moves into 24 Sussex Drive, his first home after years of living in hotels (*May 4*). Begins his Liberal campaign focusing on creating a Just Society. Receives an honorary degree from the University of Alberta in Edmonton (*May 13*). Helps open Montreal's Man and His World on the former Expo 67 site (*May 17*). Attends the funeral of friend André Laurendeau, co-chair of the B&B Commission, in Outrement (*June 4*). Joins leaders Robert Stanfield (Progressive Conservative), Tommy Douglas (NDP), and Réal Caouette (Créditistes) in Canada's first televised debate (*June 9*). Refuses to leave the reviewing stand during separatist riots at Montreal's St. Jean Baptiste celebrations (*June 24*). Canada's 28th federal election: re-elected in Mount Royal defeating Huguette Marleau (Conservative); wins a majority government (*June 25*). Receives an honorary Doctor of Laws degree from Queen's University. The Medical Care Act comes into effect (*July 1*). Befriends a neighbour on Meech Lake, legendary canoeist Bill Mason (*Summer*). Becomes first Prime Minister to visit the Arctic Islands (Banks, Melville, Cornwallis, Ellesmere and

Baffin) (*July 21-28*). The first of 11,000 Czech refugees arrive in Canada as part of a four-month $10-million federal program (*September 8*). Rebukes French President de Gaulle for comparing Canada to civil war-torn Nigeria (*September 11*). Receives an honorary Doctor of Literature degree from the University of Moncton. Chastized by opposition parties and the media for not providing aid to Biafra in the Nigerian conflict (*September*). Government announces the elimination of Saturday mail delivery (*September 27*). Unveils a statue to Louis Riel in Regina (*October 2*). Le Parti Québécois is formed during a convention of several Quebec separatist groups (*October 11-15*). Pelletier (Secretary of State) introduces the Official Languages Bill guaranteeing English and French rights (*October 17*). Indicates that the federal government will step out of Medicare within five years once it is firmly established, passing funds over to the provinces (*November 4*). Relaxes immigration restrictions to permit Canadians to adopt orphaned Biafrans (*November 15*); aid to Biafra is stalled. Supreme Court strikes down an Indian Act provision that prohibits drunkenness by Indigenous peoples off the reserve because there is no similar restriction for others (*November 20*). Second report of the Bilingualism and Biculturalism Commission is tabled, recommending federal grants to ensure all children are educated in Canada's second language (*December 9*). The House agrees to increase the authority of Parliamentary committees, creating less time spent debating details in the House (*December 19*).

1969: Reluctantly attends the Commonwealth Conference in London where the Nigerian civil war is discussed (*January 7-10*). Meets Barbra Streisand at the London premiere of her movie *Funny Girl*; they begin dating soon after (*January 15*). Meets with Pope Paul VI at the Vatican (*January 16*). Hosts the Federal-Provincial Constitutional Conference in Ottawa; agreement is reached to look at implement-ing the bilingualism and biculturalism recommendations (*February 10-12*). Michener becomes the first Governor-General to make an official visit abroad, to four Caribbean countries (*February 11-March 4*). Announces the cancellation of the Prince Edward Island causeway because of high costs (*March 5*); plans to replace it with projects to boost the province's economy. Visits Washington to meet with U.S. President Richard Nixon (*March 24-25*); only Prime Minister to swim in the White House pool. Department of Regional Economic Expansion (DREE) is established with Marchand (Forestry & Rural Expansion) as the first minister (*April 1*). Indian Affairs takes over the funding and management of residential schools (*April*). Announces a phased reduction of spending on NATO forces in Europe, shrinking Canada's troops there from 10,000 to 5,000 (*April 23*). Hellyer (Transport) resigns to protest priority given to constitutional matters over housing issues (*April 24*). House passes an omnibus bill that liberalizes abortion, birth control and homosexual restrictions (*May 14*). Appoints Gerald Le Dain to chair a federal inquiry into non-medical uses of drugs (*May 29*). Officially opens the National Arts Centre in Ottawa (*May 31*). Edgar Benson (Finance) presents his second budget, the last balanced one for nearly three decades (*June 3*). Hosts the third Federal-Provincial Constitutional Conference held in Ottawa (*June 11-12*); closed to the media for the first time. Creates a Prices and Incomes Commission to tackle inflation (*June 19*). Chrétien (Indian Affairs) releases White Paper calling for the dismantling of the Department of Indian Affairs, abolishing the Indian Act and eliminating Indian status (*June 25*); abandoned two years later after strong Indigenous backlash. Joins U.S. President Nixon at Place des Nations in Montreal to commemorate the 10th anniversary of the opening of the St. Lawrence Seaway (*June 27*). Confronted by angry farmers in Winnipeg and Regina protesting slow wheat sales (*July 14-16*); announces interest-free loans to farmers. His message, along with those of 73 other world leaders, is left on the moon by U.S. astronaut Neil Armstrong (*July 20*). Begins dating Margaret Sinclair (*August*). Freezes government expenditures in an attempt to slow down inflation (*August 13*). The Official Languages Act comes into effect, making English and French the two languages of Canada (*September 9*). Resumes diplomatic relations with Gabon, suspended under Pearson (*October 7*). His closest competitor for the Liberal leadership, Robert Winters, dies in Monterey, California, of a heart attack (*October 10*). Appoints Herb Gray as Minister Without Portfolio, Canada's first Jewish minister (*October 20*). Announces plan to ban the pesticide DDT in the new year (*November 3*). A White Paper on taxation calls for the taxing of capital gains (*November 7*). Shuffles cabinet, bringing in new ministers Jeanne Sauvé (his first female minister) and Marc Lalonde (his former secretary) (*November 27*). Hosts the fourth Federal-Provincial Constitutional Conference in Ottawa (*December 8-10*). The Bank of Canada says new currency will replace the Queen's image with former prime ministers: $5 Laurier, $10 Macdonald, $50 King and $100 Borden (*December 17*). Meets with John Lennon and Yoko Ono on Parliament Hill (*December 23*).

1970: Announces plans to convert Canada from Imperial to metric measurement (*January 16*). Accompanies date Barbra Streisand to a National Arts Centre performance (*January 28*); she visits Question Period in the House the next day. The Federal-Provincial Conference held in Ottawa reaches an agreement on anti-inflation measures (*February 16-17*). Appoints Keith Spicer as the first federal commissioner of official languages (*March 2*). Blocks the foreign takeover of Denison Mines (*March 2*); new restrictions on foreign ownership are introduced two weeks later. Welcomes Elizabeth II to Ottawa (*March 3*). The Nuclear Non-Proliferation Treaty, signed by Canada in 1968, comes into effect (*March 5*); within a year, Canada stops arming aircraft with nuclear weapons. Opens the first Arctic Winter Games in Yellowknife (*March 9*). Joined by Margaret Sinclair for a ski holiday in Whistler (*March*). Canada joins 19 other French-speaking nations to found the international La Francophonie organization (*March 20*). Responsibility for governing the eastern Arctic is turned over to the Northwest Territories (*April 1*). Supports a bill to protect Arctic waters from pollution, aimed at discouraging foreign oil tankers from using northern waterways (*April 19*). The government again unties the Canadian dollar from the gold standard and lets it float free against other currencies (*May*). Visits New Zealand, Australia, Malaysia, Singapore and then Japan for Expo 70 (*May 10-29*). The CRTC announces new regulations calling for 50% Canadian programming by Canadian networks (*May 22*). Meets with First Nations representatives who reject the government's proposed Indian policy (*June 4*). The federal voting age is lowered to 18 from 21 (*June 26*). Meets with cabinet in Winnipeg to celebrate Manitoba's centennial (*July 1*). Welcomes Elizabeth II, Prince Philip, Prince Charles and Princess Anne to Winnipeg (*July 2*). Quebec finally joins the federal medicare plan (*July 10*). His talk of marriage, at Harrington Lake, is interpreted by Sinclair as a proposal (*July*). Visits the Yukon, Northwest Territories and British Columbia (*August 2-9*). Vacations in Sardinia and the Mediterranean (*August*). Asks Guérin one more time if she'd consider marriage; her reply is 'no' (*August*). Vacations in the Bahamas with Sinclair (*August*). Dives to the Tektite Two underwater science station in the U.S. Virgin Islands (*August*). Shuswap Chief George Manual becomes the first president of the National Indian Brotherhood, renamed the Assembly of First Nations 12 years later (*August 21*). The Committee for an Independent Canada (CIC) is launched by former Finance minister Walter Gordon and others, pushing for government policies to control foreign ownership (*September 17*). Soviet ships are banned from fishing off Vancouver Island after collisions with Canadian ships (*October 1*). James Cross, the British Trade Commissioner, is kidnapped in Montreal by members of the FLQ (Front de libération du Québec), beginning the October Crisis (*October 5*). The government refuses the FLQ's demands that include releasing 23 prisoners involved in Quebec bombings (*October 6*). Disappointed that Sharp (External Affairs) has agreed to let the FLQ manifesto be read on Radio-Canada (*October 8*). His boyhood friend Pierre Laporte, Quebec's labour minister, is kidnapped in Montreal by FLQ members (*October 10*). Troops arrive in Ottawa to guard MPs and diplomats (*October 12*). Canada officially recognizes China and ends ties with Taiwan (*October 13*). Responds to the October Crisis by imposing the War Measures Act, a move approved by cabinet (*October 16*). Laporte's body found in a Montreal car trunk (*October 17*). Attends Laporte's funeral in Montreal (*October 20*). The War Measures Act is replaced by the Public Order (Temporary Measures) Act (*December 1*). Cross is released unhurt, effectively ending the October Crisis; his kidnappers are flown to Cuba (*December 3*). Royal assent is given to change the name of the Exchequer Court of Canada to the Federal Court of Canada (*December 3*). The Royal Commission on the Status of Women tables its report, recommending abortion on demand and the relaxation of divorce laws (*December 7*). Three FLQ suspects in the Laporte murder surrender in St. Luc near Montreal (*December 28*).

Whistler & Streisand

Skiing at Whistler in 1970, Trudeau received a call from former date Barbra Streisand that she was in Vancouver and planning to join him. That was a problem, because Margaret Sinclair would be skiing with him later that day. Fortunately for Trudeau, the RCMP traced the call back to three Vancouver nursing students and he quickly forgave their prank. Still, it was a surprise to his security detail later in the day when another Whistler skier noted how wonderful it was that Streisand would be joining Trudeau. Turns out the skier's sister was the telephone switchboard operator in Squamish who had taken the phony call.

1971: Visits Pakistan, India and Ceylon (*January*). Attends his second Common-wealth Conference in Singapore (*January 14-22*); suggests an eight-nation committee to study the lifting of Britain's arms embargo against South Africa. Slips away for a quiet French ski holiday with Marc Lalonde and meets Brigitte Bardot; their picture ends up on the cover of *Paris Match* (*Winter*). Hosts the Federal-Provincial Conference in Ottawa where an agreement is reached on a feasible formula for amending the constitution (*February 8-9*). Accused of mouthing a two-word expletive in the House, he indicates he said something like "fuddle duddle" (*February 16*). Marries 22-year-old Margaret Sinclair in a secret ceremony at St. Stephen's Catholic Church in North Vancouver (*March 4*). Announces a $57.8 million program for summer student employment called Opportunities For Youth (*March 16*). David Lewis elected leader of the NDP, succeeding Tommy Douglas (*April 24*). Keirans (Communications) resigns to protest growing foreign ownership of Canadian companies (*April 29*). The Dominion Bureau of Statistics is renamed Statistics Canada (*May 1*). Elizabeth II visits British Columbia for its centennial (*May 3-12*). Appoints Robert Andras (Without Portfolio) the first Minister Responsible for the Status of Women (*May 7*). Visits the U.S.S.R. where he meets with Secretary Leonid Brezhnev and Premier Alexei Kosygin (*May 17-28*). Hellyer, who resigned from the Liberal caucus, forms the Action Canada party (*May 25*). Canada Development Corporation is established to maintain Canada-owned corporations (*June 9*). Department of the Environment is created (*June 10*). A Federal-Provincial Conference on the constitution is held in Victoria where all first ministers agree to a charter of rights and an amending formula allowing a Quebec veto (*June 14-17*). Premier Robert Bourassa says Quebec will not sign the Victoria Charter (*June 23*). Signs a marriage contract with Margaret that would prevent her from sharing the Trudeau fortune (*June*). Attends British Columbia's centennial celebrations in Victoria (*July 1*). Serves as parade marshal at the Calgary Stampede (*July*). Unsuccessful in preventing the imposition of U.S. surcharges on duty goods (*August 15*). Announces a multiculturalism policy, to be more than French-English biculturalism (*October 8*). The Créditistes party reunites with the Social Credit and Réal Caouette is elected leader at the party convention in Hull, Que. (*October 9*). Meets with Soviet Premier Alexei Kosygin in Ottawa who is later assaulted by anti-Communist Hungarian Geza Matrai (*October 18*).

Mothballs the experimental hydrofoil *Bras d'Or* because of high costs (*November 2*). Meets with Yugoslavian President Josip Broz Tito in Ottawa (*November*). Meets with President Richard Nixon in Washington to try to defuse talk of U.S. protectionist policies (*December 6*). Attends Christmas Eve service with the Turners (*December 24*). His son Justin is born, the first child born to a serving Prime Minister since Macdonald (*December 25*).

1972: Capital gains tax comes into effect (*January 1*). The Le Dain Commission report recommends legalization of heroine for drug-addiction treatment (*January 26*); the government rejects the recommendation. Shuffles his cabinet, moving Turner (Justice) to Finance (*January 28*). Canada becomes a permanent observer of the Organization of American States (*February 2*). Sets aside land for the creation of Nahanni National Park and Kluane National Park (*February 22*). Announces plans for a new airport in Pickering, Ont. (*March 2*). Gives Quebec control of family allowances under certain conditions (*March 12*). Agreements are reached with Britain, France, Portugal and Denmark to phase out their traditional and treaty fishing rights on Canada's east coast (*March 27*). Meets with U.S. President Nixon who addresses Parliament (*April 14*); both sign an agreement to improve the water quality in Lake Erie. At a gala banquet in Ottawa, Nixon proposes a toast "to the future Prime Minister of Canada: to Justin Pierre Trudeau", the Prime Minister's three-month-old son (*April 14*). The government bans salmon fishing off New Brunswick and parts of Newfoundland to help conserve stocks (*April 24*). The second Le Dain Commission report recommends legalizing the possession of marijuana and hashish (*May 17*). Opens the Churchill Falls hydroelectric power project in Labrador (*June 16*). Founds the Council of Canadian American Relations with U.S. banker David Rockefeller to build awareness and appreciation between the two countries. The government says first-time offenders possessing marijuana will no longer be imprisoned (*July 31*). Indicates his intention to have a swimming pool built at the Sussex Drive residence (*August*). Oversees the opening faceoff of the Canada-Soviet hockey series in Vancouver (*September 1*); Canada wins the final game in Moscow. Heritage Canada is established (*September 12*). Canada's 29th federal election: re-elected in Mount Royal defeating Andrew Brichant (Conservative); Liberals narrowly beat the Conservatives 109 seats to 107, the closest vote in Canadian history (*October 30*). Meets with cabinet to indicate he does not intend to resign (*November 1*). The first Federal-Provincial-Municipal Conference is held in Toronto (*November 20-21*). Meets with British Prime Minister Edward Heath and Elizabeth II in London (*December 10*). Appoints Muriel McQueen Fergusson as the first woman Speaker of the Senate (*December 14*). Attends Pearson's funeral, Canada's 14th Prime Minister, at Christ Church Anglican Cathedral, Ottawa (*December 31*).

1973: Parliament votes to condemn the U.S. bombing of North Vietnam (*January 15*). His mother Grace dies in Montreal (*January 16*). Canada joins the International Commission of Control and Supervision (ICCS) to oversee the Vietnam truce (*January 24*). Canada officially recognizes North Vietnam (*January 29*). The budget includes social welfare improvements to encourage NDP support (*February 19*). Meets with Mexican President Luis Echeverria who addresses Parliament (*March 30*). Appoints Beryl Plumptre chair of the new Food Prices Review Board (*May 25*). Launches a program making it possible for illegal immigrants to gain citizenship (*June 6*); nearly 50,000 apply. Meets with India's Prime Minister Indira Gandhi who addresses Parliament (*June 19*). Elizabeth II visits Canada to celebrate the RCMP and P.E.I. centennials (*June 25-July 7*). Calls for a national energy policy at the federal-provincial Western Economic Opportunities Conference in Calgary (*July 25*). Leads 80 honorary pallbearers in Quebec City for the funeral of Louis St. Laurent, the 12th Prime Minister of Canada (*July 30*). Chairs the 19th Commonwealth Heads of Government Conference in Ottawa (*August 2-10*). Adds a 40-cent tax on each exported barrel of crude-oil, prompting a retaliatory tax by Alberta (*September 13*).

Announces the appointment of career diplomat, Jules Léger, as Canada's 21st Governor General (*October 5*). Becomes the first Prime Minister to officially visit China (*October 10-17*); meets with Chairman Mao Zedong in the Forbidden City, and later with Premier Zhou En Lai. Agrees to a support role for Canada on the UN Middle East peacekeeping force to supervise an Egyptian-Israeli ceasefire (*October 25*). Imposes another export tax on crude oil (*November 1*). Addresses the nation on television, urging Canadians to voluntarily restrict energy consumption (*November 22*). Announces the creation of a publically owned oil company to be called Petro-Canada (*December 6*). His second son Alexandre 'Sacha' is born in Ottawa (*December 25*). Appoints Bora Laskin as the 14th Chief Justice of Canada (*December 27*).

1974: His wife Margaret is treated for depression following Sacha's birth; diagnosed much later as bipolar disorder (*January*). Hosts the Federal-Provincial Conference of First Ministers on Energy where leaders override Alberta Premier Peter Lougheed's objections to keeping oil prices well below international levels (*January 22-23*). Meets with provincial premiers at 24 Sussex to hammer out a new Canadian oil price of $6.50 a barrel (*March 27*); Alberta responds by imposing an additional royalty rate. Attends the funeral of French President Georges Pompidou in Paris (*April 8*). The Canadian dollar hits a modern high of U.S.$1.0443 (*April 25*). Extends the peacekeeping mission in the Middle East for another six months (*April 25*). Loses a confidence vote in the House when the NDP joins the Conservatives to defeat the budget (*May 8*). Suspends nuclear cooperation with India after that country explodes a nuclear bomb using Canadian nuclear technology (*May 18*). Receives an honorary degree from Duke University in North Carolina (*May*). Receives an honorary Doctor of Laws degree from the University of Ottawa. Governor General Léger suffers a stroke; his administrative duties are assumed by Chief Justice Laskin (*June 8*). The government buys De Havilland Aircraft from Hawker Siddeley Aviation and nationalizes it (*June 26*). Canada's 30th federal election: re-elected in Mount Royal defeating Émile Mashaal; regains his majority but wins no seats in Alberta (*July 8*). Ed Broadbent becomes interim leader of the NDP, replacing Lewis who lost his seat in the election (*July 17*). Quebec passes its Official Language Act making French the province's only official language (*July 30*). Conservative leader Stanfield announces his intention to resign (*August 5*). Marital troubles attract media attention for the first time after Margaret's hospitalization for "emotional stress" (*September 17*). 30th Parliament opens; nominates James Jerome to be the 28th Speaker of the House (*September 30*). The RCMP prevents 200 members of the Native People's Caravan from entering Parliament (*September 30*); the natives crossed Canada earlier to publicize their demands to settle territorial claims. Meets with French President Giscard d'Estaing in Paris (*October 21-22*); also meets with leaders in Belgium and Luxembourg. Hosts a federal-provincial conference on inflation, in Ottawa (*October 30*). The government pledges $785 million in Canadian food aid to third world countries (*November 6*). Meets with U.S. President Gerald Ford in Washington (*December 4*). Again extends the Middle East peacekeeping mission (*December 12*).

1975: Joins Alberta and Ontario to invest $600 million in Syncrude's oil sands project near Fort McMurray, Alta. (*February 3*). Marchand (Transport) resigns as the Liberal's Quebec leader (*February 26*). Visits Europe to promote closer ties with the European Economic Community (*February 28-March 15*); visits the Netherlands, West Germany, Italy, Britain (where he receives the freedom of the City of London) and Ireland. Parliamentary business is televised for the first time, with cameras recording a Senate committee session (*March 4*). Shifts his international perspective from east-west to north-south in a speech in London, England (*March 13*). The beaver becomes an official symbol of Canada (*March 24*). Canada's temperature goes metric, switching from Fahrenheit to Celsius (*April 1*). Canada joins the worldwide effort to airlift war orphans from South Vietnam (*April 3*). The First

Ministers Energy Conference in Ottawa fails to agree on a future domestic price for oil (*April 10-11*). MPs vote themselves a 33% salary increase even as Parliament explores the merits of wage and price controls (*April 15*). Appoints a Royal Commission into Canadian corporate power, chaired by Robert Bryce (*April 22*). The embassy in South Vietnam is closed and consular staff members are evacuated (*April 24*). Attends his fourth Commonwealth Conference in Kingston, Jamaica (*April 29-May 6*). The Petroleum Administration Act is passed, giving the federal government the power to set domestic oil and natural gas prices without provincial input (*April 30*). The government plans to bring 3,000 South Vietnamese refugees to Canada (*May 1*). The Canadian Labour Congress rejects a federal proposal for voluntary wage and price limits (*May 7*). Meets with Denmark's Prime Minister Anker Jorgensen in Copenhagen to discuss Arctic cooperation and fisheries conflicts (*May*). Attends the NATO Summit in Brussels (*May 29-30*). Meets guitarist Liona Boyd for the first time at Harrington Lake (*June*). Ed Broadbent is elected leader of the NDP succeeding David Lewis (*July 7*). Denies the Palestinian Liberation Organization representatives entry to Canada to attend a UN conference on crime, resulting in the conference being moved to Geneva (*July 10*). Otto Lang (Justice) introduces a bill to create a federal human rights commission (*July 21*). Soviet fishing fleets are banned from Canadian ports for exceeding fishing quotas (*July 23*). The federal minimum wage is raised to $2.60 from $2.20 (*July 23*). The Petro-Canada Act is passed, creating a government-owned oil company (*July 30*). Signs the Helsinki Accord in Finland to improve relations with Warsaw Pact countries (*August 1*). Indicates intention to seek a 370-nautical-km economic coastal zone through negotiation rather than arbitrarily (*August 7*). Appoints Jim Coutts as his chief of staff (*August*). Asked by provincial premiers to call a conference to discuss possible wage and price controls (*August 22*). Pelletier (Communications) resigns to become Canadian Ambassador to France (*August 28*). Turner (Finance) resigns (*September 10*); appoints Donald Macdonald (Energy, Mines & Resources) as Finance minister (*September 26*). His third son Michel is born in Ottawa (*October 2*). Officially opens Mirabel International Airport north of Montreal (*October 4*). Announces on television three years of wage and price controls to combat inflation (*October 13*). Appoints former cabinet minister Jean-Luc Pepin as the first chair of the Anti-Inflation Board (*October 14*). The second part of the Foreign Investment Review Act takes effect, permitting government screening of investments by foreign-owned businesses (*October 15*). More than 22,000 inside postal workers begin a 43-day strike, the longest mail service disruption to date (*October 21-December 2*). The first World Conference of Indigenous Peoples takes place in Port Alberni, B.C. (*October 26-31*). Social Credit leader Caouette announces his intention to resign (*November 1*). Trudeau's leadership is endorsed at a national Liberal policy convention in Ottawa (*November 9*). The government purchases Canadair of Montreal, giving the government ownership of the majority of the country's air industry (*November 28*). His anti-inflation bill is approved by the House, creating wage and price controls (*December 3*). Cabinet overturns an Anti-Inflation Board decision that would have rejected a settlement reached in the postal strike (*December 11*). Indicates that the Company of Young Canadians, Opportunities for Youth and Information Canada will be cancelled (*December 18*). Tells a CTV interviewer that the free market system doesn't work, requiring government intervention like wage and price controls (*December 28*). Vacations in St. Lucia and British Columbia (*December-January*).

1976: Embarks on an 11-day trip to Mexico, Cuba and Venezuela (*January 19*). Becomes the first Prime Minister to visit Cuba (*January 26*). The Anti-Inflation Board gives 6,500 companies one month to file reports about prices and profits (*January 28*). Officially commissions the TRIUMF (Tri-University Meson Facility) nuclear accelerator at the University of British Columbia (*February 9*). Joe Clark wins the leadership of the Progressive Conservative party, succeeding Stanfield (*February 22*). Introduces measures offering alternatives to the death penalty (*February 24*). Calls Quebec's bill to make French the province's only official language "politically stupid" (*March 3*). Warns that his government is prepared to take unilateral steps to patriate the constitution (*March 4*). André Ouellet (Consumer & Corporate Affairs) resigns after being found in contempt of court for comments about price fixing in the sugar industry (*March 15*). Disagrees with Official Languages Commissioner Keith Spicer's report that language training for civil servants hasn't been successful and that emphasis be put on language training in schools (*March*). Presents several options to the provinces for patriating the constitution and possibly adopting the 1971 Victoria amending formula (*March 31*). The federal minimum wage increases to $2.90 an hour (*April 1*). The Canadian Radio-Television Commission becomes the Canadian Radio-Television and Telecommunications Commission with an expanded mandate (*April 1*). Cabinet approves a request by Dome Petroleum to drill in the Beaufort Sea (*April 15*). MPs vote to allow unions to appeal Anti-Inflation Board rulings (*April 20*). Parliament begins debate again on ending capital punishment (*May 3*). The U.S.S.R. formally recognizes Canada's proposed 370-nautical-km fishing zone (*May 19*). His family visits Haida Gwaii (*May*). Bars Taiwan from competing in the Montreal Olympics under the name 'Republic of China' (*May 28*). Meets with U.S. President Ford in Washington and indicates continuing support for the anti-submarine program (*June 16*). Becomes the first Prime Minister to attend a G7 Summit, in San Juan, Puerto Rico; the first meeting to involve seven countries, including Canada (*June 27-28*). Marchand (Environment) resigns (*June 30*). The Supreme Court rules that the Anti-Inflation Act is constitutional (*July 12*). MPs abolish capital punishment (*July 14*). Elizabeth II opens the Montreal Summer Olympic Games (*July 17*). Attends a state dinner for Elizabeth II in Montreal (*July 24*). Shuffles his cabinet following the resignation of ministers Sharp (Privy Council President), Bud Drury (Public Works) and Bryce Mackasey (Consumer & Corporate Affairs); Chrétien (Treasury Board) becomes the first Industry, Trade & Commerce minister. (*September 14*). Provincial premiers meeting in Toronto again can't agree on a process to patriate the constitution (*October 2*). James Richardson (National Defence) resigns because of the government's bilingualism policies (*October 12*). About one million workers participate in a day of protest against wage and price controls (*October 14*). Visits Japan (*October 21-26*). Receives an honorary Doctor of Laws degree from Keio in Tokyo (*October*). The Anti-Inflation Board takes credit for holding inflation to 8% in the past year (*October 22*). Appeals to Canadians to remain united following the success of the Parti Québécois, led by René Lévesque in the recent Quebec provincial election (*November 24*). Hosts a Federal-Provincial Conference on taxation and revenue sharing in Ottawa (*December 12-14*). Decides to hold weekly new conferences instead of impromptu media encounters (*December 16*). Former Social Credit leader Réal Caouette dies three months after suffering a stroke (*December 16*). Diefenbaker's widow Olive dies in Ottawa (*December 22*). Says the onus is on English Canada to keep Quebec in Canada (*December 23*). Vacations in St. Lucia (*December-January*).

1977: Canada's 370-nautical-km fishing zone takes effect (*January 1*). Creates Katimavik, a government charity to educate youth through volunteer work, along with Senator Jacques Hébert and Barney Danson (National Defence) (*January 26*). Tells a Quebec City audience that the Quebec provincial government needs to hold a single, clear referendum on independence; he pledges to leave federal politics if Quebec secedes (*January 28*). Second Citizenship Act passes, permitting Canadians to hold dual or multiple citizenship and reducing the residency rule from five years to three; Canadians no longer defined as 'British subjects' (*February 15*). Meets with U.S. President Jimmy Carter (*February 21*). Becomes the first Prime Minister to address U.S. Congress in Washington; assures it that Canada remains united (*February 22*). Creates Via Rail to gradually replace CN-CP passenger train routes (*March 1*). Bails out the St. Lawrence Seaway Authority by raising tolls, forgiving loans and converting costs to equity (*March 2*). His wife Margaret begins a three-month trial separation and arrives with members of the Rolling Stones for their performance at Toronto's El Mocambo club (*March 4*). Canada's jobless rate reaches 7.9%, the highest since 1958 (*March 14*). Appoints Jack Horner to cabinet (Without Portfolio) after he crosses the floor of the House from the Conservatives (*April 21*). Attends his third G7 Summit in London; performs a pirouette behind Elizabeth II at the state dinner that is captured by photographers (*May 7-8*). The Berger Commission tables its report questioning the viability of the Canadian Arctic Gas Pipeline consortium (*May 9*). The Hall Commission on grain handling and transportation tables its report calling for the retention of the Crow's Nest Pass rail rates (*May 16*). Agrees to a separation with his wife Margaret; maintains custody of their three sons (*May 27*). Flies to London, sharing sleeping quarters with Diefenbaker (*June 6*). Attends his fifth Commonwealth Conference in London (*June 6-15*). Commends the Commonwealth Secretary-General for rejecting Quebec's request for separate representation (*June 15*). Creates a national unity task force chaired by former Ontario premier John Robarts and former Anti-Inflation Board chair Jean-Luc Pepin (*July 5*). Creates a task force to look into RCMP activities, chaired by Justice David McDonald (*July 6*). Announces plans to set up an Office of National Unity to counteract Quebec separatist publicity (*July 25*). Cabinet approves an Alaska Highway natural gas pipeline route rather than one along the Mackenzie River valley (*August 7*). The Unemployment Insurance Commission is integrated with Manpower & Immigration (*August 15*). Ottawa begins closing its French language training centres, indicating they accomplished their purpose (*August 16*). Road signs are converted to metric and new cars require metric speedometers (*September 6*). Attends the signing of the Panama Canal Treaty in Washington that will return the Canal Zone to Panama (*September 7*). Moves Chrétien (Industry, Trade & Commerce) to Finance to replace Macdonald who resigned, and appoints Lalonde (National Health & Welfare) as the new Secretary of State for Federal-Provincial Relations to coordinate the federal response to the separatist government in Quebec (*September 16*). Announces the last phase of decentralizing federal civil service jobs, moving 12,000 jobs out of Ottawa in five years (*October 3*). Says he won't challenge Quebec's bill to end the use of English in the legislature, on commercial signs and in schools for new students (*October 7*). The Third Session, 30th Parliament is opened by Elizabeth II; events in the House are televised for the first time (*October 18*). Withdraws his government's support of trade with South Africa as part of a Commonwealth protest against apartheid (*December 19*).

1978: Asks Sun Life Insurance to reconsider its plan to move its head office from Montreal to Toronto, with no success (*January 5*). Seven sections of Quebec's language charter are struck down by the Quebec Superior Court for contradicting the BNA Act (*January*). Francis Fox (Solicitor General) is forced to resign after forging the signature of his girlfriend's husband on a hospital form (*January 27*). Unemployment numbers surpass one million for the first time (*March 14*). Tells New York's Economic Club that Quebec will never vote for independence (*March 22*). Begins to remove wage and price controls (*April 14*). The Royal Commission on Corporate Power tables its report, rejecting the taxing of profits if a business reinvests the money (*May 15*). Addresses the UN General Assembly, calling for nuclear "suffocation" (*May 26*). Canada orders U.S. fishing boats out of Canadian waters for exceeding quotas; U.S. retaliates with similar restrictions (*June 2*). Releases 'A Time For Action' that calls for patriating the constitution and creating a charter of rights (*June 12*). Attends the G7 Summit in Bonn, Germany (*July 16-17*). Sails with German Chancellor Helmut Schmidt in the North Sea, then vacations in Morocco (*July 18-30*). Tells Canadians on television he intends to freeze the growth of the federal civil service and turn the post office into a Crown corporation (*August 1*). First female student pages appear in the House of Commons (*October 10*). The Liberals lose 13 of 15 by-elections

(*October 16*). Hosts a First Ministers Conference in Ottawa and agrees to make distribution of powers a priority in constitution discussions (*October 30-November 1*). Canada signs the Inuvaluit Land Rights Settlement with the Committee for the Original Peoples' Entitlement (COPE) (*October 31*). The biography *Trudeau* by journalist George Radwanski is published (*November*). Vacations in Jamaica (*December-January*). Announces the appointment of former Manitoba premier Edward Schreyer as Canada's 22nd Governor General, to succeed Léger (*December 28*).

1979: Dispatches planes to airlift Canadians out of Iran following anti-Shah and anti-American riots (*January 4*). The Pepin-Robarts Task Force on Canadian Unity tables its report calling for more provincial powers and distinctive, but not special, status for Quebec (*January 26*). Hosts the Federal-Provincial Constitutional Con-ference in Ottawa (*February 5-6*). Meets Osgoode Hall law student Deborah Coyne in Toronto for the first time (*February 23*); will reconnect with her a decade later. His wife Margaret publishes *Beyond Reason* (*April*). Tells a Toronto campaign rally he will unilaterally patriate the constitution if the provinces can't reach an agreement to do it cooperatively (*May 9*). Scuba dives near the North Pole from the Lorex temporary scientific station (*May*). Canada's 31st federal election: re-elected in Mount Royal defeating David Dejong (Conservative); Clark's Conservatives win a minority government while 12 Liberal cabinet members lose their seats (*May 22*). **Trudeau government ends** (*June 4*). Liberals endorse his leadership (*June*). Lives at Harrington Lake until his sons finish school, then moves into Stornoway (*June*). Tells the media he intends to stay on as leader (*July 19*). Takes his sons on a trip to Quebec and Nova Scotia (*August*). Returns to Arctic canoeing, joining a group of MPs and others on the Hanbury and Thelon rivers (*August*). Travels to China and Tibet with architect Arthur Erickson (*September*). Flies to New York to party at discos instead of attending a Liberal policy seminar in British Columbia (*November*). Announces his intention to resign as Liberal leader (*November 21*). Buys art deco home Maison Cormier in Montreal at 1418 Avenue des Pins and rents it out (*December*). Receives a chainsaw as a parting gift at the Liberal Christmas party (*December 12*). The Conservative government loses a non-confidence vote on their budget by six votes (*December 13*). Called on by the Liberal party to stay as leader following the Clark government's defeat (*December 16*). Takes a walk in the snow and decides to remain as Liberal leader (*December 17*); announces his decision the next day.

1980: *Northern Magus*, a Trudeau biography by Richard Gwyn is published (*January 1*). His son Michel breaks up a fight between Trudeau and Margaret; they subsequently seek counselling (*January*). The play *Maggie and Pierre* premiers in Montreal, starring Linda Griffiths (*Winter*). Canada's 32nd federal election: re-elected in Mount Royal defeating Harry Bloomfield (Conservative); wins a majority government (*February 18*). **Trudeau's second government (1980-1984).** Returns as Canada's Prime Minister (*March 3*). Moves back to 24 Sussex Drive with his three sons (*March*). Asks the NDP to join a coalition with the Liberals to shore government support in the west; leader Ed Broadbent turns down the offer (*March*). Appoints Chrétien (Justice) to lead the federal opposition to the separatist forces in the Quebec referendum (*March*). Lalonde (Enegy) prohibits oilsands companies Syncrude and Suncor from selling at world prices (*March 28*); Alberta responds by restricting crude oil sales to Petrosar, a federally owned corporation. 32nd Parliament opens; nominates Jeanne Sauvé to be the 29th Speaker of the House, first female Speaker (*April 14*). Indicates that Canada and the provinces will not negotiate with Quebec if it votes for sovereignty-association (*April 15*). Announces tough conflict-of-interest guidelines for cabinet ministers (*May 1*). Meets with Japan's Prime Minister Masayoshi Ohira who addresses Parliament (*May 5*). Joins Quebec Liberal Leader Claude Ryan and former premiers Bourassa and Lesage at a 'no' rally in Quebec City (*May 7*). MPs unanimously approve patriation of the constitution from the United Kingdom (*May 9*). The government provides $200 million in loan guarantees to help bail out automotive giant Chrysler (*May 10*). Speaks at a Montreal rally for 'no' supporters (*May 14*). The Quebec referendum on sovereignty-association is defeated by 59.9% of the voters (*May 20*). Sends Chrétien (Justice) on a cross-country tour to sell the need for constitutional reform to the provinces (*May 21*). Signs an energy and industrial co-operation pact with Mexican President José López Portillo who addressed Parliament the day before (*May 26*). Meets with the provincial premiers at 24 Sussex Drive, presenting a list of 12 constitutional items to be negotiated over the summer (*June 9*). Attends the G7 Summit in Venice (*June 22-23*). He and son Justin have an audience with Pope John Paul II at the Vatican (*June*). Meets with British Prime Minister Margaret Thatcher in London to discuss patriation of the constitution (*June 25*). MPs make *O Canada* the official national anthem (*June 27*). Meets Terry Fox in Ottawa during the cross-Canada run by the fundraiser who lost a leg to cancer (*July 2*). Handily wins a Liberal leadership review (*July 5*). A First Ministers Conference on the Constitution fails to reach agreement on patriating the constitution (*September 8-13*). Visits the Arctic (*September 22-29*). Indigenous groups in British Columbia file a lawsuit to prevent Canada from patriating the constitution without First Nations' consent (*September 25*). Announces his intention to unilaterally patriate Canada's con-stitution, with or without provincial consent (*October 2*). Canada objects to the U.S. Garrison irrigation project in North Dakota (*October 9*); it is halted a year later and replaced with a scaled-down water-diversion project. Premiers meet in Toronto to try and reboot constitutional talks (*October 14*); eight premiers support a court challenge against the federal intention to move forward unilaterally. About 47,000 striking federal workers return to the job after winning a 24.7% raise (*October 14*). The government introduces its controversial National Energy Program (*October 28*). Establishes a Joint Parliamentary Committee to conduct hearings on constitutional change (*November 6*). Visits the Middle East (*November 13-23*). Meets with French President Giscard d'Estaing in Paris (*November 23*). The New Bank Act receives Assent, allowing foreign banks to operate in Canada (*November 26*). Indigenous groups present their constitutional grievances to the UN (*December 8*). British Prime Minister Thatcher brushes off a British Columbia request to stop patriation of the constitution (*December 9*). Greets the first of 18,000 Cambodian refugees who will arrive in Canada over the next 12 years (*December*).

1981: Visits Austria, Algeria, Nigeria, Senegal, Brazil and Mexico calling for efforts to bridge the gap between rich and poor nations (*January 4-18*). Britain's Kershaw Committee releases its report expressing reluctance to respond to Canada's request for patriating its constitution if the provinces aren't in favour (*January 30*). The Manitoba Court of Appeal sides with the federal government about patriating the constitution unilaterally (*February 3*); Quebec court agrees two months later, but the Newfoundland court agrees with the provinces. A Parliamentary Committee proposes 65 amendments to the constitution package (*February 13*). Alberta cuts oil production in opposition to the National Energy Program (*March 1*); Ottawa responds by adding a 'Lougheed Levy' on Alberta oil to pay for additional oil imports. A government report accuses big oil companies of cheating Canadians out of $12 billion through price fixing over a 15-year period (*March 4*). Meets with U.S. President Ronald Regan who addresses Parliament (*March 11*). Dates actress Gale Zoë Garnett for the first time (*March*). Conservatives begin a filibuster to stall the government's constitutional package (*March 24*). The Parti Québécois government is re-elected in Quebec (*April 13*). 'Gang of Eight' provincial premiers (minus Ontario and New Brunswick) meet in Ottawa and propose the Vancouver formula to amend the constitution, requiring approval of at least seven provinces representing more than half the national population (*April 16*); rejected by Ottawa. MPs pass the constitutional package (*April 23*). Visits Algeria and Italy (*May 15-19*). The government launches a program to encourage

Canadians to find alternatives to oil for heating buildings (*May 25*). Visits France, West Germany and England (*June 24-27*). His principal secretary Jim Coutts resigns to run, unsuccessfully, in a by-election (*July*). Meets with U.S. President Reagan in Washington to discuss the G7 Summit scheduled for Canada (*July 10*). Hosts the 7th G7 Summit at Montebello, Quebec (*July 20-21*). Attends the Royal wedding of Prince Charles and Diana Spencer in London (*July 29*). Visits Morocco (*July 30-31*). The Bank of Canada interest rate reaches an all-time high of 22.5% (*August*). Addresses a UN conference in Nairobi, Kenya, on renewable energy, pledging an additional $40 million in foreign energy aid (*August 12*). The Kent Commission on Newspapers calls for a break-up of media monopolies (*August 18*). The McDonald Commission inves-tigating the RCMP recommends expanded powers for covert searches (*August 25*). Forges an agreement with Alberta for a two-tier oil price system, with a higher price for newly discovered resources (*September 1*). Officially opens La Mauricie National Park in Quebec (*September 6*). Attends the opening of the Gerald Ford Presidential Library and Museum in Grand Rapids, Michigan (*September 18*). Appoints Judy Erola as the first female Status of Women minister (*September 22*). Visits South Korea, (*September 25-28*). The Supreme Court rules that Canada can patriate the constitution without agreement from the provinces, but notes it contravenes constitutional conventional practice (*September 28*). Attends the Commonwealth Heads of Government meeting in Melbourne, Australia (*September 30-October 7*). Visits Fiji (*October 8*). Co-chairs a Summit conference of 22 world leaders in Cancun, Mexico, to address global economic disparities (*October 21-22*); attempts to address Third World poverty are blocked primarily by British Prime Minister Thatcher. A First Ministers Conference convenes in Ottawa to make a final effort to cooperatively find a way to patriate the constitution (*November 2*). Rejects a compromise constitutional proposal tendered by the Gang of Eight premiers (*November 3*). Quebec Premier Lévesque breaks with the Gang of Eight by agreeing to put the constitution and charter before the voters in a referendum (*November 4*). An accord is reached to exchange the Vancouver amending formula for Ottawa's proposed charter – with a notwithstanding clause added; Quebec is not part of the negotiations (*November 4*). Reaches agreement with all provinces except Quebec to patriate the constitution (*November 5*). Receives the Family of Man award in New York, 16 years after it was awarded to Pearson (*November 5*). Quebec's Lévesque plans to boycott federal-provincial meetings unless they are essential (*November 9*). Meets with Jordan's King Hussein in Ottawa (*November 13*). Nearly 100,000 Canadians protest high interest rates, the largest demonstration yet held on Parliament Hill (*November 21*). The Metric Commission announces conversion to the metric system in all food stores over the next two years (*November 24*). The House unanimously passes a constitutional amendment to entrench Indigenous rights (*November 26*). The House passes a resolution to patriate the constitution; includes an amending formula and a Charter of Rights (*December 2*). The Senate approves the constitution package (*December 8*). Asked by his friend, architect Arthur Erickson, to intervene and support his rejected bid to design the Canadian Embassy in Washington (*December 14*); Erickson gets the job. Unemployment reaches 8.6%, the highest since the Second World War (*December 31*).

1982: The Post Office becomes a Crown corporation and regular postage rates nearly double to 30¢ (*January 1*). Visits Mexico (*January 13-16*). Statistics Canada confirms Canada is in a recession (*March 3*). Attends the Genie Awards in Toronto with best actress nominee Kim Catrall; shared a table with a former date, Gale Garnett, while one of the awards was won by yet another previous partner, Margot Kidder (*March 3*). Appoints Bertha Wilson as the first woman on the Supreme Court (*March 4*). British Parliament passes the Canada Act (*March 8*). European Parliament bans Canadian harp and hooded seal-pup skins, effectively ending the commercial industry (*March 11*). Stops weapon sales to Argentina following that country's occupation of British-governed Falkland Islands

(*April 5*). Signs the Canada Act, the patriated constitution, in Ottawa with Elizabeth II (*April 17*). Attends the funeral of auto racer Gilles Villeneuve in Berthierville, Que. (*May 12*). Receives an honorary Doctor of Laws degree from the University of Notre Dame in Indiana (*May 16*). MPs pass the Young Offenders Act, extending rights of due process of law to offenders age 12 to 18 (*May 17*). Attends the G7 Summit at Versailles, France (*June 4-6*). Visits Spain (*June 7-9*). Attends the NATO Summit in Bonn, West Germany (*June 9-10*). Canadian currency reaches a historic low of 78.6 cents (*June*). Allan MacEachen (Finance) presents his third budget, introducing the '6 and 5' (6% salary increase cap in 1983, 5% in 1984) (*June 28*). Flashes a middle finger insult to protesters during a whistle stop in Salmon Arm, B.C. (*August 8*). Moves MacEachen (Finance) to External Affairs, replacing him with Lalonde (Energy, Mines & Resources) (*September 10*). Canadian provinces are charged by the U.S. lumber industry with subsidizing the softwood export industry, touching off a 12-year dispute (*October 7*). Dominion Day renamed Canada Day (*October 27*). Visits Europe, including the Vimy Monument in France (*November 7-15*). Attends the funeral of Soviet President Leonid Brezhnev in Moscow (*November 15*). The Supreme Court rejects Quebec's claim to have a veto over constitutional amendments (*December 6*). Canada signs the international Law of the Sea Convention that recognizes Canada's 322-km (200-mile) fishing zone and sovereignty over the Continental Shelf for 565 km (350 miles) (*December 10*).

1983: Leads a trade mission to Hong Kong, Thailand, Singapore, Malaysia, Indonesia, Brunei, Philippines and Japan (*January 2-19*). Clark resigns as Leader of the Opposition following a disappointing vote of approval in a leadership review (*February 1*); replaced on an interim basis by Conservative MP Erik Nielsen. Meets with Soviet agriculture minister Mikail Gorbachev in Ottawa (*May 26-27*). Attends the G7 Summit at Williamsburg, Virginia (*May 28-30*). Receives an honorary Doctor of Laws degree from Dalhousie University. Brian Mulroney defeats Joe Clark to become leader of the Conservative party (*June 11*). Accepts a U.S. request to test cruise missiles in Canada (*June 15*). Speaks nationally on television to indicate he isn't prepared to make cutbacks to programs dealing with the struggling economy (*June 28*). Signs a new oil agreement with Alberta that freezes Canadian prices at $29.75 for 18 months (*June 30*). The Access to Information Act and the Privacy Act come into effect (*July 1*). Appoints Rosalie Abella to conduct a Royal Commission on Equality in Employment (*July 27*). Accepts the resignation of Roger Simmons (Mines) ten days after his appointment; Simmons is later charged with tax evasion (*August 22*). Meets with British Prime Minister Thatcher who addresses Parliament (*September 26*). Introduces a peace initiative at a conference in Guelph, calling for a ban on nuclear arms testing (*October 27*). Takes his peace initiative to Europe, visiting leaders in France, Netherlands, Belgium, West Germany, Britain and Vatican City (*November 8-11*) His wife Margaret files for divorce (*November 16*). Attends the Commonwealth Heads of Government meeting in New Delhi, India (*November 23-28*). Meets with China's Chairman Deng Xioping and Prime Minister Zhao Ziyang in Beijing to present his peace initiative (*November 28*); also takes his plan to Japan and Bangladesh (*November 29-December 5*). The First Session, 32nd Parliament is prorogued, the longest yet in Canadian history at 3 years, 7 months, 16 days (*November 30*). His peace initiative is endorsed by Romanian President Nicolae Ceausescu (*December 10*) and U.S. President Reagan (*December 15*).

1984: Discusses his peace initiative with UN Secretary-General Javier de Cuellar (*January 11*). Jeanne Sauvé resigns as Speaker (*January 15*) and 13 days later is appointed the first female Governor General. Nominates Lloyd Francis as the 30th Speaker of the House (*January 15*). Meets with China's Premier Zhao Ziyang who addresses Parliament (*January 17*). Attends the funeral of Soviet Union General-Secretary Yuri Andropov in Moscow (*February 14*), discusses his peace initiative while there. Decides to step down as Liberal leader, while walking in a snowstorm (*February 28*). First U.S. cruise missile is tested over Canada (*March 8*). The Supreme Court rules that the Hibernia oil field off the east coast belongs to the federal government (*March 8*). Supreme Court Chief Justice Bora Laskin dies in Ottawa (March 26). The Health Care Act is given Assent, helping to preserve the health-care system and discourage private billing (*April 1*). His divorce from Margaret is official (*April 2*). Appoints Brian Dickson as the 15th Chief Justice of the Supreme Court (*April 16*). His ex-wife Margaret marries Fried Kemper, a real estate developer in Ottawa (*April 18*). Meets with Mexican President Miguel de la Madrid who addresses Parliament (*May 8*). Legislation is introduced to create the Canadian Security Intelligence Service (CSIS) (*May 11*). Attends his last G7 Summit in London, England (*June 7-9*). Commemorates the 40th anniversary of D-Day at Juno Beach in Normandy, France (*June 6*). Receives a tribute from the party at the leadership convention that includes Paul Anka singing 'My Way' (*June 14*). John Turner wins the Liberal leadership in Ottawa (*June 16*). **Trudeau's second government ends** (*June 30*). Moves to his home in Montreal with his sons (*July*). Made a Companion of Honour by Elizabeth II (*July 4*). His last 17 political appointments are made by Turner (*July 9*). Becomes a senior counsel at Heenan Blaikie law firm in Montreal (*July*). The Liberals under Turner lose the election to Mulroney's Conservatives (*September 4*). Receives the Albert Einstein peace prize in Washington for easing global East-West tensions (*November*).

1985: Made a Companion of the Order of Canada (*June 24*). Meets aspiring actor Brooke Johnson whom he begins dating (*November 1*); she later writes the play *Trudeau Stories* based on their conversations. Receives an honorary Doctor of Laws degree from McGill (*November 5*).

1986: Represents Canada at Prime Minister Olof Palme's funeral in Sweden (*March 15*). Receives an honorary degree from the University of British Columbia.

Forgetting his full name

At a 1988 dinner marking the 20th anniversary of his election as party leader, Trudeau gamely took part in 'Trivial Pierresuit' and inevitably made it to the final round answering trivia questions about his own life. But he came in second, missing the question that asked for his full official name. Trudeau missed one of his five given names: Philippe.

1987: Publicly opposes the proposed Meech Lake Accord for shifting powers away from the federal government (*May 27*). Receives an honorary Doctor of Laws degree from Macau University, China. Receives an honorary degree from the University of Montreal. Opposes the Meech Lake agreement in six hours of testimony before a joint Parliamentary committee in Ottawa (*August 27*). Pays his respects to René Lévesque, lying in state after his death in Montreal (*November 3*).

1988: Speaks out against the Meech Lake Accord before the Senate (*March 30*). His ex-wife Margaret begins visiting him again after she separates from Fried Kemper (*May*). His former colleague, Jean Marchand, dies in Quebec (*August 28*). Helps Donald Johnston pull together articles for a book opposed to the Meech Lake Accord: *With a Bang, Not a Whimper* (*Fall*).

1989: Chairs the Ecology and Energy Options project in Montreal for InterAction, a group of former leaders (*April 29-30*).

1990: Publishes *Towards a Just Society*, calling the government's free trade deal with the U.S. "a monstrous swindle" (*March 20*). Walks out of a lunch with Liberal leadership candidate Paul Martin who supports the Meech Lake agreement (*Spring*). Chrétien succeeds Turner as Liberal leader (*June 23*). Visits China with his sons (*Summer*). *Trudeau and Our Times* is published by Stephen Clarkson and Christina McCall (*October 1*).

1991: Receives an honorary Doctor of Laws in Public Affairs from the University of Toronto and opens the Bora Laskin Law Library (*March 31*). Chairs the economic transformation of former Warsaw Pact nations project for InterAction (*April 6-7*). His daughter Sarah Elizabeth Coyne is born in St. John's (*May 5*).

1992: Visits South Africa and meets with Nelson Mandela and F.W. de Klerk (*March*). Attends the unveiling of his portrait on Parliament Hill by Myfanwy Pavelic (*May 1*). Publicly opposes the Charlottetown Accord for its concessions to nationalists (*September 21*); it is defeated a month later in a national referendum.

1993: Attends the premiere of a documentary based on his *Memoirs*; fends off persistent actor Pierre Brassard with a slap across the face and karate chop to the genitals (*August*). Publishes his *Memoirs* (*November 9*).

1994: His brother Charles 'Tip' dies (*August 8*).

1995: Canoes the Upper Stikine River in B.C. for 10 days (*Summer*). Not involved in the Quebec referendum that was narrowly defeated (*October 30*). Publishes *The Canadian Way* with co-author Ivan Head (*November 4*).

1996: Publishes a criticism of Quebec Premier Lucien Bouchard's handling of the 1995 Quebec referendum on separation (*February 3*); is on the receiving end of a Bouchard piece a week later. Takes his last canoe trip, on the Petawawa River; capsizes but is fine (*July*).

1997: Participates in a meeting of current and former western hemisphere leaders at the Carter Center in Atlanta, Georgia (*April 28-29*); reconnects with Joe Clark. Attends the funeral of his former colleague Gérard Pelletier who died of cancer in Montreal (*June 22*).

1998: Attends the Toronto launch of an English-language version of *Cité Libre* (*January 22*). His son Michel drowns in Lake Kokanee, B.C., after being caught in an avalanche while skiing (*November 13*). Trudeau is hospitalized with pneumonia, but recovers (*December*).

1999: Named the century's top newsmaker by Canadian Press (*December 5*).

2000: Dies in Montreal of prostate cancer and Parkinson's Disease (*September 28*). Lies in state on Parliament Hill (*September 30-October 2*). State funeral held at Notre Dame Basilica in Montreal (*October 3*). Buried in the family plot at Saint-Rémi-de-Napierville Cemetery, Saint-Rémi, Que.

Books about Trudeau

- **1960**: Pierre Trudeau & Jacques Hebert; *Two Innocents in Red China* (Oxford University)
- **1968**: John D. Harbron; *This Is Trudeau* (Longman Canada)
- **1968**: Martin Sullivan; *Mandate '68* (Doubleday)
- **1970**: Pierre Elliott Trudeau; *Approaches to Politics* (Oxford University)
- **1971**: Walter Stewart; *Shrug, Trudeau in Power* (New)
- **1972**: Anthony Westell; *Paradox, Trudeau as Prime Minister* (Prentice-Hall)

- **1972**: Bruce Thordarson; *Trudeau and Foreign Policy* (Oxford University)
- **1972**: *The Best of Trudeau: A Compendium of Whimsical Wit and Querulous Quip by Canada's Putative Prince* (Modern Canadian Library)
- **1977**: James Laxer; *The Liberal Idea of Canada: Pierre Trudeau and the Question of Canada's Survival* (Lorimer)
- **1978**: George Radwanski; *Trudeau* (Macmillan)
- **1979**: Rick Butler & Jean-Guy Carrier (eds.); *The Trudeau Decade* (Doubleday Canada)
- **1980**: Richard Gwyn; *The Northern Magus: Pierre Trudeau and Canadians* (McClelland & Stewart)
- **1984**: Larry Zolf; *Just Watch Me: Remembering Pierre Trudeau* (Lorimer)
- **1988**: Pierre Elliott Trudeau; *With A Bang, Not A Whimper: Pierre Trudeau Speaks Out* (Stoddart)
- **1990**: Michel Vastel; *The Outsider: The Life of Pierre Elliott Trudeau* (Macmillan)
- **1990**: J.L. Granatstein & Robert Bothwell; *Pirouette: Pierre Trudeau and Canadian Foreign Policy* (University of Toronto)
- **1990**: Stephen Clarkson & Christina McCall; *Trudeau and Our Times: Vol. 1: The Magnificent Obsession* (McClelland & Stewart)
- **1992**: Thomas Axworthy & Pierre Trudeau (ed.); *Towards A Just Society: The Trudeau Years* (Penguin)
- **1992**: Pierre Elliott Trudeau; *A Mess That Deserves A Big No* (Robert Davies)
- **1993**: Pierre Elliott Trudeau; *Memoirs* (McClelland & Stewart)
- **1993**: Kevin Christiano; *Pierre Elliott Trudeau: Reason Before Passion* (ECW)
- **1995**: Guy Laforest; *Trudeau and the End of a Canadian Dream* (McGill-Queen's University)
- **1995**: Kenneth McDonald; *His Pride, Our Fall: Recovering from the Trudeau Revolution* (Key Porter)
- **1995**: Ivan Head & Pierre Trudeau; *The Canadian Way: Shaping Canada's Foreign Policy 1968-1984* (McClelland & Stewart)
- **1997**: Stephen Clarkson & Christina McCall; *Trudeau and Our Times: Vol. 2: The Heroic Delusion* (McClelland & Stewart)
- **1998**: Pierre Elliott Trudeau, Ron Graham (eds.); *The Essential Trudeau* (McClelland & Stewart)
- **1998**: Claude Couture; *Paddling With the Current: Pierre Elliott Trudeau, Étienne Parent, Liberalism and Nationalism in Canada* (University of Alberta)
- **1999**: Andrew Cohen & J.L. Granatstein (eds.); *Trudeau's Shadow: The Life and Legacy of Pierre Elliott Trudeau* (Vintage)
- **2000**: J.L. Granatstein, Alison Gordon, Peter Gzowski, Anne Kingston, Mordecai Richler & Catherine Annau; *Trudeau Albums* (Penguin)
- **2004**: Stan Sauerwein; *Pierre Elliott Trudeau: The Fascinating Life of Canada's Most Flamboyant Prime Minister* (Lorimer)
- **2005**: Nancy Southam (ed.); *Pierre: Colleagues and Friends Talk About the Trudeau They Knew* (McClelland & Stewart)
- **2006**: Ramsay Cook; *The Teeth of Time: Remembering Pierre Elliott Trudeau* (McGill-Queens University)
- **2006**: Max & Monique Nemni; *Young Trudeau: Son of Quebec, Father of Canada 1919-1944* (Douglas Gibson)

- **2006**: John English; *Citizen of the World: The Life of Pierre Elliott Trudeau, Volume 1 1919-1968* (Knopf Canada)
- **2007**: Bruce Powe; *Mystic Trudeau: The Fire and the Rose* (Thomas Allen)
- **2007**: Robert A. Wright; *Three Nights in Havana: Pierre Trudeau, Fidel Castro and the Cold War World* (HarperCollins)
- **2009**: John English; *Just Watch Me: The Life of Pierre Elliott Trudeau, Volume 2 1968-2000* (Knopf Canada)
- **2009**: Nino Ricci; *Extraordinary Canadians: Pierre Elliott Trudeau* (Penguin Canada)
- **2010**: Canadian Press; *Trudeau: Images of Canada's Passionate Statesman* (Wiley)
- **2011**: Ron Graham; *The Last Act: Pierre Trudeau, the Gang of Eight, and the Fight for Canada* (Penguin Canada)
- **2011**: Max & Monique Nemni; *Trudeau Transformed: The Shaping of a Statesman 1944-1965* (McClelland & Stewart)
- **2013**: Bob Plamondon; *The Truth About Trudeau* (Great River Media)
- **2016**: Allen Mills; *Citizen Trudeau: An Intellectual Biography; 1944-1965* (Oxford University)
- **2016**: Robert Wright; *Trudeaumania: The Rise to Power of Pierre Elliott Trudeau* (HarperCollins)
- **2016**: Paul Litt; *Trudeaumania* (UBC)
- **2017**: Darryl Raymaker; *Trudeau's Tango: Alberta Meets Pierre Elliott Trudeau* (Gutteridge)
- **2018**: Christo Aivalis; *The Constant Liberal: Pierre Trudeau, Organized Labour, and the Canadian Social Democratic Left* (UBC)

16

Joe Clark

The Unanticipated Prime Minister

If Pearson enjoyed his greatest national successes before his term in office, Joe Clark, Canada's youngest Prime Minister, garnered most of his national respect after his time as leader. In office for less than nine months before losing a confidence vote to the Liberals, he was still able to tighten internal expenditure controls and reshape the structure of cabinet committees. Later, as Mulroney's global and constitutional cabinet minister, he'd finally assumed a role with savvy and confidence. Clark returned as party leader at the turn of the millennium and attempted unsuccessfully to prevent a unite-the-right merger with the Reform party.

Clark the Politician

Prime Minister of Canada: June 4, 1979 – March 3, 1980
Length of term: 8 months, 29 days
Parliament as Prime Minister: 31st
Age on entering office: 39
Political party: Progressive Conservative
Leader of party: February 22, 1976 – February 18, 1983; November 14, 1998 – May 31, 2003
Member of Parliament: January 4, 1973 – September 8, 1993; September 11, 2000 – October 22, 2000; January 29, 2001 – May 23, 2004
Ridings represented: Rocky Mountain [Alta.] 1973-1979; Yellowhead [Alta.] 1978-1993; Kings-Hants [N.S.] 2000; Calgary Centre [Alta.] 2001-2004
Cabinet portfolios: External Affairs (1984-1991); Privy Council President (1991-1993); Constitutional Affairs (1991-1993)
Other political post: Leader of the Opposition (1976-1979, 1980-1983)
Titles: Canadian Privy Councillor (1979); Alberta Order of Excellence (1983); Honorary Chief Bald Eagle, Samson Cree Nation (1993); Companion of the Order of Canada (1994); Commandeur, l'Ordre de la Pléiade
Quotes: "We will not take this nation by storm, by stealth or by surprise. We will win it by work." (leadership acceptance speech, 1976); "Anyone who can bring the Conservative party together can bring the country together."

Clark the Man

Name: Charles Joseph Clark
Born: June 5, 1939, High River, Alberta
Ancestry: Scottish
Religion: Roman Catholic
Education: B.A. [Bachelor of Arts in Political Science] (University of Alberta, 1960); M.A. [Master of Arts in Political Science] (Alberta, 1973)
Nickname: Joe Who?
Military service: Air cadets
Occupation: journalist; political assistant
Occupation after term: Leader of the Opposition; professor; consultant
Publications: *A Nation Too Good To Lose* (1994); *How We Lead: Canada in a Century of Change* (2013)
Appearance: "Clark had begun to look ever so slightly like a John A. Macdonald: a bit lanky, teetering slightly on his heels, arms akimbo ..." (Warner Troyer in *200 Days: Joe Clark in Power*); "The chin, the paunch, that wide-eyed look – You knew that Joe was not a crook." (opening to the poem *The Best Man* by John Allemang in the *Globe & Mail*, 2002)
Personality: "Joe Clark's style was to have no style." (Sandra Gwyn in *Saturday Night Magazine*); "Often derided as a wimp, Clark was determined to be tough." (Bob Plamondon in *Blue Thunder*)
Married: Maureen Anne McTeer, June 30, 1973, Notre Dame High School Chapel, Ottawa
Age at marriage: 34

Clark was the:

- The youngest Prime Minister (age 39)
- The youngest leader of a major federal party (age 36)
- The Prime Minister with the shortest term after being elected
- The only Minister of Constitutional Affairs for Canada
- First Prime Minister born in Alberta
- Second Prime Minister never to lead a majority government
- Second Progressive Conservative Prime Minister
- Second Prime Minister defeated by a non-confidence vote
- Third Prime Minister with no previous cabinet experience
- Fifth Roman Catholic Prime Minister (first who was not French Canadian)

Clark's legacy

- Reorganized the Cabinet committee structure
- Introduced expenditure controls
- Drafted a *Freedom of Information Act* adopted by the next government
- Permitted civil servants to talk to the media

Clark's Family

Clark's Parents

Father: Charles Archibald Clark

Born: 1910, High River, Alberta
Occupation: reporter; publisher
Died: May 10, 1982, High River, Alberta

Mother: Grace Rosaline Welch
Born: 1910
Married: 1937
Died: August 1997, Calgary, Alberta

Clark's Brother (1 sibling; Joe the oldest)

Brother: Peter M. Clark (b.1942), lawyer; judge; two sons
  Married: Marcia; Sunny Delaney

Clark's Wife

Name: Maureen Anne McTeer
Born: February 27, 1952, Cumberland (Ottawa), Ontario
Father: John J. McTeer (farmer; businessman)
Mother: Beatrice E. Griffith (insurance worker)
Occupation: author; lawyer; professor
Age at marriage: 21
Younger than Clark: 13 years

Clark's Daughter

Name: Catherine Jane Clark
Born: November 6, 1976, Ottawa, Ontario
Occupation: broadcaster; communications consultant
Married: Chad Schella (June 8, 2002)
Children: 2 – Alexandra Charmaine Maureen; Charles Roger Dennis

POLITICAL STORIES

Dark horse candidate

From the beginning, Clark indicated he was in the Conservative leadership campaign to win, not merely to make his name better known. He wasn't really considered a major candidate, but that was the case for most of the 11 candidates.

At the leadership convention in Ottawa on February 22, 1976, Clark polled third behind Quebec's Claude Wagner and Brian Mulroney with less than 12% of the vote. But in the next two ballots he received endorsements from unsuccessful candidates Heward Grafftey, Jim Gillies, Sinclair Stevens, John Fraser and Flora Macdonald, moving him ahead of Mulroney and within reach of Wagner. On the fourth ballet, he beat Wagner by 65 votes of the 2,309 cast.

Clark's momentum had come primarily from English Canada delegates. Wagner, who unlike Clark, had cabinet experience at the provincial level, was unhappy about his loss. Two years later he stepped down as an MP, frustrated by trying to work under the new leader. The following year he was dead at 54 of cancer.

Equally despondent was Mulroney. Although he had no experience in office, he entered the convention as one of the serious contenders. Losing was hard, but he soon moved on to become president of Iron Ore of Canada. In 1983, Clark unexpectedly gave him another leadership shot after resigning when he failed to get more than two-thirds of the party members to support him.

Joe Who?

The headline in Canada's largest paper, *The Toronto Star*, stretched across all eight columns on February 23, 1976. 'Joe Who?' referred to the largely unknown western MP who had just won the Conservative leadership. It was a moniker that would stick until well after Clark's term as Prime Minister.

He couldn't shake the moniker. When he was Leader of the Opposition, the media tended to focus on incidents that portrayed the earnest, young politician as hapless. He backed away from seeking election in an Alberta riding when another Conservative MP refused to make way for him. His luggge was lost on a trip to the Middle East. The miscues made news. Sometimes, Clark's efforts to project a more confident persona were complicated by the media's focus on the strength and assertiveness of his wife, Maureen.

Things didn't improve once he became Prime Minister. He announced plans to move Canada's embassy in Israel to Jerusalem, then backtracked in the face of predictable Palestinian outrage. He was outmanoeuvred by the Liberals who brought his government down. It was only when he made an impressive return as Mulroney's External Affairs minister that the lingering 'Who? putdown began to fade away.

Youngest Prime Minister

Canada's 16th Prime Minister took office one day before his 40th birthday, making him the country's youngest leader. Was age a liability for him? It appeared that way. His government was chopped short by a Liberal non-confidence vote after only six months in power.

By the time he returned as Secretary of State for External Affairs in 1984, he was in his mid-40s and demonstrated a confidence – almost a gravitas – that was absent when he was at the helm. Mulroney, his boss, was the same age as Clark and he noted in his personal journal many years later that when they both sought the leadership in 1976, they were "both too young, too inexperienced, and too ambitious and, unfortunately for him (Clark), he won."

Felled by the Budget

Clark was determined to govern as if his party had a majority, setting forth on a path marked by ambitious legislation. There was pushback. He narrowly survived two non-confidence votes in the fall of 1979, then unveiled his first budget that was going to raise oil prices by $4 a barrel and boost the tax at the gas pump to 18 cents a litre.

He knew the opposition would not like the budget as presented by his Finance minister, John Crosbie. But he also knew the Liberals had no leader (Trudeau had resigned), so were unlikely to mount much resistance.

It was a miscalculation. MP Allan MacEachen quietly marshaled every Liberal who could be found to their seats for the non-confidence vote on December 13. Meanwhile, the Conservatives made no genuine effort to court the two Créditiste votes in the House, turning down leader Fabien Roy's proposals to spend the gasoline tax on Quebec or, when that failed, on tackling poverty.

When the vote came that evening, the Créditistes abstained and the government lost by six votes. Clark, feeling combative despite an assortment of bad polls, immediately announced his intention to dissolve Parliament. The subsequent election ended what became Canada's shortest government that had been elected to power.

The Iranian escape plan

Iranian students supporting the country's new leader Ayatollah Khomeini stormed the U.S. embassy in November 1979 and held most of the staff hostage. Six escaped and ultimately found their way to the homes of Canadian Ambassador Ken Taylor and his Chief Immigration Officer John Sheardown.

Taylor quickly sought permission from External Affairs to hide the Americans. Clark was called out of Question Period in the House by his External Affairs minister Flora Macdonald and readily agreed to protect them.

For the next two and a half months, the government managed to keep the operation secret. Several media outlets were on to the story, but had agreed to postpone publication. Clark eventually shared the information with Trudeau in the vain hope of stopping the opposition's barrage against the government's perceived inaction in Iran. It was clearly becoming necessary to move the Americans out of Iran before they were discovered.

With Canadian documentation and a cover story that had them working for a fictitious Hollywood film company, all six successfully flew out of Iran on January 28, 1980. Taylor shut the embassy the same day and left with his staff.

The story was made public, making Taylor an instant celebrity. Clark received a warm thank you from U.S. President Jimmy Carter and met with Taylor the next day to convey his appreciation.

PERSONAL STORIES

Clark and Diefenbaker

Having just turned 17, Clark was living a political dream. He'd won a trip to Ottawa in a Rotary public speaking contest and had the opportunity to meet Leader of the Opposition George Drew, whom Clark greatly admired. With Drew was the feisty Saskatchewan Conservative MP John Diefenbaker, who also impressed Clark. Their paths would cross regularly until Diefenbaker's death 23 years later.

As part of the executive team of the Progressive Conservative Student Federation, Clark helped ensure that the man he looked up to was supported by the party's youth wing. He even introduced Diefenbaker at the 1964 national convention when the leader's star was on the wane. A year later, however, Clark accepted the fact that Dief had stayed too long. He told the national party executive that the Chief needed to resign and in 1967 he worked on Davie Fulton's bid to replace the Conservative leader. Fulton came in third (Dief was fifth) in the race that was eventually won by Nova Scotia's Premier, Robert Stanfield.

In 1979, Diefenbaker quipped, "Canada celebrated the year of the child by electing Joe Clark as Prime Minister." But that same 'child' freed up a larger office on Parliament Hill for him as a substitute for the small space given to him by Pearson. Later that same month, Clark delivered the eulogy at Diefenbaker's funeral in Saskatoon.

Maureen McTeer

When Maureen McTeer's boss invited her out for dinner in March 1973, she was prepared for the worst. Only a year earlier, she'd been let go from her job as an assistant in the Conservatives' parliamentary research office. It was tough work satisfying political masters while still completing university studies. But her boss, rookie MP Joe Clark, didn't see their meal in Hull as a business meeting. For him, it was a first date.

Three months later, the two were quietly married in Ottawa. In many ways, Maureen was similar to Margaret Trudeau. She was married to a much older man who became Prime Minister and she was a strong feminist. As the Prime Minister's wife, she displayed a confident, if sometimes argumentative, personality. There was no way she was going to change her last name to Clark just to satisfy worriers on the Hill.

Her time at 24 Sussex Drive was frustratingly short and she didn't recover easily from the rapid fall from power. But she started developing her career while Clark tenuously held on to the Conservative leadership. Despite having a law degree, she rarely worked as a lawyer. Instead, she produced books, for the coffee table (*Residences*), for children (*Parliament*) and for the dying (*Tough Choices*) before writing her memoirs in 2003.

Maureen was the first wife of a Prime Minister to seek a seat in the House of Commons, as the Conservative candidate for the newly created riding of Carleton-Gloucester in 1988. Although she grew up in the area, she lost to local councillor Eugène Bellemare.

Clark's Timeline

1939: Born in High River, Alta. (*June 5*). Lived in family home on MacLeod Trail.

1942: Nearly drowns when a riverbank gives way while he is fishing (*Summer*).

1944: Attends High River (now Spitzee) Public School (*September*).

1947: Was a Wolf Cub, and later a Boy Scout. Also joined the Air Cadets. Delivered the *Calgary Herald* newspaper.

1952: Begins attending High River High School (*September*).

1953: Becomes editor of the student newspaper, *The Reflector*.

1956: Wins a Rotary public speaking scholarship to visit Ottawa where he meets MP John Diefenbaker and Opposition Leader George Drew (*June*); also sits in the House Gallery to watch the pipeline debate. Elected president of the student council (*September*).

1957: Meets Diefenbaker again during an election campaign stop in High River (*May*). Works as a junior reporter at the *Calgary Herald* (*Summer*). Attends the University of Alberta in Edmonton (*September*). Spends his first term in a converted broom closet at St. Joseph College residence (*Fall*).

1958: Finishes his first year, but fails French (*April*). Attends a Conservative Youth conference in Ottawa; meets Brian Mulroney for the first time (*Spring*). Works for the *Edmonton Journal* (*Summer*). Campaigns for Alan Lazerte who comes in second in the leadership race for the Alberta Progressive Conservatives (*August*). Becomes vice-president of the campus Progressive Conservative club and managing editor of the university student newspaper, *The Gateway* (*Fall*).

1959: Works as the driver for Progressive Conservative Leader Cameron Kirby during the provincial election (*May-June*); the Conservatives end up winning only one seat. Becomes editor of *The Gateway* (*Fall*). Attends the Canadian University Press conference in Quebec City (*December*).

1960: Moves a resolution on campus demanding Kirby's resignation (*January*). Helps lead a demonstration against the provincial Social Credit government for not building student residences (*March 10*). Returns for a fourth year at university to raise his grade-point average (*September*).

1961: Serves as Conservative Leader of the Opposition in the University of Alberta's mock Parliament; a year earlier, fellow student Jim Coutts was the Liberal Prime Minister (he went on to become Trudeau's principal secretary). Receives his Bachelor of Arts in Political Science from the University of Alberta (*June*). Attends the Conservative national convention in Ottawa as a student delegate. Travels to London, England, where he works in the stock room of Harrod's department store (*Fall*). Visits Paris and Barcelona (*December*).

1962: Travels in Spain, attempts to learn French in France and visits Italy (*Winter*). Returns to Canada after accepting a job writing pamphlets and speeches for Conservative party headquarters in Ottawa (*Winter*). Begins post-graduate studies at Dalhousie Law School in Halifax (*September*). Elected president of the national Progressive Conservative Student Federation (*Fall*).

1963: Transfers to the University of British Columbia Law School in Vancouver (*September*). Campaigns unsuccessfully for B.C. Conservative leader Davie Fulton; the Social Credit government is re-elected (*September 30*). Begins dating fellow student Penny Riordin (*Fall*).

1964: Presides over the national meeting of the Progressive Conservative Student Federation in Ottawa that narrowly supports Diefenbaker's leadership (*January*). Introduces Diefenbaker at the national convention (*February 5*). Breaks up with Riordin (*Spring*). Does not pass all his law courses (*Spring*). Returns to the University of Alberta in Edmonton for post-graduate studies in political science (*September*).

1965: Tells the Conservative executive that Diefenbaker needs to resign as party leader (*February*). Hired as a reporter at Calgary's *Albertan* newspaper by managing editor David Humphreys (his later biographer) (*Summer*). Works as a strategist for Alberta Conservative leader Peter Lougheed (*Summer*). Begins dating Catriona Gibson.

1966: His father, Charles, sells the *High River Times* to one of his employees. Becomes vice-president of the Alberta Progressive Conservatives.

1967: Loses Calgary South riding in the provincial election to incumbent Arthur Dixon, Speaker of the Legislature, by 462 votes (*May 23*). Joins Davie Fulton's campaign for the leadership of the federal Conservatives, working with a team that includes Lowell Murray and Mulroney (*Spring-Summer*); Fulton polls third to Robert Stanfield (*September 9*). Asked by Stanfield to join the leader's transition team (*September*). Shares an apartment on Rideau Terrace with other Stanfield staffers Graham Scott and Murray (*Fall*). Becomes Stanfield's speechwriter (*November*).

Losing Catriona

There are perks to canvassing. Clark was stumping for Peter Lougheed in Okotoks when he was met at a door by an attractive girl wearing only a towel. He and Catriona Gibson both found it hilarious and were soon dating. Distance was a problem for them with Clark in Edmonton then Ottawa, and Catriona in Kingston then Toronto. They would meet midway whenever possible, as they did in Huntsville in the fall of 1969. Unfortunately, Catriona was tragically killed in a car accident on the way back to Toronto.

1969: His girlfriend, Catriona Gibson, is killed in an automobile accident that occurs shortly after her meeting with him in Huntsville, Ont. (*Fall*). Attends Gibson's funeral in Okotoks, Alta. (*Fall*).

1970: Resigns from Stanfield's office (*May*). Spends six months in Europe working on his thesis in Putney Heath, England, and studying French in Besançon, France (*June-November*).

1971: Begins campaigning to get the Conservative nomination in Rocky Mountain federal riding (*Summer*).

1972: Wins the Rocky Mountain nomination on the second ballot (*March 18*). Canada's 29th federal election: elected in Rocky Mountain defeating incumbent Allen Sulatycky; the Liberal government is narrowly re-elected federally (*October 30*). Rents an apartment at 300 Cooper Street in Ottawa (*Fall*). Hires Ottawa university student and government researcher Maureen McTeer as his office research assistant (*November*).

1973: Chairs an ad hoc caucus committee on youth (*Winter*). Invites McTeer on a first date and proposes that evening (*March*). Marries Maureen McTeer at Notre Dame High School Chapel, Ottawa (*June 30*). Takes a short honeymoon to Quebec City (*July*). Shows Maureen around his riding, including Banff, Jasper and Waterton Lakes national parks (*July*). Visits the Northwest Territories and the Yukon (*August*). His wife Maureen enters law school at the University of Ottawa (*September*). Becomes Conservative critic for youth (*October*).

1974: Directs Michael Meighen's successful campaign to become president of the Conservative party. Canada's 30th federal election: re-elected in Rocky Mountain defeating Arthur Yates (Liberal); the Liberal government regains its majority (*July 8*). Becomes Conservative critic for the environment (*December 20*).

1975: Begins exploring potential for support if he runs for the leadership (*June*). Conservative leader Stanfield announces his intention to resign (*August 5*). Returns to France to take French language courses in Royan (*August*). Buys his first home at 36 Rockcliffe Way in Ottawa (*August*). Announces his intention to seek the leadership (*November 18*). Vacations in Scottsdale, Arizona (*December*).

1976: Vacations in Bermuda (*February*). His small plane lands safely in Wiarton, Ont., after it flips in the air during a storm (*February*). Elected leader of the Progressive

Conservative party (*February 22*). Called Joe Who? by the *Toronto Star* (*February 23*); the name sticks. Vacations in the Bahamas (*February*). Moves into Stornoway (*March*). Receives an honorary Doctor of Laws degree from the University of New Brunswick (*May 13*). Meets with U.S. President Gerald Ford in Washington (*June*). Visits Europe where he meets with Canadian troops in Lahr, Germany, and with Pope Paul VI at the Vatican (*August-September*). Backs away from challenging MP Stan Schumacher for the Conservative nomination in the recreated Bow River riding; Schumacher later loses the nomination to Gordon Taylor, leaves the party to sit as an Independent and loses the election to Taylor. Clark's daughter Catherine is born in High River, Alta. (*November 6*).

The Stornoway-Puddicombe connection

The Clarks were living at Stornoway when their only child, Catherine, was born in High River, Alta., on November 6, 1976, delivered by Dr. Paul Puddicombe. Flashback 33 years: Stornoway was occupied by the Dutch royal family during the Second World War. On January 19, 1943, Princess Margriet, daughter of the Netherlands' Princess Julianna was born in Ottawa – delivered by Dr. John Puddicombe, Paul's father. The delivery room at Ottawa Civic Hospital had been declared Dutch territory by the King's Liberal government to avoid any future challenges about the princess's nationality or place of birth.

1977: His former Transport critic Jack Horner crosses the floor to join the Liberals and accepts a position in the Trudeau cabinet (*April 20*); His party loses all five by-elections in Quebec and Prince Edward Island (*May 24*). Another Conservative, Jacques Lavoie, crosses the floor to join the Liberals (*June*). Receives the Queen Elizabeth II Silver Jubilee Medal. Vacations in Massachusetts (*August*). Meets in Kingston with Conservative premiers Peter Lougheed of Alberta, Bill Davis of Ontario, Richard Hatfield of New Brunswick, Sterling Lyon of Manitoba and Frank Moore of Newfoundland to discuss the constitution and the economy (*September 20*). Wins a leadership confidence vote of 93% at the Conservative convention (*November*).

1978: Meets with new Quebec Liberal leader Claude Ryan in Montreal the night before Ryan is to meet with Trudeau (*May 4*).

1979: Embarks on a trip to the Middle East that includes Israel; his luggage is lost (*January*). Canada's 31st federal election: elected in Yellowhead defeating Laurie Switzer (Liberal); wins a minority government (*May 22*). **Clark's government (1979-1980).** Becomes 16th Prime Minister of Canada one day before his 40th birthday (*June 4*). Announces plans to move Canada's embassy in Israel from Tel Aviv to Jerusalem (*June 5*). Initiates a two-month hiring freeze in the federal civil service (*June 8*). Several Arab oil nations threaten to boycott Canada if it goes ahead with moving its embassy to Jerusalem (*June 9*). Moves to Harrington Lake for the summer (*June*). Informs the Social Credit leader that the party won't receive official party status because it is one MP short of the required minimum (*June 17*). Defers his decision to move the embassy in Israel and appoints Stanfield to explore it further (*June 23*). Attends the G7 Summit in Tokyo, Japan (*June 28-29*). About 300 Indigenous leaders hold a news conference in London, England, calling on Canada to include First Nations in constitutional talks (*July 2*). His primary leadership competitor, Claude Wagner, dies of cancer in Montreal (*July 11*). Canada launches a program to match private efforts to adopt refugees from Vietnam, Cambodia and Laos (*July 18*); welcomes 60,000 refugees over the next 17 months. Attends the christening in Montreal of Mulroney's third child, Mark (*July*). Becomes the first sitting Prime Minister to visit Africa, stopping in Cameroon (*July*). Attends the Commonwealth Heads of Government meeting in Lusaka, Zambia (*August 1-7*). Visits Tanzania and Kenya (*August*). Gives Diefenbaker a larger office on Parliament Hill to replace the tiny one imposed on him by Pearson (*August 8*). Promises to eliminate 60,000 federal civil service jobs over three years (*August 15*). Attends Diefenbaker's state funeral in Ottawa (*August 19*). Delivers the eulogy at Diefenbaker's funeral in Saskatoon (*August 22*). Moves to 24 Sussex Drive (*August*). Accepts a Royal Commission recommendation to permit bilingual communication in Quebec air traffic control towers (*September*). His government announces that it is getting out of the lottery business, turning Loto Canada over to the provinces (*September 25*). Survives a non-confidence vote by nine votes (*October 15*). Abandons plans to move Canada's embassy in Israel (*October 29*). Threatens to use federal powers to make inexpensive Alberta oil accessible to eastern Canada (*October 30*). The Parti Québécois unveils its platform to negotiate 'sovereignty-association' with Canada if it wins a provincial referendum (*November 1*). His Freedom of Information Act receives second reading in the House (*November 1*); fails to be passed during his term. Agrees to let Canada's ambassador to Iran, Ken Taylor, hide five (later six) U.S. embassy staff who escaped being taken hostage during the Iranian revolution (*November 4*). Indicates he has no intention of quickly calling a federal-provincial conference to discuss the constitution. Survives a non-confidence vote by two votes (*November 5*). Hosts a Federal-Provincial Conference on energy in Ottawa; premiers agree to raise the oil price by $2 a barrel (*November 12*). John Crosbie (Finance) presents his first budget, calling for a $4 a barrel increase on oil and an 18-cent hike in the gasoline pump price in 1980 (*December 11*). Loses a non-confidence vote over the budget by six votes (*December 13*). 31st Parliament is dissolved (*December 14*).

1980: Expels three Soviet embassy employees for spying (*January 21*). Indicates Canada will boycott the Moscow Summer Olympics unless Russia pulls out of Afghanistan (*January 26*). Canadian diplomats help the six U.S. embassy staff escape Iran; Canada closes its embassy the same day (*January 28*). Thanked by U.S. President Carter for Canada's role in the Iran embassy escape plan (*January 31*). Meets with Ambassador Ken Taylor to thank him for overseeing the Iranian mission (*February 1*). His wife's arm is injured by a protester at a campaign rally in Etobicoke, Ont. (*February*). Canada's 32nd federal election: re-elected in Yellowhead defeating Switzer (Liberal) again; loses to the Liberals who form a majority government (*February 18*). Submits his resignation as Prime Minister (*February 21*). Releases the final report by Ambassador-at-Large Stanfield who recommends Canada strengthen its links with the Palestinian Liberation Organization (PLO) to help encourage peace in the Middle East (*February 29*). **Clark government ends** (*March 3*). Vacations in Hawaii (*March*). Moves back to Stornoway (*April*). His wife Maureen is called to the Ontario bar (*April*).

1981: Gets 66.4% support in a leadership review held in Ottawa (*February 28*). Leads the fight in the House against Trudeau's constitutional initiative (*Fall*).

1982: His father Charles dies of a heart attack (*May 10*). École Joe Clark School opens in High River. His wife Maureen publishes a coffee table book *Residences: Homes of Canada's Leaders* (*September*). Receives an endorsement from Mulroney prior to another leadership review (*December 6*).

1983: Gets 66.9% delegate support in the leadership review held in Winnipeg, less than 1% more than the previous review; decides to call for a leadership convention (*January 28*). Resigns as Leader of the Opposition (*February 1*); replaced on an interim basis by MP Erik Nielsen. Resigns as party leader but indicates intention of trying to retain the leadership (*February 19*); interim leader is Nielsen. Loses the leadership race to Brian Mulroney 1,584 to 1,325 on the fourth ballot (*June 11*). Travels in Europe (*June-August*). Moves to John Street in Ottawa (*September*). His home's furnace explodes, covering furniture with soot (*October*). Receives the Alberta Order of Excellence.

1984: Buys a house in Aylmer, Que. (*March*). Sells the John Street house (*April*). Visits China (*May*). Canada's 33rd federal election: re-elected in Yellowhead defeating Rick Hardy; Mulroney's Conservatives win a majority (*September 4*). Moves into his Aylmer home (*September*). Becomes External Affairs minister (*September 17*). Attends the funeral for assassinated Indian Prime Minister Indira Gandhi in New Delhi (*November 3*). Becomes the first senior official from the West to visit famine-plagued Ethiopia (*November 5*). Receives an honorary degree from the University of Calgary.

1985: Becomes acting National Defence minister after the forced resignation of Robert Coates (*February 13*); two weeks later, Erik Nielsen (Deputy Prime Minister & Privy Council President) assumes the defence portfolio. Receives an honorary Doctor of Laws degree from the University of Alberta.

1986: Holds meetings with various provincial premiers to get their buy-in on U.S. free trade talks (*May*). Seals an arms deal with Saudi Arabia's King Fahd in Riyadh.

1987: Holds bilateral talks with U.S. Secretary of State George Schultz in Ottawa, while Mulroney and Reagan meet (*April 5-6*). His wife Maureen publishes a children's book *Parliament: Canada's Democracy and How It Works* (*December 27*).

1988: Canada's 34th federal election: re-elected in Yellowhead defeating Reform leader Preston Manning; Maureen is defeated in Carleton-Gloucester; the Mulroney government is re-elected (*November 21*). Becomes acting Justice minister replacing Ray Hnatyshyn who was defeated in the election (*December 8*). Maureen is appointed to the Royal Commission on new reproductive technologies (*December*).

1989: Has an audience with Pope John Paul II at the Vatican (*January 2*). Attends a foreign ministers' conference in Paris on chemical warfare (*January*). Steps down as acting Justice minister (*January 29*). Plays a major role in crafting an agreement at the NATO Summit in Brussels to reduce small nuclear arms production (*May 29-30*). Visits the Soviet Union, East Germany, Poland and Hungary shortly before the Soviet collapse in eastern Europe (*Spring*). Chairs the foreign ministers committee at the Commonwealth Heads of Government conference in Kuala Lumpur, Malaysia, where a unified position opposing apartheid in South Africa is crafted (*October 18-24*). Signs documents in Washington to make Canada the 33rd member of the Organization of American States (*November 13*).

1990: Hosts the first joint meeting of NATO and Warsaw Pact foreign ministers in Ottawa (*February 11-13*); discussion centres on the proposed reunification of Germany.

1991: Moves from External Affairs to Privy Council President in a cabinet shuffle, becoming responsible for Constitutional Affairs. (*April 21*). Agrees to a process that will permit Indigenous groups to play a more prominent role in constitutional reform (*July 5*). Attends the Commonwealth Heads of Government meeting at Victoria Falls, Zimbabwe (*October 16-21*). Receives the first Vimy Award from the Conference of Defence Associations Institute (*November*). Recalls the committee travelling cross-country to promote the government's constitutional proposals following charges of mismanagement (*November 7*). Maureen is fired from the Royal Commission on new reproductive technologies based on differences with the commission's chair (*December 16*).

1992: Convenes a series of constitutional conferences to discuss the government's proposals, in Halifax, Calgary, Montreal, Toronto, Vancouver and Ottawa (*January-*

March). Meets with provincial premiers on cross-country consultations for a new constitutional accord (*Winter*). Gets provincial premiers (minus Quebec's) to agree to try for a constitutional deal before June (*March 12*). Agrees with nine English Canada premiers to push for a triple-E Senate that would be elected, effective and equitable (*July 7*). His cabinet colleagues reject the deal reached with provincial premiers (*July 15*). Attends the signing of the Charlottetown Accord in P.E.I. (*August 28*). Receives the 125th Anniversary of the Confederation of Canada Medal. The Charlottetown Accord is defeated in a national referendum (*October 26*).

1993: Plans to retire from politics (*February 20*). Visits India, then China to restore relations after the Tiananmen Square protests and clamp-down (*Winter*). Maureen becomes the first graduate of the Health Law Institute's master's program at Dalhousie (*May*). Endorses Jean Charest for the leadership that is subsequently won by Kim Campbell (*June 7*). Resigns as Privy Council President and Constitutional Affairs minister (*June 25*). Appointed as the UN special representative to Cyprus to determine if the conflict between Greek and Turkish Cypriots might be resolved (*Summer*). His term as an MP ends (*September 8*). Becomes a visiting scholar in the University of California's Canadian Studies department in Berkeley (*Fall*). Maureen receives the Canadian Bar Association's St. Laurent award for her role in bringing eastern European lawyers to Canada to experience western law.

1994: Creates Joe Clark & Associates (*January 1*); works in partnership with Milner Fenerty law firm and Ernst & Young accounting. Leads talks in Nicosia between the Greek and Turkish Cypriot governments to resolve the political conflict (*February*); negotiations collapse two months later. His book *A Nation Too Good To Lose* is published. Moves from California to a condo in Calgary (*August*). Becomes a Companion of the Order of Canada (*October 19*). Receives an honorary Doctor of Laws degree from Concordia University (*November*).

1996: His term ends as UN special envoy to Cyprus. Stays in Pornic, France, while his daughter studies art in Paris (*Summer*).

1997: Participates in a meeting of current and former western hemisphere leaders at the Carter Center in Atlanta, Georgia (*April 28-29*); reconnects with Trudeau. Buys a house in Ottawa and opens an office in the capital (*May*). His mother Grace dies in Calgary (*August*).

1998: Charest resigns as Conservative leader to become Quebec Liberal party leader (*April 2*). Announces he will run for the leadership again (*June 25*). Wins 48% of the vote on the first ballot over Hugh Segal, David Orchard, Brian Pallister and Michael Fortier (*October 24*); all but Orchard endorse him, necessitating a second ballot. Elected leader of the Progressive Conservative party for the second time, defeating Orchard with 77% of the vote (*November 14*).

1999: Meets with Reform leader Preston Manning who encourages him to merge their two parties; he is not interested (*May*). Meets with Manning for public merger negotiations in Calgary (*September 12*). The Reform party narrowly approves the United Alternative initiative to merge with the Conservatives (*September 13*). His wife Maureen publishes *Tough Choices: Living and Dying in the 21st Century* (*November 1*).

2000: Tells a parliamentary committee that the Clarity Act will actually tie the hands of future politicians trying to negotiate separatism with Quebec (*February 23*). Challenges the winner of the Canadian Alliance leadership race to run against him in a Calgary riding (*May 8*). Announces his intention to seek election in Kings-Hants, N.S., after MP Scott Brison steps down to free up the seat for a by-election (*July 25*). Rents a house in Wolfville, N.S. (*Summer*). Wins the Kings-Hants by-election, returning to the House of Commons

(*September 11*); Canadian Alliance leader Stockwell Day wins on the west coast. Introduced at his first major campaign event by former prime minister Mulroney (*October 24*). Performs well in the leaders debate (*November 9*). Canada's 37th federal election: elected in Calgary Centre defeating incumbent Eric Lowther (Alliance) (*November 27*).

2001: Calls on Chrétien to step down as Prime Minister while the Shawinigate scandal is investigated (*March 23*). Joins Chrétien and other party leaders on a visit to Ground Zero in New York City after the 9/11 attacks (*September 29*).

2002: Downsizes in Ottawa, selling his house for a townhouse. Announces the failure of his party to unite with the Canadian Alliance following a meeting with Stephen Harper (*April 9*). His daughter Catherine marries Chad Schella in Ottawa (*June 8*). Announces his intention to resign as Progressive Conservative leader (*August 6*). Receives the Queen Elizabeth II Golden Jubilee Medal.

2003: Steps down as Conservative leader and is replaced by newly elected leader Peter MacKay (*May 31*). Becomes Conservative critic for government operations and estimates (*September 10*). His wife Maureen publishes her memoirs *In My Own Name* (*October 14*). Indicates he will not join the caucus of the newly merged Canadian Alliance and Progressive Conservative parties (*December 8*); sits as an Independent Progressive Conservative MP.

2004: Suggests Canadians vote for Martin's Liberals instead of Harper's Conservatives in the election (*April 26*). Steps down as MP for Calgary Centre (*May 23*). Becomes a distinguished statesman-in-residence at American University's School of International Service in Washington (*September 1*). Becomes a public policy scholar at the Woodrow Wilson International Center for Scholars for two months in Washington (*October 1*). Serves as an election observer in Cameroon (*October 11*).

2005: Teaches at American University's Center for North American Studies in Washington (*Spring*). Becomes a member of the Global Leadership Foundation, eventually serving as vice-chair of the board. Becomes a director on the board of Triton Logging. Receives the Alberta Centennial Medal. Joins Campbell, Turner and Mulroney to judge contestants for a CTV television show *The Next Great Prime Minister* (*Fall*).

2006: His company, Clark Sustainable Resource Development, negotiates a project to harvest underwater hardwood forests in Ghana (*February*). Sells the joe.ca web domain name to Loblaw for its Joe Fresh clothing line. His first grandchild Alexandra Schella is born (*May 26*). Becomes a professor of practice for public-private sector partnerships at McGill University's Institute for the Study of International Development, in Montreal (*October*). Joins Campbell, Mulroney and Martin to be judge again on *The Next Great Prime Minister,* moved to CBC (*Fall*).

2007: Assaulted by a pedestrian in Montreal who gives him a bloody nose (*November*).

2008: Attends the unveiling of his portrait on Parliament Hill, painted by Patrick Douglas Cox (*May 27*). Becomes a founding partner of Stratus Royalty Corporation.

2009: Receives an honorary Doctor of Laws degree from York University (*Spring*).

2010: Receives an honorary Doctor of Laws degree from Carleton University.

2012: Receives the Queen Elizabeth II Diamond Jubilee Medal. Receives an honorary degree from the University of British Columbia (*May 24*). Attends the Truth and Reconciliation Commission hearings on residential schools in Saskatoon as an honorary witness (*June 23*). Becomes a member of the supervisory board of Meridiam Infrastructure, later serving as chair. Meets with Theresa Spence, the Attawapiskat chief on a hunger strike in Ottawa to bring attention to resolving Indigenous issues (*December 29*).

2013: Flooding in High River, Alta., badly damages his childhood home (*June 20*). His book, *How We Lead: Canada in a Century of Change*, is published (*November 5*). Flies to South Africa from Ivory Coast to attend Nelson Mandela's funeral (*December*).

2014: For his 75th birthday, his family commissions a work by composer John Estacio for the musical production *I Lost My Talk* (*June 5*). Becomes the first former prime minister to register as a lobbyist under the government's six-year-old lobbying rules; represents Meridiam Infrastructure, a firm that hopes to build a Quebec bridge (*July*). Launches Canadians For A New Partnership with former prime minister Martin to foster relations with Indigenous peoples (*September 4*).

2015: Issues a letter with Turner, Chrétien and Martin calling for stricter oversight of CSIS in anti-terrorism legislation tabled by the government (*February 19*). Receives an honorary Doctor of Laws degree from McGill University (*June 3*).

2016: Receives the DreamKEEPERS Life Achievement Award for making Ottawa more inclusive and tolerant (*January 18*). Honoured in Atlanta by the Centre for International Governance and Innovation for his contributions in the field (*March 18*).

2017: Attends the 150th anniversary of Parliament's first session in Ottawa (*November 6*).

Books about Clark

- **1978**: David L. Humphreys; *Joe Clark: A Portrait* (Deneau & Greenberg)
- **1978**: Michael Nolan; *Joe Clark: The Emerging Leader* (Fitzhenry & Whiteside)
- **1980**: Warner Troyer; *200 Days: Joe Clark in Power* (Personal Library)
- **1984**: Jeffrey Simpson; *Discipline of Power: The Conservative Interlude and the Liberal Restoration* (Macmillan)
- **2013**: Joe Clark; *How We Lead: Canada in a Century of Change* (Random House)

17

John Turner

The Uncomfortable Prime Minister

Having waited more than a decade for the Liberal crown, John Turner was unable to wear it long enough to make an impact. A dashing politician and effective cabinet minister in his early political years, he returned to the fray after eight years as a lawyer, but without his earlier instincts. Turner easily assumed the Liberal leadership, but the electorate was disenchanted with the Trudeau years and took his coveted prize away after two and a half months. Defeated by the Conservatives, he stayed on as party leader and reclaimed some of his lost lustre.

TURNER THE POLITICIAN

Prime Minister of Canada: June 30, 1984 – September 17, 1984
Length of term: 2 months, 18 days
Parliament as Prime Minister: 32nd
Age on entering office: 55
Political party: Liberal
Leader of party: June 16, 1984 – June 22, 1990
Member of Parliament: June 18, 1962 – February 12, 1976; September 4, 1984 – October 25, 1993
Ridings represented: St. Laurent-St. Georges [Que.] 1962-1968; Ottawa/Carleton [Ont.] 1968-1976; Quadra [B.C.] 1984-1993
Cabinet portfolios: Minister Without Portfolio (1965-1967); Registrar General (1967); Consumer & Corporate Affairs (1967-1968); Solicitor General (1968); Justice (1968-1972); Finance (1972-1975)
Other political post: Leader of the Opposition (1984-1990)
Titles: Canadian Privy Councillor (1965); Queen's Counsel (1968); Companion of the Order of Canada (1994)
Quotes: "I'm not bidding now for your consideration at some vague convention in 1984 when I've mellowed a bit." (1968 leadership campaign speech; he ultimately won the leadership in 1984); "We built a country east and west and north ...With signature of a pen, you've reversed that, thrown us into the north-south influence of the United States ..."

(speaking in 1988 against the free trade agreement)

Turner the Man

Name: John Napier Wyndham Turner
Born: June 7, 1929, Richmond (now Richmond upon Thames), Surrey, England
Ancestry: English
Religion: Roman Catholic
Arrival in Canada: 1932
Education: B.A.Hon. [Honours Bachelor of Arts] (University of British Columbia, 1949); B.A. [Bachelor of Arts] (Oxford University, 1951); B.C.L. [Bachelor of Civil Law] (Oxford, 1952); M.A. [Master of Arts] (Oxford, 1957)
Nickname: Chick (at UBC)
Military service: none
Occupation: lawyer
Occupation after term: Leader of the Opposition; lawyer
Publications: *Politics of Purpose* (1968)
Appearance: "… he was still photogenic: tall and well built, with silver hair and patrician looks." (Paul Litt in *Elusive Destiny*); "He's Mackenzie King in a mod suit." (Tim Creery in the *Edmonton Journal*)
Personality: "His personality is a methodically achieved balance between his obsessive fears of failing or making a mistake and his heroic conceits about his ability to influence people and get things done." (Ron Graham in *Saturday Night*, 1984); "He is gregarious and affable, a man who oozes charm with every well-scrubbed pore." (Richard Gwyn in *The Northern Magus*)
Married: Geills McCrae Kilgour, May 11, 1963, St. Ignatius Church, Winnipeg, Manitoba
Age at marriage: 33

Turner was the:
- Prime Minister who served the second shortest term
- Prime Minister who met the most other Prime Ministers (about a dozen, possible tie with Diefenbaker)
- Only Prime Minister to serve ridings in three provinces
- First Prime Minister who didn't live in the official residence since 1951
- Second Prime Minister who wasn't in Parliament
- Second Prime Minister born in England
- Third Prime Minister to serve as Finance minister
- Sixth Roman Catholic Prime Minister
- Seventh Liberal Prime Minister
- Eleventh Prime Minister who was a lawyer
- First Finance minister to have his budget defeated in the House (1974)

Turner's legacy
- Reduced the size of cabinet, streamlining its operation
- Created the Department of Consumer & Corporate Affairs, the first of its kind in the Western world (as Minister of Consumer & Corporate Affairs)

- Established the federal court of Canada (as Minister of Justice)
- Removed party patronage from judicial appointment process (Justice)
- Rebuilt the Liberal party after its 1984 defeat

TURNER'S FAMILY

Turner's Parents

Father: Leonard Hugh Turner
Born: 1904, England
Occupation: journalist; gunsmith
Died: November 18, 1932, London, England
Age at death: 28

Mother: Phyllis Marie Gregory
Born: 1904, Rossland, British Columbia
Occupation: federal civil servant
Married: 1928
Second husband: Frank Mackenzie Ross (1945)
Died: April 18, 1988, Saltspring Island, British Columbia
Age at death: 85

Turner's Brothers & Sisters (2 siblings; John the oldest)

Brother: Michael Turner (1930-died shortly after birth)
Sister: Brenda Turner (b.1931)
  Married: John Norris

Turner's Wife

Name: Geills McCrae Kilgour
Born: December 23, 1937, Winnipeg, Manitoba
Father: David Kilgour (President of Great West Life Assurance)
Mother: Maria Sophia Russell
Occupation: systems engineer
Age at marriage: 25
Younger than Turner: 8 years
Note: First name pronounced Jill.
Note: Great-niece of John McCrae, author of *In Flanders Fields*.

Turner's Children (4)

Name: Elizabeth Turner
Born: March 8, 1964, Ottawa, Ontario

Name: Michael Turner
Born: October 28, 1965
Occupation: lawyer

Name: David James Turner
Born: May 14, 1968
Occupation: risk consultant

Name: Andrew Turner
Born: October 7, 1971
Children: Andrew, David

POLITICAL STORIES

From hunter to hunted

From the time he lost his leadership bid to Trudeau in 1968, the youthful Turner was seen by many as the obvious heir. He had served in Trudeau's cabinet for seven years before differences with the leader finally prompted Turner's exit from politics.

Working as a Toronto lawyer for the following decade didn't dampen speculation that Turner would be back. It's something he neither envisioned nor wanted, but the media and his close supporters (including the somewhat mythical 195 Club representing the number of delegates backing him on the final leadership ballot in 1968) wouldn't let it go. Every hiccup on the Ottawa political landscape spawned new rumours that this was Turner's moment. The result was a contrived friction that Turner was nipping at Trudeau's heels to take over.

Inevitably, when Trudeau resigned in 1984, Turner was talked into coming back to grab the prize. To do it, he had to beat Chrétien at the leadership convention. Accomplishing that, he (and everyone else) discovered he'd been away a long time and no longer had the drive and intuition to be a leader.

Chrétien was now the hunter and Turner was in his crosshairs. Like Turner, Chrétien left politics and returned to law, until coming back in 1990 to become leader. By then, Chrétien was being stalked by his own nipping dog, Paul Martin.

Campaigning instead of leading

Only Tupper spent less time as Prime Minister. And, like Tupper, Turner used most of his time fighting an election campaign. It had been Turner's choice to call an election, which he did nine days after taking office.

Initially, he would have preferred to wait until the fall and avoid a summer election. But the indicators were suggesting an economic downturn in the next few months, while the polls were showing an uptick for the Liberals after the leadership change. It was time to act fast.

Turner jetted to England to ask Elizabeth II to postpone her Canadian visit because he hoped to dissolve Parliament for an election. She was fine with that and he returned to Ottawa the next day.

And so, Turner spent 57 of his 79 days in power on the campaign trail. It was a journey plagued by the Trudeau patronage appointments, his tendency to pat bums and slap shoulders on the hustings, and other gaffs eagerly recorded by the media. He ended up losing 95 Liberal seats to the Mulroney steamroller.

"I Had No Option"

It is probably the most notable moment in Canada's many televised leaders' debates. Conservative leader Brian Mulroney attacked Turner, the new Prime Minister, for making a large number of patronage appointments that spring. Turner responded that he'd already told everyone "I had no option."

"You had an option, sir," retorted Mulroney, pouncing on the excuse. "You could have said, 'I'm not going to do it'." Turner's feeble comeback was to merely repeat "I had no option." Mulroney had the last word on the exchange: "You could have done better." It helped seal Turner's fate in the approaching 1984 election.

In many ways, Turner had no option. His predecessor, Trudeau, had warned the candidates seeking to replace him that he planned a series of appointments, offering them the chance to do it themselves if they preferred. None of them jumped at the suggestion.

Once Trudeau uncharacteristically rolled out his several hundred appoint-ments, there was a genuine reason for Turner to wait and do it himself. The list included six Liberal MPs whose disappearance from the House would chip away at the Liberal majority he would need to form his government.

Trudeau was prepared to accept the rationale, as long as Turner would assure him in writing that the appointments would be made. It was done. The irony is that the scenario Turner desperately tried to avoid never happened. He almost immediately called an election, making the need for a majority unnecessary.

Combating free trade

As Leader of the Opposition, Turner needed an issue that would resonate with Canadians. He found his answer in Mulroney's proposed free trade agreement with the U.S. Having already warned Canadians that the deal would be a lopsided arrangement, given America's much larger size, he now pointed out it would also mean snubbing Canada's other trade partners.

Emphasizing the legal details that made it a bad deal wasn't working for the opposition leader. But when an election was called for the fall of 1988, he switched to a more emotional appeal, warning of the dangers to "selling out" Canada. Even as he was fending off Liberal schemes urging him to resign before the vote, Turner kept hammering the message. "I will not let this great nation surrender its birthright."

The emotional appeal to protectionism had worked for Macdonald and Borden in their campaigns to stop free trade (then referred to as reciprocity). It worked for Turner, too, boosting his ratings in the polls. Although it raised the Liberals' fortunes in the final vote, the free-trade wedge wasn't enough to return him to power.

PERSONAL STORIES

Olympic class sprinter

He was very fast on his feet. From the age eight, when he won all four track and field sprint events at Ottawa's Normal Model School, Turner consistently outpaced the school's competition in the 100-yard and 220-yard dashes (later replaced by the 100-metre and 200-metre sprints).

As a member of the University of British Columbia's track team, he won both events at the Dominion Track and Field Championships in Edmonton in 1947. That same year he ran the 100 in 9.7 seconds, only 3/10ths of a second behind the world record set by America's Jesse Owens in 1933.

Turner had already begun training for a spot on Canada's squad at the 1948 London Summer Olympic Games when his car was hit by a train at a crossing in Vancouver. His left knee was smashed and, by the time it was repaired, his leg muscles had deteriorated. Nevertheless, he attempted the Olympic trials, collapsing on the track during the painful effort.

It didn't end his running career – he set a record at the university competition in the U.S. the following years, but his dream of winning an Olympic medal was finished. As a student at Oxford, he was a close friend of Roger Bannister who became the first person to run a mile in under four minutes. Turner had been invited to witness the feat, but was not able to make the trip from Canada back to England.

Turner and Princess Margaret

The call from Turner's mother was a plea. Could he please fly out to British Columbia and help the family entertain their houseguest, Princess Margaret. He turned her down – too much work piling up at his law firm in Montreal. However, he relented after calls from his sister and step-father.

He and Margaret met over dinner at the Ross's home, but it was a ball on the HMCS Discovery the next night that seized the British tabloid press's attention. The Princess didn't want to dance with anyone but Turner. He ended up joining her for the next leg of her 1958 British Columbia Royal tour and then showed up again as her dance partner at Rideau Hall in Ottawa a few days later.

The gossip columnists loved it. The following summer, Turner was invited to spend a few days with the Royal family at Balmoral Castle in Scotland (he shared a room with Margaret's future husband, Antony Armstrong-Jones). In 1960, he was the only Canadian outside government invited to her wedding.

In a letter Margaret wrote to a friend several years later, she described Turner as the man "I nearly married."

Geills Turner

When Turner asked computer whiz Geills McCrae Kilgour to work on his first election campaign in St. Lawrence-St. George in Montreal, he not only acquired an adept data progammer, he ended up with a partner for life.

Geills (a Gaelic name pronounced Jill) was the daughter of David Kilgour who eventually became president of Great-West Life Assurance in Winnipeg. Like Turner, Geills was a gifted athlete, having won a provincial gymnastics competition. Her mastery of mathematics took her through studies at Manitoba, McGill and Harvard before starting work with IBM in New York City.

Back in Montreal, she met Turner and developed a computer tracking system that analyzed individual poll results from the previous election; the first time high-tech scientific polling was used extensively in Canada. Turner was elected and by the end of the year they were engaged.

Geills zealously guarded her privacy and that of their four children. When Turner resigned as Finance minister and the family moved to Toronto, she finally felt she had time to indulge herself. It took the form of a four-year photography program at Ryerson, although she never worked actively in the field.

A woman who spoke her mind, Geills had little time to put it on display before Turner's two and a half months as Prime Minister were finished because of the election and they returned to Stornoway.

TURNER'S TIMELINE

1929: Born in the London suburb of Richmond, England (*June 7*).

1930: His brother Michael is born in Richmond, but dies shortly after. A sister, Brenda, is born the following year.

1932: His father Leonard dies of pneumonia following a thyroid operation (*November 18*).

1933: His family sails for Canada; moves to Rossland, B.C., his mother's home-town. Family moves to Ottawa where Phyllis gets a civil service job as an economist for the Tariff Board (*Fall*). Moves to a downtown Sparks Street apartment. Attends Normal Model School in Ottawa.

1934: His family moves to a duplex at 134 Daly Avenue in the Sandy Hill neighbourhood (*Winter*). Regularly attends St. Joseph's Roman Catholic Church, often followed by a swim and buffet at the Chateau Laurier.

1935: His mother Phyllis dates Prime Minister Bennett who may have proposed to her. His sister, Brenda contracts polio, but recovers. Takes piano lessons with neighbourhood friend Barbara Ann Scott, the future Olympic figure skater.

1936: Family moves up the street to 232 Daly. Attends Camp Temagami in northern Ontario for the first of 17 years (*Summer*).

1937: Occasionally chats with Prime Minister King while they are walking their dogs in Sandy Hill. His mother rents a cottage in Wakefield, Que., next door to the Pearson cottage (*Summer*).

1938: Family moves further up Daly Street to a detached house at 434. Wins all four sprints at his school's track and field event (*May*). Skips Grade 4 and begins Grade 5 (*September*). Occasionally invited by Lord Tweedsmuir to children's parties at Rideau Hall.

1939: His mother Phyllis becomes chief research economist at the Tariff Board. Wins his school's all-round athlete trophy after coming first in four events (*Spring*). Attends Ashbury College private school in Rockcliffe Park (*September*).

1940: His mother Phyllis is seconded to the Wartime Prices and Trade Board as oils and fats administrator.

1941: Runs the 100-yard dash in 11 seconds; wins the all-round athlete trophy again (*Spring*). Meets Winston Churchill outside Parliament after his famous "Some chicken ... Some neck" speech (*December 30*).

1942: Attends St. Patrick's College in Ottawa (*September*). Skips a grade for the second time, vaulting from Grade 8 to 10, making him two years younger than his classmates (*September*).

1943: Becomes editor of the high school newspaper, the *Patrician*, and joins the football and hockey teams.

1944: Becomes a counsellor at Camp Temagami (*Summer*).

Regular encounters with newsmakers

Turner's life seemed to move through charmed circles that brought him into contact with personalities who were celebrities or would be eventually. As a six-year-old boy in Ottawa, he often saw Prime Minister Bennett who was dating his mother. A few years later, he would stop and chat with Prime Minister King while both were walking their dogs. He also met or knew skater Barbara Ann Scott, Governor General Lord Tweedsmuir, Britain's Winston Churchill, Vancouver neighbours artist Lawren Harris and business tycoon Garfield Weston, sprinter Roger Bannister, Guinness Record Book creators the McWhirter brothers, and Australian Prime Ministers Malcolm Fraser and Bob Hawke.

1945: His mother Phyllis marries B.C. industrialist Frank Mackenzie Ross (*April*). Wins the Governor General's Award based on votes at his school's track and field events (*May*). Family moves to Belmont Avenue in Vancouver's West Point Grey area where neighbours include businessman Garfield Weston and artist Lawren Harris (*Summer*). First summer visit to the Ross farm in New Brunswick (*Summer*). Enrols in arts and science at the University of British Columbia, with an emphasis on the latter (*September*). Joins the Beta Theta Pi fraternity (*Fall*).

1946: Majors in political science (*September*). Becomes a sports columnist for the university student paper, *The Ubyssey*, writing as Chick Turner (*Fall*).

1947: Joins the university track team (*Spring*). Wins the 100- and 220-yard dash at the Dominion Track and Field Championships in Edmonton (*June*). Works at one of his step-father's plants (*Summer*). Helps rescue his step-father from an auto accident over a Fraser Canyon cliff (*Summer*). Wins his first election as coordinator of activities for the Student Council (*Fall*). Runs the 100-yard in 9.7 seconds (*Fall*).

1948: Injures his knee in a car accident in Vancouver (*February*) Attempts to run at the Canada trials for the Olympic Games, but collapses on the track (*June*).

1949: Ties a meet record for the 100-yard dash at an inter-university event. Writes his undergraduate thesis on the Senate 1924-49 (*Spring*). Graduates from UBC with an Honours BA in political science (*June 21*). Wins B.C.'s Rhodes Scholarship, earning an education at Oxford University in England. Enters Magdalen College at Oxford (*September*).

1950: At his 21st birthday party, he and friends jump from Oscar Wilde's room into the Char River in formal attire and swim to the women's college (*June 7*).

1951: Receives his BA in Jurisprudence from Oxford (*Spring*).

1952: Receives his Bachelor of Civil Law degree (*April 19*). Attends the Olympic Games in Helsinki to watch friends compete (*July*). Studies for the bar exam in London (*Fall*).

1953: Moves to Paris to study for a doctorate in private international law and learn French at the University of Paris (*Spring*). Takes his sister Brenda on a tour of France (*Summer*). Called to the bar at Gray's Inn in London (*August*). Returns to Canada to study for his Canadian bar exams in Vancouver (*Fall*). Moves to Montreal and hired as a student lawyer by the Stikeman Elliott law firm. Rents an apartment on Mountain Street.

1954: His friend Roger Bannister runs the four-minute mile; Turner regrets he didn't accept the invitation to return to see it happen (*May 6*). Succeeds in having a private bill passed by Quebec to recognize his British law admittance so he won't have to take three years of Civil Code; bill introduced by Daniel Johnson with whom he celebrates over a drink, along with Premier Maurice Duplessis. Seriously considers abandoning law for the priesthood; instead becomes a warden of St. Patrick's church and does the legal work for Archbishop Paul-Émile Cardinal Léger. Rents an apartment at 1536 Summerhill Avenue.

1955: Occasionally asked by Duplessis to join him for Montreal Canadiens hockey games. Begins organizing train trips for party weekends at the Ross property in New Brunswick with his friends. His step-father Frank Ross is appointed Lieutenant Governor of British Columbia (*October 3*).

1956: Becomes president of the junior committee of the Montreal Symphony. Rents a penthouse at 1520 McGregor Avenue. Begins his association with Harterre House for mentally and emotionally challenged children, eventually becoming president.

1957: Asked by C.D. Howe (Trade & Commerce) to help run New Brunswick MP Wes Stuart's re-election campaign; he does and Stuart wins (*June 10*). Receives his Master's degree from Oxford. Works on Jean Drapeau's unsuccessful campaign for re-election as Montreal's mayor (*Fall*).

1958: Becomes a trustee of the fund established to provide financial support for Pearson, the Liberal leader. Reluctantly visits his parents in Victoria to entertain Princess Margaret; dances with her at a ball (*July 25*) and at a second ball at Rideau Hall in Ottawa (*August 2*); speculation increases about a romance.

1959: Guest of Princess Margaret at Balmoral Castle in Scotland, renewing gossip about a romance (*August*). Lectures in law at Sir George Williams University in Montreal.

1960: Becomes president of the Montreal Junior Bar. Becomes director of the Legal Aid Bureau for three years. The only private Canadian citizen to attend the wedding of Princess Margaret to Armstrong-Jones in London (*May 6*). Attends the Liberal Study Conference on National Problems, at Queen's University in Kingston (*September 6-10*).

1961: Helps organize C.D. Howe's funeral in Montreal (*January*). Contributes a chapter about *The Senate of Canada: Political Conundrum*, based on his thesis, for the book *Canadian Issues* (*Spring*). Excerpts from his Senate chapter appear in the *Ottawa Journal* (*April 24-25*), which he sends to friends and others, including Trudeau. His mother Phyllis becomes chancellor of the University of British Columbia, the first woman chancellor in the Commonwealth. Dined by Paul Martin Sr., the first of a series of Liberals trying to entice him to enter politics (*Fall*).

1962: Wins the Liberal nomination in St. Lawrence-St. George, Que., riding (*May 1*). One of his campaign workers, Geills Kilgour, uses a computer to track and analyse voter patterns, possibly for the first time in a Canadian election (*May-June*). Canada's 25th federal election: wins in St. Lawrence-St. George defeating the incumbent Egan Chambers (Conservative) (*June 18*).

1963: Canada's 26th federal election: re-elected in St. Lawrence-St. George where he doubles his plurality over Chambers (*April 8*). His celebration photo in the Montreal Gazette includes his fiancée, Kilgour (*April 9*). Marries Geills Kilgour in Winnipeg (*May 11*). Appointed parliamentary secretary to Arthur Laing (Northern Affairs & Natural Resources) (*May 14*). Has a five-day honeymoon in Bermuda (*May*). Moves into an apartment overlooking Ottawa's Rideau River (*Summer*). Spends time at the Kilgour family cottage on Lake of the Woods in northwestern Ontario (*Summer*). Visits Canada's North with Liang (*Summer*). Buys a house in Rockcliffe Park (*Fall*). Chairs a caucus subcommittee on the role of MPs and holds meetings in ridings calling for an overhaul of the House of Commons; some of his brash recommendations are adopted (*Fall*). Vacations in Tobago and coincidently stays at the same hotel as Diefenbaker (*December-January*); a friendship develops.

1964: His first child, Elizabeth, is born in Ottawa (*March 8*). Successfully shepherds the revised Columbia River Treaty through a parliamentary committee (*Spring*); it is passed in the fall. Visits Canada's North again with Laing (*Summer*).

1965: Is given the second new Canadian flag raised on Parliament Hill (*February*). Visits U.S.S.R. with Laing (*Spring*); becomes the first Western delegation to tour Siberia since the Russian Revolution. His son Michael is born (*October 28*). Canada's 27th federal election: re-elected in St. Lawrence-St. George defeating Alfred Warkentin (Conservative) (*November 8*). In a speech to the National Water Conference in Washington, tells the U.S. Chamber of Commerce that Canada will maintain control of its water resources (*December 9*). Appointed by Pearson as Minister Without Portfolio; the youngest member of cabinet (*December 18*). Vacations in Barbados and again is at the same hotel as Diefenbaker; saves him from struggling in the undertow (*December*).

Saving Diefenbaker's life?

Diefenbaker (Leader of the Opposition at the time) was vacationing at the same Barbados resort as Turner (Minister Without Portfolio) in 1965 where the two would sometimes spend time together on the beach in conversation. Noticing Diefenbaker struggling one day in the surf, Turner dashed out to pull him to shore. He was about to begin artificial respiration when a gasping Diefenbaker sat up and said "Thanks, John."

1966: Votes against a five-year ban on capital punishment (*April 5*). Identified as the man "I nearly married" in a personal letter from Princess Margaret to a friend (*May 16*). Represents Canada at the Commonwealth Parliamentary Association Conference held in Ottawa (*September 28-October 5*). Appointed acting Registrar General until Guy Favreau's (Privy Council) health improves (*October 1*).

1967: Becomes Registrar General (*April 4*); Trudeau and Chrétien enter cabinet the same day. Expo 67, in the south end of his riding, opens (*April 28*). Acts as a host to Elizabeth II at the Parliament Hill centennial celebrations and later welcomes teens to a party on the Rideau Hall grounds (*July 1*). Introduces legislation to create a Department of Consumer & Corporate Affairs (*October 13*). Pearson announces his retirement (*December 14*). Becomes minister of the new Consumer & Corporate Affairs Department (*December 21*).

1968: Announces intention to run for the Liberal leadership (*January 17*). Comes in third at the leadership convention in Ottawa behind Pierre Trudeau and Robert Winters after four ballots (*April 6*). Continues as Consumer & Corporate Affairs minister in Trudeau's cabinet (*April 20*). His son David is born (*May 14*). Becomes a Queen's Counsel. Receives an honorary Doctor of Laws degree from the University of New Brunswick. Canada's 28th federal election: wins in Ottawa-Carleton (his old riding was lost in redistribution) defeating Kenneth Binks (Conservative) (*June 25*). Appointed Justice minister by Trudeau (*July 6*). Called to the bar in Ontario. Visits the Northwest Territories (Mittimatalik) (*Summer*). Introduces the revised omnibus Bill C-150 to permit approved abortions, decriminalize homosexual activity, legalize government-run lotteries, toughen drunk driving penalties and tighten firearm restrictions (*December 19*).

1969: Visits with provincial premiers to build support for the Official Languages Act (*February*). Attends the Federal-Provincial Constitutional Conference in Ottawa where there is general acceptance of the official languages policy (*February 10-12*). Appoints Réjane Laberge-Colas to the Superior Court of the District of Montreal, the first woman to sit on a Canadian superior court (*February 22*). Bill C-150 passes in the House after a three-week filibuster by the Créditistes (*May 14*). Receives an honorary Doctor of Laws degree from York University. The Official Languages Act, which he helped develop, passes in the House (*July 7*). Called to the bar in British Columbia (*December*).

1970: Introduces a bill to create a Law Reform Commission of Canada (*February 16*). The Supreme Court of British Columbia rules against Bill C-150's unresolved sections on drunk driving (*April 6*). His anti-hate bill is passed in the House (*April 13*). The Supreme Court of Canada upholds the drunk driving legislation (*June 26*); wins a bet with Diefenbaker that this would be the outcome. Attends the Commonwealth Parliamentary Association Conference in Australia (*October*). Represents Canada at Fiji's independence ceremonies (*October 10*). Presents proposed legislation to cabinet dealing with the FLQ October Crisis, but cabinet opts for the more immediate solution of re-enacting the War Measures Act (*October 15*). Defends the use of the War Measures Act in the House (*October 16*). Announces his intention to replace the Tax Appeal Board with a Tax Review Board that is more accessible to the public (*October 30*). Introduces the Public Order (Temporary Measures) Act to replace the War Measures Act (*November 2*).

1971: Meets Pope Paul VI at the Vatican (*January*). Attends the Commonwealth Conference in Singapore (*January 14-22*). Abandons his attempt to deliver a speech to the Vancouver Institute following noisy demonstrations by protestors opposed to his role during the FLQ Crisis (*March 6*). The Public Order Act ends after he persuades cabinet not to replace it with more extraordinary powers legislation (*April 30*). Visits the provincial premiers to hammer out an amending formula for the constitution (*Spring*). His proposed Federal Court officially replaces Ottawa's Exchequer Court (*June 1*). Attends the Federal-Provincial Constitutional Conference in Victoria (*June 14-17*). His son Andrew is born (*October 7*). Accepts Trudeau's offer to take over as Finance minister in 1972 (*November 12*). Joined by Trudeau and his wife Margaret for a Christmas Eve service in Ottawa (*December 24*); Justin Trudeau is born the next day.

1972: Becomes Finance minister (*January 28*). Attends federal-provincial finance ministers conference in Banff with just three days briefing (*January 31*). Presents his first budget, addressing high unemployment and calling for a reduction in corporate taxes (*May 8*). Meets with new U.S. treasury secretary John Schultz in hopes of easing recent trade restrictions (*September 18*), the first of numerous visits. Canada's 29th federal election: re-elected in Ottawa-Carleton defeating Strome Galloway (Conservative) (*October 30*). Urges the Liberal government to resign, given the close vote (*November 1*). Visits Pearson for last time (*December*).

1973: Presents his second budget; borrows the Conservatives indexing of income tax to get their support (*February 19*). Attends the finance ministers conference in Paris to discuss the international currency crisis (*March*). His corporate tax cuts paired with taxpayer relief win approval in principle (*June 30*). Takes part in the Western Economic Opportunities Conference in Calgary (*July*). Attends the Commonwealth Heads of Government Conference in Ottawa and meets with Elizabeth II (*August 2-10*).

1974: Presents his third budget that maintains tax incentives for corporations and introduces the Registered Home Ownership Savings Plan (*May 6*). The NDP join the Conservatives to defeat the government on the country's first non-confidence vote based on a budget (*May 8*). Canada's 30th federal election: re-elected in Ottawa-Carleton defeating Bill Neville (Conservative) (*July 8*). Crosses the country to gauge interest in calling for voluntary wage and price controls (*August-September*). Becomes chairman of the interim committee on economic policy of the International Monetary Fund, charged with addressing the global energy crisis (*October*). Presents his fourth budget, calling for a deficit in order to fund increased purchasing power by Canadians (*November 18*).

1975: Vacations in Jamaica; he and Geills have dinner several times with Pierre and Margaret Trudeau. Expresses concern about the effect high wage settlements are having on economic recovery (*March 12*). His deputy minister, Simon Reisman retires in discontent over interference from the Prime Minister's Office (*March 31*). His proposal for voluntary wage and price controls is rejected by the Canadian Labour Congress (*April*). Visits Saudi Arabia, Iran, Kuwait and Algeria to persuade oil producers to spend some of their profits on third world development (*April*). Presents his fifth budget that struggles with high inflation but rejects mandatory wage and price controls (*June 23*). Writes a column in the *Ottawa Journal* defending Reisman. Resigns as Finance minister (*September 10*). Attends Diefenbaker's 80th birthday celebration in Saskatoon (*September 20*). Trudeau announces the implementation of wage and price controls (*October 13*). Vacations in Jamaica with U.S. Treasury Secretary William Simon and also dines with Henry Kissinger and finance ministers from Germany and Belgium (*December-January*).

1976: Joins McMillan, Binch law firm in Toronto (*January*). Moves to a home in Toronto's Forest Hill neighbourhood. Resigns as MP for Ottawa-Carleton (*February 12*). Elected to the boards of directors at Canadian Pacific, Sandoz Canada, MacMillan Bloedel, Credit Foncier and Marathon Realty. Honorary pallbearer at the funeral for Olive Diefenbaker in Ottawa (*December 24*).

1977: Expresses no interest in Trudeau's offer of the External Affairs cabinet portfolio (*June*). Begins co-writing a subscription newsletter on trends in business and government with his boss, Bill Macdonald.

1978: Criticizes Finance minister Chrétien in his newsletter (*March 31*), but apologizes to him five months later.

1979: Canoes the Burnside River in the Northwest Territories (Nunavut) (*Summer*). Joins the board of Bechtel. Trudeau announces his resignation as leader (*November 22*). Indicates he will not seek the leadership (*December 10*). The Clark government is defeated in Ottawa (*December 13*). Trudeau announces his decision to stay on as leader (*December 18*).

1980: Meets with Australian Prime Minister Malcolm Fraser in Canberra (*May*). Elected to the boards of Seagram's and Massey-Ferguson. Receives an honorary Doctor of Laws degree from Mount Allison University.

1981: Holds several parties for Princess Margaret during her visit to Toronto (*July*). Canoes the Coppermine River in the Northwest Territories with his family (*August*).

1982: Elected to the board of Holt Renfrew. Attends the Liberal policy convention in Ottawa, but avoids connecting with Trudeau (*November 6*).

1983: A campaign team begins to assess the possibility of his success in an expected Liberal leadership race (*Fall*).

1984: Trudeau again announces his resignation as leader (*February 29*). Vacationing in Jamaica, Turner decides to seek the leadership. Chrétien (Energy, Mines & Resources) launches his bid to be leader (*March 16*). Announces his intention to run for leader (*March 19*). Embarrassed by a *Globe & Mail* story that he quit as Finance minister because Trudeau wouldn't back his voluntary wage and price controls; apologizes to Trudeau for the remarks (*May 11*). Wins the Liberal leadership on the second ballot (*June 16*). Receives a long list of patronage appointment requests from Trudeau (*June 26*); agrees in writing to make the appointments once he is called on by the Governor General to form a government. **Turner's government 1984**. Becomes the 17th Prime Minister of Canada (*June 30*); gives up his corporate directorships. Takes part in the Canada Day celebrations on Parliament Hill (*July 1*). Flies to London to tell Elizabeth II he is planning to call an election (*July 7*); returns the following day. The patronage appointments requested by Trudeau are announced, including 17 Liberal MPs (*July 8*). A bum-patting incident with Liberal party president Iona Campagnola on the campaign trail later becomes a media story (*July 13*). Announces his intention to seek the Liberal nomination in Vancouver Quadra riding in B.C. (*July 16*). Participates in Canada's first televised French-language leaders' debate (*July 24*). Accused of not exercising the option to say no to the patronage appointments, during the English-language leaders' debate (*July 25*). The Supreme Court rules that Quebec's legislation restricting English language schooling violates the Charter of Rights and Freedoms (*July 26*). Canada's 33rd federal election: elected in Vancouver Quadra defeating incumbent Bill Clarke (Conservative); his government is defeated by Mulroney's Conservatives who win the largest majority in Canada's history (*September 4*). Meets Pope John Paul II in Quebec City at the beginning of a 12-day papal visit to Canada (*September 9*). **End of Turner's government** (*September 17*). Moves to Stornoway. Announces his shadow cabinet of 40, to match the size of Mulroney's cabinet (*October 11*).

1985: Liberal MPs Don Boudria, Sheila Copps, John Nunziata and Brian Tobin – dubbed The Rat Pack – begin to bait the government. Hosts an 80th birthday party for Jack Pickersgill at Chateau Laurier; guests include Trudeau and Martin (*June 20*). Speaks at a seniors rally protesting the government's plan to de-index pensions (*June 25*); the government backs down. Sails around Haida Gwaii (Queen Charlotte Islands) with Haida sculptor Bill Reid and others (*September*). Attends the launch of Chrétien's autobiography *Straight from the Heart* (*September*). Squelches discontent about his leadership at the party policy convention in Halifax (*November*).

1986: Chrétien resigns as an MP (*February 27*). Receives an honorary Doctor of Laws degree from his alma mater, University of British Columbia. Opens the new Liberal National Headquarters in Ottawa (*November 26*). Receives a 76% confidence vote after delegates at the Liberal convention in Ottawa vote against calling a leadership review (*November 30*).

1987: Asks Paul Martin to coordinate candidate recruitment for the next election (*March*). Crosses the floor of the House to shake Mulroney's hand for reaching the Meech Lake Accord with the premiers (*May 3*). Meech Lake Accord is publicly denounced by Trudeau (*May 27*). Defends Meech Lake at a Liberal thinkers conference in Cobourg, Ont. (*June 20*). Publicly told by Liberal party president Michel Robert that he needs to tighten up his leadership (*August 25*); 13 of 40 Liberal MPs call for his resignation. Told he needs to communicate more effectively and tighten caucus discipline, following an emergency meeting of Liberals (*August 30*). Calls for an end to cruise missile testing, reversing his stand (*October 2*). Describes the Mulroney government's free trade agreement with the U.S. as an "absolute fraud" (*October 5*).

1988: Vows to fight the just-signed Canada-U.S. Free Trade Agreement (*January 2*). Donald Johnston leaves caucus to sit as an independent Liberal because of clashing views about Meech Lake and free trade (*January 15*). Suffers spinal cord back pain for several months (*Winter*). Attends the funeral of his mother Phyllis in Vancouver (*April 20*). Overcomes a leadership challenge sparked by 22 Liberal caucus members (*April 27*). Plans to have Liberal Senators block the free trade deal until Canadians have a chance to vote on it (*July 20*). *Reign of Error*, an unflattering biography is published by Greg Weston (*September*). Unveils his daycare policy in Montreal, but conflicting cost numbers are given to the media (*October 5*). Subject of a CBC story that his campaign committee had urged him to resign (*October 19*). Performs much better in the French and English leaders' debates (*October 24-25*). Canada's 34th federal election: re-elected in Vancouver Quadra defeating Clarke again; Mulroney's Conservative government is re-elected (*November 21*).

1989: Undergoes back surgery (*January 10*); recuperates in Jamaica. Announces intention to resign as leader (*May 3*). Turns down an offer from Mulroney to become Canadian Ambassador to the Vatican (*June*).

1990: Resigns as Leader of the Opposition and is replaced by Herb Gray; continues as Liberal party leader (*February 6*). Joins the Toronto law firm of Miller Thomson (*March 1*). Gives his farewell speech at the Liberal leadership convention (*June 21*); resigns as party leader the next day. Chrétien wins the party leadership (*June 23*). Becomes chair of the Community Foundation of Toronto.

1991: Supports sending troops to take part in the Gulf War, in opposition to the Liberal stand (*January 16*); the Liberals subsequently support the action.

1992: Takes part in a task force to help promote passage of the Charlottetown Accord (*Fall*).

1993: Steps down as chair of the Community Foundation of Toronto. Does not seek re-election, ending his tenure as an MP (*October 25*).

1994: Appointed as a Companion of the Order of Canada (*June 1*).

1996: Receives an honorary Doctor of Laws degree from the University of Toronto.

1997: Becomes a director of Northland Power (*April 29*).

2001: Attends the unveiling of his portrait on Parliament Hill painted by Brenda Bury (*May 8*).

2002: Receives an honorary Doctor of Laws degree from Assumption University in Windsor.

2003: Is the keynote speaker at The Hidden Pierre Trudeau conference at the University of Waterloo where he talks about their common beliefs in Catholicism (*May*).

2004: Becomes a director of Q9 Networks. Inducted into the University of British Columbia Sports Hall of Fame. Leads the Canadian delegation to oversee the Ukraine elections (*December*).

2005: Joins Clark, Campbell and Mulroney to judge contestants for a CTV television show *The Next Great Prime Minister* (*Fall*).

2007: Joins Campbell, Martin and Newfoundland Premier Danny Williams to judge *The Next Great Prime Minister.*

2008: His 1968 book *Politics With Purpose* is republished by McGill-Queen's University Press (*October 24*).

2009: Supports the movement to turn Kingston's Montreal Street train station into a John A. Macdonald museum (*July 14*).

2011: His biography *Elusive Destiny* is published by Paul Litt (*October 21*).

2012: Receives a Public Policy Forum award in Toronto, along with four other former prime ministers; bemoans the trend towards too much party discipline and control from the Prime Minister's office (*May 4*). Heads up the Jamaican Canadian Initiative for Disaster Resilience and Response (JCIDRR) to help Jamaica develop a natural disaster plan (*December 14*).

2013: Supports Sandra Pupatello, runner-up to Kathleen Wynne, in the Ontario Leadership vote (*January 26*). Announces his retirement from Miller Thomson, after 23 years with the firm (*February 21*). Announces plans to visit Washington to lend support to the Keystone pipeline proposal (*April 29*).

2014: Attends a Port Colborne, Ont., meeting to support a marijuana operation proposed by Mulleboom Organics; he is a board member (*March 24*).

2015: Attends the bicentennial of Macdonald's birthday in Kingston with Harper (*January 11*). Issues a letter with Clark, Chrétien and Martin calling for stricter oversight of CSIS in anti-terrorism legislation tabled by the government (*February 19*). Receives the first Environmental Leadership Award from the Niagara Peninsula Conservation Authority (*September 24*).

2016: Serves as a co-chair of The Pearson Centre's think tank called the Pursuing Justice Project, along with Campbell, Chrétien and Martin (*March 31*).

2017: Attends the 150th anniversary of Parliament's first session in Ottawa (*November 6*).

Books about Turner

- **1968**: John Turner; *Politics of Purpose* (McClelland & Stewart)
- **1984**: Jack Cahill; *John Turner: The Long Run* (McClelland & Stewart)
- **1985**: Norman Snider; *The Changing of the Guard: How the Liberals Fell from Grace and the Tories Rose to Power* (Lester & Orpen Dennys)
- **1988**: Greg Weston; *Reign of Error: The Inside Story of Turner's Troubled Leadership* (McGraw-Hill Ryerson)
- **2011**: Paul Litt; *Elusive Destiny: The Political Vocation of John Napier Turner* (UBC)

18

Brian Mulroney

The Unyielding Prime Minister

With a background more corporate than political, Brian Mulroney left a firm stamp on Canada. He negotiated a free trade agreement with the United States that was later expanded to include Mexico and nudged U.S. President Ronald Reagan to sign an agreement to control acid rain. But his abilities to bargain failed to bring Quebec into the constitutional framework, resulting in the rejection of the Meech Lake and Charlottetown accords. On the international front, Mulroney was a leading opponent of apartheid in South Africa. At home, his style could be confrontational, helping to foster the growth of two new federal parties: Reform and Bloc Québecois.

MULRONEY THE POLITICIAN

Prime Minister of Canada: September 17, 1984 – June 25, 1993
Length of term: 8 years, 9 months, 8 days
Parliaments as Prime Minister: 33rd; 34th
Age on entering office: 45
Political party: Progressive Conservative
Leader of party: June 11, 1983 – June 12, 1993
Member of Parliament: August 29, 1983 – September 8, 1993
Ridings represented: Central Nova [N.S.] 1983-1984; Manicouagan [Que.] 1984-1988; Charlevoix [Que.] 1988-1993
Cabinet portfolio: none
Other political post: Leader of the Opposition (1983-1984)
Titles: Canadian Privy Councillor (1984); Companion of the Order of Canada (1998)
Quotes: "To govern is to choose. Being prime minister requires a capacity to decide and move on." (in his *Memoirs*); "When the time for change strikes, it's lethal." (his response during a television interview to Justin Trudeau's 2015 election win).

Mulroney the Man

Name: Martin Brian Mulroney
Born: March 20, 1939, Baie-Comeau, Quebec
Ancestry: Irish
Religion: Roman Catholic
Education: B.A. [Bachelor of Arts] (St. Francis Xavier, 1959); LL.L. [Bachelor of Law] (Laval University, 1964)
Nicknames: Bones; Little Guy from Baie-Comeau
Military service: none
Occupation: lawyer; businessman
Occupation after term: lawyer
Publications: *Iron Ore Company of Canada: Three Decades of Involvement in Northeastern Quebec and Labrador* (1983); *Where I Stand* (1983); *Memoirs 1939-1993* (2007)
Appearance: "The eyes are Paul Newman blue, his hair has the swoop of the Robert Redford style and the voice has the resonance of a Lorne Greene school of broadcasting. The jaw is by Gibraltar." (*Edmonton Journal*, 1976); "Mulroney's big chin stuck out so far that the middle of his face looked pushed in." (John Sawatsky in *Mulroney: The Politics of Ambition*)
Personality: "Style not substance brought him down. The public regarded him as high living and uncaring." (J.L. Granatstein & Norman Hillmer in *Prime Ministers: Ranking Canada's Leaders*); "All the characteristics that made him likable among his friends—loyalty, industry, generosity—didn't help his politics. He was instead perceived as too well-packaged, slick, manipulative, free-spending, thin-skinned, and of course, inexperienced." (*Encyclopedia of World Biography*)
Married: Mila Pivnicki, May 26, 1973, Montreal, Quebec
Age at marriage: 34

Mulroney was the:
- Prime Minister who won the greatest number (211) of seats
- Prime Minister with the least experience as a Member of Parliament (1 year)
- First Conservative Prime Minister to win two consecutive majorities in the 20th century (Borden's second government was under the Unionist banner)
- First Prime Minister to never lose an election while leader
- First English Canadian Catholic Prime Minister from Quebec
- Third Progressive Conservative Prime Minister
- Third youngest Prime Minister
- Fourth Prime Minister with no previous cabinet experience
- Fifth Prime Minister born in Quebec
- Seventh Roman Catholic Prime Minister
- Twelfth Prime Minister who was a lawyer

Mulroney's legacy
- Negotiated the Free Trade Agreement with the U.S., later expanding it to Mexico (NAFTA)
- Brought in the Goods and Services Tax (GST)

- Negotiated the Meech Lake Accord, later defeated
- Negotiated the Charlottetown Accord, later defeated
- Negotiated an acid rain Air Quality Agreement with the U.S.
- Played a leading international role opposing apartheid in South Africa
- Alienated Quebec (Bloc) and the west (Reform)

Mulroney's Family

Mulroney's Parents

Father: Benedict Martin Mulroney
Born: October 9, 1903, Ste-Catherine-de-Portneuf, Quebec
Occupation: electrician
Died: February 16, 1965, Baie-Comeau, Quebec
Age at death: 61
Note: 12th of 13 children

Mother: Mary Irene O'Shea
Born: August 21, 1912, Shannon, Quebec
Married: October 29, 1934, Ste-Catherine-de-Portneuf, Quebec
Died: September 14, 2002, Montreal, Quebec
Age at death: 90

Mulroney's Brothers & Sisters (6 siblings; Brian the fourth)

Brother: John Mulroney (1935-1935)
Sister: Olive Mulroney (b.1936), 4 children
  Married: Richard Elliott (1958)
Sister: Peggy Mulroney (b.1937), 3 adopted children
  Occupation: nun
  Married: Joseph Fitzpatrick
Sister: Doreen Mulroney (b.1942)
  Occupation: nurse
Brother: Gary Mulroney (b.1943)
  Occupation: teacher
Sister: Barbara Mulroney (b.1948)
  Occupation: nurse

Mulroney's Wife

Name: Milica 'Mila' Pivnicki
Born: July 13, 1953, Sarajevo, Yugoslavia (now Bosnia & Herzegovina)
Father: Dimitrije 'Mita' Pivnicki (psychiatrist)
Mother: Bogdanka Ilic
Arrival in Canada: December 1958
Age at marriage: 19
Younger than Mulroney: 14 years

Mulroney's Children (4)

Name: Caroline Mulroney

Born: June 11, 1974, Montreal, Quebec
Occupation: lawyer; businesswoman; co-founder of Shoebox Project for Shelters; Attorney-General of Ontario (2018-)
Married: Lewis 'Andrew' Lapham II (2000)
Children: 4 – Lewis H. III; Pierce (twin); Elizabeth Theodora (twin); Miranda Brooke

Name: Benedict Mulroney
Born: March 9, 1976, Montreal, Quebec
Occupation: television host
Married: Jessica Brownstein (October 30, 2008)
Children: 3 – Brian Gerald Alexander (twin); John Benedict Dimitri (twin); Isabel 'Ivy' Veronica
Note: Jessica is a co-founder of Caroline's Shoebox Project.

Name: Robert Mark Mulroney
Born: April 29, 1979, Montreal, Quebec
Occupation: bank capital trader; head of equity
Married: Vanessa Miedler
Children: 3 – Maximilian Brian; Dylan James Heribert; Ronan Milo

Name: Daniel Nicolas Dimitri Mulroney
Born: September 4, 1985, Montreal, Quebec
Occupation: investment banker
Married: Katy Carlyle Brebner (August 6, 2011)
Children: 1 – Victoria Claire
Note: Katy is a co-founder of Caroline's Shoebox Project.

POLITICAL STORIES

Two free trade deals

The idea of free trade, with no tariff barriers between Canada and the U.S., had been a tantalizing scenario for political parties since before Confederation. Two elections – 1891 and 1911 – were partly lost because the Liberals promoted 'unrestricted reciprocity' while the Conservatives successfully appealed to the need for protectionism.

In 1985, the situation was reversed and it was the Conservatives now interested in free trade talks with the Americans.

The negotiations were complex and plodding, with former Finance deputy minister Simon Reisman in charge of the Canadian team. After more than a year of talks, Reisman quit in frustration. Mulroney told his cabinet that progress was being "killed by indifference" on the part of the Americans. Reisman's exit jolted the discussions back to life, with more input at senior levels.

Still, there were plenty of unresolved issues and, just before the negotiations deadline in early October 1987, Mulroney was informed that the deal was likely dead. A surprised U.S. Treasury Secretary Jim Baker asked for more time and came back a half-hour later, accepting the proposed dispute settlement process and the deal overall.

Within a year, Mulroney and U.S. President Ronald Reagan signed the agreement and it passed final reading in the House.

Both countries returned to the negotiating table in 1991 to consider adding Mexico to the partnership. This time, it all took less than two years to reach a deal. Mulroney signed the North American Free Trade Agreement (NAFTA) in December 1992.

Accord Round 1: Meech Lake

Mulroney wanted a constitutional accord that would accommodate Quebec, the only province not to sign the 1982 constitution. But, to do it, he needed the cooperation of the premiers and that meant giving more controls to the provinces over sectors like immigration. The agreement was worked out at Meech Lake in April 1987.

Politicians and others took firm stands for or against the Meech Lake Accord. Opposition leader Turner supported it; former prime minister Trudeau was vehemently opposed. After being endorsed by Parliament, the deal started to fray as a growing number of premiers began having second thoughts. Newfoundland elected a new government under Clyde Wells who was committed to stopping it.

The Accord required agreement from all 10 provinces by June 23, 1990. As the date loomed closer, Mulroney did everything possible to get those endorsements. But, in the end, it didn't happen. Manitoba's legislature required unanimous approval, which was denied by NDP member Elijah Harper, who objected to the lack of Indigenous input in the process. That meant Newfoundland didn't have to bother putting it to a vote that was certain to be defeated.

In the aftermath, interest in Quebec's sovereignty, with or without Canada, increased. And although the exercise whittled away much of Mulroney's strength in the polls (Canadians see constitutional wrangling as a sport best avoided), he wasn't finished trying to bring Quebec back into the constitutional fold.

Accord Round 2: Charlottetown

In his second attempt to amend the constitution and gain Quebec's support, Mulroney passed the job to his Constitutional Affairs minister Joe Clark who succeeded in getting a consensus with the premiers.

Although unhappy with parts of Clark's agreement, Mulroney brought the key players together in Charlottetown in August 1992 to hammer the final Accord together. It was a mammoth undertaking that involved intensive give-and-take with the premiers, the territorial leaders and representatives from the First Nations, Métis and Inuit.

This time, the Accord was to be judged in a national referendum. While there was much to like in the many proposed amendments, there were inevitably parts of the agreement that did not appeal to some groups. It was like an omnibus bill, covering everything from increased provincial powers to Senate reform to a Canada Clause embracing Quebec as a distinct society to Indigenous self-government.

Many Canadians weren't prepared to say Yes to the entire package. Nearly 55% voted against the Accord, with opposition highest in the west. Even Quebec voted against it. The outcome denied Mulroney his second chance to enshrine constitutional harmony.

Unveiling the GST

The Manufacturers' Sales Tax levied by Ottawa was invisible to consumers. That was because it was applied directly to the manufacturers at the wholesale level. Out of sight, out of mind. But businesses complained it meant exported products lost their competitive edge because it was necessary to embed the extra cost.

Mulroney's government proposed an at-the-time-of-sale Goods & Services Tax that would be revenue neutral – everything would be taxed the same. It was the way most countries levied their taxes, and the way most provinces did as well. But, with the cloak of invisibility gone, Canadians didn't like what they were seeing.

Finance Minister Michael Wilson introduced the GST as a 9% tax on all products and services sold in Canada. Voters howled and Wilson pared the pain down to 7%. Of course, consumers still weren't particularly thrilled. Nor were the Senate's Liberals who threatened to hold up the legislation. Mulroney appointed extra Conservative Senators to offset the challenge.

The GST came into effect on January 1, 1991. Long after Mulroney stepped down, some provinces began to splice their provincial taxes and the GST together to create a Harmonized Sales Tax (HST).

The Airbus affair

Air Canada bought 34 jets from France's Airbus Industrie in 1988; the kind of expenditure – $1.8 billion – that inevitably attracts scrutiny for possible biased tendering and kickbacks.

The scrutiny spawned plenty of rumours and accusations. So much so that the Chrétien government and the RCMP investigated. A letter sent to Swiss banks suggested that Mulroney accepted kickbacks related to the purchase. He, in turn, sued the RCMP and the Justice department for $50 million. A settlement reached in 1997 resulted in apologies from the federal government and the RCMP, with Mulroney's legal costs covered by the latter.

But the Airbus Affair wasn't over. Accused in 2003 of accepting money from Airbus lobbyist Karlheinz Schreiber, Mulroney urged Harper to set up an inquiry and clear the air. The inquiry, conducted by Justice Jeffery Oliphant, heard testimony from Mulroney who said the money he received from Schreiber was for an unrelated business deal. The judge's final report agreed with Mulroney's assertion, but found the $225,000 from Schreiber to be "inappropriate" because Mulroney was an MP at the time (he'd already stepped down as Prime Minister).

PERSONAL STORIES

Debut with the Cliche Commission

The Cliche Commission, examining corruption and violence in Quebec's construction industry, marked Mulroney's entry to the limelight. The inquiry was public and played daily on Quebec television, a veritable political soap opera. Mulroney, as the young crusading lawyer, became a familiar name to viewers.

Robert Cliche's team was investigating the violence by two competing unions determined to dominate the labour pool at the gigantic James Bay hydroelectric project. One of Mulroney's first moves after joining the commission was to hire Lucien Bouchard, a friend from his days at Laval, who was struggling to build a law practice in Montreal.

The commission published its report in March 1975, calling for sweeping changes to clean up the construction industry. It had uncovered the gritty underbelly of Quebec's trade unions, complete with their Mafia connections. Cliche was confident the Bourassa government would act on the recommendations and it did. It also positioned Mulroney as a viable candidate for politics.

The Iron Ore president

Bill Bennett, CEO of Iron Ore of Canada, had approached Mulroney with a job offer before the1976 Conservative leadership race. After Clark was surprisingly elected leader, the offer was extended again. Mulroney would become executive vice-president of the company with the intent of becoming president when Bennett retired. He agreed and moved up to the presidency in 1977.

As CEO, he immediately began grappling with Iron Ore's festering labour relations, nudging the corporate culture towards a friendlier work environment dedicated to improved communication. But his early successes couldn't stem the economic pressures that forced him to close the company's Sept-Iles operations.

In 1982, Mulroney announced the closing of the Schefferville, Que., location, virtually shutting down the town. He followed that up with a severance benefits package of $16,400 for each permanent employee and an offer to let them buy their company houses for $1. Even the unions were impressed by Iron Ore's desire to deal compassionately with its workforce.

Quebec set up hearings to investigate the closure. It was a public forum that gave Mulroney the chance to outline, compellingly, the economic realities that forced the shutdown. Just like the Cliche Commission had given him a profile to enter the 1976 Conservative leadership race, his performance at the provincial inquiry helped oil the wheels of his 1983 leadership bid.

Mila Mulroney

With the "sophistication of Jacqueline Kennedy" and the "warmth of the Queen Mother" – to borrow author Carol McLeod's description – Mila Mulroney had an aura about her that attracted either adoring crowds or displeased progressives.

Brian Mulroney was a 33-year-old, young-turk lawyer when he first spied attractive 18-year-old Milica Pivnicki by the golf club swimming pool. He did not make a good impression; he was pushy and already talking about being Prime Minister. But she grew to admire his determination and focus, marrying him two years later instead of completing her civil engineering degree.

Born in Sarajevo, Yugoslavia, Mila was only five when her family moved to Montreal. Money was tight for the family, but they still sent her to private school. Mila was a asset during Mulroney's elections, willing and happy to talk to the media and the public – even as she studiously avoided political thickets that could undermine his message on the campaign trail.

Mulroney's Timeline

1939: Born at Boisvert Hospital in Baie-Comeau, Que. (*March 20*). Lives at 132 Champlain St.

1944: Attends Académie Ste-Amélie Catholic School in Baie-Comeau (*September*).

1940s: His family moves down Champlain Street to #99.

1949: Attends Académie St-Viateur (*September*). Enters and wins his first Rotary public speaking contest talking about comics.

1951: Sings for Colonel Robert McCormick, the American newspaper baron who founded Baie-Comeau, earning US$50; often returns to sing for him.

1952: Wins the Baie-Comeau junior tennis championship.

1953: Attends St. Thomas High School in Chatham, N.B. (*September*).

1955: Works as a forestry reserve security guard (*Summer*). His father talks him out of considering an apprenticeship at the paper mill. Attends St. Francis Xavier University in Antigonish, N.S. (*September*); enrols in arts. Asked by senior student Lowell Murray to join the campus Conservative party; he accepts (*September*); becomes campus party whip. Starts writing sports for the *Xavierian Weekly* (*Fall*).

1956: Works as a labourer and driver at the Canadian British Aluminium construction site in Quebec (*Summer*). Dates a former Baie-Comeau classmate Mary McGrath (*Summer*). Switches to commerce at St. Francis Xavier (*September*). Works on Bill MacKinnon's Conservative provincial election campaign; Mackinnon is elected as is the Robert Stanfield government (*October 30*). Attends the Conservative convention in Ottawa as a youth delegate (*December*); is a vice-chairman of Youth for Diefenbaker supporting Diefenbaker's successful leadership bid.

The Prime Minister is on the line

Having first admired Diefenbaker during the leadership race of 1956, Mulroney nurtured a relationship with the Chief that had them crossing paths in Ottawa or by phone over the next few years. His Dalhousie classmates weren't convinced and dared him one evening to give Dief a call. He did, and silenced their scoffing as he chatted with the leader.

1957: Plays the role of Fisheries minister in Lowell Murray's cabinet in a model Parliament (*February*). Elected leader of the St. Francis Xavier Progressive Conservative party (*March*). Organizes a $1,100 relief fund for refugees of the 1956 Hungarian uprising. Switches his major to political science at St. Francis Xavier (*September*).

1958: Plays the role of Prime Minister in the model Parliament (*February*). Writes a weekly column, *A Matter of Opinion*, for the Baie-Comeau weekly newspaper (*Summer*). Becomes president of the National PC Student Conservatives (*September*). Becomes president of the university's co-operative (*September*). Attends the Conference on World Affairs at McGill University as a delegate (*November*). Receives advice from Trudeau, a University of Montreal professor, for his thesis on Quebec politics (*December*).

1959: Receives his bachelor's degree in political science from St. Francis Xavier (*Spring*). Enrols in law school at Dalhousie University in Halifax (*September*). Has a date with future singer Anne Murray who isn't interested in pursuing the relationship.

1960: Works on Stanfield's re-election campaign in Nova Scotia; visits ridings and handles radio commercials (*Spring*). His family moves still further down Champlain Street to #79 as homeowners for the first time. Works at the Cargill grain elevator in Baie-Comeau (*Summer*). Switches to law school at Laval University in Quebec City (*September*); boards at 71 St-Louis. St. Laurent is a Laval law professor, but Mulroney never has him. Begins hosting a public affairs program for Quebec City's English radio station. Often meets over drinks with Daniel Johnson, future Quebec premier. Begins dating Johanne Ross, a relationship that lasts on-and-off for five years.

1961: Greets Diefenbaker in Ottawa on the Prime Minister's return from the Commonwealth Conference where he helped remove South Africa from the Commonwealth because of apartheid (*March*). Occasionally talks with Diefenbaker by phone about Quebec issues. As executive vice-president of the Progressive Conservative Student Federation, participates on a Young Canadians panel sponsored by *Maclean's* magazine. Interviewed by Peter C. Newman and Peter Gzowski. Sends a telegram to Diefenbaker outlining how to combat separatism in Quebec (*October 19*); his ideas are ignored, but ultimately adopted by the Liberals. Helps organize the Congrès des Affaires Canadiennes at Laval that attracts many controversial speakers including Marcel Chaput, president of the Rassemblement, who is suspended from his federal government job (and later resigns) for participating in the conference (*November 15-18*).

1962: Becomes an assistant to Alvin Hamilton (Agriculture) (*May*). Campaigns with Hamilton in Qu'Appelle (Sask.) riding, providing daily radio campaign reports on CKRM Radio in Regina (*May-June*). Urges Hamilton to hire French Canadians in the Agriculture department (*August*); the minister acts on it a month later.

1963: Receives his bachelor of laws degree from Laval (*Spring*). Returns for his fourth year at Laval to prepare for the Bar exams (*September*). Elected student president of the law faculty (*Fall*).

1964: Monitors the Quebec royal commission reviewing the conviction and execution of Wilbert Coffin for murder; first meets Trudeau who assists his friend Jacques Hébert during testimony (*Winter*). Writes his Bar exams but fails to pass Civil Procedure (*June*). Articles with Howard, Cate, Ogilvy law firm in Montreal, one of the largest in the British Commonwealth (*June*); eventually specializes in labour law. Rents an apartment on Claremont Avenue in Notre-Dame-de-Grâce with fellow lawyer Bernard Roy (*September*).

1965: His father Ben dies of cancer in Baie-Comeau, Que. (*February 16*). Brings his mother, younger brother and sister from Baie-Comeau to Montreal to live with him on Addington Avenue at Notre-Dame-de-Grâce (*Spring*). Fails Civil Procedure a second time (*Spring*), but passes a rewrite several months later. Breaks up with Johanne Ross.

1966: Moves to an apartment at 331 Clarke Avenue after moving his mother to her own apartment.

1967: Successfully represents Canadian British Aluminium of Baie-Comeau in negotiations with the Confederation of National Trade Unions (*Spring*). Represents the Shipping Federation of Canada, charged with restoring business-labour harmony at eastern Canadian ports, a process that takes several years. Works on the leadership campaign for

Davie Fulton who comes in third at the Conservative convention behind Robert Stanfield and Duff Roblin; backs Stanfield on the final ballot (*September 9*).

1968: Works on the federal election campaign as a link between the federal Conservatives and Quebec premier Daniel Johnson (*May-June*). Turns down an offer to join the Montreal Catholic School Commission because he has no children. Advises Paul Martin Jr. to stay at Power Corporation rather than leave to work for a United Nations agency.

1969: Helps shipping companies form the Maritime Employers Association and serves as interim president before the first CEO is hired.

1970: Plays a role in helping 29 fired faculty at Loyola College regain their jobs based on faulty dismissal.

1971: Begins dating Paula Cinko of the Goldiggers travelling musical troupe (*January*). Switches to dating Goldigger Francie Mendenhall after Cinko returns to the U.S. (*February*); the relationship ends before the year does.

1972: Negotiates a settlement in the eight-month strike at Paul Desmarais's *La Presse* (*Winter*). Travels in France and Spain with Michel Cogger (*June*). Sees Mila Pivnicki at the Mount Royal Tennis Club in Montreal (*July*); they begin dating and become engaged at Christmas. Serves as a vice-chair of the Conservatives' Quebec campaign in the federal election (*September-October*).

1973: Becomes the youngest law partner at Howard, Cate, Ogilvy (*January*). Marries Mila Pivnicki at Ascension of Our Lord Catholic Church in Westmount, Montreal (*May 26*). Honeymoons in Europe (*September*). His wife, Mila, miscarries their first baby (*September*). Moves to a semi-detached house at 41 Devon Avenue opposite Devon Park in Westmount (*Fall*).

1974: Appointed to the Cliche Commission looking into corruption and violence in Quebec's construction industry (*May 3*). Asks his friend Lucien Bouchard to join the Cliche team as one of the lawyers (*May*). His daughter Caroline is born in Montreal (*June 11*). The Cliche Commission begins its hearings (*September*).

Working in close proximity

Contemplating a bid for the leadership, Mulroney met with his organizers for the first time in October 1975 at the Bristol Place Hotel in Toronto. Turns out, the organizing committee for Clark was meeting in the room next door. Eight years later, when Mulroney finally won the Conservative leadership, he worked and lived in a suite at the Chateau Laurier in Ottawa. The same suite of rooms was used by Turner as he organized his Liberal leadership bid a few months later.

1975: The Cliche Commission submits its report (*May 3*) and Quebec's government enacts changes to clean up the construction industry. Approached by the Iron Ore Company of Canada about being its executive vice-president (*Summer*). Stanfield announces resignation as party leader (*September*); considers the possibility of running to succeed him. Speaks about the Cliche Commission to the Empire Club of Toronto, increasing speculation he might contest the leadership (*October 16*). Announces his intention to seek the leadership (*November 13*). Not chosen as a Quebec delegate-at-large to the leadership convention (*December 6*). Gives a popular speech in Baie-Comeau saying "It is a great country where the son of an electrician can seek the highest office in the land." (*December 16*). Best man at journalist Peter C. Newman's third wedding.

1976: Implicated for his indirect role in setting up a fund for Claude Wagner to run as a Conservative candidate in 1972 (*February 6*). Bears the brunt of Diefenbaker's convention speech opposing the election of a leader who hasn't served as an MP (*February 20*). Polls second on the first ballot at the leadership convention; drops off the third ballot and Clark wins (*February 22*). His son Ben is born in Montreal (*March 9*). Becomes executive vice-president of Iron Ore Company of Canada in Sept Iles, Que. (*July*). Turns down an offer of a cabinet position in Trudeau's Liberal government (*Fall*). Moves from Devon Avenue to a bigger Westmount house at 68 Belvedere Road (*December*).

1977: Becomes president of the Iron Ore Company of Canada following Bill Bennett's retirement and also president of the Quebec North Shore and Labrador Railway. Chairs Montreal's Centraide community fundraising drive. Becomes a founding member of the Pro-Canada Committee, a coalition of 14 groups to counteract the separatist mandate of the newly elected Parti Québécois government (*December*); it eventually folds into the provincial Liberal's campaign in the Quebec referendum.

1978: Faced with a four-month strike at Iron Ore, he is prompted to improve communications and labour relations. Chairs St. Francis Xavier University's development campaign that raises $11 million.

1979: His son Mark is born in Montreal (*April*). Serves as a CBC television commentator for the federal election won by Clark (*May 22*). Honorary pallbearer at Diefenbaker's state funeral in Ottawa (*August 19*). Asked by Clark to run as a Conservative candidate; he declines, citing his commitment to Iron Ore of Canada (*December 14*).

1980: The Clark government is defeated at the polls (*February*). Appears on a CTV panel with Louis Laberge, president of the Fédération des Travailleurs de Québec, during the Quebec referendum (*Spring*). Visits Romania on a business trip and meets with President Nicolae Ceausescu who predicts he will someday be Canada's Prime Minister (*June*). Stops drinking alcohol (*June 24*). Receives an honorary Doctor of Laws degree from Memorial University (*October 25*).

1981: Quietly supports Clark in a leadership review held in Ottawa (*February 28*). Shuts down Iron Ore's concentrator and pelletizing plants in Sept-Iles. Sells his Belvedere Road house to Iron Ore.

1982: Begins a series of speaking engagements, first in Ottawa, to determine the mood for a leadership review (*April 22*). Visits Iron Ore of Canada's fishing camps with Conservative party organizers Dalton Camp, Finlay MacDonald and Bill Neville to discuss leadership possibilities (*July*). Takes a ten-day trip on Europe's Orient Express from Paris to Vienna with Mila, Paul Desmarais and his wife (*October 13*). Iron Ore of Canada announces it is closing its operations in Schefferville, Que. (*November 2*). Joins Clark at a news conference and indicates he will endorse the leader in the leadership review (*December 6*).

1983: Announces severance benefits for his Schefferville employees: $16,400 for each permanent employee and an offer to sell company houses to them for $1 (*January 26*). Clark receives two-thirds support in a leadership review and decides to call for a leadership convention (*January 28*). Successfully defends Iron Ore of Canada's reasons for closing Schefferville plant at a Quebec legislative hearing held in Schefferville (*February 10*). Announces his intention to run for the leadership the same day as John Crosbie; indicates he has resigned as president of Iron Ore and his corporate directorships and will seek a seat in the next election (*March 21*). The battle begins between the Mulroney and Clark campaigns to sign up new party members (*March 25*). A collection of his speeches is published as *Where I Stand*, targeted to convention delegates (*May*). Wins the leadership at the convention in Winnipeg 1,584 to 1,325 on the fourth ballot over former leader Joe Clark (*June 11*). A seat becomes available when MP Elmer MacKay resigns in Central Nova, N.S. (*June*). Holidays in Bermuda then moves to Pictou Lodge, N.S., to campaign (*July*). Wins the Central Nova by-election by 11,000 votes over Alvin Sinclair (Liberal) (*August 29*). Becomes Leader of the Opposition (*August 29*). Moves into Stornoway (*November*). Celebrates New Year's Eve at the Desmarais home in Palm Beach, Florida, with Pierre Trudeau (*December 31*).

1984: Gives up smoking while in Florida (*February*). Cuts his Florida vacation short when Trudeau resigns (*February 29*). Visits Winnipeg to reinforce his party's support for French rights in Manitoba (*March 29*). Meets with U.S. President Ronald Reagan in Washington (*June 21*). An election is called by Turner, the new Prime Minister (*July 9*). Indicates his intention to seek election in the Manicouagan riding that includes Baie-Comeau (*July 13*). Embarrassed after private remarks to the media are published in the *Ottawa Citizen* about his willingness to take advantage of making patronage appointments (which he had attacked the Liberals for doing) (*July 16*). Canada's 33rd federal election: elected in Manicouagan defeating André Maltais (Liberal); his party wins 211 seats, the largest majority in Canada's history (*September 4*). **Mulroney's government 1984-1993**. Becomes the 18th Prime Minister of Canada (*September 17)*. Delays moving into 24 Sussex Drive so that renovations can be carried out (*September 17*). Meets with Pope John Paul II in Hull (*September 20*). Meets with Elizabeth II in Moncton, then U.S. President Reagan in Washington (*September 22*); begins a journal following his meeting with the Queen. Dines with Elizabeth II on the Britannia yacht in Toronto, then attends the 25th anniversary of his graduation at St. Francis Xavier in Antigonish (*September 29*). Appoints Stephen Lewis as UN ambassador for Canada. Commits Canada to taking an active role in responding to the famine in Ethiopia. 33rd Parliament opens; nominates John Bosley to be the 31st Speaker of the House (*November 5*). Meets with the provincial premiers at Meech Lake (*November 14*). The Royal Commission on Equality in Employment is tabled, calling for employment equity programs (*November 29*). Meets with South African Bishop Desmond Tutu in Ottawa to ask how Canada can help end apartheid (*December 20*).

1985: Signs the Atlantic Accord with Premier Brian Peckford to share the development of Hibernia offshore oil resources with Newfoundland & Labrador (*February 11*). Removes Robert Coates (National Defence) for visiting a strip club while travelling in West Germany (*February 12*). Attends the First Ministers Conference on the economy in Regina (*February 14-15*). David Crombie (Indian Affairs) tables legislation enabling Indigenous women to keep their status when marrying non-Indigenous partners (*February 28*). Attends the funeral of U.S.S.R. leader Konstantin Chernenko in Moscow and meets his successor Mikhail Gorbachev (*March 13*). Hosts the Shamrock Summit with U.S. President Reagan in Quebec City to talk about trade relations and acid rain; both leaders sing a rendition of 'When Irish Eyes Are Smiling' (*March 17*). Attends a First Ministers Conference on Indigenous self-government where some provinces and Indigenous groups are reluctant to reach an agreement (*April 2*). Attends his first G7 Summit in Bonn, West Germany (*May 2-4*). Removes price controls on domestic and export oil, part of dismantling the National Energy Program (*June*). Investment Canada replaces the more aggressive Foreign Investment Review Agency (FIRA) (*June 20*). Backtracks on Old Age Security de-indexing following protests by seniors (*June 27*). His youngest son Nicolas is born in Montreal (*September 4*). Appoints Lincoln Alexander, formerly Canada's first black MP, as Ontario's Lieutenant-Governor, the first black to hold a vice-regal position (*September 4*). The Macdonald Royal Commission on Economic Union and Development Prospects for Canada urges the government to seek a free trade deal with the U.S. (*September 5*). Declines to participate in the U.S.'s Strategic Defence Initiative (Star Wars) that would create a North American nuclear missile protection system (*September 7*). Removes John Fraser (Fisheries) after a television exposé accuses him of permitting potentially tainted tuna to be sold (*September 23*). Removes Marcel Masse (Communications) who is part of an RCMP investigation for improper campaign spending (*September 25*); replaces him temporarily until his name is cleared. Announces his intention to seek a free trade agreement with the U.S. (*September 28*). Quebec Premier René Lévesque resigns, opposing his party's intention to fight the next election on the issue of sovereignty (*October 3*). Attends his first Commonwealth Heads of State meeting in Nassau, Bahamas (*October 16-22*) where leaders call for an end to apartheid in South Africa. Addresses the United Nations General Assembly during its 40th anniversary celebrations (*October*). Appoints Simon Reisman as chief negotiator for free trade talks (*November 8*). Attends the NATO Summit in Brussels (*November 21*). The House votes to sell Canada's stake in the Canada Development Corporation (*November 28*). Attends the First Ministers Conference in Halifax (*November 28-29*). Agrees to sell Crown-owned de Havilland Aircraft to Boeing for $155 million (*December 2*). Quebec's Parti Québécois, first elected in 1975, is defeated by the Liberals, returning Robert Bourassa to power (*December 2*).

1986: Canada imposes economic sanctions on South Africa. Meets with Japanese Prime Minister Yasuhiro Nakasone who addresses Parliament (*January 13*). The Canadian dollar falls to a low of U.S.$0.63 (*February 4*). Attends the first meeting of La Francophonie in Paris (*February 17-18*). Speaks at the funeral for Tommy Douglas in Ottawa (*February*). Cuts funding to Katimavik; Liberal Senator Jacques Hébert protests with a 21-day hunger strike (*March 10-31*). Meets with U.S. President Reagan in Washington (*March 18-19*). Opens Expo 86 in Vancouver with Prince Charles and Princess Diana (*May 2*). Attends his second G7 Summit in Tokyo, Japan, where he succeeds in persuading the leaders to keep Canada and Italy in the group (*May 4-6*). Becomes the first Prime Minister to speak in the Japanese Diet (*May 7*). Meets with China's Chairman Deng Xioping and Premier Zhao Ziyang in Beijing (*May 11*). Sinclair Stevens (Industry) resigns following conflict of interest claims involving his wife and Magna, the automotive parts manufacturer (*May 12*); an inquiry finds him guilty of conflict of interest, but the Federal Court declares the decision void in 2004. Visits South Korea (*May 14*). Writes to Reagan to protest the U.S. imposition of a five-year tariff on Canadian cedar shakes and shingles, on the day before free trade discussions begin (*May 22*). Meets with the premiers to update them on free trade discussions (*June 2*). In a televised address, seeks the support of Canadians for the free trade talks (*June 16*). Writes to provincial premiers to try to restart constitutional talks to bring Quebec into the agreement (*July 21*). Tries unsuccessfully to convince British Prime Minister Margaret Thatcher in Montreal to join the countries imposing sanctions on South Africa (*July 23*). Attends the Commonwealth Heads of Commonwealth meeting in London where Thatcher's continued opposition to sanctions creates fault lines between Britain and other Commonwealth countries (*August 3-5*). Premiers agree to restart constitutional negotiations to include Quebec (*August 12*). Indicates his intention to remove John Bosley as Speaker of the House for lack of control over proceedings (*September 5*). Second Session, 33rd Parliament opens; John Fraser elected 32nd Speaker of the House, first Speaker to be elected (*September 30*). Awards a $1.6-billion, 20-year contract to Montreal's Bombardier for CF-18 aircraft, angering opponents who felt it should have gone to the west (*October 31*). Sells Crown corporation Canadair to Bombardier for $120 million plus possible royalties of $120 million (*October 31*). His mother Irene has a heart attack (*November*). Attends the First Ministers Conference in Vancouver (*November 20-21*). A softwood lumber deal with the U.S. is reached, with a Canadian tax imposed on Canadian softwood exports (*December 30*).

1987: Asks for André Bissonnette's (State minister for Transport) resignation when he becomes the subject of an RCMP investigation into land speculation (*January 19*). Meets with U.S. Vice-President George Bush in Ottawa to encourage the U.S. to give the free trade talks more priority (*January 21*). Awards a contract to procure CF-5 aircraft to Bristol Aircraft in Winnipeg (*January 23*). Perrin Beatty (National Defence) says women can now take on most jobs in the military on a trial basis (*February 5*). Visits with leaders of Zimbabwe, Zambia and Botswana at Victoria Falls to discuss apartheid (*February*). Meets with Pope John Paul II at the Vatican (*February 24*). Meets with provincial premiers to update them on the free trade talks (*March 11*). Another First Ministers Conference fails to reach agreement on Indigenous self-government (*March 26-27*). Meets with U.S. President Reagan and pushes hard on issues like acid rain and Arctic sovereignty (*April 5-6*); Reagan addresses Parliament for the second time. Meets with provincial premiers at Meech Lake to discuss a constitutional accord that will accommodate Quebec (*April 30*); agreement is reached to consider Quebec a distinct society and to give provinces more control over immigration as well as the ability to propose names for the Senate and Supreme Court. Applauded in the House for reaching the Meech Lake Accord (*May 3*). Meets with French President François Mitterrand who addresses Parliament (*May 26*). Trudeau attacks the Meech Lake Accord publicly for diluting federal powers (*May 27*). Meets with the premiers in Ottawa to confirm agreement on the Meech Lake Accord (*June 2-3*). Announces the creation of the Atlantic Opportunities Agency (ACOA) (*June 6*). Attends the G7 Summit in Venice, Italy, where he presses the group to address apartheid (*June 8-10*). The Meech Lake Accord passes second reading in the House, requiring endorsement from all provinces by June 23, 1990 (*June 22*). A one-dollar coin replaces the paper bill and is quickly nicknamed the "loonie" because of the loon featured on the tails side (*June 30*). Meets with the premiers again to update them on free trade talks (*July 7*). Signs an agreement with British Columbia for the creation of Gwaii Haanas national park on Haida Gwaii (*July 11*). Recalls Parliament and tables the Refugee Deterrents and Detention Bill (*July*). Announces the creation of the Western Diversification Office that will provide $1.2 billion to encourage a broadening of the west's economy (*August 2*). Stiffens penalties against refugees smuggled into Canada after nearly 200 Sikhs land on the Nova Scotia coast seeking refugee status (*Summer*). Meets with the premiers in St. John's to discuss the Meech Lake Accord and free trade talks (*August 27-28*). Meets with French Premier Jacques Chirac at Meech Lake to discuss the impasse over fishing quotas (*August 30*). Hosts La Francophonie Summit in Quebec City (*September 2-4*). Free trade negotiator Simon Reisman walks away from the table because of U.S. unwillingness to address a dispute settlement process (*September 23*). Meets with U.S. representatives who revive the free trade negotiations (*October 1*). Free Trade Agreement is reached with the U.S., calling for the elimination of border tariffs within 10 years (*October 3*). Hosts the Commonwealth Heads of Government meeting in Vancouver where everyone again attempts to convince Britain to impose sanctions on South Africa (*October 13-17*). MPs vote 242-16 in favour of the Meech Lake Accord (*October 25*). The Reform party is created with Preston Manning as its first leader (*October 30-November 1*). Attends the Quebec City funeral for René Lévesque, first leader of Quebec's Parti Québécois, who died in Montreal of a heart attack (*November 5*). Lights the Calgary Winter Olympic Games torch at Signal Hill, Nfld., before 7,000 runners carry it across the country over the next three months (*November 17*). Meets with the premiers in Toronto to discuss free trade and the Meech Lake Accord (*November 26-27*). Meets agains with the premiers in an unsuccessful attempt to get Ontario, Manitoba and Prince Edward Island to support the free trade agreement (*December 11*).

1988: Signs the Free Trade Agreement with the U.S. (*January 2*); Reagan signs the same day. The Supreme Court rules that restrictions on Canada's abortion law are unconstitutional (*January 28*). Prince Edward Island voters say yes to a bridge to the mainland (*January 18*). Appoints a Senator based on a list provided by a province, in this case Newfoundland, as outlined in the proposed Meech Lake Accord (*January 26*). Svend Robinson (NDP-Burnaby) becomes the first MP to publicly declare being gay (*February 29*). Attends his second NATO Summit in Brussels (*March 2-3*). Air Canada buys 34 jets from Airbus Industrie, a French-British-German consortium (*March 30*). Appoints long-time friend and Canada's ambassador to France Lucien Bouchard to cabinet as Secretary of State (*March 31*). Meets with U.S. President Reagan and Vice-President George Bush (*April 27-29*). Addresses the U.S. Congress in Washington (*April 27*). Meets with Queen Beatrix of the Netherlands who addresses Parliament (*May 10*). Visits European leaders prior to welcoming them to Toronto for the G7 Summit (*May*). Meets with German Chancellor Helmut Kohl who addresses Parliament (*June 16*). Hosts the G7 Summit in Toronto (*June 19-21*). Margaret Thatcher, Prime Minister of the U.K., addresses Parliament for the second time (*June 22*). The Meech Lake Accord receives a second approval in the House to override a Senate amendment (*June 22*). Meets with the premiers in Saskatoon where talks include Senate reform (*August 19*). The Free Trade Agreement passes final reading in the House (*August 31*). Signs an agreement with the Dene and Métis involving royalty splitting and special rights (*September 5*). Apologizes to Japanese Canadians for their mistreatment during the Second World War (*September 22*). Addresses the UN General Assembly in New York City (*September 29*). Canada's 34th federal election: elected in Charlevoix defeating Martin Cauchon (Liberal); becomes the first Conservative leader since Macdonald to win back-to-back majorities (*November 21*). The Supreme Court strikes down Quebec's language law that restricts the use of English signage (*December 15*); Quebec Premier Bourassa uses the notwithstanding clause to override the decision. Decides not to remove Bouchard (Secretary of State) for breaking rank and supporting Quebec's use of the clause (*December*). The free trade agreement passes in the Senate; most Liberal Senators abstain (*December 30*).

1989: The free trade agreement comes into effect (*January 1*). Shuffles his cabinet to bring in new MPs including Kim Campbell as Minister of State for Indian Affairs & Northern Development (*January 30*). Meets with U.S. President George Bush in Ottawa (*February 10*); both agree to address acid rain. Hosts Prince Charles at his Florida home (*February*). Meets with the premiers, but fails to end an impasse over the Meech Lake Accord (*February 27*). Signs the Hague Declaration on the Environment in the Netherlands to deal with atmospheric pollution, along with 23 other countries (*March 11*). The Reform party wins its first federal seat in a by-election (*March 13*). Meets with British Prime Minister Thatcher in London (*March*). Has lunch with Elizabeth II (*April 1*). Speaks at the John F. Kennedy Presidential Library in Massachusetts (*May*). Opens the new Canadian Embassy in Washington and meets with U.S. President Bush (*May*). Attends La Francophonie Summit in Dakar, Senegal (*May 24-26*). Attends the NATO Summit in Brussels (*May 29-30*). Recalls Canada's China Ambassador following the massacre of Chinese students protesting in Tienanmen Square (*June 5*). Meets with Israeli President Chaim Herzog who addresses Parliament (*June 27*). Cancels an upcoming premiers meeting because little progress is being made on the Meech Lake Accord (*July 5*). Attends the G7 Summit in Paris (*July 14-16*). Hosts Prince Andrew and the Duchess of York at Harrington Lake (*July 19*). Accepts Bernard Valcourt's (Consumer & Corporate Affairs) resignation after he is in a serious motorcycle accident that costs him his eye (*August 1*). Meets with the premiers in Quebec City where the main focus is the proposed Goods & Services Tax (GST) (*August 22-23*). His family vacations in Kennebunkport, Maine, at the summer home of U.S. President Bush (*September*). Benoît Bouchard (Transport) announces plans to cancel nearly half of Via Rail's routes starting the following year (*October 4*). Meets with Jordan's King Hussein who addresses Parliament (*October 11*). Alberta holds the country's first Senate election and forwards the results to Ottawa (*October 16*); winner Stan Waters is later appointed as a

Senator. Attends the Commonwealth Heads of Government conference in Kuala Lumpur, Malaysia (*October 18-24*). Attends his first Organization of American States Summit in San Jose, Costa Rica (*October 26-27*). Hosts the First Ministers Conference in Ottawa where a growing number of premiers oppose the Meech Lake Accord (*November 9-10*). Meets with Polish leader Lech Walesa who says the aid package for his country isn't enough; Walesa later apologizes (*November 10*). Ratifies the UN Convention on the Rights of the Child in New York, along with 190 other countries (*November 20*). Meets with Soviet President Mikhail Gorbachev in Moscow (*November 20*). Signs a joint declaration with Gorbachev to respect the right of European countries to pursue change without outside interference (*November 21*). Visits the Ukraine where he announces the plan to open a consulate in Kiev (*November 24*). Audrey McLaughlin becomes leader of the New Democratic Party, the first female to lead a major national party (*December 2*). Attends the year's second NATO Summit in Brussels (*December 4*). Appoints former NDP leader Ed Broadbent as head of the International Centre for Human Rights and International Development (*December 13*). Announces the appointment of former cabinet minister Ray Hnatyshyn as Canada's 24th Governor General (*December 14*). Wilson (Finance) plans to reduce the proposed GST from 9% to 7% (*December 19*).

1990: Canada becomes the 33rd member of the Organization of American States (*January 8*). Accepts the resignation of Jean Charest (Minister of State for Youth, Fitness & Amateur Sport) for telephoning a judge who is ruling on a case affecting his ministry (*January 24*). Wilson (Finance) introduces legislation to create a Goods & Services Tax (GST) to replace the Manufacturers' Sales Tax (*January 24*). Turner resigns as Leader of the Opposition and is replaced on an acting basis by Herb Gray (*February 7*). Talks by telephone with South Africa's Nelson Mandela one day after his release from 27 years in jail (*February 11*). Wilson (Finance) presents his fifth budget and announces the intention to privatize Petro-Canada and Telesat Canada (*February 20*). Shuffles cabinet, moving Campbell (Indian Affairs & Northern Development) to Justice, returning Valcourt to cabinet in Fisheries, and elevating Lucien Bouchard (Environment) to Quebec chief (*February 23*). Meets with Mexican President Carlos Salinas in Mexico City (*March 16-17*). Attends the Commonwealth Caribbean Conference in Barbados (*March 18-19*). Newfoundland legislature votes in favour of a resolution presented by Premier Clyde Wells to rescind the province's support of the Meech Lake Accord (*April 6*). The House approves the GST (*April 10*). Meets U.S. President Bush at Toronto's SkyDome (*April 10*). Bouchard resigns from cabinet (*May 21*). Meets the provincial premiers individually to seek a Meech Lake Accord consensus (*May 25-28*). Hosts lunch for the Gorbachevs at 24 Sussex Drive (*May 29*). Meets provincial premiers again and reaches an agreement on the Meech Lake Accord, which is still subject to approval in some provinces (*June 4-9*). Meets with recently released Nelson Mandela of South Africa who addresses Parliament (*June 17*). Addresses members of the Newfoundland legislature urging them to vote in favour of the Meech Lake Accord (*June 21*). Deadline for Meech Lake Accord passes without ratification by Manitoba or Newfoundland (*June 23*). Jean Chrétien is elected Liberal party leader (*June 23*). Indicates there will be no more first ministers conferences if Quebec declines to participate, as has been suggested by Premier Bourassa (*June 24*). Appoints Antonio Lamer as the 16th Chief Justice of Canada (*June 26*). Joins Elizabeth II for Canada Day celebrations on Parliament Hill (*July 1*). Attends the NATO Summit in London (*July 5-6*). Attends the G7 Summit in Houston, Texas (*July 9-11*). Quebec police storm a barricade by Mohawks in Oka opposed to a golf course expansion onto lands considered to be Indigenous; an officer is killed and protesters later block Montreal's Mercier Bridge (*July 11*). Former cabinet minister Bouchard and other independent Quebec MPs announce the formation of a new party, the Bloc Québécois (*July 25*). Appoints Quebec Justice Alan Gold to mediate in the Oka crisis and makes Canadian soldiers available to the province (*August 1*); the crisis ends in late

September. Meets with the premiers in Winnipeg without Quebec's participation (*August 13-14*). Dispatches two destroyers to the Persian Gulf to help enforce a UN embargo against Iraq following its invasion of Kuwait (*August 24*). Federal troops begin dismantling the barricades at Oka and Kanewake (*August 28*). Puts the military on active duty if needed in the Persian Gulf (*September 15*). Unveils a statue to Pearson on Parliament Hill (*September 26*). The last Mohawk warriors at Oka lay down their arms (*September 26*). Invokes a constitutional manoeuvre to appoint eight Senators – including Meighen's grandson Michael Meighen – to overcome a Liberal intention to have the Senate block GST legislation (*September 27*). Co-chairs the World Summit for Children at the UN in New York City, involving the largest number of national leaders to attend a UN gathering (*September 29-30*). Liberals end their filibuster in the Senate against the GST (*October 5*). Apologizes to Italian-Canadians interned during the Second World War, not in the House but at an Italian-Canadian luncheon (*November*). The land agreement with the Arctic's Dene and Métis fails after lack of consensus (*November 7*). U.S President Bush finally agrees to sign a joint clean air act (*November 15*). Signs the non-aggression declaration between NATO and Warsaw Pact nations in France, signaling the end of the cold war (*November 19*). Signs an agreement with Manitoba's First Nations to give them control of education on reserves (*December 5*). Unveils the government's Green Plan to tackle environmental issues (*December 11*). Establishes a 17-member Parliamentary committee to study processes for amending the constitution (*December 13*). Chrétien becomes Leader of the Opposition, replacing acting leader Gray (*December 21*).

Mulroney and Mandela

When Nelson Mandela was freed from a South African prison after 27 years behind bars, one of his first calls was to Mulroney. Canada had been a consistent force in the efforts to free Mandela. The two men kept in touch and Mulroney ushered Mandela into Parliament four months after his release. Significantly, Mulroney also singled out his External Affairs minister, Joe Clark, for his unwavering efforts to end apartheid.

1991: The GST comes into effect (*January 1*). Joins with the UN coalition in the war against Iraq in the Persian Gulf (*January 16*). Gives Quebec responsibility for selecting its own immigrants (*February 5*). Joins U.S. President Bush and Mexican President Carlos Salinas in announcing the intention to pursue a North American Free Trade Agreement (*February 5*). The Gulf War ends when the UN coalition recaptures Kuwait from Iraq (*February 27*); there were no Canadian casualties. Signs the Air Quality Agreement on Acid Rain with U.S. President Bush on Parliament Hill (*March 13*). Rita Johnston becomes British Columbia premier, the first female leader of a province (*April 2*). Meets with Mexican President Carlos Salinas who addresses Parliament (*April 8*). Shuffles his cabinet, moving Clark (External Affairs) to the newly created Constitutional Affairs, and Don Mazankowski (Deputy Prime Minister) to Finance (*April 21*). The Multiculturalism and Citizenship department is established with Gerry Weiner as the first minister (*April 21*). Announces the creation of a Royal Commission on Aboriginal Peoples (*April 23*). Visits Hong Kong and Japan (where he meets with Emperor Akihito and Prime Minister Toshiki Kaifu) (*May*) His mother Irene undergoes emergency quadruple bypass heart surgery in Florida (*May*). Recognizes the 100th anniversary of the death of Sir John A. Macdonald at his grave in Kingston (*June 6*). Meets with German Chancellor Helmut Kohl in Bonn (*June*). The Bloc Québécois party is officially founded, with former cabinet minister Bouchard as leader (*June 15*). Meets with U.S. President Bush at the Major League Baseball All-Star Game in Toronto (*July 9*). His family visits Ireland, including

Leighlinbridge, home of his great great great grandfather Pierce Mulroney (*July*). Attends the G7 Summit in London, which includes guest Mikhail Gorbachev of the Soviet Union (*July 15-17*). Suspends aid to the Soviet Union unless Gorbachev and his family are released by a junta attempting a coup (*August 20*); Gorbachev is later returned to power. Turns down an offer by U.S. President Bush to consider the position of U.N. Secretary-General while visiting Kennebunkport, Maine (*August*). Releases his proposal for constitutional reform: *Shaping Canada's Future Together* that includes recognizing Quebec as a distinct society and implementing Indigenous self-government within 10 years (*September 24*). Addresses graduates at Stanford University's 100th anniversary in California (*September 29*). Attends the Commonwealth Heads of Government conference in Harare, Zimbabwe (*October 16-19*). Attends the NATO Summit in Rome, Italy (*November 7-8*). Attends La Francophonie Summit in Paris (*November 19-21*). Recognizes the independence of the Ukraine from the former Soviet Union (*December 2*). Allegedly calls Liberal MP David Walker a 'fucking bastard' during a House debate (*December 11*). Chats with Gorbachev the day before his resignation as the U.S.S.R.'s last president and the creation of the Commonwealth of Independent States (*December 24*).

1992: Appoints Louise Frechette to be Canada's first female ambassador to the UN (*January*). Meets with Russian President Boris Yeltsin in Ottawa (*February 1*). Meets with the premiers, minus Quebec's, in Ottawa to discuss the sagging economy (*February 2*). The Royal Commission on Electoral Reform and Party Financing tables its reports calling for shorter election campaigns and making it easier for candidates to get public financing (*February 13*). Commits Canadian forces to the UN peacekeeping in the former Yugoslavia (*February*). Supports the recommend-ations of the special Parliamentary committee looking at constitutional reform (*March 1*). Meets with the premiers in Toronto to look at ways to eliminate interprovincial trade barriers (*March 24-25*). Tells the House he is prepared to hold a referendum on constitutional proposals if the premiers don't reach an agreement in the next two months (*April 1*). Attends the 75th anniversary of the Battle of Vimy in France (*April 9*). Reaches a land claim agreement with the Gwich'in Dene nation in the Northwest Territories (*April 23*). A bill is introduced to permit the government to hold a referendum on constitutional reform (*May 15*). Meets with U.S. President Bush in Washington (*May 20*). Receives an honorary Doctor of Humane Letters degree from Johns Hopkins University in Maryland (*May 21*). Canada wins a boundary dispute with France over waters south of Newfoundland near St. Pierre & Miquelon (*June 10*). Speaks at the Earth Summit in Rio de Janeiro (*June 12*). Meets with Russian President Boris Yeltsin who addresses Parliament (*June 19*). The Supreme Court rules that implementation of the GST is legal, ending a challenge by Alberta, British Columbia and Ontario (*June 25*). Joins Elizabeth II for the 125th Canadian anniversary celebration on Parliament Hill, then hosts her for lunch at 24 Sussex Drive and dinner at the Museum of Civilization in Hull (*July 1*). Meets with British Prime Minister John Major and Japanese Prime Minister Kiichi Miyazawa in London (*July 4*). Attends the G7 Summit in Munich, Germany (*July 6-8*). Clark (Constitutional Affairs) agrees with nine English Canada premiers to push for a triple-E Senate that would be elected, effective and equitable (*July 7*). Cabinet rejects Clark's proposal for a triple-E Senate (*July 15*). Mulroney commits Canadian forces to UN peacekeeping in Somalia (*Summer*). Meets with all provincial premiers at Harrington Lake to try for a constitutional deal (*August 4, 10*). The North American Free Trade Agreement (NAFTA) is tentatively reached with the U.S. and Mexico (*August 12*). Hosts a First Ministers Conference in Ottawa to continue constitutional talks until a deal is reached (*August 18-22*). Attends the First Ministers Conference in Charlottetown and signs the Charlottetown Accord along with the premiers (*August 27-28*). Informs Parliament about the Charlottetown Accord and plans to hold a national referendum (*September 8*). A bill is passed to end the 'baby bonus' and replace it with social assistance to targeted lower income families (*September 16*). Meets with U.S. President Bush and Mexican President Salinas in San Antonio, Texas, to approve the NAFTA draft (*October 7*). The Charlottetown Accord is defeated in a national referendum with a 54% No vote (*October 26*). A land claim settlement in the eastern Arctic gives the Inuit the option to create a new territory called Nunavut (*November 12*). The Royal Com-mission on Transportation tables its report recommending the government end its $5-billion annual subsidies and make passengers pay the cost of all road, rail, water and air travel (*November 20*). The ban on homosexuals in the military is removed by the Federal Court (*November*). Signs the North American Free Trade Agreement ending barriers to free trade with the U.S. and Mexico (*December 17*).

1993: Reduces his cabinet to 35 members, moving Campbell (Justice) to National Defence and Veterans Affairs, and Pierre Blais (Consumer & Corporate Affairs) to Justice (*January 3*). Visits U.S. President Bush at Camp David one more time before he steps down as president (*January*). Meets with U.S. President Bill Clinton in Washington (*February 5*). Announces his resignation from politics (*February 24*). New Brunswick officially becomes a bilingual province (*March 12*). A Somali teen in Belet Huen, Somalia, is beaten to death by Canadian soldiers on a peacekeeping mission (*March 16*). Hosts a meeting between U.S. President Clinton and Russian President Yeltsin at the University of British Columbia (*April 4-5*). Visits Russia, Germany, Britain and France to discuss Canada's viewpoints for the next G7 meeting (*May 6*). Signs the Nunavut Land Claims Agreement in Iqaluit calling for the creation of Nunavut in the eastern part of the Northwest Territories (*May 25*). The House passes legislation to accept NAFTA (*May 27*). Meets with U.S. President Clinton in Washington (*June*). Gives his farewell speech at the Conservative leadership convention in Ottawa (*June 11*). Campbell wins the leadership (*June 13*). His last day in the House of Commons (*June 16*). Canada's peacekeeping mission in Cyprus ends after 29 years (*June 16*). Provides Campbell with a list of patronage appointments, which she later cancels (*June 17*). Takes part in the groundbreaking for the new $180-million Montreal Forum, calling it his last official function as Prime Minister (*June 22*). **Mulroney government ends** (*June 25*). Vacations with his family in London and Nice (*June 27-July*). Joins the Montreal office of law firm Norton Rose Fulbright.

1994: Receives an honorary Doctor of Social Science degree from Central Connecticut State University (*April 26*). Spends a weekend with his family at the Kennedy compound in Cape Cod, sleeping in John F. Kennedy's bedroom (*November*).

1995: Sues the RCMP and Justice department for $50 million for a letter sent to the Swiss alleging he took kickbacks in the Airbus airplane deal (*November 20*).

1997: A settlement reached on the Airbus affair will reimburse him for legal costs, later set at $2 million (*January 6*); the government apologizes and the RCMP says suggestions of wrongdoing are unjustified. Tells a Toronto audience that the government is not dealing with Quebec's grievances and must reopen constitutional talks (*April 14*); Ontario, British Columbia and Alberta express no interest in restarting talks.

1998: Awarded the Companion of the Order of Canada (*May 6*). Receives an honorary Doctor of Laws degree from the University of Missouri-St. Louis (*May*).

2001: Visits former U.S. president George Bush in Maine where they watch the 9/11 terrorist attacks on television (*September 11*).

2002: Attends the unveiling of his portrait on Parliament Hill painted by Igor Babailov (*November 19*).

2003: Attends the dedication of Brian Mulroney Hall at the University of New Brunswick in Fredericton (*August*). The *Globe & Mail* reports he was paid $300,000 by Karlheinz Schreiber to help facilitate the Airbus deal (*November*).

2004: Delivers a eulogy at the funeral of Ronald Reagan in Washington (*June 11*). Joins the board of Independent News and Media; resigns in 2011. Implicated in a book published by William Kaplan that reveals alleged details of the payments from Schreiber in the Airbus deal (*October 2*).

2005: Suffers from an inflamed pancreas following lung surgery (*March 25*); takes many months to recover. Joins Clark, Turner and Campbell to judge contestants for a CTV television show *The Next Great Prime Minister* (*Fall*). Sues former friend Peter C. Newman for releasing their interview tapes as a book: *The Secret Mulroney Tapes* (*November 24*). Receives an honorary Doctor of Laws degree from Concordia University (*December*).

2006: Harper's government considers the file about his dealings with Schreiber to be closed (*February*). Receives the Greenest Prime Minister award in Ottawa (*April*). Joins Clark, Campbell and Martin to judge contestants again on *The Next Great Prime Minister,* now on CBC (*Fall*).

2007: Sued by Schreiber for failing to provide any services for the $300,000 he was allegedly paid (*March*). Receives the Founders Award from the Fraser Institute. Receives an honorary Doctor of Laws degree from Boston College (*May 21*). Receives an honorary Doctor of Laws degree from UWO (Western) in London (*June 15*) and an honorary degree the next day from Laval. Ordered by the Ontario Superior Court of Justice to repay Schreiber (*July*); decision is set aside. Tells CTV he has been the victim of a Liberal smear campaign, but doesn't provide answers about his dealings with Schreiber (*September*). Issues a statement urging the government to conduct an inquiry into the Airbus affair (*November 12*); Harper complies. Schreiber appears before the federal ethics committee to explain his dealings with Mulroney (*November 29*).

2009: The Airbus inquiry begins (*March 30*). Testifies before the Airbus inquiry, admitting he accepted $225,000 from Schreiber after he was Prime Minister, saying it wasn't for lobbying but simply a business deal (*May 12-18*).

2010: Schreiber is convicted for tax evasion in Germany and sentenced to eight years in jail (*May 5*). Justice Jeffrey Oliphant tables his Airbus inquiry report, saying the former prime minister acted "inappropriately" in accepting money from Schreiber (*May 31*). Contracted hepatitis B following a trip to Turkey (*Summer*). Diagnosed with diabetes (*September*).

2011: *Mulroney: The Opera*, a satirical film starring Rick Miller, opens in theatres (*April 16*). Re-elected to the Independent News & Media Board of Directors, despite concerns about a possible conflict of interest (*June 3*). Receives the Order of the Rising Sun from Japan for his official apology for the internment of Japanese Canadians during the Second World War (*December 5*). His daughter Caroline and daughter-in-law Jessica launch The Shoebox Project Christmas charity (*December*).

2012: Receives the Horatio Alger Award in Washington for overcoming humble beginnings (*April 13*). Receives a Public Policy Forum award in Toronto, along with four other Prime Ministers; talks about Macdonald as Canada's greatest Prime Minister (*May 4*). A German court orders the release of Schreiber from prison due to ill health (*May 15*). Speaks at his alma mater, St. Francis Xavier University, about leadership (*November 14*).

2013: In a CTV interview, asks "what's not to like?" about the new Liberal leader, Justin Trudeau (*April 8*). Attends Margaret Thatcher's funeral in London, England, with Harper (*April 17*). Puts his Montreal mansion up for sale for $7.9 million (*September 14*). Opposes Harper's intention to boycott the Commonwealth meetings in Sri Lanka (*October 20*). Flies to South Africa with Harper to attend Nelson Mandela's funeral (*December 8*). Resigns as a Barrick Gold director (*December*).

2014: Plays a growing role in helping to bring an NHL team back to Quebec City (*March 11*). One hundred people turn out for his surprise 75th birthday party at Club Colette in Palm Beach, Florida (*March 22*). Becomes chair of Quebecor board of directors (was vice-chair) after owner Pierre Karl Peladeau becomes a Parti Québécois member of the provincial legislature (*June 19*).

2015: Awarded the Order of the Companions of O.R. Tambo for his support of South Africa's liberation movement (*April*). Gives the convocation speech at his alma mater, St. Francis Xavier (*May 3*). Announces a $10-million endowment scholarship fund from the Horatio Alger Foundation of Canada for students entering university (*May 18*).

2016: Reads a Reagan letter at the funeral for Nancy Reagan in California (*March 11*). Joins the advisory board of ARHT Media, a hologram company (*May 24*). Criticizes U.S. Republican presidential candidate Donald Trump for threatening to tear up NAFTA (*September 4*). Unveils plans for the Brian Mulroney Institute of Government and Mulroney Hall at St. Francis Xavier University in Antigonish, N.S. (*October 26*). Named a commander in the French Legion of Honour (*December 6*).

2017: Sings *When Irish Eyes Are Smiling* for U.S. President Trump at Mar-a-Lago, Florida, accompanied by Canadian music producer David Foster (*February 17*). Meets with Trudeau's cabinet to advise them about negotiations with the U.S. on the expected reopening of NAFTA (*April 6*). Attends the 150th anniversary of Parliament's first session in Ottawa (*November 6*). Joins Catherine McKenna (Environment) to mark the 30th anniversary of the Montreal Protocol (*November 20*).

2018: Defends NAFTA in testimony before a U.S. Senate committee reviewing the trade deal (*January 23*). His grandchildren, twins Brian and John, both 7, and Ivy, 4, are part of the bridal party for Prince Harry and Meghan Markle at Windsor Castle (*May 19*). Daughter Caroline becomes Attorney-General of Ontario in the Doug Ford cabinet (*June 29*).

Books about Mulroney

- **1983**: Brian Mulroney; *Where I Stand* (McClelland & Stewart)
- **1984**: Nick Auf der Maur, Rae Murphy & Robert Chodos; *Brian Mulroney: The Boy from Baie Comeau* (Goodread Biography)
- **1984**: L. Ian MacDonald; *Mulroney: The Making of the Prime Minister* (McClelland & Stewart)
- **1987**: Claire Hoy; *Friends in High Places: Politics and Patronage in the Mulroney Government* (Key Porter)
- **1988**: Eric Hamovitch, Rae Murphy & Robert Chodos; *Selling Out: Four Years of the Mulroney Government* (Lorimer)
- **1991**: John Sawatsky; *Mulroney: The Politics of Ambition* (Macfarlane, Walter & Ross)
- **1992**: Jeffrey Brooke; *Breaking Faith: The Mulroney Legacy of Deceit, Destruction and Disunity* (Key Porter)

- **1993**: Lawrence Martin; *Pledge of Allegiance: The Americanization of Canada in the Mulroney Years* (McClelland & Stewart)
- **1994**: Stevie Cameron; *On the Take: Crime, Corruption and Greed in the Mulroney Years* (Seal)
- **1995**: Marci McDonald; *Yankee Doodle Dandy: Brian Mulroney and the American Agenda* (Stoddart)
- **1998**: William Kaplan; *Presumed Guilty: Brian Mulroney, the Airbus Affair, and the Government of Canada* (McClelland & Stewart)
- **2001**: Stevie Cameron & Harvey Cashore; *The Last Amigo: Karlheinz Schreiber and the Anatomy of a Scandal* (McFarlane Walter & Ross)
- **2004**: William Kaplan; *A Secret Trail: Brian Mulroney, Stevie Cameron and the Public Trust* (McGill-Queen's University)
- **2005**: Peter C. Newman; *The Secret Mulroney Tapes: Unguarded Confessions of a Prime Minister* (Vintage)
- **2007**: Raymond B. Blake; *Transforming the Nation: Canada and Brian Mulroney* (McGill-Queen's University)
- **2007**: Brian Mulroney: *Memoirs* (Douglas Gibson)
- **2018**: Fen Osler Hampson; *Master of Persuasion: Brian Mulroney's Global Legacy* (Signal)

Leaders of the Reform Party

1. Preston Manning 1987-2000

Canadian Alliance (2000-2003)

2. Stockwell Day 2000-2001
3. Stephen Harper 2002-2003

Merges with the Progressive Conservative party

19

Kim Campbell

The Untapped Prime Minister

Canada's first and only female Prime Minister did not have much time to exert her influence. Kim Campbell inherited the leadership of Mulroney's deeply unpopular Conservative party, knowing she would have to call an election a few months later. She made changes in cabinet and created several new federal departments, but there was little time for further reorganization before the writ dropped. In the election, she lost her own seat in B.C. and the Conservatives were reduced to two seats in the House. A month later, she resigned as party leader, disappearing from federal politics after less than five years.

CAMPBELL THE POLITICIAN

Prime Minister of Canada: June 25, 1993 – November 4, 1993
Length of term: 4 months, 9 days
Parliament as Prime Minister: 34th
Age on entering office: 46
Political party: Progressive Conservative
Leader of party: June 13, 1993 – December 13, 1993
Member of Parliament: November 21, 1988 – October 25, 1993
Riding represented: Vancouver Centre [B.C.] 1988-1993
Cabinet portfolios: Indian Affairs & Northern Development (1989-1990); Justice (1990-1993); National Defence (1993); Veterans Affairs (1993); Federal-Provincial Relations (1993)
Other political posts: Vancouver School Board trustee (1980-1984); Vancouver School Board chair (1983); Vancouver School Board vice-chair (1984); British Columbia MLA (1986-1988); Consul General to Los Angeles (1996-2000)
Titles: Canadian Privy Councillor (1989); Queen's Counsel (1990); Companion of the Order of Canada (2008)
Quotes: "Charisma without substance is a dangerous thing." (refering to British Columbia's Bill Vander Zalm during her bid for the provincial leadership of the Social Credit party, 1985); "We cannot encourage women

to participate and then punish them for their successes, for the effrontery of aspiring to do more." (Women and the Media Conference, Ottawa, 1992).

Campbell the Woman

Name: Avril Phaedra Douglas 'Kim' Campbell
Born: March 10, 1947, Port Alberni, British Columbia
Ancestry: Scottish
Religion: Anglican
Education: B.A. [Bachelor of Arts in Political Science] (University of British Columbia, 1969); LL.B. [Bachelor of Law] (UBC, 1983)
Nickname: Kim (name she gave to herself in 1957)
Military service: none
Occupation: lecturer, lawyer
Occupation after term: lecturer; consul general
Publications: *Time and Chance: The Political Memoirs of Canada's First Woman Prime Minister* (1996)
Appearance: "well dressed with fluffy blond hair (Stan Persky quoted in *The Politics of Kim Campbell*); "she could charm an audience with her sisterly exuberance, the sparkle in her eyes, and her captivating smile ... In conflict situations, however ... Her facial muscles tightened, her frown appeared, her humour vanished, her eyes became icy blue" (Ron Graham in *All the King's Horses*)
Personality: "tough, disciplined, intelligent, combative, bilingual – and I think she could effectively replace me as party leader and prime minister." (Brian Mulroney in his personal journal, 1993); "she can be quite dismissive of those who do not share her view of the world. On the other hand, she is dedicated, witty and vibrant." (Robert Fife in *Kim Campbell: The Making of a Politician*)
First marriage: Nathan Divinsky, September 15, 1972, Hampstead, England
Age at first marriage: 25
Years married: 11
Divorced: 1983
Second marriage: Howard Eddy, August 23,1986, Royal Vancouver Yacht Club, Vancouver, British Columbia
Age at second marriage: 39
Years married: 7
Divorced: 1993
Third marriage: Hershey Felder (common law), September 1997
Age at third marriage: 50

Campbell was the:

- Only woman to be Prime Minister
- Only Prime Minister born in British Columbia
- Prime Minister with the shortest term as party leader
- Prime Minister with the most spouses (3)
- First female national leader in North America
- First Prime Minister born after the Second World War
- First baby boomer to be Prime Minister

- First Prime Minister to accept a diplomatic post after politics
- First female Defence minister of any NATO country
- First female Justice minister
- Second Prime Minister since 1951 who didn't live at 24 Sussex Drive
- Fourth and last Progressive Conservative Prime Minister
- Thirteenth Prime Minister who was a lawyer

Campbell's legacy
- Canada's first female Prime Minister
- Reorganized cabinet
- Created several new departments, including Human Resources
- Biggest electoral defeat in Canadian history

Campbell's Family

Campbell's Parents

Father: George Thomas 'Paul' Campbell
Born: April 3, 1920, Montreal, Quebec
Occupation: lawyer; prosecutor
Second marriage: Virginia 'Ginny' Vessey (February 1962)
Second divorce: 1969
Third marriage: Marguerite Parkinson (1969)
Died: July 17, 2002, Vancouver, British Columbia
Age at death: 82

Mother: Phyllis Margaret 'Lissa' Cook
Born: December 14, 1923, Port Alberni, British Columbia
Occupation: wartime wireless telegraphist; secretary; receptionist; salesclerk; artist
Married: May 1943, Port Alberni, British Columbia
Divorced: October 1969
Second marriage: William Vroom
Died: November 20, 2013, Vancouver, British Columbia
Age at death: 89

Campbell's Sister (1 sibling; Kim the youngest)

Sister: Alix Paula Bernadette Campbell (b.1945)
Married: David Allen; David Hambleton

Campbell's First Husband

Name: Nathan Joseph Harry 'Tuzie' Divinsky
Born: October 29, 1925, Winnipeg, Manitoba
Father: David Divinsky
Mother: Rose Polonsky
Age at marriage: 46
Occupation: mathematics professor; chess master; school trustee; municipal councillor; businessman

First marriage: Bebi "Betty" Ullman
Third marriage: Marilyn Goldstone
Children: 3 – Judy; Miriam 'Mimi'; Pamela (all with his first wife)
Died: June 17, 2012, Vancouver, British Columbia, New Westminster, British Columbia
Older than Campbell: 22 years

Campbell's Second Husband

Name: Howard R. Eddy
Born: 1937
Age at marriage: 46
Occupation: lawyer
First marriage: Sandra
Children: 3 – Jonathan; Andrew; Abby (all with his first wife)
Older than Campbell: 10 years

Campbell's Common Law Partner

Name: Hershey Felder
Born: July 9, 1968, Montreal, Quebec
Father: Jacob Felder
Mother: Eva Surek
Occupation: pianist; composer; actor; director
Common law marriage: September 1997
Age at marriage: 29
Younger than Campbell: 21 years

POLITICAL STORIES

Social Credit leadership bid

When Campbell's boss, B.C. Premier Bill Bennett, announced his retirement, she decided to apply for the job. As executive director of the premier's office, Campbell had no political experience beyond a stint on Vancouver's school board. Her one attempt to win a provincial seat in 1983 left her well behind the frontrunners.

She knew she couldn't win, but saw it as a way to "stake out some territory on the political landscape." The convention in July 1986 was held at Whistler where Campbell ran a bare-bones campaign. Her speech, which warned delegates not to be seduced by the charisma of the race leader Bill Vander Zalm, ended up getting the only standing ovation of the evening.

But it didn't translate into votes the next day. She got 14, putting her last place in a field of 12 candidates. "I have often had occasion to chuckle since then at the number of people who assured me they were among the fourteen," she says in her memoirs. "If all the people who said they voted for me had in fact done so, I'd have been on the second ballot."

Her territory had been staked. In the fall, she ran again for the Social Credit and won a seat in the legislature.

First female Justice minister

Appointed by Mulroney in 1990, Campbell tackled her job as Canada's first female Justice minister with zest. Her own law career had lasted only two years, but that didn't stop her from confidently shepherding 26 bills through Parliament in three years.

Her first challenge was responding to the massacre of 14 female students at Montreal's École Polytechnique with a bill to restrict the use of military assault weapons. She had less luck prohibiting the use of long guns, an initiative that didn't get the support of her own caucus.

Even trickier was her intention to support the Progressive Conservative plan to recriminalize abortion, an unusual move considering her opposition to British Columbia's plan to stop funding abortions. Her bill passed in the House, but was later turned down by the Senate.

Campbell didn't feel the murder conviction of David Milgaard merited a second look. However, Mulroney did, so she asked the Supreme Court to review the case. It recommended overturning the original verdict and calling a new trial. Saskatchewan decided not to retry him and Milgaard was released after 22 years in prison. Campbell didn't challenge the result.

First female Defence minister

Campbell's appointment as National Defence minister "dumbfounded" her. It made her the first female to play that role in any NATO country. But her work in Justice had already convinced Mulroney she could make tough calls when needed. The job would last only five months and had to be balanced with her cross-posting as Veterans Affairs minister and her leadership bid for the party.

There wasn't much time to absorb the complexity of Canada's military activity and defence spending. She softened her support for the government's controversial plan to spend $4.4 billion on 50 submarine-hunting helicopters, but later reverted to her unconditional backing of the purchase.

In March 1993, Canada's UN peacekeepers in Somalia – the Canadian Airborne Regiment – were mired in scandal following the deaths of several local civilians. Concerned about equipment thefts, soldiers had shot a Somali and wounded another on March 4. Twelve days later, Somali Shidane Arone was beaten to death in the compound. Campbell didn't welcome the gruesome details as she busily campaigned to replace Mulroney. Nor could she ignore them; an inquiry into the deaths was announced in late April. She had finished her short stint as Prime Minister and was no longer in politics when the Somalia Affair slowly wrapped up. Four soldiers were convicted and the Liberals disbanded the regiment.

Crippled by a quote with no context

Campaigning in Quebec, Campbell was asked by a *Globe & Mail* reporter if there was a Conservative plan to reform social programs. She wasn't aware of one, but added that the party would have a 'dialogue' with Canadians before crafting one prior to the next budget. The reporter persisted: Couldn't she carry out that consultation during the election campaign? "I think that's the worst time to have that kind of dialogue," responded Campbell.

When the reporter returned to the issue later in the scrum, Campbell intercepted the attempt. "This is not the time, I don't think, to get involved in a debate on very, very serious issues."

There was an opportunity that evening for Campbell to clarify her comments, but she felt there was no need. The *Globe* ran a story that had the Prime Minister saying elections are not the time to discuss issues. Over time, that phrase became a running gag that helped explain the pounding her party took in the 1993 election, ending her short tenure as Prime Minister.

PERSONAL STORIES

Losing her mother and her name

The fall of 1959 was a dreadful time for 12-year-old Avril Campbell. She and her sister Alix were shipped off to private school in Victoria. A month later, Alix told her that their mother had left. The staff at the Catholic school refused to pass on their mother's letters, so they had no idea where she was.

Her mother, Lissa, had met Bill Vroom at church and their secret affair had gone on for some time before they fled to London, spent a season sailing the Mediterranean, then settled on the French Riviera. Campbell wouldn't see her mother again for ten years.

It was her sister and father who took the abandonment the hardest, pushing Campbell into the role of amateur therapist. But she was also affected by the loss. She partly coped by changing her name to Kim, ironically a name her mother had considered for her. "In hindsight," says Campbell in *Time and Chance*, "the desire to flee from a name so closely associated with Mum on the one hand, but to reinforce my attachment to her on the other, indicates my natural emotional confusion towards her at that time."

Three husbands

Twice divorced, Campbell was the first Prime Minister without a spouse since King. Part way during her brief time in office, she began seeing Russian entrepreneur Gregory Lekhtman, the inventor of impact-free running shoes. But the relationship ended three years later.

Campbell met her first husband, University of British Columbia mathematics professor Nathan 'Tuzie' Divinsky, while still a student. The eclectic chess whiz was 22 years older. She followed him into elected office as a trustee with the Vancouver School Board. They were also partners on several real estate and restaurant ventures. After they separated, Campbell maintained a close relationship with one of her stepdaughters, Pamela Divinsky.

Husband number two was Vancouver lawyer Howard Eddy. Both of them worked hard, but also devoted time to recreational pursuits. They lived on a yacht docked at Vancouver Island for several years. Once they moved to Ottawa and Campbell began climbing the Tory cabinet ladder, Eddy found their interests diverging and left.

As consul general in Los Angeles after her time as Prime Minister, Campbell met multifaceted entertainer Hershy Felder at a consulate event. Although he was 21 years younger, they entered into a common law marriage in 1997 and moved to Paris nine years later. The two collaborated on the musical *Noah's Ark*, with Campbell working on the lyrics and story.

CAMPBELL'S TIMELINE

1947: Born in Port Alberni, B.C. (*March 10*); the family joins her father at the University of British Columbia in Vancouver where he is pursuing a B.A. (*June*).

1948: Develops septic laryngitis, requiring a tube inserted into her wind-pipe to enable breathing (*Winter*). Her family moves to Burnaby (*Spring*).

1953: Her father George graduates from UBC with a law degree (*Spring*).

1954: Her family moves to 2707 West 33rd Avenue in Vancouver's Kerrisdale neighbourhood (*May*). Attends Kerrisdale Public School (*September*).

1956: Sings in the Ryerson United Church choir.

1957: Her mother Lissa breaks her hip slipping in the snow (*Winter*); the surgery does not go well, leaving her mother an invalid. Becomes a regular on CBC's *Junior Television Club*, interviewing guests (*May 1-June 26*). Attends Point Grey Junior High School in Vancouver (*September*).

Junior Television Club interviewer

CBC Television was only five years old when its Vancouver station launched a news show for children, the *Junior Television Club*. Running each Wednesday afternoon in May and June 1957, the show's five hosts included 10-year-old Avril Campbell, whose specialty was interviews related to responsibility – on everything ranging from spending pocket money and looking after pets to using lipstick.

1959: Her mother Lissa has the first titanium hip replacement in Canada. Writes, produces and directs a Roaring Twenties dance concert at her school (*Spring*). Sent to St. Ann's Academy Catholic boarding school in Victoria with her sister (*September*). Her mother Lissa leaves the family, eloping with Bill Vroom to England (*October*); they sail in the Mediterranean for a year before settling in Cannes, France. Campbell changes her name from Avril to Kim (*Fall*).

1960: Attends Prince of Wales Secondary School in Vancouver (*September*). Is confirmed as an Anglican. Begins dating Ralph White.

1962: Her father George remarries, to Ginny Vessey (*February*). Begins dating Bob Jackson (*Fall*).

1963: Elected the first female student council president at Prince of Wales (*Fall*). Competes on television's *Reach For The Top* with her high school team (*Fall*).

1964: Gives the valedictorian address at her high school graduation (*Spring*). Attends the University of British Columbia (*September*). Becomes the first female president of the first-year class (*October*). Begins dating Steve Whitelaw.

1965: Works at the Royal Fish Plant boxing halibut in Prince Rupert for $1.82 an hour (*Summer*). Whitelaw moves to Ontario.

1966: Fails her second year at UBC (*Spring*). Works at Kraft Foods filling mayonnaise jars (*Summer*). Repeats her second year at UBC (*Fall*). Boards at 1270 West 11th Avenue. Begins dating UBC mathematics professor Nathan Divinsky.

1967: Becomes vice-president of the university's Alma Mater Society student council (*Spring*). Works as a clerk at The Bay (*Summer*). Attends the Canadian Union of Students conferences in Vancouver and London, Ont., and visits Expo 67 (*Summer*). Majors in political science and international relations (*September*).

1969: Receives her B.A. in political science from UBC (*Spring*); her mother is there, the first time they've seen each other in 10 years. Joins Divinsky in Oregon where he is teaching (*Summer*). Begins graduate work in international relations at UBC to qualify for a Canada Council scholarship (*Fall*). Her father George marries for a third time, to Marguerite Parkinson.

1970: Her mother Lissa and husband Bill Vroom move from Grenada to Vancouver Island; has her malfunctioning titanium hip removed and doesn't replace it. Studies international relations at the London School of Economics and Political Science (*October*). Takes part in her first women's liberation march to Trafalgar Square (*Fall*).

1972: Visits the Soviet Union as part of her thesis work on Stalinization (*April-June*). Marries Nathan 'Tuzie' Divinsky in London (*September 15*). Honeymoons in Scotland, along with her grandmother Elizabeth Cook (*September*). Joined by her stepdaughters Mimi and Pam Divinsky in London (*Fall*).

1973: Returns to Vancouver and never completes the doctoral work for her degree (*August*). Fails to get a teaching position at Simon Fraser University (*Fall*).

1974: Works on her husband's successful campaign to become a trustee of the Vancouver School Board.

1975: Becomes a sessional lecturer at UBC filling in for professors on sabbatical (*January*). Joins her husband and architect Roger Ramses in forming the University Non-Profit Building Society to develop condominiums in Kerrisdale (*Spring*).

1978: Her step-father Bill Vroom dies following open-heart surgery. Learns she won't be able to have children. Her brother-in-law David Allen dies of a heart attack at age 32 (*Spring*). Doesn't receive tenure at UBC after three years of sessional contracts (*Summer*). Teaches sessionally at Vancouver Community College's Langara campus after not secuing a full-time position (*September*).

1980: Becomes a shareholder in Bridges, a pub, bistro and restaurant complex on Granville Island owned by Divinsky and partners. Elected as a trustee to the Vancouver School Board, representing the right-leaning Civic Non-Partisan Association (*Fall*); Divinsky had left the board after four years as chair to run successfully for city council. Enrols in law school at UBC and continues to teach at Langara in the evenings (*Fall*). Writes and produces the first of three annual Law Revue satirical shows (*Fall*).

1982: Separates from Divinsky and moves to a False Creek condominium (*January*). Wins re-election and becomes chair of the Vancouver School Board (*November*).

1983: Asked to run for the Social Credit Party in Vancouver Centre in the provincial election (*February*). Reduces health services in Vancouver schools (*March*); continues to promote programs for gifted children. Begins articling with Ladner Downs law firm. Writes her final law exams (*April*). Defeated in the British Columbia provincial election in Vancouver Centre along with Social Credit co-candidate Philip Owen to NDP incumbents Gary Lauk and Emery Barnes (*May 5*). Receives her law degree from UBC (*May*). Divorces Divinsky (*August*). Buys a house in the Fairview Slopes neighbourhood. Successfully gets a court injunction to stop a teachers strike (*November*); the teachers walk out for three days despite the ruling. Steps down as chair of the Vancouver School Board to serve as vice-chair (*December*).

Divinsky's math

Nathan Divinsky was fond of observing that his first wife, Bebi Ullman, was born on March 12, while his second wife, Campbell, was born March 10. His mathematical predisposition suggested the sequence would be complete if he could find a wife born on March 11. Such a person was Marilyn Goldstone, the mother of one of his daughter's friends. They dated. They married. Tuzie and Marilyn lived together for 27 years. Mathematical harmony was achieved.

1984: Called to the British Columbia bar (*May*).

1985: Joins CBC Radio *Morningside* as an occasional B.C. commentator. Meets Victoria lawyer Howard Eddy at the annual meeting of the Canadian Bar Association and they begin dating (*Summer*). Leaves Ladner Downs to become Executive Director in the office of B.C. Premier Bill Bennett (*Summer*).

1986: Her boss, Premier Bennett, announces his retirement (*May 22*). Declares her intention to seek the leadership of the Social Credit party (*June 12*). Polls last of 12 candidates in the leadership bid won by Bill Vander Zalm (*July 30*). Marries Howard Eddy in Vancouver (*August 23*). Wins in the two-seat Vancouver-Point Grey riding along with NDP candidate Darlene Marzari in the provincial election (*October 22*). Moves with Eddy aboard their yacht *Western Yew*, moored in Sidney (*Fall*).

1987: Admonishes Vander Zalm for scheduling a two-day caucus retreat at his Fantasy Gardens theme park (*June*). Chairs the Project Pride task force reviewing heritage conservation legislation.

1988: Breaks ranks with her party by opposing Vander Zalm's intention to stop funding abortions (*February 11*). Participates in a European Community fact-finding visit to Ireland, Denmark and France (*June-July*). Turns down an invitation to seek the Conservative federal nomination in Vancouver Quadra, running against former prime minister Turner (*July*). Nominated by acclamation to succeed Pat Carney as the federal Conservative candidate for Vancouver Centre (*October 18*). Resigns from the B.C. legislature (*October 22*). Canada's 34th federal election: elected in Vancouver Centre by 269 votes; Mulroney Conservatives win a majority (*November 21*). Sublets her predecessor Pat Carney's Ottawa apartment and is soon joined by Eddy who is working as a lawyer for the Immigration and Refugee Board (*December*).

1989: Appointed Minister of State for Indian Affairs and Northern Development by Mulroney (*January 30*). Supports the cap placed on the Post-Secondary Student Assistance Program for Indigenous young people (*April*). Meets with Indian Affairs staff and Indigenous bands in British Columbia to kick-start land claims negotiations (*Summer*). Assists Pierre Cadieux (Indian Affairs & Northern Development) in Greenville, British Columbia, to sign a framework agreement with the Nisga'a, the first negotiations to take place under the new Indigenous land claims policy (*September 11*). Supports her government's plan to recriminalize abortion (*November 21*).

1990: Becomes Canada's first female Justice minister (*February 23*). Visits École Polytechnique, where 14 female students were massacred four months earlier, to promote the government's plan to ban military assault weapons but not semi-automatics (*April*). Bill C-43 to recriminalize abortion narrowly passes in the House (*May 29*). Introduces Bill C-80 to prohibit the use of long guns (*June 6*). Becomes a Queen's Counsel (*Summer*). Shelves Bill C-80 when it fails to gain enough caucus support (*November*).

1991: The abortion bill (C-43) is defeated in the Senate on a tie vote (*February 1*). Turns down request to have David Milgaard's murder conviction reviewed (*February 27*). Eddy walks out of the marriage (*March 17*). Introduces Bill C-17 to restrict the use of military assault rifles (*May*). Speaks at the symposium she organized called Women, Law and the Administration of Justice, in Vancouver (*June 11*). The Supreme Court strikes down 1983's rape shield law that restricted the use of evidence of past sexual history in a trial (*August 22*). Bill C-17 gun legislation passes in the House (*November 7*). Asks the Supreme Court to review Milgaard's conviction following Mulroney's intervention (*November 28*). Introduces a new rape law that would make a woman's sexual history relevant if proven to the judge to be critical to the case (*December 12*).

1992: Receives an honorary Doctor of Laws degree from the Law Society of Upper Canada (*February*). The federal budget eliminates the Law Reform Commission and the Court Challenges Program designed to give citizens a chance to challenge the status quo in court (*February 25*). Advised by the Supreme Court to quash the Milgaard verdict of 1970 and order a new trial based on new evidence (*April 15*). Milgaard is released from prison after Saskatchewan elects not to retry him (*April 17*). Responds to concern by lawyers about the requirement to seek a woman's consent in a sexual encounter; agrees to delete to the word "all" from in front of "reasonable steps" (*June 15*). A portrait of her holding her black judicial gown, with bare shoulders, is published by the *Ottawa Citizen* (*October 31*). Faced with a court challenge, reluctantly agrees to compensate victims of brainwashing by the CIA in Montreal (*November*). Tells attendees at a conference on women and the media that women in politics are treated unfairly (*November*). Introduces legislation to add sexual orientation and disabilities to the Human Rights Act; bill doesn't pass (*December 10*).

1993: Appointed by Mulroney to be National Defence minister and Veterans Affairs minister (*January 3*), becoming a member of cabinet's operations committee and the first female defence minister in a NATO country. Attends a security conference in Munich, Germany (*February 5-7*). Mulroney announces his resignation as party leader (*February 24*). A poll suggests the Conservatives could win the next election if Campbell was leader (*March*). Jean Charest (Environment) announces his leadership bid (*March 16*). Michael Wilson (Industry) withdraws his name as a possible leadership candidate, followed by Barbara McDougall (External Affairs), Bernard Valcourt (Employment & Immigration) and Perrin Beatty (Communications) (*March*). Attends the Juno Awards in Toronto with country singer George Fox (*March 21*). Announces her intention to seek the party leadership (*March 25*). Attends the NATO-Warsaw Pact meeting in Brussels (*March 28*). Divorced from Eddy. Announces an inquiry into the deaths of Somali citizens by Canadian Airborne Regiment soldiers in Somalia (*April 29*). Wins the Conservative leadership on the second ballot in Ottawa, defeating Charest (*June 13*). **Campbell's government 1993**. Becomes Canada's 19th Prime Minister on same day as Tansu Ciller becomes Turkey's first female Prime Minister (*June 25*). Appoints a cabinet with 15 fewer members than under Mulroney (*June 25*). The Department of Canadian Heritage is created (*June 25*). *Kim Campbell: The Making of a Politician* by Robert Fife is published (*June 25*). Moves into

Harrington Lake residence (*June 27*). Kicks off Canada Day by celebrating in St. John's, Nfld., in the morning, on Parliament Hill midday, and at Canada Place in Vancouver at day's end (*July 1*). Meets with provincial premiers in Vancouver (*July 4*). Her report commissioned three years earlier concludes that the male-dominated justice system in Canada discriminates against women (*July 5*). Attends the G7 Summit in Tokyo, Japan (*July 7-9*). The House passes the Nunavut Land Claims Agreement Act and the Nunavut Act to create the new territory in 1999 (*July 9*). Signs an agreement with Quebec that turns manpower training over to the province (*August 3*). Begins dating Russian-born entrepreneur Gregory Lekhtman (*August*). The Royal Commission on Aboriginal Peoples tables its interim report that indicates the right to self-government never disappeared and is protected by the constitution (*August 18*). Extends the east coast cod-fishing moratorium, raising the unemployment number in the Maritimes to 42,000 (*August 31*). Reluctantly reduces the purchase of military helicopters by seven (*September 2*). Croatian forces exchange fire with Canadian troops serving as part of a UN peacekeeping force, the most significant engagement by Canadian troops since Korea (*September 16*). Responds to media questions about policy plans to change social programs by saying "This is not the time, I don't think, to get involved in a debate on very, very serious issues." (*September 23*). Nelson Mandela calls on Canada to lift economic sanctions against South Africa; hours later it happens (*September 24*). Addresses the UN General Assembly in New York (*September 29*). Pulls negative television ads that focus on Liberal leader Chrétien's facial deformity caused by Bell's palsy (*October 16*). Canadian Major-General Roméo Dallaire begins his task as commander of the UN Assistance Mission in Rwanda (UNAMIR) in the war between the Hutu government and Tutsi guerillas (*October 22*). Canada's 35th federal election: defeated in Vancouver Centre by Hedy Fry (Liberal); her party wins only two seats (*October 25*). **Campbell government ends** (*November 4*). Vacations in California (*November 13-18*). Announces her resignation as Conservative party leader (*December 13*); Charest becomes interim leader the next day.

1994: Becomes a Fellow at the Institute of Politics in the John F. Kennedy School of Government at Harvard University (*January*). Becomes a Fellow at the Joan Shorenstein Center on the Press at the Harvard Kennedy School (*Fall*); her thesis is about the cynicism and mistrust between the media and politicians.

1995: Attends the Conservative party convention and votes for Charest to be the next leader (*April*). Hosts a talk show at CKNW radio in Vancouver (*Summer*).

1996: Her memoirs, *Time and Chance*, are published (*April 1*). Hosts a radio show for the BBC in Britain (*May*). Appointed Canada's consul general in Los Angeles, California, by Chrétien (*September 16*). Ends her relationship with Lekhtman (*Summer*). Meets performer-composer Hershey Felder at a consulate event (*Fall*).

1997: Receives an honorary Doctor of Laws degree from Brock University (*June 13*). Helps write lyrics for Felder's musical *Noah's Ark,* which is performed in Los Angeles (*July*). Enters a common law marriage with Felder (*September*).

1999: Elected Chair of the Council of Women World Leaders. Receives an honorary Doctor of Public Service degree from Northeastern University, Massachusetts.

2000: Steps down as consul general in Los Angeles. Receives an honorary Doctor of Laws degree from UBC, her alma mater (*November 23*).

2001: Becomes a lecturer at the new Center for Public Leadership at the Harvard Kennedy School in Cambridge, Massachusetts.

2002: Awarded the Freedom of the City award from Vancouver. Becomes a founding member of the Club de Madrid, an independent organization that fosters democracy (*May*); serves briefly as its acting president.

2003: Term ends as Chair of the Council of Women World Leaders, but she continues to serve as a Director. Becomes president of the International Women's Forum (*October*).

2004: Becomes Secretary-General of the Club de Madrid (*January 1*). Named one of history's 50 most famous people by the National Geographic Society (*April*). Receives an honorary Doctor of Laws degree from Mount Holyoke College, Massachusetts (*May 23*). Attends the unveiling of her portrait on Parliament Hill, painted by David Goatley (*November 30*).

2005: Receives an honorary Doctor of Laws degree from Chatham College, Pennsylvania. Steps down as president of the International Women's Forum (*October*). Joins Clark, Turner and Mulroney to judge contestants for a CTV television show *The Next Great Prime Minister* (*Fall*). Receives an honorary Doctor of Humane Letters degree from Arizona State University (*December 15*).

2006: Moves to Paris. Joins Clark, Mulroney and Martin to judge contestants again on *The Next Great Prime Minister,* now on CBC (*Fall*). Steps down as Secretary-General of the Club de Madrid (*December 31*).

2007: Joins Turner, Martin and Newfoundland Premier Danny Williams to judge for the third time on *The Next Great Prime Minister.* Co-chairs the International Women Leaders Global Security Summit in New York City with former Irish president Mary Robinson (*November 16-17*).

2008: Becomes a founding member of the International Center for the Study of Radicalisation and Political Violence (ICSR) (*January*).

2009: Joins former Soviet president Mikhail Gorbachev and prominent business leaders, scientists and artists calling on Harper to "dispel perceptions of defeatism" and to "rally the Canadian people" toward a clean energy economy in a joint letter delivered to the Copenhagen conference (*December 15*).

2010: Receives the Companion of the Order of Canada at Rideau Hall (*September 3*). Attends a Ukrainian Foundation for Effective Governance conference in Kiev (*September 28*). Receives an honorary Doctor of Laws degree from the University of Alberta (*November 18*).

2011: Receives an honorary Doctor of Laws degree from Trent University (*June 2*). Joins an eight-person team of Club of Madrid former world leaders in Paris to help set an agenda for France prior to the G20 Summit (*September 7-9*).

2012: Receives a Public Policy Forum award in Toronto, along with four other Prime Ministers; proposes that every riding elect a male and female MP (*May 4*). Joins the Honorary Board of the Climate Action Reserve environmental carbon offset registry in the U.S. (*May 7*). Her first husband, Nathan Divinsky, dies (*June 17*). Receives the Order of B.C. in Victoria (*September 6*).

2013: Nominated by Canada to be Executive Director of the UN Entity for Gender Equality and the Empowerment of Women (*April 18*). Joins several other prominent women to call for more gender-neutral lyrics in the national anthem (*October 3*). Addresses the alumni dinner of the Parliamentary Internship Programme marking the 20th anniversary of her term as Prime Minister (*November 5*). Flies to South Africa with Harper to attend Nelson Mandela's funeral (*December 8*).

2014: Named founding principal of the Peter Lougheed Leadership College at the University of Alberta (*April 15*). Receives an honorary Doctor of Laws degree from Simon Fraser University (*June 11*).

2015: Attends the bicentennial of Macdonald's birthday, in Kingston, with Prime Minister Harper (*January 11*). Launches the Lougheed College Lectures speaking about 'Why Do We Lead?' (*September 14*). Adds her name to a letter to Trudeau calling for a Senate that is half female (*December*).

2016: Speaks at the Canadian Museum for Human Rights in Winnipeg on the 100th anniversary of Canadian women gaining the right to vote and to hold public office (*January 27*). Attends a memorial service for former B.C. premier Bill Bennett in Kelowna (*January 31*). Serves as co-chair of The Pearson Centre's think tank called the Pursuing Justice Project, along with Turner, Chrétien and Martin (*March 31*). Appointed by Trudeau to chair the advisory committee to select future Supreme Court justices (*August 2*).

2017: Tells the CBC that U.S. President Trump's style defies many of the leadership principles taught at the Peter Lougheed Leadership College (*February 2*). Opens a meeting of 338 women in the House of Commons as part of International Women's Day (*March 8*).

2018: Receives an honorary Doctor of Civil Law degree from Acadia University (*May 13*). Becomes the first living former leader – and fifth Prime Minister – to have a statue added to the Prime Ministers Path in Baden, Ont. (*June 28*). Her term ends as principal of Peter Lougheed Leadership College (*June 30*).

Books about Campbell

- **1993**: Murray Dobbin; *The Politics of Kim Campbell: From School Trustee to Prime Minister* (James Lorimer)
- **1993**: Frank Davey; *Reading 'Kim' Right* (Talonbooks)
- **1993**: Robert Fife; *Kim Campbell: The Making of a Politician* (HarperCollins)
- **1993**: Dennis Bueckert; *Kim Campbell, Above the Shoulders* (Voyageur)
- **1996**: Kim Campbell; *Time and Chance: The Political Memoirs of Canada's First Woman Prime Minister* (Doubleday)

Leaders of the Bloc Québécois Party

1.	Lucien Bouchard	1990-1996
2.	Michel Gauthier	1996-1997
3.	Gilles Duceppe	1997-2011
4.	Daniel Paillé	2011-2013
5.	Mario Beaulieu	2014-2015
	Gilles Duceppe	2015
6.	Martine Ouellet	2017-2018

20

Jean Chrétien

The Unafraid Prime Minister

Despite his image as a simple, down-home guy from Shawinigan, Jean Chrétien was a crafty politician and the first leader since Macdonald to win three successive majority governments. He paid his dues as a long-serving cabinet minister under Pearson and Trudeau. With the help of his adversarial finance minister, Paul Martin, Chrétien eliminated annual federal deficits and began paying down some of the national debt. When the U.S. invaded Iraq, Chrétien stood firm by refusing to take part. However, when NATO and the UN were looking for military help in Afghanistan, he met Canada's obligation to act.

Chrétien the Politician

Prime Minister of Canada: November 4, 1993 – December 12, 2003
Length of term: 10 years, 1 month, 8 days
Parliaments as Prime Minister: 35th; 36th; 37th
Age on entering office: 59
Political party: Liberal
Leader of party: June 23, 1990 – November 13, 2003
Member of Parliament: 1963-1986, 1990-2003
Ridings represented: Saint-Maurice—Laflèche [Que.] (1963-1968); Saint-Maurice [Que.] (1968-1986, 1993-2003); Beauséjour [Que.] (1990-1993)
Cabinet portfolios: Minister Without Portfolio (1967-1968); National Revenue (1968); Indian Affairs & Northern Development (1968-1974); Treasury Board President (1974-1976); Industry, Trade & Commerce (1976-1977); Finance (1977-1979); Justice (1980-1982); Social Development (1980-1982); Constitutional negotiations (1980-1982); Energy, Mines & Resources (1982-1984); Deputy Prime Minister (1984); External Affairs (1984)
Other political post: Leader of the Opposition (1990-1993)
Titles: Queen's Counsel; Canadian Privy Councillor (1967); Companion of the Order of Canada (2007)
Quotes: "Canadians love Canada, but not for 52 weeks of the year." "The art of politics is learning to walk with your back to the wall, your elbows high, and a smile on your face." (in his autobiography *Straight From the Heart*)

Chrétien the Man

Name: Joseph Jacques Jean Chrétien
Born: January 11, 1934, Baie-de-Shawinigan, Quebec
Ancestry: French
Religion: Roman Catholic
Education: B.A. [Bachelor of Arts] (St. Joseph Seminary, Trois-Rivières, 1955); LL.L. [Bachelor of Law] (Laval University, 1958)
Nicknames: Ti-Jean (Little Jean); Jean Fidèle (a university name that reflected his faithfulness to girlfriend Aline); Little Guy from Shawinigan; Dr. No (his own label for his role as President of the Treasury Board)
Military service: none
Occupation: lawyer
Occupation after term: lawyer
Publications: *Straight From the Heart* (1985); *My Years as Prime Minister* (2007)
Appearance: "The battered face with the nose that looks like it's been done in by a hockey puck, the crooked grin and gangly, 6-foot frame are instantly recognizable." (Linda Diebel in the *Toronto Star*); "He always looks like the driver of a getaway car" (Dalton Camp)
Personality: "cautious and conservative by temperament and experience, [he] embraced the King philosophy of governing from the middle, day by day, avoiding the hard choices whenever possible, making deals when necessary." (J.L. Granatstein & Norman Hillmer in *Prime Ministers: Ranking Canada's Leaders*); "He could rarely relax. His metabolism wouldn't let him." (Lawrence Martin in *Chrétien*).
Married: Aline Chaîné, September 10, 1957, Sacré-Coeur Roman Catholic Church, Baie-de-Shawinigan, Quebec
Age at marriage: 23

Chrétien was the:
- Prime Minister who held the largest number of previous cabinet positions (12)
- Second Prime Minister never to lose an election while leader
- Second Prime Minister to win three majorities in a row
- Prime Minister with the second longest previous experience in cabinet (16 years)
- First French Canadian Finance minister
- Second youngest member of a Canadian cabinet as of 1967
- Fifth longest-serving Prime Minister
- Fourth Prime Minister to serve as Finance Minister
- Eighth Liberal Prime Minister
- Fourteenth Prime Minister who was a lawyer

Chrétien's legacy
- Eliminated federal deficits and paid off nearly 10% of the federal debt
- Successfully fought the second Quebec secession referendum and brought in the Clarity Act
- Appointed the first female Supreme Court Chief Justice
- Created the Millennium Scholarships, Canada Foundation for Innovation, Canadian Institutes of Health Research, and Canada Research Chairs.

- Accepted the UN request to send troops to Afghanistan, Canada's largest military engagement since Korea
- Refused the U.S. request to send troops to Iraq
- Introduced the same-sex marriage bill
- Created 10 new national parks (Indian Affairs & Northern Development minister)
- Helped successfully negotiate the Constitution of Canada (Constitutional Negotiations minister)

CHRÉTIEN'S FAMILY

Chrétien's Parents

Father: Wellie Chrétien
Born: November 16, 1887, Shawinigan, Quebec
Occupation: machinist; insurance agent
Died: September 21, 1980, Montreal, Quebec
Age at death: 92

Mother: Marie Boisvert
Born: April 3, 1892, Baie-de-Shawinigan, Quebec
Married: May 27, 1909, Baie-de-Shawinigan, Quebec
Died: June 10, 1954, Baie-de-Shawinigan, Quebec
Age at death: 62

Chrétien's Brothers & Sisters (19 children; Jean the second youngest)

Brother: Joseph Chrétien (1910-1910)
Brother: Fernand Maurice Chrétien (1911-2002), 6 children
  Married: Cécile Marcotte (1939)
  Note: Son Raymond was Canada's ambassador to France and the U.S.
Brother: Joseph Roger Marcel Chrétien (1913-1993), 6 children
  Married: Thérèse DeGrandmont (1940)
Sister: Marie Carmen Dionne Yvette Chrétien (1914-1996)
  Married: Charles-Édouard Martel (1942)
Sister: Madeleine Pauline Gabrielle Chrétien (1916-1916)
Brother: Joseph Gabriel Raymond Chrétien (1917-2015), 4 children
  Married: Françoise Lamothe (1947)
Sister: Marie Juliette Thérèse Chrétien (b.1919)
  Married: Roger Desmarais
Brother: Albert Jean Paul Chrétien (1920-1921)
Sister: Gisèle Chrétien (1921-1922)
Sister: Marie Gisèle Chrétien (1923-2015), 3 children
  Married: Jacques Suzor (1946)
Sister: Jeanine Françoise Chrétien (1924-1924)
Brother: Jean Paul Guy 'Jean-Guy' Chrétien (1925-1926)
Sister: Marie Chrétien (1926-1926)
Brother: Gilles Chrétien (1928-1928)
Brother: Jean Claude Chrétien (1930-1932)
Brother: Joseph Marc Guy Chrétien (b.1929)

Married: Maria Duras
Brother: Willie Chrétien (1932-1932)
Brother: Joseph Célestin Michel Chrétien (b.1936), 2 children
Married: Micheline Ruel (July 9, 1960)
Note: A medical researcher who received the Order of Canada.

Chrétien's Wife

Name: Aline Chaîné
Born: May 14, 1936, Shawinigan, Quebec
Father: Albert Chaîné (labourer)
Mother: Yvonne Bellemare (hairdresser)
Occupation: secretary; payroll manager
Age at marriage: 21
Younger than Chrétien: 2 years

Chrétien's Children (3)

Name: France Chrétien
Born: July 5, 1958, Quebec City, Quebec
Occupation: lawyer; businesswoman
Married: André Desmarais (1981)
Children: 4 – Olivier; Maximilien; Philippe; Jacqueline-Ariadne
Note: Companion of the Order of Canada; Chair of Canadian Olympic Foundation.
Note: Daughter Jacqueline-Ariadne married Prince Hadrien de Croy-Roeulx.

Name: Hubert Chrétien
Born: 1963
Occupation: automotive services worker; scuba instructor

Name: Michel Charles Chrétien
Born: 1968
Status: Adopted

POLITICAL STORIES

An early Liberal partisan

From his earliest days, Chrétien learned that his family members were ardent Rouges, or Liberals, particularly his father Wellie. "Politics was his favourite hobby," notes Chrétien in his memoirs. He helped his father hand out flyers during elections and, as a teen, enjoyed the exhilarating tension of partisan arguments in poolrooms and the paper mill where he worked in the summer. His reputation as a political scrapper predated his first forays into organized politics and elected office.

As a Laval law student, Chrétien honed his Liberal talents. In his first year, he confronted Premier Maurice Duplessis, without success, about having to pay for a textbook that was offered free to Union Nationale members. He also helped lead a large student demonstration calling for an overhaul to financial aid. By year three, he was president of Quebec's Young Liberals and vice-president of the Canadian University Liberal Federation.

Elected as an MP at only 29, he was added to Pearson's cabinet four years later as the second youngest Canadian up to that time to run a ministry. Only Tupper's son, Charles Hibbert, had been younger.

Constructing a Constitution

The late-night meeting in a small pantry of the Ottawa Conference Centre has, over time, taken on mythical proportions. Dubbed The Kitchen Cabinet, it involved Justice Minister Chrétien and the attorneys general of Saskatchewan and Ontario, Roy Romanow and Roy McMurtry. Together, they tweaked the premiers' proposed amending formula in return for an agreement to include the Charter of Rights and Freedoms in the recommended new constitution. The compromise helped persuade Trudeau that they could successfully patriate the BNA Act.

Of course, it wasn't quite that easy. Chrétien had been working with the provinces for more than a year trying to find constitutional consensus. But the final changes to the amending formula in November 1981 helped tip the balance towards an agreement. Trudeau backed away from his threat to take the issue to the nation in a referendum and every province agreed to the new package, except Quebec (to Chrétien's sadness, but not surprise).

As the politician who dogged the constitution to reality, Chrétien was the one who sat in the British parliament to witness its passage, presented it to Elizabeth II for Royal assent, and added his signature to the Constitution of Canada in April 1982. It was an ironic journey for someone who had no use for constitutional debates when he arrived in Ottawa, nor later when he became Prime Minister.

The second Quebec Referendum

The federal government's role in Quebec's 1980 sovereignty referendum was largely orchestrated by Chrétien, and once he became Prime Minister, he faced a another Quebec referendum in 1995. As he did in the first vote, he let the Quebec Liberal party lead the No forces rather than risk cries of federal meddling.

But his continued inaction was frustrating for many who felt Ottawa should do something to prevent a Yes vote. The Action démocratique du Québec (ADQ) party joined the No side because it wasn't willing to accept the status quo seemingly offered by Chrétien. The Prime Minister continued to maintain that his government would not recognize a close vote.

In the weeks leading up to the vote, the pendulum began swinging dangerously to the independence side. The popular leader of the federal Bloc Québécois, Lucien Bouchard, took over the campaign from the less charismatic Parti Québécois Premier Jacques Parizeau. France hinted it might recognize the results of a Yes vote (and the U.S. said it definitely wouldn't). The Quebec Liberals under Daniel Johnson were losing traction.

So Chrétien waded into the debate. In a four-day period, he spoke at rallies in Verdun and Montreal, as well as addressed the nation on television to add support to the No side. Before the vote was counted, he told a family member the No side would win by one percent. It was even closer than that (0.58), but enough to avert the disaster of deciding what the next steps would have been around Quebec's separation.

Night attack and a handshake

There was an intruder in 24 Sussex Drive wielding a knife. Aline saw him when she went to check after hearing footsteps. Waking Chrétien who was on medication for a cold, she waited anxiously with her husband for 10 minutes before the RCMP security detail arrived. In that interval, Chrétien had a firm grasp on an Inuit sculpture, ready to use it as a weapon if necessary.

André Dallaire, a disgruntled separatist, had plans to kill the Prime Minister and had evaded the RCMP guards at the residence. He was later found not guilty because of mental illness and moved into a group home near 24 Sussex.

Three months later in February 1996, Chrétien took a more aggressive stance after an address at a Hull rally. Approached by Bill Clennett, a demonstrator who was yelling, he grabbed the man around the neck with both hands and yanked him to the ground. "It had been only three months since someone had tried to assassinate me, so my reaction was instinctive and probably angrier than it would have been otherwise," he remembers. His RCMP guards christened the move "the Shawinigan Handshake".

Afghanistan yes, Iraq no

When al Qaeda terrorists attacked New York City and Washington, D.C., on September 11, 2001, Chrétien was ready to honour Canada's pledge to NATO to aid the U.S. The pact, which is premised on collective security, stipulates that an attack on one member is an attack on all members.

Al Qaeda was training many of it operatives in Afghanistan with the Taliban government's support. Canada pledged its troops to the American-led invasion, a commitment that lasted for more than 12 years and resulted in the loss of 159 soldiers.

But when the U.S., under President George W. Bush, wanted to invade Iraq a year later, Chrétien disagreed. This was not a response to an attack, but was driven by a desire to remove Iraq's leader Saddam Hussein from power. The Prime Minister faced pressure from countries joining the alliance and from the Conservative opposition, but he didn't budge.

Hindsight vindicated Chrétien's stand. The U.S. claim that Saddam was stockpiling weapons of mass destruction was groundless and the Iraq invasion left the country in ethnically divided chaos.

The Sponsorship scandal

Part of the federal government's response to the 1995 Quebec sovereignty referendum was to pour more money into the province, sponsoring local events and raising Canada's profile through advertising.

Public Works didn't keep close tabs on the money and millions of untracked dollars disappeared into unknown pockets. Sheila Fraser, the Auditor General, noted that bureaucrats broke "just about every rule in the book" in dealing with the central player, marketing firm Groupaction. Chrétien viewed it as an administrative glitch that needed fixing. If Groupaction and others broke the law, he reasoned, they should be charged.

Martin, his successor, couldn't ignore the fiasco and agreed to set up an inquiry. Chrétien testified in 2005, but was clearly disturbed by what he considered to be Justice Gomery's bias in conducting the probe.

Gomery's report said the former prime minister was not involved in the scandal, but did bear some responsibility for it. Chrétien challenged that finding and the Federal Court removed the onus of responsibility. The Harper government appealed the judgment, but it was upheld.

Personal Stories

Bell's palsy

Determined to serve as an altar boy at his sister Gisèle's wedding, 12-year-old Chrétien endured the long walk from his brother Maurice's home to the church in a bitterly cold winter wind. He arrived with frostbite, but didn't appear to be in pain.

However, his face began to change in the next few weeks as his left cheek started to tighten, pulling up the side of his mouth. Doctors have speculated that the frostbite likely damaged a nerve, paralyzing part of the left side of his face and leaving him with a condition called Bell's palsy.

The condition didn't demonstrably affect his speaking or hinder his political career. In the 1993 election campaign, he countered a Conservative attack ad that ridiculed his physical defect by saying, "When I was a kid people were laughing at me. But I accepted that because God gave me other qualities and I'm grateful." Campbell quickly pulled the ad.

Faking appendicitis

The plan seemed perfect: pretend to have appendicitis, get sent home to recover, miss so much school he would not be allowed to return. It was worth the risk for Chrétien who was unhappy with all the rules in the heavily regimented classroom at the Joliette seminary. He felt like a captive.

Step one was faking stomach pains. His performance earned him a bed in the infirmary where the local doctor determined he would have to be sent home for a second medical opinion. Back in Baie-de-Shawinigan, doctors couldn't be sure whether or not his appendix was a problem. Better to err on the side of caution, the surgeons decided, and have it removed.

The 15-year-old hadn't anticipated this wrinkle to the second step in his plan. Nevertheless, his perfectly healthy appendix was taken out. His brother Maurice, a physician, was with Chrétien at the hospital. Although angry about the deception, he agreed to keep the sham a secret and spare Chrétien the wrath of their father.

The final step left him with a mixed result. He had indeed missed enough school to prevent him from being able to return to Joliette. But instead of going to a technical school as he'd hoped, Chrétien was sent by his father to another seminary to repeat his year. After that, he was back at Joliette.

Aline Chrétien

Chrétien is usually the first one to tell people that Aline is the best thing that happened to him. In many ways, that's true. When he started dating Aline Chaîné, she was 15 and he was a 17-year-old quarrelsome hellion. She had a quiet, calm way of grounding him. No one doubted he was destined for a life of trouble had it not been for her moderating influence.

They dated for six years, with Chrétien's mother understandably encouraging the relationship until her death a few years before the couple's marriage. From the time he first entered politics, Chrétien relied on Aline as his most trusted advisor. She proved to be both perceptive and direct, a peerless sounding board.

With a strong mind of her own, Aline used the proceeds from a successful lawsuit by Chrétien to buy herself a piano. She shared a passion for golf with her husband and was the only one of the two who hit a hole in one. Well after Chrétien's time as Prime Minister, Aline took on her own challenge as the first chancellor of Laurentian University in Sudbury.

Chrétien's Timeline

1934: Born in Baie-de-Shawinigan, Que. (now part of Shawinigan), the 18th of 19 children, on Macdonald's birthday (*January 11*).

1936: His brother Michel is the last child born to the family (*March 26*).

1939: Attends Jardin de l'Enfance, a Dominican boarding school in neighbouring Shawinigan Falls (*September*).

1945: Attends Sacré-Coeur school in Baie-de-Shawinigan (*September*). Discovers he is deaf in his right ear.

1946: Suffers frostbite on his left cheek while walking to his sister Gisèle's wedding (*February 16*); damages a nerve that later paralyzes the left side of his face, leaving him with Bell's palsy.

1947: Attends high school at the Séminaire de Joliette, Que. (*September*).

1948: His nose is broken in a boxing match at school with his younger brother Michel.

1950: Fakes appendicitis to get out of the Joliette school; his healthy appendix is removed back in Shawinigan and he succeeds in missing the rest of the school year. Attends the new Séminaire Ste-Marie in Shawinigan to repeat his year (*September*).

1951: His family moves from Belgoville neighbourhood to a street near the factories in Baie-de-Shawinigan. Begins dating Aline Chaîné (*Summer*). Returns to the Séminaire de Joliette (*September*).

1952: Asked not to return to Joliette because he wasn't meeting the school's standards (*Spring*). Enrols at Séminaire Saint-Joseph in Trois-Rivières (*September*).

1954: Expelled from Séminaire Saint-Joseph for possessing a master key to the building and making it available to classmates (*Spring*). His mother Marie dies of a heart attack in Baie-de-Shawinigan (*June 10*). His brother Maurice gets him reinstated at school without his father finding out (*September*).

1955: Graduates from Séminaire Saint-Joseph (Spring). Begins law school at Laval University in Quebec City (*September*). Elected class president in first-year (*Fall*); re-elected later in second and third years. Visits Quebec Premier Maurice Duplessis to express the unfairness of being charged for a textbook because he was not a Union Nationale member; offered the book for half price (*Fall*).

1956: Helps lead a demonstration of nearly 1,000 Laval students against the provincial legislature calling for reform to the financial aid system. Successfully campaigns for the re-election of René Hamel in the Saint-Maurice provincial riding (*June*). Works at the Belgo paper mill in Baie-de-Shawinigan (*Summer*).

1957: Works again at the Belgo paper mill (*Summer*). Marries Aline Chaîné at Sacré-Coeur Roman Catholic Church in Baie-de-Shawinigan (*September 10*). Honeymoons for three days at Lake George, New York (*September*). Moves with Aline to Rue Geneviève in Quebec City (*September*). Participates in a local hoax, parading a fake Bridget Bardot in front of a believing Quebec media (*Fall*). Becomes president of the Young Liberals of Quebec (*Fall*).

1958: Attends the Liberal convention in Ottawa as a Laval youth delegate and votes for Paul Martin Sr., the underdog to successful leadership candidate Pearson (*January 14-16*). Becomes vice-president of the Canadian University Liberal Federation (*Winter*). Campaigns for Liberal MP Joseph-Adolphe Richard in St-Maurice—Laflèche who wins the biggest Liberal majority in Canada (*March 31*). Loses the election for student president of the Laval Law faculty by a few votes (*Spring*). Campaigns again for Hamel who seeks the Quebec Liberal leadership; Jean Lesage wins (*May*). His daughter France is born in Quebec City (*July 5*). Helps form the Club de Soixante (Sixties Club) for working-class labourers in Shawinigan (*Summer*). Becomes president of the Club de Soixante (*December*).

1959: Graduates from Laval with a law degree (*Spring*). Called to the bar in Quebec (*June*). Joins the Lafond, Gélinas law firm in Shawinigan (*Summer*); later forms his own law firm Chrétien, Landry, Deschênes, Trudel & Norman.

1960: Defends acquaintance Gilles Huard on a murder charge, getting the sentence reduced based on provocation (*Spring*). Works part-time as a Crown prosecutor (*Fall*).

1962: Agrees not to contest the Liberal nomination against the incumbent, family friend Joseph-Adolphe Richard, who is beaten by Social Credit candidate Gérard Lamy (*June*). Becomes a director of the Bar in Trois-Rivières.

1963: Is barely understood by La Mauricie's English voters at a federal election campaign meeting (*March 19*). Joins four friends to invest $200,000 each in the Shawinigan Transport Company; all bail out soon after seeing it as a bad investment. Canada's 26th federal election: wins over incumbent Lamy by 1,944 votes; Pearson's Liberals win (*April 8*). His son Hubert is born in Shawinigan, following two miscarriages (*Fall*).

1964: Successfully revives a private member's bill to rename Trans-Canada Airlines to Air Canada. Contemplates moving to provincial politics, but decides against it. Grabs Conservative MP Bob Coates by the lapels and pushes him against the wall after he had pushed George McIlraith (Public Works) in a hallway during the flag debate (*December*).

1965: Appointed by Pearson to be parliamentary secretary to the Prime Minister, replacing Guy Rouleau who was fired for his role in the Rivard affair (*July 16*). Canada's 27th federal election: re-elected in St-Maurice—Laflèche defeating Créditiste candidate Alphonse Poulin by 6,966 votes; Liberals end up with another minority government (*November 8*). Begins dismantling his heavy-handed election organization in La Mauricie based on his rough treatment of Liberal-turned-NDP candidate Clive Liddle.

1966: Becomes parliamentary secretary to Mitchell Sharp (Finance) (*January 7*). Gives two speeches in Quebec that tie Quebec independence strongly to economic pain (*November*).

1967: Appointed Minister Without Portfolio in Pearson's cabinet with duties tied to Finance (*April 4*); becomes the second youngest cabinet member since Confederation. Travels by train with his family to Vancouver and back (*Spring*), his first trip west of Ontario. Experiences strong backlash for a speech that says advocates for special status for Quebec "are separatists" instead of the intended "are often separatists" (*Spring*). Attends a Liberal party convention in Alberta as the federal representative because most senior cabinet ministers were grounded by Pearson while they were campaigning for the Liberal leadership (*Fall*).

1968: Appointed National Revenue minister (*January 18*). Campaigns for Sharp in the leadership contest, but after Sharp withdraws, joins him to support Trudeau (*April 3*). Remains National Revenue minister under Trudeau (*April 20*). Canada's 28th federal election: re-elected by fewer than 2,000 votes in the new Saint-Maurice riding, defeating repeat candidate Poulin of the Créditiste; Liberals win a majority (*June 25*). Becomes Indian Affairs & Northern Development minister (*July 6*).

1969: Tells cabinet it would be better if Indigenous Peoples were not involved in developing a new Indian Affairs policy (*February*). Reaches an agreement in principle with Quebec to create Forillon National Park in the Gaspé, the first national park for the province (*May*). Releases a White Paper calling for the dismantling of the Department of Indian Affairs, abolishing the Indian Act and eliminating Indian status (*June 25*); abandoned two years later after strong Indigenous backlash. Opens Kejimkujik National Park in Nova Scotia (*August 9*). Adopts Michel, a two-year-old Inuk chosen by his brother, also Michel, from an orphanage in Inuvik, Northwest Territories.

1970: Leads a crowd of residents in Fort Providence, NWT, in an off-key, French version of *O Canada*, to the embarrassment of his wife Aline and the amusement of Elizabeth II (*July*). Announces the creation of La Mauricie National Park in Quebec (*August 23*). Initially opposes the imposition of the War Measures Act as an overreaction to the October Crisis in Quebec (*October 16*); later accepts the decision.

1971: Visits Bob Rae at Oxford in England, asking him to be his legislative assistant, a job vacated by Rae's brother John; as a socialist, Rae declines. Opens Pacific Rim National Park with Princess Anne on Vancouver Island (*May 4*). Visits Moscow and Leningrad, as well as indigenous and northern pipeline development sites in the U.S.S.R. (*July-August*).

1972: Announces the creation of three new national parks in the north that eventually become Nahanni, Kluane and Auyuittuq (*February 22*). Canada's 29th federal election: re-elected in Saint-Maurice by more than 8,000 votes over boyhood friend Guy Germain (Social Credit); the Liberals barely win a minority (*October 30*).

1973: Admitted to hospital with acute indigestion and exhaustion (*Winter*). Opens Gros Morne National Park, confronting angry local residents (*August*). About 200 Cree protesters occupy the department demanding a halt to the James Bay hydroelectric power project until land claims are settled (*August 30-31*).

1974: Stops offshore drilling in the Beaufort Sea until environmental impact studies are completed (*March 13*); recommends Justice Thomas Berger to head up an inquiry. Canada's 30th federal election: re-elected in Saint-Maurice by nearly 15,000 over friend Antonio Genest; Liberals win a majority (*July 8*). Becomes president of the Treasury Board in cabinet (*August 8*).

Campaigning Saint-Maurice style

Prior to the 1972 election, Chrétien approached his friend, hotel owner Antonio Genest, to run against him as the Conservative candidate in Saint-Maurice. Genest was happy to oblige, asking nothing in return. He didn't campaign, remaining holed up in his hotel instead. With another friend, Guy St. Germaine, on the ballot as the Social Credit candidate (he apparently didn't need to be asked), Chrétien won handily. In the next election two years later, Genest had the audacity to pursue the Tory nomination again but was turned down. So he ran for Social Credit, putting in another invisible performance.

1975: Urges government departments to decentralize; one initiative sees a unit of the National Revenue department move to Matane, Que. (*August*). Joins Quebec and the reluctant Cree in signing the James Bay & Northern Quebec Agreement for the gigantic hydroelectric project (*November 11*). Pushes for government cuts that result in the demise of Information Canada, the Company of Young Canadians and Opportunities for Youth (*December*).

1976: Sues *The Globe & Mail* for accusing him of influencing a judge (*March*); eventually wins $3,000 in damages which Aline uses to buy a piano. Announces an extension of the Olympic Lottery until 1979 to help defray the costs of the Montreal Olympic Games (*May 10*). Becomes Industry, Trade & Commerce minister (*September 14*). Indicates that the Foreign Investment Review Agency (FIRA) will start offering a warmer welcome to foreign companies (*Fall*). Agrees to establish quotas for textile and clothing imports if the industry improves productivity (*Fall*). Announces a program to build the Challenger jet at Canadair in Montreal that will create 3,000 jobs (*October 29*).

1977: The Berger Commission tables its report questioning the viability of the Canadian Arctic Gas Pipeline consortium (*May 9*). Contemplates running for the Quebec Liberal party leadership following Robert Bourassa's resignation (*June*); eventually decides against it. Becomes Finance minister, replacing Donald Macdonald who resigned (*September 16*). Speaks only in French at the annual meeting of the International Monetary Fund and World Bank in Washington (*September*). Presents a mini-budget that promises a gradual rolling back of wage and price controls (*October 20*).

1978: Presents his first budget, calling for a 3% provincial sales tax reduction for six months (*April 10*); Quebec manoeuvres him into accepting restrictions on the tax cuts in that province. Attends the G7 Summit in Bonn, Germany, with Trudeau (*July 16-17*). Embarrassed when Trudeau makes an economic speech to the nation promising a $2-billion cut in expenditures, without Finance's input (*August 1*). Presents his second budget that cautiously holds the line on spending and initiatives (*November 16*).

1979: Canada's 31st federal election: re-elected in Saint-Maurice, defeating Pierre-André Hamel (Social Credit) by more than 20,000 votes (*May 22*); the Liberal government is defeated. Steps down as Finance minister (*June 4*). Becomes Liberal critic for federal-provincial relations in the lead-up to the Quebec referendum (*June*). Begins putting together a leadership bid following Trudeau's resignation announcement (*November*). Shelves leadership plans after Trudeau decides to stay on to fight the next election (*December 17*).

1980: Canada's 32nd federal election: re-elected in Saint-Maurice defeating Armand Charbonneau (Conservative) by more than 25,000 votes; Liberals win a majority (*February 18*). Becomes Justice minister and Minister of State for Social Development in Trudeau's second government (*March 3*); appointed to lead the federal opposition to the separatist forces in the Quebec referendum. Prevented by Quebec Liberal leader Claude Ryan from speaking at a 'No' victory celebration in Verdun (*May 20*). Sent by Trudeau on a cross-country tour to sell the need for constitutional reform (*May 21*). Participates in constitution talks with provincial counterparts (*Summer*). Attends the First Ministers Conference on the Constitution, but agreement is not reached on patriation (*September 8-13*). His father Wellie dies in Montreal (*September 21*). Privately opposes Trudeau's intention to unilaterally patriate the constitution without the provinces (*October 2*). Appears before the House's constitutional committee to support the proposed constitution, amending formula and Charter of Rights (*December*).

1981: Hospitalized again for a week with indigestion and exhaustion (*January*). Receives an honorary Doctor of Laws degree from Wilfrid Laurier University (*May 31*). Attends the official opening of La Mauricie National Park in his riding (*September 6*). Takes part in the First Ministers Conference in Ottawa to make a final effort to patriate the constitution cooperatively (*November 2-5*). Works with Ontario's Roy McMurtry and Saskatchewan's Roy Romanow to craft a revised amending formula for the constitution that is acceptable to all provinces except Quebec (*November 4*).

1982: Visits Britain to observe the debate and approval of the constitution and charter proposals (*March*). Announces the appointment of Bertha Wilson as the first woman to the Supreme Court (*March 4*). Takes a copy of the constitution and charter to Elizabeth II in London for Royal approval (*April*). Signs the Canada Act, the patriated constitution, in Ottawa with Trudeau and Elizabeth II (*April 17*). Misleads the House by saying cabinet had made no decision on when to involve the Supreme Court on the issue of Newfoundland's offshore resources jurisdiction, when in fact it had (*May*). Receives an honorary Doctor of Laws degree from Laurentian University. Becomes Energy, Mines & Resources minister (*September 10*). Announces a $1 billion bailout package to Alberta resource company Dome Petroleum from the government and four national banks (*September 29*).

1983: Reaches a compromise with Alberta on oil pricing in which the federal govern-ment won't lower the price if Alberta doesn't raise natural gas pricing (*June 30*).

1984: Trudeau announces his plan to resign as party leader (*February 29*). Chrétien indicates his intention to run for the leadership (*March 16*). John Turner says he also plans to run for the leadership (*March 19*). Loses the leadership to Turner on the second ballot (*June 16*). Appointed to Turner's cabinet as Deputy Prime Minister and External Affairs minister (*June 30*). Visits Southeast Asia (*July*). Canada's 33rd federal election: re-elected in Saint-Maurice, receiving the highest percentage of votes of any Liberal candidate; the Liberals are defeated by Mulroney's Conservatives (*September 4*). Joins Lang Michener law firm in Toronto, working for them one day a week (*Fall*). Becomes External Affairs critic in Turner's shadow cabinet (*October 11*).

1985: Campaigns for David Peterson's Ontario Liberals to shore up his own support in that province (*April*). Publishes his autobiography *Straight from the Heart* written with help from journalist Ron Graham (*September*).

1986: Meets with Turner to try to patch up their differences (*February 4*); believes he has Turner's support to make Francis Fox the Quebec party president, but the job is later given to lawyer Paul Routhier. Resigns as an MP (*February 27*). Intervenes to convince Senator Jacques Hébert to end his hunger strike protesting the elimination of Katimavik (*March 31*). Receives an honorary Doctor of Laws degree from Glendon College, York University (*Spring*). Begins working fulltime for Lang Michener in Ottawa as well as serving as an advisor to Gordon Capital brokerage of Montreal. A call for a leadership review at the Liberal convention in Ottawa is defeated with 76% support for Turner (*November 30*).

1987: Opens an Ottawa branch of Lang Michener with his former political staffers Eddie Goldenberg and Roger Tassé. Receives an honorary Doctor of Laws degree from the University of Alberta (*June 8*).

1988: Buys the Grand-Mère golf course with two partners for $1.25 million from Consolidated Bathurst in Shawinigan and leases the Auberge Grand-Mère hotel for $1. Joins a variety of corporate boards, including Consolidated Bathurst, Toronto Dominion Bank, Viceroy Resources, Brick Warehouse and British Columbia Forest Products. Receives an honorary Doctor of Laws degree from Lakehead University.

1990: Opposes the Meech Lake Accord in a speech at the University of Ottawa (*January*). Announces his second attempt to seek the leadership of the Liberal party (*January 23*). Heckled by his party's youth in Montreal for opposing Meech Lake (*Spring*). Wins the Liberal leadership on the first ballot in Calgary (*June 23*). Son Michel is arrested for assault. Tells a news conference he is "not a lawyer" despite the fact everyone knows he is (*September*). Directs the Liberals to end the filibuster in the Senate against the GST (*October 5*). Reluctantly adopts his party's dominant view by emphatically stating, "I am opposed to the GST"; promises to remove it if he becomes Prime Minister (*October 29*). Wins the by-election in Beauséjour, N.B., beating NDP candidate Guy Cormier (*December 10*). Becomes the 22nd Leader of the Opposition, replacing acting leader Herb Gray (*December 21*).

1991: Ambiguously opposes the government's role with the UN coalition in the war against Iraq in the Persian Gulf (*January 16*). Has a possibly cancerous growth removed from his lung and spends several weeks convalescing (*February*). Presents his process for constitutional review that would involve a Parliamentary committee and a national referendum (*March 13*). Abandons an effort at speech and image coaching and reverts to his rough-edges persona (*March*). Participates in a Liberal policy meeting in Aylmer, Que., which is when he moves from the social left to the economic right (*November*).

1992: Meets with President George Bush in Washington (*February*). Son Michel is convicted of sexually assaulting a woman in Montreal (*July*); later serves a three-year jail term. Supports the Mulroney government's Charlottetown Accord constitution initiative (*September*); it is defeated in the national referendum that is held the following month.

1993: Sells his shares in the Grand-Mère golf course and unloads his hotel lease in Shawinigan. Campbell succeeds Mulroney as Prime Minister (*June 25*). Unveils his campaign policies in the Red Book called *Creating Opportunity: The Liberal Plan for Canada* (*September 19*). Responds candidly and emotionally to a Conservative campaign ad that highlights the physical defect on the left side of his face (*October 15*). Canada's 35th federal election: elected in Saint-Maurice, his old riding, defeating Claude Rompré (Bloc

Québécois) by more than 6,000 votes; wins a majority government (*October 25*). Appoints Mitchell Sharp as his special advisor (*October*). **Chrétien's government (1993-2003).** Becomes the 20th Prime Minister of Canada (*November 4*). The External Affairs department becomes Foreign Affairs & International Trade (*November 4*). Moves into 24 Sussex Drive (*November 4*). Lucien Bouchard of the Bloc Québécois becomes the first Leader of the Opposition who does not belong to either mainstream party (*November 4*). Stops the purchase of navy helicopters at his first cabinet meeting, resulting in a $500-million contract penalty (*November 4*). Confronts a current deficit of $41 billion, adding to the national debt of nearly $500 billion (*November*). Meets with U.S. President Clinton in Seattle, Washington, to discuss the North American Free Trade Agreement (NAFTA) (*November 18*); fails to get the U.S. and Mexico to reopen the agreement for modifications. Attends the Asia-Pacific Economic Cooperation (APEC) Summit in Seattle (*November 19-20*). An inquiry into contamination in Canada's blood system begins under Justice Horace Krever (*November 22*). The Royal Commission on New Reproductive Technologies tables its report recommending a ban on surrogate motherhood and human cloning (*November 30*). Cancels a deal by the previous government to privatize Pearson airport in Toronto (*December 3*); the bail-out ends up costing $60 million. Jean Charest replaces Campbell on an interim basis as Progressive Conservative party leader (*December 14*). Meets with the premiers in Ottawa to draft a national public works program (*December 21*). Paul Martin (Finance) appoints Gordon Thiessen as Governor of the Bank of Canada; replacing John Crow who was not prepared to permit inflation (*December 22*).

1994: The North American Free Trade Agreement (NAFTA) comes into effect, superseding the Canada-U.S. Free Trade Agreement (FTA) (*January 1*). Meets with French President François Mitterrand in Paris (*January 7*). Attends his first NATO Summit in Brussels, requesting no bombing in Bosnia unless Canadian peace-keepers are removed (*January 10-11*). 35th Parliament opens; nominates Gilbert Parent to be the 33rd Speaker of the House (*January 17*); the Speech from the Throne contains a promise to replace the GST. Meets with Mexican President Carlos Salinas in Mexico City (*March 24-25*). Receives an honorary degree from the University of Ottawa. Talks begin in Quebec City between the government and Indigenous groups about self-government, but Assembly of First Nations Chief Ovide Mercredi walks out (*May 18*). Restores funding for Katimavik through Youth Service Canada (*May 20*). Tells an Edmonton audience that Canadians "are fed up with talking about the constitution" (*May 27*). Legislation is passed to reduce unemployment insurance and extend the public service pay freeze (*May 31*). Visits Juno Beach in Normandy, France, on the 50th anniversary of D-Day (*June 6*). Appoints Howard Wilson as the first ethics counsellor reporting to the Prime Minister (*June*). Visits the Canadian military position at Visoko near Sarajevo, Bosnia – the first time a Prime has been inside a war zone (although Borden made a trip to the Western Front during the First World War) (*June* 9). Consultations begin to implement a gun registry (*June*). Introduces a new ethics package that tightens up guidelines for lobbyists (*June 16*). Attends his first G7 Summit in Naples, Italy (*July 8-10*). Declines a U.S. request to join a military force to remove the three-year-old military dictatorship in Haiti (*July*); sends a police force instead. Signs an agreement with the premiers to improve interprovincial trade (*July 18*). Tells the first World Acadian Conference, held in Moncton, that Canadian unity is the best way to preserve French culture in North America (*August 16*). Asks retired hockey player Jean Béliveau to become Governor-General, but is turned down (*September*). Appoints Landon Pearson, daughter-in-law of the former prime minister, to the Senate (*September 15*). Receives an honorary degree from the University of Moncton. Indicates he will not interfere with the Quebec Liberal party's lead role in fighting next year's sovereignty referendum (*October 29*). Heads up the first Team Canada trade mission to Asia with all premiers except Quebec's (*November 4-10*). Becomes the first Prime Minister to visit Vietnam (*November*

16). Announces the appointment of former cabinet minister Roméo LeBlanc as Canada's 25th Governor General (*November 22*). Attends the AIDS Summit in Paris and addresses the French Senate (*November 30-December 2*). Opposition leader Bouchard loses his leg following an attack of necrotizing fasciitis (flesh eating disease) (*December 1*). Attends the first Summit of the Americas, in Miami, Florida, to discuss a potential Western Hemisphere free trade agreement (*December 9-11*). Marcel Massé (Intergovernmental Affairs) presents recommendations for $6.8 billion in cuts fol-lowing a half-year of consultations with all government departments (*December 20*).

English with 'Little Guy' Charm

Chrétien never formally studied English. Instead, he worked at it in conversations with political colleagues. Wanting to soften the rough edges of his English, he asked for help from his speech coach. She refused. "She said anybody in Canada who's driving his or her car open their radio, when you speak they all know it's you and Coca-Cola would pay a lot of money to have that level of recognition," he noted in his memoirs.

1995: The Airborne Regiment is disbanded following the death of a young Somalian who was beaten by Canadian troops (*January 23*). Becomes the first Prime Minister to visit Chile; meets with President Eduaro Frei (*January 24-26*). Meets with Pakistani Prime Minister Benazir Bhutto and asks for the release of Ahmen Said Khadr, accused of bombing the Egyptian embassy in Islamabad; Khadr is freed. The Canadian Tourism Commission is created, reporting to the Industry department (*January 31*). Refuses to permit Martin (Finance) to make pension reforms (*February 17*), but later agrees to accept them in the 1996 budget. Meets with U.S. President Bill Clinton who addresses Parliament (*February 23*). Martin (Finance) presents his second budget, outlining the largest budget cuts ever, $25 billion over three years (*February 27*); includes offloading many health care and other costs to the provinces. Brian Tobin (Fisheries) has the Spanish trawler *Estai* seized for turbot fishing off Newfoundland (*March 9*); ultimately wins the standoff with the European Union. David Collenette (National Defence) establishes an inquiry to look into the Somalia Affair (*March 21*). Denounces Alberta's attempts to privatize some health care services (*April 13*). Inaugurates a Canadian garden of remembrance in Caen, France, commemorating the 50th anniversary of the end of the Second World War (*May 11*); also visits the Netherlands and Moscow. Says the government will pick up the cost of a proposed gun registry (*May 24*). His inaction on Quebec's proposed referendum prompts the Action démocratique du Québec (ADQ) party to join the Parti Québécois and Bloc Québécois in supporting a 'Yes' vote (*June 12*). The gun control law that includes a registry is passed (*June 13*). Hosts the G7 Summit in Halifax (*June 15-17*). The Crow's Nest Pass Agreement is abolished (*August 1*). Plans are announced to sell most of the rest of Petro-Canada (*September 6*). Tells the House his government will not acknowledge Quebec independence if the referendum vote is close (*September 19*). Rejects a proposal from Quebec Premier Parizeau for a debate about the referendum (*September 29*). Bouchard takes over from Parizeau as the chief negotiator dealing with Quebec independence (*October 7*). Polls suggest the 'Yes' side for the Quebec referendum is leading (*October 13*). Alexa McDonough is elected leader of the NDP, replacing Audrey McLaughlin (*October 14*). Invites all five former prime ministers to take part in a large 'No' rally (*October 17*); they all agree, but the idea is later shelved. Attends the 50th anniversary of the UN in New York (*October 21*). French President Jacques Chirac indicates likely recognition of Quebec if the province votes 'Yes' in the referendum (*October 23*), while U.S. President Clinton comes out favouring the 'No' side the following day. Cree in James

Bay vote 96.3% in favour of remaining with Canada should Quebec separate (*October 24*). Agrees to having the federal government take a more active role in stopping a 'Yes' vote in the Quebec referendum (*October 24*). Speaks for the 'No' side at a Verdun rally (*October 24*). Appeals for a 'No' vote in a national televised message (*October 25*). Speaks for the 'No' side at a rally of about 100,000 in Montreal (*October 27*). Flies to Shawinigan to vote in the referendum (*October 30*). The 'No' vote against sovereignty for Quebec wins with 50.58% (*October 30*). Says Canada is prepared to designate Quebec as a distinct society (*October 31*). His plans to amend the constitution to include Quebec are dashed when Ontario Premier Mike Harris says he's not interested (*November 2*). Waits with his wife behind a locked door at their residence waiting for the RCMP to remove an intruder, André Dallaire, a disgruntled separatist who is armed with a knife (*November 5*). Attends the funeral of assassinated Israeli Prime Minister Yitzhak Rabin (*November 6*). Attends the Commonwealth Heads of Government meeting in Auckland, New Zealand (*November 10-13*). Attends the APEC Summit in Osaka, Japan (*November 18-19*). His government is sued by Mulroney over the Airbus affair (*November 20*). Bouchard indicates he will resign as leader of the Bloc Québécois to become premier of Quebec and leader of the provincial Parti Québécois (*November 21*). Unveils legislation to give each region – Maritimes, Quebec, Ontario and the West – a constitutional veto (*November 23*); the West feels under-represented. Invites Quebec professor Stéphane Dion to 24 Sussex Drive and asks him to join the cabinet (*November 25*); Dion suggests his friend Pierre Pettigrew be considered as well. Announces plans to recognize Quebec as a distinct society, give Ontario and Quebec veto power over constitutional changes, and give provinces more control over job training (*November 27*). The Canadian National Railway, Canada's largest Crown corporation, is privatized (*November 28*). A bill overhauling unemployment insurance, renamed employment insurance, is introduced (*December 1*). Attends La Francophonie Summit in Benin (*December 2-4*). Agrees to send 1,000 troops to Bosnia (*December 6*). His bill for veto powers for Canada's regions is passed (*December 13*).

1996: Leads a Team Canada trade mission to Asia for three weeks, visiting India, Pakistan, Malaysia and Indonesia (*January*). Receives an honorary doctorate degree from Meiji University in Japan. Tobin (Fisheries) resigns to become Newfoundland premier (*January 8*). Gilles Duceppe becomes acting Leader of the Opposition and Bloc Québécois party leader after Bouchard becomes Quebec premier (*January 15*). Appoints Liberal MP Shirley Maheu to the Senate, recapturing a Liberal majority in the upper house (*February 1*); the next day the Senate approves the veto bill. Grabs protester Bill Clennett by the neck, forcing him to the ground, in Hull (*February 15*); the action is nicknamed the "Shawinigan handshake". Michel Gauthier is elected leader of the Bloc Québécois, also becoming Leader of the Opposition (*February 17*). A two-dollar coin replaces the bill and is quickly nicknamed 'toonie' (*February 19*). Martin (Finance) presents his third budget, calling for a $32.7 billion reduction in the deficit (*March 6*). Attends the Summit of Peacemakers in Sharm el Sheikh, Egypt (*March 11-13*). Expels Liberal MP John Nunziata from caucus for opposing the government's budget (*April 21*). Martin (Finance) says the government made a mistake in promising to eliminate the GST (*April 23*). Copps (Deputy Prime Minister) resigns after saying she would do just that if the GST wasn't eliminated (*May 1*); she is re-elected in a by-election the following month. Alberta agrees to suspend private clinic health care billings following penalties imposed by Ottawa (*May 30*). Meets with Mexican President Ernesto Zedillo who addresses Parliament (*June 11*). Hosts a meeting with the premiers in Ottawa where a general agreement is reached to reduce the federal role in social housing and tourism (*June 20-21*). Attends the G7 Summit in Lyon, France (*June 27-29*). Announces the creation of the Canadian Information Office (*July 9*). Collenette (National Defence & Veterans Affairs) resigns after writing a letter to the refugee board on behalf of a constituent (*October 4*). Attends the state funeral for former Quebec premier Robert

Bourassa in Montreal (*October 7*). Announces an $87-million interest-free loan to Bombardier to build a new passenger jet (*October 21*). His appointed Lieutenant-Governor of Quebec, Jean-Louis Roux, resigns after admitting having worn a swastika as a student protester (*November 6*). The Royal Commission on Aboriginal Peoples tables its report calling for Indigenous self-government, or risk further violence (*November 21*). Gun-control legislation that includes a long-gun registry is approved by the Senate (*November 22*).

1997: Leads a Team Canada trade mission to Thailand, South Korea and the Philippines (*January 8-20*). Pratt & Whitney Canada in Quebec receives $147 million from Ottawa to continue building airplane engines in Canada (*January 10*). Meets with French President Chirac in Paris (*January 27*). The government presents its case to the Supreme Court that Quebec must operate through the Constitution to separate from the country (*February 28*). Gilles Duceppe, the new Bloc Québecois leader, becomes Leader of the Opposition, replacing Gauthier (*March 15*). Nova Scotia, New Brunswick and Newfoundland & Labrador become the first provinces to implement a harmonized sales tax (HST) combining the GST and provincial sales taxes (*April 1*). Makes his first official visit to Washington to meet with U.S. President Clinton (*April 7-9*). Asked by Quebec to amend the BNA Act to allow the province to switch from religious to language-based schools (*April 15*); passed later in the year. Indigenous peoples across the country rally on streets and highways to protest the lack of government action on the Royal Commission recommendations released in the fall (*April 17*). Indicates that unity will be the focus of the Liberals' approaching election campaign (*April 25*). During the leaders televised French debate, the moderator Claire Lamarche collapses and is rushed to hospital (*May 13*); the debate is rescheduled. Announces a federal Crown corporation loan of $615,000 to the Grand-Mère hotel in his riding (*May 30*). Confederation Bridge opens, linking Prince Edward Island to the mainland (*May 31*). Canada's 36th federal election: re-elected in Saint-Maurice defeating Yves Duhaime (Bloc Québécois) by about 1,600 votes; the Liberals are re-elected with a slim majority (*June 2*). Attends the first G8 (G7+Russia) Summit in Denver, Colorado (*June 20-22*). The Somalia inquiry report is released, criticizing the military for its handling of violent incidents (*July 2*). Attends his second NATO Summit in Madrid, Spain (*July* 8-9); a microphone is on as he jokes about the Americans' "horse-trading" method of government. Commends Dion (Intergovernmental Affairs) for his letter-writing campaign to counter separatist arguments (*August 28*). Lloyd Axworthy (Foreign Affairs) promotes a more aggressive international effort in Oslo to ban landmines (*September*). The English-Canadian premiers release the Calgary Declaration emphasizing a commitment to recognize Quebec's unique status (*September 14*). A court rules that the federal government and the RCMP must pay Mulroney $2 million in court costs after an out-of-court settlement over the Airbus affair (*October 7*); Rock (Justice) apologizes for the harsh wording of the original letter, but the RCMP's investigation continues for another five years. Israel apologizes for using Canadian passports in its spying activities (*October 10*). Meets with Russian President Boris Yeltsin in Moscow to urge him, unsuccessfully, to sign the landmines ban (*October 20*). Attends the Commonwealth Heads of Government meeting in Edinburgh where he convinces six smaller nations to sign the landmines ban (*October 24-27*); first Commonwealth meeting to be attended by Elizabeth II. Seven premiers meet with Indigenous leaders to expand the Calgary Declaration to recognize Indigenous peoples as also having a unique status (*November 18*). Hosts the APEC Summit at the University of British Columbia (*November 24-25*); his office is implicated in the decision to use excessive force against protesters. Justice Horace Krever tables his report recommending the establishment of a new blood service agency following a tainted blood incident involving the Canadian Red Cross (*November 26*). Meets with Chinese President Jiang Zemin in Ottawa (*November 28*). Signs the Ottawa Treaty to ban landmines, ultimately signed by 162 countries (*December 3*). The Supreme Court rules that Indigenous peoples without treaties have a constitutional right to their ancestral lands (*December 11*). Hosts a first ministers meeting in Ottawa where issues other than unity are discussed (*December 11-12*). Ralph Goodale (Natural Resources) agrees to the Kyoto Accord in Japan to reduce greenhouse gas emissions by 6% (*December 15*). Sets up the CPP (Canada Pension Plan) Investment Board to tease out greater returns on the invested money (*December*). Enjoys a ski holiday in Colorado with his grandchildren; two RCMP officers end up with broken bones trying to keep up with him on the slopes (*December*).

1998: A severe ice storm knocks out power and damages the roof at 24 Sussex Drive (*January 6*); delays his trade mission to South America. The government apologizes for mistreatment of Indigenous peoples, including abuse in residential schools (*January 7*). Leads the second Team Canada trade mission to Brazil, Argentina and Chile (*January*). Establishes the Aboriginal Human Resources Development Council to improve Indigenous employment (*January 23*). A bill to expand the Wheat Board's influence to crops beyond barley and wheat is passed (*February 17*). The Senate suspends its first member, Andrew Thompson, for poor attendance (*February 18*). Martin (Finance) presents a budget that breaks even, the first non-deficit budget in 28 years (*February 24*). Alan Rock (National Health & Welfare) presents a compensation package to victims who contracted hepatitis C from tainted blood from 1986 to mid-1990, sparking outrage from those affected before or after those dates (*March 27*). Jean Charest steps down as Conservative party leader to seek, successfully, the leadership of the Quebec Liberals (*April 2*); replaced by interim leader Elsie Wayne. Attends the second Summit of the Americas, held in Santiago, Chile, for more free trade talks (*April 18-19*). Visits Cuba and meets with President Fidel Castro (*April 26-28*). Attends the G8 Summit in Birmingham, England (*May 15-17*). Visits Canadian soldiers in Bosnia (*May*). The government buys the property adjacent to his Lac des Piles cottage for security. Nova Scotia becomes the final English province to endorse the Calgary Declaration (*June 9*); Quebec's Bouchard refers to it as 'doomed' since he will never approve it. Rejects a request from provincial finance ministers to restore health funding, although Martin says he'll consider it (*June 15*). Launches the Child Benefit that provides a tax credit to families making less than $26,000 (*June 18*). David Anderson (Fisheries) offers $1.1 billion to help east and west coast fishing industries devastated by dwindling fish stocks and tight quotas on fishing (*June 19*). The dollar hits a new all-time low of 67.77 cents U.S. (*June 22*). Joins British Columbia in reaching an agreement with the Nisga'a people to grant them 1,992 sq. km of land and self-government (*July 15*). The Supreme Court rules that Quebec cannot make a unilateral declaration of independence, but Ottawa would be obliged to negotiate terms (*August 20*). Appoints Douglas Roche as an Alberta Senator, ignoring the province's wish to elect a candidate (*September 17*). Meets with South African President Nelson Mandela who addresses Parliament (*September 24*). Canadian Blood Services is launched (*September 28*). Canada is elected to the UN Security Council for a two-year term beginning in January (*October 8*). Tells *La Presse* that "the Constitution is not a general store", jeopardizing Charest's chances against the Parti Québécois in the expected provincial election (*October*). Joe Clark returns as leader of the Conservative party (*November 14*). Andy Scott (Solicitor General) resigns following remarks on a flight early in the year that might have compromised the APEC inquiry (*November 23*). The gun registry comes into effect, requiring all firearms to be registered by 2003 (*December 1*). Gerald Morin resigns as chair of the APEC inquiry, citing RCMP interference (*December 4*). Martin (Finance) rejects plans by four major Canadian banks to merge (*December 14*).

1999: Receives an honorary doctorate from the Warsaw School of Economics in Poland (*January 26*). Signs a social union agreement with nine provinces giving them looser guidelines on spending federal grants and a commitment to remove many of the interprovincial barriers to post-secondary education, employment, health care and social assistance (*February 4*). Criticized for not interrupting his Whistler ski trip to attend the funeral of King Hussein of Jordan (*February 8*). A bill is passed to give Indigenous band councils control over reserve lands (*March 8*). Announces the Canadian Debt Initiative to forgive third-world loans at a quicker pace than the international Heavily Indebted Poor Countries program (*March*). Attends the 50th anniversary gala performance in St. John's of Newfoundland's entry into Confederation (*March 31*). The Territory of Nunavut is created in the eastern Arctic (*April 1*). Responds angrily to a *National Post* editorial that suggests he profited personally from Shawinigate (*April 9*). Plays trombone with Dan Ackroyd at 24 Sussex in a quasi Blues Brothers jam (*April 15*). Newfoundland changes its name to Newfoundland & Labrador (*April 29*). Revenue Canada merges with Canada Customs to form the Canada Customs and Revenue Agency (*April 29*); it splits again in 2003. Meets with Czech President Vaclav Havel who addresses Parliament (*April 29*). Receives an honorary Doctor of Laws degree from Michigan State University in Ann Arbor (*May 7*). The House votes to retain the definition of marriage as being between a man and a woman, despite the Supreme Court declaring earlier that a lawful marriage was between two persons (*June 8*). Appoints UN war crimes prosecutor Louise Arbour to the Supreme Court (*June 10*). Becomes the first Prime Minister to visit Austria where he addresses the Organization for Security and Co-operation in Europe (*June 17*). Attends the G8 Summit in Cologne, Germany (*June 18-20*). Sued by publisher Conrad Black who was denied a British peerage (*August*); the lawsuit fails in court and on appeal since the denial follows Canadian policy. His wife Aline hits a hole in one at the Royal Ottawa Golf Club, something he never matches (*August 13*). Builds a retirement home beside his cottage on Lac des Piles. Hosts La Francophonie in Moncton (*September 3-5*). Visits the Arctic with French President Chirac (*September*). Announces the appointment of journalist Adrienne Clarkson as Canada's 26th Governor General (*September 8*). Cancels a Team Canada trade mission to Australia after several premiers drop out (*September 9*). The Reform party narrowly approves the United Alternative initiative to merge with the Conservatives (*September 13*). Participates in an international conference on federalism at Mont Tremblant with U.S. President Clinton (lured to the event by a game of golf) and Mexican President Zedillo (lured by a private Diana Krall concert) (*October 6-8*). Visits Senegal and Nigeria (*November 7-11*). Attends the Commonwealth Heads of Government conference in South Africa (*November 12-14*). Attends the OECD meeting in Turkey (*November*). Liberal Irwin Cotler wins the Mount Royal by-election (Trudeau's former riding) with 92% of the vote, one of the highest majorities on record (*November 15*). Canadian Airlines agrees to a $92 million takeover bid by Air Canada (*December 4*). Dion (Intergovernmental Affairs) introduces the Clarity Act with its ground rules for any future Quebec secession initiatives (*December 13*). Takes part in millennium celebrations on Parliament Hill (*December 31*).

2000: Appoints Beverley McLachlin as the 17th Chief Justice of Canada, the country's first female top judge (*January 7*). An audit of Human Resources Development Canada is released, indicating that nearly $1 billion in grants was released with little or no monitoring (*January 19*). The Reform party proposes to rename itself the Canadian Reform Conservative Alliance, or Canadian Alliance party for short (*January 29*). Introduces legislation giving same-sex couples the same benefits as common-law couples (*February 11*). Plans to stay on to fight another election, although he recognizes interest in having Martin (Finance) replace him (*March 13*). Maintains control of the leadership at the Liberal convention, despite efforts by Martin's backers for a review (*March 18*). His brother Maurice publicly suggests it might be time for him to step down (*March 21*). Opposition Leader Preston Manning steps down to seek the leadership of the new Canadian Alliance party (*March 26*); replaced by acting leader Deborah Gray. Tours the Middle East, becoming the first Prime Minister to visit Israel, Gaza, Lebanon, Jordan and Syria; also visits Egypt and Saudi Arabia (*April 9-21*). Receives an honorary degree from Hebrew

University of Jerusalem (*April*). Visits Clayoquot Sound with British Columbia Premier Ujjal Dosanjh, recognizing its designation as a UNESCO biosphere reserve (*May 4*). Receives an honorary Doctor of Laws degree from Memorial University (*May 24*). The Supreme Court upholds the government's 1995 gun control legislation (*June 15*). Alberta's former treasurer Stockwell Day wins the Canadian Alliance leadership (*July 8*). Matthew Coon Come is elected National Chief of the Assembly of First Nations, replacing Phil Fontaine (*July 12*). Joins other leaders at the UN in New York to help launch eight Millennium Development Goals, including eradicating poverty (*July*). Attends the G8 Summit in Nago, Japan (*July 21-23*). Goes white water rafting on the Ottawa River to counter concerns about his advancing age (*July 27*). Hit in the face with a pie in Charlottetown by a demonstrator protesting federal economic and social policies (*August 16*). Hosts a meeting with the premiers in Ottawa; agrees to increase health care and social funding to the provinces by $23.4 billion over five years (*September 10-11*). Conservative leader Clark and Canadian Alliance leader Day win by-elections (*September 11*); Day becomes Leader of the Opposition, replacing Gray. Challenged by Day to call an election, giving him an opening to do just that (*September 25*). Attends the Caribbean Community (CARICOM) meeting in Jamaica (*September 28*). Attends the funeral of former prime minister Trudeau in Montreal (*October 3*). Announces he'll rename Canada's highest mountain, the Yukon's Mount Logan, after Pierre Trudeau (*October 4*); public outcry causes him to back down. Persuades Newfoundland Premier Brian Tobin and Royal Bank economist John McCallum to run as Liberal candidates in the next election (*October 13*). Axworthy (Foreign Affairs) resigns to accept a University of British Columbia posting and is replaced by John Manley (Industry) (*October 17*). Martin (Finance) tables a mini-budget offering the largest tax cuts in Canada's history (*October 18*). Releases his Red Book III election platform (*November 1*). Accused in a *National Post* article of calling the Federal Business Development Bank to urge them to make a decision in 1997 about a loan to the new owner of the Auberge Grand-Mère (*November 16*). Rejects a call by political opponents to launch an inquiry into his dealings with Auberge Grand-Mère (*November 20*); ethics counselor Howard Wilson says he did not violate any government rules. Media stories appear, connecting Auberge Grand-Mère with funding from the Immigrant Investor Program (*November*). Meets with Innu leaders in Shawinigan to address a crisis of glue sniffing by young people in Davis Inlet and Sheshatshiu (*November 26*). Canada's 37th federal election: re-elected in Saint-Maurice defeating François Marchand (Bloc Québécois); wins his third consecutive majority government (*November 27*). Meets for the last time with U.S. President Clinton in Washington (*December 2*). Meets with Russian President Vladimir Putin in Ottawa (*December 18*). Hosts the European Union-Canada Summit in Ottawa (*December 19*).

2001: On his birthday, marks Quebec Premier Lucien Bouchard's retirement from politics by describing him as an "able parliamentarian who has fought for his beliefs with passion and determination" (*January 11*). Discusses the creation of a Canadian Museum of Human Rights with newspaper baron Izzy Asper (*January*). Forced by Martin's (Finance) supporters to announce his intention to resign by Fall 2002 or face a leadership vote (*January 26*). 37th Parliament opens with Peter Milliken elected 34th Speaker of the House (*January 29*). Meets with U.S. President George W. Bush in Washington (*February 4*). Leads a Team Canada trade mission to China (*February*). Forces Liberals to vote in the House against their Red Book promise to appoint an independent ethics counsellor (*February 13*). The Auto Pact with the U.S. ends after the World Trade Organization declares it violates international trade laws (*February 19*). Meets with British Prime Minister Tony Blair who addresses Parliament (*February 22*). Appoints former Saskatchewan premier Roy Romanow to chair an inquiry into the health care system (*April 4*). His supporters reach an agreement with Martin's for a leadership review in February

2003 (*April 19*). Hosts the Summit of the Americas in Quebec City and invites Chief of the Assembly of First Nations Matthew Coon Come to attend (*April 20-22*). Coon Come rejects a proposed overhaul of the Indian Act unless Indigenous peoples take part in the changes (*May 10*). Eight Canadian Alliance MPs refuse to sit in the House as long as Day is leader (*May 15*). Appoints Sheila Fraser as the first female Auditor General (*May 31*). The House passes a bill giving MPs a 20% pay raise and a 42% hike for the Prime Minister (*June 7*). Attends the Canada-European Union Summit in Sweden (*June*); his flight home is forced to return to Stockholm after the aircraft malfunctions. Health Canada provides access to marijuana for medicinal purposes (*July*). Attends the G8 Summit in Genoa, Italy (*July 20-22*). The APEC inquiry report is tabled outlining evidence of RCMP incompetence and meddling by the Prime Minister's Office (*August*). The Democratic Representative Caucus, a group of 12 rebel Alliance MPs, agrees to work with Progressive Conservative MPs (*August 28*). Plays a round of golf in Montreal with Tiger Woods before the Canadian Open (*September 5*). Collenette (Transport) oversees the diversion of U.S. airplanes to Canadian airports like Gander shortly after the 9/11 terrorist attacks in New York and Washington (*September 11*). Conducts a news scrum on Parliament Hill shortly after the 9/11 attacks, offering the U.S. any support that is needed (*September 11*). Speaks at a 9/11 memorial gathering on Parliament Hill attended by 100,000 people (*September 14*). Meets with U.S. President Bush in Washington to discuss security issues (*September 24*). Visits Ground Zero in New York City with opposition party leaders (*September 29*). Announces that Canada will contribute to the UN-backed NATO force fighting terrorism in Afghanistan (*October 7*). Attends the APEC Summit in Shanghai, China (*October 21*). Nelson Mandela becomes the first living person to be named a Canadian honorary citizen (*November 19*). Anti-terrorism legislation is passed in the House (*November 28*). Day resigns as Leader of the Opposition and Canadian Alliance leader (*December 12*) and is replaced in both positions by acting leader John Reynolds.

2002: Removes Alfonso Gagliano (Public Works) from cabinet amid growing allegations of misspent funds, making him Ambassador to Denmark (*January 14*). The Canadian dollar falls to a low of 61 cents U.S. (*January 21*). Leads a Team Canada trade mission to Russia and Germany (*February*). Meets with U.S. President Bush in Washington to talk about softwood lumber duties (*March 14*); unable to prevent a permanent U.S. duty. Informed by Don Boudria (Public Works) that funding to the advertising firm Groupaction to sponsor and evaluate post-referendum recreational events is suspect (*March*); an audit is requested. Stephen Harper is elected Canadian Alliance leader (*March 20*). Meets with Nelson Mandela in Pretoria, South Africa (*April 8*). Attends the funeral of Elizabeth, the Queen Mother, in London (*April 9*). Canadian Alliance and Progressive Conservatives fail to unite their parties (*April 9*). Four Canadian soldiers in Afghanistan are killed and eight wounded by a U.S. jet during night exercises (*April 17*). A process to resolve disputes about the Canada Health Act is accepted by all provinces except Quebec (*April 24*). Sheila Fraser, auditor general, releases a report accusing Public Works of having broken "just about every rule in the book" when awarding $1.6 million in contracts to Groupaction (*May 8*); RCMP to investigate. Promises to use all of the year's predicted budget surplus to pay down the $540-billion debt (*May 9*). Meets with French President Chirac in Paris (*May 13*). Harper becomes Leader of the Opposition, replacing acting leader Reynolds (*May 21*). Reassigns Boudria (Public Works) to a lower cabinet position after he spends a weekend at a resort owned by a recipient of federal funds (*May 26*). Directs candidates to stop campaigning for the leadership (*May 30*); Martin refuses. Martin (Finance) resigns and is replaced by Manley (Foreign Affairs) (*June 2*). Many in caucus urge him to resign (*June 5*). A bill to overhaul the Indian Act is tabled, but does not have the support of various Indigenous organizations (*June 15*). Unveils a farm aid program to provide $5.2 billion in emergency funding over the next two years (*June 20*). Removes Art Eggleton (National Defence) from cabinet for hiring an ex-girlfriend (*June 25*). Hosts the G8 Summit in Kananaskis, Alta., where the focus is on addressing poverty in Africa (*June 26-27*). His son Michel is again charged with sexual assault (*July*). Meets Pope John Paul II at World Youth Day in Toronto (*July 24*). His organizers attempt to get supporters to sign letters of allegiance, getting signatures from about 55% of caucus (*August*). Announces in Chicoutimi that he intends to step down as leader in February 2004 (*August 21*). Attends the Earth Summit in Johannesburg, South Africa (*August 26-September 4*). Meets in Detroit with U.S. President Bush who is thinking about invading Iraq (*September 9*). Receives World Statesman of the Year award from the Appeal of Conscience Foundation in New York (*October 1*). Announces plans for the creation of 10 national parks and five marine conservation reserves over the next five years (*October 4*). Visits Lebanon (*October 17*). Lawrence McAuley (Solicitor General) resigns from cabinet after accusations he misdirected federal funds to relatives and friends (*October 22*). Introduces new ethics guidelines with a code of conduct for MPs and tighter requirements for lobbyists (*October 23*). Opposed by 56 members of his own party in a vote on an Alliance motion to have committee chairs chosen by secret ballot instead of by the Prime Minister (*November 6*). Attends a NATO Summit in Prague (*November 21-22*); communications director Françoise Ducros is quoted by the media calling Bush "a moron" for favouring an Iraq war and resigns from the PMO soon after. Romanow's Royal Commission on the Future of Health Care recommends $15 billion be put into medicare by 2006 to stop the growth of private medicine (*November 28*). His oldest brother Maurice dies at age 91 (*November 29*). Pledges $11.9 million to help Afghanistan rebuild its legal system and army (*December 2*). The Auditor General tables a report that indicates the gun registry, estimated to cost $2 million, could end up rising to $1 billion by 2005 (*December 3*). Signs the Kyoto Protocol approved a week earlier by the House (*December 16*).

2003: Indicates a willingness to expand Canada's role in Afghanistan as part of the International Security Assistance Force (ISAF) (*January*). Jack Layton is elected leader of the New Democratic party, replacing McDonough (*January 25*). Hosts a first ministers conference in Ottawa where a $27-billion, five-year deal is reached with the provinces on health care (*February 5*). Tells a Chicago audience that the U.S. should get UN backing for any war in Iraq (*February 13*). Informs the House that Canada will not join the Iraq war effort (*March 17*). Dines at a Chinese restaurant in Toronto to dispel the concerns about the scope of the SARS epidemic (*April 10*); reminds the media that dealing with the outbreak is a provincial responsibility. Rejects Newfoundland's call to renegotiate its terms of union with Canada (*May 14*). His son Michel is found not guilty of three sex-related charges in Yellowknife (*May 15*). Attends the 300th Anniversary celebrations in St. Petersburg, Russia (*May 29-31*). Peter MacKay is elected leader of the Progressive Conservative party, replacing Clark (*May 31*). Attends the G7 Summit in Évian-les-Bains, France (*June 1-3*). Visits Juno Beach in Normandy (*June 6*). Receives an honorary degree from Pontificia Universidad Católica Madre y Maestra in the Dominican Republic. The government provides compensation to farmers affected by mad cow disease after the U.S. prohibits beef exports (*June 17*). Premiers agree to create a Council of the Federation to provide a united front in negotiations with the federal government (*July 17*). Asks the Supreme Court to rule on the legality of his proposed same-sex marriage legislation, effectively moving the issue on to the next government (*July 11*). Phil Fontaine defeats Matthew Come Coon to become National Chief of the Assembly of First Nations (*July 16*). Criticized for keeping a low profile when a power outage blacks out Ontario and the U.S. northeast (*August 14*). Indicates he is not putting a priority on the proposed First Nations Governance Act (*August 23*). The opposition parties call for a judicial inquiry into the sponsorship scandal (*September 15*). Unveils the national Korean War memorial in Ottawa (*September 28*). The Canadian Alliance and Progressive Conservative parties announce their intention to merge

(*October 17*). Lifts his chair over his head at his last caucus meeting as Liberal party leader (*November 5*). George Radwanski, former privacy commissioner, becomes the first Canadian found in contempt of Parliament after altering documents and misrepresenting expense claims (*November 6*). The Second Session, 37th Parliament is prorogued, killing his new ethics guidelines and pre-empting the release of the auditor general's report on the sponsorship scandal (*November 12*). Gives his farewell speech to Liberals at the leadership convention in Toronto (*November 13*). Martin is elected leader on the first ballot (*November 14*). Indicates he will resign two months earlier than planned (*November 16*). The Canadian Alliance party votes 96 per cent in favour of joining the Progressive Conservative party to create a new Conservative party (*December 5*). Attends the Commonwealth Heads of Government meeting in Abuja, Nigeria (*December 5-8*). Stephen Harper steps down as Canadian Alliance leader to seek the leadership of the new Conservative party (*December 8*); Senator John Lynch-Staunton becomes the Conservative interim leader. Makes his last official visit to France (*December 9*). Resigns as leader and as MP for Saint-Maurice (*December 12*). **Chrétien's government ends** (*December 12*). Moves to a condominium not far from 24 Sussex (*December*).

2004: Hired by Heenan Blaikie law firm in Montreal, the same firm that hired Trudeau (*January 5*). Martin sets up a public inquiry into the sponsorship scandal to be headed by Quebec Justice John Gomery (*Feburary 10*). Delivers the eulogy at the funeral of Mitchell Sharp in Ottawa (*March 27*). Calls the sponsorship scandal an administrative problem in which wrongdoers should be jailed (*March 30*). Receives an honorary Doctor of Laws degree from Queen's University (*May 27*).

2005: Testifies before the Gomery inquiry and criticizes the chair for his comments in the media (*February 8*). Withdraws his court application calling for the removal of Justice Gomery as head of the sponsorship scandal inquiry (*May 30*). Receives an honorary Doctor of Laws degree from McMaster University (*June 8*). The Gomery report says that although he was not directly involved in the sponsorship scandal, he bears some of the responsibility (*November 1*). Files a challenge to Gomery's findings (*November 30*).

2006: The academic he brought into politics, Stéphane Dion, is elected leader of the Liberal party (*December 2*).

2007: Attends the funeral of former Russian president Boris Yeltsin in Moscow (*April*). Awarded the Companion of the Order of Canada (*May 3*). Receives an honorary degree from National University of Kyiv-Mohyla Academy in Ukraine (*May 24*). Undergoes emergency quadruple-bypass heart surgery in Montreal (*October 3*). His second book of memoirs, *My Years As Prime Minister*, is published (*October 16*).

2008: Becomes co-president of the InterAction Council of Former Heads of State and Government. Becomes an honorary member of the Fondation Chirac that fosters peace through advocacy programs (*June 9*). Receives an honorary joint degree with Aline from the Université du Québec à Trois-Rivières (*November 23*). The Federal Court strikes down the Gomery finding that he bore some of the responsibility for the sponsorship scandal (*June 26*); appealed by the Conservative government. Receives on honorary Doctor of Laws degree from the University of Western Ontario (*October*). Works with former NDP leader Ed Broadbent to forge a coalition agreement between the Liberals and New Democrats with Bloc Québécois and Green support to overturn the Harper government (*November*).

2009: Receives the British Order of Merit from Elizabeth II, the third Canadian after King and Pearson (*October 20*).

2010: Attends the unveiling of his portrait on Parliament Hill painted by Christian Nicholson (*May 25*). Receives an honorary Doctor of Laws degree from Concordia

University (*Spring*). Undergoes brain surgery (*August 6*). His wife Aline is appointed as the first chancellor of Laurentian University in Sudbury (*September 22*). The Federal Court upholds the appeal exonerating him from responsibility as determined in the Gomery commission into the sponsorship scandal (*October 26*).

2011: Receives an honorary degree from the University of Montreal. Attends Jack Layton's funeral in Toronto, then climbs over a barricade for a CTV interview (*August 27*). In a CBC interview, suggests a Liberal-NDP merger is possible, if it happens quickly (*September 6*). Jogs and pushes Rick Hansen's wheelchair in the Rick Hansen Relay in Ottawa (*October 27*). Awarded $200,000 from the Harper government to pay for legal costs in the sponsorship scandal (*December 22*).

2012: Attends Laurentian University's Model Parliament in Sudbury where his wife, who is the university's chancellor, plays the role of Governor General (*January 6*). Appointed by Harper to be Canada's representative on the Queen Elizabeth Jubilee Trust (*April 30*). Featured on a Le Trou du Diable beer label administering the Shawinigan Handshake choke hold on hockey broadcaster Don Cherry (*May 17*). Participates in the Fourth Congress of Leaders of World and Traditional Religions in Astana, Kazakhstan (*May 29*). The Chrétien Museum, with gifts he received as Prime Minister, officially opens in an old Shawinigan aluminum factory that used to employ his father-in-law (*June 16*). Receives the Queen Elizabeth II Diamond Jubilee medal. Swaps five properties on Lac des Piles with the city of Shawinigan for the property adjoining his cottage on the lake (*October*).

2013: Attends the funeral of Venezuelan President Hugo Chavez in Caracas (*March 8*). Visits London to provide advice to the 'No' forces in the 2014 Scotland independence vote (*May 15*). Goes wakeboarding, at 79, in North Carolina; not enough wind to go kiteboarding (*May 24*). Granddaughter Jacqueline-Ariadne Desmarais marries Prince Hadrien de Croy-Roeulx of Belgium in Montreal (*September 9*). Flies to South Africa with Harper to attend Nelson Mandela's funeral (*December 8*).

2014: Receives Russia's Order of Friendship in Ottawa (*January 24*). Moves to Dentons Canada law office in Ottawa after Heenan Blaikie folds (*February 10*). Receives an honorary Doctor of Laws degree from the University of Winnipeg (*June 12*).

2015: Joins Liberal leader Justin Trudeau in Mississauga to celebrate the 50th anniversary of the Canadian flag (*February 15*). Issues a letter with Clark, Turner and Martin calling for stricter oversight of CSIS in anti-terrorism legislation tabled by the government (*February 19*). Meets with Russian President Vladimir Putin while on business in Moscow (*April 30*). Appears in a YouTube video waterskiing at age 81 (*August 4*).

2016: Serves as a co-chair of The Pearson Centre's think tank called the Pursuing Justice Project, along with Turner, Campbell and Martin (*March 31*). Draws criticism for suggesting Cree residents of the remote northern Ontario community of Attiwapiskat, plagued with high suicide rates, may have to move (*April 13*). Meets with Chinese Premier Li Keqiang in Beijing (*April 19*). Opens the MacEachen Institute of Public Policy at Dalhousie University in Halifax (*May 9*). Attends the funeral of former Israeli prime minister Shimon Peres in Tel Aviv along with Harper and Prime Minister Trudeau (*September 30*).

2017: Sits with the Duke of Edinburgh at the Order of Merit luncheon in London (*May 4*). Meets with Vietnamese Prime Minister Nguyen Xuan Phuc in Hanoi (*May 18*). Is the first former prime minister to speak in a series of presentations for Canada 150 at the University of Saskatchewan in Saskatoon (*September 27*).

Books about Chrétien

- **1985**: Jean Chrétien; *Straight from the Heart* (Key Porter) (revised 1994)
- **1995**: Maude Barlow & Bruce Campbell; *Straight Through the Heart: How the Liberals Abandoned the Just Society* (HarperCollins)
- **1995**: Lawrence Martin; *Chrétien: The Will To Win, Vol. 1* (Lester)
- **1996**: Edward Greenspon & Anthony Wilson-Smith; *Double Vision: The Inside Story of the Liberals in Power* (Doubleday Canada)
- **2001**: Jeffrey Simpson; *The Friendly Dictatorship* (McClelland & Stewart)
- **2003**: Lawrence Martin: *Iron Man: The Defiant Reign of Jean Chrétien, Vol. 2* (Penguin)
- **2003**: Edward McWhinney; *Chrétien and Canadian Federalism: Politics and the Constitution 1993-2003* (Ronsdale)
- **2004**: Paul Tuns; *Jean Chrétien: A Legacy of Scandal* (Tristan Emmanuel)
- **2006**: Lois Harder & Steve Patten (eds.); *The Chrétien Legacy: Public Policy in Canada* (McGill-Queen's University)
- **2007**: Jean Chrétien: *My Years as Prime Minister* (Knopf Canada)
- **2017**: Bob Plamondon; *Shawinigan Fox: How Jean Chretien Defied the Elites and Reshaped Canada* (Great River Media)

21

Paul Martin

The Unoffending Prime Minister

Paul Martin Jr. is best remembered for his role in eliminating federal deficits and helping to birth the G20 international summits, achievements that dated to his time as finance minister. When he succeeded Chrétien as Prime Minister, he bore the brunt of the Liberal's sponsorship scandal in Quebec, which was a factor in reducing the party to a minority government in 2004. Before losing a confidence vote a year and a half later, Martin was able to hammer out agreements for child care, health care and relations with Indigenous peoples. Many of the proposals were axed by the next government.

Martin the Politician

Prime Minister of Canada: December 12, 2003 – February 6, 2006
Length of term: 2 years, 10 months, 6 days
Parliaments as Prime Minister: 37th; 38th
Age on entering office: 65
Political party: Liberal
Leader of party: November 14, 2003 – March 19, 2006
Member of Parliament: November 21, 1988 – October 14, 2008
Riding represented: LaSalle/Émard [Que.] 1988-2008
Cabinet portfolios: Finance (1993-2001); Federal Office of Regional Development, Quebec (1993-1996)
Other political post: none
Titles: Canadian Privy Councillor (1993); Companion of the Order of Canada (2011)
Quotes: "I have no regrets about my desire to shake things up as prime minister. That's why I wanted the job." (in his memoirs *Hell or High Water*, 2008); "I was terrible at math, but … I could intuit numbers. I don't know how (on CPAC's *Beyond Politics* with Catherine Clark, 2013).

Martin the Man

Name: Paul Edgar Philippe Martin Jr.

Born: August 28, 1938, Windsor, Ontario
Ancestry: French, English
Religion: Roman Catholic
Education: B.A. [Bachelor of Arts in History and Philosophy] (University of Toronto, 1961); LLB [Bachelor of Law] (Toronto, 1964)
Military service: none
Occupation: lawyer; business executive
Occupation after term: philanthropist
Publications: *Hell or High Water: My Life In and Out of Politics* (2008); *Canada and Aboriginal Canada Today: Changing the Course of History* (2015)
Appearance: "he's got the charm and the twinkling eyes down pat." (Patrick Gossage to Marci Macdonald in *The Walrus*, 2003); "wide eyes, visible teeth and an expression that always carried some modicum of shock." (Tristin Hopper in the *National Post*, 2016)
Personality: "Many people who are really hard-working are not great thinkers because the volume of the work gets in the way of the thinking process. He did both." (John Godfrey to John Gray in *Paul Martin: The Power of Ambition*); "He is essentially an ordinary person who has achieved extraordinary things." (Robert Chodos, Rae Murphy & Eric Hamovitch in *Paul Martin: A Political Biography*)
Married: Sheila Ann Cowan, September 11, 1965, Our Lady of the Assumption Roman Catholic Church, Windsor, Ontario
Age at marriage: 27

Martin was the:
- First Prime Minister whose father was a cabinet minister
- Second English Canadian Catholic from Quebec
- Third Prime Minister defeated by a non-confidence vote
- Fifth Prime Minister to serve as Finance minister
- Fifth Prime Minister born in Ontario
- Ninth Liberal Prime Minister
- Fifteenth Prime Minister who was a lawyer

Martin's legacy
- Produced a new tax deal for cities
- Brokered a 10-year, $41 billion health care agreement with the provinces
- Negotiated the Kelowna Accord with Canada's Indigenous peoples
- Legalized same-sex marriage
- Developed the first national child care agreement with the provinces
- Helped develop the UN's Responsibility to Protect (R2P) principle
- Helped create the G20 Summit and eliminate deficit budgets (as Finance minister)

Martin's Family

Martin's Parents

Father: Joseph James Guillaume Paul Martin
Born: June 23, 1903, Ottawa, Ontario
Occupation: MP; cabinet minister; diplomat

Died: September 14, 1992, Windsor, Ontario
Age at death: 89

Mother: Eleanor 'Nell' Alice Adams
Born: 1913, McGregor, Ontario
Married: September 8, 1937, Windsor, Ontario
Died: November 11, 1993, Windsor, Ontario
Age at death: 80

Martin's Sister (1 sibling; Paul the oldest)

Sister: Mary-Anne Martin (1944-2011), 2 daughters
Married: Michael Bellamy (1970)

Martin's Wife

Name: Sheila Ann Cowan
Born: July 31, 1943, Windsor, Ontario
Father: William Cowan (law partner of Paul Martin Sr.)
Mother: Sheila Scott
Age at marriage: 22
Younger than Martin: 5 years

Martin's Children (3)

Name: Paul William Martin
Born: September 11, 1966, Montreal, Quebec
Occupation: Chairman, CSL Group
Married: Alysia Yip-Hoi
Children: 2 – Sienna; Lara

Name: James 'Jamie' Robert Martin
Born: June 21, 1969, Montreal, Quebec
Occupation: screenwriter; film producer

Name: David Patrick Martin
Born: June 13, 1974, Montreal, Quebec
Occupation: investment banker; executive; environmentalist
Married: Laurence Duguay (July 10, 2004)
Children: 3 – Ethan; Liam; Finn

Political Stories

The deficit crusader

Four other Prime Ministers served as Finance minister before assuming the top job – Tupper, Bennett, Turner and Chrétien – but Martin's time in the position proved to be the most signficant. Seen as the man who wrestled 28 years of deficit budgeting into submission, he was never quite able to match that performance when he became leader.

Martin unwillingly accepted the Finance portfolio when it was offered by Chrétien; he really wanted Industry. But once there, he was insistent that the annual deficits and mounting national debt needed to be tamed. Chrétien backed him up and Martin began pushing cabinet colleagues into a regimen of cost cutting and service reduction.

For six months in 1994, he grilled the ministers and senior staff of almost every federal department to find those savings, coming up with $6.8 billion worth, while Marcel Massé (Intergovernmental Affairs) ensured the cuts worked. Martin's 1995 budget rolled out the largest cutbacks in the country's history -- $25 billion and 4,500 public service jobs over three years.

The pressure (in many cases, suffering) didn't let up for the next two years and, in 1998, Martin was able to offer Canadians a break-even budget. It needed to be done and Martin made it happen. His remaining budgets were also balanced, making it possible to start offering tax cuts.

An architect of the G20

Finding tools to revise the world's financial systems is a colossal challenge that has resulted in bodies like the International Monetary Fund, the World Bank and the World Trade Organization. In the late 1990s, national finance ministers and bank governors continued working to make sense of it all. Martin, Canada's Finance minister, played a key role early on in the discussions that resulted in the creation of the G20.

It was the Mexican peso crisis that convinced Martin an organization broader than the G7 needed to be considered so that more smart minds could help avert future economic calamities. Countries outside the G7 had little reason to accept the financial medicine promoted by the group. A series of meetings involving global finance ministers and officials in 1998-1999 resulted in the creation of Group of 20, or G20, adding developing countries that were not part of the original G7 thinking.

Throughout that time, Martin championed the need to embrace emerging economies, not just the money powerhouses. His active role resulted in his being chosen to chair the first gathering of the G20 finance ministers in Berlin. Meetings in the next two years were hosted by Martin in Montreal, then Ottawa. He went on to play a central role in the G20's evolution until being bumped as Finance minister in 2002.

Gomery Commission fallout

The Liberals sponsorship scandal in Quebec was an unsavory piece of business inherited by Martin. His predecessor, Chrétien, chose to ignore it as an administrative hassle. The auditor general felt there was more to it than that and Martin decided to mount an inquiry.

Justice John Gomery started his hearings in the fall of 2004, calling on both Martin and Chrétien to testify. As the inquiry and the media coverage dragged on, the Liberals could see the impact in their sinking poll rankings. Martin apologized to Canadians in a televised address, promising to call an election within a month of the release of Gomery's report.

Canadians didn't have to wait that long. Although Gomery had cleared Martin of any wrongdoing, the minority Liberal government lost a non-confidence vote, forcing an election. By the time Gomery's report was tabled, Martin had been defeated by Harper's Conservatives.

Forging the doomed Kelowna Accord

Martin got his first impressions of Indigenous peoples, and the raw hand they'd been dealt, while working as a 19-year-old deckhand plying the Mackenzie River. His desire to address this unfairness became a lifelong passion that particularly blossomed after he left elected office.

Early in his mandate, he met with 75 Indigenous organizations and MPs – 500 people altogether – to start the process. The provincial and territorial leaders agreed to discuss it further and Indigenous leaders would be part of those discussions. By the time the Summit meeting took place in Kelowna, B.C., the support of most players was secured, as was the significant financial commitment needed from the federal government. On November 24, 2005, the $5 billion Kelowna Accord achieved consensus.

Four days later, the government was defeated in the House and Parliament was dissolved. When the Harper government was elected, it refused to act on the Kelowna initiative. The deal died.

PERSONAL STORIES

Martin Sr. and Jr.

Throughout his childhood, Martin witnessed first-hand the esteem in which his father, Paul Martin Sr., was held by the people of Essex East. Whether campaigning or simply making the rounds in the riding, the personable MP and cabinet minister, often accompanied by Martin Jr., clearly loved what he was doing.

Elected office posed no lure to the younger Martin, even though he worked on his father's 1958 and 1968 leadership campaigns. When he did start to take an interest, his father urged him to wait until he was 45 and established in another career. He didn't seek office until he was 49.

No other Prime Minister had come into office with a father who had enjoyed such a prominent political career (until Justin Trudeau followed nine years later). Paul Martin Sr. was a cabinet minister with King, St. Laurent, Pearson and Trudeau. He was one of the few League of Nations delegates to play the same role in the United Nations. He ushered in medicare as the Health & Welfare minister. Two months before he died, he received the special 'Right Honourable' designation reserved for Prime Ministers.

Explaining why he was so close to his father who was busy on the national and international stages, Martin noted in his memoirs that "it is not always the quantity but the quality of the time you spend together…Dad and I would often go off into Lake Erie, or to Lake St. Clair, and laze away hours together with nothing more to disturb us than the nibbling fish."

A night in jail

Always ready to help his father on the campaign trail, Martin and others from the campus Liberal club at the University of Toronto headed to Massey Hall in March 1958 to hear Paul Martin Sr. and the man who had recently beat him for the leadership, Mike Pearson. After the rally, the students moved over to Yonge Street, deciding where to go for a drink.

Asked to move along by a Toronto police officer, Martin dug in his heels. "You can't make us go," he argued, citing his rights. By the time the paddy wagons arrived, most of the other U of T students had quietly vanished. Martin wasn't so lucky; he was locked up for the night.

Appearing before the judge the next morning, the only-somewhat chastened Martin was ready with his defence against his trampled civil liberties. Instead, the judge preempted his plea with one of his own: "Why don't you just get out of here, go home, and stop causing trouble?"

Martin's father learned about the incident the next morning on the radio. He wasn't so sure his son was helping the Liberal cause.

Sheila Martin

Martin almost literally married the girl next door. Sheila Cowan lived a few houses away in Windsor's Walkerville neighbourhood. She was a close friend of Martin's sister Mary-Ann and their fathers were law partners. He'd known her most of his life, but she was five years younger and not on his radar as he was growing up.

The neighbours reconnected at the University of Toronto. Sheila needed a ride home to Windsor for the weekend and law student Martin had a car. It was the start of a relationship that resulted in his proposal two years later, not long after she fractured her ankle on a ski trip to Blue Mountain in Ontario.

When Martin moved from the corporate world to politics, Sheila was an active and constant campaigner. Often quiet in public, her biggest political asset for him was her ardent social conscience. Part of that was demonstrated in her committee work for the Writer's Trust of Canada's Politics and the Pen annual event to promote and reward Canadian writing and writers.

Martin's Timeline

1938: Born at Hotel Dieu Hospital in Windsor, Ont. (*August 28*); his father leaves for Europe four days later as a Canadian delegate to the League of Nations.

1939: Spends first of many summers at the Adams' family cottage in Colchester on Lake Erie (*Summer*).

1945: Family moves to Goulburn Street in Ottawa because his father is Secretary of State in King's cabinet (*Fall*). Attends École Garneau, although he speaks little French (*Fall*).

1946: Rushed to hospital in Windsor with polio (*August*). Quickly begins to recover from polio (*Fall*). His father becomes Minister of National Health & Welfare in the King government (*December 21*).

1948: His father continues in the cabinet of the St. Laurent government (*November 15*).

1950: Family moves to 448 Daly Avenue in Ottawa (*Summer*).

1952: Picks tomatoes and tobacco for several weeks (*Summer*).

1953: Works on a Lake Erie fishing boat (*Summer*). Works on his father's re-election campaign in Essex East (*Summer*).

1954: Works in the office at Hiram Walker distillery, then in construction with Eastern Construction (*Summer*).

1955: Works again at Eastern Construction (*Summer*).

1956: Last year at Eastern Construction (*Summer*); accidently crashes the boss's car. Enrols in pre-entrance at the University of Ottawa (*September*).

1957: His family moves back to Windsor after the Liberal government's defeat (*Summer*), eventually moving to a house in the Walkerville neighbourhood that belonged to bootlegger Harry Low during prohibition. Receives tutoring to pass his missed course in algebra (*Summer*). Works for Coca-Cola in Windsor doing truck deliveries (*Summer*). Helps build the Mid-Canada Line, a series of defence stations just south of the Arctic Circle (*Summer*). Enrols at St. Michael's College at the University of Toronto (*Fall*). Asked to join the campus Liberal club (*Fall*).

1958: Helps organize the floor demonstration at the Liberal leadership convention in Ottawa where his father loses to Pearson (*January 16*). Attends a Liberal rally in front of Toronto's Massey Hall and is picked up by police after refusing to disperse (*March*); spends the night in jail. Hired by Canadian Industrial Gas and Oil president Maurice Strong to read gauges in the Alberta oil fields (*Summer*); accidently drives a company truck into a ditch after taking it to visit the Calgary Stampede. Works for the Yellowknife Transportation Company as a deckhand on a Mackenzie River tugboat (*Summer*). Unsuccessfully tries out for the University of Toronto Blues football team (*Fall*).

1960: Drives his sister's best friend, neighbour Sheila Cowan, to the cottage, taking her to a Shakespearean play in Stratford en route (*Summer*).

1961: Receives his honours B.A. in philosophy from the University of Toronto (*Spring*). Enrols in U of T's law school (*Fall*).

1962: Works as a cadet officer on the Canadian vessel *Sun Rhea*, shipping bauxite from Jamaica to Norway (*Summer*).

1963: Reconnects with Sheila Cowan, who is at U of T (*Fall*); they begin dating.

1964: Takes Sheila to Blue Mountain for a skiing weekend; she fractures her ankle (*Winter*). Receives his law degree from the University of Toronto. Works for the legal branch of the European Coal and Steel Community in Luxembourg (*Summer*). Articles with Osler, Hoskin and Harcourt law firm in Toronto (*Fall*). Proposes to Sheila in Colchester (*December*).

1965: Marries Sheila Cowan at Our Lady of the Assumption Roman Catholic Church in Windsor (*September 11*). Moves to an apartment in midtown Toronto (*Fall*). Former boss Strong tells him to work in business instead of law if he wants to tackle Third World issues.

1966: Called to the bar in Ontario (*Winter*). Moves to Montreal (*Winter*). Becomes executive assistant to Strong, president of Power Corporation (*March 1*). Campaigns for a first-time provincial Liberal candidate, Robert Bourassa (*May*); his nose is broken in a campaign scuffle. His son Paul is born in Montreal (*September 11*).

1967: Takes a six-month leave of absence to help run his father's unsuccessful campaign for the Liberal leadership (*December*).

1968: Helps convince his father to stay in the leadership race (*January*). His father polls fourth on the first ballot at the leadership convention (*April 6*). Returns to Power to become a troubleshooter for the new president, Paul Desmarais (*May*). Arranges the profitable sale of Power subsidiary Congoleum Nairn, a linoleum manufacturer.

1969: Becomes a Power vice-president. Seconded to Dominion Glass to help resolve labour disputes. His son Jamie is born in Montreal (*June 21*).

1970: Joins the board of Canada Steamship Lines (CSL) (*December 2*).

1971: Seconded to Consolidated Bathurst as vice president of special projects; it becomes necessary to close some plants to stop financial losses.

1973: Named vice-president of planning and development at Power. Becomes president of CSL, the shipping company. (*November 22*).

1974: Sells CSL's Davie shipyards in Lauzon, Que. His youngest son David is born in Montreal (*June 13*).

1975: Becomes chief executive officer as well as president at CSL.

1976: Advised by his father to wait until he is 45 before entering politics (*March 9*). Buys Valleystream Farms near Knowlton in Quebec's Eastern Townships.

1978: Joins Jean Chrétien, Ed Lumley and John Rae for a round of golf in Montreal, a foursome that gets together again on occasion.

1981: Announces plans to expand CSL beyond its traditional St. Lawrence River-Great Lakes corridor (*June 7*). Purchases Canada Steamship Lines (CSL) with partner Laurence Pathy for $180 million from Power Corp., the largest leveraged buyout up to this time in Canada (*August 8*). Appointed by the Trudeau government to the Canada Development Corporation board.

1982: Creates Passage Holdings to hold his CSL shares (*April 1*). Begins building ocean-going self-unloader ships. Participates in a think tank hosted in King City, Ont., by Murray Koffler of Shoppers Drug Mart that results in the creation of the Canadian Council for Aboriginal Business; he becomes a founding director.

1984: Moderates one of the federal Liberal leadership debates (*May-June*).

1986: Reluctantly closes CSL's shipbuilding operation in Collingwood, Ont., the last completed ship being the *Sir Wilfrid Laurier* (*September 12*).

1987: Asked by Turner to coordinate candidate recruitment for the next election (*March*). Sells his Kingsway Transport subsidiary (*Spring*). Completes his term as a director of the Canada Development Corporation.

1988: Buys Pathy's shares in CSL and assumes full control (*March 31*). Wins the Liberal nomination for the west Montreal riding of LaSalle-Émard (*May 29*); gives up his directorships at Fednav, Canadian Shipbuilding and Engineering, Imasco, Manufacturers Life, Redpath and CB Pak. Canada's 34th federal election: elected in LaSalle-Émard defeating the Conservative incumbent Claude Lanthier; Mulroney's Conservatives win a second majority (*November 21*). Replaced as CSL president by Jim Elder (*December 8*).

1989: Becomes the Liberal critic for Housing, Urban Affairs and the Treasury Board (*February*). Turner announces his intention to resign as Liberal leader (*May 3*).

1990: Launches his leadership bid in Montreal and Windsor (*January 17*). Many of his youth supporters heckle Chrétien in Montreal for opposing the Meech Lake Accord (*June 2*); the protest continues at the beginning of the leadership convention. Loses the Liberal leadership to Chrétien on the first ballot in Calgary; garnering 25% of the votes to come in second (*June 23*). Becomes the Liberal Environment critic (*Summer*). Co-chairs the committee to develop an updated Liberal policy platform (*Summer*)

1991: Helps organize the Liberal policy meeting in Aylmer, Que., that moves the party from the social left to the economic right (*November*).

1992: Attends the UN Earth Summit in Rio de Janeiro, chaired by his former boss Maurice Strong (*June 3-14*). His father is specially designated 'Right Honourable' by Mulroney (*July*). His father dies in Windsor (*September 14*).

1993: The Red Book he co-authored with Chaviva Hosek – called *Creating Opportunity: The Liberal Plan for Canada* – is unveiled by Chrétien (*September 19*). Canada's 35th federal election: re-elected in LaSalle-Émard with nearly 60% of the vote; Chrétien's Liberals form the government (*October 25*). Turns down Chrétien's offer of Finance minister, preferring the Industry post (*October*). Relents and accepts Finance (*November 2*). Becomes Canada's 34th Finance minister (*November 4*). Places his CSL holdings under a blind management agreement (*November*). His mother Nell dies in Windsor (*November 11*). Doesn't reappoint John Crow, Governor of the Bank of Canada, replacing him with Gordon Thiessen who is prepared to address inflation with budget cuts (*December 22*).

1994: Announces an increase in equalization payments to the seven poorer provinces by about 5% annually over five years (*January 21*). Reduces taxes on cigarettes as a way to combat smuggling (*February 8*). Attends his first G7 finance ministers meeting, in Frankfurt, Germany (*February*). Presents his first budget, making cuts in defence and unemployment insurance (rebranded as 'employment insurance') to try and tackle growing deficits (*February 22*). Gets reluctant approval from cabinet for his intention to find significant ways to make cuts in most federal departments (*June 18*). Holds consultations across Canada to prepare for spending cuts. The federal government building in Windsor is named after his father. Comes up with $6.8 billion in proposed cuts after a half-year review with Marcel Massé (Intergovernmental Affairs) (*December 20*).

1995: Considers resigning when Chrétien refuses to allow reforms to the pension plan (*February 17*); accepts a compromise to introduce reforms in the following year's budget. Presents his second budget, outlining the largest budget cuts ever, $25 billion and 45,000 civil service jobs over three years (*February 27*). Suggests in a speech in Quebec City that Quebec independence could create a loss of one million jobs in the province (*October*).

1996: Presents his third budget, calling for a targeted $32.7 billion reduction in the deficit (*March 6*). Admits the government made a mistake in its intention to eliminate the GST; he continues his efforts to replace it with a harmonized federal-provincial tax (*April 23*).

1997: Presents his fourth budget that continues to target cuts to the deficit, offers pre-election social program spending and a new child tax credit (*February 18*). Canada's 36th federal election: re-elected in LaSalle-Émard with 61% of the vote (*June 2*). Remains as Finance minister in Chrétien's post-election cabinet (*June 11*). Attends the first G8 Summit in Denver, Colorado (*June 20-22*). Tables a bill to reform the Canada Pension Plan by increasing the contribution rates and creating a CPP Investment Board to manage the funds (*September 25*). Agrees to consider giving the provinces more flexibility around tax initiatives after they complain about the impact of federal cuts to reduce the deficit (*December 9*).

1998: Indicates there will be a surprise bonus of $236 million in provincial transfer payments based on revised growth figures from Statistics Canada (*January 22*). Presents a landmark budget that breaks even, the first non-deficit budget in 28 years, and launches the Millennium Scholarship fund for post-secondary students (*February 24*). Attends the first meeting of international finance officials held in Washington where Canada plays a lead role in promoting a summit group broader than the G7 (*April*). Attends G7 meetings in Birmingham, England (*May*). His chief of staff, Terrie O'Leary, leaves to become Canada's representative at the World Bank (*August*). Receives an honorary Doctor of Laws degree from Concordia University (*November*). His friend, 50-year-old MP Shaughnessy Cohen, collapses in the House and dies soon after (*December 9*); he speaks at her Windsor funeral. Rejects merger plans by four major Canadian banks (*December 14*).

1999: Presents his sixth budget, his second balanced budget, featuring minor tax cuts and increased health spending (*February 16*). Takes part in a meeting of finance ministers and officials in Bonn, Germany, further exploring an entity broader than the G7 (*March 11*). Helps develop the Canadian Debt Initiative to forgive third- world loans at a quicker pace than the international Heavily Indebted Poor Countries program (*March*). Indicates he will seek re-election even if Chrétien remains Prime Minister (*September 28*). Chairs the first meeting of the G20 finance ministers in Berlin, Germany (*December 15-16*).

2000: Presents his seventh budget, outlining plans for lower tax rates and an increased Child Tax Benefit (*February 28*). A group of his supporters meets in Toronto to discuss his party leadership prospects, prompting Chrétien to stay and fight another election (*March 10*). At a meeting of G7 finance ministers in Prague, calls for a moratorium on the debt service payments of eligible poor countries (*September 19-28*); the initiative results in a meeting with Bono of rock group U2. Tables a mini-budget offering the largest tax cut in Canada's history (*October 18*). Hosts the second G20 meeting in Montreal (*October 24-25*). Canada's 37th federal election: re-elected in LaSalle-Émard winning two-thirds of the votes; a third Chrétien majority government is elected (*November 27*). Indicates there won't be an annual budget next February as there are no new initiatives planned (*December 13*).

2001: His supporters push for a leadership vote in Fall 2002 (*January 26*). Chrétien agrees to a leadership review in February 2003 (*April 19*). Receives an honorary Doctor of Laws degree from Wilfrid Laurier University (*June*). As chair of the G7 finance ministers, works the phones to avert a financial crisis because of the 9/11 terrorist attacks in New York and Washington (*September 11*). Says federal reserves will be used to fund security in the wake of the 9/11 attacks (*September 17*). Hosts the third G20 meeting in Ottawa, where delegates focus on stopping terrorist financing (*November 16-17*). Presents his eighth budget, with an emphasis on security spending (*December 10*).

2002: Reduces the cuts in equalization payments to some provinces because of a change in the recalculation method (*February 28*). All candidates directed by Chrétien to stop campaigning for the leadership (*May 30*); Martin refuses. Replaced as Finance minister by John Manley (Foreign Affairs) (*June 2*). Chrétien announces in Chicoutimi that he intends to step down as leader in February 2004 (*August 21*).

2003: Endorsed for the leadership by Alan Rock (National Health & Welfare) who drops out of the race (*January 12*). Files his nomination papers for the leadership (*March 6*). Says he will sell his residual shares in CSL to his three sons (*March 11*). Manley (Finance) withdraws from the leadership race, leaving only two candidates (*July 22*). Elected Liberal leader at the party convention in Toronto with 94% of the vote, beating his only competition, Sheila Copps (Heritage) (*November 14*). Meets informally with the premiers in Regina before the Grey Cup game (*November 15*). Chrétien indicates he will resign two months earlier than planned (*November 16*). Conservative MP Scott Brison joins the Liberals in opposition to the newly merged Alliance-Conservative party (*December 10*). **Martin's government (2003-2006)**. Becomes the 21st Prime Minister of Canada (*December 12*). Announces the creation of the Department of Public Safety & Emergency Preparedness with Anne McLellan as minister; creates the Canada Public Health Agency;

splits Human Resources Development Canada into Human Resources & Skills Development and Human Development (*December 12*). Andy Mitchell (Indian Affairs) pledges to review the proposed First Nations Governance Act (*December 20*); introduces self-government legislation a month later.

Sudan's Widad Isa

While leaving a refugee camp near Khartoum, Sudan, in November 2004, one of the vehicles in Martin's convoy struck a five-year-old girl, Widad Isa. Learning of the accident, Martin's wife Sheila insisted they visit Isa in hospital. Later, when her condition worsened, the Martins arranged to fly Isa and her father to London to receive better care. After her recovery, Widad and her father returned to Sudan.

2004: The Leader of the Opposition, Harper, steps down to seek the leadership of the new Conservative party and is replaced on an acting basis by MP Grant Hill (*January 8*). Martin attends the Summit of the Americas in Monterrey, Mexico, where he meets with U.S. President Bush (*January 13*). Appoints an inquiry to investigate Canada's role in the U.S. decision to deport Canadian citizen Maher Arar to Syria (*January 28*). Meets with premiers in Ottawa to confirm the transfer of budget surplus monies to the provinces for health care (*January 30*). Releases *Ethics, Responsibility, Accountability: An Action Plan for Democratic Reform*, promising more free votes for MPs (*February 4*). Appoints former MP Jean Lapierre as his Quebec lieutenant (*February 5*). Announces an inquiry into the sponsorship scandal to be headed by Justice John Gomery (*February 10*). Recalls former Public Works minister Alfonso Gagliano as Denmark ambassador following the release of the auditor general's scathing report on the "appalling" examples of alleged fraud and money laundering in the government's sponsorship programs (*February 11*). Premiers of the provinces and territories meet for the first time as the Council of the Federation (*February 23-24*). Fires Business Development Bank of Canada president Michel Vennat for his connection to the sponsorship scandal (*March 12*). Harper wins the leadership of the new Conservative Party of Canada (*March 20*); returns as Leader of the Opposition. Martin visits Alberta to announce an additional $991 million in aid to farmers dealing with mad cow disease (*March 22*). Announces his intention to work with the premiers to "fix health care for a generation" (*April 16*). Meets with over 70 Indigenous leaders and MPs to begin making changes to the Indian Act (*April 19*). Parliament passes a private member's bill that calls Turkey's 1915 massacre of Armenians genocide (*April 21*). Becomes the first Prime Minister to meet with a Tibetan leader, the Dalai Lama, at an interfaith prayer vigil in Ottawa (*April 23*). Meets with U.S. President Bush in Washington and gets a commitment to lift the ban on beef cattle (*April 30*). The government partially reopens cod fishing on the east coast (*May 4*); a crackdown on illegal fishing by foreign vessels is announced two days later. Has the parliamentary inquiry into the sponsorship programs suspended a day after the program's head, Charles Guité, and the GroupAction's CEO, Jean Brault, are charged with fraud (*May 10*). Commits his government to putting $9 billion into health care if re-elected (*May 25*). Labrador's Inuit vote in favour of a land claim agreement giving them ownership of the land and limited self-government (*May 26*). Sued by Alfonso Gagliano for wrongful dismissal as Ambassador to Denmark (*May 28*); suit is dismissed in a Quebec court five years later. Tells the Federation of Canadian Municipalities the Liberals plan to give cities a share of the federal gas tax (*May 28*). Participates in the 60th Anniversary of D-Day with veterans including his father-in-law Bill Cowan in Courselles-sur-Mer, France (*June 6*). Attends the G8 Summit in Sea Island, Georgia (*June 8-10*). Undertakes a last-day cross-country campaign swing, dipping his foot in the Atlantic in the morning and into the Pacific at the end of the day, with stops in Gatineau, Toronto, Winnipeg and Regina (*June 27*). Canada's 38th federal election: re-elected in LaSalle-Émard with about 57% of the vote; ends up with a minority government (*June 28*). Adds eight new members to his revised cabinet, including Ken Dryden (Social Development) and Ujjal Dosanjh (Health) (*July 20*). André Ouelette resigns as Canada Post president following allegations of excessive spending and questionable hiring practices (*August 13*). The Gomery inquiry into sponsorship programs begins (*September 7*). Meets with premiers and Indigenous leaders to hammer out deals to improve health care, including a commitment to increase health care transfer payments by $41.2 billion over 10 years (*September 13-16*); includes a precedent-setting side deal for Quebec as a demonstration of "asymmetrical federalism". The Canada Public Health Agency is created (*September 24*). His government is almost defeated by the Speech from the Throne vote until agreement is reached with the Bloc Québécois and later with the Conservatives (*October 5*). Meets with Russian President Vladimir Putin in Moscow (*October 14*). Participates in the Progressive Governance Summit in Budapest, Hungary (*October 15*). Mexican President Vicente Fox addresses Parliament (*October 25*). Martin meets with the premiers to reform and increase equalization payments (*October 26*); the gathering is boycotted by Newfoundland Premier Danny Williams who is unhappy about conditions requiring the sharing of oil and gas royalties. Becomes the first Prime Minister to visit Haiti where he meets with Prime Minister Gérard Latortue (*November 14*). Removes MP Carolyn Parrish from caucus for inflammatory statements about the U.S., the Iraq war and him (*November 18*). Meets with Sudan's President Omar al-Beshir in Khartoum and visits Mayo Camp for displaced persons in Darfur (*November 25*). Talks with Bush on the U.S. President's first visit to Ottawa (*November 30*). The Supreme Court reaffirms the federal government's jurisdiction over marriage rights, including same-sex marriage, should that be included (*December 9*). Announces a Northern strategy for housing, education and sovereignty with the three territorial premiers (*December 14*). Meets with Libyan President Muammar Gadhafi in Tripoli (*December 19-20*); then vacations in Morocco. Criticizes Newfoundland Premier Williams for removing Canadian flags from public buildings as part of his protest about oil and gas royalties (*December 23*). Commits $425 million to help Southeast Asian nations hit by a mammoth tsunami that kills more than 140,000 people (*December 26*).

The almost-holiday to Phuket

For the family's Christmas gathering in 2004, Martin's son Paul, who was living in Singapore, suggested Phuket, Thailand. The family gave it serious thought but ultimately opted for Morocco. On December 26, a tsunami, caused by an earthquake in the Indian Ocean, crashed into Phuket killing more than 250 tourists and workers. Martin visited Phuket in January to survey the devastation. The federal government matched funds donated by Canadians to aid the survivors in affected countries.

2005: Judy Sgro (Immigration) resigns from cabinet following allegations of expediting immigration requests in return for support on her election campaign (*January 14*). Visits Phuket, Thailand, to view the tsunami carnage (*January 16*), part of an Asian tour that includes Sri Lanka (*January 17*), India (*January 18*), Japan where he meets Emperor Akihito (*January 19-20*), China (*January 20-21*) and Hong Kong (*January 22*). Reaches an Atlantic Accord with Nova Scotia and Newfoundland & Labrador related to sharing revenues from offshore natural resources (*January 28*). Legislation is tabled to legalize same-sex marriage (*February 1*). Allocates $5 billion of the fuel tax revenues to municipal governments (*February 1*). Testifies before the Gomery inquiry into the sponsorship scandal, becoming the first Prime Minister since Macdonald to appear publicly at an inquiry (*February 10*). The Kyoto Protocol comes into effect internationally (*February 15*); Dion (Environment) says Canada's plan to reduce emissions will be unveiled sometime after the budget is passed. *The Economist* magazine posts a story calling Martin 'Mr. Dithers' for being an indecisive leader; the nickname sticks (*February 16*). Rejects participation in the U.S. ballistic missile defence system (*February 24*). Receives 88% delegate support for his leadership at the Liberal policy convention in Ottawa (*March 6*). Speaks at the Edmonton memorial service for four RCMP officers killed in Mayerthorpe, Alta., a week earlier (*March 10*). Signs the Security and Prosperity Partnership in Waco, Texas, with U.S. President Bush and Mexican President Fox (*March 23*). His poll numbers drop after the Gomery Commission releases testimony that ties missing sponsorship funds to the Quebec Liberal party (*April 7*). Releases Canada's $10 billion plan to reduce carbon emissions; it relies heavily on voluntary initiatives (*April 13*). Canada cancels the debt it is owed by Rwanda, Zambia and Honduras (*April 13*). Apologizes on television for the sponsorship scandal and indicates he'll call an election a month after Gomery issues his final report (*April 21*). Agrees to replace the budget's proposed corporate tax cuts with expenditures on education, housing and the environment (*April 26*). Signs an agreement with Manitoba for a child care program (*April 28*); all 10 provinces sign up over the next seven months. Attends the 60th Anniversary of Victory in Europe Day in the Netherlands (*May 4*). Officially opens the new Canada War Museum in Ottawa (*May 8*). Conservatives and Bloc Québécois win a motion to have a committee declare that the government should resign; opinions differ as to whether this constitutes a non-confidence motion (*May 10*). The government avoids any direct confidence votes until several budget bills are presented the following week (*May 11*). Appoints Belinda Stronach as Human Resources & Skills Development minister after she crosses the House floor from the Conservatives (*May 17*). Meets Elizabeth II at Saskatchewan's 100th Anniversary events in Regina (*May 18*). Wins the first of two votes on budget bills; the second vote is a tie broken in the government's favour by Speaker Peter Milliken (*May 19*); the government survives. Meets Elizabeth II again at Alberta's 100th Anniversary events in Edmonton (*May 24*). Meets with leaders of five national Indigenous groups and reaches an agreement to involve them in future government policy discussions (*May 31*). His government is accused by the Conservatives of attempting to bribe MP Gurmant Grewel with a cabinet seat if he crossed the floor; transcripts from a Grewel recording of the deal are released and the issue is dropped (*May 31*). Survives a series of 16 budget votes in the House, ending the threat of an immediate election call (*June 14*). Parliament votes to extend the Session to complete discussions on the budget and same-sex marriage legislation (*June 23*). Attends the G8 Summit at Gleneagles, Scotland (*July 6-8*). Attends the memorial service for Independent MP Chuck Cadman who died of cancer having prevented the government's defeat on May 19 with his vote (*July 16*). Legislation recognizing same-sex couples is passed, making Canada the fourth country in the world to do so (*July 20*). Announces the appointment of CBC journalist Michaëlle Jean as Canada's 27th Governor General (*August 4*). A NAFTA panel rules that Canada does not unfairly subsidize its lumber industry (*August 10*); U.S. ignores the ruling and maintains duties. Canada's military involvement in Afghanistan moves from Kabul to Kandahar (*August*). Officially apologizes for the internment of Ukrainian Canadians during the First World War (*August 24*). Canada provides air and sea support for victims of Hurricane Katrina in Louisiana (*September 2*). Meets with Chinese President Hu Jintao in Ottawa (*September 9*). Addresses a special session of the UN in New York that adopts the Responsibility To Protect (R2P) initiative he helped create, commiting members to prevent crimes against humanity (*September 16*). Joins Terry Fox's mother, Betty, and Rick Hansen for the annual Terry Fox Run in Port Coquitlam, B.C. (*September 18*). David Dingwall, former cabinet minister, resigns as head of the Royal Canadian Mint following revelations about lobbying activities (*September 28*). Receives the first report from the Gomery Commission that blames former bureaucrats involved in the federal sponsorship scandal and clears him of any wrongdoing (*November 1*). Attends the APEC Summit in South Korea (*November 18-19*). Sends the first combat troops to Kandahar, Afghanistan. The government announces a $2 billion compensation package for residential school victims that includes the establishment of a Truth and Reconciliation Commission (*November 23*). First ministers reach a $5 billion deal in Kelowna, B.C., with the First Nations (*November 24*); not approved before Parliament dissolves. His government will provide $1.5 billion to forestry workers adversely affected by the U.S. duties on softwood lumber (*November 25*). Refuses to accept the NDP's terms for continued support and subsequently loses a confidence vote 173 to 133 (*November 28*). The U.S. reduces duties on Canadian software lumber (*December 6*). Addresses the UN climate change conference in Montreal (*December 7*). His communications director Scott Reid says the Conservative child care subsidy gives parents money to "blow on beer and popcorn" (*December 11*); later apologizes.

2006: Liberals release an unintended attack ad saying Harper would put "soldiers with guns" on the streets of 12 Canadian cities; it is quickly pulled (*January 11*). Canada's 39th federal election: re-elected in LaSalle-Émard defeating May Chiu (Bloc Québécois); his Liberal government loses to the Conservatives (*January 23*). Announces his intention to resign as party leader (*January 24*). Learns he will become a grandfather with the birth of David's son Ethan (*January 24*). The Gomery Commission releases its report, calling for an overhaul of the decision-making process in Ottawa (*February 1*). **Martin's government ends** (*February 6*). Liberal MP Bill Graham becomes Leader of the Opposition (*February 6*). Attends the World Progressive Governance Summit in South Africa (*February 11-12*). Makes an impromptu presentation at a university in Izmir, Turkey (*February*). Meets with UN Secretary General Kofi Annan in New York and agrees to co-chair an advisory panel for the African Development Bank (*March*). Steps down as Liberal leader; replaced on an interim basis by Graham (*March 19*). Introduces a private member's bill calling on the government to honour the Kelowna Accord (*May 17*). Joins Clark, Mulroney and Campbell to judge contestants on the CBC's *The Next Great Prime Minister* (*Fall*).

2007: Becomes Chair of the multi-million-dollar Congo Basin Forest Fund supported by the United Kingdom, Norway and later Canada. Receives an honorary Doctor of Laws degree from the University of Windsor (*June 14*). Joins Turner, Campbell and Newfoundland Premier Danny Williams to judge *The Next Great Prime Minister.*

2008: Along with son David and various corporate partners, founds Capital for Aboriginal Prosperity and Entrepreneurship (CAPE) with $50 million to support First Nations businesses and entrepreneurs. Launches the Martin Aboriginal Education Initiative supporting Indigenous elementary and secondary education. His autobiography *Hell or High Water: My Life In and Out of Politics* is published (*October 28*).

2009: Receives an honorary Doctor of Civil Law degree from Bishop's University (*May 30*). Undergoes a knee replacement required because of an old waterskiing injury (*Summer*).

2010: Receives an honorary Doctor of Laws degree from Queen's University (*May 28*). Receives an honorary Doctor of Laws degree from the University of Western Ontario (*June 18*). Attends the African Capacity Building Foundation in Paris (*September 28-29*).

2011: Receives an honorary Doctor of Laws degree from the University of Toronto (*June 3*). Receives an honorary Doctor of Laws degree from McMaster University (*June 16*). His sister, Mary Anne, dies in Colchester, Ont. (*July 20*). Attends Jack Layton's funeral in Toronto (*August 27*). Receives the first Award for Excellence in Aboriginal Relations by the Canadian Council for Aboriginal Business, in Vancouver (*September 29*). Receives an award from *Corporate Knights* magazine for adding natural resources to Canada's economic indicators when he was Finance minister (*October 27*). Indicates his support for the Occupy movement opposed to the growing gap between rich and poor (*November 21*). Takes part in We Day in Winnipeg to encourage youth to lead change locally and globally (*November 23*).

2012: While attending an Aboriginal Peoples' Commission convention, says Conservative policies will send more Indigenous young people to jail than to school (*January 13*). Receives a Public Policy Forum award in Toronto, along with four other former prime ministers; indicates a wish that he'd done more for Indigenous peoples when he was Prime Minister (*May 4*). Receives an honorary degree from UBC (*May*). Is made a Companion of the Order of Canada (*May 25*). Receives an honorary Doctor of Laws degree from the University of Alberta (*June 11*). Receives an honorary Doctor of Education degree from Nipissing University (*June 13*). Leads a Sir John A. Macdonald walking tour in Kingston (*August 20*). A juvenile novel about 12-year-old Martin is published, written by 17-year-old Caroline Woodward (*November 15*). Partners with UBC and a Vancouver high school to deliver the Aboriginal Youth Entrepreneurship Program (*December 17*).

Presidential golf balls

In a golf game with U.S. President George W. Bush, Martin confessed to not being a great golfer. That's okay, said Bush, who gave him a handful of presidential-branded golf balls to use. Martin lost about half of them during the match. Playing a round of golf later near his Eastern Townships farm, Martin lost two more of the balls. He was in the clubhouse a week or two later when he overheard a golfer at a nearby table boast that the U.S. president had played the local course because the golfer had found one of his presidential golf balls in the woods. Martin didn't have the heart to tell him the actual story.

2013: Meets with Theresa Spence, the Attawapiskat chief on a hunger strike in Ottawa, to bring attention to resolving Indigenous issues (*January 5*). Serves as a commissioner on the newly launched Global Ocean Commission (*February 12*). Testifies at the Truth and Reconciliation Commission, saying "how come we didn't know" about the recently defined "cultural genocide" committed through residential schools for Indigenous children (*April 24*). Receives an honorary degree from Lakehead University (*June*). Receives an honorary doctorate from the University of Ottawa (*June*). Receives an honorary Doctor of Laws degree from the University of New Brunswick. Opens Couchiching Summer Conference on First Nations peoples in Orillia with Phil Fontaine, former chief of the Assembly of First Nations (*August 8*). Receives an honorary degree from Haifa University, Israel. Receives the Symons Medal in Charlottetown (*October 10*). Announces expansion of his Aboriginal Youth Entrepreneurship Program from two to 17 schools in Saskatchewan (*October 3*). Helps fund the sale of Universal Helicopters to the Nunatsiavut Group of Companies run by Labrador's Inuit government (*December 9*).

2014: Agrees to advise Ontario on its goal to develop its own pension plan (*January 22*). Receives an honorary Doctor of Laws degree from Mount Allison University (*May 12*). Receives the "Stop the Clock" award from the Canadian Taxpayers Association for tackling the country's growing debt (*May 31*). Helps launch Canadians For A New Partnership with former prime minister Clark to foster relations with Canada's Indigenous peoples (*September 4*). Receives an honorary Doctor of Laws degree from Dalhousie University

(*October*). Becomes a member of the Ecofiscal Commission, a group of prominent politicians and economists looking to shift taxation to polluters (*November*).

2015: His book *Canada and Aboriginal Canada Today: Changing the Course of History* is published (*January 28*). Issues a letter with Clark, Turner and Chrétien calling for stricter oversight of CSIS in anti-terrorism legislation tabled by the government (*February 19*). Publishes an article with violinist Itzhak Perlman about eradicating polio (*April 23*).

2016: Moderates a panel in Montreal that brings together five former national chiefs of the Assembly of First Nations (*February 18*). Serves as a co-chair of The Pearson Centre's think tank called the Pursuing Justice Project, along with Turner, Campbell and Chrétien (*March 31*). Delivers the eulogy at the Montreal funeral of Jean Lapierre, his former Quebec lieutenant who died in a plane crash (*April 16*). His official portrait, painted by Paul Wyse, is unveiled in the Centre Block (*May 11*). Receives an honorary Doctor of Laws degree from Brandon University (*May 27*). Becomes a charter member of the Global Risk Institute's advisory council (*November 17*).

2017: Receives an honorary Doctor of Laws degree from Trent University (*June 9*). Accepts an honorary degree for his late father, awarded by Algonquin College in Pembroke, Ont. (*June 15*). Awarded the Cunard Prize for Vision, Courage and Creativity in Halifax (*August 10*) and expresses regret for how some of the Omar Khadr case was handled. Attends the 150th anniversary of Parliament's first session in Ottawa (*November 6*).

Books about Martin

- **1998**: Robert Chodos, Eric Hamovitch & Rae Murphy; *Paul Martin: A Political Biography* (J. Lorimer)
- **2003**: John Gray; *Paul Martin: The Power of Ambition* (Key Porter)
- **2003**: Susan Delacourt; *Juggernaut: Paul Martin's Campaign for Chétien's Crown* (McClelland & Stewart)
- **2003**: Murray Dobbin; *Paul Martin: CEO for Canada?* (Lorimer)
- **2007**: Paul Wells; *Right Side Up: The Fall of Paul Martin and the Rise of Stephen Harper's New Conservatism* (Douglas Gibson)
- **2009**: Paul Martin; *Hell or High Water: My Life In and Out of Politics* (Emblem)

22

Stephen Harper

The Unfathomable Prime Minister

Fiercely partisan, Stephen Harper shifted the needle in a number of ways during his time as Prime Minister. He moved the country to the political right by cutting taxes, and reducing and decentralizing federal regulations, services and responsibilities. Geographically, he moved the focus more to the west, where he and the Reform movement were based. His biggest achievement was uniting the Progressive Conservative and Reform parties to create a powerful alternative to the Liberals, but once in power he was not always able to push the country to the right as fast as many in his party had hoped.

HARPER THE POLITICIAN

Prime Minister of Canada: February 6, 2006 – November 4, 2015
Length of term: 9 years, 8 months, 29 days
Parliaments as Prime Minister: 39th; 40th; 41st; 42nd
Age on entering office: 46
Political party: Conservative (Reform 1993-2000; Canadian Alliance 2000-2004)
Leader of party: Canadian Alliance: March 20, 2002 – January 21, 2004; Conservative: March 20, 2004 – October 19, 2015
Member of Parliament: October 25, 1993 – January 14, 1997; May 13, 2002 – August 26, 2016
Ridings represented: Calgary West [Alta.] 1993-1997; Calgary Southwest [Alta.] 2002-2015; Calgary Heritage [Alta.] 2015-2016
Cabinet portfolio: none
Other political post: Leader of the Opposition (2002-2004, 2004-2006)
Title: Canadian Privy Councillor (2004)
Quotes: "In the stale air of politics, what Canada really requires is the sweeping wind of change." (his 1987 address to delegates creating the Reform party). "I believe that all taxes are bad." (during the 2006 election)

Harper the Man

Name: Stephen Joseph Harper
Born: April 30, 1959, Toronto, Ontario
Ancestry: English
Religion: United; Christian and Missionary Alliance
Education: B.A. [Bachelor of Arts in Economics] (University of Calgary, 1985); M.A [Master of Arts in Economics] (Calgary, 1991)
Nickname: Steve
Military service: none
Occupation: legislative assistant; lecturer; association executive
Occupation after term: consultant
Publication: *A Great Game: The Forgotten Leafs & The Rise of Professional Hockey* (Simon and Schuster Canada, 2013)
Appearance: "He was tall, really heavy, with a helmet of graying medium-brown hair. Fleshy, almost pouty lips. Intense blue eyes." (John Ibbotson in *Stephen Harper*); He's about six feet two inches tall, and according to data compiled by British newspaper the *Guardian*, he is one of the tallest world leaders *ever*." (CBC, 2015)
Personality: "To some, he seems cold, aloof and cruelly partisan. To others, he is decent, loyal, compassionate, even funny." (Mark Kennedy in *Rebel To Realist*); "The cool, aloof politician can erupt in explosive rages in private, sink to dark depths, crack up his caucus with imitations of his foes, or rock out to a Beatles tune." (Tondra MacCharles in the *Toronto Star*).
Married: Laureen-Ann Teskey, December 11, 1993, Calgary, Alberta
Age at marriage: 34

Harper was the:

- Prime Minister who ran the longest uninterrupted minority government
- Prime Minister who appointed the most Senators (59)
- First Conservative Party of Canada Prime Minister
- First Prime Minister who was not a member of a mainstream religion
- Second-longest serving Conservative Prime Minister
- Second Prime Minister to win a majority after losing a non-confidence vote
- Third Prime Minister to represent Alberta
- Fifth Prime Minister with no previous cabinet experience
- Sixth longest-serving Prime Minister
- Sixth Prime Minister born in Ontario

Harper's legacy

- United a fractured political right by merging the Progressive Conservative and Canadian Alliance parties to co-found the Conservative Party of Canada
- Presided over Canada's most ideological partisan-driven government
- Shifted government's focus from the east to the west
- Shifted taxing powers from federal to provincial governments
- Created an environment of lower taxes and reduced regulation
- Chopped the GST by 2%

Harper's Family

Harper's Parents

Father: Joseph Harris Harper
Born: September 20, 1927, Moncton, New Brunswick
Occupation: chartered accountant
Died: April 12, 2003, Calgary, Alberta
Age at death: 75

Mother: Margaret Frances Johnston
Born: August 6, 1933
Occupation: secretary
Married: September 18, 1954, Toronto, Ontario

Harper's Brothers (2 siblings; Stephen the oldest)

Brother: Grant Harper
Brother: Robert Harper, 2 daughters
  Married: Elan

Harper's Wife

Name: Laureen-Ann Teskey
Born: 1963, Turner Valley, Alberta
Father: Dennis Teskey (rancher; electrician)
Mother: Barbara
Occupation: graphic designer
First husband: Neil Fenton (New Zealand) (April 1985)
Divorced: 1988
Age at second marriage: 29
Children: 2 (with Harper)
Younger than Harper: 3 years

Harper's Children (2)

Name: Benjamin S. Harper
Born: April 19, 1996

Name: Rachel Harper
Born: 1999

Political Stories

Uniting the right

The wave of Reformers elected to Parliament in 1993 included a very pleased Stephen Harper. But the party juggernaut – 52 seats – split the vote on the right. The trend continued in subsequent elections. There was no way to defeat Chrétien's Liberals unless Reform could find a way to merge with the gutted Progressive Conservatives. But the new Reform party held little appeal for voters east of Manitoba. By rebranding itself as Canadian Alliance, it attracted the support of the Mike Harris neo-Conservatives in Ontario.

However, Joe Clark, once again leader of the PCs, would have nothing to do with amalgamation, fearing the disappearance of his dozen MPs after bonding with Alliance's four dozen. Harper knew the right couldn't be united without the Tories, but he also publicly acknowledged that wouldn't happen until Clark was gone.

He got his wish when the Conservatives picked Peter Mackay as leader in 2003. But there was a problem. Mackay won with the help of candidate David Orchard who extracted a written assurance from Mackay that he would not cooperate or merge with Alliance. Despite that, Mackay agreed to explore collaboration with Harper.

Then the Tories went further. They were willing to leapfrog right to merger talks. Harper was prepared to give them anything to make the union work. His negotiators agreed to accept universal health care, official bilingualism, and a pro-rated leadership selection process that would give the tiny Conservative faction a fighting chance. Mackay achieved everything he requested. The deal was a go.

Harper went on to win the leadership of the new Conservative Party of Canada on the first ballot. His united party of the right defeated the Liberals in 2006 and Mackay ended up serving in his cabinet for the entire ministry. Clark turned his back on the new party, sitting as an Independent, while Orchard attempted unsuccessfully to sue Mackay for breaking their contract.

Cutting taxes

It was a mantra of the Reform/Alliance/Conservative party. Canadians were overtaxed, it felt, and the intrusive money grab needed to be reversed. As the Official Opposition, Harper's Conservatives campaigned in 2004 on a promise to slash the middle class's taxes by 25%. It wasn't enough to win, but they would only prop up Martin's minority government with an agreement to cut taxes for low-income earners.

Once in power, Harper used his first budget surplus to introduce tax breaks. The Tax-Free Savings Account (TFSA) and corporate tax reductions followed. Only the 2008 recession that walloped the government's budget piñata stopped the Conservatives' intention to continue cutting.

As Ottawa was lowering taxes, the provinces were raising theirs. With the help of health care transfer payments and equalization handouts, Harper gradually shifted the financial fulcrum for taxation away from the federal government.

Census and the climate

The Harper team was always receptive to changes that would reduce the government's interference in people's – and businesses' – lives. Two initiatives achieving that were the elimination of the long-form census and bailing out of the Kyoto Accord.

When the census is conducted every 10 years, 20 percent of the population are randomly picked to fill out the detailed long-form census – a mandatory requirement seen by Harper as unnecessary prying. What he didn't anticipate when the long-form census was scrapped was the ensuing backlash from analysts and the public who recognized the role this information played in helping to plan realistically for the future. When the Liberals returned in 2015, so did the long-form census.

With the Kyoto Accord, it was Chrétien's Liberal government that had agreed to reduce Canada's greenhouse gas emissions by 6% between 1990 and 2012. Harper knew it couldn't happen (actually, the Liberals knew that, too) and wasn't prepared to devote time and money to the attempt.

Instead, he reduced spending on environmental projects and sought international allies in an effort to create a watered-down version of the ambitious Kyoto benchmarks. As environmental activity dwindled in Ottawa, so did Canada's image as a champion promoting green issues.

Outflanking the coalition

Nothing brings political adversaries together more effectively than the threat of a common enemy. In 2008, it was Harper's threat to eliminate subsidies to political parties that kick-started exploratory talks between the Liberals and the NDP. Although Harper backed away from cutting off funds, it was too late.

On December 1, the leaders of the two opposition parties announced their agreement to form a coalition to defeat the Conservative minority. They also had the support of the Bloc Québécois and Green parties. Harper took the offence, calling the move a betrayal to Canadians and unconstitutional – although coalitions can and do occur in parliamentary systems.

More importantly, he visited Governor General Michaëlle Jean and convinced her to prorogue Parliament until the new year. As a strategy, it worked. By the end of the following January, Liberal leader Stéphane Dion had been replaced by Michael Ignatieff who didn't support the coalition. When Parliament reopened, the Liberals voted for Harper's revised budget, which had removed the clause about no party subsidies.

The Israel fixation

Joe Harper instilled in his sons a profound respect for the resilience of the Jewish people despite a history of persecution. The Jews deserved to have their own homeland, he suggested. It was a lesson not lost on his son and it helped explain Stephen's resolute support for Israel that tilted Canada's position on the Middle East away from the middle.

Harper insisted Israel had every right to retaliate against the terrorist tactics of Hamas and Hezbollah, often at odds with his G8 colleagues. The Prime Minister felt any peace talks should recognize Israel's claim for already-occupied Palestinian lands and he opposed Palestine's recognition by the UN.

These were strident stands on one side of the conflict that didn't sit comfortably with Canadians who were used to the country's traditionally neutral position. But it did play well with many voters in Jewish communities. Harper was seen as a good and loyal friend by the Israeli leader, Binyamin Netanyahu. A bird sanctuary and university research chair are named after Harper in Israel.

The Senate frustration

The Conservatives came to power armed with a clear mandate to either reform or scrap the Senate. But over the next nine years, Harper sent out mixed messages about how to tackle the problem.

The intention took a hit at the very beginning of his administration when he appointed his election campaign chair, Michael Fortier, to the Senate so he could include him in cabinet. It wasn't one of the better uses of the Red Chamber. The Prime Minister was determined to revamp the upper house and make it an elected body. But he wasn't willing to negotiate for the support of the provinces, a requirement that the Supreme Court ruled was a necessary step toward any changes.

He recaptured a Conservative majority in the Senate by appointing more Senators than any Prime Minister in Canada's history, then reversed his strategy by refusing to make any more appointments at all.

Many of the Senate reform ideas floated by the Conservatives didn't materialize. The final irony was the scandal surrounding improper spending by some Senators (most of them Harper appointments) and the Prime Minister's Office attempts to make it go away. The fallout contributed to the Conservatives' defeat.

PERSONAL STORIES

A hockey connoisseur

It was childhood asthma that derailed Harper's hope to play the game he loved: hockey. Instead, he became a spectator and a stats hoarder. Growing up in Leaside, he avidly followed the Toronto Maple Leafs; his father's cousin was married to defenceman Carl Brewer. With a classmate, he invented 'foot' hockey that didn't require sticks, and he began devoting more time to analyzing any data he could acquire about the game.

As opposition leader, Harper would often spend part of the evening on the history he was writing about the early years of professional hockey and the Leafs. It's a book project that spread out over nine years before being published as *A Great Game: The Forgotten Leafs & The Rise of Professional Hockey* by Simon & Schuster in 2013.

A member of the Society for International Hockey Research, he took particular pride in unveiling Canada's first 3D postage stamps to mark the 100th anniversary of the Montreal Canadiens hockey team. He also wrote the foreward to Paul Henderson's book *How Hockey Explains Canada*.

Harper and Williams

Cynthia Williams was a journalism student at Calgary's Mount Royal College living in residence at the University of Calgary. Harper was a third-year economics university student who spied Williams in the cafeteria and asked her out. Extroverted and boisterous, Williams was the opposite of introspective Harper, but it seemed to work.

It was Williams who steered Harper into political campaigning. As Progressive Conservatives, they worked on the re-nomination battles for two Calgary MPs, Jim

Hawkes and Harvie Andre, spending most of their time together. By the end of 1984, they were engaged.

Harper moved to Ottawa without her to work for Hawkes and, by the time he returned, ended the relationship. They remained friends and she eventually introduced him to her friend Laureen Teskey.

Having shifted further to the right in his political thinking, Harper ran against Hawkes in the 1988 election as the Reform candidate. That pitted him against his friend and former boss Hawkes as well as Conservative campaign workers Williams and Teskey (his future wife). Williams went on to become a Calgary event and video producer.

Laureen Teskey Harper

Growing up on a ranch in Turner Valley, Alta., Laureen Teskey developed a free-spiritedness that was often masked much later by the pressures that go with living at 24 Sussex Drive. However, even those confines didn't prevent her from hiking the Harrington Lake property or motorbiking.

At 25, she had already travelled from Cairo to Capetown on an African bus trip and wrapped up a three-year marriage with New Zealander Neil Fenton. Laureen campaigned for Conservative Jim Hawkes against his former aide Stephen Harper in 1988, but didn't really meet the latter until she'd moved to the Reform party.

They met at a Reform convention and soon after, Laureen applied her graphics skills to help package Harper's university thesis. The two were married in a Calgary civil ceremony in 1993. When Harper became Leader of the Opposition, Laureen folded her graphic design business and moved to Ottawa, gradually adopting Harper as her last name instead of Teskey.

Despite her sociable nature, Laureen preferred to stay in the background, raising Ben and Rachel, as well as stray cats – about 150 over a five-year period. Or taking kick-boxing lessons with Governor General Jean. She also managed to weather a barrage of unfounded rumours about her crumbling marriage and a purported affair with a female RCMP officer.

Harper's Timeline

1959: Born in Leaside, a suburb of Toronto; lives at 332 Bessborough Drive (*April 30*). Family attends Leaside United Church.

1963: Suffers his first asthma attack; the bouts persist for the next decade.

1964: Attends Northlea Public School in Leaside (*September*).

1968: Joins the Scouting movement as a Wolf Cub, later becoming a Scout.

1971: His family moves to 57 Princess Anne Crescent, Etobicoke (Toronto) and begins attending St. Luke's United Church. Starts classes at John G. Althouse Middle School in Etobicoke (*September*).

1973: Attends Richview Collegiate in Etobicoke (*September*).

1976: Talked by a friend into joining the school's Liberal club.

1977: Works as a clerk at the LCBO (Liquor Control Board of Ontario) (*Summer*).

1978: Appears on CBC's *Reach for the Top* quiz program representing Richview (*March*). Graduates from Richview Collegiate with the top academic standing (*Spring*). Spends six weeks in French immersion at the University of Victoria (*Summer*). Joins some Richview classmates and a teacher for a weeklong canoe trip in Algonquin Park (*August*). Enrols in Trinity College, University of Toronto, but quits a few weeks later (*September*). Starts a job, through his father's influence, as a mailroom clerk at Imperial Oil in Edmonton (*Fall*); lives at the Edmonton YMCA before moving on to boarding houses.

1979: Moves from the mailroom to computer systems work at Imperial Oil.

Missing a grandfather

Nine years before Harper was born, his grandfather Harris Harper left his doctor's office in Moncton, N.B., after a routine injection and was never seen again. The local high school principal had recently had a nervous breakdown, but none of his colleagues anticipated his disappearance. Harris Harper's body was never found.

1980: Transferred to Calgary by Imperial Oil to work with computers.

1981: Leaves Imperial Oil and enrols at the University of Calgary to pursue a degree in economics (*September*).

1982: Works at Imperial Oil (*Summer*).

1983: Works at Imperial Oil (*Summer*). Begins dating Cynthia Williams, a Mount Royal College journalism student (*Fall*). Attends a town hall forum of local MP Jim Hawkes and starts getting involved in Conservative constituency politics (*Fall*).

1984: Joins the Progressive Conservatives with Williams and successfully campaigns for Hawkes's re-nomination in Calgary West (*Winter*). Campaigns for Harvie Andre's nomination in Calgary Centre (*Spring*). Becomes president of the Youth Wing of the Calgary West Progressive Conservative Association. Works at Imperial Oil (*Summer*). Works on Hawkes's successful re-election campaign (*Summer*). Completes his BA in economics (*Fall*). Proposes to Williams (*Fall*).

1985: Becomes legislative assistant to Hawkes in Ottawa (*January*); rents an apartment in the Sandy Hill neighbourhood. Graduates from the University of Calgary.

1986: Quits his Ottawa job and returns to Calgary (*June*). Enrols at the University of Calgary for a master's degree in economics. Breaks up with Williams and leaves the Calgary West PC organization (*Summer*). Becomes an economics instructor while doing postgraduate work at the University of Calgary (*Fall*).

1987: Introduced to Preston Manning who is creating a Western Canada political party (*April*). Is a substitute delegate at the Western Assembly on Canada's Political and Economic Future held in Vancouver (*May 29-31*); votes in favour of forming a new political party. Resigns from the Progressive Conservative party (*June*). Establishes the Calgary West Reform Constituency Association with friend John Weissenburger (*October 7*). Addresses delegates at a session on political economics at the convention in Winnipeg that names the new party (Reform) and elects its first leader (Manning) (*October 30*). Becomes chief policy officer for Reform (*Fall*).

1988: Becomes the founding president of the Calgary West Reform Association (*January 16*). Teaches his last term at the University of Calgary (*Winter*). Is nominated as the Reform candidate for Calgary West by acclamation (*June 28*). His Reform policies are endorsed by a party assembly in Calgary (*August 12-14*). Canada's 34th federal election: loses to incumbent Hawkes in Calgary West, but polls second with 17% of the vote; Reform wins no seats (*November 21*).

1989: Writes a 20-page memorandum to Manning indicating why it's wrong for Reform to dilute its right-wing roots in order to attract more supporters (*March 10*). Becomes legislative assistant to the first Reform MP, Deborah Grey, in Ottawa (*Spring*). Attends the Reform convention in Calgary to hear his policy speech on ending appeasement of Quebec read by Manning (*October 27-29*).

1990: Returns to Calgary and shares an apartment with his brother Grant. Serves as master of ceremonies at the Calgary wedding of his close friend John Weissenberger to Angela Tu, whom he had introduced (*May 12*). His new Reform policy boss is Calgary professor Tom Flanagan (*Fall*).

1991: Addresses a Reform convention in Saskatoon urging the party to expand nationally and seconds the successful motion to field candidates east of Manitoba (*April 4-6*). Meets Laureen Teskey at the convention (*April 4*). Works on his master's thesis, with Teskey doing the charts and graphs (*Summer*); graduates with his MA.

1992: Helps develop Reform's opposition to the Charlottetown Accord (*August*), but is not asked to sit on the steering committee for the party's 'No' campaign.

1993: Helps develop Reform's policy to bring the deficit to zero in three years. Buys a house in northwest Calgary with Teskey. Steps down as a policy advisor for Reform. Threatens to publicly withdraw as the Reform candidate for Calgary West; talked into staying (*Summer*). Canada's 35th federal election: elected in Calgary West defeating Hawkes with 52% of the vote; Reform wins 52 seats (*October 25*). Rents a furnished suite in an apartment-style hotel in Ottawa. Indicates he will join some fellow Reform MPs in taking a salary cut. Marries Laureen Teskey in a civil ceremony in Calgary (*December 11*).

1994: Attends East Gate Alliance Church in Ottawa. Publicly criticizes Manning for expense account abuses (*April 6*); partially resolved in caucus. Appointed by Manning as critic for Intergovernmental Affairs, focusing on the approaching Quebec referendum (*September*).

1995: Adds Finance critic to his shadow cabinet role with Reform (*June*). Helps write Reform's New Confederation proposal calling for more provincial powers if Quebec secedes (*October*).

1996: His son Benjamin is born (*April 16*). Attends the Winds of Change conference in Calgary that fails to find connections between the Conservatives and Reformers (*May*). Moves to a larger house in Calgary. Presents an unsuccessful private member's bill to declare unilateral secession from Canada unlawful and calling for a clear question to be presented – three years before the Liberal Clarity Act (*October 30*).

1997: Announces his resignation as MP for Calgary West (*January 14*); becomes vice-president of the National Citizens Coalition, working for David Somerville. Co-writes an article with Flanagan in *Next City* magazine calling for a reunion of the 'three sisters' of conservatism: traditional Tories, Western populists and Quebec nationalists (*January*). Launches an NCC ad campaign against targeted MPs who would benefit from government pension plans (*April*).

1998: Approached about seeking the leadership of the Progressive Conservatives after Jean Charest steps down; declines (*Spring*). Becomes president of the National Citizens Coalition, to 2001.

1999: His daughter Rachel is born.

2000: Opposed to the Reform party's rebranding as the Canadian Reform Conservative Alliance since the Progressive Conservatives refuse to join (*January 29*). Launches an NCC court challenge against the government's prohibition on third party advertising in elections (*May*); wins the case, but three years later loses it on appeal. Nominally supports Tom Long for leader of the Canadian Alliance, but Stockwell Day wins, defeating Manning (*July 8*). Writes a *National Post* op-ed piece calling for *Separation, Alberta-Style* (*December 8*).

2001: Publishes a letter, with others, to Alberta's premier saying it's time "to build firewalls around Alberta" to stop a "hostile federal government from encroaching on provincial jurisdiction" (*January 26*). Day avoids a non-confidence vote in caucus by expressing a willingness to step down as leader (*July 17*). Indicates he plans to resign as NCC president (*August 13*). Speaks at an Alliance economic policy conference (*September 8*). Fires his campaign team when his leadership bid appears to stall; Laureen and the team talk him into persevering (*November*). Announces his bid for leadership of the Alliance party (*December 2*).

2002: His main competitor, Stockwell Day, launches his bid for re-election as party leader (*January 7*). Elected leader of the Canadian Alliance party, defeating Day (*March 20*). Secures the Alliance nomination in Calgary Southwest after Ezra Levant reluctantly drops his candidacy (*March*). Persuades Alliance to soften some of its more extreme stands like favouring a flat income tax and abolishing the Charter of Right and Freedoms, at its policy convention in Edmonton (*April 4*). Announces the failure of his party to unite with the Progressive Conservatives following a meeting with Clark (*April 9*). Welcomes most of the rebel Democratic Representative Caucus MPs back to Alliance (*April 17*). Elected MP for Calgary Southwest in a by-election with 72% of the vote (*May 13*). Sworn in again as an MP, becoming Canada's 28th Leader of the Opposition, replacing acting leader John Reynolds (*May 21*). Moves into Stornoway (*Spring*), with his family following in the summer. Alienates Atlantic Canadians after telling a reporter that federal development programs in the area foster a "culture of defeat" (*May 30*). His wife Laureen gives up her Calgary design and publishing business (*Summer*) and gradually begins going by 'Harper' instead of 'Teskey'.

2003: Denounces the government in the House for not joining the war against Iraq (*March 20*). Delivers the eulogy at his father's funeral at Westminster Presbyterian Church in Calgary (*April 16*). The Conservatives elect Peter Mackay as their new leader, replacing Clark (*June 1*); Mackay signs an agreement with candidate David Orchard to ensure there would be no merger with Alliance. Meets with Mackay and agrees to exploratory cooperation talks (*June 26*). Conservatives willing to negotiate a full merger (*August 21*). Negotiates to reach a merger agreement, giving the Conservatives most of their demands (*September 22-October 11*). Writes to 26,000 religious groups asking for support to oppose the government's proposed same-sex marriage legislation (*October 1*). Publicly announces the creation of the proposed new Conservative Party of Canada (*October 16*). Canadian Alliance votes 96% in favour of joining the Progressive Conservatives to create a new Conservative party (*December 5*); the next day the PCs vote 90% in favour. Resigns as the last leader of the Alliance party (*December 7*); replaced by interim leader of the new Conservative Party of Canada, Senator John Lynch-Staunton.

2004: Steps down as Leader of the Opposition (*January 8*); replaced by interim House leader MP Grant Hill. Launches his bid for leader of the new party (*January 12*). Wins the leadership of the Conservative Party of Canada, defeating former Magna International CEO Belinda Stronach (*March 20*); becomes Leader of the Opposition again. Releases an election platform that offers a 25% tax cut to middle-income earners (*Spring*). Refuses to apologize for a release saying "Paul Martin Supports Child Pornography" (*June 17*). Canada's 38th federal election: re-elected in Calgary Southwest with 68% of the vote; the Liberal government is reduced to minority status (*June 28*). Announces his intention to stay on as party leader (*July*). Negotiates tax cuts for low-income families and other minor Throne Speech amendments in return for his party's support of the government (*October 5*).

2005: Attends the first policy convention of the new party in Montreal, where delegates agree to pursue tax cuts, review the Kyoto Protocol commitment and not reopen the abortion debate (*March 17-19*). His amendment to the same-sex bill, that would define marriage as limited between a man and woman, is defeated (*April 17*). Joins with the Bloc Québécois on a motion to have a committee declare the government should resign; opinions differ as to whether this constitutes a non-confidence motion (*May 10*); the government avoids a confidence vote indicating there will be votes on several budget bills the following week. Former leadership opponent, MP Belinda Stronach crosses the floor to become a Liberal cabinet minister (*May 17*). His non-confidence vote in the Commons triggers an election (*November 28*). Says a Conservative government would give Quebec a stronger international voice (*December 19*).

2006: Launches his election campaign with a promise to cut the GST by 2% (*January 2*). Canada's 39th federal election: re-elected in Calgary Southwest with 72% of the vote; wins 124 seats to form a minority government (*January 23*). As Prime-Minister-designate, asserts Canada's sovereignty in the North in response to U.S. comments that regard Arctic waters as neutral (*January 26*). **Harper's government (2006-2015).** Becomes the 22nd Prime Minister; his 26-member cabinet is sworn in, including former Liberal cabinet member David Emerson as International Trade minister (*February 6*). Announces the cancellation of the national day care plan launched by the Martin government (*February 6*). Moves into 24 Sussex rather than wait for renovations to be undertaken (*February*). The NORAD treaty is expanded to include Canada-U.S. maritime as well as air defence (*February 21*). Meets informally with the premiers to discuss equalization payments and aid to cities (*February 24*). Appoints Michael Fortier (Public Works & Government Services) – co-chair of the Conservative election campaign – to the Senate (*February 27*). Appoints Manitoba judge Marshall Rothstein to the Supreme Court (*March 1*); the first justice required to be vetted by an all-party committee. Announces his intention to hold Senate elections in the next federal vote, with or without provincial approval (*March 1*). Refuses to cooperate with an Ethics Commission inquiry into the ethics behind luring Emerson to the Conservatives (*March 8*); later exonerated. Meets with Afghanistan President Hamid Karzai in Kabul and Pakistani Prime Minister Shaukat Aziz in Islamabad (*March 14*). Cuts funding for the Canadian Unity Council, a non-profit organization supporting federalism (*March 18*). Martin resigns as Liberal leader, replaced by interim leader Bill Graham (*March 19*). Ends Canada's peacekeeping mission in the Golan Heights between Israel and Syria (*March 25*). Cuts off funding to Palestine after the Hamas takeover of Gaza, becoming the first nation other than Israel to do so (*March 29*). Meets with U.S. President George Bush and Mexican President Vicente Fox in Mexico (*March 30-31*). Begins reducing funding for environmental initiatives, redirecting Kyoto Protocol funds to domestic solutions to reduce greenhouse gases (*April 6*). Warns Alberta that its Third Way health care proposal to accommodate private medicine will encourage queue jumping and medical advantages for the wealthy (*April 8*); Alberta abandons the idea under threat of withheld transfer payments.

Tables the Federal Accountability Act to ban corporate and union political donations, limit lobbyist influence and track Indigenous band spending (*April 11*). Assumes the role of appointing MPs to chair committees (*April 18*). The government bans the media from covering ceremonies for soldiers killed in the Afghanistan mission (*April 25*). Reaches a seven-year agreement with the U.S. to resolve the software lumber dispute, including repayment of duties to Canada and flexibility in how provinces comply (*April 27*). Appoints a Commission of Inquiry into the Investigation of the Bombing of Air India Flight 182 in 1985 (*May 1*); its 2010 report blames errors by the government, RCMP and CSIS for enabling the terrorist attack. Introduces a criminal law reform bill to stiffen mandatory minimum sentencing and eliminate conditional sentences for some crimes (*May 4*). Begins managing news conferences by deciding which reporters can ask him questions (*May*). Signs an agreement with Quebec Premier Jean Charest giving the province a formal role in UNESCO (*May 5*). The House votes to extend the Afghanistan military role for two years (*May 17*). Meets with Australian Prime Minister John Howard who addresses Parliament (*May 18-19*). Apologizes to Chinese Canadians for the Head Tax levy, 1885-1923, and the exclusion of Chinese immigrants, 1923-1947 (*June 22*). Meets with U.S. President Bush in Washington to discuss border crossing requirements and terrorism (*July 6*). Attends the G8 Summit in St. Petersburg, the first meeting held in Russia (*July 15-17*). Recognizes Israel's right to retaliate against Hamas and Hezbollah after seven Canadians killed in Lebanon (*July 16*). The premiers announce their support for the Kelowna Accord reached with Indigenous peoples by previous prime minister Martin (*July 25*). Visits Iqaluit, Nunavut, to reinforce Canada's sovereignty of the North (*August 12*); subsequently visits the North once every year while in office. Elizabeth May is elected leader of the Green party, replacing Jim Harris (*August 26*). Announces plans to arm Canada's border guards (*August 31*). Becomes the first Prime Minister to speak before a Senate committee, outlining his proposal to limit Senate appointments to eight years (*September 7*). Backs out of the Kyoto Protocol agreement to help developing nations find ways to cut greenhouse gas emissions (*September 10*). The government announces there was a $13.2 billion surplus under the Liberals (*September 25*). Receives the Woodrow Wilson Award for Public Service, in Calgary (*October 5*). Suspends MP Garth Turner from caucus for criticizing the leader on his blog (*October 18*). Jim Flaherty (Finance) announces intention to tax income trusts, despite an election promise not to touch them (*October 31*). Attends the APEC Summit in Hanoi, Vietnam (*November 18-19*). Introduces a motion to recognize Quebec as a nation within a nation (*November 22*); passes five days later, but Michael Chong (Intergovernmental Affairs) resigns in protest. Attends a NATO meeting in Riga, Latvia, to encourage NATO support in Afghanistan (*November 28-29*). Plans to close 12 of 18 regional offices of Status of Women Canada over the next six months (*November 29*). The Liberal party chooses Stéphane Dion to be its new leader, replacing interim leader Bill Graham (*December 2*); the last leadership contest where delegates are physically present. Jim Prentice (Indian Affairs) is booed on Parliament Hill by Indigenous peoples protesting the $155 million cut to the Kelowna Accord provisions (*December 5*). MPs defeat an attempt to reopen the same-sex marriage debate and return to the traditional definition (*December 7*). Introduces legislation to allow Canadians to vote for individuals being suggested as Senate appointments (*December 13*).

2007: Staying at Harrington Lake when a woman crashes her car into the fence surrounding the residence (*January 1*); the woman is later declared unfit to stand trial. Officially apologizes to Maher Arar for Canada's role in his deportation from the U.S. to Syria and subsequent torture (*January 26*); Arar receives $10 million in compensation. The Supreme Court strikes down key parts of the government's legislation to detain and deport suspected foreign-born terrorists (*February 23*). Survives a confidence vote on the budget when the Bloc Québécois supports the government (*March 26*). Liberal leader Dion and

Green leader May reach a deal to avoid fielding competing candidates in ridings in the next election (*April 22*). Agrees to have Canadian officials monitor prison conditions in Afghanistan after charges of torture of prisoners handed over by Canadian forces (*April 24*). The Fixed Election Dates Act is passed (*May 3*). His residence is shut down by the RCMP after a bag is tossed over the wall; it merely contains personal items (*May 13*). Indicates he will meet with the premiers in early June (*May 15*), but cancels two weeks later. Establishes a tribunal to help speed up resolving Indigenous land claims (*June 12*). Aboriginal Day of Action includes blockades to protest relations with the government (*June 29*). Peter MacKay (Foreign Affairs) is moved to National Defence (*August 14*). Attends the APEC Summit in Sydney, Australia, where he signs a less-binding agreement on climate change to replace the Kyoto Protocol (*September 2-9*). Becomes the first Prime Minister to address the Australian Parliament (*September 11*). The Indian Residential Schools Settlement Agreement comes into effect (*September 19*); offers nearly $2 billion for compensation to former students and establishes the Truth and Reconciliation Commission to chronicle the experiences of residential school survivors. The Canadian dollar reaches par with the U.S. dollar for the first time since the 1970s (*September 20*). Canada votes against the UN Declaration on the Rights of Indigenous Peoples, saying it conflicts with the constitution and lacks clear implementation guidelines (*September 20*). Says Canada will join the Asia-Pacific Partnership, a competing environmental accord to the Kyoto Protocol (*September 24*). Announces a larger-than-expected surplus, with plans to use $725 million of it for tax breaks (*September 26*). Appoints Mark Carney as Governor of the Bank of Canada (*October 4*). Announces an offshore revenue sharing deal with Nova Scotia (*October 10*). The government creates the Lake Superior National Marine Conservation Area, the largest protected, fresh underwater area in the world (*October 25*). Meets with the Dalai Lama in Ottawa, despite protests from China (*October 29*). Suggests a national referendum on abolishing the Senate if the House can't reform it through legislation (*November 6*). Orders a public inquiry into the Airbus affair involving former prime minister Mulroney; to be chaired by academic David Johnston (later Governor General) (*November 13*). Flaherty (Finance) tables a bill for $60 billion in tax cuts (*November 22*). The Nunavik self-governing region agreement is signed by Canada, Quebec and the Malvik Corporation (*December 5*).

2008: Lowers the GST to 5% from 6% (*January 1*). The U.S. requires passports for Canadians crossing the border (*January 1*). Fires Canadian Nuclear Safety Commission president Linda Keen after she accuses Gary Lunn (Natural Resources) of interfering with the watchdog organization's independence (*January 16*). Acts on the Manley Report to extend the military operation in Afghanistan to 2011 (*February 25*). Flaherty (Finance) proposes the Tax-Free Savings Account (TFSA) in his budget (*February 28*). Visits Electro-Motive in London, Ont., to tout federal corporate tax breaks (*March 19*); four years later, Electro-Motive locks out its employees after demanding a 55% wage cut. Conservative party headquarters is raided and searched by the RCMP looking for evidence of improper election expenses (*April 15*). The Truth and Reconciliation Commission is appointed (*April 28*). Flaherty announces that gas tax revenues will be shared with municipalities (*May 5*). Announces the Canada First defence strategy and increased military spending (*May 12*). Meets with Ukrainian President Victor Yushchenko who addresses Parliament (*May 26*). Accepts the cabinet resignation of Maxime Bernier (Foreign Affairs) who left confidential NATO papers at the home of a former girlfriend linked to a motorcycle gang (*May 30*). Joins Ontario in providing a $250 million bail-out to General Motors in Oshawa (*June 4*). Officially apologizes to Indigenous peoples for abuses suffered in residential schools (*June 11*). Has the 39th Parliament dissolved; ignoring the fixed election date law by triggering an earlier vote (*September 7*). Unsuccessfully appeals a Federal Court decision to strike down the Gomery Commission's finding that Chrétien bore some of the responsibility for the sponsorship scandal (*September 26*). A Conservative campaigner resigns for his role in writing a 2003 speech plagiarized from an address by Australia's prime minister (*September 30*). Blasts Stéphane Dion for indecision after CTV runs an interview that includes outtakes of the Liberal leader struggling to understand a question about hypothetical leadership (*October 9*). Assures voters that Canada will not have a recession in 2009 (*October 10*); prediction turns out to be incorrect. Canada's 40th federal election: re-elected in Calgary Southwest with 73% of the vote; wins a second minority term with 143 seats; the lowest voter turnout ever (58.8%) (*October 14*). Dion announces his resignation as Liberal leader (*October 20*). Ontario officially becomes a 'have-not' province, qualifying for equalization money for the first time (*November 4*). Meets with the premiers to discuss the economy (*November 10*). Attends an emergency G20 Summit meeting in Washington to discuss steps needed to stimulate the economy and tackle the international financial crisis (*November 14-15*). Attends the APEC Summit in Lima, Peru, despite sickness after drinking tainted water on the flight (*November 22-23*). Acknowledges Canada is slipping into a recession and considers the need for government stimulus (*November 23*). A Conservative proposal to eliminate political party subsidies prompts coalition discussions by the opposition parties (*November 27*). Retracts decisions to eliminate party subsidies and ban strikes by the civil service (*November 30*). The Liberals and NDP agree to a coalition supported by the Bloc Québécois and Greens (*December 1*). In a televised national address, describes the coalition as an attempt to overturn the results of the last election (*December 3*). Asks Governor General Michaëlle Jean to prorogue the 40th Parliament until January 26 (*December 4*); first time prorogation has been used to evade a confidence vote since Macdonald did it in 1873. Statistics Canada reports the worst monthly job losses in a quarter century: 70,600 in November (*December 5*). Announces a $4 billion bailout with Ontario to automakers General Motors and Chrysler (*December 7*). Michael Ignatieff becomes leader of the Liberal party and Leader of the Opposition, to be ratified by the party membership in six months (*December 10*). Appoints 18 new Senators, saying his efforts to reform the Senate have been resisted by some provinces (*December 22*); the Conservative appointments include Patrick Brazeau, Mike Duffy and Pamela Wallin.

2009: Meets informally with the premiers for the third and last time (*January 16*). Appoints an investigator to look into the listeriosis outbreak at Maple Leaf Foods (*January 20*). Abandons his $3.5 million defamation lawsuit against the Liberals for their claim that he knew the Conservatives offered terminally ill Independent MP Chuck Cadman money to change parties (*February 6*). Tony Clement (Industry) announces $50 million to support the G8 Summit in Huntsville, Ont., his riding (*February 6*). Meets with U.S. President Barack Obama during his first foreign visit since assuming office (*February 19*). Canadian workers in any province or territory are allowed to work anywhere in the country thanks to an agreement by all Canadian governments (*April 1*). Attends the G20 Summit in London, England (*April 2*). Attends the Summit of the Americas in Port of Spain, Trinidad (*April 17-19*). Environment Canada indicates carbon dioxide emissions have increased 26% since 1990, as opposed to the Kyoto promise to reduce them by 7% (*April 29*). Launches an education program to deal with the international pandemic H1N1 swine influenza (*May 1*). Attends the Canada-European Union Summit in Prague, Czech Republic, to launch free trade negotiations (*May 6*). Kicks off a negative ad campaign against Liberal leader Ignatieff, accusing him of Just Visiting after being out of the country for 34 years (*May 12*). A free trade agreement with the European Free Trade Association (Iceland, Liechtenstein, Norway and Switzerland) comes into effect (*July 1*). Canada cancels the remaining $2.3 million debt owed by Haiti, the last forgiven debt from Latin American and Caribbean countries (*July 2*). Attends the G8 Summit in L'Aquila, Italy (*July 8-10*). Attends two days of Summit talks in Guadalajara, Mexico with U.S. President Obama and Mexican President Felipe Calderón (*August 9-10*). Signs a free trade agreement with Panama and visits the

Panama Canal (*August 11-12*). Holds a cabinet meeting in Iqaluit, Nunavut, during a five-day tour of the Arctic (*August 18*). Appoints nine more Conservatives to the Senate (*August 27*). Meets with UN General Secretary Ban Ki-Moon and others in New York for environment talks before the international meeting in Copenhagen (*September 22*). Makes his public performance debut at a National Arts Centre charity event singing and playing keyboard to the Beatles' *With a Little Help From My Friends,* accompanied by cellist Yo-Yo Ma (*October 3*). Doubles the budget for prison construction to accommodate more inmates anticipated under tougher laws (*October 16*). As a member of the Society for International Hockey Research, unveils Canada's first 3D postage stamps celebrating the 100th anniversary of the Montreal Canadiens hockey team (*October 18*). Joins Prince Charles for the Remembrance Day ceremonies in Ottawa (*November 11*). Attends the APEC Summit in Singapore for climate change talks; the primary discussions are about reducing trade protectionism (*November 13*). Visits India to discuss nuclear deals and trade pacts (*November 15*); visits the Golden Temple in Amritsar (*November 18*). A former senior Canadian diplomat in Afghanistan tells a House committee that all Afghan detainees turned over to officials by Canadian soldiers were likely tortured (*November 18*). Meets with Elizabeth II at the Commonwealth Conference in Trinidad (*November 27*). Visits China (*December 2-6*); publicly rebuked by Chinese Premier Wen Jiabao for taking so long to visit. Greenpeace protesters breach Parliament Hill security and hang large banners from the Centre and West blocks reading 'Stop the Tar Sands' and 'Climate Inaction Costs Lives' (*December 7*). The Olympic torch is carried into the House by former Olympic skater Barbara Ann Scott (*December 10*). Attends the UN Framework Convention on Climate Change in Copenhagen and commits to reducing greenhouse gases by 20% by 2020 (*December 17-18*). The Second Session, 40th Parliament is prorogued for the Olympics and to avoid questions about the torture of Afghan detainees (*December 30*).

Left wing, right wing

Harper's love of hockey was passed on to his son Ben, who played minor league hockey in Ottawa. On the same team was the son of NDP MP Paul Dewar. The rink was not the place for politics. Ben Harper played left wing; Nathaniel Dewar played right wing.

2010: Attends the Haiti donors conference in Montreal following a devastating earthquake in the Caribbean country earlier in the month (*January 25*); Canada pledges $135 million in relief funds, along with $40 million from private donors. Opposition Leader Jack Layton announces he has prostate cancer (*February 5*). Harper becomes the first Prime Minister to address the British Columbia legislature (*February 11*). Takes part in the opening of the Winter Olympic Games in Vancouver (*February 12*). Governor General Jean apologizes in Rwanda for Canada's part in failing to stop the 1994 genocide (*April 21*). Meets with Mexican President Felipe Calderón who addresses Parliament (*May 27*). Replaces the mandatory long-form census questionnaire with a voluntary one (*June 17*). Hosts the G8 Summit in Huntsville where he pushes for global maternal health and reduced infant mortality, then takes part in the G20 Summit in Toronto where he pushes for deficit reduction (*June 25-27*); nearly 1,000 people are arrested during protests at the Toronto meetings. Welcomes Elizabeth II in Halifax for an eight-day visit to include Ottawa, Winnipeg, Toronto and Waterloo, Ont. (*June 28*). Ontario and British Columbia introduce the harmonized sales tax (HST) to replace the GST and provincial sales taxes (*July 1*); three years later, B.C. returns to the GST/PST following a referendum on the issue. Announces the appointment of academic David Johnston as Canada's 28th Governor General (*July 8*). A man is arrested for starting a small fire outside 24 Sussex Drive (*August 14*). His effort to abolish the long-gun registry is defeated in the House by two votes (*September 22*). Speaks for the second time in a week to the UN General Assembly in an unsuccessful bid for a Canadian seat on the Security Council (*September 23*). Ontario Supreme Court Justice Susan Himel strikes down Canada's prostitution laws for posing a danger to sex-trade workers (*September 28*). Attends La Francophonie conference in Switzerland (*October 23*), then visits the Ukraine (*October 25*). Jim Prentice (Environment) resigns to become vice-chair of CIBC (*November 4*). Attends the G20 and APEC meetings in South Korea and Japan (*November 9-14*). Indicates Canada will extend its military time in Afghanistan beyond 2011, but only to train Afghan soldiers (*November 12*). Visits Japan's Imperial Palace (*November 14*). Conservative senators defeat the climate change bill passed by the House, without debate (*November 17*). Attends a NATO meeting in Lisbon and indicates support to remain in Afghanistan until 2014 (*November 19-20*). Hosts the first Hannukah party held at the official residence, for 50 Jewish guests (*December 1*). Canada joins Russia and Japan at a climate change conference in Mexico to prevent extending the Kyoto Protocol beyond 2012 (*December 12*). Performs a five-song rock set at the Conservative's Christmas party, playing keyboard and singing *Share the Land, Jumpin' Jack Flash* and others (*December 8*). Appoints two more Senators, giving the Conservatives a majority in the Senate for the first time since 1997 (*December 20*).

2011: Flies to Geneva, Switzerland, to co-host a UN commission establishing benchmarks to help Third World mothers and children (*February 1*). Meets with U.S. President Obama in Washington and announces a joint perimeter border plan (*February 4*). Meets with world leaders in Paris who agree to launch air strikes against Libyan forces loyal to President Muammar Gadhafi (*March 19*). The government is defeated in a non-confidence vote that cites it for contempt of Parliament – a first for a Commonwealth government (*March 25*). Marches in Vancouver's Vaisakhi Parade with 10,000 Sikhs (*April 15*). Canada's 41st federal election: re-elected in Calgary Southwest with 75% of the vote; wins a majority government (*May 2*). Gilles Duceppe resigns as Bloc Québécois leader, replaced by interim leader Vivian Barbot although she lost her seat in the election (*May 2*). Liberal leader Michael Ignatieff resigns, replaced by interim leader Bob Rae (*May 25*). Attends the G8 Summit in Deauville, France, where he is the only leader opposed to Israel accepting pre-1967 borders as a pre-condition to peace talks with Palestine (*May 26*). Meets with Greek Prime Minister George Papandreou in Athens (*May 28*). Makes a surprise visit to Afghanistan to mark the approaching withdrawal of Canadian troops (*May 30*). 41st Parliament opens; Andrew Scheer is elected the 35th Speaker of the House (*June 2*). A parliamentary page holds up a 'Stop Harper' sign during the Speech from the Throne (*June 3*). Uses Facebook to let Canadians suggest names for his family's cat (*June 6*); the winning name is Stanley. Tells the Conservative policy convention he intends to continue steering Canada to the right (*June 10*). Appoints Prince Philip an honorary admiral and general in the Canadian Armed Forces to mark his 90th birthday (*June 10*). Appears on the television show *Murdoch Mysteries* as a simple-minded policeman (*July 20*). Jack Layton steps down temporarily as Leader of the Opposition following a second bout with cancer (*July 25*); Nycole Turmel is appointed interim NDP leader a month later. Meets with Brazilian President Dilma Rouseff in Brasilia (*August 8*) on a Latin American trip that includes signing a free trade agreement with Colombia (*August 10*) and announcing a free trade deal with Honduras (*August 12*). Extends trade sanctions against Syria for its oppressive measures against protesters (*August 13*). Jack Layton, Leader of the Opposition, dies of cancer in Toronto (*August 22*); replaced by Turmel. Attends the state funeral for Layton at Roy Thomson Hall in Toronto (*August 27*). Attends dedication of the British Garden in New York City, commemorating the lives lost in the World Trade Center attacks 10 years earlier (*September 11*); declares the day to be a National Day of Service. Meets with Israeli Prime Minister Benjamin Netanyahu in New York and supports opposition to Palestine's bid for state recognition by the UN (*September 21*). Meets with British Prime Minister David Cameron in Ottawa who addresses Parliament (*September 22*). Asked by eight Nobel Peace Prize winners to halt the Alberta oil sands expansion, two days after 117 protesters opposed to the Keystone pipeline from Alberta to Texas are arrested on Parliament Hill (*September 28*). The Supreme Court rules against the government's attempt to close down a safe-injection drug centre in Vancouver (*September 30*). Writes the foreword for Paul Henderson's book *How Hockey Explains Canada* (*October 1*). Tables legislation to dismantle the Canadian Wheat Board (*October 18*). Attends his fourth Commonwealth Heads of Government Meeting, in Perth, Australia (*October 28-30*). Attends the G20 Summit in Cannes, France (*November 3-4*). Told by Obama that the Keystone pipeline won't receive U.S. approval in its current form (*November 10*). Attends the APEC Summit in Hawaii, where Canada opts out of the Trans-Pacific Partnership trade agreement in order to protect its dairy, egg and poultry farmers (*November 12*). Meets with Chinese President Hu Jintao in Honolulu (*November 12*). Orders an audit into the chronic living conditions in the northern Ontario Cree community of Attawapiskat (*November 30*). Former MP Daniel Paillé is elected leader of the Bloc Québécois (*December 11*). Peter Kent (Environment) tells the House that Canada is withdrawing from Kyoto Protocol on climate change (*December 12*). Sued for $1.3 million by former cabinet minister Helen Guergis for defamation connected to her dismissal from caucus (*December 22*); thrown out the following August.

2012: Accuses environmentalists opposed to the Northern Gateway pipeline of being funded by foreign money (*January 6*). Holds his first Summit with First Nations peoples in Ottawa to discuss improving Indigenous self-sufficiency (*January 24*). Speaks to the World Economic Forum in Davos, Switzerland (*January 26*); suggests raising Old Age Security qualifications to age 67 instead of 65. Visits China for trade talks (*February 7-11*). MPs vote in favour of abolishing the long-gun registry (*February 15*). Denies any knowledge of the 'robocall' misleading phone calls in the last election that directed non-Conservative voters to fictitious polling stations in Guelph, Ont. (*February 22*). Shuts down the embassy in Damascus, Syria, because of escalating violence (*March 5*). Meets with Thailand's Prime Minister Yingluck Shinawatra in Bangkok to explore the potential for free trade discussions (*March 23*). Thomas Mulcair is elected leader of the New Democratic party, becoming Leader of the Opposition (*March 24*). Meets with Japanese Prime Minister Yoshihiko Noda in Tokyo to begin discussions for a free trade agreement (*March 25*). Attends the North American Summit with U.S. President Obama and Mexican President Calderón in Washington to discuss trade and Mexico's drug wars (*April 2*). Auditor General Michael Ferguson says the Conservatives have been misleading Parliament about the soaring costs for 65 Lockheed Martin F-35 fighter jets (*April 4*). Attends the Summit of the Americas in Cartagena, Colombia, where he opposes initiatives to invite Cuba to the next meeting and recognize Argentina's claim to the Falkland Islands (*April 14-15*). Announces an agreement with Chilean President Sebastian Pinera in Santiago to update the 15-year-old free trade agreement between the two countries (*April 16*); unaffected by an earthquake in Chile early the next morning. Introduces a 400-page omnibus bill that includes about 70 legislative changes (*April 26*). Meets privately with the Dalai Lama in Ottawa (*April 27*). Appoints former prime minister Chrétien to be Canada's representative on the Queen Elizabeth Jubilee Trust (*April 30*). Meets with Israeli President Shimon Peres in Ottawa (*May 8*). A painting of him reclining in the nude, by Margaret Sutherland, is part of a Kingston library exhibit (*May 10*). Meets with other G8 leaders at Camp David, Maryland, to discuss Europe's continuing debt crisis (*May 18-19*). Attends the NATO Summit in Chicago (*May 20-21*). Luca Magnotta is charged with threatening him by mailing a severed foot to Conservative headquarters (*June 2*). Attends Elizabeth II's Diamond Jubilee in London (*June 4-6*). Presents Elizabeth II with a gigantic portrait of her to hang at Rideau Hall (*June*

6). Meets with new French President François Hollande in Paris *(June 6*). The Ominbus Bill is passed following closure imposed after 24 hours of debate (*June 14*). Attends the G20 Summit in Mexico City and secures Canada's invitation to join Trans-Pacific Partnership trade talks (*June 18-19*). Scientists protest on Parliament Hill against Conservative environmental policies that put ideology ahead of science (*July 10*). Former advisor Bruce Carson is charged with fraud by the RCMP *(July 27*). Visits Kindersley, Sask., to mark the official end of the Wheat Board's monopoly (*August 1*). Turns down the premiers' request that he attend an economic first ministers meeting in the fall (*August 1*). Meets with German Chancellor Angela Merkel in Ottawa to discuss a trade deal between Canada and the European Union (*August 16*). Severs relations with Iran, closing the Canadian embassy in Tehran (*September 7*). Attends the APEC conference in Vladivostok, Russia; holds meetings with Russian President Vladimir Putin and Chinese President Hu Jintao (*September 8-9*). A motion to re-open the abortion debate is defeated in the House *(September 26*). The government suspends XL Foods' licence after e-coli, discovered in its products, poisons 15 consumers (*September 27*). Receives the World Statesman of the Year Award from the Appeal of Conscience Foundation in New York (*September 27*). Omar Khadr, captured while fighting for al-Qaida in Afghanistan in 2001, is transferred from U.S. Guantanamo prison to Millhaven prison in Ontario (*September 29*). Attends La Francophonie conference in Kinshasha, Congo (*October 13-14*); meets with Quebec's PQ premier Pauline Marois. Hull's Museum of Civilization will be renamed the Canadian Museum of History (*October 16*). Rejects a $5.18 billion bid to take over Progress Energy Resources of Calgary by Petronas of Malaysia (*October 20*). Crashes an Ottawa wedding photo shoot in Rockcliffe Park and poses with the married couple (*October 20*). Visits India (*November 3-9*); sees the Taj Mahal in Agra (*November 5*); meets with President Pranab Mukherjee and Prime Minister Manmohan Singh (*November 6*); attends the World Economic Forum near New Delhi (*November 6-8*). Meets with President Benigno Aquino III in Manila, Philippines (*November 10*). Marks Remembrance Day at the cemetery of Canadian soldiers in Hong Kong (*November 11*). A Senate committee begins examining possible improper use of the housing allowance by Senator Patrick Brazeau (*November 22*); later expands the audit to Senators Mike Duffy and Mac Harb, and to Senator Pamela Wallin for travel expenses. Presents the Queen's Diamond Jubilee Medal to singer Justin Bieber in Ottawa (*November 23*). John Baird (Foreign Affairs) votes against a resolution to upgrade Palestine to non-member observer status, approved by the UN (*November 29*). Approves the $1.5 billion buyout of Calgary-based Nexen energy company by the Chinese government company CNOOC, and the Malaysian Petronas purchase of Progress, previously rejected (*December 7*); indicates future approvals will not occur except in special circumstances. Refuses to meet with Chief Theresa Spence of Attawapiskat, Ont., who begins a hunger strike on an island in the river at Ottawa to focus attention on Indigenous issues (*December 11*); the strike sparks a series of Idle No More demonstrations and blockades by First Nation peoples across the country.

2013: Meets with Thomas Yayi Boni, President of Benin and the African Union, who requests Canadian involvement in an international mission to Mali; declines to send troops (*January 8*). The Supreme Court rules that 600,000 Indigenous peoples living off reserve are still 'Indians' (*January 8*); the government plans to appeal the decision. Meets with First Nations leaders to discuss treaty rights and reduce rising tensions (*January 11*). Records his day through comments and photos on Twitter, from breakfast with his cat Stanley to the opening of the Session of Parliament to "a few minutes of writing before calling it a night" (*January 28*). John Duncan (Indian Affairs & Northern Development) resigns after lobbying a tax judge on behalf of a constituent (*February 15*); replaced by Bernard Valcourt (Atlantic Canada Opportunities Agency). Announces the establishment of the Office of Religious Freedom, to be led by Dr. Andrew Bennett (*February 19*). The Supreme Court rules that Canada failed to implement the land grant provision to Métis set out in the 1870 Manitoba Act (*March 8*). Peter Penashue (Privy Council; Intergovernmental Affairs) resigns for accepting ineligible election campaign contributions (*March 14*). Participates in a video chat with Canadian astronaut Chris Hadfield who is in command of the International Space Station (*March 15*). Justin Trudeau becomes leader of the Liberal party, replacing interim leader Bob Rae (*April 14*). Attends Margaret Thatcher's funeral in London, England, with former prime minister Mulroney (*April 17*). Speaker Andrew Scheer rules that the Speaker has the ability to override party whips' lists of who can speak during Question Period (*April 23*). Attends the 100th anniversary of Leaside, the Toronto community where he grew up (*April 27*). Visits New York City to promote the Keystone XL pipeline (*May 9*). Accepts the resignation of his chief of staff, Nigel Wright who wrote a $90,000 personal cheque to Senator Duffy as compensation for improperly claimed Senate expenses (*May 19*). Visits Peru to meet with President Ollanta Humala Tasso (*May 21-22*). Attends the Pacific Alliance Leaders Summit in Cali, Columbia (*May 22-23*). Becomes the second Canadian Prime Minister to address British Parliament (*June 13*). Meets with Irish Prime Minister Enda Kenny in Dublin (*June 16*). Attends the G8 Summit in Northern Ireland (*June 17-18*); says Russia should not be part of the group because of its invasion of the Ukraine. Views flooding in Calgary with Alberta Premier Alison Redford and Mayor Naheed Nenshi (*June 21*). The Senate blocks a bill that requires disclosure of union leaders' salaries and outside donations (*June 26*). Helps with flood clean-up in High River, Alta, and attends the Calgary Stampede (*July 5*). Visits Lac-Mégantic, Que., scene of a major train derailment and resulting explosion (*July 7*). Senator Duffy is charged with bribery, fraud and breach of trust (*July 17*). Indicates Canada supports but has no plans to join a military mission against Syria for its alleged use of chemical weapons (*August 29*). Attends the G20 Summit in St. Petersburg, Russia, to discuss the Syrian conflict and the global economy (*September 5-6*). Leona Aglukkaq (Environment) avoids attributing climate change to human activity, despite a recommendation to do so from an intergovernmental panel (*September 27*). Meets with Malaysia's Prime Minister Datuk Nazak in Kuala Lumpur (*October 6*). Attends the APEC Summit in Bali, Indonesia (*October 7-8*). Announces a free trade agreement in principle with the European Union (*October 13*). His office building, Langevin Block, is evacuated by police following discovery of a suspicious package that later turns out to be no threat (*October 16*). The government challenges the constitutionality of Quebec's Bill 99 that lets the province set the rules for its secession (*October 16*). Accused by Duffy of participating in a cover-up in the growing Senate scandal (*October 28*). The Conservative convention in Calgary endorses policies designed to pull the party firmly back to the right (*November 2-3*). His book, *A Great Game: The Forgotten Leafs & The Rise of Professional Hockey*, is published (*November 5*). The Senate suspends Brazeau, Duffy and Wallin for two years without pay for spending irregularities (*November 5*). Boycotts the Commonwealth leaders meeting in Sri Lanka based on concerns about that country's human rights record dealing with its Tamil minority (*November 15*). Flies to South Africa to attend Nelson Mandela's funeral (*December 8*). Canada claims the Arctic up to the North Pole in a submission to the UN Convention on the Law of the Sea (*December 9*). Paillé resigns as leader of the Bloc Québécois for health reasons (*December 16*). The Supreme Court rules against federal laws prohibiting brothels, streetwalking and making a living through prostitution, giving the government a year to replace the legislation (*December 20*).

2014: Launches construction of a road between Inuvik and Tuktoyaktuk in the Northwest Territories (*January 8*). Appears in the first episode of *24/Seven*, weekly videos about his job, produced by his office (*January 9*). Visits Israel, the West Bank and Jordan (*January 19-24*); lays the cornerstone for the Stephen J. Harper Hula Valley Bird Sanctuary and Education Centre in northern Israel and receives an honorary Doctor of Philosophy degree at Tel Aviv University. Addresses the Knesset (*January 20*). Meets with Abdullah II of Jordan in Amman (*January 23*). Liberal Leader Justin Trudeau removes all 32 Liberal Senators from his caucus in an effort to make the Senate less partisan (*January 29*). Senator Patrick Brazeau, already suspended, and retired senator Mac Harb are charged with fraud relating to travel and living expense claims (*February 4*). The Fair Elections Act is introduced, tightening the restrictions that allow citizens to vote (*February 4*). Changes to the Citizenship Act are introduced to make it easier to strip citizenship from people guilty of terrorism or treason (*February 6*). Drummer Phillip Nolan, part of his band Herringbone, is charged with sexual assault (*February 6*); sentenced 11 months later to two years. Meets with Mexican President Enrique Peña Nieto and U.S. President Obama for his sixth North American leaders summit, in Toluca, Mexico (*February 19*). Wins a bet for a case of beer from Obama after the Canadian men's hockey team beats the U.S. at the Winter Olympics in Sochi, Russia (*February 23*). Meets with the Aga Khan who addresses Parliament (*February 27*). Concludes a free-trade deal with South Korea, meeting with President Park Gaun-Hye in Seoul (*March 9-11*). Marks the official end of Canada's military mission in Afghanistan (*March 12*). Flaherty (Finance) resigns from cabinet to return to the private sector and is replaced by Joe Oliver (Natural Resources) (*March 19*). His nomination of Marc Nadon as a Supreme Court justice is rejected by the Supreme Court (*March 21*). Visits the Ukraine to meet with Acting President Oleksandr Turchynov and Prime Minister Arseniy Yatsenyuk, reaffirming Canada's support following Russia's occupation of the Crimea (*March 22*). Attends the Nuclear Security Summit and an emergency G7 Summit in The Hague, Netherlands, to discuss the Russian takeover of the Crimea (*March 23*). Meets with Merkel in Berlin and visits Munich (*March 26-27*). Removes Dimitri Soudas as the party's executive director for interfering in his girlfriend MP Eve Adams's bid to win the nomination in a new Ontario riding (*March 30*). Introduces a Victims Bill of Rights (*April 3*). Announces the First Nations Control of First Nations Education Act to provide funding and guidelines (*April 10*); withdrawn following opposition from many chiefs. Former Finance minister, Jim Flaherty, dies of a heart attack in Ottawa (*April 10*). His former chief of staff, Nigel Wright, won't face charges for paying Senator Duffy to cover his falsely claimed expenses (*April 15*). Delivers the eulogy at Flaherty's state funeral at St. James Cathedral in Toronto (*April 16*). The U.S. extends its review of the Keystone XL pipeline rather than make a decision (*April 18*). Abandons Senate reform after the Supreme Court unanimously rules that any changes require the support of most or all provinces (*April 25*). Shawn Atleo resigns as leader of the Assembly of First Nations (*May 2*). Accuses Chief Justice McLachlin of inappropriately calling him about a judicial appointment (*May 2*); she and others in the legal community dispute the charge. Announces the appointment of the Prince of Wales, who is beginning a four-day Canadian visit, to the Privy Council (*May 18*). Joins the Prince of Wales in Winnipeg for the last day of the Royal couple's Canadian visit (*May 21*). Sued by the National Council of First Nations chiefs who reject proposed changes to Indigenous education (*May 27*). Hosts a three-day conference on maternal, newborn and child health, in Toronto (*May 28-30*). Meets with Polish Prime Minister Donald Tusk in Warsaw while participating in Poland's 25th anniversary of independence from Soviet influence (*June 4*). Attends the G7 Summit in Brussels, Belgium (*June 4-5*). Attends the 70th anniversary of D-Day in Normandy, France (*June 6*). A new prostitution law is introduced making it illegal to buy sexual services (*June 6*). Attends the swearing-in ceremony of Petro Poroshenko, the new President of Ukraine (*June 7*). The Bloc Québécois chooses Mario Beaulieu to succeed Paillé as leader (*June 14*). Conditionally approves the Northern Gateway Pipeline project to move Alberta oil sands through northern British Columbia to the Pacific (*June 17*). Celebrates the 150th anniversary of the Charlottetown Conference in P.E.I. (*June 19*). The Supreme Court rules in favour of First Nations having more control over use of their lands along pipeline routes (*June 28*). Geneva-based

International Commission of Jurists indicates Chief Justice McLachlin acted appropriately in communicating with the Prime Minister about an appointment to the Supreme Court (*July 23*). Blames Hamas after Israel bombs a UN school in Gaza (*July 30*). A Conservative worker in Guelph is convicted of fraudulent robocalls during the 2011 election (*August*). Joins the search for the lost Franklin expedition, aboard the *Sir Wilfrid Laurier* coast guard ship (*August 25*); announces the discovery of one of the ships (the *Erebus*) 15 days later. Commits up to 100 soldiers in advisory roles to the Middle East fight against Islamic State (*September 4*); sends combat aircraft a month later. Attends the NATO Summit in Wales to discuss the Russian invasion of the Ukraine (*September 4-5*). Opens the Aga Khan Museum in Toronto (*September 12*). Meets with Ukrainian President Poroshenko in Ottawa (*September 17*). Signs the Canada-South Korea free trade agreement with President Park Geun-hye in Ottawa (*September 22*) Addresses the UN General Assembly in New York, focusing on preventable deaths of mothers, newborns and children (*September 25*). Signs the free trade agreement with the European Union during the Canada-European Union Summit in Ottawa (*September 26*). Holds his first meeting with new Alberta Premier Jim Prentice, a former member of his cabinet (*October 10*). Named the recipient of Rotary International's 2014 Polio Eradication Champion Award (*October 18*). Quickly moved out of a caucus meeting and eventually offsite after gunman Michael Zehaf-Bibeau enters the Centre Block before being shot (*October 22*); the gunman had killed Nathan Cirillo, a corporal on duty at the National War Memorial, earlier. Delivers the eulogy at Cirillo's funeral in Hamilton (*October 28*). Announces tax cuts that include income-splitting for couples with children (*October 30*). Canadian airstrikes in Iraq begin (*November 2*). Meets with French President François Hollande in Ottawa (*November 3*). Visits Hangzhou and Beijing in China (*November 5-10*). Attends the APEC Summit in Beijing (*November 10-12*). Visits New Zealand (*November 13-14*) before attending the G20 Summit in Brisbane, Australia (*November 16-16*); tells Russian President Putin to get his troops out of the Ukraine. Attends the 15th La Francophonie Summit in Dakar, Senegal (*November 28-30*); former governor-general Michaëlle Jean is appointeed as the group's Secretary General. Attends the funeral for hockey legend Jean Béliveau in Montreal (*December 10*). Thanked by Obama for his role in facilitating meetings in Canada between the U.S. and Cuba aimed at restoring relations (*December 17*).

2015: Attends the bicentennial of Sir John A. Macdonald's birthday, in Kingston; introduces a commemorative Macdonald stamp and coin (*January 11*). Meets with the new national chief of the Assembly of First Nations, Perry Bellegarde; little achieved (*January 28*). Unveils his Anti-Terrorism Act, giving expanded powers to law enforcement and intelligence agencies (*January 30*). John Baird (Foreign Affairs) resigns (*February 3*); replaced by Rob Nicholson (Defence). Meets with German Chancellor Merkel in Ottawa (*February 9*). Conservative MP Eve Adams crosses to the Liberals after being denied a chance to seek election as a Tory in the next election (*February 9*). Introduces a plan for legislation that would eliminate any chance of parole for some prisoners convicted of first-degree murder (*March 4*). Indicates the intention to extend and expand Canada's military mission in Iraq against Islamic State (*March 18*). Canada's (and Britain's) Succession to the Throne acts are changed from 'eldest son' to 'eldest child' (*March 26*). Canada sells the last of its stock in General Motors that it purchased as part of a 2009 bailout package (*April 10*). Attends the Summit of the Americas in Panama City (*April 10-11*); includes a meeting with Cuban President Raoul Castro. Meets with India's Prime Minister Narendra Modi in Toronto (*April 15*). Sued by B.C. lawyer Aniz Alani for refusing to fill Senate seats (*April 23*). Meets with Iraqi Prime Minister Haider al-Abadi in Baghdad, then visits the front lines in northern Iraq and meets with Kurdish regional president, Massoud Barzani (*May 2*). Visits Canadian soldiers at a Kuwait air base (*May 3*). Meets with Dutch Prime Minister Mark Rutte before helping to mark the 70th anniversary of the liberation of the Netherlands during the Second World War, at Holten Canadian War Cemetery (*May 4*). The Alberta NDP, led by Rachel Notley, win the provincial election to end the Conservative dynasty (*May 5*). Unsuccessful in preventing the release from jail of Khadr, accused of terrorism by the U.S. (*May 7*). Meets with Philippines President Benigno Aquino III in Toronto (*May 8*). Rejects the tradition of participating in a televised leaders' debate organized by a consortium of Canadian television networks (*May 12*). Announces that a new Windsor-Detroit bridge will be named after hockey star Gordie Howe (*May 14*). MacKay (Justice) indicates he will not seek re-election (*May 29*). Takes part in the closing ceremony at Rideau Hall of the Truth and Reconciliation Commission that released its report about Indigenous residential schools the previous day (*June 3*). His office halts the processing of UN-approved Syrian refugees, presumably to audit the process (*June*); the embargo lasts two months. Visits Kyiv, Ukraine (*June 6*). Attends the G7 Summit in Schloss Elmau, Germany (*June 7-8*); backs the U.S. and Germany in supporting continued sanctions against Russia; works with Japan to water down efforts to deal with climate change. Visits Warsaw, Poland (*June 8-10*) then Rome and the Vatican City where he meets with Pope Francis (*June 10-11*). Beaulieu steps down as Bloc Québécois leader and is replaced by former leader Gilles Duceppe (*June 10*). Makes 98 patronage appointments prior to the election campaign (*June 18-19*). Attends the opening of the Pan American Games in Toronto (*July 11*). Vows not to appoint any more Senators until the provinces agree to reforms (*July 24*). The 41st Parliament is dissolved, triggering the longest election campaign since 1872 (*August 2*). Refuses to provide federal assistance for a proposed Ontario Retirement Pension Plan, calling it a 'tax hike'', intensifying his ongoing conflict with Ontario Premier Kathleen Wynne (*August 3*). During the Senator Duffy trial, it becomes clear that the Prime Minister's current chief of staff, Ray Novak, knew about former chief of staff Nigel Wright's secret $90,000 payment to Duffy (*August 18*). Statistics Canada confirms Canada is in a recession (*September 1*). Attracts social media criticism for describing non-immigrants as "old stock Canadians" during a televised leaders debate (*September 17*). Attends a party rally in Toronto with former city mayor Rob Ford in an effort to court the populist vote referred to as 'Ford Nation' (*October 17*). Canada's 43rd federal election: elected in the new riding Calgary Heritage with 64% of the vote; his government is defeated (*October 19*). Informs party president John Walsh he plans to resign, but doesn't refer to it in his election night speech (*October 19*). His family moves out of 24 Sussex Drive with the intention to return to Calgary (*October 27*). Sends a letter to public service employees thanking them for their work; the Public Service Alliance of Canada union responds that it's "unfortunate" he didn't recognize their contribution during his mandate (*November 3*). **Harper's government ends** (*November 4*). Attends a caucus meeting that chooses Rona Ambrose, former Health minister, as interim leader (*November 5*). Incorporates as Harper & Associates Consulting with former staffers Ray Novak and Jeremy Hunt (*November*). Accused by Senator Duffy of insisting the former broadcaster represent P.E.I. although he didn't actually live there (*December 8*).

2016: Makes a rare public appearance speaking at the Republican Jewish Coalition in Las Vegas (*April 7*). The Ontario court clears Duffy of all 31 charges related to fraud, bribery and breach of trust, and calls the orchestration of the Senator's problems by the former prime minister's office "mind-boggling and shocking" (*April 21*). His legislation for minimum two-year compulsory sentences for drug trafficking by those under 18 is ruled unconstitutional by the B.C. Court of Appeal (*April 25*). Appointed as a director of Conservative Fund Canada, the party's fundraising arm (*June*). Endorses Jason Kenney's candidacy for the Alberta Conservative leadership (*July 9*). Awarded the Order of Liberty by the Ukraine (*August 25*). Resigns as MP for Calgary Heritage (*August 26*). Joins the roster of the Worldwide Speakers Group (*September*). Joins Denton's law firm as a global markets and economic risk advisor; the same firm that hired Chrétien (*September 12*).

Becomes a director of Colliers International Group real estate company (*September 15*). Attends the funeral of former Israeli prime minister Shimon Peres in Tel Aviv along with Chrétien and Prime Minister Trudeau (*September 30*). Speaks at the memorial service for his former cabinet colleague, Jim Prentice, who died in a plane crash earlier in the month (*October 28*). Joins the Alberta Progressive Conservative party to support former colleague Jason Kenney who seeks the party's leadership, with plans to merge it and the Wildrose party (*November*).

2017: Visits Asia and Australia on speaking engagements (*January-February*). Indicates plans to join the U.S. venture capital company 8VC as an advisor (*April 19*). Joins former U.S. president George W. Bush for dinner in Texas the same evening Prime Minister Trudeau has dinner in Montreal with former U.S. president Barack Obama (*June 7*). Calls the Trudeau government's payout to Omar Khadr "simply wrong" (*July 7*). Warns that U.S. President Trump could very well tear up NAFTA, currently under renegotiation *(October 11*); later criticizes the Liberal government for "napping on NAFTA" renegotiations.

2018: Elected chairman of the International Democratic Union (IDU), an alliance of right-of-centre political parties around the world (*February 21*). Adds his name to a full-page ad in the *New York Times* endorsing Trump's withdrawal from the Iran nuclear deal (*May 10*). Indicates his book on populism, *Right Here Right Now*, will be released in the fall (*June 4*). Receives an honorary degree from Jerusalem College of Technology at a Toronto fundraiser (*June 13*).

Books about Harper

- **2005**: Lloyd Mackey; *The Pilgrimage of Stephen Harper* (ECW)
- **2006**: William Johnson; *Stephen Harper & the Future of Canada* (Douglas Gibson)
- **2006**: Bob Plamondon; *Full Circle: Death and Resurrection in Canadian Conservative Politics* (Key Porter)
- **2007**: Chantal Hebert; *French Kiss: Stephen Harper's Blind Date With Quebec* (Vintage)
- **2007**: Paul Wells; *Right Side Up: The Fall of Paul Martin and the Rise of Stephen Harper's New Conservatism* (Douglas Gibson)
- **2009**: Tom Flanagan; *Harper's Team: Behind the Scenes in the Conservative Rise to Power* (McGill-Queen's University)
- **2009**: Garth Turner; *Sheeple: Caucus Confidential in Stephen Harper's Ottawa* (Key Porter)
- **2009**: Barry Cooper; *It's the Regime, Stupid!: A Report from the Cowboy West on Why Stephen Harper Matters* (Key Porter)
- **2010**: Lawrence Martin; *Harperland: The Politics of Control* (Penguin)
- **2011**: Christian Nadeau; *Rogue in Power: Why Stephen Harper is Remaking Canada by Stealth* (Lorimer)
- **2011**: Paula Mallea; *Fearmonger: Stephen Harper's Tough on Crime Agenda* (Lorimer)
- **2012**: Yves Engler; *The Ugly Canadian: Stephen Harper's Foreign Policy* (RED, Fernwood)
- **2012**: Paul Adams; *Power Trap: How Fear and Loathing Between New Democrats and Liberals Keep Stephen Harper in Power – and What Can Be Done About It* (Lorimer)

- **2013**: Paul Wells; *The Longer I'm Prime Minister: Stephen Harper 2006-* (Random House Canada)
- **2013**: Mark Kennedy; *Rebel to Realist: How Politics Changed Stephen Harper and How He is Changing Canada* (Postmedia News ebook)
- **2014**: Michael Harris; *Party of One: Stephen Harper and Canada's Radical Makeover* (Viking)
- **2014**: Mark Bourrie; *Kill the Messengers: Stephen Harper's Assault on Your Right to Know* (HarperCollins Canada)
- **2014**: Bruce Carson; *14 Days: Making the Conservative Movement in Canada* (McGill-Queen's University)
- **2014**: Donald Gutstein; *Harperism: How Stephen Harper and His Think Tank Colleagues Have Transformed Canada* (Lorimer)
- **2015**: John Ibbotson; *Stephen Harper* (Signal)
- **2015**: Mel Hurtig; *The Arrogant Autocrat: Stephen Harper's Takeover of Canada (Lightning Source)*
- **2015**: Jeffrey Brooke; *Dismantling Canada: Stephen Harper's New Conservative Agenda* (McGill-Queen's University)
- **2015**: Les Whittington; *Spinning History: A Witness to Harper's Canada and 21st Century Choices* (Hill Times Books)
- **2016**: Jennifer Ditchburn & Graham Fox; *The Harper Factor: Assessing a Prime Minister's Policy Legacy* (McGill-Queen's University)

23

Justin Trudeau

The Unstuffy Prime Minister

With charisma, a famous last name and the promise of an enlightened government that harkened back to Laurier's 'sunny ways', Justin Trudeau catapulted the Liberal party from third-party status to government in 2015. Like his father, he was welcomed by adoring crowds in his early years as Prime Minister. He embraced deficits and began to swing Canada back to the left by boosting social spending, confronting climate change and legalizing marijuana. Trudeau was an antidote to stodgy politics, describing himself as a feminist (he gave women equal representation in cabinet) and readily engaging in hugs and selfie photos with world leaders and citizens alike.

Trudeau the Politician

Prime Minister of Canada: November 4, 2015 –
Parliament as Prime Minister: 43rd
Age on entering office: 43
Political party: Liberal
Leader of party: April 14, 2013 –
Member of Parliament: October 14, 2008 –
Riding represented: Papineau [Que.] 2008 –
Cabinet portfolio: Intergovernmental Affairs & Youth (2015-)
Other political post: none
Title: Canadian Privy Councillor (2015)
Quotes: "I don't care if you thought my father was great or arrogant. It doesn't matter to me if you were a Chrétien-Liberal, a Turner-Liberal, a Martin-Liberal or any other kind of Liberal. The era of hyphenated Liberals ends right here, tonight." (Trudeau's leadership acceptance speech, 2013); "whether you're trying to assert your will in a barroom confrontation or a political altercation, the biggest obstacle to overcome is the ego … The trick is to try and find a way for your opponent to save face." (from his autobiography *Common Ground*).

Trudeau the Man

Name: Justin Pierre James Trudeau
Born: December 25, 1971, Ottawa, Ontario
Ancestry: French, Scottish
Religion: Roman Catholic
Education: B.A. [Bachelor of Arts in English Literature] (McGill, 1994); B.Ed. [Bachelor of Education] (University of British Columbia, 1998)
Nickname: The Tornado (coined by future New Brunswick premier Brian Gallant after observing Trudeau's frenetic canvassing pace)
Military service: none
Occupation: teacher; public speaker
Publication: *Common Ground* (2014)
Appearance: "Strikingly young and wavy-haired … dashing in his blue suit and jaunty brown shoes—a stylistic riposte to the old world of boringly black-shoed politicians." (John Powers in *Vogue*, 2015); "Handsome and boyish, his dark curls flopping into his blue eyes … with his mother's good looks and warmth and his father's élan" (Diane Solway in *W Magazine*, 2008)
Personality: "He has a charisma and a magnetism that draws people to him, like his father. But like his mother, he's exuberant, warm and affectionate. Justin likes the spotlight, craves it." (Althia Raj in *The Contender*); "What he had was just a controversial last name, youthful vigour, and an understanding of people. It is proving more than enough." Samuel Getachew on *Leaders and Legacies* website
Married: Sophie Grégoire, May 28, 2005, Sainte-Madeleine d'Outremont Church, Montreal, Quebec
Age at marriage: 33

Trudeau is the:
- Only Prime Minister to grow up at 24 Sussex Drive
- First Prime Minister who was the child of a Prime Minister (Pierre Trudeau)
- First Prime Minister to win an election from third party position
- First Prime Minister born in Ottawa, the capital city
- Second youngest Prime Minister (43)
- Sixth Prime Minister with no previous cabinet experience
- Seventh Prime Minister born in Ontario
- Tenth Liberal Prime Minister

Trudeau's legacy
- Changed mood in government to emulate Laurier's 'sunny ways'
- Appointed a cabinet with equal male-female representation

Trudeau's Family

Trudeau's Parents

Father: Pierre Elliott Trudeau
Born: October 18, 1919, Montreal, Quebec

Occupation: lawyer; civil servant; professor; journalist; politician; MP; Prime Minister of Canada (1968-1979, 1980-1984)
Died: September 28, 2000, Montreal, Quebec
Age at death: 80

Mother: Margaret Joan Sinclair
Born: September 10, 1948, Vancouver, British Columbia
Occupation: author; speaker
Married: March 4, 1971, North Vancouver, British Columbia
Divorced: April 2, 1984
Second marriage: Fried Kemper, April 19, 1984 (div. 1999)

Trudeau's Brothers (2 siblings; Justin the oldest)

Brother: Alexandre 'Sacha' Emmanuel Trudeau (b.1973), 3 children
Married: Zoë Bedos (2007)
Brother: Michel 'Micha' Charles-Émile Trudeau (1975-1998)
Half-Brother: Kyle Kemper (b.1984)
Half-Sister: Alicia 'Ally' Mary Rose Kemper (b.1988)
Half-Sister: Sarah Elisabeth Coyne (b.1991)

Trudeau's Wife

Wife: Sophie Grégoire
Born: April 24, 1975, Montreal, Quebec
Father: Jean Grégoire (stockbroker)
Mother: Estelle Blais (nurse)
Occupation: broadcaster
Age at marriage: 30
Younger than Trudeau: 4 years

Trudeau's Children (3)

Name: Xavier James Trudeau
Born: October 18, 2007, Montreal, Quebec
Note: Shares his birthday with his late grandfather Pierre Trudeau.

Name: Ella-Grace Margaret Trudeau
Born: February 5, 2009, Montreal, Quebec

Name: Hadrien Grégoire Trudeau
Born: February 28, 2014, Ottawa, Ontario
Note: Born exactly 30 years after Pierre Trudeau's "walk in the snow".

POLITICAL STORIES

A leadership edge

After Michael Ignatieff stepped down as Liberal leader, and long before he declared himself as a leadership candidate, Justin Trudeau was the person to beat in the eyes of most party members. He was the son of Pierre, which suffused him with a charismatic, mystical aura other hopefuls couldn't to bring to the contest.

While he weighed the merits of making a bid, other potential candidates began to decline rather than take him on. One significant politician taking a pass was interim leader Bob Rae. Twice, he'd lost a chance to be Liberal leader and he didn't want to lose a third time against a magnetic candidate like Trudeau. Others weren't interested, including former Liberal premiers Frank McKenna, Dalton McGuinty, Robert Ghiz and Jean Charest.

By the start of the leadership race, there were nine candidates: David Bertschi, Martin Cauchon, Deborah Coyne (mother of Trudeau's half-sister), Martha Hall Finley, Marc Garneau, Karen McCrimmon, Joyce Murray, George Takach and Justin Trudeau.

It was a stacked deck with 24 MPs and 18 Senators backing Trudeau. The next best showing was Garneau with 3 MPs in his camp. When Takach, Garneau and Bertschi dropped out, only the latter did not support Trudeau's bid.

Instead of a convention, 127,000 registered party members voted electronically, their votes assigned to a convoluted system involving districts and a point system. If there wasn't a clear winner, the candidate with the lowest tally would be dropped from the ballot with the second preferences of his or her supporters added to the other candidates' tallies. It wasn't necessary. On the first ballot, Trudeau took 80% of the points (and more than 78% of actual votes cast), followed by Murray with 10%.

The Syrian refugee crisis

The spectre of hundreds of thousands of refugees fleeing war-torn Syria and other troubled areas in Asia and Africa competed for news time during the 2015 federal election. With the Harper government showing a reluctance to respond quickly to the crisis, Trudeau and the Liberals seized on the issue by committing to bring in 25,000 Syrian refugees by the end of the year.

The compassionate response struck a nerve with many Canadians and played a part in the Liberal victory at the polls. But delivering on the promise in less than two months was impossible. The new government quickly revised the plan, extending the deadline by two months to February 2016 and adding privately sponsored refugees to the desired tally.

There was an intense effort to ramp up the processing and security screening of refugees in Lebanon, Jordan and Turkey. On his 37th day as Prime Minister, Trudeau greeted the first wave of arrivals at Toronto's Pearson airport. Two days before the end of February, the 25,000th refugee had entered Canada. The undertaking wasn't without its problems, but the goal had been achieved.

A visible Prime Minister

Justin Trudeau was fond of saying Canada "was open for business". The mantra started with him. After a decade of government characterized by secrecy, Trudeau's alternative was pronounced. He seemed to be everywhere and keen to talk to everyone – a politician open for business.

He readily addressed international summits and made the first official visits to Toronto and Washington in decades. Here was a Prime Minister who liked to hug, liked to pose for selfies, liked to chat. It was an affableness that carried the Trudeaumania revival through his first year in office.

The summer of 2016 felt more like an election campaign. He marched in the Montreal, Vancouver and Toronto Pride parades; turned up at the celebrated final concert of Canadian rock group The Tragically Hip; stumbled into a beach wedding while surfing in Tofino, B.C.; attended a community breakfast in St. John's, N.L.; and participated in Old Home Week in Charlottetown, P.E.I. The media loved it.

Personal Stories

An emotional eulogy

The eulogy for his father, delivered at his state funeral on October 3, 2000, suggested to many that Justin might have a future in politics. Trudeau maintained that wasn't the intent. Indeed, he wouldn't enter politics for another six years.

The eulogy, televised nationally, was charged with emotion. Despite its reliance on stirring clichés, it was clearly heartfelt. In French, he said, "We need a genuine, deep respect for every human being, whatever their thoughts, their values, their beliefs, their origins. That's what my father demanded of his sons and that's what he demanded of his country."

In his memoir, *Common Ground*, Trudeau "knew that the newspapers and television tributes would be filled with my father's political accomplishments, so I wanted to share … how great he was as a father." He began his remarks with the recollection of the first official trip he took with his father, to Alert in the Arctic. The visit included a "top-secret mission" to a red building with frosted windows. Peering through a cleared windowpane, six-year-old Justin saw a man with a red suit lined with furry, white trim working industrially at a cluttered table. "And that's when I understood just how powerful and wonderful my father was."

An interest in boxing

Trudeau's charity boxing match with Senator Patrick Brazeau in March 2012 became a metaphor for the approach he took to politics. He entered the ring as the underdog. Few expected he could win. But after enduring a round of aggressive assaults by Brazeau, he had the stamina in the subsequent rounds to beat his exhausted opponent by technical knockout.

The public – particularly anyone putting money on the Trudeau-Brazeau match – was mostly unaware that the Liberal MP was ready for the fight. He had been training vigorously for six months with mentors in Montreal and Ottawa. After all, it was Trudeau who first issued the challenge for a Conservative sparring opponent to raise money for cancer research.

His interest and experience in amateur boxing stretched back to his 20s when he was a student at McGill. Once he became Prime Minister, Trudeau would still find time to practice in the ring when possible – as he did at the legendary Gleason Gym while in New York to sign the Paris climate-change agreement.

Sophie Grégoire Trudeau

As chair of Katimavik, Trudeau teamed up with local broadcaster Sophie Grégoire in June 2003 to co-host the Starlight Children's Foundation gala in Montreal. He had first met Sophie when she was a classmate of his youngest brother years earlier and welcomed the chance to share with her fond remem-brances of Micha who had died in a B.C. avalanche four and half years earlier.

Sophie followed up by email, but Trudeau was "too chicken to reply. I sensed … that even just meeting for coffee would quickly escalate into *the rest of my life*." They met on the street a few months later and he persistently worked at getting a date with her. Like Joe Clark with Maureen McTeer, he proposed on that first date. "It took Sophie a few weeks to realize I was serious, and a few more to realize I was right." A formal proposal followed a year later and they were married in 2005.

Full of energy and a sense of fun, Sophie had an opportunity to exercise her incisive sense of humour at the 2016 Press Gallery dinner in a skit with Trudeau embellishing her need for staff and nannies. Passionate, articulate and used to the limelight, she has served as a spokesperson for Plan, WaterCan and numerous other charities. Her fondness for Canadian fashion gets a boost from her advisor Jessica Mulroney, daughter-in-law of the former prime minister.

Like Trudeau, she attended Collège de Jean-de-Brébeuf and McGill University. Sophie worked in advertising before switching to broadcasting, ending up as a correspondent on CTV's *eTalk* entertainment show.

TRUDEAU'S TIMELINE

1971: Born at Ottawa General Hospital, Ottawa (*December 25*).

1972: Christened at Notre Dame Basilica in Montreal (*January 15*). At a gala banquet in Ottawa, U.S. President Richard Nixon proposes a toast "to the future Prime Minister of Canada: to Justin Pierre Trudeau", the Prime Minister's three-month-old son (*April 14*). His father's government is reduced to a minority in the federal election (*October 30*).

1973: Meets Elizabeth II at the Commonwealth Heads of Government meeting in Ottawa (*August 2*). On his second birthday, his brother Alexandre is born in Ottawa (*December 25*).

1974: His father's government regains a majority in the federal election (*July 8*).

1975: Attends Rockcliffe Park Public School in Ottawa (*September*). His brother Michel is born in Ottawa (*October 2*).

Ottawa delivery

Pierre Trudeau witnessed the birth of his son Justin at Ottawa General Hospital on Christmas Day, 1971, a remarkable opportunity. Remarkable because hospitals didn't permit fathers in the delivery room. Margaret Trudeau was outraged by the restriction and the hospital promptly removed it. More hospitals quickly followed suit.

1976: Made an honorary member of the Children of the Raven on Haida Gwaii during a family visit (*May*). At a meeting his father is having with the premiers at 24 Sussex Drive, sits on the lap of the only premier he recognizes: René Lévesque (*December*).

1977: His parents separate with his father retaining sole custody of the boys (*May 27*).

1978: Catches chicken pox on a family vacation in Jamaica, requiring his father to arrange their return on a government jet instead of a commercial airline (*January*). Beaten up by older Rockcliffe Park student (and future actor) Matthew Perry.

1979: His father's government is defeated by Clark's Conservatives (*May 22*). Moves with his father and brothers to Stornoway (*June*). His parents separate permanently (*Fall*).

1980: His father is re-elected and the Liberals return to power (*February 18*). The family moves back to 24 Sussex Drive (*March*). Joins his father on a trip to the G7 Summit in Venice, which includes an audience with Pope John Paul II (*June 22-23*).

1983: Attends Lycée Claudel d'Ottawa French private school (*September*). Visits China with his father (*November 28*).

1984: His father announces his resignation as Prime Minister (*February 29*). His parents' divorce becomes official (*April 2*). His mother Margaret marries Ottawa real estate developer Fried Kemper (*April 18*). Attends his father's tribute at the convention that elects Turner as the new leader (*June 14*). Moves with his father and brothers to Maison Cormier at 1418 Avenue des Pins in Montreal (*July*). Attends Collège Jean-de-Brébeuf in Montreal, his father's alma mater (*September*). His half-brother Kyle Kemper is born in Ottawa (*November*).

1985: Switches from skiing to snowboarding after seeing a ski used as a snowboard in the James Bond movie *A View To a Kill* (*Winter*).

1986: Succeeds in changing Brébeuf's dress code against shorts by wearing a kilt to class (*June*).

1988: His half-sister Alicia (Ally) Mary Rose Kemper is born in Ottawa. Elected to the student council at Brébeuf (*Fall*).

1989: Enters the CEGEP section of Brébeuf (*September*).

Partisan respect

Spying Opposition Leader Joe Clark in the parliamentary cafeteria while having lunch with his father, eight-year-old Justin sought to impress Trudeau Sr. with a joke he'd heard about Clark. His father saw nothing funny in personal attacks on individuals and sternly told him so. Pierre Trudeau then took his son across the room to introduce him to Clark and daughter Catherine.

1990: Visits China for a second time with his father and brothers (*Summer*). Begins dating his first girlfriend Zully Leon on and off for five years. Speaks unsuc-cessfully for the federalist side in his college's debate as part of a province-wide series of CEGEP debates (*November*)

1991: His half-sister Sarah Coyne is born in St. John's, Nfld, to his father and Deborah Coyne (*May 5*). Attends McGill University (*September*). Convinced by McGill friend Gerald Butts to join the Debating Union (*Fall*).

1992: Promotes the 'No' side on campus prior to the referendum on the Charlottetown Accord (*Fall*). Becomes a facilitator at the McGill Sexual Assault Centre (*Fall*).

1994: Graduates from McGill with a B.A. in English literature (*Spring*). Begins a trip with friends that takes him to France (*Summer*), England (*September*), Morocco, Mauritania, Mali, Burkina Faso, Ivory Coast, Ghana, Togo, Benin (*Fall*), Nigeria, Finland and Russia (*December*).

1995: Continues his trip through Russia, China, Hong Kong, Vietnam and finally Thailand where he acquires a tattoo of a globe on his left shoulder (*Winter-Spring*). Returns to McGill to pursue a Bachelor of Education degree (*September*). Takes part in the large 'No' rally before the second Quebec referendum that rejects separation (*October 27*).

1996: Drops out of McGill (*December*).

1997: Moves to Whistler, B.C., to join his brother Michel and become a snowboard instructor (*January*); also becomes a doorman at the Rogue Wolf nightclub. Returns to McGill to take prerequisite courses to continue his education degree in the West (*Spring*). Enrols in a one-year education program at the University of British Columbia in Vancouver (*Fall*); continues to teach snowboarding on weekends at Whistler.

1998: Graduates from UBC with a Bachelor of Education degree (*Spring*). Moves in with UBC classmate Chris Ingvaldson and his wife. Works as a substitute teacher in Coquitlam, B.C. (*Fall*). His brother Michel dies in an avalanche while skiing in Kokanee Glacier Park, B.C. (*November 13*).

1999: Begins teaching French and mathematics at West Point Grey Academy private school in Vancouver (*January*). Becomes a Founding Director of the Canadian Avalanche Foundation (*May*).

2000: Spends the summer with his father who has prostate cancer. His father Pierre dies in Montreal (*September 28*). Delivers the eulogy at his father's funeral at Montreal's Notre Dame Basilica (*October 3*). Inherits the family cottage near Morin Heights and his father's Mercedes-Benz convertible.

2001: Begins teaching at Sir Winston Churchill high school in Vancouver (*September*).

2002: Returns to Montreal and enrols in engineering at the University of Montreal's École Polytechnique (*September*). Joins Katimavik's board of directors, soon becoming its chair.

2003: Defends Wayne Johnston's novel *The Colony of Unrequited Dreams* on CBC Radio's *Canada Reads*, but casts his vote for Hubert Aquin's *Next Episode* (*April*). Co-hosts a Starlight Children's Foundation gala in Montreal with local broadcaster Sophie Grégoire, a childhood friend of his brother Michel (*June*). Joins his mother for the re-opening of Kokanee Glacier Cabin where his brother Michel spent his last night (*July 12*). Canoes the South Nahanni River (*July 21-27*); becomes an unpaid spokesperson for the Nahanni Forever project of the Canadian Parks and Wilderness Society (CPAWS) (*Fall*). Begins dating Grégoire (*September*). Starts a weekly broadcast about current affairs on French radio station CKAC. Shares an apartment with Grégoire (*Fall*).

2004: Drops out of École Polytechnique (*Spring*). Introduces the Dalai Lama to a crowd of 30,000 in Toronto (*April 25*). Attends the Summer Olympic Games in Athens as a correspondent for CKAC radio (*August 13-29*). Buys an apartment with Grégoire near Avenue Van Horne in Montreal.

2005: Marries Grégoire at Église Sainte-Madeleine d'Outremont (*May 28*); honeymoons in Morocco. Enrols in the graduate environmental geography program at McGill (*September*). Hires a firm to help organize his speaking engagements (*Fall*). Takes part in the two-month Nahanni Forever campaign sponsored by the CPAWS (*November*).

2006: As a public speaker registered with Speaker's Spotlight, gives his first paid speech at UBC for $5,000 (*January 14*). Chairs the Youth Task Force of the Liberal Party Renewal Commission (*Spring*). Steps down as chair of Katimavik. Writes the foreward for Nancy Southam's book *Pierre: Colleagues and Friends Talk about the Trudeau They Knew* (*September 19*). Buys a house in Outremont. Drops out of the McGill geography program (*Fall*). Campaigns for Gerard Kennedy in the Liberal leadership campaign, introducing him at the convention in Montreal (*December 1-2*); switches his support to ultimate winner Stéphane Dion when Kennedy drops out after the second ballot. Tells Dion he's interested in running as a candidate in Outremont riding (*December*).

2007: Appears as soldier Talbot Papineau in the four-part CBC television docudrama *The Great War* (*January*). Turned down by the party to run in Outremont (*January*). Announces his intention to seek the nomination in Papineau (*February 27*). Wins the Liberal nomination in Papineau riding (*April 29*). Takes part in the Generation II Global Peace Initiative in London involving children and grandchildren of famous peace advocates including Gandhi, Tutu, Kennedy and King (*July 16-17*). His first child Xavier is born in Montreal on Pierre Trudeau's birthday (*October 18*).

2008: Visits Israel as part of a junket sponsored by the Centre for Israel and Jewish Affairs (*February*). Canada's 40th federal election: elected in Papineau by 1,189 votes over Bloc Québécois incumbent Vivian Barbot (*October 14*). Rents an apartment in Ottawa (*Fall*). Indicates he has no intention of seeking the leadership after Dion announces plans to step down (*October 20*). Appointed by Dion to be associate youth critic for the Liberals (*November 14*). Dion resigns as party leader and Michael Ignatieff becomes interim leader (*December 10*).

2009: His daughter Ella-Grace is born in Montreal (*February 5*). Tables a motion calling for a national policy to encourage volunteerism (February 25); it is defeated. Makes his first speech in the House about the budget (*March 2*). Co-chairs the leadership convention in Vancouver where Ignatieff is confirmed as Liberal party leader (*April 30-May 2*). Generation II group meets a second time, in Toronto (*August*). Appointed youth and multiculturalism critic (*October 6*).

2010: Sells his Outremont home for $1.6 million and buys a semi-detached house near Mont Royal. Begins living in hotels while staying in Ottawa. Appointed citizenship and immigration critic (*September 7*). His mother Margaret's book *Changing My Mind* reveals her battle with bipolar disorder (*October 12*). Weathers controversy over wearing fur in the family photo on his Christmas card (*December*).

2011: Canada's 41st federal election: re-elected in Papineau defeating NDP candidate Marcos Radhames Tejada by over 4,000 votes, one of only two Liberals to increase their vote count; Liberals reduced to a historical low of 34 seats (*May 2*). Ignatieff resigns as leader after Liberals sink to third-party status (*May 3*); Liberal caucus chooses Bob Rae as interim leader. Appointed post-secondary education and sports critic by Rae (*June 1*). Calls Peter Kent (Environment) a "piece of shit" and later apologizes (*December 14*). Acquires a Haida-influenced raven tattoo on his left shoulder for his 40th birthday (*December*).

2012: Beats Senator Patrick Brazeau in a charity boxing match to raise funds for cancer research (*March 31*). Interim Liberal leader Rae indicates he will not seek the leadership

(*June 13*). His half-sister Sarah's mother, Deborah Coyne, is the first leadership candidate to declare (*June 27*). Decides to seek the leadership during a weekend planning retreat with supporters at Mont Tremblant (*July*). Announces his bid to seek the Liberal party leadership (*October 2*). Backs the controversial takeover of the Nexen oil company by a Chinese company (*November 20*). Apologizes for a two-year-old remark that suggests Quebecers are better at running government than Albertans (*November 23*).

2013: An ebook biography *The Contender: The Justin Trudeau Story* by Althia Raj is published by Huffington Post Canada (*March* 5). Gets the support of leadership candidate Marc Garneau who withdraws (*March 13*). Liberals vote electronically for a new leader (*April 7-14*). Wins the Liberal leadership with more than 78% of the votes (*April 14*). Proposes to legalize marijuana (*July 25*).

2014: Removes all 32 Liberal Senators from his caucus in an effort to make the Senate less partisan (*January 29*). His son Hadrien is born in Ottawa (*February 28*). Says all Liberal candidates in the next election must agree to support abortion rights (*May* 7). His autobiography *Common Ground* is published (*October 20*). Caught in a Parliament Hill lockdown while lone gunman Michael Zihaf-Bibeau roams the hallways before being shot (*October 22*). Suspends two MPs from caucus for alleged sexual misconduct with two female NDP MPs (*November 5*).

Nixon prediction

Justin Trudeau was only three months old when he met U.S. President Richard Nixon. After the encounter, Nixon proposed a toast at a gala banquet for the American. "To the future Prime Minister of Canada: to Justin Pierre Trudeau." Everyone was amused.

2015: Liberal MPs reluctantly support the government's anti-terrorism bill (*May 6*). Unveils his plans to focus on helping the middle class (*May 4*). Prepared to run deficit budgets for several years if it will help to restart the economy (*August 27*). Announces his intention to bring in 25,000 Syrian refugees (*September 3*). Canada's 42nd federal election; re-elected in Papineau defeating broadcaster Anne Lagacé Dowson (NDP); wins a majority government (*October 19*). His family moves into Rideau Cottage while his government decides the fate of 24 Sussex Drive; becomes the first Prime Minister to live on the grounds of the Governor General's residence (*October*). **Trudeau's government (2015-).** Becomes the 23rd Prime Minister of Canada and first Minister of Intergovernmental Affairs & Youth (*November 4*). Appoints a cabinet that has equal representation of females and males (*November 4*). The Conservatives choose Rona Ambrose to be interim leader, replacing Harper (*November 5*). The government reinstates the long-form census (*November 5*). Attends the G20 Summit in Anatalya, Turkey (*November 15-16*). Attends the APEC meeting in Manila, Philippines (*November 18-19*). Meets with the provincial premiers to discuss climate change before the international meeting in Paris (*November 23*). The government extends its original pledge to settle 25,000 Syrian refugees to the end of February (*November 24*). Meets with Elizabeth II and British Prime Minister David Cameron in London (*November 25*). His new desk, which was used by his father, Laurier, Pearson, Chrétien and Martin, arrives at Parliament Hill (*November 27*). Attends the Commonwealth Heads of Government meeting in Malta (*November 27*). Meets with French President François Hollande in Paris (*November 29*). Attends the international climate change conference in Paris (November 30). The government asks 33 of Harper's patronage appointees to step down voluntarily to permit their jobs to be filled through the regular hiring process (*December 8*). Announces a public inquiry into the murder or disappearance of hundreds of Indigenous women over the past few decades (*December 8*). Joins Ontario Premier Kathleen Wynne to welcome the first wave of Syrian refugees in Toronto (*December 11*). His family vacations on Nevis in the Caribbean (*December-January 11*).

2016: Becomes first Prime Minister to officially visit Toronto since its amalgamation in 1996 (*January 13*). Holds a cabinet meeting in St. Andrews-by-the-Sea, N.B. (*January 17-19*); the first in a pattern of regional cabinet retreats. Attends the World Economic Forum in Davos, Switzerland (*January 20-23*). Says his government won't be a 'cheerleader' for pipeline projects (*January 26*). Visits La Loche, Sask., site of a mass shooting that left four dead the previous week (*January 29*). Announces plans to end bombing by Canadian fighter planes in Iraq and Syria within two weeks, focusing instead on a "train, advise and assist" mission (*February 8*). Meets with UN Secretary General Ban Ki-moon in Ottawa (*February 11*). Indicates the government will not likely be able to balance the budget within four years as promised because of the lagging economy (*February 11*). Meets with the premiers in Vancouver to discuss the economy and carbon emissions reduction (*March 3*). Receives an honorary headdress from Tsuu T'ina nation southwest of Calgary (*March 4*). Meets with U.S. President Obama in Washington on the first official U.S. visit by a Prime Minister in nearly 20 years (*March 9-11*). Speaks out for gender equality at a UN women's conference in New York (*March 16*). A motion to save the former government's Office for Religious Freedom is defeated in the House (*March 21*). The budget calls for spending $8.4 billion over five years for Indigenous peoples (*March 22*). His family visits Fogo Island, N.L. (*March 26-27*). Attends the Nuclear Security Summit in Washington (*April 1*). NDP leader Thomas Mulcair becomes the first leader of a major federal party to lose a confidence vote by party members, receiving 48% support (*April 10*). Signs the Paris climate-change agreement in New York (*April 22*). Tours the fire damage in Fort MacMurray, Alta., that displaced more than 80,000 residents (*May 14*). Tables a bill for the protection of transgender people (*May 17*). Issues a formal apology for the 1914 *Komagata Maru* incident when Canada turned the ship away with 375 mostly Sikh refugees on board (*May 18*). Elbows NDP MP Ruth Ellen Brosseau on the House floor while hurrying MPs to their seats for a vote (*May 18*). Visits Japan and meets with Emperor Akihito and Prime Minister Shinzo Abe (*May 23-25*). Attends the G7 Summit in Ise-Shima, Japan (*May 26-28*). Appoints Domenic LeBlanc (House Leader) as Fisheries minister to replace Hunter Tootoo who resigns to deal with addiction-related problems (*May 31*). The House votes to modify the English lyrics of *O Canada* from "all thy sons command" to "all of us command" (*June 15*). Meets with U.S. President Obama and Mexican President Enrique Peña Nieto in Ottawa where they agree to work together towards a goal of 50% clean energy by 2025 (*June 29*); Obama addresses Parliament. A task force is launched to look at the process of legalizing the use of marijuana, chaired by Anne McLellan, former deputy prime minister (*June 30*). Becomes the first Prime Minister to march in Toronto's Pride parade (*July 3*); marches three weeks later in the Vancouver parade and then Montreal's in August. Attends the NATO Summit in Warsaw, Poland (*July 8-9*). Visits Auschwitz-Birkeneau concentration camp (*July 10*) and the Ukraine (*July 11-12*). Announces a new process for picking Supreme Court judges that leaves selections to an advisory committee chaired by former prime minister Campbell (*August 2*). Attends the final concert of rock group The Tragically Hip in Kingston (*August 21*). Is a guest on the first episode of the new CTV show *Your Morning*, interviewed by Ben Mulroney (*August 22*). Visits China (*August 30-September 6*). Featured as a comic book character in Marvel's *Civil War II: Choosing Sides* (*August 31*). Attends the G20 Summit in Hangzhou, China (*September 4-5*). His brother Alexandre publishes *Barbarian Lost: Travels in the New China* (*September 13*). Hosts the Global Fund initiative in Montreal to raise $13 billion to help eradicate AIDS, malaria and tuberculosis (*September 15*). Addresses the UN General Assembly in New York, warning against the politics of fear, a veiled reference to Donald Trump's U.S. presidential bid; also attends several summits about refugees (*September 20*). Welcomes Prince William and Kate to Victoria (*September 24*). Approves the Petronas Pacific Northwest liquefied natural gas pipeline, with nearly 200 environmental protection conditions attached (*September 27*). Attends the funeral of former Israeli prime minister Shimon Peres in Tel Aviv along with Chrétien and Harper (*September 30*). Announces that provinces have until 2018 to adopt either carbon pricing or a cap-and-trade system, or the federal government will impose a program (*October 3*). His comments in *Le Devoir* that the need for electoral reform is "less compelling" spark concern he doesn't plan to make changes (*October 19*). Postpones his trip to Brussels to sign the Canada-European Union Comprehensive Economic and Trade Agreement (CETA) after Belgium's Wallonia region raises objections to the deal (*October 27*); attends the signing three days later after resistance is resolved through compromise. Appoints nine independent Senators, the first ones chosen using a merit-based system (*October 28*); appoints 12 more for Ontario and Quebec soon after. Indicates he is willing to renegotiate NAFTA with U.S. president-elect Donald Trump (*November 10*). Visits Cuba, Argentina and Peru (*November 15-20*); attends the APEC summit in Lima. Visits Liberia (*November 24*) and attends the La Francophonie summit in Madagascar (*November 26-27*). Experiences public backlash over his laudatory comments about recently deceased former Cuban leader Fidel Castro (*November 26*). Approves tripling the capacity of the Kinder Morgan pipeline to Vancouver and extending the Enbridge main export line to Wisconsin, but turns down the Enbridge Northern Gateway line through B.C. to Kitimat (*November 29*). Defends his government's cash-for-access fundraising events despite growing concern about the practice (*December 12*). His government fails to reach a deal on future health care funding with the provinces and territories (*December 19*); over the next week, New Brunswick, Nova Scotia and Newfoundland & Labrador reach separate agreements with Ottawa. His family vacations on the Aga Khan's island in the Bahamas (*late December-early January*).

2017: Shuffles his cabinet, removing former Liberal leader Stéphane Dion (Foreign Affairs) and replacing him with Chrystia Freeland (International Trade); former Somali refugee, Ahmed Hussen, becomes Immigration, Refugees and Citizenship minister (*January 10*). Launches a cross-country tour to meet with Canadians (*January 12*); includes a two-day cabinet retreat in Calgary. Commits to continue accepting refugees from the Middle East after U.S. President Trump bans visas for people from seven predominantly Islamic countries (*January 28*). Attends a vigil in Quebec City for six worshippers shot at a mosque by an extremist (*January 30*). Abandons his promise to seek election reform before the next election (*February 1*). Meets with U.S. President Trump in Washington (*February 13*). Addresses the European Parliament in Strasbourg, France, following the ratification of CETA (*February 16*). Meets with German Chancellor Merkel in Berlin and speaks at the St. Matthew's Day banquet in Hamburg (*February 16*). Introduces the opening performance of the *Come From Away* musical on Broadway (*March 15*). The government eliminates Canada Savings Bonds (*March 22*). Introduces the tribute to Leonard Cohen at the Juno Awards in Ottawa (*April 2*). Addresses the nearly 25,000 people attending the 100th anniversary at Vimy, France (*April 8*); follows with a visit to Juno Beach in Normandy. Meets with Pakistani youth activist Malala Yousafzai on whom he confers honorary Canadian citizenship (*April 12*). Introduces legislation to legalize the recreational use of marijuana (*April 13*). Joins Mexican President Enrique Pena Nieto to urge U.S. President Trump not to pull out of NAFTA (*April 26*). Appoints a cabinet task force to fix the costly Phoenix computer pay system for civil servants (*April 26*). Appoints Stéphane Dion as Ambassador to Germany and special envoy to Europe (*May 1*). Rona Ambrose, interim Conservative leader, announces her resignation as an MP to join a Washington think tank (*May 16*). His proposed dinner with Conservative Senator Stephen Greene prompts the Conservatives to remove the Nova Scotia Senator from caucus (*May 16*). Attends the

NATO leaders meeting in Brussels (*May 25*); followed by the G7 Summit in Taormina, Italy (*May* 26-27). Andrew Scheer becomes leader of the Conservative party, defeating Maxime Bernier after 13 ballots (*May 27*). Meets with Pope Francis to discuss a possible Roman Catholic apology for residential schools (*May 29*). Addresses the Italian Parliament (*May 30*). Meets with Daw Aung San Suu Kyi of Myanmar in Ottawa (*June 7*). The Senate rejects the government's appeal to separate the proposed Canada Infrastructure Bank Act from the budget bill to move it forward (June 19). Designates the Wellington Street building across from Parliament Hill to be a space for Indigenous peoples (*June 21*). Renames National Aboriginal Day to National Indigenous Peoples Day (*June 22*). Appoints Jennifer Macintyre as the first Ambassador for Climate Change (*June 27*). Attends security-intense Canada 150 celebrations on Parliament Hill, along with Prince Charles (*July 1*). Meets with Elizabeth II at Holyroodhouse in Edinburgh (*July 5*). Participates in the Global Citizen concert in Hamburg to thank people who have been pushing for sustainable development (*July 6*). Attends the G20 Summit in Hamburg (*July 7-8*). Issues an apology and a $10.5 million settlement to Omar Khadr for human rights violations he suffered at the U.S.'s Guantanamo Bay (*July 7*). Delivers the keynote address at the U.S. Governors Summit in Rhode Island (*July*). Announces the appointment of astronaut Julie Payette as Canada's 29th Governor General (*July 13*). Meets two-month-old namesake Justin-Trudeau Adam Bilal, son of Syrian refugees, at the Calgary Stampede (*July 17*). Rides the Canada150 train from Revelstoke, B.C., to Calgary (*July 29-30*). Shuffles his cabinet, splitting the Indigenous portfolio in two: Indigenous Services (Jane Philpott, former Health minister) and Crown-Indigenous Relations & Northern Affairs (Carolyn Bennett) (*August 28*). Meets with British Prime Minister Theresa May in Ottawa; both indicate a desire to maintain strong trade relations after Britain leaves the European Community (*September 18*). Receives the Atlantic Council's Global Citizen Award from Jordan's Queen Rania in New York (*September 19*). Speaks to more than 6,000 youth at WE Day in New York City, aimed at involving young people in tackling the world's problems (*September 20*). Addresses the UN General Assembly in New York, calling Canada a "work in progress" as it tries to right the wrongs done to Indigenous peoples (*September 21*). Launches the Invictus Games in Toronto with Prince Harry; the games are for soldiers and veterans in recovery (*September 23*). Inaugurates the National Holocaust Memorial in Ottawa (*September 27*). Jagmeet Singh wins the leadership of the NDP (*October 1*). Visits Washington to help convince U.S. President Trump not to pull the plug on NAFTA (*October 10-11*); speaks at the Most Powerful Women's Summit. Visits Mexican President Nieto in Mexico City to strengthen bilateral relations (*October 12-13*). His government agrees to pay $600 million to help fund legal settlements for Indigenous children who were separated from their families and put up for adoption, known as the 'Sixties Scoop' (*October 13*). Marks the 150th anniversary of Parliament's first session, noting that, "Within these walls, Canada has been reborn countless times." (*November 6*). Travels to Vietnam (*November 6*) and attends the APEC summit in Da Nang (*November 10-11*) where he temporarily derails attempts to revive discussions about the 11-nation Trans Pacific Partnership trade agreement. Raises concern in the Philippines about its brutal anti-drug campaign (*November 14*). His likeness in wax is unveiled at the Grevin wax museum in Montreal (*November 21*). Announces a 10-year, $40-billion national housing strategy that will require contributions from the provinces (*November 22*). Receives the Symons Medal for contributions to Canadian life, at Confederation Centre in Charlottetown, P.E.I. (*November 23*). Apologizes to the Inuit survivors of Labrador residential schools (*November 24*). Apologizes for past wrongs to the LGBTQ community (*November 28*). Visits China (*December 3-7*); meets with Premier Li Keqiang and President Xi Jinping. Announces the appointment of Richard Wagner as the 18th Chief Justice of Canada, succeeding McLachlin (*December 12*). Accused by Ethics Commissioner Mary Dawson of violating conflict of interest laws by accepting a 2016 family holiday in the Bahamas from the Aga Khan (*December 20*).

2018: Conducts town hall meetings in Halifax, Hamilton, London, Quebec City, Edmonton and Nanaimo (*January 9-February 2*). Kent Hehr (Sports & Disabilities) resigns over allegations of sexual misconduct (*January 25*). Visits Chicago, San Francisco and Los Angeles to promote the benefits of NAFTA (*February 7-10*). His visit to India leads to criticism about too many photo-ops, being largely ignored by Indian leaders, and hosting a banquet that included a convicted terrorist (*February 17-23*). The U.S. agrees to postpone heavy tariffs on Canadian steel and aluminum while NAFTA negotiations continue (*March*). Announces the appointment of Brenda Lucki as the first female RCMP Commissioner (*March 9*). Trump boasts he made up his response to Trudeau's assertion that the U.S. has a trade surplus with Canada: "I said, 'Wrong, Justin, you do." I didn't even know … I had no idea." (*March 14*). Exonerates six Tsilhquot'in chiefs who were hanged by B.C.'s colonial government in 1864 after being lured to 'peace talks' to resolve the killing of 14 construction workers during the Chilcotin War; seven Tsilhqot'in perform a drum ceremony in the House (*March 26*). Attends a vigil in Humboldt, Sask., for 15 people killed in the local Broncos hockey team bus crash (*April 8*). Attends the eighth Summit of the Americas in Lima, Peru (*April 12-14*). Attempts unsuccessfully to break the deadlock over Kinder Morgan's Trans Mountain pipeline project, in an Ottawa meeting with B.C. Premier John Horgan and Alberta Premier Rachel Notley (*April 15*). Visits Paris and meets with French President Emmanuel Macron (*April 15-17*); becomes the first Prime Minister to address the French National Assembly. Visits London and meets with British Prime Minister Theresa May and Elizabeth II, then attends the Commonwealth Heads of Government meeting (*April 17-20*). Takes part in a Toronto vigil for 10 people slain in a van attack along Yonge Street (*April 29*). Receives an honorary Doctor of Laws degree from New York University at Yankee Stadium (*May 16*). Blocks China's $1.5-billion takeover of Aecon construction company, citing security concerns (*May 24*). Intends to buy the $4.5-billion Trans Mountain pipeline to move more Alberta oil to the Pacific coast (*May 29*). Calls Trump's proposed tariffs on Canadian steel and aluminum "insulting and unacceptable" (*June 3*); indicates later that Canada will retaliate with tariffs on selected U.S. imports on July 1. Appoints Patricia Fuller as the first Ambassador of Climate Change (*June 5*). Hosts the G7 Summit in Charlevoix, Que. (*June 8-9*); marred by Trump who has imposed tariffs on the U.S.'s allies, wants Russia to rejoin the group, and reneges on the summit's final communique. Announces that October 17 will be the date for the legalization of marijuana in Canada (*June 20*). Spends Canada Day in Leamington, Ont., Regina, and Dawson City, Yukon, instead of in Ottawa (*July 1*).

Books about Trudeau

- **2013**: Althia Raj; *The Contender: The Justin Trudeau Story* (ebook, Huffington Post Canada)
- **2014**: Justin Trudeau; *Common Ground* (Harper Collins)
- **2015**: Paul Tuns: *The Dauphin: The Truth About Justin Trudeau* (Freedom Press Canada)
- **2016**: Huguette Young; *Justin Trudeau: The Natural Heir* (Dundurn)
- **2016**: Candice Malcolm; *Losing True North: Justin Trudeau's Assault on Canadian Citizenship* (Magna Carta)

Bibliography

General

- Ralph Allen; *Ordeal by Fire: Canada 1910-1945* (Doubleday, 1961)
- Sally Armstrong; *Mila* (Macmillan, 1992)
- J.M. Beck; *Pendulum of Power: Canada's Federal Elections* (Prentice Hall, 1968)
- Réal Bélanger & Ramsay Cook (ed.); *Canada's Prime Ministers, Macdonald to Trudeau: Portraits from the Dictionary of Canadian Biography* (University of Toronto, 2007)
- Pierre Berton; *The Great Depression 1929-1939* (McClelland & Stewart, 1990)
- Michael Bliss; *Right Honourable Men: The Descent of Canadian Politics from Macdonald to Mulroney* (Harper Collins, 1994)
- George Bowering; *Egotists and Autocrats: The Prime Ministers of Canada* (Penguin Canada, 1999)
- R. Craig Brown & Ramsay Cook; *Canada 1896-1921: A Nation Transformed* (McClelland & Stewart, 1974)
- D. Owen Carrigan; *Canadian Party Platforms 1867-1968* (Copp Clark, 1968)
- Jean Chevrier (ed.); *The Prime Ministers of Canada* (2nd ed., New Federation House, 2005)
- Edgar Andrew Collard; *Passage to the Sea: The Story of Canada Steamship Lines* (Doubleday Canada, 1991)
- Greg Donaghy; *Grit: The Life and Politics of Paul Martin Sr.* (UBC, 2015)
- Gordon Donaldson; *Eighteen Men: The Prime Ministers of Canada* (Doubleday, 1985)
- John Duffy; *Fights of Our Lives: Elections, Leadership and the Making of Canada* (HarperCollins, 2002)
- Patrice Dutil; *Prime Ministerial Power in Canada: It's Origins Under Macdonald, Laurier and Borden* (UBC, 2017)
- Patrice Dutil & David MacKenzie; *Canada 1911: The Decisive Election That Shaped the Country* (Dundurn, 2011)
- Patrice Dutil & David MacKenzie; *Embattled Nation: Canada's Wartime Election of 1917* (Dundurn, 2017)
- Will Ferguson; *Bastards & Boneheads: Canada's Glorious Leaders, Past and Present* (Douglas & McIntyre, 1999)
- Raul de L. Furtado; *Prime Ministers of Canada, 1867-1980* (D.S. Sodhi)
- Ron Graham; *One-Eyed Kings* (Collins, 1986)
- Ron Graham; *All the King's Horses: Politics Among the Ruins* (Macfarlane, Walter & Ross, 1995)
- J.L. Granatstein & Norman Hillmer; *Prime Ministers: Ranking Canada's Leaders* (Harper Collins, 1999)
- Edward Greenspon & Anthony Wilson-Smith; *Double Vision: The Inside Story of the Liberals in Power* (Doubleday Canada, 1996)
- Simma Holt; *The Other Mrs. Diefenbaker: A Biography of Edna Mae Brouwer* (Doubleday, 1982)
- Bruce Hutchison; *Mr. Prime Minister 1867-1964* (Longmans Canada, 1964)
- Martin Lawrence; *The Presidents and the Prime Ministers: Washington and Ottawa Face to Face: The Myth of Bilateral Bliss, 1867-1982* (Doubleday Canada, 1982)

- Jim Lotz; *Prime Ministers of Canada* (Bison, 1986)
- Carol McLeod; *Wives of the Canadian Prime Ministers* (Lancelot, 1985)
- Preston Manning; *Think Big: My Adventures in Life and Democracy* (McClelland & Stewart, 2002)
- Paul Martin; *The London Diaries 1975-1979* (University of Ottawa, 1988)
- Paul Martin; *A Very Public Life: Volume 1 Far From Home* (Denau, 1983)
- Maureen McTeer; *Residences: Homes of Canada's Leaders* (Prentice-Hall Canada, 1982)
- Maureen McTeer; *In My Own Name* (Random House, 2003)
- Knowlton Nash; *Kennedy and Diefenbaker: Fear and Loathing Across an Undefended Border* (McClelland & Stewart, 1990)
- Christopher Ondaatje; *The Prime Ministers of Canada: Macdonald to Mulroney, 1867-1985* (Pagurian)
- Bob Plamondon; *Blue Thunder: The Truth about Conservatives from Macdonald to Harper* (Key Porter, 2009)
- Louise Reynolds; *Agnes: The Biography of Lady Macdonald* (Carleton University, 1990)
- Charles Ritchie; *Storm Signals: More Undiplomatic Diaries, 1962-1971* (Macmillan, 1983)
- Heather Robertson; *More Than a Rose: Prime Ministers, Wives and Other Women* (Seal, 1991)
- Raymond Samuels; *Prime Ministers of Canada: Selected Speeches 1867-2002, Profiles, Bibliography with Commentary* (Agora Cosmopolitan, 2002)
- J.D.M. Stewart; *Being Prime Minister* (Dundurn, 2018)
- Margaret Trudeau; *Beyond Reason* (Paddington, 1979)
- Margaret Trudeau; *Changing My Mind* (HarperCollins Canada, 2010)

Juvenile/Children

- Rennay Craats; *Prime Ministers* (Weigl, 2000)
- Pat Hancock; *The Kids Book of Canadian Prime Ministers* (Kids Can, 1998)
- Shane Peacock; *Unsung Heroes: Canada's Prime Ministers and Fathers of Confederation* (Puffin Canada, 2002)
- Martin Spigelman; *Wilfrid Laurier* (Fitzhenry & Whiteside, 2000)
- Warts & All series (Jack Fruit)
    - Jacqueline A. Brown; *Sir John A. Macdonald: The rascal who built Canada* (2005)
    - Elle Andra-Warner; *Sir John S.D. Thompson: The pushover who died too soon* (2007)
    - Johanna Bertin; *Sir Charles Tupper: The bully who battled for Canada* (2007)
    - Heather Stewart; *Sir Wilfrid Laurier: The weakling who stood his ground* (2006)
    - Irene Gordon; *Sir Robert Borden: The shy guy who challenged an empire* (2007)
    - Nate Hendley; *William Lyon Mackenzie King: The loner who kept Canada together* (2006)
    - Lanny Boutin; *John Diefenbaker: The outsider who refused to quit* (2006)
    - Gordon Gibb; *Lester B. Pearson: The geek who made Canada proud* (2006)
    - Sandra Phinney; *Pierre Trudeau: The prankster who never flinched* (2006)
    - Heather Stewart; *Kim Campbell: The keener who broke down barriers* (2007)

- Nate Hendley; *Jean Chrétien: The scrapper who climbed his way to the top* (2005)
- Prime Ministers of Canada series (Weigl)
  - Bev Cline; *The New Nation: Sir John A. Macdonald* (2007)
  - Bev Cline; *Turn of the 20th Century: Sir Wilfrid Laurier* (2007)
  - Douglas Baldwin & Patricia Baldwin; *Time of Turmoil: William Lyon Mackenzie King* (2007)
  - Douglas Baldwin & Patricia Baldwin; *Time of Transition: Lester Pearson* (2007)
  - Douglas Baldwin & Patricia Baldwin; *Trudeau Era* (2007)
  - Bev Cline; *Contemporary Canada: Stephen Harper* (2007)
- Leaders & Legacies series (Fireside)
  - Roderick Benns; *The Legends of Lake on the Mountain: An early adventure of John A. Macdonald* (2011)
  - Barbara Martin; *The Hero of Hopewell Hill: An early adventure of Richard Bennett* (2014)
  - Roderick Benns; *The Mystery of the Moonlight Murder: An early adventure of John Diefenbaker* (2009)
  - Steve Pitt; *The Wail of Wendigo: An early adventure of Pierre Trudeau* (2015)
  - Caroline Woodward; *Showdown at Border Town: An early adventure of Paul Martin* (2013)
- Canadian Prime Ministers series (Weigl)
  - Anita Yasuda; *John Diefenbaker* (2015)
  - Anita Yasuda; *Lester Pearson* (2014)
  - Anita Yasuda; *Pierre Trudeau* (2014)
  - Anita Yasuda; *Stephen Harper* (2015)

Television
- Holly Doan; *The Prime Ministers* (CPAC, 2009)
- Catherine Clark; *Beyond Politics*; interviews with Joe Clark, John Turner, Brian Mulroney, Kim Campbell, Jean Chrétien, Paul Martin, Justin Trudeau (CPAC, 2013)

Websites
- *www.prime-minister.ca* The Prime Ministers of Canada by 7th Floor Media
- *www.biographi.ca/en* Dictionary of Canadian Biography
- *www3.sympatico.ca/goweezer/canada/canpms.htm* Canadiana Prime Ministers of Canada
- *www.lop.parl.gc.ca/ParlInfo/Compilations/FederalGovernment/PrimeMinisters/Gallery.aspx* Prime Ministers of Canada, Parliament of Canada
- *www.craigmarlatt.com/canada/government/pms.html* CanadaInfo by Craig Marlatt
- *www.collectionscanada.gc.ca/primeministers/h4-3000-e.html* First Among Equals by Library and Archives Canada

Index

34537055R00252

Made in the USA
Middletown, DE
31 January 2019